The Enemy in Contemporary Film

Culture & Conflict

Edited by
Isabel Capeloa Gil and Catherine Nesci

Editorial Board
Arjun Appadurai · Claudia Benthien · Elisabeth Bronfen · Joyce Goggin
Lawrence Grossberg · Andreas Huyssen · Ansgar Nünning · Naomi Segal
Márcio Seligmann-Silva · António Sousa Ribeiro · Roberto Vecchi
Samuel Weber · Liliane Weissberg · Christoph Wulf

Volume 12

The Enemy
in Contemporary Film

Edited by
Martin Löschnigg and Marzena Sokołowska-Paryż

DE GRUYTER

ISBN 978-3-11-070908-7
e-ISBN (PDF) 978-3-11-059121-7
e-ISBN (EPUB) 978-3-11-059003-6
ISSN 2194-7104

Library of Congress Cataloging-in-Publication Data
Names: Loschnigg, Martin, editor. | Sokoowska-Paryz, Marzena, editor.
Title: The enemy in contemporary film / edited by herausgegeben von Martin Loschnigg, Marzena Sokoowska-Paryz.
Description: Berlin ; Boston : De Gruyter, [2018] | Series: Culture & conflict ; band/volume 12 | Includes bibliographical references and index.
Identifiers: LCCN 2018023453 (print) | LCCN 2018029336 (ebook) | ISBN 9783110591217 (electronic Portable Document Format (pdf)) | ISBN 9783110589924 | ISBN 9783110589924¬(print :¬qalk. paper) | ISBN 9783110591217¬(e-book pdf) | ISBN 9783110590036¬(e-book epub)
Subjects: LCSH: Enemies in motion pictures.
Classification: LCC PN1995.9.E54 (ebook) | LCC PN1995.9.E54 E64 2018 (print) | DDC 791.43/653--dc23
LC record available at https://lccn.loc.gov/2018023453

Bibliographic information published by the Deutsche Nationalbibliothek
The Deutsche Nationalbibliothek lists this publication in the Deutsche Nationalbibliografie; detailed bibliographic data are available on the Internet at http://dnb.dnb.de.

© 2020 Walter de Gruyter GmbH, Berlin/Boston
This volume is text- and page-identical with the hardback published in 2018.
Cover image: Dimitris66 / E+ / getty images
Printing and binding: CPI books GmbH, Leck

www.degruyter.com

Table of Contents

Marzena Sokołowska-Paryż and Martin Löschnigg
Introduction —— 1

Part I: **The 'Faces' of the Enemy: Film Aesthetics and Contemporary (Geo)Politics**

Gunnar Iversen
New Enemies, New Cold Wars: Reimagining Occupation and Military Conflict in Norway —— 19

Angela Brintlinger
'A Murky Business': The Post-Soviet Enemy —— 35

Holger Pötzsch
Of Monsters and Men: Forms of Evil in War Films —— 53

Janet Harris
The Domestic Enemy in British TV Documentaries on the Iraq War —— 73

Maryam Jameela
Britain's Muslims as the Enemy Within in Contemporary British Cinema —— 91

Florian Zappe
(Re)Framing the Disembodied Public Enemy: The 'War on Drugs' in Contemporary Narrative Screen Media —— 105

Part II: **Who are the Perpetrators? Who are the Victims? Confronting Difficult Pasts and the Crisis of Identity**

Petra Rau
From 'Ivan' to Andreij: The Red Army in German Film and TV —— 121

Niina Oisalo
Enemies Within: Reimagining the 'Fallen Women' of World War II in Contemporary Finnish Documentary —— 145

Caroline Perret
The Collaborator as Enemy during the French Occupation in (Auto-) Biographical and Post-Memory Cinema —— 159

Noah McLaughlin
False Idyll: Siri's *L'Ennemi intime* —— 177

Marcelline Block
"Femme, je ne vous aime pas": The Enemy Within in Joachim Lafosse's *A perdre la raison* —— 197

Mario Ranalletti
The Past as Enemy in Argentine Cinema, 1983–2000 —— 219

Maria Kobielska
Who Attacked Whom? The Year 1981 in Twenty-First Century Polish Feature Films —— 233

Part III: **Do Nations Need Enemies? Transcending/Perpetuating Nationalisms**

Daniel Reynaud
Redefining the Enemy in Contemporary Australian Anzac Cinema —— 253

Andrejs Plakans and Vita Zelče
The Fading of Enemy Images in Contemporary Latvian Cinema —— 271

Francesca de Lucia
Looking for an Invisible Enemy in Israeli Film —— 293

Miri Talmon
Bonds Across Borders: A Fictional Enemy in Motion on the Israeli Screen —— 309

Stephen Harper
Bosnia Beyond Good and Evil: (De)Constructing the Enemy in Western and Post-Yugoslav Films about the 1992–1995 War —— 327

Marek Paryż
Forbidden Bonding at the Time of the War on Terror: The Enemy as Friend in *Camp X-Ray* **and** *Boys of Abu Ghraib* —— 345

Martin Löschnigg
Canadians and the Pacific War 1941–1945 in Anne Wheeler's *A War Story* **and** *The War Between Us* —— 361

Jonathan Rayner
Lost Pasts and Unseen Enemies: The Pacific War in Recent Japanese Films —— 377

Contributors —— 395

Index —— 401

Marzena Sokołowska-Paryż and Martin Löschnigg
Introduction

Cultural memory, in Jan Assmann's definition, "has its fixed points; its horizon does not change with the passing of time. These fixed points are fateful events of the past, the memory of which is maintained through cultural formation (texts, rites, monuments) and institutional communication (recitation, practice, observance)" (2011: 213). Since the later twentieth century, film has become dominant among the "cultural formation[s]" which convey cultural memory and its coordinates in the sense of Assmann. Accordingly, one may detect in contemporary international cinema a surge of 'returns' to the defining moments of national history and of a nation's cultural memory. Very often, these defining moments (or "fixed points") are constituted by conflicts and will thus involve an 'enemy.' These conflicts may be either military, uniting a national community in opposition to an external enemy, or socio-political, ethnic and/or racial conflicts dividing a nation into 'us' and an internal enemy. In the cinema, adherence to a dominant national interpretation of the past may result in a 'resurrection' of past antagonisms, problematic in strikingly different geopolitical and socio-political states of affairs. Concomitantly, a counter-tendency may be observed, with contemporary filmmakers offering a radical re-interpretation of "fateful events," and thus also offering a different perspective on the enemy, attempting to construct a historical consciousness which "focuses on the historicity of events – that they took place then and not now, that they grew out of circumstances different from those that now obtain" (Novick, 1999:4).

The focus of this volume is on the "enemy image" as generated by "a belief held by a certain group that *its security and basic values are directly threatened by some other group*" (Luostarinen 1989: 125; original emphasis). These images have been constructed (as well as de- or re-constructed) in contemporary film in response to current geopolitical situations and/or socio-political needs, either to reassert or to redefine a national identity in the present. Films produced by different national cinematographies reveal symptomatic tensions between the requirements of political correctness and historically determined conventions in the representation of past and present conflicts, and of the enemy in particular. Being a densely contextualized narrative construct, the "enemy image" triggers not only a dialogue between former and current horizons of historical perception, but also raises the issue of the role of race, ethnicity, and gender in the construction of national identities.

The chapters in *The Enemy in Contemporary Film* adopt various methodological approaches such as surveys of the changing images of the enemy in a national cinematography over a span of time, analyses of films produced in a particular period that continue to have an impact on representations of the enemy within a national culture, discussions of a particular film that is either representative of a nation's current historical politics or a significant attempt at its redefinition, and, finally, analyses of recent films in connection to past productions. The volume brings together discussions on the enemy in various national cinemas: Norwegian, Finnish, Latvian, Russian, Kazakh, Polish, German, French, Belgian, Bosnian, Serbian, Israeli, American, Argentinian, British, Australian, Canadian and Japanese. Considering the number of military and socio-political conflicts in the twentieth and twenty-first centuries, and their even more numerous filmic (re)imaginings, this volume necessarily had to be very selective with regard to geopolitical regions. However, we have tried to be as comprehensive as possible with regard to representative filmic strategies underlying the (de)(re)constructions of the "enemy image" in transnational contexts.

The readings of filmic representations of the enemy included in this volume address the dominant trends in a given nation's politics of memorialization. If "we accept that [...] personal or group identities include a system of self-esteem maintenance that balances dichotomous feelings such as pride or humiliation, giving emotional texture to international relations considerations," then it is obvious that "every national culture in itself is engaged in its ongoing process and acknowledging this difference would help us understand so-called misinterpretations" (Femenia 1996: 24, 32). According to Debra Merskin, "nations 'need' enemies [...] as a hegemonic device," for "a common enemy can serve to distract attention and divert aggression and energy toward a common threat. In addition, a common enemy is important in organizing evolutionary-based survival strategies that rely on perceptual and behavioral patterns that are a fundamental part of human nature" (2004: 159). However, Heikki Luostarinen (within the specific context of Finland, yet highly relevant to other national contexts) emphasizes that "relative affluence and prosperity, democratization, and rapid, social mobility [...] [are] all factors that tend to take the edge off enemy images, [whereas] unemployment, lack of future perspectives, and despair tend to support the growth of violence, war, and enemy images" (134). Thus, the enemy as a political as much as a philosophical category also provokes questions about the ways in which the historical concerns manifesting themselves in different parts of the world are related to Western standards of liberal democracy.

It needs to be underscored that the actual or assumed global threats of today's world have also had a decisive impact on cultural representations of the enemy in relation to national identities, all too often effectively overriding socio-economic concerns. The greater the real or perceived-as-real threat stemming from current geopolitics, the greater the rise of populist nationalisms requiring both politically and culturally constructed "enemy images" which substantiate the dominant national narratives. At the same time, there will also always be significant cultural endeavors aiming to question – more or less explicitly – the dominant national identity-politics. Rather than confirming "enemy images," these will prefer mechanisms of 'de-enemization' for the purposes of a common good, i.e. promoting a vision of the past that allows for national or ethnic reconciliation on the basis of an understanding of the motivations of the 'enemy' and an acknowledgement of the humanity of the 'Other.'

Robert Rosenstone has distinguished between those "standard historical film[s]" which "deliver the past in a highly developed, polished form that serves to suppress rather than raise questions [...] rarely [...] push[ing] boundaries of what we already know," and "the postmodern historical film," which "utilizes the unique capabilities of the media to create multiple meanings." As Rosenstone goes on to say, "Such works do not [...] attempt to recreate the past realistically. Instead they point to it and play with it, raising questions about the very evidence on which our knowledge of the past depends, creatively interacting with its traces" (1995: 11–12). It should be emphasized, however, that "standard" and "postmodern" historical films, though diverse in their aesthetics and narrative formulas, are similar insofar as their depictions of the past are both ideological constructs, inevitably written into the socio-political and geopolitical contexts in which they were produced. The present volume engages with such constructs and their respective contexts. Discussing a number of genres that deal with history and/or politics, including popular films based on original screenplays, film adaptations of novels, TV series, and documentaries, it aims to show the enemy as represented in contemporary global cinemas as a multifaceted ideological concept. In particular, the chapters will show how filmic imaginings of the enemy either pose the risk of linking film to specific nationalistic agendas, or alternatively promote a trans-national or even a trans-continental global empathetic historical awareness and understanding.

Why the focus on film? Because "ours is a world in which films rank second only to photographs as the means by which people claim to connect with the past" (Hughes-Warrington 2009: 1). One may venture the claim that to understand a nation's (re)definition of its identity in the present, one needs to be acquainted with its film productions. As a result, most publications in the field of film and cultural memory have tended to focus on national cinemas – let it suffice to mention, for example, *Nordic National Cinemas* (Gunnar Iversen, Astrid Soderbergh Widding, Tytti Soila), *Israeli Cinema: Identities in Motion* (eds. Miri Talmon and Yaron Peleg), *Russian War Films: On the Cinema Front, 1914–2005* (Denise J. Youngblood), *Keeping It Real: Irish Film and Television* (eds. Ruth Barton and Harvey O'Brien), *A History of Pain: Trauma in Modern Chinese Literature and Film* (Michael Berry), *French War Films and National Identities* (Noah McLaughlin), or *Guts and Glory: The Making of the American Military Image in Film* (Lawrence Howard Suid). In contrast, *The Enemy in Contemporary Film* brings together, for the first time, various national cinematographies, underlining both the common transnational and trans-temporal paradigms which underlie constructions of the enemy figure, as well as the differences stemming from the impact of the current historical politics of a given nation. The historian, as Rosenstone writes, may well have problems with both the ideological and/or aesthetic (mis)interpretations of the past in film, yet he acknowledges that even "standard historical films may do something for history by showing, personalizing, and emotionalizing the past, and delivering it to a new audience" (1995: 11). Furthermore, as Alison Landsberg adds, "the cinema offers spectators from diverse backgrounds and ancestries a shared archive of experience" (2004: 14).

Our volume aims at uniting two goals: first, to enhance an understanding of various national cinemas, which in spite of their diversity all prove that "the production, circulation and consumption of the moving image is constitutive of the national collectivity;" second, to augment the fact that "this internalism is necessarily tempered by an awareness of exteriority as a shaping force" (Schlesinger 2000: 24). "In the past two decades," John R. Gillis writes, "memory has [...] become more global [...]. Events and places with international meaning, such as Hiroshima, Chernobyl, Auschwitz, and Nanjing capture the world's attention even when nations responsible may wish to forget them" (1994: 14). Unquestionably, in the era of a global film market, depictions of the enemy in film have the power to necessitate transnational discussions of burdensome pasts, shared or diverse, with a view to creating shared futures: "a commodified mass culture opens up the possibility that people who share little in the way of cultural or ethnic background might come to shared memories" (Landsberg 2004: 9). The focus of the volume thus lies on (re)configurations of the enemy in contemporary global cinemas which, beside the two world wars, explore regional military conflicts, ethnic, racial and gender conflicts, socio-political conflicts (also within totalitarian regimes), as well as both external and internal forms of terrorism.

The choice of Gunnar Iversen's discussion of the Norwegian TV-series *Okkupert* for the opening paper seemed appropriate, as the generic hybridity of the series serves as a perfect reminder that the kind of political feature film dealt with in most of the chapters belongs to the realm of the imagination more than that of fact. However, it is mostly by inciting the workings of the imagination that film, as Landsberg writes, can provide the possibility of "suturat[ing] [oneself] into a larger history, [...] the person does not simply apprehend a historical narrative but takes on a more personal, deeply felt memory of a past event through which he or she did not live." This is what Landsberg has defined as "prosthetic memory," "a new form of memory" which "emerges at the interface between a person and historical narrative about the past, at an experiential site," and which "has the ability to shape that person's subjectivity and politics" (2004: 2). In a global world, a trans-national perspective on (de)(re)constructions of the enemy figure in film is urgently needed in order also to promote an understanding of national cultures other than one's own. It is also important to see how the concept of the enemy is either imaginatively/ideologically re-instituted or has become prone to significant imaginative/ideological reconfigurations, in response to both the historical politics of a given nation as well as the threats posed by the contemporary world. According to Landsberg, "prosthetic memory creates the conditions for ethical thinking precisely by encouraging people to feel connected to, while recognizing the alterity of the 'other'" (2004: 9). This is a very idealistic attitude: while films may indeed advocate a need for the reconciliation of former enemies, they may equally effectively promote nationalist politics, even if they do not explicitly demonize the enemy. Thus, films need to be approached with an awareness that all have intended messages that need to be approached critically. Hence, the volume ends with Jonathan Rayner's analysis of contemporary Japanese war films which reflect the dangerous recourse to extreme nationalism by evoking an allegedly glorious military past.

The first part of this volume, "The 'Faces' of the Enemy: Film Aesthetics and Contemporary (Geo)Politics," comprises chapters accentuating the interdependence of overt ideologies of genre, underlying philosophies of film style, and current political agenda. The focus is thus on the correlation of form and meaning, the underlying questions being to what extent filmic representations of the enemy are interpretations of the actual threats menacing today's world, or, alternatively, to what degree they may be considered ideological evocations of fear for the (geo)political needs of the 'here and now' of a nation's self-interest. In "New Enemies, New Cold Wars: Reimagining Occupation and Military Conflict in Norway," Gunnar Iversen argues that the particular combination of alternate history, dystopia and political thriller in the series *Okkupert* (*Occupied*) proved an effective formal strategy for both interpreting the present and conveying a warning for the future. The highly improbable fictive scenario that both 'revives' and 'rewrites' the histories of World War II and the Cold War perfectly underscores contemporary concerns over Russia's expansionism as well as fears of extremist nationalist movements and terrorism, concomitantly raising questions on the role of the EU and the US in today's geopolitical reality. "'A Murky Business': The Post-Soviet Enemy" by Angela Brintlinger focuses on allegorical uses of fog in three films representing three difference genres, Ermek Tursunov's nature drama *Shal* (*The Old Man*), Sergei Loznitsa's war film *V tumane* (*In the Fog*) and Georgii Gitis's animated fairy-tale for children *Prikliucheniia Alënushki i Erëmy* (*The Adventures of Alënushka and Erëma*). The different national backgrounds of the filmmakers (Kazakh, Belarusian/Ukrainian and Russian) are of significance, for, though the past echoes strongly in all the films, this is a past filtered through the anxieties which emerged in the aftermath of the collapse of the USSR. As this chapter proves, the inevitable and necessary redefinitions of national identities in a post-Soviet order, as well as Russia's increasing isolationism, could not remain without impact on the "enemy image" in popular culture.

"When increasingly our identity is invented, dispersed, disseminated, as the communities that we inhabit become more imagined, constellated, ethereal," Rick Altman writes, there remains "a continuing chain of genres offering a type of communication particularly well suited to the perpetually reimagined communities in which we live" (2004: 205). "Of Monsters and Men: Forms of Evil in War Films" by Holger Pötzsch begins with an overview of the intricate relationship between history and genre. The subsequent comparative analysis of Clint Eastwood's *American Sniper* and Nick Broomfield's *Battle for Haditha* focuses on the ethical and epistemological effects of embedding, respectively, the military career of the 'all American hero' Christopher Scott ('Chris') Kyle and the actual massacre of 24 Iraqi civilians by US forces in Haditha in 2005 within the dialectics of the conventional war film. Despite the fact that the two films are concerned with the conduct of US soldiers during a specific military conflict, it is genre – as a transnational category – that allows a reading of both films in more universal contexts of the 'cosmology' versus the 'banality' of evil. If, as Altman says, "genre is a contract" which determines "the viewing position required by each genre film of its audience" (2004: 14), the question posed in this chapter is what moral "position" is induced by the filmmakers on the 'us' versus 'them 'dichotomy. Accordingly, Janet Harris's "The Domestic Enemy in British TV Documentaries on the Iraq War" offers a radically different take on the same conflict, the national perspective being British this time, and the mode of representation analysed the documentary film. One of the chief "concern[s]" regarding the documentary film is that "[it] not only involves artifice and craft, but that it exerts ideological or political pressure on its viewers" (Kahana 2016: 6). However, Harris's discussion of over twenty television documentaries shows how these (hi)stories of the political and military causes of the British presence in Iraq 2003–2009, as well as its after-effects, serve as an ethical indictment of the decision to engage in this preventive war, the questioning of its legitimacy having a crucial impact on (re)definitions of the enemy.

The final two chapters in this section focus on the geopolitical and socio-political intricacies at the heart of convention-bound filmic representations of the internal 'domestic' enemy. The constant threat of terrorist attacks and the ongoing so-called 'immigrant crisis,' so readily exploited in current populist political rhetoric, have cast a dark shadow on the ideal of multiculturalism, an ideal that incorporates the necessary prerequisites for "empathy in the global world": the first of these prerequisites is "to recognize the Other as a moving, breathing, and living human being;" the second is that of "imaginative placement," as "empathy relies heavily on being able to understand mental states that the other may not have experienced first-hand," and the third "involve[s] understanding and communication," i.e. "a human's ability to explain, predict, and describe the sentiments of others" (Calloway-Thomas 2010: 14–15). Maryam Jameela's chapter on "Britain's Muslims as the Enemy Within in Contemporary British Cinema" illustrates what insights cultural phenomenology may provide into the uses of the drama genre on the examples of Kenneth Glenaan's *Yasmin* and Sarah Gavron's *Brick Lane*. These are films that highlight the post 9/11 issue of the dominance of the 'Western' gaze in cultural depictions of Muslims as 'terrorists' and at the same time also problematize the concept of the 'enemy' by underscoring the religiously and/or culturally determined relationships between Muslim men and women. As Jameela shows, it is the latter aspect in particular which shapes the 'image,' in the films she discusses, of Muslims as the 'unassimilable' enemy within Western/British society.

While the filmic depictions of the 'enemy' discussed in the previous chapters stand in the context of the enduring memory of World War II and the consequences (military, political, social, and in terms of gender) of the declared "War on Terror," Florian Zappe adds another significant perspective on the 'faces' of the enemy in contemporary film: drugs. In his "(Re)Framing the Disembodied Public Enemy: The 'War on Drugs' in Contemporary Narrative Screen Media," Zappe analyses Steven Soderbergh's *Traffic*, Michael Mann's *Miami Vice*, Oliver Stone's *Savages* and the TV series *Narcos* with reference to the ideological borders delineated by the tropes of the 'war on drugs' film genre, a genre which situates itself in-between the traditional war film and crime drama and which also problematizes conventional depictions by rendering a 'disembodied' version of the enemy.

The second part of this volume, entitled "Who are the Perpetrators? Who are the Victims? Confronting Difficult Pasts and the Crisis of Identity," includes contributions on filmic representations of the enemy within the frames of ethically and/or politically necessitated returns to a past that continues to be seen as a national burden in the present. As Nyla B. Branscombe and Bertjam Doosje emphasize, "National and other social groups have histories. Reminders of group history can have important consequences for present-day emotional experience" (2004: 3). The chapters included in this section analyse popular and documentary films which testify to the fact that pasts, distant or more recent, continue to have an impact on contemporary understandings of national identity, the roots of ongoing or emergent crises of such an identity residing in a complex intertwining of collective guilt and shame. In psychoanalytical theory, there exists a clear-cut distinction between the two emotions: "The experience of shame is directly about the *self*, which is the focus of evaluation. In guilt, the self is not the central object of negative evaluation, but rather the *thing* done or undone is the focus" (Lewis 1971: 30; original emphasis). The mechanisms underlying cultural constructions of national identities work along different lines, for, in the sphere of historical politics, "emotions can be ephemeral," and the way in which "events are appraised and the subjective experience they generate can rapidly shift with changes in the social context" (Branscombe, Slugoski, and Kappen 2004: 16).

Max Färberböck's *Anonyma: Eine Frau in Berlin* (*Anonyma: A Woman in Berlin*), as discussed in Petra Rau's "From 'Ivan' to Andreij: The Red Army in German Film and TV" clearly belongs to post-reunification German cinema, which probes the set assumptions of historical guilt by exposing the hitherto suppressed national shame (mass rapes of German women by Red Army soldiers). The film writes itself into the "place and meaning fascism holds in the contemporary cultural imagery" (Rau 2013: 3), as "with the onset of a *post-cold-war phase*, beginning in the late 1980s and lasting up to the present, the tendency towards triumphalism returned, alongside the ongoing tendency towards self-critique" (Rosenfeld 2005: 24; original emphasis). Max Färberböck's film, although an adaptation of a real-life victim's memoir, is a fictional re-framing of actual events for the purposes of emphasizing Germany's victimhood. This allows for situating the nation's problematic past within a more universal context of gender-oriented violence in wartime, yet at the same time the manner in which the Soviet soldiers are depicted testifies to a national need for overcoming past enmities. Similarly, Niina Oisalo's analysis of Virpi Suutari's *Auf Wiedersehen Finnland* ("Goodbye Finland"), with reference to Mari Soppela's autobiographical *Kuka piru pimeässä näkee* (*Who the Devil Can See in the Dark*), in "Enemies Within: Reimagining the 'Fallen Women' of World War II in Contemporary Finnish Documentary" unearths hitherto suppressed personal histories of Finnish women who fell in love with German soldiers. She thereby problematizes the simplified version of the nation's difficult past that was politically necessary and officially propagated in the years after World War II. The historical complexities of Finland's history, including the ethical ambivalences of the political motivations underlying the military alliances during the Continuation War, rendered it a past that needed re-definitions for the purposes of a post-World War II present in which war time coalitions with the Third Reich were ethically and legally rejected. Hence the need, as Oisalo shows, for construing an ideological scapegoat, a trans-national and trans-temporal defensive social mechanism. In the words of René Girard, "The rite aims at the most profound state of peace known to any community: the peace that follows the sacrificial crisis and results from the unanimous accord generated by the surrogate victim. To banish the evil emanations that accumulate within the community and to recapture the freshness of the original experience are one and the same task" (2013: 108). Girard's concept of a "generative mimetic scapegoating mechanism" denotes the constructions of post-event (hi)stories that need an 'enemy' for the symbolic 'purification' of a national community. The films discussed in Petra Rau's and Niina Oisalo's chapters reveal the mechanisms of constructing enemies of the past and, concomitantly, confront these strategies of (hi)story-telling with contemporary understandings of enemy and gender.

In turn, Caroline Perret's "The Collaborator as Enemy during the French Occupation in (Auto-)Biographical and Post-Memory Cinema" and Noah McLaughlin's "False Idyll: Siri's *L'Ennemi intime*" raise the interrelated issues of national guilt and shame in relation to films which challenged official versions of French history. Perret deals with the figure of the French citizen as collaborator during the Nazi occupation of France. Drawing on Marcel Ophüls's documentary *Le Chagrin et la pitié: chronique d'une ville française sous l'occupation* (*The Sorrow and the Pity: Chronicle of a French Town under the Occupation*), she concentrates on two films by Louis Malle, *Lacombe Lucien* and *Au revoir les enfants* ("Goodbye Children"), analysing their portrayal of the ambiguities that often underlie the issue of collaboration *versus* resistance in the historical, political and cultural context of the Occupation. In particular, she emphasizes how Malle's filmic renderings reflect contemporary discourses surrounding fascism, the occupation, collaboration and resistance. The film discussed by McLaughlin, Florent-Emilio Siri's *L'Ennemi intime* (*Intimate Enemies*), deals with an equally troubled issue, although one which is not as overwhelmingly present in the French popular memory as the two World Wars, namely that of the Algerian War for Independence. Here too, as McLaughlin shows, boundaries between enemy and ally are sometimes not so sharply drawn as one might expect. Siri's film is analysed in the light of Hayden White's concept of "historiophoty," i.e. the visual (filmic) rendering of history and views on historical events, and, with regard to its genre, that of a 'transnationalism' which transcends the dominant aesthetics of national cinematic traditions. As McLaughlin shows, *L'Ennemi intime* is indebted to Hollywood types of action films (Westerns and platoon movies) as well as to counter- or anti-hegemonic styles, combining action sequences with the profound analysis of milieu and its psychological effects that is prominent in the French cinematic tradition. The film emphasizes the transformative powers of war, visible in the brutalizing of ordinary human beings that renders them capable of committing atrocities, and critiques the violence connected with colonial domination.

The colonial past of francophone countries stands as a shadow behind the depiction of a dysfunctional family in Joachim Lafosse's film *A perdre la raison* (*Our Children*). Based on a true case of multiple infanticide which shocked Belgians in 2007, the film centres on the murder of four young children by their mother, a Belgian woman married to a Moroccan immigrant. Marcelline Block's discussion of the film ("'Femme, je ne vous aime pas': The Enemy Within in Joachim Lafosse's *A perdre la raison*") focuses on the figure of an internal enemy in the shape of the sinister and menacing Dr Pinget, who has made the family dependent on himself by housing and supporting them, and by arranging 'green card marriages' for their relations. By analogy, his domination over the family, which gives rise to repeated instances of domestic violence, re-enacts the colonial oppression especially of women, embodying the socio-political forces which encroach on women in (post)colonial societies. As the 'enemy' of Murielle in particular, he thus contributes to the mental illness that will eventually cause her to commit the atrocious act.

Internal enemies, although in an overtly political sense, are the subject of the films discussed by Mario Ranalletti ("The Past as Enemy in Argentine Cinema, 1983–2000") and Maria Kobielska ("Who Attacked Whom? The Year 1981 in Twenty-First Century Polish Feature Films"). Ranalletti discusses the search for truth and justice in Argentinian cinema since the end of the military dictatorship in 1983. He focuses on notions of 'subversion' and of subversive (internal) enemies cited by the *junta* in order to legitimize repression, as various groups (notably 'communists') were accused of de-stabilizing the country. As he shows, the transition to democracy brought a new manifestation of this 'subversive enemy' that is prominent in recent Argentine film, namely the former perpetrators living hidden among their victims. Kobielska deals with the contested interpretations of the martial law introduced on 13 December 1981 by the authoritarian communist government of Poland, analysing the significance of that year in Polish cultural memory on the example of contemporary feature films. In particular, Kobielska is interested in different narrative patterns or forms of 'emplotting' the events, from the "martyrological" to the picaresque or the kind of domestic realism which 'de-heroises' the conflict by concentrating on its effects on people's everyday lives. The focus on genre (including the shifting identifications of the 'enemy' it may entail) is particularly illuminating, as Kobielska shows, with regard to the complex portrayal of Lech Wałęsa in Andrzej Wajda's film of 2013.

The third part of this volume, entitled "Do Nations Need Enemies? Transcending/Perpetuating Nationalisms," focuses on films which work to alleviate past antagonisms by downplaying and/or problematizing the concept of the enemy. However, as the final chapter makes clear, there are also those films which render disturbingly nationalistic interpretations of the past, showing that "there are ample reasons to suppose that people will be strongly inclined to protect their social identity by perceiving their group's actions from the vantage point of the 'moral high ground'" (Branscombe and Doosje 2004: ix). Analyses of representative examples from cinematographies across nations underscore divergent trends: on the one hand, films aim at 'de-enemizing' the past and present, the underlying question being to what extent such reconfigurations of the enemy serve the purposes of trans-national and/or trans-ethnic reconciliation; on the other hand, films show to what degree the "enemy image" is constructed in a manner so as to serve as a "screen memory," shrouding uncomfortable truths about the national pasts and presents.

Daniel Reynaud's "Redefining the Enemy in Contemporary Australian Anzac Cinema" investigates shifting conceptions of the enemy in Australian films about the First World War, and especially the disastrous yet amply mythicized Gallipoli campaign, from two periods, the 1980s and the years since 2010. As Reynaud illustrates, the 1980s films (foremost among them Peter Weir's *Gallipoli*) are inspired by anti-imperialism and a national Australian ideology which celebrates the Anzac myth, also in view of the 1988 bicentenary. Accordingly, the enemy are British hierarchism, arrogance and military incompetence rather than the Turks and Germans, if their role is accentuated at all. In contrast, the later wave of films challenges the Anzac myth for instance by focusing on marginalized topics like divided loyalties among German Australians, desertion, and others. Above all, however, the enemy is now the war as such, and the nationalism and hatred it produces.

While Reynaud focuses on films about the First World War, Andrejs Plakans and Vita Zelče ("The Fading of Enemy Images in Contemporary Latvian Cinema") discuss Latvian films whose temporal settings represent a broad historical sweep from the Inter-War Period 1919–1939 to the present. After a brief outline of Latvian film-making in the post-Soviet era, the chapter discusses Aigars Grauba's *Baigā vasara* (*Dangerous Summer*), *Sapņu komanda 1935* (*Dream Team 1935*), *Rīgas sargi* (*Defenders of Riga*); Arvids Krievs's *Dancis pa trim* (*Three to Dance*); Jānis Streičs's *Cilvēka bērns* (*The Child of Man*); and Juris Poskus's *Kolka Cool*, whose enemy images range from the external and internal enemies in a history marked by intricate (and changing) political and ethno-cultural allegiances, to the internal enemies (in a broader sense) within contemporary Latvia, like social strictures or the negative effects of Western consumerism.

The following chapters by Francesca de Lucia and Miri Talmon are both concerned with filmic representations of the conflict in the Middle East. De Lucia's

"Looking for an Invisible Enemy in Israeli Film" analyses three feature films on the First Lebanon War of the early 1980s, all dating from the twenty-first century (*Beaufort*, *Vals im Bashir* and *Lebanon*). All three are characterised by an elusive, undefined enemy, virtually eclipsing the people of Lebanon as enemies and/or victims. As a result, they render a 'de-historicized' picture of the war, concentrating instead on conflicts within the Israeli soldiers, emphasizing the mental traumas induced by war. This is especially striking, as de Lucia shows, in *Vals im Bashir* (*Waltz with Bashir*), where the use of animation creates a hyper-reality and a hallucinogenic dreamscape that stand in for the enemy, while *Lebanon* uses consistent focalization through rendering the perspective of Israeli soldiers in a tank. Miri Talmon's "Bonds Across Borders: A Fictional Enemy in Motion on the Israeli Screen" focuses on the Egyptian enemy of the Six Day War in June 1967 against the background of the tradition of the Jewish (Israeli) society to define their own identity in opposition to the Arab 'Other.' Accordingly, Talmon's analysis of the films emphasizes the oblique expression of Israeli anxieties, desires and identitary concerns that emerge from their depiction of the Arab enemy. Dating from three different points in Israel's political and cultural history, these films deal with the enemy in a remarkably different manner. While *Ha-Matarah Tiran* (*The Sinai Commandos*), produced in the immediate aftermath of the war, conveys its nationalist agenda through a traditionally heroic style, *Avanti Popolo* adopts the perspective of the vanquished Egyptian soldiers, and *Bikur Ha-Tizmoret* (*The Band's Visit*) projects images of a final reconciliation with a former enemy with whom a peace treaty has since been concluded.

Stephen Harper's "Bosnia Beyond Good and Evil: (De)Constructing the Enemy in Western and Post-Yugoslav Films about the 1992–1995 War" deals with another notoriously conflict-ridden region. Critically discussing a representative selection of films about the war in Bosnia-Hercegovina, Harper shows how the historical, political and cultural complexities of this "massively over-determined event" have mostly been simplified and portrayed one-sidedly in film fictions. Indeed, as Harper emphasizes, "in both the East and the West the cinema of the Bosnian war [...] is heavily compromised by nationalism and racism and is strongly invested in the creation of enemy Others." Western mainstream films, for instance by Michael Winterbottom and Angelina Jolie, while taking a humanitarian and liberal stance, reinforce images of the enemy Other by rendering a dichotomy between Serb villainy and Muslim innocence. On the other hand, there is the determinedly pro-Serbian political and nationalist bias of Emir Kusturica. Obviously, such stereotyping is aggravated in action melodrama, but even a film like Bosnian Muslim Danis Tanović's, *Ničija zemlja* (*No Man's Land*), hailed as an impartial accusation of the war as such, does not entirely escape nationalist framings.

Prison drama as an important type of 9/11 cinema stands in the centre of Marek Paryż's "Forbidden Bonding at the Time of the War on Terror: The Enemy as Friend in *Camp X-Ray* and *Boys of Abu Ghraib*." Both films deal with growing friendships between a guard (female in the case of *Camp X-Ray*) and the enemy in the shape of a detainee at Guantanamo and Abu Ghraib respectively. In both cases, the friendships begin with feelings of guilt on the side of the guard, and are fraught with anxiety. However, they develop differently as in the first instance, the detainee's guilt remains uncertain, while in the second the friendship is based on deception on the side of the prisoner. The figure of the enemy thus remains fluctuating in these films, with *Boys of Abu Ghraib* also dealing directly with mistreatment and torture.

The concluding two chapters of this volume deal with aspects of the Pacific War 1941–1945. Martin Löschnigg's "Canadians and the Pacific War 1941–1945 in Anne Wheeler's *A War Story* and *The War Between Us*" discusses two films by the Canadian director, one a documentary on her father's ordeal in a Japanese POW camp, the other a feature film on the displacement of Japanese Canadians during the war. In the documentary, the Japanese enemy are not individualized, yet the film, like other films and books on the subject, stresses the importance of dealing with trauma by overcoming personal hatred. This is also played out in *The War Between Us*, which exposes the xenophobic hatred directed against an internal 'enemy that never was.' The film thus represents one of many recent attempts in Canadian arts to expiate a troubled history of racially motivated discrimination in a country whose present (self-)image is that of a model multicultural nation. Conversely, Jonathan Rayner deals with Japanese perspectives on the war ("Lost Pasts and Unseen Enemies: The Pacific War in Recent Japanese Film"). He shows how contested interpretations of the Pacific War in Japan have shaped the contents and perspectives of Japanese films on that war up to the present. In particular, Rayner deals with two films on the Kamikaze tactics adopted by the Japanese in 1945, when defeat was approaching: *Ore wa, kimi no tame ni koso shini ni iku* (*For Those We Love*, a.k.a. *Assault on the Pacific: Kamikaze*), and *Eien no O* (*The Eternal Zero*, a.k.a. *The Fighter Pilot*). Both films, he argues, are informed by a national pride and a potentially revisionist tendency to celebrate the sacrifice made by the pilots that appeals to the patriotic among Japanese audiences. The American enemy in these films largely remains faceless, reduced to distant aircraft or ships. As Rayner goes on to discuss, this creates significant ambiguities as wartime enemies have become post-war allies and trading partners.

Is it better to remember or to forget conflicts of the past? When interviewing survivors of the Rwandan genocide, Susanne Buckley-Zistel met with the view that "we should stop memorial sites because they are nonsense, they generate trauma and hate" (2006: 138). There is always the danger that films may enhance rather than decrease nationalistic sentiments, reignite rather than alleviate past antagonisms or – even – create new tensions in the present. One may cite here the example of the controversies sparked by the release of Wojciech Smarzowski's *Wołyń* (*Volhynia*), a war drama about the massacres of Polish civilians by the Ukrainian Insurgent Army (UPA) in 1943, and the following Polish reprisals on Ukrainian citizens. Some Polish and Ukrainian reviewers saw this film as a problematic 'resurrection' of an ethnic conflict in a time when Ukraine remains in a state of quasi-war with the Russian Federation – and, symptomatically, the first showing of the film in Kiev was called off under the pressure of the Ukrainian Foreign Ministry. Not all films arouse such heated debates, of course, yet the manner in which the enemy is depicted in national cinematographies bespeaks far more about present identities and international relations than it does about history. Films are part and parcel of "the global nature of mass communications," allowing "people [to] learn how other groups have confronted their troubled pasts" (Branscombe 2004: 328). Most importantly, however, the perspective of the 'Other' as rendered by national cinema is an incentive to also critically evaluating one's own.

Works Cited

Altman, Rick (2004) *Film/Genre* (London: BFI Publishing).
Assmann, Jan (2011) From "Collective Memory and Cultural Identity," in *The Collective Memory Reader*, eds. Jeffrey K. Olick, Vered Vinitzky-Serousssi, and Daniel Levy (Oxford: Oxford University Press), 212–215.
Branscombe, Nyla R., and Bertjan Doosje (2004) "Preface," in *Collective Guilt: International Perspectives*, ed. Nyla R. Branscombe and Bertjan Doosje (Cambridge: Cambridge University Press), ix–x.
Branscombe, Nyla R., and Bertjan Doosje (2004) "International Perspectives on the Experience of Collective Guilt," in *Collective Guilt*, ed. Branscombe and Doosje, 3–15.
Branscombe, Nyla R. (2004) "A Social Psychological Process Perspective on Collective Guilt," in *Collective Guilt*, ed. Branscombe and Doosje, 320–334.
Buckley-Zistel, Susanne (2006) "Remembering to Forget: Chosen Amnesia as a Strategy for Local Coexistence in Post-Genocide Rwanda," *Africa: Journal of the International African Institute* 76, 2, 131–150.
Calloway-Thomas, Carolyn (2010) *Empathy in the Global World* (Los Angeles, London, New Delhi, Singapore, Washington DC: SAGE).
Femenia, Nora (1996) *National Identity in Times of Crisis: The Scripts of the Falklands/Malvinas War* (New York: Nova Science Publishers).
Gillis, John R. "Introduction," in *Commemorations: The Politics of National Identity*, ed. John R. Gillis (Princeton: Princeton University Press), 3–24.

Girard, Rene (2013 [1988]) *Violence and the Sacred*, trans. Patrick Gregory (London, New Delhi, New York, Sydney: Bloomsbury).

Hughes-Warrington, Marnie (2009) "Introduction: History on Film: Theory, Production, Reception," in *The History on Film Reader*, ed. Marnie Hughes-Warrington (London and New York: Routledge), 1–12.

Kahana, Jonathan (2016) "Editor's General Introduction," in *The Documentary Film Reader: History, Theory, Criticism*, ed. Jonathan Kahana (Oxford and New York: Oxford University Press), 1–9.

Landsberg, Alison (2004) *Prosthetic Memory: The Transformation of American Remembrance in the Age of Mass Culture* (New York and Chichester, West Sussex: Columbia University Press).

Lewis, Helen B. (1971) *Shame and Guilt in Neurosis* (New York: International Universities Press).

Luostarinen, Heikki (1989) "Finnish Russophobia: The Story of an Enemy Image," in *Journal of Peace Research* 26. 2, 123–137.

Merskin, Debra (2004) "The Construction of Arabs as Enemies: Post-September 11 Discourse of George W. Bush," *Mass Communication and Society* 7. 2, 157–175.

Novick, Peter (1999) *The Holocaust in American Life* (Boston: Houghton Mifflin).

Rau, Petra (2013) *Our Nazis: Representations of Fascism in Contemporary Literature and Film* (Edinburgh: Edinburgh University Press).

Rosenfeld, Gavriel D. (2005) *The World Hitler Never Made* (Cambridge: Cambridge University Press).

Rosenstone, Robert (1995) *Visions of the Past: The Challenge of Film to Our Idea of History* (Cambridge, MA, and London: Harvard University Press).

Schlesinger, Philip (2000) "The Sociological Scope of 'National Cinema,'" in *Cinema and the Nation*, ed. Mette Hjort and Scott MacKenzie (London and New York: Routledge), 19–31.

PART I: **The 'Faces' of the Enemy: Film Aesthetics and Contemporary (Geo)Politics**

Gunnar Iversen
New Enemies, New Cold Wars: Reimagining Occupation and Military Conflict in Norway

On 5 October 2015, the Norwegian TV series *Okkupert* (*Occupied*) premiered. The series is a political thriller set in a near future. Oil production is low in the Middle East, and the United States has withdrawn from NATO after having achieved energy independence. In Norway, after a devastating natural disaster, the Green Party wins the election, and Norway decides to cut off all fossil fuel production. In desperation, the EU calls on Russia to initiate a velvet glove invasion of Norway, forcing the Norwegian government to resume oil and gas production. *Okkupert* depicts how the government as well as a number of ordinary people react to the Russian occupation and the growing presence of Russian secret agents and soldiers in Norway.

The series was based on an idea by popular Norwegian crime novelist Jo Nesbø, who also wrote an outline for the first episodes. The ten episodes in the first season were directed by well-known Norwegian film directors: Erik Skjoldbjærg, Pål Sletaune, John Andreas Andersen, Eva Sørhaug and Erik Richter Strand. *Okkupert* is the most expensive Norwegian TV drama production to date, and it has been sold to numerous European countries. It is also available on Netflix in North America. Internationally, *Okkupert* is the best-known Norwegian TV series besides *Lilyhammer* (2012–2014), a mild social critique of both Norway and the US in the form of a crime comedy. The series has been categorized as an example of a special "high-end drama" and "event television" (Engelstad 2016). It was not only given a prominent spot in the prime time schedule of the public service broadcaster TV2 in Norway, but also worked to build competitive brand identity for the broadcaster through production values and controversial themes.

A big success in Norway, despite lukewarm reviews in the major newspapers, *Okkupert* immediately attracted international attention and protest, especially from Russia. The Russian ambassador to Norway, Vyacheslav Pavlovsky, wrote a statement immediately after the first episode was broadcast, protesting against the depiction of a Russian occupation: "It is certainly a shame that, in the year of the 70th anniversary of the victory in World War II, the authors have seemingly forgotten the Soviet Army's heroic contribution to the liberation of northern Norway from Nazi occupation and decided, in the worst traditions of the Cold War, to scare Norwegian spectators with the nonexistent threat from the east" (Tjernshaugen 2015; qtd in Engelstad 2016). In his statement, the Russian ambassador

https://doi.org/10.1515/9783110591217-002

links the series not only to the Cold War but also to World War II, and these two historical periods form the backdrop for the events in the series. The international controversy did not change the popularity of the series in Norway, and a second season was broadcast in the autumn of 2017.[1]

This chapter analyzes the representation of occupation, resistance, political pressure, and the moral dilemmas of politicians and ordinary people in *Okkupert*. It compares the new political thriller with the way Norwegian films from 1946 to 2016 have depicted the five-year German occupation as well as the Cold War. The chapter will also briefly discuss the new series in the light of the representation of the Cold War in Norwegian film culture more broadly. It argues that the representation of the Russian occupation of Norway in *Okkupert* is a reimagining of the German occupation during World War II, while at the same time Cold War images are used in a complex way to depict the new enemy. The series also comes after the Russian takeover of the Crimea, and although the series does not seem to suggest any deliberate warning about new Russian aggression, this is an important context for the viewers. Past and future merge with the present, as this new enemy is seen through the representations of older enemies, also reimagining new political and legal concerns like the questions of justified terrorism and the threat of fanaticism.

1 *Okkupert*

The first episode of the series *Okkupert* starts with a close-up of a shaken prime minister of Norway, Jesper Berg, played by Henrik Mestad, who walks along a path in the woods, following a trail of blood in the snow. After a very brief introduction to some of the central characters in the series, the events that have led to the prime minister being on the path in the woods are shown.

After the public announcement of the end of the age of oil and other fossil fuels in Norway, and the opening of a first new power plant driven by Thorium, a new and sustainable climate-friendly energy source, the Norwegian prime minister is kidnapped by unknown men. He is taken by helicopter to an isolated area in a forest, where he receives video calls from the EU commissioner and the Swedish prime minister. They tell him that the Russian government has agreed to help the EU in making sure that Norway restarts oil and gas production. At the same time, Russian military forces take control over oil and gas installations in the North Sea. The prime minister does not want to cooperate until an old man

---

[1] During the printing of the present volume (the editors).

with a dog appears on the snowy path close to the spot where the helicopter has landed. He leans out of the window and shouts to the man for help, but the armed Russians immediately shoot the old man. The witnessing of the cold-blooded killing of an innocent bystander convinces the prime minister that military resistance is useless. Returning to the capital Oslo and a government meeting, he avoids an armed conflict and issues a second public announcement, acknowledging the presence of Russians in the country but toning down the invasion of the Russian troops. "We are completely alone," he says to his fellow cabinet members, and this forces the Norwegian government to sit still while the country is slowly being taken over by Russian military forces.

The first episode of *Okkupert* sets the tone for the whole series. An invasion takes place, but in the beginning few notice anything. The only immediate result is the fact that the prime minister and government change their policy, from turning off all oil and gas production to turning it back on again because of the desperate need for fossil fuel energy in the EU countries. In addition, the number of Russians in Norway increases.

In the first season of the series, the invasion is rendered either through events involving the prime minister and his cabinet, or a small number of ordinary citizens: a restaurant owner who is about to go bankrupt and lose her restaurant, her husband, who is a journalist with a small newspaper, one of the Secret Service men that guard the prime minister, and the leader of the Secret Service, a middle-aged woman suffering from an incurable disease. These protagonists all react to the invasion in different ways. However, as the presence of the Russian military becomes more and more visible, and the pressures on ordinary people as well as the elected government become more tangible, the theme of resistance becomes increasingly important. Early on, a lone soldier acts, and the King's Guard protest, while a small number of soldiers and citizens form a resistance movement. People from the army and the police slowly start helping out what at first is a small group of young men.

Half way through *Okkupert*, the theme of resistance becomes the main motif. The Norwegian police try to hunt down these resistance fighters in order to avoid a direct military conflict between Norway and Russia, but the Russian intelligence and military forces are also looking for the small group, whose numbers grow steadily. However, the first season of the series comes to a dramatic ending when some of the most fanatic resistance fighters kidnap the Russian ambassador Sidorova. The first season ends dramatically upon the hunt for the cell of fanatics that keep the Russian ambassador as hostage, threatening to kill her unless the Russians leave the country. If the Norwegian police and the Secret Service cannot find Sidorova in time, war will break out. However, a Secret Service man manages to locate the group on a ship and rescues the Russian ambassador, preventing an open military conflict on Norwegian soil. At the same time, in a dramatic cross cutting, the Norwegian Prime Minister is taken by a group of men and once more forced into a helicopter. This time, though, it is not an enemy group, but the resistance movement who are taking the Prime Minister to a safe area. In the very last scene of the season, the Prime Minister walks up to a waiting Norwegian general who says to him: "Are you ready to fight for your country?" The last image is a close-up of the Prime Minister, with a look of ambivalence on his face, surrounded by the bustle of military personnel and vehicles in the background.

2 Norwegian Occupation Drama

The most important context in which to situate *Okkupert* is Norwegian occupation drama. In many ways, this is the lens through which the future Russian occupation is seen. The series uses this Norwegian film genre, and the different motifs that run through its depiction and discussion of the 1940 to 1945 German occupation of Norway as a way of discussing current political concerns and anxieties. In this sense, occupation drama is the main background for the reimagining of military conflict and occupation in the TV series.

Between 1946 and 2016, nearly 30 occupation dramas were made in Norway, focusing on the collective struggle on the home front. In addition, a number of other fiction films have dealt more briefly with the war years and the war experience, and there have also been a number of feature-length as well as shorter documentaries about World War II. In particular, fictionalized versions have been important in interpreting the war and disseminating images about this pivotal period in modern Norwegian history. The Norwegian occupation drama genre includes highly symbolic stories of heroism, combat, resistance, ethnicity and identity, but also collaboration, lack of heroism, everyday life under the occupation, and specifically male and female experiences. The most famous occupation dramas have been staged in highly symbolic national landscapes, often the barren mountains, but also in everyday urban milieus (cf. Iversen 2011: 145–155, Iversen 2012, Haugland Sørensen 2015).

Even though there have been a number of war films made in Norway, the genre of the occupation drama has gone through significant changes. Its development can be divided into four distinct phases, each representing a different interpretation of the war years with a particular focus: on trauma (1946), on ordinary collective heroism (1948–1962), on revisionism and the critique of earlier heroic stories (1962–1993), and on extraordinary individual heroism (1993–2016). Although these categories are not all-inclusive, and there is a short transitional period in the late 1950s and early 1960s, very few films can be said to contradict the general trend of the period during which they were made (Iversen 2012: 239–240). The most recent phase focuses on extraordinary individual heroism, and some of the greatest Norwegian feature film successes in recent years belong to this category. Examples are *Max Manus* (*Max Manus: Man of War*) (dirs. Espen Sandberg and Joachim Rønning, 2008), about the real-life resistance fighter Max Manus, and *Kongens nei* (*The King's Choice*) (dir. Erik Poppe, 2016), about the choice of King Haakon VII not to surrender to the German occupation forces and go into exile in England.

Okkupert combines aspects of all four types of occupation drama. It deals with the trauma of occupation, when all boundaries are unclear, and also discusses different types of collaboration, a central aspect of the revisionist phase. However, the TV series also blends ordinary collective heroism with extraordinary individual heroism. The beginning of the series focuses on trauma, and it ends by focusing on single characters that act bravely and responsibly in the new traumatic situation. World War II is present in the series in the many allusions to the war years as well as the themes and motifs that the series takes from occupation drama but reimagines in the context of a vague future situation. The connections between the series and World War II events were also part of the public discussion in Norway after the premiere of the series. Historian Bård Larsen, of the liberal think-tank Civita, was one who made this direct connection in a comment in the newspaper *Dagbladet* on the day of the premiere: "The series scratches at our own history of war, carrying distinct references to the period of occupation during World War II, and how matters could have turned out, if we had chosen the Danish solution – that is, to accept a kind of cooperation with the forces of occupation, as the Danes did until 1943" (qtd. in Engelstad 2016). *Okkupert* as well as recent occupation dramas like *Max Manus* or *Kongens rei*, put an emphasis on the Norwegian resistance to the German occupation, both in the period just after the invasion in 1940 and during the war. The series and the films focus on heroic resistance in the small country against the big enemy, but in contrast to the films, *Okkupert* is also concerned with collaboration in different forms. In this way, the series touches upon a still not fully healed wound, the extent of the collaboration in Norway during World War II.

Okkupert also stages highly symbolic scenes in places that are linked either to World War II or the remembrance and commemoration of the war, especially Akershus castle in Oslo. In many ways, the TV series, like much science fiction, uses the premise "What if ..." to work through what could happen if Norway were once more occupied by foreign troops. In this way, events during the war as filtered through the fictional accounts of highly successful and popular occupation dramas, are the lens for the reimagining of occupation and resistance. The attempt to replace the past enemy, the Germans, with a new future enemy, the Russians, does not reflect a large actual fear of Russia in Norway, among ordinary citizens as well as the political leadership, and is more of a play on an alternate scenario.

3 The (Real) Moral and Political Dilemmas of (a Fictional) Occupation

When does cooperation become collaboration? When, if ever, is it necessary to go from passive opposition to active resistance? When and what type of violence is morally justifiable in a situation of occupation? These are three of the most important questions posed by the TV series. The main theme in *Okkupert* centers on the moral and political dilemmas represented by the lives and situations of the main characters. The dramatic nerve in the series are the tensions created not only by the different moral and political dilemmas embodied by the characters, but also between personal moral dilemmas and the larger political dilemmas.

Politics are personal in the TV series, and the moral dilemmas are primarily discussed through four of the main characters: the Prime Minister, Jesper Berg, the restaurant owner Bente Norum, her husband, the journalist Thomas Eriksen, and the Secret Service man Hans Martin Djupvik. In different ways, these characters try to negotiate the situations that arise when the Russian presence becomes more and more obvious, and the most interesting case is that of Bente Norum (Ane Dahl Torp). She owns a fancy restaurant in the center of Oslo, but at the start of the series she is about to face bankruptcy. All her employees leave because she can no longer pay their wages. The miracle that makes it possible for her to restart her restaurant and pay all her debts is the Russian presence in the city. Significantly, the first time she benefits from the occupation comes when some wealthy Russians hire the whole restaurant on the Norwegian Independence Day.

Instead of celebrating independence, she and her whole family, including her husband, who is a journalist, have to work in the kitchen or help out as waiters. Bente soon benefits from all the Russians who frequent her restaurant. Her moral dilemma is obvious: if she makes the Russians comfortable, she will save her restaurant, if not, she will lose her livelihood, and the family will face debt and hard times. In the beginning, she makes sure that the Russians will return to her restaurant to dine in peace. She thus becomes the equivalent of a World War

II "economic collaborator," a profiteer who benefitted economically from the German Occupation.

The question of economic collaboration has been an important part of Norwegian post-war history, and the neglect of economic collaborators during the years of reconciliation after the war has been discussed until recent years. The dilemma Bente faces captures these questions and forces the audience to think about how her moral dilemma has changed over time. When does she tip over from desperately using the Russian presence to save her restaurant to becoming more affluent because of her active accommodation of the occupants? And when does she become aware of her economic collaboration and start reacting to the occupation of her country?

The story of Bente's restaurant becomes particularly important in the series because the restaurant is situated just across the street from the headquarters of the Russian intelligence officers. The restaurant is rendered in warm tones of yellow and is usually filled with the 'warmth' of people eating and working quietly, while the Russian headquarters are in greyish blue, evoking large uninviting spaces. This is where the Russians direct their velvet glove occupation, illegally questioning Norwegian citizens, and where the Russian ambassador plays her game of power politics, forcing the Norwegian government to act against its policy and the wishes of the people.

"For me you are just a waiter," one of the wealthy Russians says to the journalist Thomas, when he helps his wife at the restaurant but also tries to get information about the activities of the Russians. This sums up the relationship between the Russians and the Norwegians. Even the Norwegian prime minister is often treated like a waiter by the Russian ambassador, Irina Sidorova, and Bente's relationship to the Russians goes through four stages. First, she is desperate and does not really think about what she is doing when she tailors her restaurant to their needs. Second, she becomes aware that her acts are seen as morally reprehensible by many around her, even her own husband and her step-son Petter, who experiences pressure from the other kids because his mother is too friendly with the Russians. Third, she becomes erotically involved with a Russian agent, when her relationship to her husband seems to disintegrate because of their different attitudes to the Russians. The final stage comes when she is convinced that Russians killed her journalist husband while he was investigating irregularities in the Russian workforce at the Norwegian oil installations. Although Bente's trajectory is from an innocent profiteer to a willing one and, finally, to becoming a 'good Norwegian' by getting information from her Russian lover that makes it possible for the Resistance to kidnap the Russian ambassador, the audience is forced to think about her dilemmas and the question of when her choices are right or wrong. Bente forces the spectators to think about the relationship between the personal and the political, and between collaboration, opposition and resistance.

Another protagonist that experiences a personal moral and political dilemma is the Secret Service agent Hans Martin Djupvik (Eldar Skar). Having saved the life of the Russian ambassador, he becomes a go-between, linking the Norwegian government and Secret Service to the Russian intelligence officers and occupation forces. "It has been a good day," he says at the very end of episode two, when he recounts his experiences. In particular, the praise and special treatment he receives from the Russians create a personal moral dilemma for him. For whom is he really working? Whose interests does he really represent? Both sides see him as another 'waiter,' a pawn in the great game, but praise from the Russians makes him more favorable to the occupation forces.

Djupvik's situation makes it possible for the Norwegian Secret Service to get more information from the Russians, since they trust him more than anybody else, even if it is never really clear what his motives are. Although he becomes a double agent, working undercover as a friendly Norwegian in order to get information from the Russians, he is more favorable to the Russians than most other Norwegians, and his Secret Service leader does not really trust him. To others he says that his main motive is to prevent an open conflict and war, but this stands in contrast to how gratified he is by praise from the ambassador and other Russians on numerous occasions.

The only central character that from the very start opposes the occupation and also uses the word 'occupation' when the Prime Minister and others try to cloud the issue by using words like 'assistance' and 'helping,' is the journalist Thomas Eriksen (Vegard Hoel). Ironically, he also initially benefits from the occupation. He represents a small independent newspaper struggling to keep its readers, but Thomas' articles and his fierce stand against the Norwegian Prime Minister as well as the Russians result in rising circulation numbers. As a consequence, his editor in chief starts treating him differently. However, Thomas quits his job when he realizes that the editor wants him to stop being too critical because of political pressure, and he is killed by the Russians when he illegally crosses the Russian border in order to disclose how the Russians are using criminals as workers on the Norwegian oil installations.

The situation of Prime Minster Berg is also personal as well as political. On the one hand, his new policy aims at preventing war and bloodshed; on the other hand, he is forced not only to implement a different policy than the one he promised voters when he was elected. Just quitting, however, would seriously jeopardize the country and result in open military conflict. He tries to oppose the Russians but always ends up not only compromising but also defending the opposite of what he wants to do. Instead of saving the world from environmental disaster he is forced to compromise in order to prevent war. Obviously, his position is far from the situation of the fascist collaborator Vidkun Quisling, who led a puppet government in Norway during World War II, but there are still many connections between the two that the series plays upon in the first part of the season. In a different context, Jesper could be seen as illustrating how during the Cold War the Norwegian government provided a tool for the Americans for establishing illicit listening posts and military installations, and helping US surveillance by allowing U2 airplanes to land at Bodø, in the north of Norway, after flying over Soviet Union territory.

Jesper Berg also faces problems in his own cabinet and on the home front. His wife is pregnant and wants to leave the country and fly to safety, but Jesper initially succeeds in making her stay and give birth to their child in Norway. He also succeeds in keeping the government together, even though they are actively implementing a policy that is hostile to the environment and their political platform.

Through these four protagonists, a number of important issues and questions is expressed. *Okkupert* points out the impossibility of staying neutral in an occupied country, yet at the same time it compares personal dilemmas to political dilemmas. The protagonists are continually put in positions that make decisions problematic and will usually result in different forms of deceit or misinformation. The personalization of political and ethical dilemmas is highly effective because it refers back to World War II. Even if the film is a fiction, and a fiction that takes place in the future, the dilemmas the main protagonists face are the same as those faced by politicians and ordinary people during the German occupation. The very connection to a concrete past makes the blurring of enemies and heroes a central theme in the series.

4 Justified Terrorism?

The second episode of *Okkupert* starts with a failed attack on the Russian ambassador in Norway. Against the will of the Norwegian Prime Minister and the military, she attends a military ceremony at the old castle of Akershus in Oslo on the morning of 17 May, Norway's independence day. A young soldier tries to shoot her, but she is saved by Hans Martin Djupvik. The Russian ambassador sees this as a violation of the agreement that Norwegian police should protect Russians in Norway, and the Russians tighten their control over the state apparatus as well as Norwegian territory.

Two important aspects of the first period of the Russian occupation of Norway in *Okkupert* are the use of an Orwellian "newspeak" to redefine power relations and violence in a totalitarian state, and the attempt to reformulate armed resistance as the work of extremists beyond moral and legal boundaries. Most of the Russians in Norway are obviously from the very start of the series either soldiers or members of the Secret Service. However, they are just called "The Russian Energy Administration." The occupation and the role of the Russians are also most often defined by the Russians as well as the Norwegian political elite as either "peace" or just "assistance." In this way, the series problematizes the question of when a takeover can be called an occupation. Throughout the series, life seems nearly to go on as before, and the EU calls the Russian presence a way of kindly "assisting" Norway to reach an agreed goal.

The use of language and words as disinformation is an important theme in the series, and links the linguistic motif with the question of who has the power to define concepts and interpret reality. When does a takeover become an occupation or a situation of war? This is an obvious concern in the series, and the different characters give different answers through their actions. Some see the Russian presence as an occupation from the very beginning, while others come to the same conclusion only much later. The word used for the first Norwegian resistance by the Russians is "extremists." In a central scene in the second episode, the Russian ambassador tries to downplay the effect and role of the first lone assassin by calling him such. To Djupvik, who is allowed to question the soldier, she says: "Extremists exist in all countries, but we can't allow them to decide our behavior."

In episode three of the series, the question of extremism and of justified terrorism is highlighted through the story of a political refugee from Chechnya and his young son. The Chechnyan accidentally kills a Russian in a hit-and-run accident while driving his son home from an Independence Day party. While the Norwegian court sentences him to a short term in prison, and initially protects him from the Russians, who want him extradited, the Russians force the legal system to adapt to the new situation. Against Norwegian law he is about to be extradited, and this leads him to commit suicide in his cell. This becomes important in the later episodes, as it results in the radicalization of his young son Iljas.

By adding the side-plot of Iljas' radicalization, the Chechnyan opposition and resistance are used as a way of problematizing extremism and justified terrorism. Iljas is an ordinary young man, and it is the ill treatment and death of his father that turn him into an 'extremist' and resistance fighter. Together with the young soldier who tried to assassinate the Russian ambassador, Iljas becomes the main face of the young resistance. In this way, *Okkupert* links the Norwegian resistance movement in World War II to the opposition and resistance in Chechnya. This is intimated frequently throughout *Okkupert*, comparing Norway to former Soviet Union republics that are now either threatened or occupied by Russia.

As the resistance to the new occupation grows, the series focuses more and more on the effects of a small resistance movement as well as on two different forms of active resistance. At the very end of the series, the small cell that Iljas belongs to is officially incorporated into a larger resistance movement sanctioned by the Norwegian military. Through the World War II history of resistance fighters, in Norway often just lovingly called "the boys of the forest," contemporary themes of radicalization and terrorism are reformulated in an interesting but increasingly problematic way.

From the beginning, the actions of the resistance movement harm innocent bystanders, as for instance when a bomb placed in a Secret Service car nearly kills an innocent young boy, yet by the end of the series another context is introduced. Iljas and others kidnap the Russian ambassador Sidorova and threaten to kill her. They send out the message live and signal their will to use violence by executing one of her captured bodyguards. In this part of *Okkupert*, episodes nine and ten, the resistance is seen as using a number of methods or symbolic acts that today are associated more strongly with Al-Qaeda than with resistance fighters in Chechnya or from World War II. Disturbingly, the bodyguard is executed by a small group of masked men while the Norwegian national anthem is playing in the background, thus linking the resistance to nationalism – and maybe also terrorism.

In this way, *Okkupert* uses not only World War II and the generally positive attitude towards the role of resistance fighters during the German occupation, but also nationalism and national symbols like the national anthem and the Norwegian flag to ask questions about justifiable terrorism and violence as well as nationalist pathos. The series does not give any answers, but just like the discussion of personal, moral and political dilemmas it poses a number of questions that the spectators need to resolve by themselves. The past is used to question the present and the future, and the present casts a special light on the events of the past, and on the remembrance and commemoration of World War II in contemporary Norway.

5 The Role of the EU and the US

In *Okkupert*, the EU plays a major role, one which has shifted from that of an ally to that of an enemy. The US plays a minor role, not an enemy but not an ally either. Rather, it tries not to take part in the conflict. In this way, *Okkupert* imagines a very different situation in the near future than today, a situation when allies are enemies, and friends behave indifferently or even in a hostile manner.

The political as well as the moral landscape are redrawn in order to imagine a future different from the past and the now.

As a political scenario set in the near future, the series is an experiment in thought, asking "What if?" in order to serve as a mirror for contemporary society. This kind of speculative fiction usually functions as a way of enlarging contemporary issues and questions, the future being a pretext for describing and questioning the present (cf. Parrinder 1980, Roberts 2000). "What sort of enemies and allies does Norway *really* have?" is another question the series asks its viewers to reflect upon. Do the real enemies come from without or from within the nation?

Even though the Russians are the invaders in *Okkupert*, the EU is just as much of an enemy. After all, it is they who have asked Russia to 'assist' Norway in resuming oil and gas production and export and have thereby created the political scenario presented in the series. Even though there are some sequences towards the end where it seems obvious that Russia has started overacting, or acting on its own accord, the EU is in fact the main enemy. The contemporary situation of Norway not being a member of the EU but at the same time being economically dependent on the European market is thus turned on its head: the EU, a friend and ally, becomes an aggressor and an enemy.

The role of the US is very interesting in *Okkupert*, too. The premise of the TV series is that in the future the US is no longer a member of NATO and has stopped playing the role of 'world police.' In episodes eight and nine, the Norwegian Prime Minister seeks refuge from the open Russian aggression and threat, after yet another attack on him, and stays for a period with the American ambassador. However, instead of treating him well and giving him a safe haven, the American ambassador rids himself of this burden by slipping liquid nicotine into the Prime Minister's coffee, so that he has to be taken from the safety of the embassy to a Norwegian hospital.

"The US is always happy to help a friend," the American ambassador says. However, when the Norwegian Prime Minister tries to force the US to choose sides in the conflict and help Norway by flying illegal Russians to the Arctic island of Svalbard, the US just gets rid of the Norwegian 'problem' in order to stay out of the conflict. This is done in yet another highly symbolic context, Christmas. While a crooner on the radio sings a happy Christmas song, the Norwegian Prime Minister is poisoned. Another former ally turns out to be an enemy.

By framing the Russian occupation (and possible annexation) of Norway in the manner of the Russian aggression in Ukraine, and by reversing traditional enemies and allies, *Okkupert* not only uses the past (in particular World War II) as a model for understanding and questioning the present, but also deliberately invokes the Cold War situation in Norway, yet without the country's allies in NATO or the US. The reaction of the Russian ambassador to Norway after the premiere is one example of how the Cold War has also become a prism through which contemporary anxieties and discussions may be viewed.

6 Cold War Enemies: The Soviet Union and Russia

Even though World War II is the most important frame for imagining a future occupation in *Okkupert*, the Cold War is also a significant backdrop. The promotion of the series by the production company and the broadcaster included the question: "How will society respond to a Russian occupation?" with a promotional poster that shows the Russian flag atop the Norwegian Royal Castle. The anxieties of the Cold War are thus combined with iconic images of the Norwegian Parliament covered in Nazi slogans during World War II, or with a Nazi flag for the production of the occupation drama *Max Manus* in 2009.

As Norwegian film scholar Audun Engelstad has pointed out, *Okkupert* could also be seen as a conspiracy thriller in which the international community takes the part of the conspirators, and Norway is a country all alone (cf. Engelstad 2016). *Okkupert* shares with the conspiracy thriller an atmosphere of paranoia and blurred boundaries, where it is hard to define enemies and allies, and ordinary people are caught up in larger political plots. In Norway, as in the US, the conspiracy thriller is usually linked to the situation and geopolitics of the Cold War (cf. Cook 2000: 197). One of the most significant and popular films in modern Norwegian film history, *Orions belte* (*Orion's Belt*) (dir. Ola Solum, 1985) takes place on the Svalbard archipelago, and in this film American and Norwegian Secret Service agents get rid of a troublesome witness in order not to upset the Soviet Union. Even though the US is supposed to guarantee the safety of Norwegians, in this film the US becomes just as much an enemy as an ally.

The problematic role of the US during the Cold War years is also an important theme in films by director Knut Erik Jensen. In the spy thrillers *Brent av frost* (*Burnt by Frost*) (1997) and *Iskyss* (*Kiss of Ice*) (2008), Jensen reimagines Norway's participation in the Cold War. However, few films in Norway have tackled Norway's role as an interstitial state between West and East during the Cold War. Throughout this period, the US was Norway's ally, and the political establishment in Norway was extremely anti-communist. Norway took a substantial part in the Western intelligence effort against the Soviet Union due to its geographical location and close military ties to Britain and the US. As Norwegian historian Olav Njølstad has pointed out, Norwegian authorities in this period "were always concerned that the visible presence of Allied military forces in Norway would trigger hostile reactions from Moscow, increase East-West tensions in the region, and deepen the split within the Norwegian population between those who favored and those who were critical of Norway's membership of NATO" (Njølstad 2006: 654).

Okkupert depicts a well-known Cold War scenario, namely that of Russia invading and annexing Norway, but this time without the US as an ally. The series also plays on contemporary concerns that figure as frequent news items on Norwegian television and in the press, concerns about territorial disputes in the Arctic, violations of Norwegian air space by Russian military airplanes, naval maneuvers close to or on the Norwegian border, as well as the discussions to solve the lack of delineation of the maritime border between Russia and Norway in the South-Eastern Barents Sea and the Arctic Ocean. Although the historical situation of the Cold War and the international political situation of *Okkupert* are very different, many of the scenes in *Okkupert* link the future to the Cold War past. The many secret activities, the blurring of the boundaries between legal and illegal surveillance, the lack of freedom for the press or ordinary people, and the role of Norway as a pawn in the game of the superpowers, bring to mind the Cold War period. The TV series reimagines both World War II and the Cold War in order to work through the thought-experiment of "what if" that links the present to the past and the future.

7 New Enemies, New Cold Wars

Both directly and indirectly, *Okkupert* addresses pressing contemporary conundrums and anxieties in Norway about environmental crisis and disaster, political pressure and loss of sovereignty, national identity, and extremism and terrorism. Even though the series takes place in the future, the past is a more important background for the interpretation of its actions and events. *Okkupert* uses World War II as the main prism for reimagining occupation and the loss of sovereignty, the moral dilemmas of ordinary people as well as the political elite, and resistance, justifiable terrorism and violence. The TV series combines elements from Norwegian occupation drama with highly symbolic places and events associated with World War II. At the same time, the film uses elements from Cold War political thrillers and real-life anxieties and scenarios from that period. World War II and the Cold War become tools for a reimagining of contemporary anxieties.

Okkupert is highly effective exactly because it does not give answers, using ambiguity in order to force viewers to ask questions instead. The moral and political dilemmas of ordinary people caught up in large-scale political confrontations and conflicts are foregrounded, pointing out that the personal is also political. The TV series not only offers a different perspective on allies and enemies but also to a certain degree erases the historicity of past events by restaging the *then* in the *now* and the *future*. However, the very end of the series opens up new concerns, when the occupation seems to unite the national community in opposition and resistance to an external enemy. *Okkupert* became a big success in Norway as well as internationally. Its concerns and questions may be posed upon the example of a small country such as Norway, but the series speaks to larger audiences through the discussions of justified terrorism, and the use of violence and extremism in general. Norway becomes a prism for looking at larger international concerns, new images of new enemies, and new Cold Wars.

Works Cited

Bastiansen, Henrik G. (2014) "Norwegian Media and the Cold War 1945–1991," *Nordicom Review* 35, 155–169.
Cook, David A. (2000) *Lost Illusions: American Cinema in the Shadow of Watergate and Vietnam 1970–1979* (Berkeley: University of California Press).
Engelstad, Audun (2016) "Sensation in a Serial Form: High-End Television Drama and Trigger Plots," *Kosmorama* 263. <www.kosmorama.org> (accessed March 2, 2017).
Haugland Sørensen, Tonje (2015) *The Second World War in Norwegian Film: The Topography of Remembrance* (Bergen: Universitetet i Bergen).
Iversen, Gunnar (2011) *Norsk Filmhistorie – Spillefilmen 1911–2011* (Oslo: Universitetsforlaget).
Iversen, Gunnar (2012) "From Trauma to Heroism: Cultural Memory and Remembrance in Norwegian Occupation Dramas, 1946–2009," *Journal of Scandinavian Cinema* 2, 3, 237–248.
Njølstad, Olav (2009) "Atomic Intelligence in Norway during the Cold War," *The Journal of Strategic Studies* 29, 4, 653–673.
Orwell, George (1979 [1949]) *Nineteen Eighty-Four* (London: Penguin).
Parrinder, Patrick (1980) *Science Fiction: Its Criticism and Teaching* (London: Methuen).
Roberts, Adam (2000) *Science Fiction* (London and New York: Routledge).
Tjernshaugen, Karen (2015) "Russland fordømmer ny norsk TV-serie," *Aftenposten*, August 8.

Filmography

Brent av frost (*Burnt by Frost*) (1997) Dir. Knut Erik Jensen (Barentsfilm AS).
Iskyss (*Kiss of Ice*) (2008) Dir. Knut Erik Jensen (Baltic Film Group).
Kongens nei (*The King's Choice*) (2016) Dir. Erik Poppe (Paradox).
Lilyhammer (2012–2014) Created by Eilif Skodvin, Anne Bjørnstad (Rubicon TV AS).

Max Manus (*Max Manus: Man of War*) (2008) Dir. Espen Sandberg and Joachim Rønning (B&T Film).
Okkupert (*Occupied*) (2015–2017) Created by Karianne Lund, Erik Skjoldbjærg, and Jo Nesbø (TV2 Norge).
Orions belte (*Orion's Belt*) (1985) Dir. Ola Solum (Filmeffekt AS).

Angela Brintlinger
'A Murky Business': The Post-Soviet Enemy

During the Cold War, the Soviet Union was engaged in battles with foreign powers on diplomatic, economic, cultural and political fronts, and even during athletic engagements (see Guttmann 1988 and Riordan 1988). So it was no surprise when the opening ceremony of the 2014 Winter Olympics in Sochi featured the cultural, scientific and intellectual achievements of the Russian and Soviet past. After all, opening ceremonies of the Olympic Games are a great opportunity for hosting countries to lay out their identities and make their claims on the world stage. The Brits gently lampooned their Queen, their fiction, and their secret services by having Her Majesty leap out of a helicopter with James Bond during the 2012 London Summer Games opening ceremony; the Russians showed no such sign of self-deprecating humor.

What did impress in the Sochi opening ceremony was the Cyrillic alphabet, which the organizers used to create an *azbuka*, an alphabet book, celebrating achievements of the Russians and/or Soviets. Perhaps the most extraordinary and cryptic choice for foreign spectators was the representative of the letter Ё (pronounced YO) – the shy and sweet hedgehog from Iurii Norshtein's ten-minute 1975 animated film *Ëzhik v tumane* (*Hedgehog in the Fog*) (fig. 1).

Why a hedgehog, some viewers of the opening ceremony asked themselves? In fact, the tradition of animated film in Russia hearkens back to this classic short, and as we shall see below, the hedgehog continues to play a part in contemporary Russian film. But in the context of the other letters of the alphabet – representing Russian writers, composers, scientists, engineers and military leaders – the hedgehog looked positively, well, cute.

In Norshtein's film the hedgehog is perpetually caught in a dense fog, a fog that makes him timid and careful, that immerses him in a murky atmosphere and gives him only glimpses of his surroundings and the other creatures therein. Though the Olympic organizers surely did not realize it, this condition turns out to be a metaphor for contemporary Russian and post-Soviet political and cinematographic life. In this chapter I argue that the complexities of portraying the relationship of Russian and post-Soviet citizens with the outside world and with each other in this current era of nationalism and isolation emerge precisely through the representation of fog in films of various genres by three recent filmmakers working in post-Soviet republics.

Kazakh director Ermek Tursunov uses fog as a main motif in his lyrical film *Shal* (*The Old Man*) (2012), in which the title Kazakh character interacts with Russian hunters on a winter safari in an SUV. The fog also serves to pit the old man

Fig. 1: Hedgehog in Fog (Norshtein, *Ëzhik v tumane*)

against such intangible adversaries as time, cultural loss, and nature itself. Sergei Loznitsa's *V tumane* (*In the Fog*) (2012) reprises a story by Belarusian writer Vasil' Bykau of life during WWII to lay out the difficulties of loyalty, collaboration and survival for Belarusian peasants under German occupation and to imply that in a society where no one trusts anyone, everyone is a potential enemy. Finally, Georgii Gitis's animated film for children, *Prikliucheniia Alënushki i Erëmy* (*The Adventures of Alënushka and Erëma*) (2008) actually references *Ëzhik v tumane*, bringing the hedgehog character into an updated Russian fairytale that also features specific foreign enemies such as the evil German knight von Zwetter (whom the gentle hedgehog encounters and instinctively labels a "psycho").

All three filmmakers evoke fog in their representations of human relationships, suggesting that the enemy can emerge suddenly and without warning, usually from the outside but sometimes from within one's own community. Enemies can be foreign or native traitors. They can be natural predators or nature itself, and the paranoia spread by such a concept becomes even thicker and more incapacitating when complicated by fog. Both the meteorological and metaphorical conditions of fog are disorienting, confusing. Fog can increase a sense of isolation, close people off from each other, and even set them against themselves.¹ Whenever fog is evoked in these films, both viewers and protagonists struggle to identify the way forward. Perhaps in the post-Soviet world truth itself is a murky business.

Fog has a special role to play in Russian and Russian-influenced cinema, in great part thanks to the work of Soviet animator Norshtein. In his pictures, as film scholar Mikhail Iampol'skii has argued, the "delimitation of the world is realized slowly through the veil [of fog], [and] the world turns out to be a puzzle" (Iampol'skii 1990: 99).² Norshtein's plot is magnificent in its simplicity. As Iampol'skii summarizes it:

> A little hedgehog is going to meet up with a bear cub to count the stars together, but along the way he encounters fog, gets lost in it, runs into unfamiliar – or rather transformed-by-the-fog – objects and creatures, he falls into the river and almost drowns, but is brought to the shore by a fish and in the end finds the bear cub. [...] the whole story is the history of the hedgehog's immersion in the fog. His mishaps lack any trace of adventurism and represent a series of appearances and disappearances of a world that offers living and dead forms encased in whiteness. (1990: 102)

This idea that the world is transient and the creatures within can be transformed has relevance not just for Norshtein's hedgehog but for contemporary film generally. Perception – of nature, of culture, of the enemy within and without – in many cases is what drives film today.

By drawing on these three very different genres (nature drama, war film and animated feature film) from filmmakers of three different nationalities working within the Russian and post-Soviet film industry, the chapter will highlight stark, ambiguous, and parodic portrayals of the enemy and argue that simple binaries (us/them, native/foreign, nature/culture) do not apply in the murky ethical world of the twenty-first century, where the fog obscures everything: locations, operations, even intentions.

---

1 The phrase "fog of war" originated in the nineteenth century with the German expression *Nebel des Krieges* and designates the inability of combatants to make good decisions in conditions of war. See Errol Morris's 2003 documentary film about the war in Vietnam, *The Fog of War: Eleven Lessons from the Life of Robert S. McNamara*.
2 "Очертания мира медленно реализуются сквозь пелену, мир оказывается загадкой." Unless otherwise noted, all translations from the Russian are mine [AKB].

1 The Sheep are (Mostly) Dead, and the Wolves are (Mostly) Dead

> Man is not made for defeat. A man can
> be destroyed, but not defeated.
> Ernest Hemingway, *The Old Man and the Sea*

Iampol'skii's summary of *Ëzhik v tumane* resembles to an uncanny degree the journey undertaken in *Shal*, a film directed by Ermek Tursunov (b. 1961). Tursunov has in recent years risen to the top of Kazakh cinema. *Shal* was his third feature film and won "Best Film of the Year" in his native Kazakhstan as well as the grand prize at *Kinoshok*, a festival for cinema of the former republics of the Soviet Union. It was also nominated for the 2013 Oscar in the best foreign film category ("Vybor goda"; Stishova). In the film, the title character embarks upon his yearly expedition to take his sheep to their winter pasture and encounters complications when an unprecedented fog descends upon the steppe, obscuring the familiar landmarks. He struggles to find his way and has to spend two nights in makeshift shelters in the steppe. The journey includes circling aimlessly in search of his path, an episode with a river and a near-drowning, plenty of unfamiliar creatures and objects in the fog, some dream sequences where fog represents the atmosphere of transitioning from the real world to the world of the dead, and a final encounter with a mother wolf and her cub that seems to underline his own fierce love of family. There is an old Russian proverb about the need to compromise that is hard to translate into English. It would sound something like: "the sheep are safe and the wolves are sated."[3] But in contemporary Kazakhstan, proverbs cannot help navigate the clash of civilizations: traditional Kazakh culture, leftover Soviet habits (including the presence of alcohol and the absence of religion), and "new Russian" aspirational recreation all collide. This film chronicles Russian-Kazakh interactions, and it may be that the fog rolls in precisely in retribution for Russian violation of the Kazakh natural world.

Kazakh cinema is among the 'youngest' of traditions in post-Soviet space, with the republic's first film produced only in 1939, and it continues to be tied to Russian production and education systems even in post-Soviet times (Micciché 1992: 299, 300).[4] As Sylvie Dallet has written, through the 1980s non-Russian So-

---

[3] "И овцы целы и волки сыты."
[4] Tursunov, like many of his compatriots in the Kazakh film business and indeed in the cinematic world across the former Soviet Union, was educated at VGIK (The All-Russian State Institute of Cinematography in Moscow).

viet cinema had its own view of history, "usually limited to traditional and local philosophies" (1992: 303). Although Kazakh cinema has since grabbed the world's attention, one of Dallet's observations about Central Asian film is particularly appropriate for *Shal*. She writes: "Producers tend to stress the importance of children and elderly people, who in the collective imagination represent the virtues of innocence and wisdom" (1992: 310). This film, which is in part about generations, and about negotiating the cultural past and the unknown future, chronicles that closeness between its protagonists, grandfather Kasym and grandson Yeraly. Their bond survives generation gap problems, physical trials, and significant suffering, and they come to a place of true kinship by the last frames of the film.

In *Shal*, we find portrayed a hybrid society. The old man Kasym is a skilled herdsman and former head of a Soviet kolkhoz, who lives for his horse, his sheep, and his televised soccer matches, while young Yeraly sits still all day, eyes glued to the hand-held electronic device on which he plays hunting video games. Yeraly's mother, Kasym's daughter, keeps house for both of them. Time is rhythmic, with cyclical agricultural time in synch with nature, and 'outside' time represented by the weekly soccer transmissions religiously viewed by Kasym.[5] The old man's love of soccer leads him to name each of his sheep after a cherished player, and his odyssey to take the sheep to their winter pasture features a funny broadcaster-style monologue as he urges them along by name.

In the film, daily life is interrupted by two incursions of outsiders. When a Kazakh acquaintance shows up with a Jeep full of Russian hunters, local hospitality requires that Kasym point the way to the hunting grounds, though he warns them that now is not a good time, as the female wolves have just given birth. Similarly when Kasym's neighbor has relatives descend unexpectedly, he has to opt out of their joint trip to move their sheep; if he leaves on the eve of the guests' arrival he will seem a poor host, so instead he asks Kasym to move his sheep for him and offers to pick him up the next day in a car. Timing, one might suggest, is everything. The old man is old indeed, but tough as nails, and he heads out by himself with his horse (fig. 2).

---

[5] His interest in television is limited to these games; we watch in the first part of the film as he falls asleep during the seduction scene of the 1967 American coming of age film *The Graduate*, being rebroadcast with Russian voiceover. This is only one of the jokes inserted into the film as if for an American viewer. The other revolves around Kasym's choice for his grandson's education. Comparing the effort to study in the US to his ancestors' trips on foot to Mecca, he pronounces the name of his chosen institution of higher learning: Yale University. "In their language that means 'People's.'"

Fig. 2: Grandfather and Sheep in Fog (Tursunov's *Shal*)

Under normal circumstances, his expertise would have enabled him to safely deliver both small herds. But this year is different, and when the fog rolls in, Yeraly senses that his grandfather may be in trouble. The boy tries to get the neighbor to go on a rescue mission, but the neighbor, busy drinking toasts with his relatives, puts him off until morning.

Though the Russians are perceived as the primary enemy, who violate Kazakh natural space and rhythms and perhaps bring on the fog with their untimely hunting trip, their time on screen is fairly limited and the film presents several other possible enemies. A 'righteous' adversary is the steppe itself and its inhabitants, the wolves: one of the most powerful scenes in the film is the staring contest between Kasym and the mother wolf, who backs down after having seen him kill several other wolves with only an ax and his bare hands. Nature is a worthy opponent and both wolf and old man respect and admire each other despite their conflict. Yeraly disdains soccer and hard work around the ranch, preferring his electronic games, and through his youthful impatience the viewer gets a sense that the trappings of the contemporary world are a social 'enemy' portending the end of traditional Kazakh ways. However, that enemy is vanquished when Kasym goes missing and his grandson shows dogged persistence in pursuing him until he finds him half-dead in a ravine and is able to rescue him.

Kazakh commentator Al'mira Naurzbaeva believes that this film aims to subvert the traditional Western binary of nature/culture which posits "eternal enmity between wolf and man." Instead, she maintains, both man and wolf are children of nature which is not subject to categories of good and evil:

> The invasion of civilization, of people armed with super-contemporary attributes (a Jeep, rifles with telescopic sights) and who are deaf to the traditions of living according to the laws of nature is what destroys the harmony of life and leads to catastrophe. (Naurzbaeva, qtd. in Abikeeva 2012)

The film's protagonist, Kasym, is alone in the steppe through much of the film, and thus the plot is moved along both by his actions and his monologues and harangues. He converses with his sheep, with the wolves, with the Russian hunters whose dead bodies he happens upon, and with god. "Why are you doing this to me? After all, I never believed in you," he shouts at the sky. "I don't know any prayers – do they punish people for that?" This loss of religion and religious habits among the Kazakhs during the Soviet era is another of the themes of the film, but Kasym's relationship with the steppe and its inhabitants seems to be plenty sacred. "My god," he says to the Russians' Kazakh guide, "is the steppe." Later he notes, recognizing his own responsibility for the deaths of both wolves and Russian hunters: "I should never have shown you the way."

Kasym understands how things should be, and at one point states: "No. It's not that the wolves have gone crazy. The people have gone crazy." His endurance and will, and stubbornness, might remind viewers of Ernest Hemingway's old man, and his challenge to the mother wolf sounds like a Hemingway line: "You can kill me, wolf. But you will not beat me." Indeed, although not all reviewers saw the connection, Tursunov labeled the film "Hemingway Kazakh-style," evoking *The Old Man and the Sea*. "Everyone has read and knows Hemingway," he said. "Instead of the sea, I have the steppe. All the poetic elements remain, but they are thought through in a new way" (qtd. in Abikeeva).[6] Even though the old man's life is endangered by the weather, the environment, and the wolves, in this film the natural world is not a true enemy of man; it is simply the place in which he lives. When man honors the land, the rhythms of the steppe, and his ancestors, Tursunov argues through his protagonist, he is effectively worshipping god. Kasym is able to maintain an admirable equilibrium, one his grandson comes to understand and embrace. The virtues of innocence and wisdom – in Dallet's words a highlight of Central Asian film – come together to triumph over any and all enemies in this clash of civilizations.

---

6 "Хемингуэя все читали и знают. Просто у меня вместо моря степь. Все элементы поэтики остались, но переосмыслены по-другому."

2 Partisans and Patriots, Redux: *V tumane* (*In the Fog*)

> The past is never dead. It isn't even past.
> William Faulkner, *Requiem for a Nun*

Sergei Loznitsa's film version of Bykau's World War II story came out in 2012 and thus predated Russia's 2014 invasion of Ukraine and takeover of Crimea, but the questions raised in the film are similar to those with which Russians and Ukrainians struggle today.[7] Who is the enemy in post-Soviet space? Who is to be trusted, and who is ready to betray his nation, his family, his detachment to save his own skin? As Zoya Abdullaeva has written, the "dramatic conflict of *V tumane* diagnoses the hardest truth of our time: our lack of trust toward fellow human beings." She goes on to note that discussions of this topic can get by "without partisans or fascists" (Abdullaeva 2012). The most fascinating development of Russian political attitudes toward the 'near abroad' today, though, is just how quickly the mudslinging and name-calling begin to evoke WWII terminology. Watching Loznitsa's film we once again feel the truth of William Faulkner's famous aphorism.

With a background as a documentary filmmaker, Loznitsa (b. 1964) made his debut on the feature film scene in 2010 with *Moë schast'e* (*My Joy*), a bleak film portraying corruption and hopelessness which, like the period piece *V tumane*, implied that current social problems in Russia have their roots in WWII.[8] Although he draws financial support for his films from across Europe (*V tumane* is a co-production of Germany, Russia, Latvia, Holland and Belarus) and currently lives in Germany, there is no doubt that Loznitsa can be considered a 'Russian' filmmaker. He was born in Belarus of Ukrainian descent, attended school in Ukraine, and like Tursunov studied at VGIK in Moscow. As he states: "my native language is Russian, I write my screenplays in Russian, I film in the Russian language" (Maliukova 2012a). And *V tumane*, as one critic wrote, was "worthy of representing Russia" at Cannes: "filmed [...] (in the genre of existential drama using partisan material), there is nothing particularly shocking about the film,

---

[7] Set in 1942, Bykau's story was originally published in Belarusian in 1988. It was translated into Russian in 1990, and Loznitsa read it in the early 2000s. He worked on the screenplay for eleven years before making the film.
[8] *Moë schast'e* received mixed reviews in Russia, particularly because it was seen as an indictment of contemporary society. Andrei Plakhov (2012) noted that reactions were violent, sometimes leading to fistfights. For more on Loznitsa's first feature film see Liashchenko.

nor anything unpatriotic" (Plakhov 2012).[9] In interviews Loznitsa refuses to claim a homeland, but given that he comes from the geographic area that has been contested over the centuries by various national entities and empires, he also insists that the label "occupiers" is a complicated one and the relationships among nationalities, ethnic groups, and state power are not unambiguous (Maliukova 2012b).[10] In every case, he suggests, those who "think differently," whether dissidents or other minority groups, find themselves marginalized. In his discussion, Loznitsa references terminology usually applied only to Native Americans:

> Even now anyone with a different world view is sooner or later driven onto a reservation. Further we could add the word, say, 'destabilization,' and it becomes clear to everyone why you are the enemy. (Loznitsa, qtd. in Maliukova 2012b).

Thus it is that the fairly historical film *V tumane* expands beyond its WWII theme to be applicable to today's world in Russia, Ukraine, and beyond.

Though the title *V tumane, In the Fog*, lowers a curtain of ambiguity over the entire production, the film's plot is straightforward: a Belarusian lineman named Sushchenia refuses to work for the German occupying forces until people from his village explain that he has to. If he does not comply, his fellow villagers will suffer; the Germans will simply shoot them. So Sushchenia gives in to pressure and goes against the clear-cut ethical lines he would prefer, thus launching himself into a metaphorical fog. Working on the rail line with some comrades, Sushchenia resists a plot to commit sabotage, knowing they will be caught. His fellow workers derail a train anyway, and they are all arrested by the Germans, but when Sushchenia tries to remain neutral, he is let go while the others are punished. Added to his own ethical fog is this lack of clarity as to why he remains free.

Sushchenia returns to his village and family, where everyone, including his beloved wife, assumes he is now a German collaborator. The film's plot highlights the ambiguity of this particular historical moment when questions of "us/them" (referred to in Russian as "svoi/chuzhoi") were problematic, since Soviet customs and loyalties were still under construction when the Nazis occupied Belarusian territory. Identifying the enemy was no easy task.

---

[9] *V tumane* won the Golden Apricot at the 2012 Yerevan International Film Festival and competed for the Palme d'Or that year at Cannes.

[10] Especially interesting are Loznitsa's comments, quoted in Maliukova 2012b, on Ryszard Kapuściński's 1993 book *Imperium*. It is easy to see the parallel Loznitsa might make between Native American 'reservations' and, say, the Pale of Settlement for Jews in the Russian empire.

But though the war clearly interests him, Loznitsa locates the resonance of Bykau's story for him in his own childhood experience, when he came to understand that

> You can't do anything to restore fairness. That's what the film is about. About the border between each of us and the surrounding world, which you cannot cross; you cannot penetrate the thoughts and feelings of others [...]. (Loznitsa, qtd. in Maliukova 2012b)

Ostensibly about the complications of life in an occupied zone, the film demonstrates that trust in another human being is impossible, and that once a man's honor has been impugned, he can never restore it. Sushchenia is kidnapped by partisans, who have an order to execute him as a traitor, but they are trapped in the woods with occupying German troops all around. One after the other the partisans are picked off, and Sushchenia as the only survivor recognizes that he will be unable to prove his innocence (fig. 3).

Fig. 3: Sushchenia with Partisans (Loznitsa's *V tumane*)

With crisp, vivid cinematography and an often eerily silent soundtrack, the film ends with a dense fog rolling in and the sound of shots – the viewer assumes that Sushchenia has taken his own life. Here, one critic claims, Loznitsa portrayed a "heroic death," and in so doing demonstrated that what some saw as an "old-fashioned" picture was actually very brave and contemporary (Plakhova 2012).

3 Knights, Tsars, and *Kompromat*[11]

> We make no distinction between knights
> and infidels, as long as they pay up on time.[12]
> *Prikliucheniia Alënushki i Erëmy*
> (*Adventures of Alënushka and Erëma*)

Georgii Gitis (b. 1977) reaches further back into history when he creates the setting for his animated film *Prikliucheniia Alënushki i Erëmy* (*Adventures of Alënushka and Erëma*), but the rather bizarre aesthetic which resulted emerged from a compromise between the director and his producers.[13] Apparently for this film and its 3D sequel Gitis – also a VGIK graduate – was encouraged to use elements of the fairytale world, which were seen as guaranteeing commercial success. "The action takes place in Rus'," the director points out, and we see that in some of the costumes (traditional fabrics, the Russian folk headdress known as *kokoshnik*) and architectural elements as well as the presence of a *tsar* and his daughter. At the same time, as Gitis explained, he was able to convince the producers to allow him to parody Russian folktales (fig. 4), to "make a postmodern *mul'tik* in which the protagonists and conditions of various eras and genres collide. [...] Erëma is wearing Keds and the *tsarevna* invents spacecraft."[14]

The fairytale world of *Prikliucheniia* exists sometime in the mythical past. The *tsar*'s daughter Vseslava is a kind of giant who resembles Peter the Great, both in her stature and her penchant for inventions. She spends all her time thinking of new methods to move vehicles through space, utilizing steam, coal, and even a special "black water" which she gets from the rival Eastern potentate. In the meantime her inventions – a flying machine, a car-like vehicle

---

[11] "Kompromat" is what's known in linguistics as a clip compound, formed from the words *kompromatiruiushchii material* (compromising material), and while the word probably came into existence in the 1940s, there was a huge spike in usage in the 1990s and 2000s. See the google Ngram: https://books.google.com/ngrams/graph?content=%D0%BA%D0%BE%D0%BC%D0%BF%D1%80%D0%BE%D0%BC%D0%B0%D1%82&year_start=1800&year_end=2010&corpus=25&smoothing=3&share=&direct_url=t1%3B%2C%D0%BA%D0%BE%D0%BC%D0%BF%D1%80%D0%BE%D0%BC%D0%B0%D1%82%3B%2CcO. Accessed 25 August 2016.
[12] "Нам что рыцарь, что басурманин, лишь бы платили исправно." In colloquial speech, *basurmanin* is an offensive appellation that primarily refers to Muslims.
[13] The sequel, *Novye prikliucheniia Alënushki i Erëmy* (*New Adventures of Alënushka and Erëma*) (2009), was the first Russian 3D animation film.
[14] All quotes from Gitis's interview with Fedina (2010). *Mul'tik* is the common shortened nickname in Russian for *mul'tiplikatsionnyi fil'm*, or cartoon.

Fig. 4: The folkloric figure of Erëma plays rock music on his balalaika (Gitis's *Prikliucheniia Alënushki i Erëmy*)

with pedals – inspire von Zwetter, who decides he can drop bombs from the air and really make a big impression. Her poor relation, Alënushka, is more interested in hairstyles, cosmetics, and her boyfriend Erëma, and she struggles with Erëma's preference for rock music and his band mates over romantic assignations and a future with her.

As in *Shrek*, a film Gitis cites as highly influential for the Russian animation market, the features of the characters are exaggerated, often hideously so. The *tsar* is short and fat and loves to make *bliny* for his beloved daughter; the aunt, a stand-in matriarch, is tall, thin, and too clever by half. Most horrifying for a Western viewer are the outdated and racist caricatures of foreigners – Africans dance half-naked on the beach and prepare a cannibal stew; the Chinese are single-mindedly devoted to competing in the development of technology, especially train travel; and the Eastern shah is a cross between Robin Williams's genie from Disney's 1992 film *Aladdin* and a plump, lovesick village boy who happens to live in a palace. But the presence of so many foreign "others" dilutes their power and creates ambiguity. There is no one adversary.

The most obvious enemy in the film is the ridiculous Frauenlob von Zwetter, a knight who speaks with a heavy German accent and has an obsession with explosives. These features are played for laughs in this romantic musical comedy. That the enemy is German is to be expected in post-WWII Russia, and even though von Zwetter wears the armor of a Teutonic knight, his evil cackle marks him as a typical bad guy, the enemy from without. More importantly, though, in the film von Zwetter buys his equipment to attack the Russians from the local *voevoda*, Gordei, who holds a trusted position at the *tsar*'s court but resembles nothing more than an arms dealer.[15] This internal enemy, willing to sell munitions to the external enemy, undermines his own state, and in his greed for personal wealth betrays *tsar* and country.[16]

Thus a dynamic is set up between the German enemy and the internal one, who are actually partners. The greedy *voevoda* Gordei is utterly corrupt and has stashed a trunk containing his loot in coins along with a ledger keeping track of all his financial shenanigans. When the knight discovers the buried treasure, he looks through the book and recognizes it for the prize it is. He utters a word that certainly did not exist back in the days of Rus', although its popularity soared in the late Soviet period and it continues to be common in media and politics today: *KOMPROMAT!!* This word, short for compromising material, i. e. information or "dirt" that can be used to influence people in power, has real contemporary resonance. Extortion schemes based on *kompromat* have proliferated in the post-Soviet world and riddle Russian society today.[17] In that sense, the internal enemy can easily infiltrate and sway the very structures of government, depending on who uses the *kompromat* and for what purpose. The political and business practices portrayed in *Prikliucheniia* overshadow the singing-and-dancing and the parodic girl-inventor scenes and move the film out of the "kind, simple" category of animated film – the genre that Gitis believes he practices – and into the "murky, complicated, adult" category (a category he reserves for *auteur* animated cinema).

To justify his own actions in the film, the *voevoda* utters a vivid slogan, which the adult viewer 'reads' as a coded message for the oligarchs of Putin's Russia: "It's not the one who steals who's a thief, it's the one who gets caught."[18] Convinced that he deserves all that he pockets, this internal enemy facilitates von Zwetter's access to Russian society and keeps his own interests firmly in view, not even noticing the damage his client inflicts. Fortunately for the fairy-

---

15 Interestingly, in his interview with Anna Fedina, Gitis argues that independent animators make films inappropriate for children: "often murky, complicated, adult" ["часто [...] мутная, сложная, взрослая"]. He seems to connect his own work to that of official Soviet directors of old: "kind, simple" ["доброе, простое"]. See Fedina 2010.
16 There are no overt references to political events here, but an adult viewer might recall the tragedy of the Russian wars in Chechnya, when soldiers regularly sold their own armaments to the enemy who then used them in combat with the Russians. See, for example, Babchenko 2009.
17 Ukrainian society too. See Yaffa 2016, esp. 46.
18 "Не тот вор, кто ворует все, а тот кто попадёт."

tale world of Rus', the German knight lacks intelligence, and the young Russian Erëma saves the day (along with the clever inventor-*tsarevna* and her busybody Aunt Evrosinia).

Though Gitis has lamented that Russians "have not yet created our own cinematic language," in fact he draws on Soviet cinematic language and history specifically by featuring Norshtein's hedgehog, who wanders through the film. Made enormous accidentally by Alënushka in her careless use of magic, the hedgehog bumbles about in the landscape, seeking her attention for help returning to his original shape and size in vain until the very end of the film (fig. 5).

Fig. 5: The enormous hedgehog looking alarmed at his fate (Gitis's *Prikliucheniia Alënushki i Erëmy*)

As film historian David MacFadyen argues,

> *Hedgehog in the Fog* had by the end of the [twentieth] century acquired a legendary status in its ability to express and prompt [...] dissolution [in the world of desire], through the manipulation of rhythmic sounds and interwoven sentiments across the emptiness of fog or a perspectiveless expanse. It had the social status of an act of revolutionary subjectivity. (2005: 170)

Ëzhik v tumane, MacFadyen further argues, "was heralded as an especially successful work in its reduction of a folkloric tradition to the essence of a pure spatiotemporal freedom, one of express relevance and application to children's own development" (164). In contemporary film, folkloric tradition has taken on new parameters – the hip hop and rap music of Erëma being but one example – but the hedgehog remains, connecting Russian animated film to its past and evoking that groping in the fog from the 1975 short. "Even my paw is obscured," the hedgehog notes in surprise in Norshtein's classic film. Not being able to see the nose on their own faces is a common occurrence for characters in all three of these films, which implies that everyday life has been penetrated by the 'fog of war.'

Conclusion

Indeed, there is nothing murkier than the 'fog of war.' It gets in the way of seeing one's true enemy, and it permits enemies to emerge from nowhere. As we see today in the Russo-Ukrainian conflicts, brothers kill brothers and aunts betray grandfathers, when everything is immersed in a deep murk of nationalism, fear, and paranoia.

In 2008 Oleg Sulkin published an article entitled "Identifying the Enemy in Contemporary Russian Film." Surveying a plethora of late twentieth- and early twenty-first-century Russian films, Sulkin argued that three discourses of the enemy could be identified: 1) that the enemy never slept and that Russians needed to remain vigilant and destroy him wherever he was; 2) that in contrast, the enemy was deep undercover, perhaps in a sleeper cell, and must be sought and ruthlessly rooted out; and 3) that the enemy was really just a phantom, a "vestige of the past," or perhaps was located within the Russian people themselves, and again needed to be discovered and purged in order that Russian society could heal itself (125). Despite naming three discourses, Sulkin placed post-Soviet film into a framework of binaries. As he maintained:

> Deeply rooted in Russia's protracted experience of serfdom and intensified by the Bolshevik doctrine of class antagonism, the dichotomous Russian mentality still pulsates to the anxious binary rhythm of Us and Them, Our Guys and Their Guys, Russian and Foreign. (2008: 114)

Analyzing the three films above, *Shal*, *V tumane*, and *Prikliucheniia Alënushki i Erëmy*, this chapter argues that the contemporary cinematic landscape has mostly dispensed with binaries in favor of a much more nuanced picture of the post-Soviet world. If the early 2000s saw a return to Soviet-style World War II-themed films featuring Soviet heroes and portrayed their attitude toward the German enemy unambiguously (see i.e. *Zvezda* [*The Star*], *Kukushka* [*The Cuckoo*]), and though Loznitsa depicts cruel and clever Nazis who use the innocent lineman to help trick the Belarusian partisans into betraying their positions, in the second decade of the twenty-first century revisiting WWII means more than just scapegoating the foreign enemy (see Sulkin 2008, esp. 117–120). Or it can mean that, unless the murk gets in the way.

Of the films, *Prikliucheniia*, influenced by contemporary American animation trends and with conflicting commercial and artistic goals, features the most stereotypical representations of "foreign" and "other," yet still manages to locate the internal enemy as well and to highlight corrupt practices as central to the weakening of the Russian state. For a children's film billed as a "romantic musical comedy," this is no small accomplishment. What's more, Gitis's play with Norshtein's hedgehog gives the film a historical depth that his faux-Rus' setting fails to deliver. Though the fact that Alënushka is incapable of handling her magical powers is tragic for the hedgehog character, it is quite telling as one of the hallmarks of how power is portrayed in this film generally. It is not just the frivolous girl who fails here. Tsar Dormidont and other bumbling male characters in the film demonstrate their own inabilities to handle power as well. In what might easily be dismissed as a rip-off of American *mul'tiki* or as pandering to spoiled post-Soviet children who live in a consumer world, Gitis harkens back to models of Russian patriarchy and nationalism birthed by Tsar Peter the Great himself – even if he does so in a pseudo-feminist way, through the inventor-*tsarevna* daughter Vseslava.

These filmmakers were all educated at the same film school, Moscow's famous All-Russian State Institute of Cinematography (VGIK). However, each has moved in his own direction in the post-Soviet era, and thus the films examined illuminate different aspects of the post-Soviet contemporary cinematic scene. Tursunov's *Shal* – shot in Kazakh with some Russian speech as well – is the least "Russian" of the three (though Russian critics, in describing the film, make the representation of "new Russian" hunters – with their cell phones and their high-powered rifles – seem more central to the film than it is). But since in the film Tursunov openly and specifically confronts not just Russian hunting tourists but also the legacy of Soviet culture (atheism, soccer fandom), it too belongs in the group. Cinematically it is perhaps the most beautiful and simultaneously unambiguous of the films, praising lost virtues of family, honor, and life in harmony with the natural world.

One theme uniting the films is that the individuals portrayed must come to terms with their personal responsibility for the circumstances in which they find themselves. In that sense these films imply that it's time to act like a grown-up. Instead of repeating the traditional Russian 'accursed questions' (who is to blame? what is to be done?), these characters – in some cases even the animated ones – try to act to address their problems.[19] And when the situation is hopeless, as it is with poor Sushchenia, doomed to be thought a traitor, he still chooses to act as ethically as possible. He carries a wounded partisan – formerly his captor – through the woods on his back even after the partisan has died, not wanting to leave the corpse to the Germans. When the second partisan also dies, he recognizes that there is only one possible ending to his story. The filmmaker mercifully sends him fog to mask his bravery/cowardice in committing suicide. Even in ethical behavior, ambiguity remains, and though this is an extremely honest film, given its natural audience of Soviet patriots who still cling to the somehow more simple oppositions of World War II, *V tumane* can be read in numerous ways by Belarusian, Ukrainian, Russian nationalists, all of whom are trying to find their way in the post-Soviet murk.

When fog, a natural phenomenon, enters these films, the protagonists find themselves confused and disoriented. But though their sight is compromised, that is only an outward manifestation of what is going on in their souls. Cultural and ethical principles have been distorted, and on one hand the search for an enemy frequently fits Sulkin's third scenario – the enemy is within them. On the other hand, because there are enemies all around as well, simple binaries do not suffice. In the bloody conflicts of *V tumane* and *Shal* in particular, the victims are us and them, nature and culture – humans, sheep and wolves alike.

Works Cited

Abdullaeva, Zoya (2012) "Postklassicheskii film," *Iskusstvo kino* 4. <http://www.kinoart.ru/blogs/inthefog> (accessed 29 August 2016)

Abikeeva, Gulinara (2012) "Nazad k budushchemu: novyi vektor kazakhskogo kino," *Iskusstvo kino* 4. <http://kinoart.ru/archive/2012/04/nazad-v-budushchee-novyj-vektor-kazakhskogo-kino> (accessed 25 August 2016)

Babchenko, Arkady (2009) *One Soldier's War*, trans. Nick Allen (New York: Grove Press).

Dallet, Sylvie (1992) "Historical Time in Russian, Georgian, Armenian and Kirghiz Cinema," in *The Red Screen: Politics, Society and Art in Soviet Cinema*, ed. Anna Lawton (London and New York: Routledge), 303–314.

Fedina, Anna (2010) "Svoego iazyka ne pridumali." <http://www.peoples.ru/art/cinema/director/george_gitis/> (accessed 24 August 2016).

---

[19] The so-called 'accursed questions' (*prokliatye voprosy*) ran through nineteenth-century Russian social thought. Originally explored in novels such as Alexander Herzen's 1846 *Who is to Blame?* and Nikolai Chernyshevsky's 1863 *What is to Be Done?* and in review essays such as Nikolai Dobroliubov's "What is Oblomovism?" (1859) and "When Will the Real Day Come?" (1860), they remain relevant in discussions of political and ethical dilemmas in post-Soviet space today.

Guttmann, Allen (1988) "The Cold War and the Olympics," *International Journal* 43.4, Special Issue: Sport in World Politics, 554–568.
Iampol'skii, Mikhail (1990) "Palitra i ob"ektiv: o fil'makh Iuriia Norshteina," *Iskusstvo kino* 2, 94–104.
Liashchenko, Vladimir (2011) "Schast'e moe, ia tvoi khaos: v prokat vykhodit *Schast'e moe* Sergeia Loznitsy," *gazeta.ru.* <http://www.gazeta.ru/culture/2011/03/29/a_3568857.shtml> (accessed 29 August 2016).
MacFadyen, David (2005) *Yellow Crocodiles and Blue Oranges: Russian Animated Film since World War Two* (Montreal: McGill-Queen's University Press).
Maliukova, Larisa (2012a) "Sergei Loznitsa: 'Kann – luchshee mesto dlia prem'ery fil'ma'" <http://kinote.info/articles/7260-sergey-loznitsa-kann-luchshee-mesto-dlya-premery-filma> (accessed 15 May 2013).
Maliukova, Larisa (2012b) "Sergei Loznitsa: Okkupatsiia – eto prikhod vlasti, diktuiushchei narodu svoiu voliu," *Novaia Gazeta.* <http://www.novayagazeta.ru/arts/52592.html> (accessed 29 August 2016).
Micciché, Lino (1992) "The Cinema of the Transcaucasian and Central Asian Republics," in *The Red Screen: Politics, Society and Art in Soviet Cinema*, ed. Anna Lawton (London and New York: Routledge), 291–302.
Plakhov, Andrei (2012) "Rossiia okazalas' 'V tumane': Fil'm Sergeia Loznitsy v konkurse Kannskogo festivalia," *Gazeta Kommersant.* <http://www.kommersant.ru/doc/1919382> (accessed 29 August 2016).
Plakhova, Elena (2012) "Gde ravny liubov' i krov'," *SEANS* 26. <http://seance.ru/blog/summer-festivals-total/> (accessed 31 August 2016).
Riordan, Jim (1988) "The Role of Sport in Soviet Foreign Policy," *International Journal* 43.4, 569–595.
Stishova, Elena (2013) "Kinoshok-13. Pobediteli," *Iskusstvo kino* 9. <http://kinoart.ru/blogs/kinoshok-2013-pobediteli> (accessed 26 August 2016).
Sulkin, Oleg (2008) "Identifying the Enemy in Contemporary Russian Film," trans. Timothy Sergay, in *Insiders and Outsiders in Russian Cinema*, ed. Stephen M. Norris and Zara M. Torlone (Bloomington, IN: Indiana University Press), 113–126.
Yaffa, Joshua (2016) "After the Revolution," *The New Yorker* (5 September), 40–49.
n.a. "Vybor goda – 2012" <http://www.np.kz/index.php?newsid=12199> (accessed 28 November 2016)

Filmography

Ëzhik v tumane (Hedgehog in the Fog) (1975) Dir. Iurii Norshtein (Soiuzmul'tfil'm).
Prikliucheniia Alënushki i Erëmy (The Adventures of Alënushka and Erëma) (2008) Dir. Georgii Gitis (Paradis)
Shal (The Old Man) (2012) Dir. Ermek Tursunov (Kazakhfil'm).
V tumane (In the Fog) (2012) Dir. Sergei Loznitsa (MA.JA.DE Fiction, Rija Films, Lemming Film, Belarus'fil'm, GP Cinema Company).

Holger Pötzsch
Of Monsters and Men: Forms of Evil in War Films

The present chapter engages with the formal framing of friend and foe in the war genre. Asserting the significance of film for cultural forms of memory and a politics of the past, I sketch out the generic conventions through which particular notions of self and other are inscribed, before I conduct an analysis of Clint Eastwood's *American Sniper* (2014) to flesh out what I term a cosmologic form of evil at play in the genre. Secondly, a reading of Nick Broomfield's *Battle for Haditha* (2006) introduces an understanding of evil as a systemic property of war independent of individual intentions. Finally, I suggest an inherent banality of systemic evil that becomes conceivable as embedded in mundane everyday routines rather than bound towards the exceptional.

1 War, Film, and History

Film, including fiction film, has emerged as an important medium for historical thinking and practice, and has attracted corresponding scholarly attention. From Rosenstone's (2006) inquiry into the medium-specific characteristics of film as a conveyer of historical knowledge, via Erll's (2010) and Landsberg's (2002) notions of movies as memory-making media and origins of prosthetic memories respectively, to Adkins and Castle's (2013) experimentally backed assertion of movies' ability to influence and change political attitudes, the moving image has acquired growing salience for studies of the interrelation between cultural expressions, history, collective identity, and cultural memory. Films about history, it seems, matter for politics of the past and as such merit "careful examination" (McCrisken and Pepper 2005: 8).

In his inquiry into the forms and functions of the historical Hollywood film, Burgoyne (2008:6) has argued for the genre's polysemic nature that enables both inscription and negotiation of various possible pasts in the light of the present. Drawing upon the thought of Mikhail Bakhtin, Burgoyne (2008:14) applies the concept of "genre memory" to assert a wider socio-political significance of formal aspects of Hollywood cinema. Rosenstone (2006) provides a similar argument when he states that historical films, in spite of their dramatic structure and ambiguous relation to historical research, "have an effect on the way we see the past" (5). The present chapter builds on these advances and investigates a specific subset of the genre of the historical film – the war film.

Due to the significant sufferings inflicted by wars on both civilians and combatants, the need arises to retrospectively assign value to the devastations caused and to re-frame apparently arbitrary deaths and destruction as meaningful sacrifices suffered in the name of a collective greater good. Such acts of legitimizing wars, however, are not only retrospectively bound. As scholars such as Zur (1987) or Der Derian (2009) point out, culturally produced biased perceptions and attitudes are important ingredients in the planning and waging of wars, as well as in the retrospective inscription of value. Mainstream visual culture, argues Kozol (2014), is contested terrain where regimes of visibility and disappearance are inscribed, negotiated, and potentially subverted.

The generic war film plays an important role in the formation and challenging of a hegemonic visuality in relation to violent conflict. Westwell (2006), for instance, has argued that, "for all their protestations to the contrary, Hollywood movies tend to show war as necessary, if not essential, and present the armed forces as efficient, egalitarian and heroic institutions" (3). Eberwein (2010) adopts a more balanced position when he asserts that the Hollywood war genre functions like a myth that provides a way for a culture to productively "deal with the contradictions it experiences" and to "understand and negotiate current experiences" (7). Both authors, however, connect war films to the formation of particular worldviews and therefore treat them as important media of cultural memory.

How can the potential effects of war films be analyzed? Erll (2010) has introduced the valuable distinction between intra-, inter-, and pluri-medial levels of analysis to address possible memory-making potentials of films. The intra- and inter-medial levels invite for formal interrogation of the technical means and narrative tropes applied to cue a particular form of engagement with the past. While the intra-medial register focuses on how particular films predispose engagement with key characters, establish a particular structure of sympathy, or cue certain emotional and affective responses, an inter-medial analysis investigates how connections to preceding historical events are drawn and how issues of verisimilitude and authenticity are negotiated.

In historical films, the intra- and inter-medial levels create memory-making potentials by inviting audiences to perceive of the depicted persons and events as if they were realistic reflections of the past, and by emotionally and ideologically charging the presented historical narrative. However, as Erll (2010) suggests, only a third level of analysis – the pluri-medial dimension – can provide insights into whether, and if yes how, these potentials for memory-making are realized in specific individual or collective contexts of reception. Reviews, box office numbers, educational packages, as well as empirical audience research, or studies of social media responses all fall within the purview of this contextual level as they allow for a cautious assessment of actual patterns of distribution, reception, and further dissemination. In the present chapter, I will limit my analysis to an assessment of the memory-making potentials motivated at the intra- and inter-medial levels of war films.

Erll's (2010) approach is indebted to a neo-formalist strain within contemporary film theory. Building her argument on Russian formalism, Thompson (1988) has argued that cultural expressions, film among them, have the inherent capacity to either reinforce or question received ways of seeing, thinking, and acting. According to her, one characteristic of artworks is that they can de-familiarize habitualized cognitive and perceptual schemata and force spectators to re-think and re-assess largely automated response patterns. On the other hand, however, mainstream works often acquire popularity by responding to, and thus strengthening, pre-established expectations and frames. I will here argue that popular war films adhere to conventionalized depictions of friend and foe and in this way not only ensure popularity, but also play into and reinforce received cultural and political frames of war.

2 The Genre of the War Film

What constitutes the genre of the war film? Tudor (1974) identifies one key problem regarding the concept of genre. The author argues that studies of film genres face an "empiricist dilemma" in that they are "caught in a circle that first requires that the films be isolated, for which purpose a criterion is necessary, but the criterion is, in turn, meant to emerge from the empirically established common characteristics of the films" (138). As a pragmatic solution Tudor suggests to "lean on a common cultural consensus as to what constitutes a particular genre and then go on to analyze it in detail" (138). In this reading, film genres emerge as contingent cultural conventions that constantly evolve in and through social practice, and that shape audience expectations. Regardless of the weaknesses of Tudor's (1974) framework, which for instance Neale (2000) pinpoints as a set of unanswered questions regarding how a common cultural consensus can be established or, what role the industry or other societal interests can be seen to play in the process, Tudor's pragmatic framework constitutes an applicable approach.

As such, the question of what constitutes a war film seems to entail an intuitive answer possibly reflecting a common cultural consensus: a war film is a film that deals with war, that is, with organized military endeavors of a certain magnitude that involve the use of direct violence on a massive scale. Such a pragmatic definition seems applicable enough, but would refer to a wide set of films including historical dramas and reenactments, action flicks, science fiction and fantasy movies, as well as homecoming movies and movies about the home front.

For the purpose of the present chapter, I will follow Eberwein (2010), who provides a more limited definition that asserts a productive middle ground between excessively wide and extremely focused positions, and that gestures towards a common cultural consensus suggested by Tudor (1974). Eberwein (2010: 45) argues that the war genre includes films that either 1) focus directly on war and combat, 2) that follow soldiers' activities off the battlefields, or 3) that address the effects of war on civilians and human relationships. Eberwein connects the war film to preceding historical events and argues that their claims to verisimilitude entail certain potentials for socio-political impact. Similar considerations lead Burgoyne (2008) to treat the war film as a subgenre of the historical film.

As historical representations, many war movies are based on autobiographical accounts by soldiers and privilege their particular point of view on incidents of great collective significance. Often these partial perspectives are left unchallenged and are therefore implicitly objectified. This generic structure has two related discursive implications; firstly, it implicitly assigns secondary status to the experiences and competing points of view of non-combatants and enemies, and secondly, it translates the living and dynamic "communicative memory" (Assmann 2010) of a particular group of people who were directly involved in the represented events – in this case groups of soldiers – into a static and implicitly prescriptive cultural memory with implied relevance for an entire collective. In most generic war films such filters transform contingent and often contradictory war stories recounted by variously situated subjects into an objectified account of the war as it allegedly took place. This streamlining of messy and contradictory historical recollections into implicitly objectified, quasi-authoritative accounts has direct implications for the presentation of the friend and foe in these films.

3 Biased Structures of Engagement: Enemies in the War Genre

War films are "genre hybrids" (Pötzsch 2012: 158). They present what is framed as authentic reenactments of actual past wars, yet at the same time signal their own fictionality. This peculiar in-between position is negotiated at an inter-medial level during opening sequences that connect the story-universe of the film to preceding historical events and that provide normative and ideological orientation to viewers.

Pötzsch (2012) has introduced three rhetorical modes of memory-making in the war film: 1) an objectifying rhetoric that raises the impression of presenting a historical incident as it actually happened, thus tacitly excluding competing or problematizing positions, 2) a subjective rhetoric that presents past events as experienced through a particular diegetic character, however without giving pretense of this being the only possible version of the events, and 3) a reflexive rhetoric that invites an active form of reception and critical questioning of the medial frames of the presentation. According to Pötzsch (2012), mainstream war films usually cue an objectifying rhetoric that enables a clear distinction between friend and foe and allows for a disambiguating normative structure.

While the inter-medial level predominantly targets audiences' intellectual faculties and negotiates the relation between the diegetic universe of the film and an extra-diegetic historical-political reality, the intra-medial level employs a series of generic formal devices to enable an emotional and affective engagement of the audience with particular diegetic characters and events. In general, generic war films exhibit a biased structure of sympathy that enables access to and involvement with only one side of the depicted conflicts (Pötzsch 2011, 2013). A biased distribution of such means as slow motion, dwelling close-ups, sad or valorizing music, and certain narrative tropes, and figures such as the main adversary or the evil deed invite perceptions of only one side as human and worthy of empathy, while the respective opponents emerge as "ubiquitously absent" (Pötzsch 2013: 136) – invisible, inaccessible, and incomprehensible, yet at the same time potentially omnipresent as a deadly threat that can actualize anywhere at any minute.

In sum, the formal properties of the genre draw an "epistemological barrier" (Pötzsch 2011: 77) that veils the various subjectivities and the rationality of the other and that preclude affective engagement and empathy with this group. This rhetoric of othering invites for the perception of the respective enemies of the various soldier-selves populating mainstream war films as less than human – as "ungrievable life" in the sense of Butler (2009: 22) that can be killed or harmed without remorse or sanctions.

By such means, the generic Hollywood war film predominantly cues what Erll (2010) terms antagonistic and mythical memory-creating modes that invite for monolithic conceptualizations of historical wars as embedded in timeless Manichean struggles between mutually exclusive normative positions. Specific conflicts are thus re-articulated within cosmologic and religious frames that veil their concrete socio-economic and political contexts, while the respective enemies of the various soldier-selves are framed as motivated by an absolute form of evil that disables any form of interaction between self and other except massive violence deployed with the rightful objective of eradicating an unambiguous and immediate deadly threat.

Through its widespread adoption in war and action cinema, this particular biased representational frame plays into and potentially reinforces established cultural schemata and paradigm scenarios that aid and structure the conceptualization of new enemies and threats in real life and politics. Anker (2005) and Pötzsch (2011, 2013, 2014), for instance, have shown that the mythical-antagonistic rhetoric of generic film spills over into political discourse by habitualizing ultimately ideological positions and providing implicit plausibility to bellicose articulations by political actors.

The next section will conduct an analysis of Clint Eastwood's Iraq war movie *American Sniper* (2014). I will argue that the film predominantly reiterates generic conventions and transcodes the ambiguous politics and economics of the invasion into a cosmologic struggle between good and evil; however, I shall also suggest an alternative reading based on a re-interpretation of some of the cues and indices presented in the film.

4 The Good, the Bad, and the Helpless: Cosmologic Evil in Fallujah

Clint Eastwood's *American Sniper* tells the story of highly decorated US Navy SEALs operative Christopher Scott ('Chris') Kyle, who gained notoriety for being the most lethal sniper in US military history. Kyle served four tours of service in Iraq in the period 2003 to 2008 and allegedly killed approximately 160 enemies. He was highly decorated and was honorably discharged in 2009. Kyle was shot dead by a fellow veteran in 2013. Eastwood's film is based on Kyle's autobiography (Kyle, McEwen, and DeFelice 2012) and focuses mostly on combat sequences connected to his tours of service in Iraq, but interrupts these with sequences set in the Unites States that show his growing estrangement from family and civilian life.

In his earlier war films, *Flags of our Fathers* (2006) and *Letters from Iwo Jima* (2006), Eastwood thoughtfully addresses the various ambiguities and contradictions inherent in an apparently morally clear-cut struggle such as the Pacific theatre of World War II and carefully balances US and Japanese perspectives in a unique double-take on the events. In *American Sniper*, on the other hand, the director sets a quite different and far more assertive tone that transforms the various ambivalences and contradictions of contemporary urban counter-insurgency operations into a monolithic battle between good and evil. While *Flags of our Fathers* critically interrogates the power-laden processes of translating the memories and traumas of individual soldiers into cultural forms of memory that serve particular socio-political and economic purposes (Pötzsch 2013b), Eastwood's recent take on the Iraq War objectifies the individual experiences of a US special forces operative and transforms it into a metaphorical stand-in for the Iraq war and the global war on terror as such.

American Sniper cues a dichotomous moral universe that draws clear and unambiguous distinctions between friend and foe, good and evil, us and them. The film opens with a black screen and a distant voice chanting 'Allahu akbar,' thus indicating a Middle Eastern setting. As the churning sound of tank tracks blends with the voice, the image fades in and reveals a US armored vehicle advancing through an Arab cityscape. The opening scene then cuts to a rooftop where it adopts the perspective of a US sniper, Chris Kyle, surveying the slow advance of the US column. As he witnesses a young woman handing a grenade to an adolescent boy who starts running toward the US unit, Kyle is left with the difficult decision to trust his perception and shoot, or to risk the lives of his fellow soldiers.

The intense scene employs eyeline matches to focalize the situation through Kyle and thus align audiences to his perspective. This way, spectators are confined to the same set of information as the protagonist to evaluate what happens. As a result, a moral dilemma is created that makes audiences oscillate between two possible readings regarding the memory-making rhetoric of the film. Either, the film will deliver indices that Kyle's perception can be trusted, thus implicitly objectifying his gaze, or it will insert doubts framing his point of view as subjective and undermining the authority of his vantage point. A series of subsequent flashbacks that bring the viewer back to the time before Kyle's deployment on the roof remove such ambiguities and anchor the evolving narrative to a clearly normative moral and ethical frame. The repeatedly invoked trope of evil plays a key role in this process last but not least in preventing audience allegiance with the Iraqi enemy-other.

The first time evil becomes an issue is during a scene set in Kyle's childhood home, where an adamant and authoritative father-figure preaches a simple moral universe consisting of sheep, wolves, and sheep dogs. He claims that "there are people who believe that evil does not exist and if it moves over their doorstep, they wouldn't know how to protect themselves," before he explains that theirs is a family of sheep dogs containing evil and fighting on behalf of the weak. This simplifying triad is then extended to serve as a moral template for the evaluation of Kyle's pending decision on the rooftop and of US counterinsurgency operations in occupied Iraq in general.

The connection of childhood morals to global politics is achieved during a scene showing Kyle's initial deployment to Iraq immediately prior to the scene on the roof. While the camera follows US soldiers approaching an urban battle space, a speech by the commanding officer anchors the ensuing narrative historically, geographically, politically, and morally. The man states, "Welcome to Fallujah. The new wild west of the old Middle East," thus invoking the mythical-ideological frame of an expanding frontier of civilization familiar from the Western genre, before he moves on to morally disambiguate the situation. Among other things he determines that the city of Fallujah has been evacuated and that those left "are here to kill you," before he restates the immediate objective of US snipers to protect and safely bring home Marines. As such, the scene reiterates the simple cosmology of sheep, wolves, and sheep dogs introduced through the figure of Kyle's father, and redeploys it as a frame to evaluate US military conduct in Iraq.

Implied in this particular disambiguation of both battlefield and war discourse is an epistemological grand claim, namely the unquestioned ability of key actors – personified through sniper Kyle – to clearly distinguish between sheep, wolves, and sheep dogs at any given time and place. The story thus circumvents the truly difficult issue of a contingent nature of perception that would make someone's sheep dog another person's wolf and avoids the troubling possibility of misapprehension. Instead, a specific, religiously inspired moral-ideological cosmology developed in the context of a 1970s patriarchic nuclear family in rural Texas is extrapolated to frame ethical decisions on the battlefield and to predispose understandings of issues pertaining to international relations and military interventions in general.

The subsequent decision by Kyle to kill first the advancing boy and then the mother running after him and picking up the grenade is thus disambiguated and implicitly justified. Conveniently, the grenade carried by the boy actually explodes in safe distance from the advancing Marines, leaving the audience in no doubt regarding the accuracy of Kyle's perception and the ethical viability of his decision. In addition, during a verbal exchange with another soldier after the incident, Kyle's only reaction to his deed is that "this is evil like I've never seen before," thereby effectively deflecting such pressing and challenging questions as to what severe grievances and despair might bring a young woman to do something like sending a little boy to death in this manner. As usual, the invocation of a cosmologic and absolute category of evil effectively confines critical thinking, disables conscious deliberation, and precludes any form of empathy with opponents who are narrowly framed as monstrously threatening subhumans. By these means, *American Sniper* cues a deeply antagonistic mode of memory-making in the sense of Erll (2010) and establishes unambiguous normative poles that structure and predispose audience evaluation of the depicted characters and events.

From this initial kill-scene onward, Eastwood's film follows a predictable generic script that puts the unchallenged hero Chris Kyle up against a comic book-like motley crew of evil "main adversaries" (Pötzsch 2013a) such as the militant Zarqawi, who is "financed by Bin Laden, trained by Bin Laden, loyal to Bin Laden," his enforcer 'the butcher' with the unpleasant habit of (among other things) slowly killing children with an electric drill, the supposedly superior enemy sniper Mustafa with the ability to hit US soldiers across vast distances, and the inevitable rows of faceless opponents in menacing advance toward US held positions. These characters not only brush over the manifold subjectivities and complex socio-political interests of the Iraqi resistance, they also create the (wrongful) impression of a symmetrical struggle between equally equipped, trained, and motivated groups of combatants.

The rhetoric of enemizing deployed in *American Sniper* becomes palpable in several later scenes, as well. One example is the encounter with Sheik Al-Obeidi, who after an intense argument agrees to help the US soldiers locate their main adversary Al-Zarqawi. In the scene, the Sheik's acting reveals an almost metaphysical fear, not of the US soldiers, but of Al-Zarqawi's deputy. With eyes wide open and heavily gesticulating, Al-Obeidi employs religiously inspired terms when referring to 'the butcher' for instance as "the despaired one" or as "son of the devil." This way, the figure of an Iraqi spiritual and cultural authority, a sheikh, is employed not only to frame the enemy as a monstrous band of subhumans of mythical qualities, but also to present Iraqi society and traditions as incapable of efficiently resisting the evil growing in their midst, thereby reiterating the implied need for a band of sheep dogs to enter the scene and re-establish order.

A second illustrative scene merits mentioning in this context. Later on in the movie, Kyle and his men advance into 'the butcher's' stronghold – a small urban shop. Through the choice of setting, lighting, and deployed props this scene blurs the boundary between the war film and the horror genre. Upon entering the narrow and darkened rooms of what appears more like a subterranean den than an urban building, the US soldiers encounter among other things the tortured remains of a man hanging in heavy chains from the ceiling and long rows of severed human heads and limbs that are neatly stapled on shelves.[1] Together with the sequence where 'the butcher' takes revenge on the cooperating sheikh, Al-Obeidi, by slowly drilling the latter's teenage son to death, the scene in the shop most clearly reframes the complex socio-political, economic, and cultural antagonisms and interests behind the Iraqi insurgency as a simple Manichean struggle between timeless and mythical forces of good and evil. Through these "evil deeds" (Pötzsch 2013a:130–131), a normative frame is put into place that effectively disables any approach to conflict resolution except the total annihilation of either the one side or the other, thereby implicitly justifying the massive violence deployed by the protagonist as ultimately benevolent, necessary, and without an alternative.

Both Burgoyne (2008) and Eberwein (2010) have used Bakhtin's concepts to assert an inherently polysemic and multi-vocal nature of cultural expressions that, regardless of their possible dominant rhetoric, always leave spaces for negotiated or oppositional readings (Hall 1977). This observation retains its validity in relation to the ways through which generic films predispose understandings of shared pasts, including the framing of the Iraq war in *American Sniper*. As I will argue below, in spite of the dominant rhetoric of othering that has been outlined above, Eastwood's movie also opens certain potentials for contradictory experiences and critical rearticulations that invite for a more reflective treatment of Kyle's life story and the US invasion of the country.

American Sniper predominantly focalizes the diegetic universe through Chris Kyle and does little to challenge, problematize, or de-naturalize his particular outlook. This way, the protagonist's individual vantage point is implicitly objectified and left standing as the only valid account of what actually happened. As has been argued above, this rhetorical choice also confines the other to the one-dimensional roles of either evil adversary or helpless victim. There are, however, a few scenes in particular in the second part of the film that invite a more reflective stance by presenting counter-perspectives without immediately undermining these with reference to Kyle's hegemonic worldview. I will briefly describe three such scenes that invite a questioning of the hegemonic regime of visuality outlined above – including the way the Iraqi other is framed.

During a mission briefing at the beginning of Kyle's second tour to Iraq, one soldier compares war to an electric wire "that makes it difficult to hold on to anything else" and asks the question "what are we doing here [in Iraq]?" The protagonist immediately tackles the mounting doubt in a familiar, assertive manner,

---

[1] Of course, after the ensuing shoot-out, 'the butcher' finally succumbs to Kyle's righteously deployed firepower.

once again invoking evil as the paramount justification of a US (and his own) presence in the country: "There is evil here. We have seen it!" This time, however, the articulation of Kyle's hegemonic outlook on the world is not left unchallenged. Instead, the soldier sarcastically responds that "there is evil everywhere" and only reluctantly follows Kyle's prompt to commence the next mission. The whole scene inserts a notion of hollowness into Kyle' discourse and introduces an inert, gnawing opposition that, however, remains unacknowledged by the protagonist.

A second scene that raises doubts regarding the ultimate validity of Kyle's perspective on things is set during the funeral of one of the soldiers who died under his command. The mother of the deceased asks in tears the by now more than rhetorical question of "when does glory fade away and become a wrongful crusade, or an unjustified means that consumes one completely?" This speech can be seen as counter articulation directly aimed at both the religiously inspired main supporting narrative of the war on terror and the objectified self-understanding of Chris Kyle. In presenting this fundamental challenge from the elevated enunciatory position of the grieving mother of a US soldier who had died in service of his country charges it with significant memory-making potential. More importantly, however, this time the words remain standing without any opposition while Kyle, who himself had been identified with a crusader's cross on insurgent leaflets, is filmed standing stiff and apparently incapable of processing the mother's words. A similar counter-perspective is launched in a later scene by a soldier who lost his eyesight under Kyle's command and who responds to the protagonist's assertion that "the bad guys will pay for what they did [to you]" with a bitter "Hooray! Legend!" Again, this challenge remains without objections from Kyle.

Finally, after Kyle's third tour of duty the homecoming episode ends with another brawl between him and his wife in the course of which Taya once again demands of him to become "human again." The scene hints at the fact that throughout his tours of service, Kyle's multiple identities as father, husband, lover, and more might have been reduced to a one-dimensional militarized subjectivity not entirely unlike his various evil opponents. As such, the religiously inspired discourse of violence, de-humanisation, and evil apparently has come full circle, devouring its hero in the process.

All the sequences described above serve to undermine the reliability of the protagonist and thus invite a possible transition from an objectifying to a subjective memory-making rhetoric that opens for other than one dominant vantage point on the presented events. The scenes not only cast doubt on Kyle's role as an unquestionable hero and efficient sheep dog in a dichotomous narrative of good and evil, but also enable a re-reading of the sequences caricaturing and demonizing the Iraqi other. In light of the now undermined position of Kyle, the exaggerated scenes demonizing his enemies emerge not as providing access to the true nature of the other, but as a mere reflection of Kyle's ultimately idiosyncratic view of the world. What *American Sniper* thus makes accessible are the protagonist's various filters put into place to sustain his sanity and self-esteem in face of his own growing de-humanisation, and which make it possible for him to continue functioning under increasingly unbearable pressure.

When presenting Kyle's final tour of duty, however, Eastwood's film does much to brush over such potentials for ambiguity and contingency. The protagonist overcomes significant obstacles and without losing any more men kills his second main adversary, the sniper Mustafa. This deed finally enables him to come home, indicating that not war as a system has estranged him from civilian life, but the continued threat to his fellow soldiers posed by the mythical insurgent sniper. This apologetic frame is further supported in a conversation between Kyle and a psychiatrist, where the former states that what haunts him are not the people he killed, but the US soldiers he could not save, thus again framing Iraqi lives as ungrievable (Butler 2009) and effectively preparing the protagonist for his post-service career as supporter of veterans struggling with civilian life. This scene in particular makes Barker's (2011) criticism of Katheryn Bigelow's *The Hurt Locker* (2008) applicable to *American Sniper* as well. Barker (2011: 157) writes that "what this film [*The Hurt Locker*] celebrates, is a character who is *the living embodiment of post-traumatic stress disorder*, but who is treated by the film as not disordered at all" (original emphasis). As such, paraphrasing Barker, it can be argued that both Bigelow's William James and Eastwood's Chris Kyle function as "poster-boy[s] of the Iraq war generation" (157).

I will now turn to Nick Broomfield's *Battle for Haditha* and show how the technique of multi-focalization makes accessible the various subjectivities and complex interests of the enemy. By these means, the film enables a transition from a cosmologic to a systemic notion of evil in war.

5 Refocalizing Friend and Foe: Systemic Evil in Haditha

Nick Broomfield's *Battle for Haditha* (2007) is a fictionalized re-enactment of an incident in the Iraqi town of Haditha on 19 November 2005, when US soldiers killed 24 civilians during a protracted raid to apprehend insurgents responsible for an IED attack. In his film, Broomfield largely refrained from shooting on a set and predominantly relied on non-professional actors – US veterans formerly stationed in Iraq and Iraqi refugees who had fled the country. This led to a peculiar authenticity of the presentation and entailed some stunning accomplishments by the cast. As Broomfield explains on the commentary track of the DVD edition, he often simply let the camera run to capture performances that quickly developed their own unintended dynamics.

From the beginning, *Battle for Haditha* cues a reflexive engagement with the past. The film opens with a sequence of mid shots showing the faces of individual US soldiers speaking directly into the camera as if in a documentary. The men present their idiosyncratic views on the Iraq War and voice a nihilistic outlook, void of national pathos. They exhibit a profound inability to express any vital reasons for or positive consequences of a US presence in the country, but at the same time de-humanize the Iraqi opponents. This doubleness indicates at once critical distance to, and total immersion in, a discourse of war. The next scene, showing the same men in Humvees driving full speed through the desert reiterates this ambivalence. While use of language and performances exhibit a hegemonic form of militarized masculinity, the song the soldiers listen to – *Lies, Lies, Lies* by the industrial metal band *Ministry* – clearly articulates a damning critique of the instrumentalization of the events of 9/11 for the sake of constructing US national unity and justifying wars and foreign interventions.

In stylistically oscillating between conventions of documentary and drama and in deferring audience allegiance through the double-framing of diegetic characters, Broomfield's film cues a reflexive memory-making mode that invites for critical distance from the events presented on screen. As such, *Battle for Haditha* motivates active audience engagement with representational frames and with the film's various possible relations to political and historical context. This critical focus extends to the presentation of US soldiers, Iraqi civilians, and insurgents at an intra-medial level.

Broomfield's film employs a form of triple focalization to develop its narrative. The camera consistently invites viewers to engage and ally with three different groups involved in the depicted conflict. Formal devices such as shot/reverse-shot sequences, eyeline matches, dwelling shots, or close-ups are used to carefully introduce and enable empathy and understanding with US soldiers, Iraqi civilians, and Iraqi insurgents alike. The viewer is provided with an inside perspective on the rational considerations, varying objectives, constraining factors, and contextual limitations that mould each group's behaviour in the evolving escalation, thus precluding the emergence of a simple dichotomous narrative.

Battle for Haditha carefully explains reasons and context behind the specific conduct of each party. The film shows that the US soldiers are forced to operate under severe pressure, with lack of sleep and support increasingly causing psychological problems and hampering their ability to make responsible decisions. When one US soldier asks for medical assistance, the film reminds him (and the audience) of Marine Corps policy that only allows for visiting a psychiatrist in Iraq after the respective tour of duty is over, meaning the soldier would have to stay in the country for an additional period of time to receive treatment. The presentation of such facts effectively undermines a hegemonic discourse of war framing military units as brotherhoods of equals guided by compassionate and responsible leaders, while at the same time providing the necessary context to absolve the ground forces of the ultimate responsibility for the subsequent escalation.

The Iraqi insurgency is similarly presented as composed of various different factions and identities – religious fanatics, cynical politicians, and individuals who were deprived of social status and economic means of sustenance – and their performances are carefully contextualized. The main insurgent character, for instance, despises both Bush and al-Qaeda as he attempts to manoeuvre through the complex terrain of post-invasion Iraq with the single objective of sustaining himself and his family. In particular the scenes where he, after the successful attack on US forces, returns home and meets his little daughter strongly invite for audience allegiance with this character. His subsequent dialogue with the local Sheikh (and military and spiritual leader of the insurgency) reveals the former's contempt for the means adopted by his superiors, who remorselessly sacrifice local families to unite the factions of the city behind their cause against US forces, and exploit his own economic hardships for the same purpose. Here, war becomes conceivable as a complex political economy that develops its own unintended dynamics and increasingly predisposes the performances of all involved actors.

Battle for Haditha also focalizes through Iraqi civilians and in this way refrains from framing them as helpless victims. When the Iraqi family central to the narrative observes the deployment of an IED on the road bordering their property, Broomfield films their discussions and debates concerning the issue. This allows for a detailed presentation of the various pressures predisposing the family's response and provides sound explanation to the apparently hostile decision not to warn US troops. The Iraqi civilians are presented as making conscious and informed decisions promising the least damaging outcome in a messy and confusing political situation. Also, in contrast to a generic presentation of Middle Eastern settings, the family's deliberations include men and women at an equal footing, thus effectively precluding the emergence of a gendered stereotype regarding Iraqi civilian life.

During the scenes of violent escalation in Broomfield's film, the camera repeatedly jumps back and forth between the subjective perspectives of all three involved parties, allowing constant access to the considerations, motivations, doubts, and fears of characters belonging to each faction, and illustrating the quickly narrowing paradigm of available actions. Long dwelling shots, sorrowful music, and short sequences showing mutual care are distributed equally among the three groups, humanizing each side and facilitating emotional involvement with each involved character.

In formally inviting for distribution of audience loyalties and emotional attachment between three opposing groups, Broomfield motivates critical reflection and enables an analytic distance to the drama presented on screen. As a result of the employed multi-focalisation, the audience is overdetermined by three competing and, indeed, mutually exclusive normative frames. *Battle for Haditha* constantly defers the formation of an ultimate audience allegiance and reinserts a notion of contingency into mediated accounts of history that preclude the formation of an overarching hegemonic perspective. History with a capital 'H' is thus dispersed into a multitude of competing idiosyncratic histories.

In doing this, the film also enables the emergence of a new perspective on evil in war as independent of the malicious intentions of individual perpetrators. Rather, evil emerges as the result of complex patterns of support and restraint that systematically reduce the paradigm of available options for all involved groups and individuals until only wrongful decisions can be made. In a manner comparable to Philip Haas' *The Situation* (2006), Broomfield's *Battle for Haditha* remorselessly exposes how war as a system fosters violence, frustrates even the best intentions, and therefore inevitably leads to disaster. Raising awareness of this peculiar logic is a precondition for a fundamental challenge of war's peculiar hegemonic visuality emanating from mainstream representations.

Battle for Haditha assigns ultimate responsibility for the depicted atrocities to the socio-political and cultural entities preparing and overseeing war. In the film, both US and insurgent leaderships are depicted as coldly assessing the unfolding events from a distance – the elevated positions of drone footage and a minaret respectively. This remote access brings forth a new epistemological barrier as characteristic of war – a barrier not between good soldiers and evil insurgents, but between abstracted and abstracting US *and* insurgent authorities attempting to control, and gain advantages from, the tragic situation on the one hand, and concretely situated individuals enmeshed in, and directly affected by, the escalation on the other.

Broomfield's film highlights the ultimate necessity of an abstracting, remote perspective for the justification of violence and profoundly challenges the ethical and epistemological basis of military leadership on both sides. Even though individual soldiers and insurgents effectuated the killings, the film assigns ultimate responsibility to the positions of power that motivate and predispose each individual subject's destructive performances. As such, rather than following the examples of Stone or de Palma, who in *Platoon* (1986) and *Redacted* (2006) launch a pseudo-criticism of war by safely confining the depicted atrocities to the malicious intentions of a few evil men among US forces, Broomfield humanizes the perpetrators and presents US soldiers as equally exploited and caught up in the destructive logics of war as their Iraqi counterparts, thus sensitizing audiences for the self-perpetuating nature of all forms of violence.

Through the technique of multi-focalization, *Battle for Haditha* brings forth the individuality and humanity of *all* sides in war and undercuts simplifying dichotomizations that legitimize massive violence as necessitated by a timeless and incomprehensible, cosmologic form of evil. As such, the film enables the emergence of the ethical requirements posed by encounters with the unique face of the other in the sense of Levinas (1999) – the face that makes "the invisible death of the other [...] 'my business'" (24), and facilitates an "ambivalent witnessing" in the sense of Kozol (2014) that loosens the representation of suffering from a sentimental gaze as the legitimizing frame for liberal interventionism. Thus, the film constitutes a profound challenge to the rhetoric of demonization characteristic of the Hollywood war film.

6 Forms of Evil in War: From Cosmology to Banality

The present chapter has presented two possible readings of Clint Eastwood's Iraq war movie *American Sniper*. A dominant reading draws upon generic cues that invite for an objectification of protagonist Chris Kyle's subjective, idiosyncratic perspective on the war that is transcoded into a deeply antagonistic, religious-mythical understanding of US military endeavors as directed against unambiguously evil, threatening adversaries. An oppositional approach, on the other hand, homes in on the, arguably few, scenes that allow for a gradual undermining of the reliability of the protagonist's vantage point, and that therefore enable a cautious critique of received discourses of self and other at war. Each reading is structured by a different notion of evil in war – either cosmologic and dwelling in particular malicious individuals, or systemic and the result of extra-individual pressures and frames.

This second understanding of evil in war – evil as a result of systemic patterns of supports and constraints – is the theme of the second film discussed in the present contribution – Nick Broomfield's *Battle for Haditha*. Here, external socio-political and economic frames emerge as the ultimate source of evil acts in war. Broomfield's film highlights how war recontextualizes the well-meaning intentions and daily practices of situated individuals, transforming them into apparently evil acts. As such, war as a system becomes conceivable as fostering the very performances and subjectivities it retrospectively claims to be directed against. War becomes conceivable as a self-enforcing, vicious circle – the result of dynamic interplays between biased representations, false justifications, and misguided performances.

In such a systemic understanding, evil in war acquires yet another quality – it can be seen as banal in the sense of Arendt (2006). In her report from the 1963 trial of Adolf Eichmann in Jerusalem, she consistently denies the Nazi leader and prime organizer of the Nazi concentration camps the status of arch-villain in a mythical-religious sense. Rather, Arendt points to the non-spectacular nature and inherent mundaneness of Eichmann's acts and highlights the plain bureaucratic routines and rationality behind the atrocious system of death developed in the Nazi state. According to Arendt (2006), Eichmann's deeds did not require any form of evil genius or hate, but only "remoteness from reality, [...] thoughtlessness" (288) and an "extraordinary diligence in looking out for [one's] personal advancement" (287) within a system that was entirely taken for granted and not questioned.

In this manner, then, evil requires a form of selective blindness that disregards the humanity and singularity of particular human beings and enables their processing as an abstracted, anonymous mass through culturally and politically sanctioned mundane routines. This understanding of evil acts as the result of structural misrepresentation and systematic misperception merits a truly troubling question to Eastwood's *American Sniper*. On the basis of what has been said so far, do not Chris Kyle's celebrated killings resemble precisely banal acts of evil? Do his self-aggrandizing actions, justified through caricatured constructions of the other as comic-book like villains, not ultimately serve his own career more than the people of Iraq or the security of the United States? Is the mindset of alleged heroes such as Chris Kyle – and of those sanctioning his deployment both politically and culturally – really as distinct from Eichmann's as we would like to believe?

Works Cited

Adkins, Todd and Jeremiah J. Castle (2013) *"Moving* Pictures? Experimental Evidence of Cinematic Influence on Political Attitudes," *Social Science Quarterly*, 95.5, 1230–1244.
Anker, Elisabeth (2005) "Villains, Victims, and Heroes: Melodrama, Media, and September 11," *Journal of Communication*, 55.1, 22–37.
Arendt, Hannah (2006) *Eichmann in Jerusalem: A Report on the Banality of Evil* (London: Penguin Classics).
Assmann, Jan (2010) "Communicative and Cultural Memory," in *A Companion to Cultural Memory Studies*, ed. Astrid Erll and Ansgar Nünning (Berlin: Walter DeGruyter), 109–118.
Barker, Martin (2011) *A 'Toxic' Genre: The Iraq War Films* (London: Pluto Press).
Burgoyne, Robert (2008) *The Hollywood Historical Film* (Oxford: Blackwell Publishing).
Butler, Judith (2009) *Frames of War: When is Life Grievable?* (London: Verso).
Der Derian, James (2009) *Virtuous War: Mapping the Military-Media-Entertainment- Network* (London: Routledge).
Eberwein, Robert (2010) *The Hollywood War Film* (Oxford: Wiley-Blackwell).
Erll, Astrid (2010) "Literature, Film, and the Mediality of Cultural Memory," in *A Companion to Cultural Memory Studies*, ed. Astrid Erll and Ansgar Nünning (Berlin: Walter DeGruyter), 389–398.
Hall, Stuart (1977) "Encoding, Decoding," in *The Cultural Studies Reader*, ed. Simon During (London: Routledge), 91–103.
Kozol, Wendy (2014) *Distant Wars Visible: The Ambivalence of Witnessing* (Minneapolis: University of Minnesota Press).
Kyle, Chris, Scott McEwen, and Jim DeFelice (2013) *American Sniper: The Autobiography of the Most Lethal Sniper in U.S. Military History* (New York: William Morrow).
Landsberg, Alison (2002) "Prosthetic Memory: The Ethics and Politics of Memory in an Age of Mass Culture," in *Memory and Popular Film*, ed. Paul Grainge (Manchester: Manchester University Press), 144–162.
Levinas, Emmanuel (1999) *Alterity and Transcendence* (New York: Columbia University Press).
McCrisken, Trevor and Andrew Pepper (2005) *American History and Contemporary Hollywood Film* (Edinburgh: Edinburgh University Press).
Neale, Steve (2000) *Genre and Hollywood* (London: Routledge).
Pötzsch, Holger (2011) "Borders, Barriers, and Grievable Lives: The Discursive Production of Self and Other in Film and Other Audio-Visual Media," *Nordicom Review*, 32. 2, 75–94.
Pötzsch, Holger (2012) "Framing Narratives: Opening Sequences in Contemporary American and British War Films," *Media, War, and Conflict*, 5. 2, 155–173.
Pötzsch, Holger (2013a) "Ubiquitously Absent Enemies: Character Engagement in the Contemporary War Film," *Nordicom Review*, 34. 1, 125–144.
Pötzsch, Holger (2013b) "Beyond Mimesis: War, Memory, and History in Clint Eastwood's 'Flags of our Fathers,'" in *Eastwood's Iwo Jima: A Critical Engagement With 'Flags of our Fathers' and 'Letters from Iwo Jima,'* ed. Anne Gjelsvik and Rikke Schubart (London: Wallflower Press), 119–138.
Pötzsch, Holger (2014) "The Ubiquitous Absence of the Enemy in Contemporary Israeli War Films," in *The Philosophy of War Films*, ed. David LaRocca (Lexington: University Press of Kentucky), 313–333.

Rosenstone, R.A. (2006). *History on Film/Film on History* (Harlow: Pearson Education Limited).
Thompson, Kristin (1988) *Breaking the Glass Armor: Neoformalist Film Analysis* (Princeton: Princeton University Press).
Tudor, Andrew (1974) *Theories of Film* (London: Secker and Warburg).
Westwell, Guy (2006) *War Cinema: Hollywood on the Front Line* (New York: Wallflower Press).
Zur, Ofer (1987) "The Psychohistory of Warfare: The Co-evolution of Culture, Psyche and Enemy," *Journal of Peace Research*, 24. 2, 125–134.

Filmography

American Sniper (2014) Dir. Clint Eastwood (Warner Bros).
The Battle for Haditha (2007) Dir. Nick Broomfield (Channel Four Films).
Flags of our Fathers (2006) Dir. Clint Eastwood (DreamWorks).
Letters from Iwo Jima (2006) Dir. Clint Eastwood (Warner Bros).
Platoon (1986) Dir. Oliver Stone (Hemdale).
Redacted (2006) Dir. Brian DePalma (Film Farm).
The Situation (2006) Dir. Philip Haas (Shadow Distribution).

Janet Harris
The Domestic Enemy in British TV Documentaries on the Iraq War

When President Bush declared 'mission accomplished' in May 2003, he obviously understood the invasion of Iraq in terms of traditional warfare, where the 'coalition of the willing' went to defeat another regular armed force and where the mission was to destroy that force by overwhelming firepower and physical manoeuvre. He thought this war had finished, but another type of war was underway. Even during the invasion the British soldiers found it difficult to identify an enemy as Iraqi soldiers melted into the population, and after the disbanding of the Iraqi army by Paul Bremner, many ex-soldiers took up arms against the occupation, not fighting for the old regime, but against the new. It became even more difficult to identify who the enemy was. Kiszely writes of post-modern warfare where "war and peace are not easily delineated [...] the contest takes place not on a field of battle, but in a complex civilian environment: 'amongst the people' and most importantly takes place where "the enemy is not obvious, nor easily identifiable, literally or figuratively, and may change on an almost-daily basis" (2007: 7). If the 'enemy' cannot be identified, it is then very difficult to know when and how they are defeated, or when one side has won, or indeed, what victory is. The problem for documentary makers becomes, how do you tell that confused and confusing story?

This chapter looks at how this framing of different enemies is constructed in British television documentaries on the British military in Iraq 2003–2009. I examined 21 documentaries on British network television which were specifically about the British military in Iraq. They fall roughly into three categories. Documentaries as investigations into what the British military was doing in Iraq include: *Real Story with Fiona Bruce*, BBC1 29/11/04; *Sweeney Investigates: Death of the Redcaps*, BBC2 10/2/05; *Newsnight* 19/9/05; *Tonight: Our Boys in Basra*, ITV 21/11/05; *Panorama: The Battle for Basra Palace*, BBC1 10/12/07; *Brothers in Arms*, Sky 17/11/09. The second category of programmes examined the effects of war on the British military fighting in Iraq: *Panorama: Bringing our Boys Home?*, BBC1 19/3/06; *Dispatches: Battle Fatigue*, C4 22/5/06; *When Our Boys Came Home*, BBC2 1/6/06; *Tonight: War Wounds*, ITV 30/1/06; *Panorama: For Queen and Country?*, BBC1 19/2/07; *Panorama: Soldiers on the Run*, BBC1 26/3/07; *Dispatches: Battle Scarred*, C4 7/9/09. The third category examines the legacy of the British occupation in Iraq: *Panorama: Basra – The Legacy*, BBC1 17/12/07; *Dispatches: Iraq – The Betrayal*, C4 17/3/08; *Iraq: The Legacy*, C4 13/12/08; *The*

Fallen: Legacy of Iraq, BBC4 19/6/09. I also looked at the series *Andy McNab's Tour of Duty* (ITV, June 2008), which contained three programmes, and the BBC series *Soldier Husband Daughter Dad* (BBC1, April 2005). This series had seven programmes, and I produced one of the programmes in this series and directed two programmes.

Winston writes that "narrative is never absent in documentary films" (1995: 119), and stories seek coherence and meaning. They define causes and list consequences. The documentary makers as well as the military needed to define the main characters of the war and post-war story, the heroes, the enemy and the victims to give the war meaning and to justify its cost. The ambivalence about the justification of war, the changing nature of war, the increasing importance of emotional over a more rational truth, the change of 'authoritative' sources from experts to 'ordinary people,' and the increasing entertainment value of television documentary in a competitive viewing market all converge to offer a more complex and different enemy from that of many past wars.

1 Framing the Enemy

Framing is defined as "selecting and highlighting some facets of events or issues, and making connections among them so as to promote a particular interpretation, evaluation, and/or solution" (Entman 2004: 5), as well as "the process by which people develop a particular conceptualization of an issue or reorient their thinking about an issue" (Chong and Druckman 2007: 2). In the traditional ideological dualistic "framing" the war is presented as a battle of good and evil, where the enemy is often simplified and monolithic: "There is always one right, justified, and innocent side – ours, even if we are committing unprovoked genocide – and the other side is always actuated by evil motives" (Hold and Silverstein 1989: 171). As a traditional war, the First Gulf War (1990–1991) was articulated as a struggle between two fundamental forces: "From the outset of the crisis in the Gulf, the media employed the frame of popular culture that portrays conflict as a battle between good and evil" (Kellner 1992: 62).

Although the Iraq War was also initially portrayed and fought as a traditional war where the coalition forces were going in to fight military forces loyal to Saddam Hussein, the discourse which ultimately gained dominance was one of intervention in Iraq for humanitarian reasons (Hoskins and O'Loughlin 2007). The Iraq War can also seem to be framed through an orientalist lens where the West was seen to be morally superior and acting from the best motives in contrast to 'the other,' which is morally degenerate. Coverage of wars in the Middle East has been notable for the emerging narratives that construct a form of 'Muslim terrorism' (Karim 2003: 81). These reinforce the orientalist view of Islam noted by Edward Said, where "malicious generalizations about Islam have become the last acceptable form of denigration of foreign culture in the West" (1997: 12).

In the Gulf War and Iraq War, the US media positioned the Iraqi people as victims of the brutal dictatorship of Saddam Hussein, with Iraqi society being fragmented and separate from the regime, which is also defined as a threat to its own people (Carpentier 2007: 107), but by late 2003 the people that the soldiers had gone to help had become those fighting the occupation, and the understanding and representation of the causes of war, and of the aggressors and enemies in the war became confused. The defining of who was evil and who was good was becoming less clear. 179 British service personnel were killed in Iraq. The war of liberation quickly became a messy war of occupation, and as the occupation became a counterinsurgency and other ambiguities became apparent, the simple master narrative seemed to come unstuck.

Beck argues that in a risk society relations of definition are to be conceived as analogous to Marx's relations of production. Risk becomes a mathematicised morality and becomes a socially constructed phenomenon: "This discourse carries the power to define and set the risk" (Beck 2000, qtd. in Shaw 2005: 97). The construction of a value in the willingness of the soldier to die was held not to be equal to the perceived poor treatment that the soldiers were receiving. The price and value of this risk in earlier wars was balanced in that the cause seemed morally equal to death, but with the growing realisation that in Iraq the cause was not worth the deaths being paid, the risk had to be re-defined and the narrative re-framed. For some the narrative began to eat itself.

"Why are we always fighting? Because we always have enemies. How do we know we always have enemies? Because we are always fighting" (Chernus 2006: 211). With doubts about the worth of the causes of war, the value of the deaths must be re-aligned. Death remains the same, but the reason for the sacrifice must have equal value to society. So, new enemies must be found to justify the fight, and new causes sought to compensate the nation for the loss of lives.

It is not just wars and their framing that are changing, but also society and soldiers. King notes that state authority over the armed forces seems to have been attenuated, and soldiers no longer die for their country. The structure and form of the obituaries from Iraq and Afghanistan are the same, and the dead of Helmand are "primarily commemorated as personalities, defined through their unique professionalism, not honoured as individual sacrifices for a collective national cause" (King 2010: 10). The state now acts through identifiable personalities and families (King 2010). Chouliaraki also notes a transformation in the understanding of war and the identity of soldiers in that "warfare is itself constituted as meaningful and legitimate precisely through the soldiers' own performance of the self, [...] and the development of the empathetic self be this in relation to a fallen fellow soldier or an ambivalent connectivity to suffering locals" (2016: 69).

If wars are fought for personal and domestic values then arguably the enemies have also changed to be those who oppose these values; that is the bureaucrats who break up families by the injury or death of the soldiers, or those who fail to let them achieve their potential as professionals or family members. In a humanitarian war the Iraqi who is being helped by the soldier is now seen as a sympathetic body, who is also a victim of war, facing the same enemy as the soldier. The ambivalence comes when the sympathetic local starts laying IEDs to blow up the helping soldiers, but the enemy is still the same. The two-dimensional framing of the enemy is thus no longer sufficient in this complex war where the old enemy is both enemy and friend, where the justification for fighting is no longer clear, but death and suffering still has to be paid for, so a different enemy must be identified.

2 Defining the Enemy

The definition of an enemy is someone "harmful or deadly [...] seeking to injure, overthrow, or confound an opponent" (Webster's dictionary). However, in war the definition and construction of an enemy is more complex. Like the military, documentaries and the media need an enemy to justify what the soldiers are doing. As story-tellers, journalists and programme makers frame war in a way that evokes a previously established story line, or scripts that depict war in mythic terms, westerns, fairy stories telling narratives of victimisation, heroism and villainy (Aalai 2014). The mythic structure is not just one of good and evil, but of issues which are seen to be forces of good. The British forces were heroes because they were helping the Iraqi people overcome the tyrant Saddam Hussein. The narrative frame of good against and overcoming evil is a fundamental justification for war, familiar to all cultures and not just presented by the media. A corollary to being good is to be seen to *do* good, which constructs the humanitarian discourse, but if the soldiers' purpose is to 'do' good, then as seen above, arguably the enemy becomes those who try to prevent them from doing good.

The enemy thus becomes not only those 'militia' (not soldiers) in Iraq who are fighting the British soldiers, but also the forces at home who can be identified more easily and held to account. The narrative demands payment from those who do wrong to the soldiers and achieving this from recognisable groups is easier and gives sight of a clearer way to resolve the problem than from a force whose wrong doing is morally uncertain. The domestic enemy is impeding the military from carrying out their duty to 'do good,' as well as being seen not to provide the funding or the adequate strategy which leads the soldier into danger and to failure in war. The suffering soldier who is prevented from doing good becomes a victim of war:

> The increasing celebration of victimhood within British society and public disquiet over the use of force, coupled with the nature and objectives of conflicts in Afghanistan and Iraq, have ensured that the soldier is easily pigeonholed as a victim of poor strategy and underfunding of the Armed Forces. (McCartney 2011: 43)

The image of the soldier as victim deprives them of agency and thus responsibility. They become less the perpetrators of violence against 'an enemy,' but the recipients of poor policy, lack of planning and care by the government, which can then be condemned, while the troops continue to be supported (McCartney 2011). Kleykamp and Hipes' study on the US media coverage of veterans of the Iraq and Afghan wars finds that as in the Vietnam war, veterans are portrayed as victims 'emphasizing the harm done to them by combat abroad and bureaucracy at home' (2015: 351). If the bureaucracy that caused the soldiers suffering can be held to account, the enemy is defeated and the war is won.

Juergensmeyer identifies a constructed enemy as an abstraction, and writes of the "faceless collective enemy" (2003: 179) where in many religious wars the ordinary people are targeted as representatives of a collective that is a corporate foe: "The amorphous foe asserts the triumph of order over disorder" (179). He notes that in conflicts where religion plays a part there is often a primary and a secondary enemy: "The primary enemy is the religious rival or local political authority that directly threatens the activist group [...] the secondary enemy is a less obvious threat [...] a governmental authority who is trying to be fair-minded" (179).

It is difficult to argue that the MoD/Government is a direct threat to the soldiers in the documentaries examined in this chapter, but they are clearly identified as a group which impedes 'our boys' from winning a war which heroes, and especially heroes with such technical advantages, should be able to win. In June 2005, US Secretary of Defense Donald Rumsfeld announced that "this insurgency is going to be defeated not by the coalition – it is going to be defeated by the Iraqi security forces." Paul Rogers comments that it is an astonishing moment when "one of the war's leading architects, publicly accepts that the world's most powerful military forces [...] cannot counter 20,000 or so determined insurgents backed by a minority of the population of Iraq" (2006: 255). Failure of coalition soldiers is a difficult concept to swallow, but failure partly due to the ineptitude of an amorphous, bureaucratic MoD/Government body is easier to accept.

Allied to the incomprehension that the biggest, most advanced army in the world was being defeated by a group of insurgents was the problem of the changing nature of the war in Iraq. Fighting was moving from traditional to asymmetric warfare, with the involvement of different groups and players, which meant that the identification of an enemy became equally shifting. In wars which involved nations, the enemy is perhaps easier to identify. In 2005 General Sir Rupert Smith, who had been Deputy Supreme Commander Allied Powers Europe in 1998–2001, wrote that "we fight amongst the people" (2005: 278) who are "an entity but not a monolithic block [...] they form entities based on family, tribe, nation, ethnicity, religion, ideology, state, profession, skill, trade and interests of many different kinds" (2005: 279). The fragmentation of war meant a fragmentation of the enemy. This fragmentation can perhaps be broken down even further to the individual. King writes in his study of obituaries that "The dead are remembered for their individual professionalism" (2010: 20). They have personalities and families. If these are today's heroes, the villains are perhaps amorphous bodies, the collective who impede the individual's path to winning, again the faceless bureaucrats in the Ministry of Defence, or 'the Army.'

3 Documentaries about Iraq

Specific genres have their own requirements which influence the way stories are told, and thus the representation and portrayal of the enemy. Genre may be defined as a "system of codes, conventions and expectations" (Ekström 2002: 277). For Corner, the documentary has always been defined in a "loose, contingent kind of way" (2001: 125), and Nichols claims that documentaries "adopt no fixed inventory of techniques, address no one set of issues, display one single set of forms or styles" (2010: 21). However, the codes and expectations of documentary can also be divided into the categories of 'current affairs' and documentary films. Both forms are documentaries in the traditional sense of being actuality, or factually based films, but as Michalski and Gow (2007) write, current affairs documentaries are treated separately because of the increasing short term focus they have. In the BBC current affairs documentaries are also commissioned from the News and Current Affairs department, thus have a more journalistic intent, and often draw on reporters and producers from news (Schlesinger, Murdock and Elliott 1983). Hill classifies current affairs and investigations as a broad category which "encompasses both long form journalism, political debate, consumer-based stories and investigative journalism" (2007: 5). In current affairs programmes the reporters are frequently news journalists who often present themselves as "populist spokesmen articulating what they take to be the prevailing fears and preoccupations of 'ordinary viewers." They base their questions on "some supposed common sense consensus on the issue" (Schlesinger, Murdock and Elliott 1983: 40). The question of who is the enemy is thus the product of discursive practices (Tagg 1988). Nichols states that these practices are the "vehicles of domination and conscience, power and knowledge, desire and will" (1991: 3). So the documentary maker constructs and makes sense of events, and tells stories about conflicts, of winning and losing through an organising idea, often drawing on cultural texts and ideology to do so.

Similar to the structuring of news into narrative frames, stories are intrinsic to documentary. Knudsen writes that a story has no inherent form: "it can be a series of feelings and emotions, a cluster of memories [...] the underlying emotional currents of someone's life, a series of events imagined, historical events communally remembered, or even a history of ideas" (2012: 91). It is in the selection of these that the documentarist tells her story, and tells it through tools of fiction such as character, dialogue and plot. The selection of facets of the events or issue is also noted by Nichols, who argues that the "post-structural critique of Western humanist thought [...] relegates all discourses to the category of master narrative [...] [i.e., to] accounts that subsume all that they survey to one controlling story line, leaving little if any room for anomaly, difference of otherness" (1991: 207). In films about war, this 'master narrative' leaves little room for an exploration of the other, and perhaps contributes to the lack of a satisfactory portrayal of 'the enemy.'

Aufderheide (2007) categorises US documentaries on Iraq into three types; the "Why we are in Iraq" films which are essay films that analyse and extrapolate motives for the US government's decision to invade Iraq; the "grunt docs," where the enemy is mostly faceless, and the "Learning from Iraqis" ones, which are overwhelmingly civilian stories. The television documentaries on the British military in Iraq fall mainly into the second category, where the "usual choice for narrative structure is to follow the course of a deployment" (Aufderheide 2007: 57). She writes that, unlike in the UK, television is off-limits for much of this material in the US, but what makes it on to public and cable television is marked by very powerful emotional narratives. Stories of the grunt soldiers are also a feature of the cinema. Luckhurst notes that of the twenty-three Hollywood films released between 2004–2009 that focused directly on the Iraq war, many were "structured around the model of a returned veteran suffering post-traumatic stress, building toward the narrative revelation of a repressed event from the war" (2012: 714). This is also a feature of the British TV documentaries, where a third of those examined are about the returned suffering soldiers.

The majority of the documentaries examined are part of news and current affairs output, with news journalists as presenters: *Panorama*; *Sweeney Investigates*; *The Real Story with Fiona Bruce* and *Newsnight* from the BBC; *Dispatches* from C4; and *Tonight* from ITN. The underlying remit of these programmes is investigative journalism: "These popular, long running series have, at various points in their history, acted as the 'conscience of the nation,' seeking to expose social injustice, investigate misdemeanours by the powerful and take on venal or corrupt vested interest" (McQueen 2011: 677). The format therefore requires a villain whose misdemeanours must be revealed.

The other documentaries on the British military in Iraq also had a traditional documentary theme of finding alternative voices and raising issues of social concern. The BBC output has a public service remit of social concern and providing information. The publicity for the BBC documentary *When Our Boys Came* home states that the film "captures the suffering of three men who served our country when we sent them to Iraq, but whose voices are seldom heard when the rights and wrongs are discussed" (BBC 2009). The BBC series *Soldier Husband Daughter Dad* brief was also to tell the stories of the military in Iraq and the concurrent experience of the families in the UK. The BBC4 documentary *No Plan no Peace* was an investigative documentary directed by Fiona Bruce, a producer for Panorama.

4 The Enemy in British TV Documentaries

To research the programmes I undertook a qualitative research approach, as this can "reveal underlying themes and contexts of the messages" (Wimmer and Dominick 2013: 422). I examined the "concepts, metaphors and themes" (Jensen 2013: 277), and transcribed all the speech and commentary from the documentaries. From this I noted who was directly spoken of as 'the enemy,' over what visuals, and who was accused of being to blame for an issue, or who was responsible for a particular event or problem experienced by the soldiers and their families to assign the identification of an enemy.

The enemy is not often directly named, but three major opponents for the British soldier are identified. The first are the British government and politicians. This is a major theme in half of the documentaries (*Real Story with Fiona Bruce*, BBC1 2004; *Sweeney Investigates: Death of the Redcaps*, BBC2 2005; *Tonight: Our Boys in Basra*, ITV 2005; *Panorama: Bringing our Boys Home?*, BBC1 2006; *Dispatches: Battle Fatigue*, C4 2006; *When Our Boys Came Home*, BBC2 2006; *Tonight: War Wounds*, ITV 2006; *Panorama: For Queen and Country?*, BBC1 2007; *Brothers in Arms*, Sky 2009). The second is the 'army,' a confused amalgam of senior officers and the Ministry of Defence, and the third, as Basra descended into violence and the British lost all control in the south, is the 'militias,' an amorphous collection of armed people who are given no nationality until 2009, when the British forces had withdrawn from Iraq.

In accordance with traditional representations the enemy are those people killing or harming the friend (that is the British military). In visual media, having pictures to illustrate the enemy is obviously vital, but this presented a problem with films made after the invasion. Part of the difficulty for those documentaries studied is the lack of footage of the Iraqis. Programmes resorted to archive footage of Fedayeen soldiers marching before 2003, and this is used to represent the enemy as when Jane Corbin states in *Panorama: For Queen and Country?* (BBC1 2007) that "the enemy the British army was sent to fight had been defeated." After the invasion, 'the enemy' is often referred to in the passive mode, in that they are not identified visually. Commentary which mentions 'the enemy' is placed over pictures of British soldiers, as in "these men are also a target for their ever watchful enemy [...] Insurgency comes to Iraq by many routes [...] the enemy is doing it with the help of the Bedouin on 'the other side'" (*Tonight: Our Boys in Basra*, ITV 2005).

After the invasion, when most journalists had left Iraq and the security situation deteriorated, it became more difficult to film on the street. Before the contribution of social media to programmes on war, getting pictures of any Iraqi opposition was problematic. When I was in Basra in 2004 I obtained a militia DVD which pictured various insurgents firing RPGs and AK47s. The tape was obviously also bought by news outlets in Basra and the footage became ubiquitous in most reports from southern Iraq.

The third type of naming the enemy is commentary over pictures from this DVD, where the 'enemy' is again clearly bent on killing British soldiers: "The enemy are changing [...] the ever watchful enemy [...] the enemy is doing it (insurgency) with the help of the Bedouin" (*Tonight: Our Boys in Basra*, ITV 2005); "in a conflict like Iraq, where the enemies are often numerous and often invisible" (*Tonight: War Wounds*, ITV 2006); "the lads were facing an enemy that didn't know when to stop" (*Andy McNab's Tour of Duty*, ITV 2008).

The "humanitarian war" (Boyd Barret 2009) continues into the occupation, where the nation-building role of the British Army is also highlighted. Five of the documentaries (*Soldier Husband Daughter Dad*, BBC1 2005; *Sweeney Investigates: Death of the Redcaps*, BBC2 2005; *Tonight: Our Boys in Basra*, ITV 2005; *Panorama: Bringing our Boys Home?*, BBC1 2006; *When Our Boys Came Home*, BBC2 2006), made before the major violence became apparent, all give reasons such as "training, and keeping the peace" to explain why the military is there. It is significant that an enemy is seldom actually named even by the soldiers. The ambivalence towards the Iraqis and hence the role of the soldiers and the nature of their enemy is apparent when looking at these documentaries over time. The early programmes reflect the dominant framing of the Iraq war as being one of liberation, where the Iraqis are represented as needing the help of the British, and of being unable to help themselves. They are mostly described as "locals, Iraqis and people," as in *Sweeney Investigates: Death of the Redcaps* (BBC2 2005). As the British military loses control of the south, the term 'enemy' is seldom used, and descriptions of the Iraqis change to 'militia' and 'insurgents,' implying their illegality and thus the irrational nature of their fight against the 'humanitarian' occupiers.

In 2004, 16,800 civilians were killed; in 2005, 20,200 and in 2006, 34,500. By October 2006, 3,709 civilians were murdered in a single month (O'Hanlon and Livingston 2010). By the end of 2005, the country was descending into civil war and the term 'insurgent' was being used in the television programmes (*Real Story with Fiona Bruce*, BBC1 2004; *Tonight: Our Boys in Basra*, ITV 2005). The Iraqis also become "heavily armed home grown militia" (*Dispatches: Iraq – The Reckoning*, C4 2005) when it has become clear that the aim of improving the lot of the Iraqis was not being achieved, and the justification for the war becomes increasingly ragged. By early 2006, those attacking the British are identified as the 'militia,' as well as the 'Shia population,' which is then categorised as "Shia insurgents or militia" (*Panorama: Bringing our Boys Home?*, BBC1 2006).

As the situation deteriorated in Basra, the enemy of the British military becomes the Iraqi militias, who are mostly portrayed as religiously fundamental maniacs who are represented as impossible to defeat because they are the irrational 'other,' playing to Orientalist stereotypes of the Middle East. They fight each other as well as the British (*Panorama: For Queen and Country?*, BBC1 2007; *Panorama: Basra – The Legacy*, BBC1 2007; *Andy McNab's Tour of Duty*, Episodes 1, 2 and 4, Sky 2009; *Iraq – The Legacy*, C4 2008; *Brothers in Arms*, Sky 2009). Brigadier Marriot states that "heavily armed home grown militia are waging a vicious battle with each other and with the coalition troops" (*Dispatches: Iraq – The Reckoning*, C4 2005). He talks about the evilness of the previous regime which "made it more difficult to give them democracy and give them their freedom because they don't know how to use it yet."[1]

Part of the problem for both programme-makers and the military is also that of identifying the enemy generally and especially as time progresses, the wider ignorance of who is the enemy. One of the officers talking about the situation in Al Majar asks: "How do you identify someone who was a gunman and someone

---

[1] See Butler's comments about the Iraq war being fought as a 'civilizing mission' (2009: 14).

who was just in the crowd with a weapon?" (*Sweeney Investigates: Death of the Redcaps*, BBC2 2005). Brigadier Marriott talks about the violence in Basra to Jane Corbin in 2006:

> [...] the direct attack against the British could be for a lot of reasons. It could be that we have arrested a member of the political militia and that's reduced their power, it could be that they want us out, it could be that orders from afar have come, just to poke them in the eye. There are so many different reasons. (*Panorama: Bringing our Boys Home?*, BBC1 2006)

Phil Hindmarch, a former Sergeant in the Royal Regiment of Fusiliers says that "There's more than one enemy in Iraq, whether that be the locals, the terrorists, or keeping an eye on the Iraqi police as well" (*Dispatches: Iraq – The Betrayal*, C4 2008). The question of whether the violence in Iraq was nationalist, religious or tribal was heavily debated, both by the military, media and by academia (Hashim 2006). Peter Galbraith, for example, states that "the fundamental reality of Iraq is that there are not very many people who consider themselves Iraqis" (*Dispatches: Iraq – The Reckoning*, C4 2005).

The second 'enemy' in the television documentaries on the British military in Iraq is the Ministry of Defence, and the military itself. This discourse is clear from the first programme that was broadcast, a year and a half after the invasion. The opening introduction to the following programmes sets the theme. In 2004, Fiona Bruce asks: "Injured, traumatised and suicidal: is enough being done for British troops?" (*Real Story with Fiona Bruce*, BBC1 2004). In 2005, John Sweeney states that the Red Caps were "betrayed by equipment that didn't work and a command and control system that forgot all about them. And even when they were dead the British Army betrayed them" (*Sweeney Investigates: Death of the Red Caps*, BBC2 2005). In 2006, "tonight we tell the shocking story of an army that can't even properly care for its own wounded and a government that's trying to cover it up" (*Dispatches: Battle Fatigue*, C4 2006). These introductions accuse both the government and the army of betraying the soldiers, but the MoD is also frequently accused. Fiona Bruce reports that "the family say the MoD hasn't been there enough [...]." John Sweeney reports that the British Army betrayed the Red Caps and "it failed to have the courage to admit to its own mistakes and the responsibility for that lies not with the six dead men but with Whitehall and the MoD" (*Sweeney Investigates: Death of the Red Caps*, BBC2 2005). Daniel Twiddy, an ex-soldier, says "my regiment have been brilliant [...] I just feel that I think the MoD should be doing more" (*When Our Boys Came Home*, BBC2 2006).

The identification of the MoD both confuses and conflates the origin of the responsibility for this dereliction. Is the enemy the MoD as part of the government, as civil servants, or is it the senior officers in the army who work at the

MoD? This confusion allows the MoD to say in response to ITV's *Tonight* programme's accusation of lack of care "Damian has received the full support of the army" (*Tonight: Our Boys in Basra*, ITV 2005). Responsibility is handed over by the MoD to the army as a separate organisation. This also allows the army to point a finger at the Government when the discussion about equipment and funding arises. It is the fault of the MoD, that is the government, for not providing enough equipment, but it is not seen as the fault of the army for deciding how and where to spend the money, for example on what equipment to buy or not to buy. This division between the political masters and the army emerges with the arrival of General Sir Richard Dannatt as Chief of the Defence Staff in October 2006, and his criticisms of government policy and strategy in Iraq and towards the treatment of the wounded British (Ellner 2010).

However, in *Dispatches: Battle Fatigue*, the presenter Andrew Gilligan talks of the soldiers being betrayed, "failed by the government, by the legal system and even by its own leaders," and says that the soldiers "should have the nation's backing," as they made "sacrifices on our behalf' (*Dispatches: Battle Fatigue*, C4 2007). The soldiers are now also denied "our help" and "we have a duty" to support them because of the "legal contract" to do so, although technically it is a covenant, not a contract. Most of the documentaries do not specify what should be done, or who should do it, but criticise the Government and the 'army' for not doing enough in a diagnostic framework. These programmes are often framed as investigative, where the reporter's role is to uncover the failure in responsibility by the government and the 'army.' The 'enemy' in the documentaries becomes the army itself, but who exactly the 'army' is, is never specified.

The fate of the Iraqis becomes part of the discourse of betrayal, of a country betrayed by British politicians in spite of the "bravery and sacrifice of our armed forces" (Vine: *Panorama: Basra – The Legacy*, BBC1 2007). As the occupation continues, the British military is not accountable, as their withdrawal strategy claims that what is happening is now in the hands of the Iraqis, and an internal matter to be sorted out by their security forces and government. The discourse of Iraqis betrayed by the British government becomes stronger as the security situation deteriorated in Basra (*Panorama: For Queen and Country?*, BBC1 2007; *Panorama: Basra – The Legacy*, BBC1 2007; *Panorama: On Whose Orders?*, BBC1 2008; *Dispatches: Iraq – The Betrayal*, C4 2008; *Dispatches: Iraq – The Legacy*, C4 2008) but it is not the soldiers who are responsible.

Both *Panorama* and *Dispatches* made programmes on the betrayal of the Iraqis. The former in *Basra: The Legacy*, where Jane Corbin "reveals the true legacy Britain is leaving the people of Basra" (BBC1 2007). At the end of the programme, the responsibility is laid in the hands of the government, again foregrounding domestic politics, with the coverage of the fate of the translators, where Corbin states that Denmark has given eleven of their interpreters asylum, but that after public outcry the UK has now promised to let some settle in Britain. One of the translators says: "We feel that the British forces are responsible for our lives," but the juxtaposition of General Binns next to this charge refutes this argument: "the government has indicated, we're discharging our moral obligation". The tricky problem also arises that the lack of security provided by the British leads to the abandonment of the Basrawi citizens to the militia, and they too are made responsible for the situation leading to the betrayal. Corbin states that "now the British are bowing out, handing over to Basra and its problems to the Iraqis", but then excuses the British forces by stating "further north the American troops took them [the militias] on, but the British army lacked the manpower and the political will back home". So, the increasing violence in Basra is laid at the feet of the militia who forced people to leave Basra, "hundreds [...] lawyers, professors, educated people Basra couldn't afford to lose" (all quotes *Panorama: Basra – The Legacy*, BBC1 2007).

This contrapuntal reading of the betrayal (Said 1994) is a reflection of the many and sometimes discordant voices which provide meaning together, thus enriching the discourse of betrayal. The betrayed are the soldiers, the Iraqis and the British public, who all mesh to provide a dominant discourse of general betrayal. In the following programmes analysed, it is not just the Iraqis and the soldiers who have been betrayed, but also the British public (*Real Story with Fiona Bruce*, BBC1 2004; *Sweeney Investigates: Death of the Redcaps*, BBC2 2005; *Dispatches: Iraq – The Reckoning*, C4 2005; *Panorama: Bringing our Boys Home?*, BBC1 2006; *Tonight: War Wounds*, ITV 2006; *Panorama: The Battle for Basra Palace*, BBC1 2007; *Dispatches: Iraq – The Betrayal*, C4 2008). The betrayers are mostly the government, but towards the middle of the occupation Tony Blair and Gordon Brown become the main perpetrators of this betrayal. For example in *Dispatches* (2008), which is actually subtitled "The Betrayal," Peter Oborne states that the public have been "deceived about the reasons for entering the war and about what is left behind" and that "the Government told us that the Iraq war would make us safer, but we have brought back the cult of the suicide bomber to Britain." This forms part of the tactic of using foreign politics for domestic political uses, in that the war forms a mechanism to criticise Tony Blair and other politicians. The Iraqis, British public and the British army are united in their fate and their betrayal by the politicians. In *Panorama: For Queen and Country?* (BBC1 2007), Sue Smith, the mother of a dead soldier, says: "I feel sorry for the Iraqi people. I sit and cry when I see how they have been massacred. Philip's blood runs on them streets, the same as theirs." The dead are thus united, and the guilt about the legitimacy of killing Iraqis can be assuaged.

Conclusion

In British TV documentaries, the certainties of allocating roles of enemy/friend, victim/perpetrator have become complex, much like the fog of war. In traditional war, the enemy is, on the whole, the person killing the British soldier. However, framing war as a humanitarian effort blurs the dynamics of the soldier as killer and the soldier as helper/protector. Are you shooting to kill or to protect? And who are you killing, a friend or an enemy? When the sanction of legitimised force is debatable because the legitimacy of the action is unclear, the delineation of the enemy also becomes confused. If the documentary stories need a justification for war, they also need a justified enemy. If the Iraqis are friends but they are also killing you, who is to blame? In the later stages of the war the enemy reverted to the traditional orientalist foe, the fundamentalist Iraqi militia, but the equally amorphous and generalised foe, the 'MoD' was still the enemy, not only of the heroic and betrayed British soldier, but the betrayed Iraqi civilian. Iraqis and soldiers became victimised individuals suffering from PTSD, and 'those who kill and those who are killed, by sharing a common humanity, may both qualify as victims of trauma' (Scandlyn and Hautzinger 2015: 557). Thus with the enemy positioned as an amorphous group of bureaucrats who not only betray the soldiers but who also betray the soldiers' friends, the Iraqis, the narrative proffers an enemy who can be held accountable for the military failure of the war. The sticky problem of defeat can thus be resolved without having to place any blame on the individual heroic soldiers, whose values are the same as ours. The politicians and military who work at the MoD can be voted out, questioned or submitted to an enquiry, so as the enemy is defeated, the war can be won.

Works Cited

Aalai, Azadeh and Victor Ottati (2014) "The Mythical Framing Effect: Media Coverage and Public Opinion Regarding the Iraq War," *Journal of Mass Communication & Journalism* 4, 217.
Aufderheide, Patricia (2007) "Your Country, My Country: How Films About The Iraq War Construct Publics," *Framework* 48. 2, 56–65.
Bernazzoli, Richelle M. and Colin Flint (2009) "Power, Place, and Militarism: Toward a Comparative Geographic Analysis of Militarization," *Geography Compass* 3. 1, 393–441.
Boyd-Barrett, Oliver (2007) "Positioning the News Audience as Idiot," in *Communicating War: Memory, Media and Military*, ed. Sarah Maltby and Richard Keeble (Bury St. Edmunds: Arima Publishing), 90–102.
Carpentier. Nico 2007 "Fighting Discourses: Discourse Theory, War and Representations of the 2003 Iraqi War," in *Communicating War: Memory, Media and Military*, ed. Maltby and Keeble, 103–116.
Chouliaraki, Lillie (2016) "Authoring the Self: Media, Voice and Testimony in Soldiers' Memoirs," *Media, War & Conflict* 9. 1, 58–75.
Chong, Dennis, and James N. Druckman (2007) "Framing Theory," *Annual Review of Political Science* 10, 103–126.
Coker, Christopher (2001) *Human Warfare: The New Ethics of Postmodern War* (London and New York: Routledge).
Douglas, Mary (2002) *Purity and Danger* (Harvard: Harvard University Press).
Corner, John (2001) "Documentary," in *The Television Genre Book*, ed. Glen Creeber (London: BFI), 124–129.
Ekström, Mats (2002) "Epistemologies of TV Journalism. A Theoretical Framework," *Journalism* 3. 3, 259–282.
Ellner, Andrea. (2010) "Civil-Military Relations under Strain – A Comparative Analysis of Britain and the US," Paper for the 60th Anniversary Conference of the Political Studies Association and the British International Studies Association, Edinburgh, 29 March–1 April 2010 (PSA).
Entman, Robert M. (2004) *Projections of Power: Framing News, Public Opinion and US Foreign Policy* (Chicago: University of Chicago Press).
Fowler, Roger (2013) *Language in the News: Discourse and Ideology in the Press* (London and New York: Routledge).
Hammond, Philip (2004) "Humanising War: the Balkans and Beyond," in *Reporting War: Journalism in War Time*, ed. Barbie Zelizer and Stuart Allan (London and New York: Routledge).
Hill, Annette (2007) *Restyling Factual Television: Audiences and News, Documentary and Reality Genres* (London and New York: Routledge).
Hoskins, Andrew, and Ben O'Loughlin (2007) *New Security Challenges: Television and Terror: Conflicting Times and the Crisis of News Discourse* (Basingstoke: Palgrave Macmillan).
Jensen, Klaus (2012) "The Qualitative Research Process," in *A Handbook of Media and Communication Research: Qualitative and Quantitative Methodologies*, ed. Klaus Jensen (London and New York: Routledge), 265–282.
Juergensmeyer, Mark (2003) *Terror in the Mind of God: The Global Rise of Religious Violence*, 3rd edition (Berkeley, Los Angeles, and London: University of California Press).

Karim, Karim H. (2003) *Islamic Peril: Media and Global Violence* (Montreal: Black Rose Books).

Kellner, Douglas (1992) *The Persian Gulf TV War* (Boulder, San Francisco, and Oxford: Westview Press).

King, Andrew (2010) "The Afghan War and 'Postmodern' Memory: Commemoration and the Dead of Helmand," *The British Journal of Sociology* 61. 1, 1–25.

Kleykamp, Meredith, and Crosby Hipes (2015) "Coverage of Veterans of the Wars in Iraq and Afghanistan in the US Media," *Sociological Forum* 30. 2, 348–368.

Kiszely, John (2007) *Post-Modern Challenges for Modern Warriors* (*The Shrivenham Papers* 5).

Lewis, Justin (2001) *Constructing Public Opinion* (New York: Columbia University Press).

Luckhurst, Roger (2012) "In War Times: Fictionalizing Iraq," *Contemporary Literature* 53. 4, 713–737.

Mcqueen, David (2011) "A Very Conscientious Brand: A Case Study of the BBC's Current Affairs Series *Panorama*," *Journal of Brand Management* 18. 9, 677–687.

McCartney, Helen (2011) "Hero, Victim or Villain? The Public Image of the British Soldier and Its Implications for Defense Policy," *Defense and Security Analysis* 27. 1, 46–47.

Michalski, Milena, and James Gow (2007) *War Image and Legitimacy: Viewing Contemporary Conflict* (London and New York: Routledge).

Nichols, Bill (1991) *Representing Reality: Issues and Concepts in Documentary* (Bloomington and Indianapolis; Indiana University Press).

Nichols, Bill (2010) *Introduction to Documentary*, 2nd edition (Bloomington and Indianapolis: Indiana University Press).

Rogers, Paul (2006) *A War Too Far: Iraq, Iran and the New American Century* (London and Ann Arbor: Pluto Press).

Said, Edward (1991) *Orientalism, Western Conceptions of the Orient* (London: Penguin).

Scandlyn, Jean, and Sarah Hautzinger (2015) "'Victim/Volunteer': Heroes versus Perpetrators and the Weight of US Service-Members' Pasts in Iraq and Afghanistan," *The International Journal of Human Rights* 19. 5, 555–571.

Schlesinger, Philip, Graham Murdock, and Philip Ross Courtney Elliott (1983) *Televising Terrorism: Political Violence in Popular Culture* (London and New York: Comedia Publishing Group).

Shaw, Martin (2005) *The New Western Way of War: Risk-Transfer War and its Crisis in Iraq* (Cambridge and Malden, MA: Polity).

Silverstein, Brett, and Robert R. Holt (1989) "Research on Enemy Images: Present Status and Future Prospects," *Journal of Social Issues* 45. 2, 159–175.

Smith, Christina (2016) "Gaze in the Military: Authorial Agency and Cinematic Spectatorship in 'Drone Documentaries' from Iraq," *Continuum* 30. 1, 89–99.

Smith, Rupert (2005) *The Utility of Force: The Art of War in the Modern World* (London: Allen Lane).

Tagg, John (1988) *The Burden of Representation: Essays on Photographies and Histories* (Basingstoke and New York: Palgrave Macmillan).

Wimmer, Roger, and Joseph Dominick (2013) *Mass Media Research: An Introduction* (Boston, MA: Wadsworth, Cengage Learning).

Filmography

Andy McNab's Tour of Duty (3 episodes). Sky, June 2008.
Brothers in Arms. Sky 17/11/2009.
Dispatches: Battle Fatigue. C4 22/5/2006.
Dispatches: Iraq – the Betrayal. C4 17/3/2008.
Dispatches: Battle Scarred. C4 7/9/2009.
The Fallen: Legacy of Iraq. BBC4 19/6/2009.
Iraq: The Legacy. C4 13/12/2008.
Newsnight 19/9/2005.
Panorama: Bringing our Boys Home? BBC1 19/3/2006.
Panorama: For Queen and Country? BBC1 19/2/2007.
Panorama: Soldiers on the Run. BBC1 26/3/2007.
Panorama: The Battle for Basra Palace. BBC1 10/12/2007.
Panorama: Basra – The Legacy. BBC1 17/12/2007.
Real Story with Fiona Bruce. BBC1 29/11/2004.
Soldier Husband Daughter Dad (7 episodes). BBC1, April 2005.
Sweeney Investigates: Death of the Redcaps. BBC2 10/2/2005.
Tonight: Our Boys in Basra. ITV 21/11/2005.
Tonight: War Wounds. ITV 30/1/2006.
When Our Boys Came Home. BBC2 1/6/2006.

Maryam Jameela
Britain's Muslims as the Enemy Within in Contemporary British Cinema

In this chapter, I will be using a phenomenological and intersectional approach to examine the constructions of British Muslims as aliens or enemies in contemporary British cinema, with specific attention paid to the construction of South Asian Muslim women. This will require an intersectional outlook cognizant of the simultaneities and overlaps embedded within depictions of multiply layered identities. Intersectionality and cultural/social phenomenology are useful tools for pulling out patterns of contemporary British cinema with regard to the representation of Muslims, as both have the methodological value of pushing for context-based analysis. Given the polarising rhetoric of post 9/11 politics, this will be fundamental for painting a more nuanced picture of both ideological conflicts and internal enemies.

9/11 has come to characterise the contemporary political moment through the so-called 'war on terror,' fought through invasions in Iraq and Afghanistan, drone attacks, illegal detainments and torture along with, recently, white supremacist and US president Donald Trump's attempts at implementing a Muslim ban. Such an environment of global and institutional Islamophobia has naturally bled into smaller interactions involving discrimination, hate crimes and racist media depictions. This context is central to how films concerning Muslims post 9/11 are both produced and disseminated; to ignore contexts is to ignore the social, political and cultural commentaries that inextricably form the foundation and structure of their production. Clint Eastwood's *American Sniper* (2014), Kathryn Bigelow's *Zero Dark Thirty* (2012), and Gavin Hood's *Eye in the Sky* (2016) are notable examples of films that use George W. Bush's rallying cry of the "war on terror" as the backdrop for their treatment of Muslim terrorists. All three concern themselves with the 'difficult decisions' army personnel take, whilst framing Muslims as either collaborators with Western intelligence agencies or bodies that exist to be shown in abject poverty, dying or dead. These films are a microcosm of the suspicion that Muslims have been tarred with after 9/11, alongside various other terrorist attacks carried out under the name of Islam. They disregard any real life issues of Muslims that do not gravitate solely around 9/11, and this single-axis focus reduces Muslim people to a highly homogenous group that can exist only within the context of 9/11 as enemy bodies.

My understanding of 'enemies within' is greatly indebted to Sara Ahmed's *Strange Encounters*, wherein Ahmed explores the familiarity of strangers as well as the boundary of 'stranger' as one that is determined by the position (and outlook) of the person who encounters the stranger. Ahmed posits that "if we think of 'home' purely as proximity and familiarity, then we fail to recognise the relationships of estrangement and distance within the home" (2000: 139). In this line of argument, the 'enemy' or 'stranger' is a figure that has to have some proximity to the 'home' in order to be encountered: "aliens allow the demarcation of spaces by belonging: by coming too close to home, they establish the very necessity of policing the borders of knowable and inhabitable terrains [...] through strange encounters, the figure of the 'stranger' is produced, not as that which we fail to recognise, but as that which we have already recognised as 'a stranger'" (2000: 3). As Ahmed argues, for a body to be designated as 'enemy,' it is necessary for that body to occupy a space close to bodies which hold the gaze, and can thereby designate others as enemy.

Both films I am comparing use 9/11 as a central event which irrevocably alters the lives of the protagonists, and it is this alteration which is a function within a larger narrative of 9/11 as a turning point for Muslims and, in this instance, Muslims living in the West. Kenneth Glenaan's *Yasmin* (2004) depicts a Pakistani woman struggling with conforming to her family's wishes for her life and her desire to assimilate into a white Britain. Sarah Gavron's *Brick Lane* (2007) concerns a young Bangladeshi woman moving to London with her new husband and confronting the demands of the men in her life. This selection will engage with the status of Muslim women as ostensibly oppressed symbols of a barbaric Islam for non-Muslim Westerners, and how this dehumanisation is assembled within the larger context of Muslims as suspicious foreigners that can only be internal enemies.

I am reminded at this juncture of Laura Mulvey's seminal film theory on the male gaze. Mulvey posits that "the image of woman as (passive) raw material for the (active) male gaze takes the argument a step further into the structure of representation, adding a further layer demanded by the ideology of the patriarchal order as it is worked out in its favourite cinematic form – illusionistic narrative film" (2003: 52). While Mulvey's work is still critical and important for contemporary cinematic analysis, in keeping its focus along a single axis it universalizes, and thereby restricts, the impact it can have on gender relations. For my analysis, gaze theory and focalisation will be central in having a structured and direct impact in discussing films that revolve around 9/11; such a structured approach is necessary in order to apprehend the context of the films without getting mired in their contemporaneity, and their highly prescient nature. I will be arguing that analysing the representation of Muslim women requires attention to be paid to who is holding the gaze; this argument is itself underpinned by Mulvey's influential assertion, but it is nonetheless an assertion which imagines only white bodies in the exchange of signifiers.

1 *Yasmin*

Yasmin was released soon after 9/11, and its proximity to the early rhetoric of the war on terror is reflected throughout the film by frequent voiceovers from George W. Bush and Tony Blair that bleed from a diegetic standpoint to extra-diegetic sound. The choice to include Bush and Blair is a choice that demonstrates the film's engagement with contemporary political rhetoric as one which remains mired in the initial calls for a "war on terror" against so-called "Islamist terrorism." For example, whilst Yasmin secretly changes into a pair of jeans at a roadside, which itself depicts a Muslim woman leading a double life, an excerpt from the radio reveals Bush stating that "the United States will hunt down and punish those responsible for these cowardly acts." The narrative is framed with the notion that Yasmin has to live a double life, itself a tagline of the film – "one woman, two lives" – positioning her as an example of a Muslim woman whose life is dominated by the opposition between Western life, apparently having a job, driving a car, wearing jeans, leaving hair uncovered, against her Muslim family's expectations that she will remain at home, not wear jeans, not drink and cover her hair. The juxtaposition of Yasmin changing into jeans with Bush's voiceover in the background is one which has permeated post 9/11 representations of Muslim women and is more symbolic and stereotypical than it is documentary.

The next instance of a voiceover from Bush occurs after Yasmin's father berates his son for claiming that 9/11 had "style." The interaction draws out the impact of generational difference in framing 9/11; Yasmin's father claims to be ashamed of the terrorists, tying his shame with how grateful he is to Britain for providing a "home" for him. Nasir, Yasmin's brother, claims they are about to be "sent back home" and positions himself, and by implication the terrorists who committed 9/11, as "freedom fighters." This fraught scene is immediately followed with shots of children playing outside in the backstreet with Bush's voice moving from the television to a voiceover, "the attack on our nation was also an attack on the ideals that make our nation [...] we value every life, our enemies value none, not even the innocent." The insertion of the voiceover undercuts the complexity of the earlier scene; Yasmin's father's opinions are conveyed from the position of an angry father berating a son. They are not made in the spirit of an engagement with a difficult issue, and Bush's polarising politics both underline and undercut the narrative. Bush's comments have to be understood in their moment – the immediate aftermath of 9/11 was one of shock, horror, and terror. The 'our' he references carries with it an implication of being non-Muslim, as well as an ideological attack that separates 'our' very ways of life from the implied 'them' of the "enemies." Bush paints a picture of a brutal, uncompromising, and cohesive enemy –no symbolic subtleties necessary here. The core of the film is thus concerned with engaging with a way of life for Muslims that is framed around a 'clash of civilisations' narrative wherein Muslims in the West are positioned as insider outsiders.

Sara Ahmed comprehensively explores the notion of the stranger and which bodies can be at home in her work *Strange Encounters*. She argues that:

> Orientations are about the direction we take that puts some things and not others in our reach. So the object, which is apprehending only by exceeding my gaze, can be apprehended only insofar as it has to come to be available to me: its reachability is not simply a matter of place or location [...] but instead is shaped by the orientations that I have taken that mean I face some ways more than others (2000: 56).

Here, the "object" in question is the depiction of Muslims that purports to represent the realities of the war on terror. In foregrounding the process of watching or encountering, Ahmed's model is one that serves to highlight the position of the person holding a gaze, particularly in filmic terms. In other words, the conditions of possibility that lead to an encounter encompass intersectional contexts that irrevocably colour *how* the object is seen, as well as *what* is seen. The recognition of people seeing different things when looking at the same object is an important one, especially when thinking through racial politics.

The repetitive function of a structure such as racist orientalism is one which serves as a backdrop to the film as a whole; the presence of Bush's voiceover verbalises the clash of cultures which the film envisions itself as depicting, and the voiceovers are a decisive reminder of an institutional, social, and cultural position taken in regards to Muslims. It is a separation between who is at home and who is an enemy that is based upon an orientalist view of Islam, and of non-white ethnicities as hailing from an exotic 'other' background. Yasmin and her family are only reachable on the screen because of their depiction as oriental objects, framed within a narrative of Muslim representation. In particular, their construction as enemies in the film is largely created through the aforementioned voiceovers.

Before I proceed with an analysis of how this creation of enemies determines focalisation, it will be useful to examine the presentational context of the film in order to consider who this film has positioned itself as being *for*. The *Daily Mail* is quoted on the cover of the DVD, reviewing the film as "a superlative and utterly convincing production." This in itself is an indication of damnation by association. The *Daily Mail* has routinely and notoriously painted Muslims in a racist, xenophobic and reactionary manner, and its labelling of the film as "convincing" is suspect at best, and tenuous at worst. The tagline for the film, as mentioned earlier, is "one woman, two lives," and this plays into a rather basic stereotype that has its roots in orientalist views that presume life as a Muslim to be one that can be characterised by a "clash of civilisations." It presents the life of this one woman, and thereby other women similar to her, as one which is a constant struggle between the values or 'ideology' of Western civilisation and the presumed influence of conservative, patriarchal, Muslim society.

The DVD cover faces a mid-close-up of Yasmin's face as she is wearing a scarf, with the colouring adjusted to a harsh black and white. The blurb of the DVD cover claims that the story is about a "goat-herder" meeting "the vivacious, Westernised Yasmin. After the shocking events of 9/11, Yasmin's life begins to change," according to the blurb, and she must confront "what it means to be Asian, Muslim and British in the 21st century." Already the film has explicitly set its parameters, claiming to represent the obviously wide-ranging and multi-faceted experience of being Asian and Muslim in Britain.

This ill-conceived drive for authenticity, grittiness, or even truth is one that leads back to the question of who this film is for. It could not be for Asian and Muslim people living in Britain, since despite what the *Daily Mail* would argue, people belonging to those groups would know what it is to exist as such. The obvious conclusion here is that the film's presentational context guides us to expect an audience of white, Western and non-Muslim people, not because those identifiers are any sort of 'opposite' to Asian and Muslim people, but because those former categories are structurally dominant in a global system of white and Western supremacy. This is further compounded in the film itself in the manner in which the characters move between Punjabi and English. There are no subtitles available on the DVD for either language, and this means that in the instances where characters speak Punjabi, monolingual speakers of English would be shut out. Whilst on the surface this may indicate that sections of the dialogue are *for* Punjabi speakers, the language is not used so simply. For example, there are disjointed phrases or half-sentences exchanged between Punjabi-speaking characters that are not the primary focus of dialogue. It is extremely rare for a speaking character to proceed in Punjabi. This indicates that the film is happy to include Punjabi as an element of 'authenticity,' while leaving the majority of the dialogue in English for an English-speaking audience. Sara Ahmed's theories of orientation are useful here as, once again, what can be seen is dependent upon where one stands. This film orientates itself *around* Muslim and Asian identity, but does so *for* non-Muslim and Western audiences, as an insight into the lives of Muslims in Britain. Their identities are thus positioned as alien, as distinctly separate from what can be considered 'normal' or 'every day.'

This can be further elaborated upon with Ahmed's exploration of the use of "objects" when discussing orientalism and white supremacy, where "objects" become an extended metaphor as the Orient itself is the object being faced. She states:

> The Orient is not only reachable, but "it" has already been reached if "it" is to be available as an object of perception in the first place [...] the object function of the Orient, then, is not simply a sign of the presence of the West – of where it "finds its way"– but also a measure of how the West has "directed" its time, energy, and resources. (2006: 117)

Here, 'reachable' indicates the ability to grasp something, be it knowledge or more tangible materials. For the Orient to be reachable, it must be grasped at, or at the very least faced, by the one who grasps, i.e. the West. Ahmed goes on to argue that "we can begin here to rethink how groups are formed out of shared direction. To put this in simple terms, a 'we' emerges as an effect of a shared direction toward an object" (2006: 119). Whilst appearing to be rather oblique, Ahmed is actually being fairly direct here – it is not only that the West defines itself against the Orient, but that, through repetition, it has positioned itself as capable of holding the Orient, of grasping it, naming it, and being the lens through which it is viewed. The proximity of Yasmin and her family, or more accurately the minorities they represent, are reachable to a Western, white, and non-Muslim audience and it is this positioning of who holds the gaze which determines what can be seen.

Ultimately, *Yasmin* is a complicated film which provides a blinkered and stereotypical gaze that presumes a specific ending for Muslims by rendering them as an unassimilable enemy that can be apprehended, understood, but ultimately kept at a distance. For example, Yasmin decides to learn more about her faith by the end of the film, and whilst on her way to the mosque she bumps into John. John claims not to have recognised her in her "get up" (a scarf), and says he is on his way to the pub. Both invite the other to their activities, both decline and move off in separate directions. The message, then, is that someone who is 'too' Muslim (Yasmin's husband, walking off into the sunset with his pet goat) cannot be successfully incorporated into British society. As to Yasmin, she is shown to become 'more' Muslim and therefore choosing not to engage with a representation of white, non-Muslim, Britishness. The film's choice of frame for its engagement with being British Muslim is restricted, presenting their situation as that of an opposition. Regardless of the film's intention, the effect is to orientate Muslim men and women in traditionally patriarchal roles, seen through varying degrees of assimilation, into a 'white' way of life. Their 'enmity' turns upon their capacity of being reached as enemy bodies, which is itself enabled through a white supremacy that functions upon positioning, in this scenario, Muslim, Pakistani, and brown men and women as objects of suspicion and exotic aliens.

2 Brick Lane

This film represents a significant departure from the conventions used in *Yasmin*, despite also depicting a South Asian Muslim woman. Nazneen is married to a significantly older man, and moves with him from Bangladesh to London. Unlike the book, the narrative opens with the couple living in a small flat with their two daughters. Whilst Nazneen's husband is a central figure in her life, much of the plot is concerned with developing a nuanced picture of her life both in London and back in Bangladesh. From the outset, Nazneen's relationship with her sister Hasina conveys most about her character; one of the opening scenes is of their mother drowning herself while her two daughters are playing nearby, and the figures of Nazneen's mother and sister are central to her motivations and the development of her character throughout the film.

Her mother's tenet "we cannot run from our fate" is frequently quoted throughout the film. Indeed, it haunts the first half of the narrative as Nazneen is shown to be timid, silent, and passive. By opening with her mother's death and allowing her belief in succumbing to fate permeate the film, a generational difference is gradually being built. As Nazneen's timidity stands against the challenges of her husband's desire to move to Bangladesh as a family unit, her mother's words hold less influence. It is troubling that we never see Nazneen's mother – we only ever see the back of her body as she slowly walks into a lake, drowns, and is removed by a group of women. There are a number of suggestions as to the representational power of Nazneen's mother's suicide: a generalisation about attitudes of older generations of South Asian people that focus on surviving rather than thriving; of the impact it has on Nazneen, who takes to heart a certain meaning of her mother's words and shrinks herself to be as small as possible. The very possibility however, of the film guiding us to the importance and influence of her mother upon Nazneen, is testimony to the film's engagement with nuance. The creation of possibilities, of showing Nazneen's mother's worldview and giving Nazneen the space to engage with it throughout the film is a choice of focalisation that allows the gaze to be held by women; in doing so, the film positions Nazneen and her mother not as objects, but as subjects.

This effect is further enhanced by its construction of Nazneen as a person. If Ahmed's argument in *Strange Encounters* that the repetition of objects both creates and solidifies positions holds true, then an expression of claims to white supremacy is the repeated positioning of white bodies and white lives as deserving of humanity. Racialised systems of power do not grant the same right to bodies that are usually seen as non-white (e. g. refugees, immigrants). Therefore, the work of asserting humanity is one that is not typically universalised and, certainly for the type of films under analysis here, it is the case that depictions of non-white and non-Western groups are consumed as indicative of a larger truth about the aforementioned groups in a thoroughly dehumanising manner. For example, Rey Chow asserts that "the original that is supposed to be replicated is no longer the white man or his culture but rather an image, a stereotyped view of the ethnic" (qtd. in Puar 2007: 92). Surrounding Nazneen with women from her racial group in *Brick Lane* to build her character is thus a choice that does the work of countering stereotypes. Not only her mother, but her sister whom she frequently writes to, cares for and whom she is shown to love; her two daughters, Shanana and Bibi, whom she respects and loves; her neighbour Shazia; the domineering moneylender Mrs Ahmed; various white and South Asian women in the background of shots – all contribute to a picture that is exactly that: contributory. This is in direct contrast to *Yasmin,* where only one background character who is also South Asian is shown to interact with Yasmin. Most of the time devoted to women in Yasmin's life is given to a group of white women at work who racially abuse her by asking her to apologise for 9/11, calling her Osama, and accusing her of being in the Taliban.

The women around Nazneen, however, are an indication of the politics of the film, a politics that builds towards her character without attempts at totalizing or universalising narratives. The effect of this is to build a strong foundation that can hold the possibility of representing women as subjects by way of focalising events through their experiences. Here, the construction of subjects is well explained through a comparison with *Yasmin*. In the latter film, many of Yasmin's actions are not well explained, going so far as to appear inexplicable because her world is not conveyed in a manner conducive to believability. In *Brick Lane,* however, there are elements of choice – of narrative, of focalisation, of time spent on world building – that work to paint a believable and convincing depiction of who Nazneen is, where she comes from and where she may go. In other words, she is a woman who has the potential, from the opening of the film, not to be an enemy. Even if the status of 'not enemy' is nothing particularly meaningful, it still stands that, as the discussion will go on to demonstrate, the designation of 'enemy' is one which operates in shades of grey rather than around clearly drawn boundaries. It is never a consideration in the beginning of this film that Nazneen *could* be an enemy, whereas Yasmin, as demonstrated earlier, is about hackneyed binary oppositions before the film even begins. *Brick Lane* provides context through building up layers of focalisation that position Nazneen as within a conflict about her position in her family, her marriage, and her country of residence, but never as innately in conflict by virtue of presumed 'facts' of existence. She is a person and not only an object of representation, even if this is tested throughout a film which is set in the same political environment as *Yasmin*, and whose protagonist is thus subject to the same questions of reachability and intention. The crucial difference with *Brick Lane* is that by simply depicting multiple South Asian and Muslim women it subtly confronts a white only gaze, in turn allowing itself to open up its engagement with Muslim life and categorisation after 9/11.

Another element which *Brick Lane* does, however, share with *Yasmin* is that it also uses 9/11 as a plot device which complicates and disrupts the narrative equilibrium. In this instance, Nazneen and Karim's eyes meet on a crowded street, and they allow themselves a rare moment of publicly acknowledging their relationship, at least among themselves. This is disrupted by people rushing into a shop to see the now familiar sight of the twin towers collapsing. As with *Yasmin*, characters in the background and the protagonists express shock and horror at what is unfolding in front of them. Interestingly however, the very next scene shows Channu's reaction as the family watch the news at home, which is to insist that they pack their bags and go 'home' to Bangladesh. 9/11 accelerates a process that for Channu had already begun. Nazneen had wanted to return to Bangladesh to be with her sister, and, while still watching the news footage of 9/11, Nazneen states that "the world has gone mad." As with *Yasmin*, voiceovers from Bush and Blair punctuate the narrative, with Blair stating that "there are no adequate words of condemnation. Their barbarism will stand as their shame for all eternity." The mention of barbarism connotes racialised stereotypes of non-White people as savage and uncontrollable. However, here this is undercut with Channu racing around the flat, declaring that they must leave as soon as they possibly can because of the 'backlash' he anticipates. Channu's fear of a racist backlash is one that many Muslims felt in the immediate and continued aftermath of 9/11, yet, depicting it in a film which is not directly 'about' the terrorist attacks is an unexpected choice. A voiceover from a newsreader goes on to state that "many claim in the last seven days 'Muslim' has become a dirty word," interspersed with shots of the family's neighbours yelling at Muslims "Go! You fucking terrorists! Get out!" along with an anti-Iraq war rally shown on screen. By including this context of a racist backlash and anti-war rallies, the film complicates any straightforward readings of post 9/11 environments, and it is here that *Yasmin* and *Brick*

Lane radically diverge due to their different basic patterns. *Brick Lane* has done the work to build up its characters' humanity, while *Yasmin* is concerned with no such thing. *Brick Lane* largely constructs its protagonists as people, by giving a range of focalisations to a range of individuals, thus positioning them as capable of existing within Britain, even if that existence is troubled by the post 9/11 demonizing of Muslims.

Meanwhile, Nazneen's daughter Shanana is begging to be left behind, to be adopted by a family remaining in England, or for her mother to stay – in short, any scheme that will mean she does not leave what she thinks of as her home. The question of home continues to rear its head as Karim proposes marriage to Nazneen. He had earlier explained that his attraction to her had been because he believes there are two types of girls, those that are "Westernised and religious," whom he finds to have excessive expectations, and those "from the village," whom he calls the "real thing." Until this point in the narrative, Nazneen and Karim have found themselves to be rather compatible with one another, and so it is a little surprising when Nazneen tells him, "I do not want to marry you. I am no longer the real thing. I am no longer the girl from the village" and clarifies what their relationship meant to her: "I just wanted to feel like I was at home." For Nazneen, Karim represented a kind of home in a number of ways – partly that she loved him and enjoyed the sex, but also that his English nationality meant that she could connect to England through him, and thus to her physical home. Her use of "I am no longer" indicates that she has undergone a change wherein her understanding of herself, and therefore of what home means to her, has shifted in some fundamental way.

It is important to note that directly after this scene Nazneen has her first narration in the film. After Channu has consistently filled space with his meaningless chatter, she begins to take up space herself and talks of her understanding of love as something that can grow over time, the implication being that she loves Channu in her own way but that she cannot be with him. She tells him he must go to Bangladesh alone, and she will remain on Brick Lane with her daughters. Channu pretends it was his decision, and the girls are clearly overjoyed to be able to stay. Both scenes show Nazneen rejecting the men in her life, and her choosing for herself as well as choosing her daughters are moments which result from the fact that here are women, and varied representations of women, who are subjects that demonstrably have their own gaze. Focalising their narratives through their eyes, and thus rendering them from specific rather than from overarching and universalised viewpoints, makes these scenes powerful moments of reclamation. Nazneen's choices of relationships and lifestyle also mirror the film's attitude towards politics – ultimately she rejects, or at the very least disregards, Karim's anti-racist politics as well as Channu's, which are critical of calls for unity. She chooses to be with her daughters, and the film, from a distance, is about Nazneen empowering herself, an empowerment which is convincingly conveyed to the audience. As much as 9/11 functions as a plot device, it is not a plot device that decisively and wholly changes the lives of all Muslims in the film, as is the case in *Yasmin*.

In choosing to represent 'home' as a fluid and changeable entity, *Brick Lane* goes some way towards acknowledging that Nazneen's reality simultaneously involves attacks by racists in Brick Lane and that there are things that can make her feel comfortable, like the friends she has made and the home their daughters have built. For Nazneen, home is simultaneously England, Bangladesh, the love of a man, the love of her sister and mother, and the love of her daughters. At the very end, Nazneen reflects that "I am torn between two worlds, leaving you [Hasina] behind. But then I wake and see that it is not you but me who has been running, searching for a place that has already been found." The conclusion the film guides us towards, then, is one which suggests that Nazneen was home all along, and that all she had to do was realise this. This neat ending carries with it a troubling undercurrent, as it orientates audiences towards a politics of assimilation. While assimilation is not exclusively negative, it is still the case that in order to assimilate, some element must have been outside the norm, strange or alien. Nazneen's process of realising that she can stay 'at home' is an internal one, and the implication is therefore that her memories of 'back home' in Bangladesh drew her away from considering England as her home. Assimilation requires an alien characteristic that can be brought into the fold and, for much of the film, Nazneen and her family were strangers/outsiders/enemies by virtue of being brown and Muslim. 9/11 exacerbated these tensions and heightened their differences, and so Nazneen's choice to remain 'at home' is both a sign of empowerment and testimony to the difficult politics of those bodies designated as enemy or strange.

These contradictory conclusions hold the centre of *Brick Lane* together. There is certainly a strong basic assumption that makes the film position both men and women as subjects who are attributed focalisation, which in turn allows for complicated representations. However, there is also a thread running through the film that positions Nazneen as outside the 'norm,' a norm that is white and non-Muslim. Indeed, in order for her to feel at home she is required to let go of her memories of Bangladesh, and she happily lies back in the snow with her scarf falling off her head, a very particular choice. This moment communicates that it took Nazneen an effort to make the decision of remaining in England, and rejecting the 'brown men' in her life, before she could smile freely, allowing herself to enjoy time with her daughters. The cost of her assimilation leaves us with the conclusion that while she may no longer explicitly be an 'enemy,' she is certainly still a 'stranger' and 'other.'

Yasmin and *Brick Lane* are useful counterpoints to one another, as the former constructs a narrative that claims to represent all of South Asian, Muslim and British culture, while the latter takes a more tentative and constructive approach to representing those kinds of identities. Reviewing any kind of post 9/11 cultural product is a difficult task precisely because the moment of post 9/11 has not yet come to pass. For both films, the question of who they have been made for is central in determining the types of enmity foregrounded in them. *Yasmin*, without question, has been designed for white and Western audiences who have experienced both 'the Orient' and Islam as consumable and understandable in a specifically Western context of globalisation. This is not to say that *Brick Lane* is in any way a 'better' or even 'good' representation, but rather that it complicates understandings of home, and thereby of enemies, on the example of women who are British Muslims coming from South Asia. This in itself is an act of complication which allows the film to avoid some of the convenient stereotyping in which *Yasmin* becomes entrapped. *Yasmin* forces 9/11 into serving as a plot device, as an easy and cohesive signifier of enmity; it represents a seismic change for Muslims in this narrative world and is constructed as the manifestation of a choice for British Muslims between country and religion. *Brick Lane*, and while this may well indicate the low standards of filmic representations of Muslims, does not force the issue of Muslims as enemies by including references to Islamophobia. Rather, and however troublingly, it presents a conclusion wherein a Muslim woman is shown to be happy with her own choices in life, choices that have been informed by her experiences and character rather than solely through the use of 9/11 as a plot device.

For contemporary audiences, Muslims are the painfully obvious choice for designations of enemy, and specifically of internal enemies when those Muslims are situated in the West. As discussed earlier, Sara Ahmed categorises the functions of white supremacy relevant to studying the stranger: "whiteness becomes a social and bodily orientation given that some bodies will be more at home in a world that is orientated around whiteness. If we began instead with disorientation, *with the body that loses its chair,* then the descriptions we offer will be quite different" (2006: 138). It is an expression of notions of white supremacy to position certain, white, bodies as emblematic of safety and trust, and to label deviations from this line as 'enemy.' With this argument in mind, then, it is easy to see, not least upon the examples of the two films discussed in this chapter, how and why Muslims have come to be labelled as the enemy within.

Works Cited

Ahmed, Sara (2000) *Strange Encounters* (London and New York: Routledge).
Ahmed, Sara (2006) *Queer Phenomenology* (Durham and London: Duke University Press).
Collins, Patricia Hill, and Sirma Bilge (2016) *Intersectionality* (Cambridge and Malden, MA: Polity Press).
Mulvey, Laura (2003) "Visual Pleasure and Narrative Cinema," in *The Feminism and Visual Culture Reader*, ed. Amelia Jones (London: Routledge), 42–53.
Puar, Jasbir (2007) *Terrorist Assemblages: Homonationalism in Queer Times* (Durham and London: Duke University Press).

Filmography

Brick Lane (2007) Dir. Sarah Gavron (Film4).
Yasmin (2004) Dir. Kenneth Glenaan (Parallax Independent).

Florian Zappe
(Re)Framing the Disembodied Public Enemy: The 'War on Drugs' in Contemporary Narrative Screen Media

> America's public enemy number one in the United States is drug abuse.
> In order to fight and defeat this enemy,
> it is necessary to wage a new, all-out offensive.
> (Richard M. Nixon, 17 June 1971)

> In this crusade, let us not forget who we are.
> Drug abuse is a repudiation of everything America is.
> (Ronald Reagan, 14 September 1986)

We see the body of a naked man, hanging by his knees from a bar highly elevated above the floor, his hands tied in front of his shins – a stress position that has been in the arsenal of torturers for centuries. A soldier, apparently the officer in charge of the operation, approaches the victim, pours hot coffee in his face and threatens to kill him slowly if he does not provide the information he is interrogated for. The visual vocabulary of this scene (the setting, the uniforms etc.) is familiar to the cinephile viewer, who will immediately recall films about the shady sides of military conflicts –films of war crimes in Vietnam and other combat theaters, POW dramas or thrillers about military coups. But the presence of two civilians disturbs the seemingly military setting. Their shabby leisure wear and the badge on the belt of one of the men indicates that they are members of a law enforcement agency rather than of a military force. Taken completely out of its narrative context and reduced to the purely visual information (like in a series of film stills), this constellation raises the question of the status of the tortured man: is he a suspect in a law enforcement operation and are we, the audience, witnessing an act of severe police brutality? Is he an enemy combatant abused by the member of an adversary army (which would make us witnesses of a war crime)? And what is the significance of the naked body in the scene, literally stripped of any sign that might allow to identify him?

Of course, the context might help to get some of the answers: The scene is taken from the fourth episode of the first season of the celebrated Netflix series *Narcos* (started in 2015), which is probably the critically most highly acclaimed depiction of the so-called 'war on drugs' in American popular culture in recent years. The tortured man is a low-ranking member of the Columbian drug trafficking mob. He is mistreated in order to reveal the whereabouts of Pablo Escobar, the equally demonized and mythologized drug lord that haunted the entire

https://doi.org/10.1515/9783110591217-007

American continent throughout the 1970s and 1980s. The torturer is Horacio Carrillo (played by Maurice Compte), a colonel in a special military force the Colombian government has sent out on the hunt for Escobar. But while many elements of the *mis-en-scène* are inevitably associated with a military context, the scene also reaches beyond this framework as Carrillo's obviously illicit abuse of the victim's body (and soul) is observed by the two civilian bystanders, who are members of a foreign law enforcement agency: Steve Murphy (Boyd Holbrook) and Javier Peña (Pedro Pascal), two agents of the US Drug Enforcement Administration (DEA), who also function as the protagonists of *Narcos*. This constellation renders the legal status of the tortured man trapped in the ambiguous no man's land between being a suspect or a combatant, but the scene leaves no doubt about how the protagonists see him – to them he is, in the profoundest sense of the word, an *enemy*.

In many ways the scene provides a fruitful starting point for the following inquiry of how films and (web) television series dealing with the 'war on drugs' actually represent the enemy in this conflict. Narrative films and TV shows on violent conflicts conventionally tell their stories by depicting bodies, and of course these bodies are more than just material entities. They are carriers of multi-layered meanings, and deciphering their semiotics can help us to understand the ideological, cultural and political preconditions that shape them. This holds especially true for depictions of the enemy in traditional war films, where the antagonists on the other side of the front are rarely defined by individual character traits but rather as anonymous bodies marked as the 'Other,' e.g. by highlighting ethnic differences or by presenting the foreign uniform as an explicit signifier of enmity. However, any cinematic or televisional engagement with the 'war on drugs' faces a dilemma that is also inherent to the inner logic of this particular conflict: the process of identifying the enemy is a highly complex endeavor, as the term 'drugs' denotes a literally *disembodied enemy* – an elusive and yet resilient transnational hydra with the ability to replace every head, every visible manifestation of her power immediately after it has been chopped off by her adversaries. So in order to be able to produce narratives about this crusade, filmmakers have to 'incarnate' this abstract adversary into bodies that can be (re)presented on the screen. Based on Steven Soderbergh's *Traffic* (2000), Oliver Stone's *Savages* (2012) and the TV series *Narcos* (since 2015), this chapter will reflect on the ideological implications of these on-screen figurations of the disembodied enemy since the turn of the millennium, and on how these works relate to the historical traumas caused by the insight that the ceaseless crusade against 'drugs' is an ostensibly Sisyphean task never to be completed.

1 Ideological Frames

In her book *Frames of War*, Judith Butler reminds us that there is one fundamental philosophical question at the heart of the logic of warfare, which every ideological narrative aiming at legitimizing war has to relate to: "Whose lives are regarded as lives worth saving and defending, and whose are not?" (2009: 38) The answer to this question depends "on cultural modes of regulating affective and ethical dispositions through a selective and differential framing of violence" (1). Such frames "structure modes of recognition, especially during times of war [...] according to which certain lives are perceived as lives while others, though apparently living, fail to assume perceptual form as such" (24). The resulting hierarchical stratification of human existences is defined by what Butler calls a "differential distribution of precarity [that] is at once a material and a perceptual issue, since those whose lives are not 'regarded' as potentially grievable, and hence valuable, are made to bear the burden of starvation, underemployment, legal disenfranchisement, and differential exposure to violence and death" (25).

Our scene from *Narcos* is an exemplary representation of this hierarchy. The body of the naked man is depicted in a state of utmost precariousness and vulnerability, and his life – from the perspective of the tormentors – is 'ungrievable' and unworthy of pity or empathy. In order to understand the discursive dynamics that 'frame' the tormented man as the fully dehumanized 'Other,' undeserving of even the most basic form of compassion, we have to look at the ideological framework of the American 'war on drugs,' which is characteristically marked by an obliteration of the dividing line between the realms of the criminological and the military, between law enforcement and warfare.

The concept of war, in the first place, is highly precarious in itself, and if we want to talk about it we might start with another fundamental philosophical question that was formulated by Ian Clark: "What specifically does it imply to say that we are waging war, rather than engaged in some other violent enterprise?" (2015: 13) Clearly, as Clark points out, history has seen many attempts to answer that question in innumerable political and ideological contexts, but most have one common denominator: in order to be accepted as such by those who are supposed to wage it, war has to be *justified*. Clark notes that "there are at least three normative sources for justness in this area: morality, legality, and the normative bundle of 'war.' The last embraces an irreducible political dimension (just as the case of legitimacy), whether injected on the part of representatives of states or their would-be challengers" (16). If we apply these markers to the 'war on drugs,' we can clearly locate the historical moment of its inception. Although the criminalization of narcotics in American culture can be traced back to the beginnings of the twentieth century, it was not until the second half of the century that the major protagonists of the post-1960s conservative turn in US politics succeeded in rhetorically elevating the struggle against drugs into a morally highly charged 'crusade,' and in establishing an enduring ideological nexus with the question of national security.

The figurehead of this ideological turn was Richard Nixon, who in his "Special Message to the Congress on Control of Narcotics and Dangerous Drugs" on 14 July 1969 set the tone for the fight to come by rhetorically inflating an existing socio-medical problem to a fundamental hazard to the entire social fabric of the United States:

> Within the last decade, the abuse of drugs has grown from essentially a local police problem into a serious national threat to the personal health and safety of millions of Americans. A national awareness of the gravity of the situation is needed; a new urgency and concerted national policy are needed at the Federal level to begin to cope with this growing menace to the general welfare of the United States. (1969)

By hoisting drug (ab)use from the street-level realm of criminality to the sphere of national security politics, Nixon provided the *moral* justification for his full-fledged campaign against the widespread consumption of intoxicating substances that allowed his administration to establish the *legal* and institutional arsenal to tackle this allegedly existential threat to the imagined 'national body':

> [T]he Nixon administration proposed the Comprehensive Drug Abuse Prevention and Control Act in 1969. Put into force on May 1, 1971, it replaced more than fifty pieces of drug legislation and established a single system of control for both narcotic and pychotropic drugs for the first time in U. S. history. [...] It created federal and state legislation to strengthen law enforcement procedures and initiated education and rehabilitation programs. (Marcy 2010: 9)

Two years later followed the outright declaration of war: "America's public enemy number one in the United States is drug abuse. In order to fight and defeat this enemy, it is necessary to wage a new, all-out offensive" (Nixon 1971).[1] Since the sites of large scale narcotics production were mostly located outside of the United States, the Nixon administration was aware that it "had to confront

---

1 The exact beginning of this war is hard to identify. Whitford and Yates point out that Nixon did not use the term 'war on drugs' before 1972 (2009: 42). Kathleen J. Frydl has remarked that "Richard Nixon's declaration of a 'war on drugs' [...] only gave a name to changes that had taken place during the preceding two decades. Between World War II and 1973, the United States transitioned from a regulatory illicit drug regime to a prohibitative and punitive one" (2013: 1). For a concise and comprehensive overview of the history of America's drug war between the 1890s and the 1990s see McWilliams.

the narcotics supply from foreign sources. As a result, the domestic War on Drugs spilled over into the international arena" (Marcy 2010: 10).

In the light of the "historically predominant view of war as something that happens (more or less exclusively) between states" (Clark 2015: 71), this shift towards the international stage posed a significant dilemma for the ideologists, propagandists and strategists of the anti-narcotics crusade. Camilla Fojas notes correctly that "[t]he very phrase 'war on drugs,' generates the idea of an enemy rather than a set of conditions and a complex dynamic in which many different players are complicit" (2008: 112–113). Consequently, as a heterogenic, rhizomatic and, in the end, primarily economic system of multiple producers, distributors and consumers located all over the world, the "public enemy number one" (see above) cannot be defined exclusively in the traditional terms of warfare, as it lacks a territory, an ideology and the institutionalized political body of a state. So on the one hand, one is apt to agree with Fojas's claim that "[t]he phrase 'war on drugs' [...] does not refer to an actual war or warfare with a designated or organized enemy, but it does refer to the U.S. government's emphasis on militarization rather than other, more socially driven goals" (2008: 112). However, one has to assess that this militarized approach clearly follows the logic of *warfare* rather than the logic of social reform or law enforcement. While the latter can only aim at keeping the harmful social effects and the crime rate at the lowest possible level, war – according to its inherent logic – is "pursued for 'total' ends" (Clark 2015: 25), that is for an irrevocable victory over the enemy. Regardless of the question if such an ultimate defeat of 'drugs' – a demand first voiced by Nixon and later reformulated by other administrations, especially those of the Republican presidents Ronald Reagan and George Bush senior – is actually feasible, the advocates of this crusade had to argue according to the logic of warfare, namely that of framing the life of every individual associated with the producers' or distributors' side of 'drugs' (as a system) as fully ungrievable in the Butlerian sense in order to justify a crusade aiming at extinction.

"'To be framed,'" as Butler notes,

> is a complex phrase in English: a picture is framed, but so too is a criminal (by the police), or an innocent person (by someone nefarious, often the police), so that to be framed is to be set up, or to have evidence planted against one that ultimately 'proves' one's guilt. When a picture is framed, any number of ways of commenting on or extending the picture may be at stake. [...] If one is 'framed,' then a 'frame' is constructed around one's deed such as one's guilty status becomes the viewer's inevitable conclusion. (2009: 8)

By implicitly framing the enemy as 'always already guilty,' the ideology of the 'war on drugs' establishes an emblematic example of the aforementioned hierarchy with regard to precarity and grievability – usually along the lines of class and ethnicity. As Butler notes,

> [f]orms of racism instituted and active at the level of perception tend to produce iconic versions of populations who are eminently grievable, and others whose loss is no loss, and who remain ungrievable. The differential distribution of grievability across populations has implications for why and when we feel politically consequential affective dispositions such as horror, guilt, righteous sadism, loss, and indifference. (2009: 24)

With regard to anti-drug policies, the differential distribution of 'grievability' has a long tradition in American culture. The domestic dimension of the threat as embodied by the addict has mostly been defined in terms of his or her low and therefore less 'grievable,' socio-economic status, as Timothy A. Hickman has shown in his book *The Secret Leprosy of Modern Days. Narcotic Addiction and Cultural Crisis in the United States, 1870–1920* (2007: 10). This framing of the addict's identity started around 1900 and still echoes in contemporary stereotypes such as the underclass meth head. The figurations of the foreign dimension of the threat have been predominantly defied through racial stereotyping. This also began at the beginning of the last century, "[w]hen stories about blacks using cocaine or Asians smoking opium began to circulate [and] much of the white population became more intolerant of those who used the drugs" (McWilliams 1992: 9), before Middle and South America became the origins for the dominant stereotypical incarnations of the disembodied enemy.

To conclude this section, we can assess that there is an inherent cultural logic within the ideology of the 'war on drugs' which selects certain lives (usually but not always white middle or upper-class American lives allegedly under threat by the specter of narcotics) as those which deserve empathy, protection and treatment, whereas others (defined either by class or ethnicity as the 'Other' of White upper- and middle-class America) are framed as the already guilty (no proof necessary), ungrievable foe who is selected for extinction.

2 Framing Cinematic Tropes

Because of these ideological implications, the structural logic of the genre of the 'war on drugs' film bears a greater similarity to the traditional war film than to the crime drama. When the crusade against narcotics became a popular topic for film and TV productions in the 1980s,[2] producers, writers and directors could al-

---

2 As the 'war on drugs' has become a widely treated subject in American popular culture, the

ready resort to a set of ideologically prefabricated images to incarnate the disembodied enemy on the screen. Although *Traffic*, *Savages*, and *Narcos* use these framings in very different ways, they also share the basic generic commonalities of what Fojas has defined as the "narcotrafficante film" (2008: 4). These films center around the ideological construction of the 'war on drugs' as an endeavor to protect the United States from a creeping subversive power threatening to infiltrate the nation through its southern border and therefore "tend to locate a clear enemy in the Latin/o American drug traffickers and the corrupt state that colludes with or harbors their efforts" (113). Since the disembodied enemy 'drugs,' unlike the enemy in conventional warfare, lacks a localized territory that could be attacked, invaded or occupied, the ideology of the conflict has framed an imaginary space of enmity – a vaguely defined 'South' – which demarcates the realm of the (presumably) more grievable American lives from those allegedly less grievable lives beyond the border which are constructed as the cultural and ethnic 'Other.'

Steven Soderbergh's *Traffic* draws heavily on these frames and reworks them within a complex narrative structure. The film is an ambitious project that "attempts to provide the 'full picture' in terms of drug trafficking, dealing, use and enforcement" (Shaw 2005: 212) and aims at a comprehensive transnational, multilingual (the dialogues between the Mexican characters are in Spanish and subtitled in English) and multi-focalized overview over the 'war on drugs' at the turn of the millennium. This approach bears resemblance to the classic D-Day epic *The Longest Day* (produced by Darryl F. Zanuck and collaboratively directed by Ken Annakin, Andrew Marton and Bernhard Wicki in 1962), which was "[c]oncerned with reconstructing an authentic documentary look as well as giving an objective, multiperspectival cronicle [...] introduc[ing] [...] the perspective of those about to lose" (Bronfen 2012: 122–123).[3] Like the directors of the *The Lon-*

---

following list of films and TV shows addressing this topic in one way or the other is by nature fragmentary: *Scarface* (dir. Brian De Palma, 1983), *Miami Vice* (NBC, 1984–1989), *Extreme Prejudice* (dir. Walter Hill, 1987), *Tequila Sunrise* (dir. Robert Towne, 1988), *Clear and Present Danger* (dir. Phillip Noyce, 1994), *Blow* (dir. Ted Demme, 2001), *Maria Full of Grace* (dir. Joshua Marston, 2004), *Miami Vice* (dir. Michael Mann, 2006), *American Gangster* (dir. Ridley Scott, 2007), *Escobar: Paradise Lost* (dir. Andrea di Stefano, 2014), and *Sicario* (dir. Dennis Villeneuve, 2015). In addition to these fictional works, the 'war on drugs' has also been the topic of a number of (mostly independently produced) documentary films: *Border* (dir. Charles Burghard, 2007), *American Drug War: The Last White Hope* (dir. Kevin Booth, 2007), *The War on Drugs* (dir. Sebastian J. F., 2007), *How to Make Money Selling Drugs* (dir. Matthew Cooke, 2012), *The House I Live In* (dir. Eugene Jarecki, 2012), *Cartel Land* (dir. Matthew Heinemann, 2015).
3 While *Traffic*'s panoramic narrative structure tries to achieve the effect of a fairly balanced documentary, its visual aesthetic decidedly does not aim at mimetic realism: "Director Stephen

gest Day, Soderbergh introduces the viewpoints of all parties involved and on all levels of the hierarchy, ranging from the 'generals' down to the 'footsoldiers' on both sides of the front line by spinning a web of several plot lines in which the distribution of precarity and grievability circulates.

On the highest level of the chain of command, the film tells the story of Robert Wakefield (played by Michael Douglas), a former judge who has just taken over the function of head of the Office of National Drug Control Strategy, the highest government official overseeing the American government's multifaceted crusade against drugs, colloquially referred to as 'drug czar.' As Fojas has pointed out, *Traffic* makes tacit references to the most recent history of the war here, as this character is at least partly inspired by Barry R. McCaffrey, a former U.S. Army general who had been appointed to that office by the Clinton administration in 1996 (Fojas 2008: 131–132). The same historical innuendo is to be found in the depictions of Wakefield's Mexican equivalent and alleged ally in the war against the cartels, General Salazar (Tomas Milian), who in the course of the film turns out to be on the secret payroll of the drug lords: "The film cites a well-known corruption scandal involving the Mexican drug enforcement chief, who was discovered to be in cahoots with Amando Carrillo Fuentes, the biggest cocaine trafficker in the country, just days after drug czar McCaffrey had praised the chief for his successful and admirable work in the anti-drug campaign" (Fojas 2008: 132).

Douglas's character clearly embodies those traditional WASP elites which have declared and defined the 'war on drugs,' although Soderbergh tries to portray Wakefield as a crusader with a capacity to doubt his mission, especially when he has to face the fact that his own daughter has a drug problem. Wakefield's antagonist on the highest level in the hierarchy is Helena Ayala (Catherine Zeta-Jones), who – in a remarkably matriarchal act of revolution within the macho world of the cartels – takes over her husband's large scale drug trafficking operation after the authorities had him arrested and indicted early in the movie. The ranks of the foot-soldiers are represented by Javier Rodriguez (Benicio del Toro) and Manolo Sanchez (Jacob Vargas), two Mexican policemen, and by Montel Gordon (Don Cheadle) and Ray Castro (Luis Guzmán), two DEA agents as their Amercian counterparts. In addition to that, the film features a number of mid-level protagonists, working for both sides and sometimes even crossing the line.[4]

Soderbergh himself explains that he shot all scenes in Mexico through a 'tobacco filter' and then oversaturated the film, which gives Mexico the look of the Old West" (Fojas 2008: 134).

4 For a detailed summary of the film's complex plot structure, see Fojas 2008: 132–135.

Although it is obvious that the producers of *Traffic* were aware of the racist implications of many earlier onscreen depictions of the 'war on drugs,' and in spite of the film's sincere attempt to challenge "racial and ethnic hierarchical categories that have traditionally characterized many mainstream Hollywood films" (Shaw 2005: 213), it does not overcome the 'differential distribution of grievability' between those to be defended and those who represent the enemy threat along these lines. While I would hesitate to agree fully with Fojas's conclusion that "[a]lthough there are no targeted 'enemies' in the war on drugs, *Traffic* depicts Mexico as the real enemy" (2008: 135), it is evident that the film never leaves the established moral coordinate system: the grievable lives are those of the characters who abide with the doctrines of America's official anti-drug policies. This includes also non-American characters – such as Javier Rodriguez – as well as Americans who diverge from the 'right path' but are considered worthy of 'salvation.' This is embodied in the subplot of Wakefield's daughter, who at the end of the film, after a downfall from her expensive private school environment into the precarity of an inner city slum, is literally rescued by her father (here the 'general' descends from the headquarters to fight on the front line) in order to redeem herself in therapy. Ultimately, although aiming at the 'big picture' in all its complexity, by not impugning the traditional distribution of grievability, *Traffic* remains locked within the ideological framework it set out to scrutinize and tells the story of the 'war on drugs' as a drama of the White middle-class.

3 (Re)Framing Trauma

In her book on *The Specters of War*, Elisabeth Bronfen asserts that

> cinema functions as a privileged site of recollection, where American culture continually renegotiates the traumatic traces of its historical past, reconceiving current social and political concerns in the light of previous military conflicts. As a shared conceptual space, cinema sustains a reflection *of* and *on* the past. Indeed, in the course of the twentieth century, Hollywood emerged as *the* site where American culture thinks about its implication in the traumatic history of war by offering personalized narratives of rites of passage that reflect (and reflect on) the ever-shifting stakes in this collective conversation about national identity. (2012: 2, original emphasis)

In many regards, the 'war on drugs' films of the new millennium have a similar function. They are also haunted by the specter of history as they renegotiate the traumata (both on the individual and the collective level) that America has suffered in the decade-long conflict with the disembodied enemy – especially in the light of the growing realization that this struggle cannot be won.

Oliver Stone's *Savages* is a particularly interesting example in this context, not only because of the director's penchant to create "movies that attempt to take the major symbols of late twentieth-century history and reconfigure (some would say revise) them into epic tales of the battle for America's soul" (Guarnieri 2016: 310). The film links the traumatic experience of the 'war on drugs' with that of another, seemingly unwinnable struggle against a different (and – to a certain extent – also disembodied) enemy: the 'war on terror.' In a 2012 interview with the *Huffington Post*, Stone, recalling Richard Hofstadter's famous argument, states that he sees both conflicts as structurally similar products of a paranoid trait prevalent in American politics:

> I think it [the 'war on drugs'] was a mistake to begin with, and it shouldn't be called a war. I remember when it started with Nixon in his first term, in 1971. And it was a huge mistake to declare it a war. The terminology exacerbates the situation. It started small; it was a $100 million operation. And now it's grown into close to a $25 to 30 billion D.E.A. bureaucracy, as well as overcrowding the prisons with victims. It's turned into an American crusade like Iraq, Vietnam, Afghanistan. And in Mexico, particularly, we have exacerbated the Mexican situation by sending our paramilitary troops down there, which is the D.E.A. It's become an immigration issue; it's become a Homeland Security issue; it's blended into the terrorism issue. We have created this Frankenstein, as we always tend to do, out of our paranoia, and we've made this thing into a monstrosity. (Hogan 2012)

Stone's film tries to grapple with this monster by appropriating and revamping the established tropes regarding the 'war on drugs' in that particular style of postmodern hyperbole which has become his trademark since *Natural Born Killers* (1994). *Savages* tells the story of three young Americans – Chon (Tylor Kitsch), Ben (Aaron Taylor-Johnson) and Ophelia (nicknamed O and played by Blake Lively) – who are not only emotionally and sexually connected in a love triangle but also joined in a successful marihuana start-up in Southern California. This operation is founded on high-quality cannabis seeds which Chon – a highly traumatized veteran, who, according to Ophelia's voice-over narration, tries to "fuck the war out of himself" whenever they make love – brought back from his tours in Afghanistan. After Chon and Ben reject a business offer by a Mexican drug cartel, its leader Elena Sánchez (Salma Hayek) tries to enforce their cooperation by abducting and imprisoning Ophelia. Using Chon's military expertise as a former marine and veteran, the two young men unleash a private vigilante-style war against the cartel in order to save their loved one.

Savages features a number of points that invite comparison with *Traffic*, not only because parts of the cast starred in both films: Benicio del Torro plays Miguel Arroyo, a heavily stereotyped strong-arm man for Salma Hayek's (who had a short cameo appearance in *Traffic)* character, who in turn seems to mirror Catherine Zeta-Jones's character in Soderbergh's film. Like Soderbergh, Stone turns the macho-chauvinistic world of the drug mob upside down and transforms it into a matriarchy (in the true sense of the word, as both characters are portrayed as hyper-protective mother figures). In their politics however, both films differ substantially. Stone's film detaches the distinction between 'grievable' and 'ungrievable' lives from the official narratives of the 'war on drugs,' which is depicted as an empty doctrine devoid of any legitimacy. In *Traffic*, institutions of American anti-drug activities might be portrayed as overstrained, yet they remain – unlike their Mexican counterparts – financially and morally incorrupt. In *Savages*, the same institutions have lost the authority over the image of the enemy. They are shown to be in a severe moral crisis, which is personified in the character of Dennis Cain (John Travolta), a venal DEA agent on the payroll of Chon's and Ben's as well as of other opaque forces (probably the cartel).

Chon's and Ben's private war against the drug mob, depicted in explicitly violent scenes of carnage and torture (no life is grievable here, except Ophelia's), is not fought to protect middle-class America from the 'Southern' threat of narcotics. And especially in that, their story is an example of those "personalized narratives of rites of passage" (see above) which, according to Bronfen, negotiate the traumatic war experiences of America. This passage takes the protagonists "on a journey through darkness, getting in touch with the ugliest and most evil parts of themselves. Ben – a pacifist and Buddhist, like Stone – allows himself to become a murderer to get back the woman he and his best friend love equally" (Guarnieri 2016: 312). Chon, the traumatized ex-marine and Ben, the ex-hippie, both become allegorical figures for the increasing dehumanization and moral vacuity of the 'war on drugs,' which is also emphasized by a narrative twist at the end of the film:

> O, who narrates the film, initially presents us with an ending in which all three characters get pulled into a literal Mexican standoff and die, beaten and bloodied, in each others' arms. Then O and Stone reveal that what we saw is not what happened, but O's fantasy. The real ending is Ben and Chon getting arrested by the US Drug Enforcement Administration, spending a few weeks in jail due to their status as confidential informants, then moving to an unnamed Third World Country with O and living, as she puts it, as "savages": "cruel, crippled, regressed back into a primal state of being." (Guarnieri 2016: 312–313)

Ultimately, Stone references the established tropes of the 'war on drugs' in the service of his postmodern spectacle but, as usual with this director, they are not without a political tinge. By depicting the conflict as a private or privatized crusade, *Savages* is in many regards the fitting narcotrafficante film for the neoliberal age. Deprived of the official moral narrative, and (albeit loosely) linked to the trauma of the war in Afghanistan, the film makes a firm statement on the futility and ideological arbitrariness of many of America's 'wars' and on their traumatic effects on American society.

4 (Re)Framing History

In his review of *Narcos*, the American historian Jorge Cañizares-Esguerra asserts that its narrative centers around one fundamental ethical question: "[W]hose blood should be spilled in the global war on drugs and whose bodies incarcerated" (2015). This brings us back to the tortured man, who was the starting point for the reflections in this chapter. It is evident that he belongs to the category of those 'ungrievable' lives whose spilled blood seems not deplorable, neither from his torturers' perspective, nor from that of his employers. However, the narrative structure of *Narcos*, other than that of *Traffic* and *Savages*, is teleologically tailored towards the extinction of the clearly defined kingpin of the 'ungrievables.' And while the two feature films only made casual references to the history of the 'war on drugs,' the flamboyant, eccentric and publicity-hungry personality of Pablo Escobar provided the producers of the Netflix series with a factual template to pin a face and a name to an otherwise abstract and elusive enemy. The first two seasons, produced in 2015 and 2016, use this historical reference to tell the story of a manhunt in the context of a proxy war. Although Escobar's Medellin Cartel was predominantly involved in a conflict (which had every characteristic of a civil war) with the society and government of Colombia, the focalization is clearly American, personified in Agent Murphy, who is the first-person voice-over narrator of the show. Even if the action is set in South America, most of the dialogues are in Spanish and most of the protagonists on both sides of the 'drug front' are Latin/o, *Narcos* is essentially another narrative about the endeavor to save allegedly more deplorable American lives by combating a stereotyped enemy. Its pseudo-historical accuracy never leaves established tropes, as it "explicitly suggests that there is a fundamental difference between an uncivilized Latino south and a peaceful Anglo north that is bridged when Anglos get to live for a long time among the savages" (Cañizares-Esguerra 2015). And Murphy's crossing of the threshold between these two worlds is the story of another rite of passage:

> *Narcos* describes the transformation of both Colombia and Murphy. Before Escobar, Colombia was corrupt but poor. But with the arrival of Escobar's billions, Colombia became a bustling, cosmopolitan hellhole. The narrative arc of Murphy's metamorphosis is also

cast in very simple terms. He was originally a naïve agent chasing after potheads in Miami. Once in Colombia, however, Murphy goes native. In the last episode, Murphy resolves the dispute over a mild car accident by shooting at the other driver, while his *gringa* wife and Colombian baby girl (who had been left orphaned in a murderous rampage by Escobar's minions and who Murphy casually picked up to raise) witness in horror Murphy's new penchant for blood and lawlessness. It is in the wake of this shooting that Murphy's wife begs Murphy to take the baby and go back home (to the US). A nonchalant Murphy replies that home is now Colombia. (Cañizares-Esguerra 2015)

Murphy's moral corruption spells out the effects of the militarization of the United States' efforts to cope with its narcotics problem. The martial logic, aimed at the ultimate defeat of the enemy, is not only in stark contrast with the highly moralized rhetoric with which it is legitimized. It also has a profoundly dehumanizing effect upon the individuals who have to wage the 'war.' Agent Peña's story, on the other hand, reveals the Sisyphean character of the crusade. After Escobar is finally killed and his body displayed as a trophy, the story is not over. We see agent Peña in a hearing with his superiors at the DEA, who ask him if he would be willing to accept a new mission against the so-called Cali cartel, which is about to take over Escobar's market shares. The most eminent embodiment of evil may have been annihilated, but the decapitated hydra persists and will inevitably grow the next head.

Conclusion

Wars are always, as we have seen, fought to achieve complete victory over the enemy. This was also the goal of the 'war on drugs' when it was declared by the Nixon government and pursued further by other presidential administrations. *Traffic*, *Savages* and *Narcos* take different aesthetic, narrative and political approaches to reflect upon this conflict that has been fought for more than four decades now. Notwithstanding their serious attempt to do justice to the complexity of their topic, one has to assert that they do not succeed in transcending the ideologically rendered stereotypes of the opponent. The distribution of grievability that frames the enemy and is inscribed in the official doctrine of the conflict is largely reproduced without substantial scrutiny. And yet these works are important as they negotiate the effects this conflict had and still has on American society by addressing a traumatic realization: that the goal of defeating the disembodied enemy is unattainable and that the 'war on drugs,' in spite of tremendous material, political and military efforts, is one of the United States' lost wars.

Works Cited

Bronfen, Elisabeth (2012) *Specters of War. Hollywood's Engagement with Military Conflict* (New Brunswick: Rutgers University Press).
Butler, Judith (2009) *Frames of War. When Is Life Grievable?* (London and New York: Verso).
Cañizares-Esguerra, Jorge (2015) "Magical Realism on Drugs: Colombian History in Netflix's *Narcos*" *Not Even Past* <https://notevenpast.org/magical-realism-on-drugs-colombia-in-netflixs-narcos> (accessed 28 May 2017).
Clark, Ian (2015) *Waging War. A New Philosophical Introduction*, 2nd edition (Oxford: Oxford University Press).
Fojas, Camilla (2008) *Border Bandits. Hollywood on the Southern Frontier* (Austin: University of Texas Press).
Frydl, Kathleen J. (2013) *The Drug Wars in America, 1940–1973* (Cambridge: Cambridge University Press).
Guarnieri, Michael (2016) "The World belongs to Savages. The Oliver Stone Crime Film," in *The Oliver Stone Experience*, ed. Matt Zoller Seitz (New York: Abrams), 310–313.
Hickman, Timothy A. (2007) *The Secret Leprosy of Modern Days. Narcotic Addiction and Cultural Crisis in the United States, 1870–1920* (Amherst: University of Massachusetts Press).
Hogan, Michael (2012) "Oliver Stone, 'Savages' Director, On Graphic Sex Scenes, The War On Drugs and Barack Obama," *The Huffington Post* <http://www.huffingtonpost.com/2012/06/20/oliver-stone-savages-war-on-drugs_n_1613 496 .html> (accessed 9 May 2017).
Marcy, William L. (2010) *The Politics of Cocaine. How U. S. Foreign Policy Has Created a Thriving Drug Industry in Central and South America* (Chicago: Lawrence Hill Books).
McWilliams, John C. (1992) "Through the Past Darkly: The Politics and Policies of America's Drug War," in *Drug Control Policy. Essays in Historical and Comparative Perspective*, ed. William O. Walker III (University Park: Pennsylvania State University Press), 5–41.
Nixon, Richard (1969) "Special Message to the Congress on Control of Narcotics and Dangerous Drugs," in *The American Presidency Project* <http://www.presidency.ucsb.edu/ws/?pid=2126> (accessed 23 October 2016).
Nixon, Richard (1971) "Remarks About an Intensified Program for Drug Abuse Prevention and Control," in *The American Presidency Project* <http://www.presidency.ucsb.edu/ws/?pid=3047> (accessed 2 September 2016).
Shaw, Deborah (2005) "'You Are Alright, But …': Individual and Collective Representations of Mexicans, Latinos, Anglo-Americans and African Americans in Steven Soderbergh's *Traffic*," in *Quarterly Review of Film and Video* 22. 3, 211–223.
Whitford, Andrew B. and Jeff Yates (2009) *Presidential Rhetoric and the Public Agenda. Constructing the War on Drugs* (Baltimore: The Johns Hopkins University Press).

Filmography

Narcos (2015) Created by Chris Brancato, Eric Newman and Carlo Bernard (Netflix).
Savages (2012) Dir. Oliver Stone (Universal Pictures).
Traffic (2000) Dir. Steven Soderbergh (USA Films).

PART II: **Who are the Perpetrators?
Who are the Victims?
Confronting Difficult Pasts and
the Crisis of Identity**

Petra Rau
From 'Ivan' to Andreij: The Red Army in German Film and TV

The war on the Eastern Front (1941–1945) claimed more lives than all the casualties in the rest of the conflict added together. Exact figures are still hard to come by but Soviet military losses exceeded Germany's by three to one, and stand at over 8 million; civilian Soviet losses suggest a further 17 million (Müller and Ueberschär 1995: 142–143; Overy 1997: 287–288; Merrivale 2005: 252). This war was fought by both sides with ideological ferocity and by Nazi Germany, with genocidal intent against combatants, civilians and partisans. The German invasion and occupation of the western Soviet Union brought 'ethnic cleansing,' the ghettoisation and extermination of local and deported Jews, the starvation and death from epidemics of millions of Soviet prisoners of war, and the deportation of further millions of male and female slave labourers to German-operated factories and farms further west. Advancing and retreating armies destroyed historic cities such as Minsk, Smolensk, Odessa, Warsaw, and Kiev. Germany's occupation deprived the civilian population of food, livestock and anything portable or usable by army and administration. On retreat Germany's 'scorched earth' policy left Belorussia and Ukraine devastated and depopulated. In turn, the rage of the Red Army advancing towards Berlin generated its own ideologically-stoked lawless behaviour not just in German territories but also in Romania and Hungary, war crimes against civilians on a massive scale, and the largest number of refugees in modern history (Merrivale 2005: 259–289). On both sides, the unpalatable truths of this war would produce resilient myths of astonishing longevity. Despite its spectacular and unprecedented scale, and despite bestselling novels or accounts by notable writers on either side about this theatre,[1] the war on the Eastern Front does not seem to have translated well onto the big or small screen: however ubiquitous the Bolshevist enemy had been in Nazi propaganda, there were, until recently, very few 'Ivans' in German film and on TV.

In this chapter, I want to examine the discrepancy between the magnitude of this campaign and its marginalisation on the screen. To this end, we need to cast an eye on the iconography of anti-Bolshevist Nazi propaganda and reflect on the narrative templates of 1950s war films (i.e. before the Soviet Union becomes the

---

[1] See for instance Plivier 1954; Kirst 1954; Kaiser 1958. On the Russian side, many accounts could only be published with great delay or abroad: Kopelew 1976 [1975]; Solschenizyn 1976 [1974], Grossmann 1985 [1980].

generic foe in blockbuster spy films and Cold War cinema). When the war resurfaces in contemporary German television and cinema after reunification, the context and the audience have changed yet again: two well-publicised and well-travelled Wehrmacht exhibitions (1995–1999/2001–2004) have informed the public of the participation of the regular army in war crimes and the Holocaust on the Eastern Front; Holocaust commemoration has now been institutionalised, but there is also room for revisiting the discourse on German suffering[2] through carpet bombing, mass rapes, and flight and expulsion. Among the flurry of docu-dramas, commercialised TV 'events' and historical films about the Third Reich and the Second World War that have appeared in the past quarter century in Germany alone, I want to focus on *Anonyma: Eine Frau in Berlin* (*Anonyma: A Woman in Berlin*). Directed by Max Färberböck (2008), no other German production has given so much screen space to the representation of Soviet soldiers. The film chronicles the Red Army's assault on and occupation of Berlin from the point of view of an educated, middle-class German woman. As the only Russian-speaker in her tenement block, she becomes a default mediator, helping to negotiate how this community moves from mere survival to fragile accommodation in their increasingly pragmatic interactions with Red Army soldiers over several weeks. *Anonyma* makes unusual demands on the audience, not just because it is a film about horrific sexual violence. Its version of the final days of the war eschews several cinematic clichés and templates on which other war films could draw. As a film about female civilians it cannot mobilise the usual uniform-clad Nazis as the familiar-and-fascinating iconography of evil; as a film about defeat, it cannot entertain a male audience with spectacular combat and valorous male bodies; as a film about rape it cannot make war more palatable through a romance plot. Despite a stellar cast and considerable critical acclaim, *Anonyma* struggled to find an audience – unlike, for instance, Joseph Vilsmaier's *Stalingrad* (1993) or the recent 3-part TV series *Unsere Mütter, Unsere Väter* (*Generation War*), produced in 2013 by Teamworx and ZDF. *Anonyma*'s exceptionality, I argue, lies in the interest it takes – highly unusual for a German film – in communicating, rather than merely depicting, the suffering of others. In fact, the film offers us a retroactive rationale for pushing the Eastern Front off the post-war cinema screen.

---

[2] See analyses by Niven 2006, Schmitz 2008, Taberner and Berger 2009.

1 From Asiatic Bolshevist Hordes to Reluctant Russian Sweethearts

Nazi propaganda benefitted from an already established anti-Communist iconography after the First World War, much of it widely distributed in leaflets and exhibition posters by the ultra-right wing nationalist Anti-Bolshevist League. This material habitually demonised and de-humanised communists in the shape of a snake, a hydra, a dragon, a monumental spider crawling all over the planet, a Kraken sprawling over the European continent, the Russian bear draped in red, a wolf lapping blood, a man-eating devil, a walking skeleton, and the well-known Asiatic horde marching relentlessly towards the west. Once war against the USSR was declared, these images could simply be reused.

The existential threat ostensibly posed by communism was aggravated by conflating it with the mortal peril of world Jewry in order to underline that the war on the Eastern Front had as its expressive purpose the necessary eradication of both groups. This them-or-us binary underpins the gender politics of Hans Schweitzer's 1943 poster *Sieg oder Bolschewismus* (fig. 1): victory against communism ensures progress and continuity (symbolised by mother and Aryan child), defeat means regression to a dark age of starvation and penury under a Semitic-looking Bolshevist.

By implication, then, the citizens of the Soviet Union were seen as largely backward and primitive, either victims of communism or susceptible to its contamination (and therefore easily persuaded to become partisans). War propaganda did not suddenly 'declare' Soviet citizens enemies; that work had already been done comprehensively by the racial and imperialist dimension of fascist ideology. To cast themselves as liberators from Soviet oppression, embedded Nazi propaganda corps on the Eastern Front exploited the population's recent memory of collectivisation, famine, and the persecution of non-Russian ethnicities such as Kulaks or Tatars.[3] The Soviet Union was a space meant to serve the German people and its military force as *Lebensraum* once the preventative campaign against Jewish Bolshevism had been won. The declared inferiority of Slavic peoples reduced them, at best, to cheap labour. At worst they were simply expendable. Communism in home front propaganda, however, was also marked as racially other, dark, and economically detrimental. Its sheer otherness was much more pronounced to emphasise that defeat would mean the end of civili-

---

[3] For a more comprehensive view of German propaganda on the Eastern Front see Buchbender 1978.

Fig. 1: Sieg oder Bolschewismus (Plak 003–029–049, Bundesarchiv Koblenz)

sation: the Red Army was a marauding bestial horde of inferior *Untermenschen* leaving raped, battered and murdered civilians in their wake. Since January 1945 the Nazi newsreel *Deutsche Wochenschau* had been showing graphic images of the civilian victims[4] of the advancing Red Army that projected for the female audience what their fate would be in case they felt inclined to surrender (Grossmann 1995: 50). As late as February 1945, the propaganda ministry exhorted Germans to fight on lest they be engulfed by Jewish Bolshevism (fig. 2).

Perhaps even more important than propaganda images are the encounters of German soldiers with the civilian populations since these experiences – deeply coloured by Nazi ideology – furnished letters home, determined the gaze through the camera and later shaped family memory.[5] The initial impression German soldiers formed, buoyed by swift victories over unprepared and ill-equipped opponents, was that of a vast but backward space, predominantly agrarian and 'primitive.' Many private photographs present the early stages of this campaign as a touristic adventure snapped for the family album (fig. 3), suggesting that war offered soldiers a unique opportunity to travel. The folkloristic framing of 'the primitive' would later frame much cinematic depiction of Soviet citizens. The gaze is curious, ethnocentric, orientalist – and it remains in this mode even when the object of the photograph or the topic of the letter is no longer a folkloristic portrait of locals but an execution, a prisoner-of-war camp with Asiatic 'specimens' (fig. 4), or a mass grave: these are all exotic 'sights.'

What this also means is that the German home front was by no means entirely innocent of the nature of the war on the Eastern Front (and therefore doubly fearful of retribution); a vast photographic archive of executions of 'partisans' and Jews, official military reports, and soldiers' letters home communicated that this was not 'regular warfare.'

Yet regular warfare is precisely the version offered in the German cinema of the 1950s. Although the moral ambivalence and formal complexity of this decade has recently received much needed attention,[6] its principal concern remained the fashioning of what Robert G. Moeller has called a "usable past" – a highly selective narrative of war and fascism (2001: 20). In the West, this narrative helped to reconcile society with itself by establishing a "new German decency" that incriminated the guilty few and exonerated many ordinary citizens through the redeeming force of their own suffering (Stern 2001: 274–275). It explained military

---

[4] See for instance *Deutsche Wochenschau* 754/9 (1945) and 755/10 (1945).
[5] For first-hand accounts see Kuby 1999 or Klee and Dreßen 1989.
[6] For recent reassessments of postwar German film beyond the dismissive verdicts of German New Cinema see Bliersbach 1989, von Moltke 2005, Wilms and Rasch 2008, Groß 2015 as well as Blachut 2015.

Fig. 2: Should we fail to win the war (Plak 003–029–048: Christian Minzlaff, Das droht uns wenn wir versagen – darum Kampf bis zum Sieg; Bundesarchiv Koblenz)

Fig. 3: Local family and occupation soldiers. (Author's private collection)

Fig 4: Soviet prisoners of war. (Author's private collection)

defeat to the post-war audience; rehabilitated German masculinity by discarding bellicose authoritarianism in favour of a humanitarian paternalistic ideal; and swapped the valorisation of death for the virtues of homosocial camaraderie (see Kapczynski 2007: 138; Hake 2002: 97). British and American imports understandably focused on different theatres of war, shifting the focus to Western Europe, North Africa or the Pacific. As a result, 1950s cinema did as much as the expediencies of Cold War politics to normalise this war as 'regular' combat: a country joining NATO in 1955 and re-establishing its military would not, and could not, be reminded of its genocidal, ideological war.

In fact, German films about the Second World War were remarkably devoid of *any* military opponents. In the 1950s, the heyday of the war film, the real struggle was between ordinary, decent Germans and ideologically driven, fanatical Nazis; or between soldiers without agency and inept military leaders. The genre appeared to explain defeat by suggesting that the German protagonist(s) had to tackle two enemies: the internal foe often helpfully clad in SS-uniform and easily recognisable through incompetence, corruption and callousness, and then some external threat hovering on the margins of the plot, furnishing a spectacular backdrop of mortar fire, rolling tanks or exploding bombs but rarely credited with anything so substantial as a speaking part or a plausible character. Germany's post-war introspection literally pushed its military opponents off the screen.

A mere four post-war West German films were set on the Eastern front, all of them adaptations of bestselling novels. All of them reduce the Soviet Union to a mere setting in which the Red Army is a shadowy presence and Soviet citizens furnish romantic subplots. Geza von Radvanyi's *Der Arzt von Stalingrad* (1958) is set in a Soviet POW camp and Harald Philipp's *Strafbataillon 999* (1960) describes a punishment battalion somewhere in Russia. In both films ordinary German soldiers' suffering is pitched against communist or fascist brutal ideologues. Frank Wisbar's *Hunde, wollt ihr ewig leben* (1959), about the battle of Stalingrad, lays the blame for this colossal defeat at the feet of obsequious careerists and poor military leadership. Paul May's *08/15* trilogy (1954–1955) helped to consolidate the idea of the decent ordinary German soldier, bullied by fascist superiors and a victim of harsh fate but devoted to his comrades. The second instalment features a romantic subplot between Captain Witterer and Natascha (Ellen Schwiers), who rewards his kindness by passing classified information to the local *politruk* as revenge for her parents' death. The folkloristic element of this misguided romance is underlined by her basic dwelling, a thatched wooden hut of simple construction. Witterer cannot bring himself to execute her because both he and his superior realise that civilian resistance is a corollary of the draconian measures by intelligence services and SS. Romance, in other words, is a way of exculpating regular officers as both gallant and decent. A more platonic middle-class version of romance hovers on the margins of Wisbar's *Hunde* and benefits from star-studded casting: Joachim Hansen's manly Senior Lieutenant Wisse falls for translator Katja, played by Sonja Ziemann, known to audiences from blockbuster Heimatfilms. (Like Schwiers, Ziemann sported a notable Slavic accent to underline exotic appeal.) The local German administration rejects Ziemann's services – unwisely, it turns out, because she, too, will end up working for the other side. Again, the implication of the subplot is that badly managed occupation undermines military victory. However, Wisse's assertive demeanour is quite in keeping with an administration that sets out to bring (rather than restore) order: the scene outside the administration suggests the arrest of a petty criminal rather than a tête-a-tête (fig. 5). Unless Katja has a penchant for authoritative masculinity there's little to suggest she actually has a choice about how to respond to his advances. Similarly, in *Der Arzt von Stalingrad*, Alexandra Kasalinskaja's rank as Captain does not protect her from the fierce advances of Dr Sellnow, which a modern audience might find hard to distinguish from sexual harassment.

Fig. 5: Romance German style? Oberleutnant Gerd Wisse (Joachim Hansen) with Katja (Sonja Ziemann) and dog (Wisbar, *Hunde, wollt ihr ewig leben*; Deutsche Film Hansa)

These cinematic romances, according to Jennifer Kapczinsky, re-masculinised German soldiers for an audience whose real-life manhood often lay in tatters after years in POW camps and other war traumas (2007: 138). They also served to feminise Russia and implied that the German advances had literally been welcome. Perhaps most important is their contribution to a narrative of German decency, even gallantry, that exonerated the Wehrmacht.

In the East, DEFA's war films served a younger audience with a more didactic albeit ambivalent approach, offering a 'melancholic anti-fascism' as Sabine

Hake calls it in her overview of DEFA war films: indebted to communism but caught up in German loyalties (2012: 118). Although both Joachim Kunert's *Die Abenteuer des Werner Holt* (1965) and émigré Konrad Wolf's autobiographical *Ich war 19* (1968) discredited fascism as criminal by showing or recounting German atrocities on the Eastern Front, the Red Army's fury against civilians escaped the cinematic record, presumably because anti-Soviet representation would have courted censorship.[7] Whatever the Red Army has done, these films suggest, was a necessary corollary of bringing the Radiant Future to (East) Germany. Unsurprisingly, Frank Wisbar's *Nacht fiel über Gotenhafen* (1959), about the sinking of the Wilhelm Gustloff by Soviet torpedoes with thousands of refugees on board, was never shown in East Germany.

2 Sepia Fascism:
War and Nazism as Regular Period Drama

Critics have been noticing the resurgence of war and fascism in German-language cinema and TV productions since the early 1990s, as if Germans could finally resume control over telling their own story. Indeed these films were made by post-war producers and directors who had wrenched narrative control and authority from the (ostensibly silent and compromised) wartime generation and addressed an even younger, late born audience (Assmann 2013: 38). But what kind of story was now being told? German resistance engaged notable film directors: Margarethe von Trotta's *Rosenstraße* (2003), Jo Baier's *Stauffenberg* (2004), Volker Schlöndorff's *Der neunte Tag* (2004), Niko von Glasow-Brücher's *Edelweisspiraten* (2004), and Mark Rothemund's *Sophie Scholl* (2005). Children's experiences in Nazi schools featured in Schlöndorff's *Der Unhold* (*The Ogre*, 1996) and Dennis Gansel's *Napola* (2004). Much ink was spilt over Hirschbiegel's *Der Untergang* (*Downfall*, 2004) and Färberböck's *Aimée & Jaguar*, and Best Foreign Language Film Oscars went to Caroline Link's *Nirgendwo in Afrika* (*Nowhere in Africa*, 2003) and Stefan Ruzowitzky's *Die Fälscher* (2006). Guido Knopp's TV-documentaries for ZDF became so ubiquitous (Hitler's generals, Hitler's helpers, Hitler's children, Hitler's warriors, and Hitler's women) that one could be forgiven for thinking that if history did not involve Hitler it simply did not happen. Increasingly TV channels marketed the twelve years of fascism in the format of the 'event movie' or the mini-series: Hans-Christoph Blumenberg's *Die letzte*

---

[7] This was certainly true for the literary representation of rape by Soviet soldiers. See Dahlke 2000.

Schlacht (TV, 2005), Roland Suso Richter's *Dresden* (Teamworx, 2006). Kai Wessel's two-parter *Die Flucht* (Arte/BR, 2007) and Joseph Vilsmaier's *Die Gustloff* (Ufa, 2008) were effectively TV-remakes of Wisbar's *Nacht fiel über Gotenhafen* (1959). The list could go on.

For Axel Bangert, modern production values and hybrid media formats aimed at the home cinema setting created (and depended upon) an "imagined community of German television viewers" for whom war and fascism were channelled into "unifying legacies of the Nazi past." In other words, these films offered "surrogate experiences of violence and suffering," intimate and immersive, that shaped the public view of the Nazi era post-unification (2014:164–165). Lutz Koepnick sees them as little more than "sweeping historical melodramas that reproduce the national past [...] as a course of nostalgic pleasures and positive identifications" (2004: 192). Hence presumably the absence of the enthusiastic (or perhaps even merely opportunistic or passive) fascist protagonist, probably the most realistic of historical points-of-view. Sabine Hake, even less charitable about the effects of event culture, spoke of the "gradual disappearance of history into simulation and spectacle" (2002: 186–187). Using *Der Untergang* (*Downfall*) as a case study, she argued that making Germany's difficult history consumable also allowed the audience to own it "through the imaginary experience of 'we Germans' and 'our history'" – a first person plural that appeared to include a variety of subject positions (2012: 251). Put bluntly, this sepia fascism is the product of a *desire* for normalisation since these films are clearly not formally innovative or aesthetically provocative in ways that might signal to the audience that such a past is precisely not reducible to costume drama.

Sepia fascism may also be an unintended side effect of the institutionalisation of Holocaust commemoration in public discourse. There certainly is a discernible generational shift in millennials' attitudes towards the wartime generation, a receptiveness to a more empathetic narrative in which German suffering had its place alongside Jewish victimhood and Nazi crimes. As sociologist Harald Welzer has pointed out, the latter's acknowledgement often depends on familial exoneration: others may have been enthusiastic, opportunistic, sadistic or casual Nazis, but one's own family was relatively blameless. Just how hard it has been to accept the possibility of one's own parents or grandparents as participants in war crimes on the Eastern Front, for instance, was revealed by the controversies over the Wehrmacht exhibition and its documentaries by Ruth Beckermann (*Jenseits des Krieges*, 1996) and Michael Verhoeven (*Der unbekannte Soldat*, 2006). Anonymous perpetration alongside familial integrity continues to shape broad public attitudes to the Nazi past in Germany.

Sepia fascism has kept contemporary German war film remarkably introspective, arguably more so than the films of the 1950s. Recent films featuring military or ideological enemies, such as Vilsmaier's *Stalingrad* (1993) or the recent mini-series *Unsere Mütter, unsere Väter* (*Generation War*) (2013) offer Hake's all-inclusive first person plural ('our' history,' 'our' parents). They leave little screen (or script) space for the other side. In *Stalingrad*, the first visual encounter with Soviets reduces them to specks on the screen, remote labourers in vast spaces. Private 'Rollo' glosses this view of Ukraine from his train window: "After the war, everyone can just ask for what they want; I've ordered ten wives and a hundred hectares. Look, they're already working for us." The battle scenes diminish enemies to nameless faces in dark corners, mute characters in sewers or thatched huts. Where 1950s films reassured the audience of the German officers' normality by offering a romantic interest, *Stalingrad* uses this subplot to confirm the depravity of the fascist Captain Haller, who keeps a captured resistance fighter as a sex slave. In *Unsere Mütter, unsere Väter*, nurse Charlotte betrays Lilja, a Jewish medic volunteering in the German field hospital. This character reappears miraculously towards the end as a Captain of the Red Army in order to discipline a marauding Soviet soldier who shoots casualties and rapes Charlotte. Later she will dispatch Charlotte's Ukrainian assistant Alina as a collaborator and argue for Charlotte's survival since she has nursing skills the Soviets need. This captain is the only face of the Red Army the camera dwells on and who consequently becomes its synecdoche: multi-ethnic, inclusive, ruthless, pragmatic. The mystery of her survival probably adds 'implausibly ingenious' to this list of compact characterisation.

Both productions offer greater historical veracity about crimes committed on the Eastern Front against Soviet soldiers and civilians: the maltreatment of POWs, the persecution and killing of Jews, the retributive executions of civilians as 'partisans,' the involvement of the *Wehrmacht* in genocidal SD and SS campaigns, the effects of the 'scorched earth' policy on civilians. Yet these films tackle neither deep-seated anti-Semitism nor anti-Communism, precisely the conflation that framed the war on the Eastern Front as ideologically motivated genocide. In fact, they insist that the audience identify with the 'band of brothers' – the Spielberg template for the plot – and this means that at best we can see the protagonists as a group of blithe youngsters who know no better, and who will, should they survive, be educated out of the error of their ways by the brutalisation of war.[8] The Red Army is incidental to the plot, often implied in combat noises rather than personified on the screen.

---

[8] On the consternation such introspection produces in audiences abroad see for instance Saryusz-Wolska and Piorun 2014.

3 *Anonyma:* Soviet Bodies and German Silence

Max Färberböck's *Anonyma* is the only exception to this marginalisation of the Soviet enemy in the introspective sepia fascism of the era, but it also explains this marginalisation. The book on which the film is based had a difficult publication history. Edited and expanded from wartime notebooks into diary form, *Eine Frau in Berlin* was first published in translation in 1954; its success abroad persuaded the author of a release in West Germany in 1959, where it had little impact, but one oft-cited reviewer deemed its portrayal of women's survival strategies in the face of relentless multiple sexual assault an insult to the "honour of German women" (qtd. in Redmann 2008: 194). When the book was re-released in 2003, precisely in this media context of normalised/normalising period drama and rediscovered German war trauma, it became a bestseller, not least because of its literary qualities. Yet despite a star-studded cast – Nina Hoss (*Das Mädchen Rosemarie; Yella*) as the protagonist; Juliane Köhler (*Der Untergang* and *Aimée & Jaguar*); Fassbinder's Irm Hermann; Werner Herzog's Rüdiger Vogler – the film failed at the box office.

Anonyma is a film of unusual and perturbing honesty that leaves the audience suspended in ambivalence towards the Soviet enemy and the German protagonist. It is the only German film that attempts to represent the Red Army precisely at the moment when Nazi propaganda clichés and the psychological effects of years of warfare seemed to converge, as the Soviet soldiers encountered the women of Berlin. The Soviet characters, like the tenants in the apartment block, have names, accumulate back stories and characterisation, and participate individually and collectively in the narrative. Consequently the cinematography negotiates between panning and tracking shots (the collective), close-ups (individuals) and over-the-shoulder frames with close-ups (interactions between individuals). Where *Generation War* shows the audience German atrocities on the Eastern Front, *Anonyma* implies their effects on Red Army soldiers in the manner in which they conduct themselves against German soldiers and civilians. In other words, the Eastern Front is an unseen prequel to *Anonyma*, and the subtlety of the film lies in the fact that the audience – from the point of view of the civilian protagonist – gradually realise that the events on the screen unfold as a corollary of German fascism and genocidal warfare.

From the start we are under no illusion about the enthusiasm Anonyma felt for the Nazi regime and its successes, but the first frame shows us where that regime and its mass support led the Germans: to the bombed streets of Berlin into which the Red Army marched on 27 April 1945. Anonyma's voiceover tells us that she was a widely travelled journalist who had voluntarily returned to Germany to be "part of it all." The subsequent flashback takes us back to her spacious attic flat in the early days of blitzkrieg, military victories and Operation Barbarossa. "I was just one of many who believed in our country's destiny. Doubts were for weaker temperaments. [...] We were convinced we were on the right side of history. We breathed the same air as everyone else, and we were right in the thick of it," runs the voiceover when she kisses her husband Gerd goodbye as he leaves for the Eastern Front, full of bravado.[9] At the party she then throws in his honour she toasts our men 'all over Europe.' We will see the final days of the Third Reich not from the point of view of Nazi big wigs or naïve secretaries in the bunker (*Downfall*) but through the eyes of an educated nationalist, a polyglot, middle-class journalist dodging mortar fire and sitting out air raids in the ill-lit cellar of her apartment block, starving and filthy. What tempts the women of the apartment block into the open is the promise of food. A low-angle shot moves the audience into the position of these emerging troglodytes facing an enemy of whom Nazi propaganda has taught them to expect the worst. What they (and we) see is not a modern, mechanised army but horses, carts with potatoes piled on, men cleaning boots, waiting or carrying valuables out of houses, smoking and staring (fig. 6). The first medium-range tracking shot of this collective of 'Sovietness' comments on this backward army with Anonyma's voiceover: "So here they are, our Soviet liberators. Overjoyed. Obviously they're amazed at how far they've come. I know them. I know their sandals, their villages and the jerry-built flats they take such pride in. They're not shy." Here, too, is the vocal framing of the Soviet citizen as primitive: a peasant who has to be dragged into the modern age in which he only clumsily accommodates himself.

The camera then presents individual soldiers going about their business, cleaning guns, carrying furniture out of houses, laughing at rude jokes, building fires, before panning over the whole street scene, or offering a tracking shot of a soldier on a bike. This initial emerging into the street to face the enemy as a collective is replayed several times in the film in montages in which the audience inhabits the point of view of the protagonist: looking, being stared at and mocked. Each time the sequence replays the emotional journey from tense anxiety to hope, from temporary relief to eventual frustration, and this prefigures the narrative arc of the film as a whole: the women's interaction with the occupiers evolves as a pragmatic response to the total lack of control they have over the

---

[9] The translations of the voiceover are my own. I have departed from the subtitles on several occasions. Anonyma's real name seems to have been Marta Hiller, a journalist who although no party member wrote brochures and pamphlets for the German Labour Service (DAF) and the Nazi Association of Teachers (NS-Lehrerbund) (Redmann 2008: 198).

Fig. 6: "I know their sandals and their villages." (Färberböck, *Anonyma*; Constantin Film)

situation, in which threats of death and multiple rapes alternate with good-natured suppers, dancing and singing and some sort of economic exchange.

The street in particular is a locus of danger. The camera conveys this time and again with tracking shots in which we follow Anonyma through groups of staring soldiers, or see her in an aerial shot as if from a sniper's position, a single woman walking through a uniformed crowd. The repetition of this scenario throughout the film reminds the audience that whatever the women manage to negotiate with the soldiers inside their domestic spaces, is a fragile, temporary truce: they are never safe. The crowd scenes are significant, though. Each time Anonyma negotiates a group of Soviet soldiers she sees them slightly differently, and the camera conveys that knowledge and that changed context simply through position, motion and degree of close up: if the first frame of the collective shows a generic image of soldiers and a potential source of food (fig. 6), the second one suggests the certainty of violence. By the time she makes her way to Major Andreij Rybkin she knows they taunt and casually rape. Later she will make her way through different crowds: men (and women) jubilant with the end of the war and singing their national anthem; men mocking Rybkin for his misguided chivalry; chagrined soldiers at attention, sending off Rybkin after Captain Andropov reported him for a disciplinary offence. Perhaps the most important encounter with the Soviet collective comes as the *mise-en-scène* of the protagonist's realisation of what fascism really means. Called to a neighbour's flat where a young, agitated soldier asks her to translate for the benefit of the female residents, she stands before them as if on trial. The frames that set up this halting exchange divide the room diagonally, with over-the-shoulder shots, between male soldiers and female civilians, before close-ups hone in on his face, distorted by anger and pain, and her face, trembling in shock and disbelief (figs 7 and 8).

Fig. 7: The mediator on trial (*Anonyma*)

The young soldier recounts that the Germans came to his village and killed the children. The camera cuts to two German children playing with wooden blocks in the next room: no one has killed them. She translates: "They stabbed them and smashed their heads against the walls." Here the script pitches fascist and communist propaganda against one another: the Soviet rapist against the Nazi sadist, a murderer of mothers and babies. According to Catherine Merrivale, propaganda "played an active part in shaping [Soviets'] perceptions of the enemy and in justifying vengeance. The Sovinformburo stoked the collective rage with manufactured images that could score themselves so deeply into a man's mind that he came to think of them as part of his own experience. The universality of the men's own tales is evidence of this" (2005: 270; see also Grossman 1995: 51). The wartime idolization of the Soviet wife and mother will also have contributed to heightening the effect of such propaganda. Warily, the protagonist asks the soldier whether he has merely heard this or witnessed it.

When the soldier confirms that he witnessed such an atrocity, Anonyma returns to the street, overwhelmed by what she has just heard.

Fig. 8: German atrocities: 'I saw it.' (*Anonyma*)

She sees a Soviet soldier drag a woman away who pleads with her, a Russian-speaker, to intervene (as she did at the start of the film). This time Anonyma sits impassive, watching the scene as if paralysed, observing an old woman in a moth-eaten fur coat lick crude oil from a barrel. Walking home she tries to avoid the Major who tells her Germany is close to defeat. From his jealous front wife Masha she learns that the Germans hung his wife. The next scene is another panning shot of the street, with Soviet soldiers looking at her (fig. 9) overlaid with the broadcast of Hitler's suicide.

This sequence of frames communicates the dejection of military defeat (we remember the arrogance of the earlier party scenes) alongside the growing realisation that Germany's devastation is the result of her own aggression. While the broadcast prepares a collective myth of victimhood – Hitler betrayed us – Anonyma's point of view asks us to see the soldiers, their rage, their violence, their looting, their mockery, in the light of Germany's genocidal ideological war on the Eastern Front. The panning shot (fig. 9) echoes the first scan over the enemy as the women emerged from the cellar (fig. 6). Now, however, the foreground focus directs the gaze to individuals who may each have their own story of suffering, whose country was invaded and ravaged, whose family may have been killed. This enemy is also a victim. We see how tired they are, how young or, conversely, how old. Sharing potatoes now seems an act of supreme magnanimity. We see in their gaze not predation but stoicism, indifference and above all bewilderment: not about how far they've come but how far they had to go. Their scrutinizing

Fig. 9: The Führer killed himself. (*Anonyma*)

gaze, directed at Anonyma and reflected by her (and projected into every scene since), finally translates into the question of what kind of people Germans – and fascists – are. For a German audience this means that the already uncomfortable point of view of the protagonist is being expanded, through her and the probing Soviets' gaze, into a first person plural ('we Germans' and 'our history') that refutes any notion of Koepnick's "nostalgic pleasure" or "positive identification." To be looked at thus and called to account, is extraordinarily rare in German cinema.

Anonyma also uses the 1950s clichés of German-Russian romance only to expose them as expedient myths. Given the power differential between invader and invaded, romance is at best an accommodation, a pragmatic negotiation of powerlessness. If such cinematic plots helped to restore German masculinity after the war, *Anonyma* unravels the de-masculinisation that necessitates later repair: the German men in Berlin are elderly and unable to protect their women; sidelined, they hover out of focus in the background, in the margins of the plot, or ruminate in kitchens, watching the goings-on from afar. Anonyma's friend Elke reports that her husband has been 'disturbed' since watching her rape. A neighbour, returned from the front and newly domesticated into his civilian cardigan, remains mute in the presence of the collective virility of the Soviet army; while his wife wishes to survive at all cost, he commits suicide after watching her enjoy a raucous party with Soviet soldiers (fig. 10). His muteness, like

Anonyma's silence, leaves the audience room to draw their own conclusions about the effects of Germany's defeat and occupation on German men.

Fig. 10: Too many men: Soviet joie-de-vivre (*Anonyma*)

During this party, as in several mid-distance panning shots, the camera revels in the sheer physicality and vitality of these men. Their bodies frame the German's suicide before and after his desperate act. They literally reverse the 1950s iconography of decent, physically imposing German officers who push Soviets into the margins of screen and plot by dwelling repeatedly on these strong Slavic bodies that have decimated, emasculated and killed German men. Some of these images are certainly folkloristic and treat the audience, among other things, to Caucasian folk songs and Mongolian throat vocals.[10] Yet their overall purpose is clearly to humanise the Red Army, to suggest that these are not the *Untermenschen* of Nazi posters and *Wochenschau* propaganda but ordinary people from diverse ethnic groups with local traditions. The soldiers repeatedly marvel at the reasons for the invasion given that these Germans are manifestly rich and can be robbed of objects so modern or refined they defy soldiers' comprehension. Major Rybkin once pulls Anonyma to the window in view of troops celebrating victory only to tell her that the Russian beasts of Nazi propaganda are a *product* of fascist aggression: the responsibility for Soviet behaviour lies squarely on Germany's shoulders. This may seem like a heavy-handed dialogue

---

10 A love of music also humanizes the camp commandant Worotilow in *Der Arzt von Stalingrad*.

in the manner of DEFA's anti-fascist war films. In fact, it reinforces earlier scenes during which the protagonist had to be brought face-to-face with Soviet suffering: how often, the scriptwriter seems to ask us, do we have to remind her of Nazi Germany's brutality before the penny drops?

Rybkin asks her twice whether she is a fascist. The first time she can fob him off with etymological flannelling, but the second time she remains silent, too respectful of him to lie, too ashamed to deny it. At no point is Anonyma able to reply to accounts of German atrocity and aggression. Her silence is a response that prefigures post-war structures of feeling (women won't talk about bombing and rape; men won't talk about the front) but it is also the most powerful, perhaps the most cinematic, response to convey what 'breathing the same air' and being 'in the thick of it' led to: an intoxicating ideological fog that rendered one supremely indifferent to others' suffering. One could also read it as an ironic comment on contemporary German war film and the near-compulsive introspection of sepia fascism: this is obtuseness masquerading as introspection.

Anonyma's third silence returns us to the narrative patterns of German-Soviet romance. A German soldier has been hiding in the attic flat and this deception endangers the civilians in the tenement, ultimately leading to Rybkin's transfer precisely when the protagonist has learnt to respect his view. This is not a romance. Rather, consensual sex here seals an understanding about commitments and differences that make romance impossible. Returning to her flat, Anonyma finds herself literally caught between the defeated Wehrmacht and the victorious Red Army (fig. 11). We look at this scenario from the over-the shoulder point of view of Captain Andropov, who takes some pleasure in delivering Rybkin's farewell note. The *mise-en-scène* shrinks Anonyma's returned husband into the background, where he will be ignored until she has read the note. The muteness with which she greets him echoes the street scene after the disclosure of German atrocities on the Eastern Front, and her muteness before Rybkin's lecture. He sees a horizontal collaborator; she sees a weary, visibly aged and bedraggled Wehrmacht soldier once cocksure of storming Moscow, having done God knows what on the Eastern Front. This marriage, and the Germany of old, are beyond resuscitation. The question Anonyma asks Rybkin in their last meeting is an existential one her husband could not possibly answer: 'how shall we live?'

Rybkin's departure is of course not the end of Soviet occupation. In East Germany Anonyma's question will be tackled increasingly unsuccessfully during the subsequent forty years and it requires the cinematic acknowledgement of the Red Army as a liberating force. In the West, it results in a questionable rehabilitation of the military and a long education into democracy that requires the exact opposite, a normalisation of the war on the Eastern Front and the margin-

Fig. 11: Between Wehrmacht and Red Army (*Anonyma*)

alisation of the Red Army into the introspective shadows of the plot. That *Anonyma* resists these patterns and cinematographically explains how they came about lifts it beyond the usual fare of sepia fascism into the category of a genuinely illuminating war film.

Conclusion

What kinds of conclusions can be drawn from a history of the Soviet enemy's marginalisation from which one recent, more nuanced film stands out? The emergence of a more comprehensive visual narrative about the nature of the genocidal war on the Eastern Front since the 1990s (the touring Wehrmacht exhibitions, Verhoeven's and Beckermann's documentaries) has in fact shifted little in Germany's popular screen victimology. Different types of knowledge about perpetration and victimhood are compartmentalised and rarely brought into dialogue as if commercially successful film and TV formats could not deliver such complexity or as if audiences could not be trusted to engage with them. The influence of Hollywood storylines and Nazi stereotypes has certainly shaped viewers' tastes in ways that may make it hard to tell a historically plausible story which deviates from the generic template of the war film. The Soviet as sniper, anonymous civilian villager, *politruk*, rapist or generic soldier remains a useful external enemy, secondary to the uniformed SS-officer as the internal one:

here Germany's war story is ultimately a struggle against both forms of totalitarianism, external communism and internal fascism.

Yet the marginalisation of the Soviet enemy in most German war films also has a degree of accuracy that reaches beyond mere exculpation or ongoing introspection. This was not an enemy who was regarded as a racial equal in Nazi ideology; no aspect of language, culture or way of life was worth engaging with beyond the requirements of conquering *Lebensraum* in the East – this is why the 1950s Slavic romances seem so implausible. The expulsions, the Cold War and the division of Germany did little to encourage a revision of this idea of a Slavic communist other, at least in the West. What makes *Anonyma* so unusual is that despite the violence of the encounters some of its characters have the chance to *engage* with Soviets as individuals. That is a small miracle.

Works Cited

Assmann, Aleida (2013) *Das neue Unbehagen an der Erinnerungskultur: Eine Intervention* (Munich: C.H. Beck).

Bangert, Axel (2014) *The Nazi Past in Contemporary German Film: Viewing Experiences of Intimacy and Immersion* (Rochester, NY: Camden House).

Blachut, Bastian, Imme Klages, and Sebastian Kuhn (eds) (2015) *Reflexionen des beschädigten Lebens? Nachkriegskino in Deutschland zwischen 1945 und 1962* (Munich: text + kritik).

Bliersbach, Gerhard (1989) *So grün war die Heide … Die gar nicht so heile Welt im Nachkriegsfilm* (Weinheim: Beltz).

Buchbender, Ortwin (1978) *Das tönende Erz: Deutsche Propaganda gegen die Rote Armee im Zweiten Weltkrieg* (Stuttgart: Seewald Verlag).

Dahlke, Birgit (2000) "'Frau, komm!' Vergewaltigungen 1945 – zur Geschichte eines Diskurses," in *Literaturgesellschaft DDR: Kanonkämpfe und ihre Geschichten*, ed. Birgit Dahlke and Martina Langermann (Stuttgart: Metzler), 275–311.

Groß, Bernhard (2015) *Die Filme sind unter uns: Zur Geschichtlichkeit des frühen deutschen Nachkriegskinos: Trümmer-, Genre-, Dokumentarfilm* (Berlin: Vorwerk 8).

Grossmann, Atina (1995) "A Question of Silence: the Rape of German Women by Occupation Soldiers," *October* 72, 42–63.

Grossmann, Vasily (1985 [1980]) *Life and Fate*, trans. Robert Chandler (London: Harvill).

Hake, Sabine (2002) *German National Cinema* (London: Routledge).

Hake Sabine (2012) *Screen Nazis: Cinema, History and Democracy* (Wisconsin: University of Wisconsin Press).

Kapczynski, Jennifer M. (2007) "The Treatment of the Past: Geza von Radvanyi's *Der Arzt von Stalingrad* and the West German War Film," in *Take Two: Fifties Cinema in Divided Germany*, ed. John E. Davidson and Sabine Hake (New York: Berghahn), 137–151.

Kirst, Hans-Hellmut (1954) *08/15* (Cologne: Lingen).

Klee, Ernst, and Willi Dreßen (1989) *"Gott mit uns": Der deutsche Vernichtungskrieg im Osten, 1939–1945* (Frankfurt/M.: Fischer).

Koepnick, Lutz (2004) "'Amerika gibt's überhaupt nicht': Notes on the German Heritage Film," in *German Pop Culture. How ‚American' Is It?*, ed. Agnes C. Mueller (Ann Arbor: University of Michigan Press), 191–208.
Kopelew, Lew (1976 [1975]) *Aufbewahren für alle Zeit*, trans. Heddy Pross-Weerth (Hamburg: Hoffmann & Campe).
Kuby, Erich (1999) *Mein Krieg: Aufzeichnungen aus 2129 Tagen* (Berlin: Aufbau).
Merrivale, Catherine (2005) *Ivan's War: The Red Army 1939–45* (London: Faber & Faber).
Moeller, Robert G. (2001) *War Stories: The Search for a Usable Past in the Federal Republic of Germany* (Berkeley: University of California Press).
Moltke, Johannes von (2005) *No Place Like Home: Locations of Heimat in German Cinema* (Berkeley: University of California Press).
Müller, Rolf Dieter and Gerd R. Ueberschär (1995) *Hitler's War in the East, 1941–1945: A Critical Assessment* (Providence: Berghahn).
Niven, Bill (ed) (2006) *Germans as Victims: Remembering the Past in Contemporary Germany* (Houndmills: Palgrave).
Overy, Richard (1997) *Russia's War* (London: Allan Lane).
Plivier, Theodor (1954) *Moskau, Stalingrad. Berlin: Der große Krieg im Osten* (Stuttgart: Fackel-Verlag).
Redmann, Jennifer (2008) "'Eine Frau in Berlin': Diary as History or Fiction of the Self?," *Colloquia Germanica* 41. 3, 193–210.
Saryusz-Wolska, Magdalena, and Carolin Piorun (2014) "Verpasste Debatte: *Unsere Mütter, unsere Väter* in Deutschland und Polen," *Osteuropa* 64.11–12, 115–132.
Schmitz, Helmut (ed) (2008) *A Nation of Victims? Narratives of Wartime Suffering from 1945 to the Present* (Amsterdam: Rodopi).
Solschenizyn, Alexander (1976 [1974]) *Ostpreußische Nächte*, trans. Nikolaus Ehlert (Frankfurt/M.: Luchterhand).
Stern, Frank (2001) "Film in the 1950s: Passing Images of Guilt and Responsibility," in *The Miracle Years: A Cultural History of West Germany, 1949–1968*, ed. Hanna Schissler (Princeton: Princeton University Press), 266–280.
Taberner, Stuart and Karina Berger (eds) *Germans as Victims in the Literary Fiction of the Berlin Republic* (Rochester: Camden House).
Welzer, Harald, Sabine Moller and Karoline Tschuggnall (2002) *Opa war kein Nazi: Nationalsozialismus und Holocaust im Familiengedächtnis* (Frankfurt/M.: Fischer).
Wilms, Wilfried, and Wilhelm Rasch (eds) (2008) *German Postwar Films: Life and Love in the Ruins* (New York: Palgrave Macmillan).
Wöss, Fritz (1958) *Hunde, wollt ihr ewig leben* (Klagenfurt: Kaiser).

Filmography

08/15 (1954–1955) Dir. Paul May (Divina Film).
Anonyma: Eine Frau in Berlin (*Anonyma: A Woman in Berlin*) (2008) Dir. Max Färberböck (Constantin Film).
Der Arzt von Stalingrad (1958) Dir. Geza von Radvanyi (Divina Film).
Der Untergang (*Downfall*) (2004) Dir. Oliver Hirschbiegel (Constantin Film).

Unsere Mütter, unsere Väter (*Generation War*) (2013) Creators Philip Kadelbach and Stefan Kolditz (Teamworx/ZDF).
Hunde, wollt ihr ewig leben (1959) Dir. Frank Wisbar (Deutsche Film Hansa).
Jenseits des Krieges (1996) Dir. Ruth Beckerman (Josef Aichholzer).
Stalingrad (1993) Dir. Josef Vilsmaier (Bavaria Film).
Der unbekannte Soldat (2006) Dir. Michael Verhoeven (ARTE/BR).

Niina Oisalo
Enemies Within: Reimagining the 'Fallen Women' of World War II in Contemporary Finnish Documentary

It is estimated that tens of thousands of children were born to German soldiers all over Europe during World War II, most of them out of wedlock. In Finland, according to cautious approximations, around 1,000 children were fathered by German soldiers. The number is likely to be much higher, as there were no records, and the fathers' identities were in many cases kept secret for fear of judgement.[1] Some of the women also travelled to Norway or Germany to give birth.[2] Children born outside marriage were often condemned by society, let alone if the father had been an enemy soldier, or even worse: a Nazi. These women and their children became easy targets – enemies within – upon whom people could unleash their disappointment after the lost wars and externalize the shame felt over the alliance with Nazi-Germany. It was not until 2006 that an association called *Saksalaisten sotilaiden lapset* ("Children of the German Soldiers") was founded in Finland, with the goal of finding the missing fathers and creating contacts between the fathers, their children and other relatives. The association also hopes for an official apology or acknowledgement from the Finnish state because of these women's discrimination by the society (Sundström 2010).

This chapter looks at Virpi Suutari's documentary film *Auf Wiedersehen Finnland* ("Goodbye Finland") (2010), dealing with the repercussions of Finnish-German love affairs during World War II. In the film, the experiences of the women who travelled to Germany with the *Wehrmacht* soldiers in the final stages of the war unfold through interviews, dramatized scenes and archival footage. The film reveals a fundamental ambivalence at the very core of the concept of the enemy, underscoring how the quickly changing national constella-

---

[1] On the difficulties of retrieving the exact number of children born to German soldiers, see Junila 2000: 268–270.
[2] In Europe, estimations of the total number of *Wehrmachtskinder* (children born to German soldiers) vary from 250,000 to 2 million (Drolshagen 2005: 235). All around Europe, the children born to foreign soldiers during World War II have received more attention in research and public discussions during the last two decades. In addition to the German soldiers' descendants, also children fathered by the American and other allied soldiers have been researched (see Simonsen 2015).

tions of 'friend' and 'enemy' can affect people's everyday lives in devastating ways. As in other European states, in Finland the discussions on World War II have exuded a "pungent smell of hypocrisy" (Stenius, Österberg and Östling 2011: 9). The memory work related to World War II is still going on, and cultural memory is produced in constantly changing forms. It is, in fact, the instability of memory which allows for the renewal and redemption of a culture or a nation (Sturken 1997: 17). In order to redeem the past, we must reimagine it.

1 Reimagining the War

World War II, and especially the Winter War against the Soviet Union (1939 – 1940), has been a key event in the construction of a Finnish collective memory and national identity.[3] The iconic figure of the wars continues to be the unyielding heroic soldier, who fights persistently against an overpowering enemy. Documentary (and fiction) films on World War II have also been dominated by the male/soldiers' point of view, with only few exceptions.[4] Other war stories, which do not fit into the national grand narrative, have received less attention in film as well as in other popular media until recent years. Alisa Lebow names documentaries looking awry at war or dealing with war experiences outside the battlefield as "unwar films" (2015: 460). This definition could also be suited for *Auf Wiedersehen Finnland*, as it maps the less visible aspects of wars, and engages the viewer with events left in the shadows, beside the field of the "frenetic action" of warfare. Unwar films thus set out to create a more ambiguous image of the repercussions of wars in order to destabilize the centrality of militarist imagery in documentary.

Another recent Finnish documentary, which could also be thought of as an unwar film, is Mari Soppela's autobiographical *Kuka piru pimeässä näkee* (*Who the Devil Can See in the Dark*) (2014), where the director convinces her father to begin a search for his missing father, an unknown Nazi soldier whose photograph

---

[3] One symbolically valuable example of the appreciation and significance of the Winter War as a national memory site is the erection of a monument *Valon tuoja* (*Bringer of Light*) by sculptor Pekka Kauhanen in 2017, when Finland celebrated 100 years of independence.

[4] A notable exception in documentary film is Elina Kivihalme's *Tuntematon emäntä* (*The Unknown Mistress*) (2011), which depicts life on the Finnish home front during World War II. Also, the experiences of the women who belonged to the Lotta Svärd voluntary organisation, which served the army's needs, have been depicted in several fiction and documentary films, though representations of the 'Lottas' in films are mostly very 'immaculate' and idealized, as for example in Ilkka Vanne's *Lupaus* (*Promise*) (2005).

they find from Soppela's grand-mother's family album. Films such as *Auf Wiedersehen Finnland* or *Kuka piru pimeässä näkee* open up an uneasy chapter in the national memory building, contesting the grand narrative of the "great unifying wars." Filmmaking is thus considered here as an act of re-telling and remembering the past in order to establish other narratives alongside the 'official' (war) history. This kind of cinematic memory work has been done extensively especially in the US (connected to the Vietnam War for example), but also in Germany, related to the period of Nazism and especially the Holocaust (cf. e. g. Elsaesser 1996: 145– 146). In Finland, candid cinematic memory work on World War II is only now beginning to catch up.

According to Marita Sturken, camera images "play a vital role in the development of national meaning by creating a sense of shared participation and experience in the nation." At the same time, these images have the "capacity to create, interfere with, and trouble the memories we hold as individuals and as a nation" (1997: 20, 24). Documentaries operate in the tumultuous field of memory work by offering the audience, the filmmakers, as well as the film's subjects, a way to remember *with* the images, while potentially harassing, conversing and creating new layers to the collective cultural imageries and imaginaries. Technologies of memory, such as film, "embody and generate memory and are thus implicated in the power dynamics of memory's production," and furthermore, this embodiment of memory is "an active process with which subjects engage in relation to social institutions and practices" (Sturken 1997: 10). In *Auf Wiedersehen Finnland*, private and public memories are intertwined, and the past is summoned and reinvented in the present through "imaginative investment, projection and creation" (Hirsch 2012: 5). *Auf Wiedersehen Finnland* and *Kuka piru pimeässä näkee* contribute to the on-going discussions in Finland over the meanings and consequences of World War II for the lives of contemporaries and for later generations: "The sense of living connection" that we still carry to the wars is mediated through a multiplicity of images, objects, stories, behaviors, and affects related, and these possess the ability to transfer traumas within the family and the culture at large (Hirsch 2012: 1, 5).

Since the 1990s, there has been a growing interest, in research and in the arts, in the hitherto marginalized emotional landscapes of war, including the trauma of women who were branded the nation's 'enemy' within the frame of the dominant historical politics.[5] Particularly the "postmemory" generation

---

[5] Also the 'unheroic' sides of World War II have been depicted in several recent documentaries describing the traumatization of soldiers and the mental marks that the war left also to the later generations, such as Ari Matikainen's *Sota ja mielenrauha* (*War and Peace of Mind*) (2016) or Timo Korhonen's *Sodan murtamat* (*The Wages of* War) (2016).

(Hirsch 2012: 5), who do not possess firsthand experiences of war, yet bear the personal, collective, and cultural trauma of the former generations, have been eager to search for their own interpretations, bringing to light aspects of Finnish wars that had been treated in the public discussions rather biasedly before.[6] In film, most of the depictions of Finnish-German wartime relations have been in documentary form, such as in Heikki Huttu-Hiltunen's *Himmlerin kanteleensoittaja* (*Instrument of Himmler*) (2014), focusing on the Nazi scientists' interest in finding the origins of the 'Aryan race' in Finnish Karelia, or Pia Andell's *Göringin sauva* (*Göring's Baton*) (2010), where a young Finnish photographer is given a confidential assignment in Nazi Germany. In literature, the sexual relations between German soldiers and Finnish women has been a persistent topic (much before historians were to tackle the subject). For example, Katja Kettu's *Kätilö* (*The Midwife*) (2011), turned into a film, *Wildeye*, in 2015, describes the stormy relationship taking place right before and during the Lapland War between a Finnish midwife working for the Germans and an SS officer. The story is inspired by the life of Kettu's grandparents. However, the women themselves have not been active in this memory work.

2 'Fallen Women': Shame and Silence

After Finland lost the Winter War (1939–1940) to the Soviet Union, the country had preserved its independence, but it had to cede large regions of Karelia and Lapland. After that war, Soviet occupation was still a potent threat, and hoping to win back the lost territories, Finland sought backing from a military alliance with Nazi Germany (Meinander 2011: 56). During the Continuation War (1941–1944), over 200,000 German soldiers arrived in the country to strengthen the Finnish defense against the Soviet army, mostly in Northern Finland. At the time, they outnumbered the local population of 144,000, who were mostly women and children, as nearly all the men had been called to the front (Tuominen 2015: 39). The relations between the German soldiers and the local Finnish people during wartime were for the most part friendly, and the majority of the Northern Finnish people accepted the German presence as it was thought to be "beneficial to the homeland" (Junila 2012: 357).[7] While most of the (young) men were at the front, Finnish women were given more freedom and responsibility in ev-

---

[6] Even today, the wars are commemorated as "national experiences," fundamentally positive and indispensable for the nation's self-understanding (Kinnunen and Jokisipilä 2012: 436).
[7] All translations are mine.

eryday life than they had ever before experienced. Many unmarried women began to work outside the home, and they gained more independence. Women learned how to take care of themselves, and to "get through everyday life without men" (Nevala and Hytönen 2015: 152). The German troops offered well-paid jobs, reasonable working hours and a private room. This economic independence freed the young women from the control of family, home village and landladies, and they also had more freedom to choose who to go out with (Junila 2006: 249). After three years of warfare, the Continuation War ended in armistice. The German troops were to be rapidly driven off the country by the Finnish, which led to the swift but shattering Lapland War (1944–1945) against the former brothers-in-arms. In almost one night, "the good Germans" became "the evil Nazis" (Kinnunen and Jokisipilä 2012: 455). Many of Lapland's towns and bridges were burned to the ground as part of the German scorched earth policy.

The disillusionment left by the lost wars and the sorrow over lost territories meant a bitter end to the alliance with Nazi Germany. The massive destruction which the Germans' retreat had left behind in Lapland cut the wounds even deeper, especially in the minds of Northern Finnish people. The 'Nazi brides' who had socialized with the Germans and especially the ones left with their 'bastard' children, became easy scapegoats for all the negative emotions: the disappointment and grief over crippled minds and bodies, and the lost land. They were treated like an enemy within, and some of the women were shamed in public after the news of Hitler's defeat had reached Finland. During and after the war, official enemies can change quickly, more quickly than people can keep up with. The experiences of these 'fallen women' and their children reveal how political strategies affect people's everyday lives in subtle, embodied, traumatizing and sometimes violent ways. They were not among the ones who were allowed to take part in what counts as the 'national story,' yet through their dismissal from the memory work, and through the active process of forgetting, they were part of the creation of the cultural memory of World War II. As Marita Sturken writes, "memory and forgetting are co-constitutive processes," where that which is forgotten is just as crucial as that which is remembered (1997: 2).

Interpretations of history always include a "struggle about remembrance, acknowledgment and recognition" (Tuominen 2015: 40). Actively forgetting the time of war was essential during the reconstruction period in Finland, as remaining silent about the traumas was for many the only way to stay sane and keep on living. The bleak memories of wars were replaced by a strong ethos of work, self-discipline and the intention to move on with life, to marry and start a family. The precondition for moving on was 'tidying up" the past, and for that, certain aspects of the war had to be swept under the rug or treated as internal enemies. In the Finnish grand narrative of World War II, the women who fraternized with the Germans tarnished the understanding of the war as the "noble battle against Nazism and fascism." The horrific acts carried out by the Nazi regime seemed to contaminate even the men and women who had been in contact with them (Ericsson 2005: 3). There was an even greater need for wiping out the traces of Nazi presence in Finland, as the country had been a co-belligerent of Germany in the war – an episode which people would rather have forgotten as quickly as possible after the war. It was a deviation, a horrible mistake which should never be made again.

As Marianne Junila notes, in this aspect, the nationalist discourse, especially in times of war, associated women's bodies with strong symbolic meanings. Women are the "reproducers of the nation" but – because of their assumed "moral strength," – they should also embody "the purity of the nation." As the men were supposed to practice virtues of warfare at the front – bravery, patriotic sacrifice and loyalty – women should act virtuously too and "tend to the hearth" (2012: 220). According to Tiina Kinnunen and Markku Jokisipilä, the women who were associated with the Germans became symbols of the morally troublesome alliance, "as Finnish women and especially the mothers have been important icons for the whole nation in cultural imagery" (2012: 477). These "promiscuous" women aroused intense public debate in the Finnish media, concerning their "appetites," "indecency" and upfront "vileness." The women's 'shameful' conduct was commonly thought to be detrimental to the morale of the men at the battlefront. A well-known columnist, 'Valentin,' (i.e. the writer Ensio Rislakki), wrote that it was other women who should have "taken action, to prevent their reputation to be spoilt as well" (qtd. in Junila 2000: 147).[8] The condemnation was thus extended to the Finnish women as a collective group.[9] After the war, the German soldiers who had fathered children could not be criticized for political reasons, so the anger was directed at the women, even if they had only worked for the Nazi army (Junila 2008: 35).

As an act of memory politics, women were labelled as 'stained,' and were ostracized with their children. Thus, the illusion of national integrity and the heroic narrative of a patriotic war could be left intact. In the case of the children who were brought up in public and private silence, it was commonly thought

---

[8] The column became a very influential propaganda article and was published by 42 newspapers and magazines (Junila 2000: 147).
[9] The sexually active but deceitful woman was a popular figure in the war propaganda and films made right after the wars. Anu Koivunen has written on the roles that women were typically assigned in Finnish films during and after the wars. They included the mother, the fallen woman, the daydreaming woman, and the modern woman. The fallen woman, threatening the social and moral order, is of special interest with regards to this chapter (see Koivunen 1995).

that this silence was only maintained in order to protect them. As Kjersti Ericsson notes, however, it was not an "empty silence" but a silence filled with meaning, wrapped in shame and guilt (2005: 1). "The internalized shame" meant that the "child was left with a deep feeling of shame, but with no clear idea of what there was to be ashamed of" (Ericsson and Ellingsen 2005: 104). Out of loyalty to the mother and family, the quest for the unknown father might actually be undertaken only later in life, as in Soppela's film, or for some, never.

3 Recollection-Images, Gaps and Frozen Emotions

In Virpi Suutari's *Auf Wiedersehen Finnland*, four women speak openly and for the first time in public about their decision to leave for Germany in the turmoil of the Lapland War. The director Virpi Suutari, who is known for documentaries with a strong social consciousness, often depicting people who have been marginalized in society, wanted to delve into the histories of the Finnish-German relations in Lapland, as she had heard many colourful stories about the women who left with the Germans as a child, growing up in Rovaniemi, Lapland (Seppälä 2010). Suutari searched for her protagonists for two years. She met many women, but they all refused to be filmed. For most of the women, who were around 90 years at the time of filming, the traumas were still too vivid to be shared. After much persuasion, four women and one man agreed to tell their stories to Suutari's camera. When the film was completed, "the women felt immense relief for opening up," the director tells in an interview (Blåfield 2016). After the film screenings, many other women have also stepped forward to tell their stories, but as Suutari describes it, "the film also seemed to reopen painful wounds in many viewers" (Seppälä 2010).

The women in the film had different reasons for leaving; Terttu and Roosa followed their German boyfriends, Kaisu escaped the feared Russian invasion, and Elma the cruel words of her mother. Later on, the women were all condemned as "traitors" by the society and even by their own families, leading to a silence which is now finally broken. In the film, Elma recollects, visibly still upset, how on the verge of their evacuation from Lapland her mother called her "whore" and refused to take her along with the rest of the family. "And that's when Elma decided that she will leave, and will not listen to the [one] calling her 'whore,' as she is not one," Elma recounts in voice-over, talking of herself in the third person. The anger that Elma felt has visibly not evaporated even after 70 years, and she has not forgiven her mother. Her daughter sits beside her, consoling and asking questions. The story of her mother seems to weigh heavily on her as well. "I have put her into the bottom of hell," Elma cries, cursing her mother, and puffing with resentment, while the camera zooms slowly into an embroidery on the wall that reads: "Forgive and forget."

The main storyline in the film revolves around the women as a group, and their individual *her*stories blend into one main narrative of the women's journey to Germany, alternating with the story of Frans. He is the son of Roosa, who abandoned him as a child and never revealed the true identity of his father, although Frans found it out later on his own. He travels to Germany in the present to visit his father's grave and the town where he used to live. In the beginning, the women look back to the final stages of the Lapland War, their life situations and decisions to leave for Germany, then the journey through Norway, the time of working first for the Germans and later for the Allied forces, the horror of learning about the concentration camps, the return to Finland, interrogations by the state police, and finally the troublesome return home.

The women's stories of their journey merge into one collective, elliptic narrative, where their images and voice-overs intermingle with miscellaneous archival imagery from the war, and dramatized scenes: "When remembrance fails, the story must be creatively falsified in order to reach the truth" (Marks 2000: 50). The hazy, intimate dramatized scenes, shot on grainy color film stock, always (apart from the very end) without recognizable faces, bring to life delicate moments and atmospheres from the women's trip to Germany and back, and allow the viewer to plunge into the story and the moods on the women's journey. They present a woman standing on a ship's deck, looking from a cabin window, leaning onto a man's chest, with snowy mountains in the background, walking on a sea shore. Combined with the women's testimonials, these scenes create resonant moments where the women's feelings of expectation, hope, disappointment and shame are enacted. The film turns into an intense voyage where the memories once left to the past are reawakened, and, perhaps at the same time, redeemed in the present, with the audience.

The testimonials of the women are presented in the film with a distance between the narrator in voice-over and the image of the narrator, as the women's voices are rarely matched with an image of the person talking, apart from the very beginning. Instead, the voice-over is juxtaposed with archival and dramatized footage and scenes where the women are filmed mostly in their homes, sitting on a bed, doing exercises, or listening to the radio. The women are often filmed through a mirror, inside window frames or other carefully staged scenes, creating a 'gap' between the one who speaks and the one who is in the image. This choice accentuates the performative nature of the film's ethos, separating the women from the shame of talking about their experiences.

The felt sense of the archival images emerges also from the temporal gap that distances the viewer in the present from the events in the past. The archival clips offer classic motives of war: bombers flying over, cities burning, soldiers marching, ruins of cities, civilians searching the ruins, war prisoners, bodies in the gutters and fields. They appear like flashes of vision or hallucinations. The images follow loosely the women's stories, but the viewer is not informed of their exact context; it is not known from which country, or from which year they are, or who the people in them are. They could be thought of as images of recollection, embodying past events that have no match in any single person's memory, "floating loosely from history" (Marks 2000: 50, 71).[10] Recollection-images also testify to the partialness and incompleteness of memory. They do not represent a particular memory or an event, but embody the traces of an event, unreachable in the present moment. Thus, such images require an imaginative investment, "a leap of meaning-making" from the viewer. From these leaps over the temporal and signifying gaps, grows the affective power of the images.

In a particularly evocative archival scene towards the midpoint of the film, when the women describe in voice-over the moments of the collapse of the Third Reich, a young woman walks in slow-motion alongside a road, with wobbly steps, towards the camera. She wears men's trousers and a worn-down shirt, her hair is messy and she has a heavily bruised face, her left eye has almost sealed up – she looks defiant at first, then desperate, lowering her face abruptly, and her hair falls on the face. In the next image her face is filmed from up-close, uncomfortably close for her and the viewer. This scene becomes an accentuated moment also because of its silence; there are no music, sound effects, or dialogues accompanying the image. After her, soldiers' bodies are shown by the side of a road, while a tank passes them, raising dust into the air. The woman's haunting figure, expressing the confusion in the middle of a disaster, stays with the viewer for a long time. What has happened to her? Why? And what is she going through? The woman in the archival clip embodies the emotional devastation of war in a much more visceral way than any words could describe – she is the image of an enemy to some, an enemy within.

Then we see Frans sitting in a car, at a German gas station, talking in voice-over about how he was very angry with his mother as a child: "Why did she not leave me to Germany, as she did not take care of me when we were in Finland either?" He was adopted later by his aunt, and abused verbally and physically by her husband: "I can't say that I would have any love for my mother, or for

---

10 Marks' understanding of the recollection-image relies on its theorizing in Gilles Deleuze's *Cinema 2: The Time-Image*.

my foster mother." In the penultimate scene of the film, mother and son sit around the same table, but their relationship is visibly very difficult. "I thought it was better, for the child," Roosa says, looking affectionately at a photo of Frans as a little boy, and continues quickly: "Let's not talk anymore." Yet Frans insists, telling about his investigations in Germany and taking out another photo, of Roosa and a German soldier, Frans' father. She then recounts, in very short sentences, how their relationship ended in Hamburg, and after a moment of silence: "It has all been endured." Yet, the sorrow visible on the faces of the mother and the son tells another story, and the image becomes silent and grained, freezing into their distressed faces. It is as if the past has swiped over them and frozen their emotions. There is no resolution, and the traumas do not entirely dissolve; ambivalence thus also pertains to the process of facing the past. Perhaps, in order to redeem the past, it has to be faced eye to eye. This gesture is enacted in the final act of the film, in a dramatized scene where a young woman leans on a man, and then looks up, straight to the camera. This is the last image of the film.

Conclusion: The Haunting Past

The most iconic memory of a woman in love with a German soldier in Finnish popular film culture might be from Mikko Niskanen's film *Pojat* (*The Boys*) (1962), based on a novel by Paavo Rintala. In the last scene of the film, a young boy, Jake, runs desperately after a train carrying his mother, who is leaving him for a German soldier. The camera follows intensely the face of the boy, who stumbles and cries uncontrollably. However, during the long investigations that Virpi Suutari made for *Auf Wiedersehen Finnland*, she found out only about few women who had abandoned their families; most of those who left had nothing to lose (Nykänen). However, the image can be stronger than the truth – it can reveal what people want to remember, how they wish to see the past, and themselves as part of that past. The image of a 'fallen woman' running off with the Germans is a persistent one; she is an enemy of the idea of a unified and idealized nation.

The war never ends when the armistice is signed. The collective legacies of World War II in Finland are manifold, but one of the most prevailing ones was the culture of silence: that traumas should be kept to oneself, as Soppela's film also suggests. Among those traumas is cooperation with Nazi-Germany. Ari Matikainen, the director of *Sota ja mielenrauha* (*War and Peace of Mind*) (2016), a documentary on the emotional ramifications of the Continuation War, claims that a reconciliation process and public discussions of World War

II's significance in Finland have never really taken place. That is why later generations now have an enormous need to go through their history, to remember, and find out what their families went through during the wars (Matikainen 2016).

Auf Wiedersehen Finnland combines mediated events of the past, told by the women in interviews made in the present, with dream-like archival footage and dramatized scenes, bringing together the public and private memories of the war. The four women's and Frans's stories reveal incidents of discrimination, mistreatment, and emotional catastrophes they have been trying to come to terms with throughout their lives. The film participates in the ongoing debates on national belongings, changing enemy constellations and cultural memory. It reveals the social mechanisms through which some people are included and excluded from the hegemonic historical narrative, and how the ambivalent enemy figures keep on shifting in the Finnish collective memory. The violence that the discussions on national histories necessarily include is presented in the film as subtle, multilayered affective practices – such as silences, internalized taboos and shame that have had, and continue to have, profound effects on people's lives.

Documentary film could be considered as an effective arena for reconsidering national narratives, as it collides different perspectives in an evocative and sensitive way within a film world, where the marginalized voices can be placed in the center. Perhaps for the first time, and at the very last moment it was still possible, in history, as it happened in the case of *Auf Wiedersehen Finnland*. Generally the film was considered in the press as a respectful and subtle depiction of war stories which rarely get told (Holm 2010, Juntto 2010). Some of the reviewers criticized the film for "lacking in substance," referring to the fact that the women in the film do not reveal that much of themselves (Maskula 2010, Vaarala 2010). However, there lies also the strength of the film, since what Suutari in fact does is to frame the silence and the shame that the women still feel and make it tangible for the viewer. As the film critic of *Helsingin Sanomat,* Leena Virtanen (2010) notes, "one can dwell in the film as if in a dream, in a quiet nightmare."

Works Cited

Blåfield, Ville (2016) "Palkittu dokumenttiohjaaja Virpi Suutari: 'En ole koskaan tuntenut tarvetta kuulua mihinkään ryhmään,'" *Gloria* <https://www.gloria.fi/artikkeli/ihmiset/palkittu_dokumenttiohjaaja_virpi_suutari_en_ole_koskaan_tuntenut_tarvetta_kuulua> (accessed 18 July 2016).

Drolshagen, Ebba D. (2005) "Besatzungskinder and Wehrmachtskinder: Germany's War Children," in *Children of World War II: The Hidden Enemy Legacy*, ed. Kjersti Ericsson and Eva Simonsen (Oxford and New York: Berg Publishers), 229–248.

Elsaesser, Thomas (1996) "Subject Positions, Speaking Positions: from *Holocaust, our Hitler,* and *Heimat* to *Shoah* and *Schindler's List*," in *The Persistence of History: Cinema, Television, and the Modern Event*, ed. Vivian Sobchack (New York and London: Routledge), 145–183.

Ericsson, Kjersti (2005) "Introduction," in *Children of World War II: The Hidden Enemy Legacy*, ed. Kjersti Ericsson and Eva Simonsen (London: Berg Publishers), 1–12.

Ericsson, Kjersti, and Dag Ellingsen (2005) "Life Stories of Norwegian War Children," in *Children of World War II*, ed. Ericsson and Simonsen, 93–111.

Hirsch, Marianne (2012) *The Generation of Postmemory: Writing and Visual Culture After the Holocaust* (New York: Columbia University Press).

Holm, Saija (2010) *Lapin Kansa*, in *Elonet* (Finnish National Audiovisual Institute) <http://www.elonet.fi/fi/elokuva/1489950> (accessed 13 February 201).

Junila, Marianne (2000) *Kotirintaman aseveljeyttä: Suomalaisen siviiliväestön ja saksalaisen sotaväen rinnakkainelo Pohjois-Suomessa 1941–1944* (Helsinki: SKS).

Junila, Marianne (2006) "Isä: 'Saksalainen sotilas,'" in *Ihminen sodassa: Suomalaistenkokemuksia talvi-ja jatkosodasta*, ed. Tiina Kinnunen and Ville Kivimäki (Helsinki and Jyväskylä: Minerva), 243–259.

Junila, Marianne (2008) "Eri maata: vieraiden naiset ja lapset kansallisessa kertomuksessa,"*Nuorisotutkimus* 26.2, 32–45.

Junila, Marianne (2012) "Wars on the Home Front: Mobilization, Economy and Everyday Experiences," in *Finland in World War II: History, Memory, Interpretations*, ed. Tiina Kinnunen and Ville Kivimäki (Leiden and Boston: Brill), 191–232.

Juntto, Anssi (2010) *Kaleva*, in *Elonet* (Finnish National Audiovisual Institute) <http://www.elonet.fi/fi/elokuva/1489950> (accessed 13 February 2017).

Kinnunen, Tiina, and Markku Jokisipilä (2012) "Shifting Images of 'Our Wars': Finnish Memory Culture of World War II," in *Finland in World War II: History, Memory, Interpretations*, ed. Tiina Kinnunen and Ville Kivimäki (Leiden and Boston: Brill), 435–482.

Koivunen, Anu (1995) *Isänmaan moninaiset äidinkasvot: sotavuosien suomalainen naistenelokuva sukupuoliteknologiana* (Turku: Suomen elokuvatutkimuksen seura).

Lebow, Alisa (2015) "The Unwar Film," in *A Companion to Contemporary Documentary Film*, ed. Alexandra Juhasz and Alisa Lebow (Malden, MA and Oxford: Wiley Blackwell), 454–474.

Marks, Laura U. (2000) *The Skin of the Film: Intercultural Cinema, Embodiment, and the Senses* (Durham and London: Duke University Press).

Maskula, Tapani (2010) *Turun Sanomat*, in Elonet (Finnish National Audiovisual Institute) <http://www.elonet.fi/fi/elokuva/1489950> (accessed 13 February 2017).

Matikainen, Ari (2016) Q&A after the film screening, DocPoint Film Festival, Helsinki, 30 January 2016.

Meinander, Henrik (2011) "A Separate Story? Interpretations of Finland in the Second World War," *Nordic Narratives of the Second World War: National Historiographies Revisited*, ed. Henrik Stenius, Mirja Österberg, and Johan Östling (Lund: Nordic Academic Press), 55–77.

Nevala, Seija-Leena, and Kirsi-Maria Hytönen (2015) "Toimet, työt ja taakat: Perhe-elämämaaseudulla sodan jälkeen," in *Rauhaton rauha: Suomalaiset ja sodan päättyminen 1944–1950*, ed. Ville Kivimäki and Kirsi-Maria Hytönen (Tampere: Vastapaino), 151–172.

Nykänen, Anna-Stina (2010) "Matka, josta piti vaieta," *Helsingin Sanomat*.
Seppälä, Anni (2010) "Virpi Suutari kaivoi vaiennetut muistot esiin," *Kainuun Sanomat* 3 <http://archive.is/fQPB> (accessed 22 September 2016)
Simonsen, Eva (2005) "Children in Danger: Dangerous Children," in *Children of World War II*, ed. Ericsson and Simonsen, 269–286.
Stenius, Henrik, Mirja Österberg, and Johan Östling (2001) "Nordic Narratives of the Second World War: An Introduction," in *Nordic Narratives of the Second World War*, ed. Stenius, Österberg, and Östling, 9–30.
Sturken, Marita (1997) *Tangled Memories: The Vietnam War, the AIDS Epidemics and the Politics of Remembering* (Berkeley, Los Angeles and London: University of California Press).
Tuominen, Marja (2015) "Lapin ajanlasku: Menneisyys, tulevaisuus ja jälleenrakennushistorian reunalla," in *Rauhaton rauha: Suomalaiset ja sodan päättyminen 1944–1950*, ed. Ville Kivimäki and Kirsi-Maria Hytönen (Tampere: Vastapaino), 39–70.
Vaarala, Kalle (2010) *Karjalainen*, in *Elonet* (Finnish National Audiovisual Institute) <http://www.elonet.fi/fi/elokuva/1489950> (accessed 13 February 2017).
Virtanen, Leena (2010) *Helsingin Sanomat, Nyt-liite*, in *Elonet* (Finnish National Audiovisual Institute) <http://www.elonet.fi/fi/elokuva/1489950> (accessed 13 February 2017).

Filmography

Auf Wiedersehen Finnland ("Goodbye Finland") (2010) Dir. Virpi Suutari (For Real Productions).
Kuka piru pimeässä näkee (*Who the Devil Can See in the Dark*) (2014) Dir. Mari Soppela (Cinatura).

Caroline Perret
The Collaborator as Enemy during the French Occupation in (Auto-)Biographical and Post-Memory Cinema

Seventy years since the end of the French Occupation by the German Nazis, this paper chapter will explore three films – a documentary, an (auto-)biographical and a fictional feature film – which reflect upon the collaborator as the enemy of democratic France and of the Resistance movement. At the Liberation, political and social division had reached its highest point in France during the national squaring of accounts which divided former Resistance members and collaborators, known as the *épuration*. From the autumn of 1944 to the autumn of the following year, *épuration* trials occupied the headlines of national newspapers. Some resulted in the execution of Pierre Laval (the head of government of the Vichy regime), Joseph Darnand (the founder of the Milice) and Robert Brasillach (the former chief editor of the collaborationist newspaper *Je Suis Partout*). In particular, intellectual *épuration* divided the *Comité National des Écrivains* (National Committee of Writers) into two factions. On the one hand, some, for the most part of Resistance background and/or of Communist belief, such as Vercors, the author of *Le Silence de la mer*, advocated a total responsibility, and as a consequence, the interdiction for the offender from ever publishing again, and in some cases, the death penalty. On the other hand, other resistants like Jean Paulhan, argued for the supremacy of literary talent and the right to political error (Goetschel and Loyer 1995: 108). Estimating that around 400,000 French citizens were victims of the *épuration*, his essay "Au Mépris des Lois" ("In Contempt of the Law") in his *Lettre aux directeurs de la résistance* (1951) claimed that their condemnation was pronounced illegally as the *Code pénal à l'article 75* used for the purpose targeted individuals who had acted against the French legal government of the time (Paulhan 1987 [1951]: 11–22). According to him, because the Vichy administration represented France between 1940 and 1944, it should have been its legal responsibility to judge the treasons committed in its name in the occupied zone before being trialed next. In this sense, he qualified the death condemnations during the *épuration* as assassinations. Moreover, in *Contre toute justice* (*Against all Justice*), he deplored the partial selection of the jury-panel in the trials, for the most part Communists and resistants, and other individuals who had been unfairly imprisoned, tortured, skinned or deported, and were therefore unlikely to remain fair in their judgement (Paulhan 1987 [1951]: 23–33). In addition, he condemned the enormous number and cruelty of succinct executions that took place even without any trials: an estimated 11,000 were tortured, shot dead and burnt alive between June 1944 and February 1945.[1] Thus in the immediate post-war period, the collaborator was considered to be a traitor of democratic France, but, endangering social cohesion as a violation of trust and loyalty (Ben-Yehuda 2001), soon became a taboo that would only be addressed in historical publications, feature films and documentaries a few decades later.

In his seminal *Le Syndrome de Vichy*, historian Henry Rousso distinguishes three stages in the post-war memory of the Vichy regime: the 'mourning phase' of 1944–1954; the period of 1954–1971 when the Gaullist myth about the French as a nation of resistors was formulated – the unifying myth of 'resistantialism,' located in between a Gaullist reading of fighting France and the militant analysis by the Communist Party; and the time after 1971 which he termed 'the return of the repressed,' when the 'resistantialist' myth was destroyed and the Vichy regime unmasked in all its horror, the nation of resistors becoming a nation of collaborators and traitors. Up until the 1960s/1970s, cinematic response reflected such official memory: with the (image of the) French Resistance being for many years a defining element in French post-war identity, great directors usually focused on its 'heroes' and their struggle in some of the most acclaimed films of French cinema of the last 60 years. For Foucault, "it was the end of Gaullism, signified by the election of Giscard d'Estaing to the French Presidency in 1974, which allowed the whole topic of the Occupation to be addressed in the cinema. For as long as De Gaulle or his political inheritors ruled France, the war was always presented in terms of resistance, since this was the only way of writing this particular history in terms of an honorable nationalism" (qtd. in Forbes 1992: 244). Early post-war films include two films by René Clément: *Le Père tranquille* (*The Quiet Father*) (1946), which uses a family as a metaphor to represent French opposition to the Occupation, and *La Bataille du rail* (*Battle of the Rails*) (1949), which shows the French railway workers' endeavor to sabotage the trains transporting German troops. Jean-Pierre Melville's first film *Le Silence de la mer* (*The Silence of the Sea*) (1949), based on famous resistant Vercors's novel, examines the question of moral responsibility in the Resistance to evil exemplified by the presence of a German occupant in a French household.

For French politicians at the beginning of the 1950s, major political issues included economic recovery, German rearmament and European integration. Moreover, their attitude vis-à-vis decolonization in Indochina, the Maghreb (Algeria, Tunisia and Morocco) and Black Africa (in particular Madagascar and the

---

[1] This number is confirmed by the *Comité d'Histoire du Temps Présent* (Noviek 1985).

Ivory Coast) also reflected their belief in the French political sovereignty being dependent upon a unilateral and inflexible French Union (Prost 1992: 65). Still extremely popular in the elections of 17 June 1951, the Communists and Gaullists both agreed to refuse any politics (whether European, German or Colonialist) that would threaten such national unity (Prost 1992: 68–69). The films of the 1950s reflect this focus on national unity. *Un Condamné à mort s'est échappé (A Man Escaped)* (1956), directed by Robert Bresson, recollects the memoirs of André Devigny, a member of the French Resistance who was held in Montluc prison by the occupying Germans during World War II, while *Marie-Octobre (Secret Meeting)* (1959), directed by Julien Duvivier, is based on the eponymous novel by Jacques Robert charting the search for the traitor among a group of ex-resistance fighters.

While in Indochina the war was continuing, only the radical Pierre Mendès France – also an interviewee in *Le Chagrin et la pitié (The Sorrow and the Pity: Chronicle of a French Town under the Occupation)* (1969) – contended the necessity to end it as soon as possible in order to focus on a sustainable French economic recovery: he achieved this in July 1954 with the Genève agreements. While Tunisia gained its autonomy in June 1955 and Morocco became independent in March 1956, the progressive decolonization of Black Africa started in June 1956 with a new framework law. The political situation was the most complex of all in Algeria, which crisis in May 1958 led De Gaulle to come back to power and to form the fifth *République:* after a violent and controversial process, Algerian independence would be recognized in March 1962 with the Évian agreement (Prost 1992: 70–71, 73, 75–76, 78). During the De Gaulle era of 1958–1962, the exaltation of the Resistance in films gained a new impetus, which is hardly surprising given De Gaulle's prominent role as the leader of the Free French during WWII, and his aim of consolidating his own legitimacy as president. In the 1960s, Melville's *Léon Morin, prêtre (Léon Morin, Priest)* (1961) subtly employs the historical context of the Occupation (by Italian and German forces) as a backdrop for a study of moral and sexual temptation. In 1966, René Clément's *Paris brûle-t-il? (Is Paris Burning?)* put an emphasis on the role played by the Free French Forces and the French Resistance in the Liberation of Paris in August 1944; Alexandre Astruc's *La longue marche* deals with the French Resistance in 1944; and Claude Chabrol's *La Ligne de démarcation* depicts the subversive actions of a French village which straddles the boundaries between the occupied and free zones. Jean-Pierre Melville's classic *L'Armée des ombres (Army of Shadows)* (1969) evokes the violence and daily menace faced by the Resistance movement and experienced by its director himself as a member of the French liberation forces.

While Alon Confino in his "Collective Memory and Cultural History: Problems of Method" (1997) finds Rousso's exploration of the mobilization of Vichy memory for political purposes useful, he is critical of his investigation as failing to discuss popular memories of Vichy and their responses to everyday experiences under the Nazi Occupation. Cinema addressed such a gap. For instance, François Truffaut's *Le Dernier métro* (*The Last Metro*) (1980) demonstrates passive resistance through culture in the story of a small Parisian theatre overcoming censorship, anti-Semitism and material shortages for the whole period of the Occupation, while Jean-Marie Poiré's cult comedy *Papy fait de la résistance* (*Gramps is in the Resistance*) (1983) is set in a Parisian mansion owned by a family of musicians who would do anything to get rid of their occupants. During the 1990s, after a focus on the main participants in history, the focus was on the responsibility of the French individual in his/her attitude and citizenship, with for instance Claude Berri's biopic of Resistance fighter *Lucie Aubrac* (1997) and Claude Lelouch's 1998 critical up-dating of Victor Hugo's novel *Les Misérables* to occupied France about the nature of French collaboration and resistance. This trend continued in the first decade of the new millennium with an emphasis on specific groups, in particular women and cultural minorities. While the documentary *Soeurs de résistance* (*Sisters in Resistance*) (2000) by Maia Wechsler and Jean-Paul Salomé's historical drama *Les Femmes de l'ombre* (*Female Agents*) (2008) tell the story of young women Resistance fighters, Bertrand Tavernier's *Laissez-passer* (*Safe Conduct*) (2002) explores the struggle of French filmmakers covertly supporting the Resistance by circumnavigating stringent Nazi censorship. Rachid Bouchareb's *Indigènes* (*Days of Glory*) (2006) deals with the discrimination of North African soldiers participating in the Free French Forces (with the film's release resulting in a partial recognition of their rights to a pension); Robert Guédiguian's *L'Armée du crime* (*Army of Crime*) (2009) questions the presentation of resistant Algerians and Jews by Nazi propaganda; Ismaël Ferroukhi's *Les Hommes libres* (*Free Men*) (2011) recounts another largely untold story about the role that Algerian and other North African Muslims played in the French Resistance in Paris and as rescuers of Jews during the German Occupation.

Thus from the earliest post-war years, French films about the Nazi Occupation have touched raw nerves. While traditionally the national memory in French films has expressed a dichotomy in the collective portrait of French society between selfishness, pragmatism and bigotry on the collaborationist side, and the courage, idealism and solidarity of the resistant side, this chapter is interested in a more subtle interpretation of history: it will innovatively present an analysis and cinematic insight into the most sensitive aspect of French history, the French citizen as collaborator. On the one hand, the seminal documentary by

Marcel Ophüls, *Le Chagrin et la pitié* of 1969, combining interviews and newsreels, will provide the historical, political and social context of such a study. On the other hand, two films by Louis Malle will illustrate the fictional depiction of the collaborator in French (auto-)biographical and post-memory cinema. His controversial *Lacombe Lucien* (1974) portrays an uneducated gun-toting farm boy who joins the Gestapo, thereby becoming a blank-faced participant in violence, torture and corruption as the war nears its close. The film had an important role in the passionate discussion on revising French history in either documentary or fiction films in the early 1970s; it was accused of scratching at old wounds and drew outrage and denunciation from various quarters. Malle's later *Au revoir les enfants* ("Goodbye Children") (1987) deals with the ordeal of Jewish children during the Occupation, their hiding and eventually being denounced. Such a revisionist presentation of history will be contextualized within the political and ideological situation of France at the time, and the debate about popular memory. This chapter will therefore consider the growing ambivalence between collaborator/resistant, as well as the evolution of French film production in the context of the culture politics of each historical period.

With the end of the De Gaulle government in 1969 and his death in 1970, as well as the impact of the 1968 protests, previous official memory was re-assessed at the beginning of the 1970s and its analysis became more critical with the work of film directors, journalists and historians. All destroyed the 'resistantialist' myth: it was then established that Vichy was a collaborationist, xenophobic, anti-Semitic and reactionary regime, which divided the French population, although the majority, eager to survive, found itself in between the two minorities of the Resistance and the Collaboration. The events of May 1968 started with students rebelling against institutional authorities and norms, adopting slogans such as "it is forbidden to forbid" or "imagination at the helm." This took concrete form in Paris with a week of unrest at the Sorbonne campus and violent confrontations in the streets with the C.R.S. (the anti-riot section of the French national police), followed in many French cities by a general strike (railways, post, education, and all sectors of industry) and demonstrations organised by trade-unions. It all ended in a political crisis and change of government. 1968 therefore accelerated the process of liberalisation of values already latent in French society, with a more permissive style of education among families, a claim for equality with men from women and the legitimisation of a more libertarian form of individualism (Prost 1992: 94–95).

The influence that the events of May '68 had specifically on French cinema resulted in a move towards a more realistic approach. Louis Malle, director of *Lacombe Lucien* and *Au revoir les enfants*, "who had worked as Bresson's assistant and co-directed the underwater documentary *Le Monde du silence*, with Jacques-

Yves Cousteau in 1956, visited India and returned in 1969 with a feature-length documentary study, *Calcutta*, and a seven-part television series. A few years later, he applied a similar documentary detachment to everyday subjects of French life in two short features, a study of a square in Paris, *Place de la République*, and an examination of the psychological dimensions of work on an assembly line," *Humain trop humain*, both of 1974 (cf. Armes 1985: 166, 223). The latter is a direct response to the great upheaval of May '68 in its treatment of one of the crucial issues raised by the events: the socio-political situation of factory workers. However, it should be stated that Malle, despite possessing a sense of history and having studied political sciences never viewed cinema as a means of political agitation, unlike Karmitz or Godard, for instance (cf. Williams 1992: 341). However, since his experience of the Algerian war, against which he had strongly militated, he had made the decision not to translate his political engagement into his films, which for him would have resulted in artistically simplistic works. He was more interested in showing the contradictions and complexities of a political situation – and of individual choices – rather than in demonstrating a specific point of view (cf. French 1993: 119).

After the events of May '68 and the end of Gaullism, the 1970s saw several compilation films which looked at aspects of recent French history in a new and questioning way. Importantly, "this exposure was not limited to the more marginal militant cinema, but extended to what could be called 'civic' mainstream cinema" (Hayward 1993: 250). Besides André Harris's and Alain De Sédouy's *Français, si vous saviez* of 1973, *Le Chagrin et la pitié* is the most important of these. While it was made in 1968, it first came out in a small left-bank theatre, incidentally owned by the Malle brothers. Moreover, it was only shown on French television in 1981, "so shocking were its revelations thought to be," according to Marcel Ophüls, its director in an interview. He added that this was only possible because of the new presidency of "socialist" François Mittérand, and thus led to twenty million viewings. Subtitled *Chronique d'une ville française sous l'occupation*, it "takes as its subjects the town of Clermont-Ferrand under the German Occupation, investigating it by means of interview material interspersed with contemporary news footage" (Armes 1985: 224). Sixty hours of interviews were pieced together by Marcel Ophüls, and the result obliged a re-appraisal of the prevalent myths about the Resistance, the sorrow and the pity of the Occupation. One specific example is the intervention in the film of Mr Leiris, former Mayor of Combronde and member of the Resistance, who almost seems to interrupt Emile Coulaudon, or Colonel "Gaspard," Head of the Auvergne Maquis and to oppose his resistantialist mythologising of the period: "'There is one thing we often tend to forget. [...] But were the French any better than the Nazis?' –

Gaspard: 'Stop!' – Mr Leiris: 'I had a 60-year old woman, who had sold me [and my son] to the Gestapo [...] to have us shot.'"

In this sense, I would argue with John Pilling and his *Autobiography and Imagination: Studies in Self-Scrutiny*, that these interviews are testimonial forms of autobiography, as they encompass memoirs, confessions, and sometimes apologies for past and memorized events (cf. Pilling 1981: 1). As such, these practices put into play the relationship of the private to the public, itself associated with the issue of the link between the personal and the political. Ophüls's collage of interviews therefore provides a site where memory is produced and represented, a notion which theorist Pierre Nora describes as *lieux de mémoire*. In effect, the privileging of memory over history in *lieux de mémoire* accesses knowledge in a liberated and flexible fashion, and allows a transformation "from the historical to the psychological, from the sociological to the individual, from the objective message to its subjective reception, from repetition to rememorisation" (Nora 1989: 18–20, 15). In addition, contemporary newsreels, with their more historical and social viewpoints, enable an interesting dialogue within this process. In the specific events of the Occupation, this practice provides a radical alternative to the narrative conventions that had thus far predominated in French historical discourse. Moreover, these *lieux de mémoire* also seem to be the only valid practices when re-historicising and questioning the Occupation, as they are dealing with traces of events and experiences.

Such is also the case of *Lacombe Lucien*, directed by Louis Malle in 1974. It is the story of a seventeen-year-old youth in 1944, during the Occupation, near Toulouse. Its portrayal is altogether very strongly located in the context of his region and nation: in the title sequence, Lucien is shown with his beret, cycling through a quaint landscape of rolling fields and villages of stone houses typical of the south-eastern regions of France. While Lucien has the "accent of the county," his life and relationship with animals before his engagement with the Gestapo is emblematic of a young French farmer (French, 1993: 119). For instance, he is able to hunt wild rabbits pitilessly and to stroke an old dying horse tenderly; to run playfully after a hen which, when caught, he kills with his own hands, and plucks out immediately afterwards. First rejected by the local Resistance when he visits its leader, the community school-teacher, and more through ignorance than intent, Lucien is recruited by the German Police, the French division of the Gestapo, thus becoming a collaborator.

Lacombe Lucien became one of the most important films made at about that period, "first because of the controversy surrounding it, and second, because it attracted such a large audience," ranking at number six the year of its release (Hayward 1993: 251). When it came to reviewing *Lacombe Lucien*, compatriot critics, mostly of the Left, were vitriolic in their denunciation: while the newspaper

Le Monde initially praised the film for its innovative point of view, the socialist *Libération* "accused its message of being 'fascisant' in its portrayal of a young man who accidentally joins the militia" (Hayward 1993: 251). Outside France, the film won international acclaim from film critics who understood it for what it was: a reflection on the nature and the "banality of evil" rather than an unusually sympathetic study of a collaborator (French 1993: 116). Indeed, several juxtaposing scenes in the film demonstrate the mundane nature of everyday life at the Gestapo headquarters in which Lucien now "works" (his own words): as the secretary reads the numerous informants' letters, Lucien is having breakfast and the Head of the Gestapo is having a hair-cut; hearing the school-teacher scream while being tortured, we observe children playing on the stairs of the mansion; while a couple are playing table-tennis and discussing holidays, the former cyclist champion cleans a range of guns and then teaches Lucien how to use one; the actress of *Night Raid* (presumably depicting the rounding-up of Jews in the night), Betty Beaulieu, discusses cocktails while Vichy news radio is giving an over-positive account of the current state of the war.

Rather than being 'fascist' in its innovatively objective portrayal of a young collaborator, I would argue that the film ought to be interpreted as being *about* the "discours fascisant" (Hayward 1993: 251). Firstly, the film exposes the mechanism of fascism in investing those without identity and social status, but desperate to obtain these, with a sense of "power" (French 1993: 121). The character of *Lacombe Lucien* is introduced to the viewer in the film as sweeping the floor of the local nursing home, emptying the bowls of urine of the patients, and removing absent-mindedly a framed photograph of Marshal Pétain in order to clean the bed-side table on which it has been resting. Lucien, therefore, does not seem to engage with the historical subject, also present acoustically through Philippe Henriot's (the Minister in the French Government at Vichy who directed propaganda broadcasts) anti-Communist and anti-Gaullist "Revanche de l'histoire" speech on the radio. Lucien is then shown on leave at his parents' farm, where he understands (and the audience with him) that his prisoner father has been replaced by the farm assistant in both his authority and his wife's bed: Lucien is told that he is not wanted there anymore. Back in the district town for work, and after the curfew because of a flat tyre, Lucien discovers the headquarters of the local Gestapo situated in a grand hotel and bursting out classical music. His attraction is immediate, and his welcome warm. Drunk after a long night, he is manipulated to give too much information on his local Resistance network, which leads to the arrest of the school-teacher who had rejected him.

While it is a common assumption that "it is by chance, not conviction that Lucien finds himself on the wrong side of the fence taking the revenge of the peasant against the town, the poor against the rich, the humiliated against the proud" (French 1993: 120), it is evident that Lucien was not aware of the consequences of his words, as he apologizes to the Resistance leader and expresses worry about what is going to happen to him. Moreover, when the secretary asks him: "Do you want to work for the police?," he replies that he does not know, highlighting the lack of a conscious decision-making process. Secondly, in addition to showing the fascists as giving Lucien a sense of self and belonging, the film points to the fact that Fascism is an "attraction" (Hayward 1993: 251), very literally at first when Jean-Bernard (the wealthy son of a Parisian count) takes him on a ride in his luxurious car to his private tailor, the refugee Jew, Mr. Horn. The beautifully-crafted suit Lucien obtains there will later act as the emblem of his transformation into a man and a collaborator, with Jean-Bernard commenting: "It is his first suit. An important step in a man's life." Thirdly, Lucien's first encounter with Fascism is as a voyeur (cf. Hayward 1993: 251): through a door ajar, he witnesses the bathtub torturing of the school-teacher. Bit by bit, however, he gets his hands dirtier and bloodier: while first helping Jean-Bernard in a pretense mise-en-scène for Dr Vaugeois to unmask himself as a supporter of the Resistance, Lucien takes initiative and becomes active in the violence.

It is for this reason that Lucien's joining of the militia is not that accidental: it is "the result of a feeling of rejection and humiliation by a member of the under-class who finds social revenge and satisfaction in collaborating" (French 1993: 120). Thus, the significance of *Lacombe Lucien* and no doubt the source of its public success, is its profound humanity in revealing how an individual can understand history as a personal experience without even being aware of the collective pursuit of politics around him. In the middle of the film, he states clearly that for him, Jews and Bolsheviks are the same. This statement is revelatory of the confusion maintained by fascist propaganda among the masses during the Occupation. Most collaborationists believed in preserving the peace and in fighting what they saw as the threat of Communism at all costs. The fear of such a menace is tangible in a speech of Jacques Doriot, Head of the Fascist French Popular Party in 1942, presented by Ophüls in his *Le Chagrin et la pitié* (part two): "England victorious? Half of its merchant navy has sunk. England has been defeated. [...] England's only way out is to call in the Bolsheviks. But as a French man, I'd be afraid they'd stab us in the back." In this sense, the invasion of the Soviet Union by the German army demonstrated for collaborationists the *Reich*'s total commitment to the regeneration of a decadent Europe through the definitive destruction of Bolshevism and the application of the universal model of National Socialism. Moreover, the collaborationists considered Bolshevism to be a Jewish enterprise and conspiracy. It is of no surprise, therefore, that Lucien could confuse Jews and Bolsheviks. The film also shows that the manipulation by populist parties of the most deprived social classes in a society and the branding of 'others' as scapegoats for all of society's evils is not a new political strategy. Indeed, in Ophüls's *Le Chagrin et la pitié*, Christian de la Mazière, an aristocratic ex-fascist veteran of the French division of the Waffen SS, presented the new fascist regime with the idea that "Marshal Pétain guaranteed a new order." In addition to being anti-parliamentary and anti-communist, he added that the Vichy propaganda "suspected certain employers" to be "foreign, cosmopolitan, not to mention dagos/dark-skinned."

We know of the horrific consequences that such ideologies would have on the persecution of the Jewish community during WWII, but for one to try and draw lessons from history for the current state of affairs in the world, one must acknowledge the premises at the *Origins of Totalitarianism*, which seem to apply to all forms of tyranny, past and present. Hannah Arendt argues in *Eichmann in Jerusalem: A Report on the Banality of Evil* that one "cannot choose with whom to share the earth without engaging in genocide" (qtd. in Butler 2013: 122). According to Judith Butler in *Dispossession: The Performative in the Political*,

> [f]or Arendt, the interdiction against genocide is a consequence of the normative value that comes from the unchosen character of earthly cohabitation. This means that we have obligations to preserve the lives of others whether or not we have contractually agreed to do so. If a normative demand to refuse genocide follows from the unchosen character of cohabitation, then we must accept and preserve this unchosen dimension of our lives and also realize that whatever actions we do take must be limited by the norms furnished by this unchosen condition. [...] [Arendt's] argument against genocide was [...] the embrace of a universal "unchosenness." She joins the "unchosen" [...], and this relates as well to the important work she did on the *Origins of Totalitarianism* and on the rights of refugees. (2013: 122–123)

It is the perverse and discreetly convincing power of fascist ideology which is also at play in *Lacombe Lucien*. As in so much early 1970s French cinema, there is no point from which the social and political issues raised can be judged: "Lucien's drift into fascist activities is depicted" honestly without "the usually glossed-over ambiguities of life in occupied France" (Armes 1985: 230). There is, however, a passing comment on the Drancy transit camp for Jews, the prolific market for forged papers and clandestine passages to Spain (of which Mr Horn is clearly an abused victim), as well as on the abundant black market and war-loot dealings in the Gestapo headquarters: "What interested Louis Malle was the idea of the role chance plays in historic events" (Biggs 1996: 159): Lucien could just as easily have joined the Resistance rather than the Gestapo (French 1993: 127). It was this premise, which precluded Malle's attempt at objectivity in wanting "to tell the story without judging Lucien, which was at the root of the scandal in France" (Biggs 1996: 159). *Lacombe Lucien* refuses to take any stance outside the consciousness of the central figure and totally adopts the viewpoint of its adolescent anti-hero: "The film shows the strength of the classic narrative tradition: it offers no flashbacks or visually emphatic sequences, contenting itself simply with showing, without explanation or apology. In this it recalls Malle's early work as assistant to Cousteau and Bresson and his [contemporary] concern with documentary approaches" (Armes 1985: 229–230). In this sense, Malle's emphasis on the relationship between subjectivity and history is a direct product of the philosophical developments which occurred in the 1970s.

Indeed, Louis Malle's *Lacombe Lucien* questions the possibility of examining this period of French history within a dualistic system of ideas, "for in the 1970s, the issue in France was still a black and white one, with no room for grey interpretations" (Biggs 1996: 159). The film transgressed the assumed opposition between resistance and collaboration, between Jewishness and anti-Semitism, between love and hate. At its centre is the "powerful clash between the over-civilised Jew Horn and the suspicious peasant" (Armes 1985: 230), and what stands opposed to Lucien's collaboration is not the Resistance, but "the Jewish tailor and his prodigious dignity and integrity" (French 1993: 122). Malle's characters are not clear-cut and stereotyped figures, being neither entirely good nor bad individuals, but are on the contrary very human in the illogicality and inexplicability of their behavior and decisions. Aware of Lucien's involvement in the Gestapo, his mother explains to Mr. Horn: "But he isn't a bad boy," and later in the torture room, the tortured resistant comments: "You don't look like a thug." Lucien is not fundamentally bad in that it is only "through a series of hazards," not through a conscious decision, that he becomes a collaborator; he is horrible and moving at the same time (French 1993: 117). There is also a certain provocation in showing a Caribbean torturer among the fascists, which was actually the case with the Gestapo in Bordeaux (cf. French 1993: 124). Together with Lucien, this character illustrates the fact that collaboration touched all social classes, from the socially-excluded to the powerful. Moreover, Malle refuses the concept of a fixed Jewish identity in his representation of three generations of the same family: the grand-mother, who has spent most of her life in an Eastern-European ghetto and who is rebelliously unhappy about her situation in this French rural environment; the son, who has become a prosperous Parisian tailor, but whose accent and behavior still belong to Central Europe; and his daughter France, who is totally Parisian and cannot bear to endorse her own Jewish identity anymore.

With a focus on the memory of the Shoah and the accusation of individuals who had directly or indirectly taken part in those crimes, the 1980s were more specific in their attack on the Vichy regime than the 1970s and were characterised by a will to compensate for the crimes committed during the Occupation. In the 1980s and 1990s, the long shadow of national trauma finally fell on the storms of recrimination and assertion which surrounded the major trials of infamous collaborators: police chiefs Klaus Barbie (Head of Gestapo in Lyons, infamous for his torturing of resistance leaders), Paul Touvier (regional director of the Milice in Lyons) and Maurice Papon (the secretary general for police in Bordeaux responsible for mass deportations). *Au revoir les enfants* (1987) thus came out when the French civic authorities were starting to recognise their participation in the Holocaust and legislators sought scapegoats for the national humiliation of 1940: while Barbie was arrested in Bolivia by the newly elected government in 1983 and extradited to stand a filmed jury trial starting in 1987, his French equivalents were only convicted a decade later for crimes against humanity, respectively in 1994 and 1998. Moreover, it would not be until 1995 that President Jacques Chirac officially apologized for the responsibility of the French police in the infamous 1942 roundup of the "Vél d'Hiv." With regards to the memory of the Occupation, the 1990s were therefore the most conflicting: while demonstrating progress in both memory and justice, the media became deeply involved in the debate about this sensitive period of French history, which made public again the 'black years' of the Occupation, attracting hostility and bitterness.

Au revoir les enfants is Louis Malle's most strongly autobiographical work. While receiving a highly traditional Catholic education during the Occupation, the director had "witnessed the arrest of some Jewish children who had been hidden in the Jesuit College of Fontainebleau" where he was studying (Williams 1992: 340–341). This incident profoundly impressed him, as he returned in his film to the ordeal of Jewish children under the Occupation and the people who hid or denounced them. His concluding remark in the film proves this point: "More than forty years have passed, but I shall remember every second of that January morning until the day I die." Based on his own boyhood experience, therefore, Malle's film begins in January 1944, when a doting mother sends a privileged, precocious twelve-year-old boy to a provincial Catholic boarding school. Julien holds aloof from loutish schoolmates until another new boy, Bonnet, joins his class. Bonnet is cultivated, clever, but reticent about his background. Julien wants to humiliate a potential rival before antagonism turns to friendship and Bonnet's secret is revealed: he is a Jew, hiding from the Gestapo under constant threat of betrayal.

As stipulated by the historical context provided in the first part of Ophüls's *Le Chagrin et la pitié*, such a danger took concrete form as early as in autumn 1940 with the implementation of Jewish decrees taken by the Vichy regime, which led to the arrests of Jews on French territory. While the first part of *Le Chagrin et la pitié* provides an overview and introduction to the historical and political context of the Occupation, the second takes a moral stance with the presentation of more challenging and denouncing interviews (French 1993: 129). It is hard to believe today that Count René de Chambrun, international lawyer and son-in-law of Pierre Laval (Head of the Vichy government between April 1942 and August 1944) would have fallen into such a trap. In his defense of Laval, he is seen as touring the local villages, whose inhabitants had had the very rare privilege of being repatriated from prisoners' camps in Germany: "[...] not one single person is willing to accuse Laval of any outrageous crime." But what are these testimonies worth when the inferiority of their social position and dependency are clearly portrayed? The answer seems to be provided later in the documentary by Georges Lamirand, Minister of Youth for the Pétain regime between 1941–1943: "Laval's policies were pro-German, because he believed in them."

This is one blatant instance of an imperceptible, yet highly charged gap between interviewer and interviewee, 'a space of release' that is 'heavily impregnated with memory,' following Neville Wakefield and his "Separation Anxiety and the Art of Release." This space in which signification is mediated and memories are figured is indeed very slim, just like Duchamp's notion of the *infra mince*. This is because memories are only present in the form of traces and indices and are dependent upon the viewer to decipher them, even more so as the object of the memory and its representation, imaginings and associations overlay one another. In addition, the subtlety of meaning occurs through the contrast which it creates through an almost caricature-like editing of juxtaposed interviews. The actual mise-en-scène is close to the aesthetic of (re)enactments, and as such, opens a critical gap between an original event and its simulation. Thus, *Le Chagrin et la pitié* enabled the viewer of the 1970s (as it does today) to follow a process from the personal memories of others to the new collective remembrance of social and political history, or rather histories. This seems to be the most effective strategy for dealing with the atrocities of WWII and the Occupation, and for reconciling cinema and history in order to create 'counter-memories' which had hitherto been so controversial for the French audience.

Moreover, Ophüls's interviewer takes the opportunity of the false report of a higher survival rate of deported Jews from France by Count Chambrun to highlight the fact that these statistics only referred to the French Jews who had not lost their citizenship, a consequence of one of the many anti-Semitic policies implemented by the Vichy regime. This is corroborated by the interview given by Dr Claude Lévy, author and biologist, as well as former resistant: "The French government agreed to turn in French nationals. [...] France was the only country in Europe to have collaborated and voted laws which were even more racist than the Nuremberg Laws [...]. France was full of concentration camps [...]. Along with the Jews, there were Spanish Republicans, Freemasons and Gypsies. And all these people were delivered to the Germans at their request." His explanation of the "Rafle du Vél d'Hiv" of July 1942, well known in the history of racial persecution and also the subject of other more recent films such as Gilles Paquet-Brenner's *Elle s'appelait Sarah* (*Sarah's Key*) and Rose Bosch's *La Rafle* (*The Round Up*), both of 2010, is particularly relevant to our discussion of *Au revoir les enfants*, as it touches children too. The Paris police, under the supervision of the SS and the Gestapo, organized two days of Jewish arrests in the capital. "At that time, the Germans had only planned on arresting people over 16 years of age. [...] Yet, the Paris police [...] began arresting children." As a result, 4,051 children found themselves in the Vélodrome, separated from already deported parents: "Laval would have advised to deport the children too."

Similarly, as in *Lacombe Lucien*, Malle is more interested in showing the contradictions and complexities of a situation, be it personal, political or historical, rather than in demonstrating a specific point of view (cf. French 1993: 128): he goes beyond the usual dualistic analysis of occupied France and reveals the ambiguities between collaboration and resistance. Firstly, Malle demolishes a common pre-conception about the period by showing in the restaurant scene that "French collaborators were generally more zealous and aggressive than the German soldiers" (French 1993: 207). He thus implicitly suggests the fact that "in France, 90 per cent of the people working for the Gestapo were in fact French" (Forbes 1992: 243). When in the film, a young member of the Milice asks an elderly and long-standing Jewish customer for his papers, a German officer furiously tells him to "Get the Hell out of here!" This is echoed by Jacques Duclos, Secretary of the clandestine Communist Party, in part two of *Le Chagrin et la pitié*: "I say that if the Germans had only their own Gestapo, they couldn't have caused half the harm they did, [...] it was the French police who helped [to] seek out the Communists [and] other patriots." In addition, Malle demystifies the German lie at the centre of collaboration. At the end of *Au revoir les enfants*, the German officer of the Gestapo responsible for the arrests of the three Jewish children and Father Jean states: "We're not your enemies." This was the manner in which the Gestapo usually portrayed itself and was believed by a majority of the French population, even if a few intellectuals, such as Germaine Tillion rebelled against such a notion. In her essay "De la collaboration" (1942), she had clearly explained the German position vis-à-vis the French population, and thus enabled the latter to affirm their juridical position towards their occupants: the Germans were indeed enemies, the armistice was a form of war rather than peace, and the collaboration a hypocritical invention (Tillion 2001 [1942]: 79–80). In this sense, the release of the film was timely, as it was simultaneous with the trial of Klaus Barbie, the infamous torturer of resistants, in particular Jean Moulin, and in addition to its extraordinary dramatic dimension, this probably contributed to its enormous success.

Secondly, the denunciator in *Au revoir les enfants*, Joseph, is very similar to Lucien: he is an "ambiguous" figure, a simple, immature youth, who is not fundamentally bad (French 1993: 121). His outright involvement with the Gestapo results from his own very specific situation of disability rather than from any historical or political awareness: his timing, six months before the Occupation was over, emphasises this point. A very secondary character in the film, Joseph, who has a limp, is the handy-man in the Carmelite convent, where he is stigmatized by the other members of staff and pushed around and kicked, defenseless, to the cold, wintery ground by the students. He feels, rightly, that he is treated like a dog. In addition, he complains about the fact that he is economically exploited and treated without dignity: "Rich, on what they pay me here? If I could find another job [...]." When he is brutalized in the playground, he states: "They yell: 'Sit, Joseph! Back to your kennel, Joseph!' I'm sick of this, I'm not a dog." Thus, stealing supplies from the convent in order to sell them on the black market, and trafficking heavily with the students, who exchange their private food supplies, he is eventually found out and rejected by those who took him in. Also unwanted by the woman, Fernande (a prostitute?), whom he has courted all along with money and rare products, he then feels an enormous sense of injustice, because the students were taking part in his dealings, too. Even Father Jean is aware of using him as the scapegoat of the situation: "I must sack Joseph, even though it's unfair." Joseph cries: "Where am I going to go now? I don't even have a place to sleep. [...] I end up taking the blame. It's not fair." Informing the Gestapo of the hiding of Jewish children in the college, he thus believes that he has acquired a share in the current real power, and has achieved pride and social re-integration and not so much vengeance, but justice. Denunciation therefore is just a tool for him to become a part of a group. Unlike Lucien, Joseph thus has a motive for his action. When Julien asks him "What is he doing with them?," Joseph replies: "You guys are to be blamed! I got the sack for doing business with you."

Between the excesses of the *épuration* after the Liberation and the major trials of infamous French collaborators in the 1990s, the collaborator as enemy of democratic France has usually taken the traits of a German officer amidst French popular opinion. While in French national politics, the Gaullist resistantialist myth still holds strong, French international affairs have focused since 1945 on economic stability and European integration in the face of globalization. Rare are the exceptions in films and documentaries which depict the traitor as French and analyse the reasons which have led him (or her) to Fascism. All three films studied here – *Le Chagrin et la pitié: chronique d'une ville française sous l'occupation*, *Lacombe Lucien* and *Au revoir les enfants* – demonstrate that fascist propaganda is characterized by its perverse and discreetly convincing power and is at its most effective with the most vulnerable members of society. Despite their popularity among the French audience, these films, putting into play French historical guilt, develop a (leftist) intellectual rather than a populist point of view. Pierre Mendès-France, French Prime Minister between 1954 and 1955, was well aware of the dangers that a lack of educated opinions might eventually mean for French society. In part two, "The Collapse," of *Le Chagrin et la pitié*, he warned: "It showed me that there are certain tendencies and demagogies which, when they are fired up, fed or stimulated, crop up like weeds, and we must always be on the defensive. We have to protect our youth from this type of propaganda." Through the recognition of the existence of nationalist discourse, these films are therefore already a first step towards opposition. They still stand today as rare examples of resistance in the face of the rise of nationalism in France, as they explain and deconstruct its social and political mechanisms. Such a social and political awareness is today crucial for those who do not wish the specters of tyranny to re-emerge and continue rearing their ugly head.

Works Cited

Armes, Roy (1985) *French Cinema* (London: Secker and Warburg).
Ben-Yehuda, Nachman (2001) *Betrayal and Treason: Violations of Trust and Loyalty* (New York: Avalon Publishing).
Biggs, Melissa E. (1996) *French Films* (Jefferson NC: McFarland).
Butler, Judith, and Athena Athanasiou (2013) *Dispossession: The Performative in the Political* (Cambridge: Polity).
Confino, Alon (1997) "Collective Memory and Cultural History: Problems of Method," *The American Historical Review* 102. 5, 1386–1403.
Forbes, Jill (1992) *The Cinema in France after the New Wave* (London: BFI & Macmillan).
French, Philipp (1993) *Conversations avec Louis Malle*, trans. Martine Leroy-Battistelli (Paris: Editions Denoël).
Goetschel, Pascale, and Emmanuelle Loyer (1995) *Histoire culturelle et intellectuelle de la France au xxè siècle* (Paris: Armand Colin Éditeur).
Hayward, Susan (1993) *French National Cinema* (London and New York: Routledge).
Nora, Pierre (1989) "Between Memory and History: les Lieux de Mémoire," *Représentations* 26, 7–24.
Noviek, Peter (1985) *L'Épuration Française. 1944–49* (Paris: Éditions Balland).
Paulhan, Jean (1987) *Lettre aux directeurs de la résistance* (Paris: Éditions Ramsay).
Pilling, John (1981) *Autobiography and Imagination: Studies in Self-Scrutiny* (London and New York: Routledge and Kegan Paul).
Prost, Antoine (1992) *Petite histoire de la France au xxè siècle* (Paris: Armand Colin Éditeur).
Rousso, Henry (1987) *Le Syndrome de Vichy: de 1944 à nos jours* (Paris: Éditions du Seuil).

Tillion, Germaine (2001) "De la collaboration" (1942), in *À la recherche du vrai et du juste* (Paris: Éditions du Seuil), 79–80.
Wakefield, Neville (1994) "Separation Anxiety and the Art of Release," *Parkett* 42, 77–78.
Williams, Alan (1992) *Republic of Images. A History of French Film-Making* (Cambridge, MA: Harvard University Press).

Filmography

Au revoir les enfants ("Goodbye Children") (1987) Dir. Louis Malle (MK2 Diffusion).
Lacombe Lucien (1974) Dir. Louis Malle (Cinema International Corporation).
Le Chagrin et la pitié: chronique d'une ville française sous l'occupation (*The Sorrow and the Pity: Chronicle of a French Town under the Occupation*) (1969) Dir. Marcel Ophüls (Télévision Rencontre).

Noah McLaughlin
False Idyll: Siri's *L'Ennemi intime*

The Algerian War for Independence (1954–1962) is more complex than an indigenous uprising against their colonial oppressors. After more than 150 years under French rule, Algeria has become a *département*, an official part of the French government and its European territory. Ethnically Gallic and Mediterranean French citizens have lived there for generations, naturalizing themselves to the region and adopting the moniker Pieds-noirs. This does not prevent the exploitations of colonialism, but the imbrication of French and Algerian cultures leads to a unique situation where Arabic and Berber Algerians volunteer to fight for France in both World Wars. During the Algerian War, matters of loyalty and identity swiftly become unstable. Several factors further complicate this constant uncertainty of enemy and ally. The war itself is traumatically brutal: more than eight years of guerrilla warfare, officially sanctioned torture and the bombing or wholesale massacre of civilians by both the French Army and the Algerian insurgence known as the National Liberation Front, or FLN. The war results in some 25,600 French casualties and 700,000 Algerian dead. Two million more are uprooted, placed into camps by French forces or fleeing to the hinterland of the Kabyle Mountains; the French defeat in 1962 leads to an exodus of some 900,000 Pieds-noirs and 91,000 of their Harki allies into metropolitan France. Within the Hexagon, matters are further complicated both during and after the war. Leftists, led at times by philosopher Jean-Paul Sartre, oppose the horrors of colonialism in general and the war specifically. Meanwhile, the French government simultaneously conscripts troops and heavily censors all news about the conflict. This combination of two divided houses pitted against each other, with civilians often caught in the crossfire, and a "nameless" war not officially recognized for half a century, creates a difficult legacy for the Algerian War and those who fought in it (Horne 2006).

It is within this context that Florent-Emilio Siri's *L'Ennemi intime* (*Intimate Enemies*) appears in 2007. Despite mixed critical reviews and an indifferent shrug from audiences in France and abroad, this is a masterfully constructed film about the Algerian War for Independence whose intertextual richness, meta-cinematic reflections and transnational character contribute to its historiophotic value. A greater appreciation of *L'Ennemi intime* must begin by first framing it within Elizabeth Ezra and Terry Rowden's take on transnationalism along with Hayden White's notions of "historiophoty" and by then addressing a common misconception that the Algerian War is almost absent from Francophone cinema. On the contrary, not only has interest in this subject recently intensified on

French screens, but *L'Ennemi intime* is also part of a rich tradition of French-language movies about the war for Algerian independence.

Constructions of the enemy have an important place among these complexities. *L'Ennemi intime* is a war film, so the figure of the opposing force, the FLN or *fellaghas*, is an essential component of the movie's verisimilitude. However, other kinds of opposition overshadow this Manichean division: divergent ideologies within the French ranks, the complexities of loyalty and identity among their *Harki* allies, and the traumatic psychological struggles of the film's protagonist, Lieutenant Terrien. The enemy is not just close: he is within.

In this context, a close analysis of Siri's use of cinematographic form and of a plethora of intertexts that transcend nation and culture demonstrates how film can combine disparate elements to depict an enemy who is more internal than external, mirroring in cinematic form the notions of 'us' and 'them' that the Algerian War exploded. Siri combines stylized cinematography and sound design to create engrossing psychological effects. Significant intertexts include Théodore Géricault's *Le Radeau de la Méduse*, Martin Scorsese's short film *The Big Shave* and Abel Gance's World War I epic *J'accuse!* Finally, metacinematic moments highlight the power of cinema as a historiophotic tool. *L'Ennemi intime* is a transnational production that suffers from a "both-and/neither-nor" crisis of identity, but this analysis seeks to recuperate Siri's film because it illustrates historical complexities that have long been ignored or misunderstood.[1]

1 Some Definitions: Transnationalism and Historiophoty

Concerned with "the global forces that link people or institutions across nations" the transnational "comprises both globalization – in cinematic terms, Hollywood's domination of world film markets – and the counterhegemonic responses of filmmakers from former colonial and Third World countries" (Ezra and Rowden 2006: 1). While Siri is strongly influenced by mainstream Hollywood productions, he brings to that mode a French cinematic tendency of critical self-re-

---

[1] Ringo Ma characterizes those with a transnational or intercultural identity as being "both-and" and "neither-nor;" that is, they can function natively in two cultures, but that hybridity also constantly labels them as outsiders (2006: 308). *L'Ennemi intime* draws successfully from both American and French traditions, but its unique Franco-American combination is problematic.

flection as well as an aspiration to transcend the artisanal towards the artistic.² This hybridity is exactly what makes transnationalism a beneficial tool for examining *L'Ennemi intime*. It problematizes traditional notions of "national cinemas" and their inherent "investment in cultural purity or separatism" (Ezra and Rowden 2006: 4). Moreover, transnationalism imagines a cosmopolitan spectator, one who can appreciate the unparalleled spectacle of Hollywood productions, but who simultaneously has a critical cinematic literacy that goes beyond the desire for escapism. Both transnational films and their characters are often liminal, their expressions and experiences interstitial and hybrid. Their condition is migrant, either by choice or by circumstance, but either results in a sense of loneliness, loss and deterritorialization. Nonetheless, the binary nature of cultural identification persists: "The drive to distinguish among groups never truly disappears; it just gets displaced periodically to reflect the shifting geopolitical landscape" (9). This constantly shifting identification is precisely the case both during the Algerian War for Independence and within Siri's film.³

"Historiophoty" is our best tool for examining this shifting historical landscape as it appears on film. Hayden White's seminal essay coining the term in 1988 argues strongly in favor of its equivalency with traditional historiography. The "representation of history and our thoughts about it in visual images and filmic discourse" is more than capable of adequately conveying "the complex, qualified and critical dimension of historical thinking about events" (1193). For, not only is it "a discourse in its own right" (1193), but it excels in many areas, capable of far greater visual and auditory verisimilitude, stronger emotive effect, less ambiguity and more accuracy than the written word (1194). These strengths are particularly true of cinema as a document of actuality. The images of Allied forces liberating Nazi concentration camps convey simultaneously more tragedy and greater exactitude than any report on the page. However, neither does White dismiss the narrative nature of most historical films, arguing that both filmed and written representations of history are products of "condensation, displacement, symbolization and qualification" (1194). That is to say, they are both inherently constructed, and thus predicative interpretations of past events whose labeling as "facts" should not be self-evident.

---

2 Before *L'Ennemi intime*, Siri directed the Miramax production of the Bruce Willis actioner *Hostage* (2005).
3 Transnationalism is a force unto itself for Ezra and Rowden: "By refusing to privilege the top [...] or the bottom [...], transnationalism unfolds as an essentially self-motivated, and apparently amoral, cultural force [that] both reflects and mediates power relations in the postindustrial, digital age" (2006: 9).

White suggests a two-part methodology for the investigation of historiophotic works. Firstly, while historical films have as much claim to historical truth as written monographs, it is important to "reflect upon the ways in which a distinctly imagistic discourse can or cannot transform information about the past into facts of a specific kind" (1196). This transformation is generally accomplished through typification rather than at the level of concreteness (1197). Secondly, because the truthfulness of a historical film is found at the interpretive level, it is "the nature of the claims made for the images considered as evidence that determines both the discursive function of the events and the criteria of their veracity as predicative utterances" (1198). Siri makes a straightforward claim about his purpose for *L'Ennemi intime:* "I used to wonder why American directors made great action films about the Vietnam War, while nobody in France made films about Algeria. We need to be talking about our own history in this form" (James 2006: 11). Movies like *Platoon* or *Rambo* emphasize spectacle and violence over intimacy and contemplation, but they also excel in communicating visceral, often personal experiences. They are exciting, but not necessarily less critical or insightful for it. Similarly, the strength of *L'Ennemi intime* lies within its ability to represent types of experiences through its formal elements and intertexts; these experiences often include an inward focus and are characterized by critical self-awareness rather than jingoistic stereotypes. Film form as much as characterization and dialogue call into question assumptions about identity, loyalty and even morality.

2 Cinemas of the Algerian War

The idea that the Algerian War is absent from French cinema is one ironically touted by many critics (and even scholars) every time a new film about the conflict appears. Correcting this misconception is necessary to better appreciating Siri's 2007 contribution to a tradition which began in the late 1950s, during the war itself, and which today includes some forty works of diverse styles and ideologies.[4] Faced with state censorship, filmmakers of the 1950s and 1960s often opt for abstraction or circumspection; early films in this tradition are not so much "about" the Algerian War as they include its shadowed presence. Jean Luc Godard's *Le Petit Soldat* (*The Little Soldier*) (1960) deploys allegory to reflect upon the occulted horrors of torture and the moral conundrums of con-

---

4 I am indebted to the works of Benjamin Stora (2007, 2008) and Matthieu Menossi (2007), whom I paraphrase in this section.

scription.[5] More often, mobilized soldiers are paradoxically almost missing, as in *Ascenseur pour l'échafaud* (*Elevator to the Gallows*) (dir. Louis Malle, 1958), *Cléo de 5 à 7* (*Cleo from 5 to 7*) (dir. Agnès Varda, 1962) and *Les Parapluies de Cherbourg* (*The Umbrellas from Cherbourg*) (dir. Jacques Demy, 1964). Alain Resnais's *Muriel* (1963) is one of the few early films to grapple with a soldier's traumatic memories, but still in a stylized manner and within a work more interested in memory than the interrogation of specific past events.

Through this tendency towards occultation, coupled with a generally critical attitude espoused by leftist New Wave filmmakers, French cinema "participates in a mythological reconstruction of a mass refusal of colonial war" (Stora 2008), and this popular myth is amplified by the engaged cinema of the late 1960s and early 1970s.[6] René Vautier's *Avoir 20 ans dans les Aurès* (*To Be Twenty in the Aures*) (1972), Yves Boisset's *R.A.S.* (1973) and Laurent Heynemann's *La Question* (*The Question*) (1977) feature graphic depictions of torture in the context of the Algerian War. They function as powerful critiques of colonialist doctrine and its indelible link with violence. However, this anti-colonialist myth fades by the late 1970s, replaced largely by the more apolitical action films of Pierre Schoendoerffer. *Le Crabe-tambour* (*Drummer-Crab*) (1977) and *L'honneur d'un capitaine* (*A Captain's Honour*) (1982) are centrally concerned with recuperating the honor of the French military and a will towards realistic *mise-en-scène*.

Films produced in Algeria about that nation's war for independence initially face two obstacles. First, it is a cinema with no indigenous tradition; secondly, it has the difficult task of giving voice to the colonized subject without falling into the tar pits of colonialist discourse. Benjamin Stora characterizes early efforts as often "moralizing and clumsy, between intense sentimentalism and political discourse" (2008). Early films such as *Le Vent des Aurès* (*The Winds of the Aures*) (dir. Mohammed Lakhdar-Hamina, 1965) and *L'Opium et le bâton* (*Fighting Opium*) (dir. Ahmed Rachedi, 1969) aim to establish the Algerian nation-state as such, sketching a close rapport between the Algerian authorities and *le peuple en marche*. From these straightforward efforts of nation-building, Algerian cinema quickly grows in self-critical complexity. Okacha Touita's 1982 *Les Sacrifiés* (*The Sacrifice*) investigates not only the miserable conditions of Algerian immigrants in France, but how these immigrants were caught in the crossfire of conflicts between the FLN and partisans for nationalist leader Messali Hadj. *Les Folles Années du Twist* (*The Crazy Years of the Twist*) (dir. Mahmoud Zemmouri,

---

5 Though produced in 1960, state officials delayed the release of Godard's spy thriller until 1963.
6 Many articles and interviews I use are in French; I have translated them for citation. All translations are my own.

1985) takes places during the 1965 signing of the Evian Accords and contrasts the insouciance of a young Algeria with stories of erstwhile Harkis and *attentistes* who join the winning side in the final hours of the war. Unfortunately, the tragic unrest which shook Algeria in the 1990s brought film production to a close for many years.

During this same period, movies about the Algerian War continue to appear in the Hexagon, including *Liberté la nuit* (*Liberty at Night*) (dir. Philippe Garrel, 1983) and *Cher frangin* (dir. Gérard Mordillat, 1989). The 1990's give us Gilles Béhat's *Le Vent de la Toussaint* (1989), Serge Moati's *Des feux mal éteints* (*Poorly Extinguished Fires*) (1994) and *Le Fusil de bois* (*The Wooden Gun*) by Pierre Delerive (1994). While these films attest to a sustained French cinematic interest in the war, none of them leave a particular mark on audiences, critics or historians. No one has satisfactorily parsed the reasons for this lack of interest, though French journalist, critic and film historian Michel Frodon posits that the story of the Algerian War, with its heavy government censorship and stigmatized veterans who struggled to relate their experiences, has never entered the French public consciousness and so does not speak to the French people, saying anything to them about themselves (2004: 76).

At end of the twentieth century, two events return the question of Algeria, the war, and the use of torture to popular attention. Firstly, in 1999, the French National Assembly permits the presence of the Algerian War, as such, on French syllabi. Previously, it had commonly been known as *la guerre sans nom*, "the war without a name," and was often officially referred to as the "Algerian events" or "Algerian dispute." The military's presence in the French département was designated a "pacifying" and "stabilizing" force against FLN "criminals" and "terrorists." Secondly, in 2000 and 2001, Generals Bigeard and Aussaresses confirm the systemic, authorized use of torture during the war, upending 40 years of official denial and governmental silence.[7] Shortly thereafter, the Algerian War returns in force to French screens with greater nuance, diversity and interrogative spirit than ever. In 2006, the destructive psychological effects of torture are put on trial in Laurent Herbiet's *Mon Colonel* (*The Colonel*); in that same year, Phil-

---

[7] General Marcel Bigeard (1916–2010) and General Paul Aussaresses (1918–2013) both served in World War II, the First Indochina War and the Algerian War. In a 2000 interview with the major French newspaper *Le Monde*, Bigeard characterized FLN members as "savages" and claimed that, while he had not engaged in it, torture was a "necessary evil" widely practiced by French forces during the Algerian War. Aussaresses's 2001 book, *Services spéciaux, Algérie 1955–1957*, confirms Bigeard's claims. Aussaresse describes the systematic use of torture upon FLN prisoners and how it was condoned, if not ordered, by high-ranking officials of the French state, including then Minster of Justice François Mitterrand.

ippe Faucon makes the most of low-budget simplicity in *La Trahison* (*The Betrayal*) to focus on characters struggling within the conflicted psychological landscape of the war, where the allegiance and motives of one's allies are perpetually in question. But the scope of recent films goes far beyond the experience of the French military. *Hors-la-loi* (*Outside the Law*), Rachid Bouchareb's 2010 follow-up to the smash hit *Indigènes* (*Days of Glory*), features controversial depictions of the 1945 Sétif riot and follows three Algerian-born brothers in Indochina, the Pigalle district of Paris and in the FLN. *Cartouches gauloises* (*Summer of '62*) (dir. Mehdi Charef, 2007) is an autobiographical work set in the late stages of the war that investigates the massive shifts in Algerian society alongside difficult questions of identity. The Harki immigrant experience has been an important element of three films: *Harkis* (dir. Alain Tasma, 2006), *Nuit noire* (*October 17, 1971*) (dir. Tasma, 2005), and *Caché* (*Hidden*) (dir. Michael Haneke, 2005). Each investigates the difficult, even violent ways in which Algerian-born allies of the French forces attempted to integrate into life in the Hexagon.

It is into this nearly 50-year-old tradition that Siri's *L'Ennemi intime* appears in 2007. There is a fair amount of fanfare in the French press just prior to its October debut, articles often touting the supposed dearth of French films about the Algerian War and lauding *L'Ennemi intime* for broaching a taboo and difficult subject. However, for all this initial praise and promise, its reception by critics and audiences on both sides of the Atlantic is far from celebratory.

3 *L'Ennemi intime:* Critical Receptions

Algeria, 1959. After four years of fighting, French military operations intensify, often supported by local Harkis. In a skirmish high in the Kabyle Mountains, two French patrols mistake each other for FLN forces and their commanding officer dies in the crossfire. His replacement, Lieutenant Terrien, is a liberal idealist who initially clashes with the platoon's Sergeant Dougnac, a cynical veteran of Indochina, as well as his commanding officer, Major Vesoul and the amoral Captain Berthaut. The film proceeds like a series of reports on the platoon's missions, which center upon finding and assassinating the leader of the FLN, Slimane. The first two missions, to the village of Taïda, introduce the cruel injustices of the war. After the first visit, the FLN massacres the village, suspecting its citizens of giving information to the French forces. Even in the face of such atrocities, Terrien refuses to torture prisoners for information or to fire on civilians – though the seasoned Dougnac reveals the 'civilians' in question to be *fellaghas* in disguise, transporting weapons.

Though Terrien refuses to torture prisoners, Berthaut has no such compunctions. His grisly methods yield intelligence about Slimane's whereabouts, and the subsequent mission contains a sad first in cinematic history. Terrien's forces are outflanked, pinned down by enemy forces on open ground; from the safe distance of his command post, Vesoul orders the delivery of *les bidons spéciaux* – a code name for barrels of napalm whose use in the Algerian War had never before been featured on screen. Their effect is literally breathtaking, jarring even the imperturbable Berthaut. The use of napalm also makes it impossible to determine if Slimane was among the incinerated. So, the missions continue and the unforgiving terrain, frequent ambushes and incessant atrocities of guerrilla warfare relentlessly wear upon Terrien. He eventually snaps, torturing a prisoner to death, executing another, and calmly watching a village of civilians gunned down because an old hunting rifle was found in a home.

Remy Besson characterizes the various French receptions of *L'Ennemi intime* as "profoundly polysemous," and this applies to their Anglophone counterparts as well. Critics' opinions range from a dismissive blurb in *Cahiers du Cinéma* that laments an overused plotline and videogame-like special effects (Frodon 2004: 34) to an effusive review by YouTube film critic "Monsieur Bobine" (2014), who lauds Siri's film as an accessible and elegant work that touches upon universal questions of the human condition. Between these two extremes, most reviews praise the film's pedigree (*Platoon*, *La 317e section*) alongside its polished production values and sense of epic scale. *Variety*'s Dennis Harvey applauds its "credibly gritty microcosm" of the war and hails it as "visceral and engrossing" (2007). However, critics also unfavorably compare it to other francophone films such as *Mon Colonel* and *Indigènes*, and to the Italian-produced *La battaglia di Algeri*. Its accessibility, in the guise of its slick production, action-movie explosions and generic characters, are also a chief liability. Guy Westwell of *Sight and Sound* finds that it plays "very generically" (2008: 70). Moreover, while Siri's "avowedly commercial aesthetic might enable the film to reach a wider audience [...] it inevitably draws it away from [screenwriter and documentarian] Rotman's more valuable historical approach" (71). *L'Ennemi intime* wants to play against expectations by combining deep thought with explosive action, but critics fail to find synergy there. What they do find remarkable is the film's portrayals of the various participants in the Algerian War, from the tragic transformations of French conscripts and their ideological battle fought by their officers, to the complexities of loyalty and identity faced by the Algerian people.

4 L'Ennemi intime: Ambiguous Enemies

For a film that purportedly transcends national boundaries, *L'Ennemi intime* seems to marginalize the native Algerian experience of their own war for independence. Siri purportedly focuses on French and Harki soldiers in order to avoid having too many characters (Alion 2007: 104), but this lacuna perpetuates a tradition of ethnocentrism that may be compounded by its will to participate in the action war movie paradigm of *Platoon* and *La 317e section*, which almost uniquely feature the Western experience of colonial wars. Indeed, French academics take *L'Ennemi intime* to task for lacking both an authentic representation of Algerian characters as well as information to contextualize their historical and personal choices (Besson 2013).

However, we should re-evaluate and nuance this broad criticism. *L'Ennemi intime* has "a range of characters that stand for diverse points of view about the war" (Honeycutt 2007), and it raises important questions about their historical experiences and motivations (Stora 2007). After two World Wars, characterized by tragedy and triumph on epic scales, what is the mindset of the French soldier, sometimes conscripted, in a small-scale war of paranoia and skirmishes? What motivates an Algerian to join the Free French forces and storm Monte Cassino against the Axis powers, only then to pitch in with the FLN? Or, rather, why would a Harki sympathize with the French Resistance but later join forces with an oppressive foreign occupier against their own people?

L'Ennemi intime focuses on the first question, but three significant native Algerian characters help us to begin exploring the latter ones. Harki soldier Saïd speaks triumphantly of his experience in World War II, fighting fascism alongside the French; during his storytelling, he proudly displays the scars he received in battle. In contrast to his usual joviality, Saïd's vehemence against the *fellaghas* is profound. He considers the FLN to be traitors of the highest order, and not simply because they betray the sacrifices that were necessary for victory against fascism; the FLN murdered Saïd's family. His tragic doppelgänger is Idir, an FLN prisoner. As the platoon marches Idir to his execution, Saïd learns that they both fought with the Free French forces and they both even stormed Monte Cassino! When he asks why Idir would join with men who massacre entire villages, the latter lights both ends of a cigarette. One burning end is the French, he says, the other end is the FLN. Haplessly caught between two destructive forces, it does not matter which agent of holocaust you join.[8]

---

8 This is a deeply cynical moment, followed shortly by Saïd shooting Idir in the back as he is

Amar is the third significant Algerian character, the lone survivor of the Taïda massacre rescued by Terrien. His character arc is a bitterly ironic one. Initially a quintessential "[h]alf devil, and half child" from Kipling's "The White Man's Burden," Amar is a witness to Terrien's spiraling descent from idealist to vengeful murderer, and this experience radicalizes the boy.[9] Eventually, he not only deserts the platoon, but also kills his erstwhile savior. While Amar's character is more a sketch than a portrait, he is in many ways Terrien's counterpart: an ingénue, thrust into the brutal absurdity of the Algerian War where he first transforms into a survivor but eventually becomes a radicalized warrior. Anton Bitel of Film4 remarks upon "how fundamentally similar the two sides are to each other in motive, method and madness, and how easily – indeed, how naturally – they both become dehumanized within the escalating orgy of violence and paranoia" (2007). The crucible of the Kabyle Mountains seems to create only agents of death and destruction.

The term "enemy" is more complex than its common connotation of "an armed foe" or the collectivity of a "hostile force." According to the *Oxford English Dictionary*, it also has the broader meaning of "adversary, antagonist, opponent." This ambiguity is important when we consider the complex figurations of opposing forces in *L'Ennemi intime*. True to past fact, dividing lines between enemies do not strictly adhere to notions of nationality, ethnicity or even ideology. The initial conflict between Berthaut and Terrien mirrors the debates happening within France during the Algerian War. Indigenous Algerians like Saïd and Idir are equally at odds. Amar and Terrien undergo similar transformations that nonetheless place them in opposite camps. Rotman's script gives voice to a variety of viewpoints, painting a complex portrait where impossible decisions result in horrible transformations.[10]

---

actually set free. Dougnac cannot bring himself to execute a fellow soldier of honor but Saïd sees only an agent of the terrorists who murdered his family.

9 Kipling's 1899 poem calls for those of the industrialized West to take care of their colonial subjects, whom he depicts as childlike and uncivilized: "Take up the White Man's burden– / Send forth the best ye breed– / Go, bind your sons to exile / To serve your captives' need; / To wait, in heavy harness, / On fluttered folk and wild– / Your new-caught sullen peoples, / Half devil and half child."

10 This kind of ambiguity was not well received by popular audiences. Revenues from French receipts barely cover half the film's budget of 9.7 million euros and it fares less well abroad. In the end, *L'Ennemi intime* only partially realizes lead actor Magimel's aim to "raise awareness" about the war (Besson 2013).

5 L'Ennemi intime:
Special Effects, Intertexts and Metacinema

This film is practically nonexistent in Anglophone academic literature. The present analysis aims to begin a dialogue about *L'Ennemi intime* within academic and public spheres in three ways. Firstly, we will reexamine the elements that make its "emotive punch" (Davies 2008) so effective: a combination of sound design and cinematography used to replicate the psychological experience of the French soldier. Secondly, beyond the much-recognized influence of Ford and Peckinpah's Westerns, there are several intertexts that may give us greater appreciation of this film's method and message. Finally, Siri places films within his film, metacinematic moments that evince a critical spirit essential to historiophoty.

Veterans of the World Wars are memorialized in the French public consciousness almost to the point of beatification. The country dedicates an official civic holiday to each war; statues, plaques and various memorials can be found in fields and street corners alike; French cinema is thoroughly enamored with their heroes, villains and complexities. But this is not the case for the tens of thousands of French soldiers who served in Algeria. The struggles and triumphs of their war never really reached metropolitan France, and even after it was all over, most found it nearly impossible to speak about what happened, either because their experiences were so traumatic or because the veterans themselves were stigmatized by a populace that viewed them with either apathy or disdain. Addressing this lacuna in popular memory is a significant part of *L'Ennemi intime*'s historiophotic worth. Though the focus on a French character reduces its polyphony, it nonetheless gives voice to a previously silent victim of the war.

In order to help the spectator understand the psychology of a French soldier during the Algerian War, Siri employs a variety of cinematic tactics to create an engrossing sensorial experience. Sound design gives us a sense of presence and place and Eisensteinian montage illustrates Terrien's shock when he discovers the massacre in Taïda. During the combat scenes, shoulder-cams bring the spectator directly into the action. A body-mounted camera expresses disorientation and existential vertigo in moments of extreme stress for Terrien, and the artificial fluidity of that cinematographic technique is mirrored in two sequences that soar over the landscape.

A sense of psychological authenticity in *L'Ennemi intime* begins with sound design. The characters' breathing was all done in post-production and it is present in the soundtrack even during long-shots. This generates a sense of nearly constant human presence. In contrast, Siri creates an otherwise sparse soundscape similar to the Kabyle Mountains during the Algerian War, one where the spectator can be ambushed at any moment. One such aural ambush happens during the second mission to Taïda, when the platoon warily enter the suddenly deserted village. Only natural atmospheric sounds are present: the scuffle of boots, the creak of a door, the nervous breath of the soldiers.

Terrien's discovery of the villagers' fate is related through another tactic, a rapid alternance of images: his face, dead bodies, his wide eyes, mutilated villagers, each shot getting closer to its respective subject, silently conveying Terrien's horror while simultaneously illustrating it for the audience without grisly voyeurism. In an Eisensteinian manner, two perfectly still images are animated by their rapid juxtaposition. Terrien (who is becoming our proxy in the movie's universe) is paralyzed with shock, and his mind is violently shaken.

Of course, violence is physical as well as mental in this war, and Siri often shoots with a shoulder-mounted camera to bring the spectator directly into the chaos of combat. A shoulder-cam's wobble helps to connote a sense of immediacy and the imprecision of human movement. It also reduces our field of vision; our sight of enemy forces is usually little more than shadows bobbing behind cover on a distant hilltop. The enemy is nameless, but their guns are as loud as their fire is constant, anonymous and terrifying.

Turning the shoulder cam on oneself creates a wholly different effect, and *L'Ennemi intime* uses a body-mounted camera to indicate important moments. After a long series of traumatic encounters, including the Taïda massacre, the napalm bombing of Slimane's forces and countless FLN ambushes that slowly whittle away the soldiers in his command, Terrien makes the wrong call and guns down two innocent women. His mental break is captured with the film's first use of a body cam, a rig mounted on the actor's hips and shoulders with the camera pointed towards him. The effect is as disorienting as it is expressive, an unwieldy and unforgiving close-up.

However, this moment merely sets the stage for a second deployment of the body camera, a scene in which Terrien completely dissociates. Giving in to righteous anger at his own powerlessness to prevent the murder and mutilation of his comrades, he tortures a Berber prisoner to death. In addition to connoting an abnormal psychology, the use of a body cam in this scene performs an important reversal. The film does not focus on the victim's torture and murder, but rather on the murderous torturer himself: Terrien, the erstwhile idealist and, let us not forget, our proxy in this film, the most relatable character with whom we have allied our sympathies and interests. Siri admits that the use of a body camera risks pulling the spectator from the story ("Body Cam," Region 1 DVD extras), but here, such a dissociation is precisely illustrative of the horrible transformations visited upon French soldiers deployed in the Algerian War.

The strange fluidity of a body cam relates in a striking way to a final cinematographic tactic: the dreamlike, soaring sequence that opens the film. In the age of drone strikes, this moment is both anachronistic and, ironically, instantly recognizable, a symbol of the physical and psychological disconnect which characterizes contemporary warfare. There is no clear subject in here, just a pure point of view from a humanly impossible height, moving with elegance and speed over the Kabyle Mountains. In many contexts, this would be a wondrous moment of beauty and even awe. However, this effect is taken up later in the film during "Operation Slimane," and like Terrien, it is transformed. Its looming, oneiric idyll proves to be devastatingly ironic: the point of view is that of a French bomber, its cargo *les bidons spéciaux*, whose terrible tactical efficacy leaves nothing but an eerie garden of ashen corpses.

While the drone-like flyover of the opening sequence gives us our first view of the Kabyle landscape, their photography by Coltellacci is clearly influenced by the Westerns of John Ford and Sam Peckinpah. The presence of one genre's iconic tradition in another is just the first of many intertexts for *L'Ennemi intime*, including the beautiful horror of Géricault's *Le Radeau de la Méduse* (*The Raft of the Medusa*), and the visceral irony of Scorsese's anti-war short *The Big Shave* (1967). Siri's film also engages with some of its francophone war film predecessors in unique ways.

The presence of a Western's tableau long shot in a French war film is one significant sign of its transnational nature, but it grew from Siri's choice to use 2.35:1 format. The very wide aspect ratio was pioneered by CinemaScope in the 1950s and is nearly synonymous with it today, regardless of the lens or film actually used. Siri chose 2.35:1 in order to give *L'Ennemi intime* an epic quality, locating its human characters in better scale to the massive mountains of Kabylie.[11]

The influence of Ford and Peckinpah's majestic expository camerawork is clear in several shots throughout Siri's film, though it is especially so as the platoon slowly traverses the landscape during their final, futile mission. The carefully composed long shots evoke an idyllic stillness. In the American (or even Spaghetti) Western these shots promise an agrarian serenity and symbolize the romantic notion of an untouched wilderness whose raw, rugged beauty must be defied, survived and loved. In *L'Ennemi intime*, however, the idylls are false: the defiance is entirely human, survival is unlikely and love is not a

---

11 Which are actually the Atlas mountains of Morocco, Algeria being considered too politically unstable for shooting.

word considered by anyone. The gorgeous vistas are cruelly ironic, lovingly photographed graves of the nameless and forgotten.

We can further explore and understand this tension between beauty and death when considering an extraordinary intertext for a film: *Le Radeau de la Méduse*. In Géricault's 1819 depiction of the wreck of a French naval frigate off the coast of Mauritania, romantic notions inherent to the genre are overturned by the hypotext. The beauty of the painting's composition attracts the viewers towards the horrific, aestheticizing grisly deaths at sea. It does this with a carefully considered palette of muted earth tones (something that it shares with Siri's film) and a dual pyramidal structure that draws the eye from top to bottom, from hope (waved clothes attempting to signal a distant ship) to despair (the dead and dying at the edge of the raft).

Siri points to *Le Radeau de la Méduse* as a touchstone for *L'Ennemi intime*'s approach to the horrors of the Algerian War, and the analyses above carry this out. The massacre of Taïda is rendered not only bearable but gripping with Einsteinian quick cuts, and the unthinkable stress of torturing another human being to death becomes a disorienting experience rather than one of either revulsion or voyeuristic spectacle. Even the effects of the napalm air strike are compelling: men transformed into statues of grey ash in an apocalyptic landscape. Importantly, while this aestheticizing of the grotesque is powerful, it is neither exculpatory nor sensational. These horrors are mitigated only to the point of being bearable.

Considerably less bearable is the metaphor at work in Martin Scorsese's 1967 short film *The Big Shave*. Set uniquely in a small apartment bathroom, a young man begins his morning shave in front of the mirror to the big band tones of Bunny Berigan's "I Can't Get Started." The violence of his quotidian ritual becomes increasingly bloody, to the point of covering his entire face, chest and sink with gore. With a subtitle of "Viet '67," scholars commonly understand Scorsese's short as a critique of the American war in Vietnam. *L'Ennemi intime* shares this critical spirit and visceral *mise-en-scène*. Though Siri avoids polemics and simple didacticism, by emphasizing the cruel difficulties of a soldier's experience in the Algerian War, his film undoubtedly leaves a bad taste in the audience's mouth, and a revolting sensation upon our skin: the grit of the desert, the heat of its sun, the dry whipping of wind, the terrible sound of a man's screams in the night as he is slowly electrocuted, the stench of mutilated bodies piled in a mud hovel.

With *L'Ennemi intime* Florent-Emilio Siri proves to be more than just a fan of big Hollywood. He also calls upon important moments in a long line of French and Francophone war films. While much hay has been made with its obvious similarities to *Platoon* (dir. Stone, 1985), there are also interesting parallels with Pontecorvo's 1966 *La battaglia di Algeri* (*The Battle of Algiers*), Schoendoerffer's *La 317e section* (*The 317th Platoon*) and Abel Gance's 1919 epic *J'accuse!*

La battaglia di Algeri pioneered a newsreel-like aesthetic, and so artfully and convincingly tells the story of Algeria's fight for independence from the point of view of the FLN that it has been used as a case study of modern insurgencies. It has such a seminal status, especially among film scholars and critics, that perhaps no film about the Algerian War could avoid being compared to it. So, Siri leans into the expectation. Major Vesoul is a clear echo of *Algeri*'s Colonel Mathieu, right down to the reflective sunglasses. However, by the end of the film, Terrien's transformation brings him to the same place, at least aesthetically: cool, clean cut, and using the same kind of reflective sunglasses to avoid looking at the victims of his righteous, indignant brutality.[12]

In interviews and DVD extras, Siri often mentions the influence of *La 317e section*. Based on director Schoendoerffer's semi-autobiographical novel, the film features the doomed final mission of a platoon during the First Indochina War. Shot on location with documentary-like simplicity (perhaps anticipating or paralleling Pontecorvo's aesthetic), it focuses on a theme of sacrifice. With this rare cinematic treatment of France's involvement in Indochina, *L'Ennemi intime* shares a focus on the human element and the horrors of modern warfare, along with a preference for shoulder-mounted camera-work to give battle scenes a sense of immediacy and shaky chaos.

On balance, much more separates rather than connects Siri's 2007 film from Abel Gance's 1919 *J'accuse!* The latter is a silent melodrama about World War I, shot in black and white, with an episodic plot that the director constantly tinkered with in the cutting room. What these movies share, however, is a powerful, silent dance of the dead. In the penultimate sequence of *J'accuse!*, fallen soldiers arise from their trench-side graves and march upon those in France who are beginning to forget them. It is a powerful and poetic message about the survivors' duty of memory, a memory that honors those lost and keeps fresh the horrors visited upon them in war. The dead also return in *L'Ennemi intime*, traipsing ghost-like across a sheet in the outpost barracks on Christmas Eve. Lefranc's

---

12 With this transformed state in mind, Terrien's first appearance becomes a moment of foreshadowing. When he arrives at the platoon's outpost for the first time, he is wearing those same sunglasses, but he is covered in dirt and grime from the road, having just traversed the Kabyle Mountains in an open jeep. By the end of his transformation, he learns to hide his moral corruption, and thus both characterizing moments are ironic: the pure soul covered in grime versus the black-hearted torturer in a clean uniform. The first uses the sunglasses as an honest practicality; the other uses them to deny the humanity of his victims.

home movie is more than a sentimental moment honoring fallen comrades so common in war films. Addressing critiques that movies cannot take part in historical debate, Hayden White posits that "the historical film draws attention to the extent to which it is a constructed [...] representation of reality" (1988: 1195). Therefore, a good, even necessary measure of a film's historiophotic value is its capacity to be self-critical, and one of the most artful ways to carry this out is to feature film within a film, subtly indicating the constructedness of the first-level work. Together with the newsreel propaganda that Terrien watches on leave, the Christmas Eve screening of Lefranc's film forms the metacinema in *L'Ennemi intime*. These two instances provide Siri's movie with the necessary self-reflection to concretize it as a critical examination of events whose goal is a better understanding of the past so that we may make good decisions in the future.

One of those decisions may be to distrust the news media, especially when they are under government control and uniquely report pastoral, peacekeeping missions by armed forces in a land fighting for its independence. The bald mistruths perpetuated by the Fourth Republic are bitterly ironic for Terrien and the spectator alike, but they are more than a contribution to *L'Ennemi intime*'s sustained acerbic mode. They provide an important explanation about one of the chief paradoxes of the Algerian War, namely that despite some eight years of armed conflict and hundreds of thousands of casualties, the war itself never enters into popular French consciousness. It is a silent, dirty war, whose victims and veterans remain outside a sphere of comprehension in French culture. This occurs, says *L'Ennemi intime*, because the state lied to its citizenry.

Because Siri's film so clearly draws a parallel between what is on a movie screen and blatant prevarication, I feel that this implies the necessity of critical reflection not just about news media, that front line of shaping history, but about movies as well. No matter how pleasing, what we see on-screen may only be part of the story; and the other parts left off-screen or on the cutting room floor may create an entirely different truth.

In *L'Ennemi intime*, much of that truth surfaces in Lefranc's home movie. Clearly, it has a memorializing function and does so with thick sentimentality and humor. But the jubilant dances that it captures are the obverse of a tragic coin. The human element of the Algerian War is marked by violent and senseless loss. The film replays the lost lives as silent, grainy, ghostly images projected imperfectly upon a dirty sheet. Just as important to *L'Ennemi intime*'s metacinema are the reactions of the living to the apparition of their fallen comrades, for they are also projected upon the screen, cavorting alongside the dead. And we, as the spectators of Siri's film, are part of this necromantic farandole as well. We watch people watch themselves, or rather, a story of themselves in a past caught between the glow of nostalgia and the shadows of regret.

Conclusion: The Liabilities of Being Transnational

Despite its masterful construction, rich intertexts and strong historiophotic function, *L'Ennemi intime* was a commercial flop. While a film's financial success or failure relies on many factors, I suspect that one of *L'Ennemi intime*'s most significant liabilities is its transnational nature: its subject matter and intellectual approach are too French to interest international audiences, while its style is too American to appeal to French moviegoers. It struggles to blend big-action directness and moralizing meditation.

Big-budget action spectacles like *Platoon* or the *Rambo* series are clearly an inspiration for director Florent-Emilio Siri, but this seems to take for granted that the action film genre has something important to bring to a historiophotic venture. Benjamin Stora sees the "hyperviolence" of *L'Ennemi intime* as its weakest point, for it creates a

> [...] universe where extreme violence spreads out constantly. The film accentuates the cruelty of man on both sides, the unconscious desires of its characters, unbearable acts of barbarism, a corporeal cinematic language, 'physical,' close to the American films about Vietnam in the 1980s or the films of Quentin Tarantino in the 90s. (2007)

Because the combat sequences are so compelling, because the torture is so visceral and grotesquely beautiful, they threaten to overshadow other, equally important elements of historical understanding that the film offers.

In Anglophone distribution, especially in the United States, the French provenance of *L'Ennemi intime* works against it in the opposite direction as its Hollywood inspiration did within the Hexagon. That is, American audiences tend to equate French cinema with a stereotype of *le cinéma du milieu:* modestly budgeted, narratively ambiguous, character-driven think pieces. The directness of Siri's plotting, the broadness of Rotman's characters, so easily identified as an almost clichéd "type" (the ingénue officer, the cynical sergeant, the amoral commanding officer, the wide-eyed kid), the shaky camerawork and adept cutting of the combat scenes are all things that seem almost derivative to American critics; and I think we can safely assume US audiences felt the same.

Siri's work struggles the most to combine action with reflection. Its didacticism and moralizing happen far from combat, and the lion's share of a debate about the war happens between two Frenchmen, Terrien and Berthaut. There is some uncomfortable, awkward and unexamined colonialism at work in a scene where two white Europeans, literally lording over the Kabyle landscape, debate the fate of a land in which they are both armed invaders. However, Rotman's script also gives the Algerians their own moment. The scene between Saïd and Idir is one of the few times *L'Ennemi intime* spotlights the Algerian experience of the war, and to its credit, the film does so with success. But, we are best to judge it as Hayden White suggests, according to the "the nature of the claims made for the images considered as evidence" (1988: 1198), and Siri has clearly made his aims known in several venues: "The main idea was to understand why a young, idealistic officer, sworn enemy of torture, becomes himself a torturer" (Alion 2007: 103) and "I wanted to show how war can transform us, how it can turn a relatively pure human being into a monster" ("Memory," Region 1 DVD Special Features). The transformative nature of war is evident in the figure of Terrien, but also in that of Amar, and that transformation is always into something ugly and murderous.

Some film critics object that this "war is hell" message is clichéd, but in a world where Guantanamo Bay continues to exist, where Russian forces bomb Syrian schools, where swimwear on French beaches is subject to legislation, one may wonder if this is a lesson we have actually learned or if it has just become an inconvenient truism we attempt to render meaningless through repetition.

L'Ennemi intime struggles to hybridize action and contemplation, and it focuses on the European experience of the Algerian War instead of seeking a balance of perspectives.[13] Nonetheless, even acknowledging these faults advances our historical understanding of a conflict that merits not only investigation but contemplation. Central in this contemplation should be the complexities of designating one's "enemy." It may be simple to hate (or fear) the shadowed figure who hails you with bullets, or who incinerates your comrades with napalm. But what of your fellow countryman whose ideology you find abhorrent – or dangerously naïve? What of your brother in faith who has allied himself with your family's murderers? With those who torture your friends? Massacre innocents? Siri's false idyll draws from disparate works in order to aestheticize horrific acts of war and bring us closer to them, capturing our attention. With that attention, it models a connective mode of thought that revives the dead, memorializing their sacrifices while also questioning both the motives and the actions of the survivors.

---

13 We might surmise that Siri's film is transnational in an unproductive way, that to be an engaging portrait of the Algerian War for Independence, a movie needs to transect the national and cultural boundaries across the Mediterranean instead of the Atlantic. Certainly, that is the kind of movie that Benjamin Stora (2008) would like to see.

Works Cited

Alion, Yves (2007) "À propos de *L'Ennemi intime*: Entretien avec Florent-Emilio Siri," *Avant-Scène cinéma* 564, 102–105.
Aussaresses, Paul (2001) *Services spéciaux, Algérie 1955–1957: Mon témoignage sur la torture* (Paris: Perrin).
Besson, Remy (2013) "L'Ennemi Intime (2007) – Une réception non-consensuelle," *Cinémadoc*, <cinemadoc.hypotheses.org/2745> (accessed 11 September 2017).
Bitel, Anton (2007) "Intimate Enemies," *Film*4 <www.film4.com/reviews/2007/intimate-enemies> (accessed 8 June 2016).
Davies, Sophie (2008) "Intimate Enemies," *The Times* (Features: The Knowledge), 10.
Ezra, Elizabeth, and Terry Rowden (2006) *Transnational Cinema: The Film Reader* (New York: Routledge).
Frodon, Jean-Michel (2004) "De l'Algérie au Vietnam: Le film de guerre n'existe pas," *Cahiers du cinéma* 593, 74–76.
Harvey, Dennis (2007) "Review: Intimate Enemies," *Variety* <www.variety.com/2007/film/reviews/intimate-enemies-2-1200556539> (accessed 11 September 2017).
Honeycutt, Kirk (2007) "Intimate Enemies," *The Hollywood Reporter* <www.hollywoodreporter.com/review/intimate-enemies-158426> (accessed 11 September 2017).
Horne, Alistair (2006) *A Savage War of Peace: Algeria 1954–1962* (New York: NYRB Classics).
James, Alison (2006) "Gaul Tackles War Taboos," *Variety* 404. 8, 11.
Kipling, Rudyard (1899) "The White Man's Burden: The United States and the Philippine Islands," *McClure's Magazine*, 290.
Ma, Ringo (2006) "'Both-And' and 'Neither-Nor': My Intercultural Experiences," in *Among US: Essays on Identity, Belonging and Intercultural Competence*, 2nd edition, ed. Myron W. Lustig and Jolene Koester (Boston: Pearson), 308–315.
Menossi, Mathieu (2007) "La Guerre d'Algérie dans le cinéma français: Une histoire sans fin?," *Le Figaro*, FigaroScope <evene.lefigaro.fr/cinema/actualite/guerre-algerie-cinema-francais-ennemi-intime-siri-1021.php> (accessed 11 September 2017).
"Monsieur Bobine" (2014) "*L'Ennemi intime*," YouTube, Le cinéclub de M Bobine <youtube/jK95nKOLCbY> (accessed 11 September 2017).
Ruscio, Alain (2012) "Deux ou trois choses que nous savons du général Bigeard," *Cahiers d'histoire: Revue d'histoire critique* 118 <http://chrhc.revues.org/2647> (accessed 11 September 2017).
Schager, Nick (2009) "Intimate Enemies," *Slant* <www.slantmagazine.com/film/review/intimate-enemies> (accessed 11 September 2017).
Stora, Benjamin (2007) "Avoir 20 ans dans la Kabylie," *L'Histoire* 342, 28.
Stora, Benjamin (2008) "La guerre d'Algérie dans les médias: l'exemple du cinéma," Cairn.info, *Hermès, La Revue* 3. 52, 2008. <cairn.info/revue-hermes-la-revue-2008-3-page-33.htm> (accessed 11 September 2017).
Westwell, Guy (2008) "Film Reviews: Intimate Enemies," *Sight and Sound* 18. 3, 70–71.
White, Hayden (1988) "Historiography and Historiophoty," *American Historical Review* 93. 5, 1193–1199.

Filmography

L'Ennemi intime (*Intimate Enemies*) (2007) Dir. Florent-Emilio Siri (Les Films du Kiosque).

Marcelline Block
"Femme, je ne vous aime pas":
The Enemy Within in Joachim Lafosse's
A perdre la raison

Joachim Lafosse's acclaimed French-language film *A perdre la raison* (*Our Children*) (2012), is based upon/inspired by a true infanticide that occurred in Belgium. In February 2007, five years before *A perdre*'s release, a former schoolteacher, Geneviève Lhermitte (b. 1966, Brussels), murdered her five children – four daughters and a son, who ranged in age from 4–14 years old – by slashing their throats. This incident, which rocked Lafosse's native Belgium (Brey 2014: 232), forms the basis for his narrative fiction film *A perdre la raison*. Lafosse's film re-creates/re-imagines a similar infanticide in contemporary Belgium as perpetrated by a young Belgian mother, Murielle (Emilie Dequenne), who, as in the Lhermitte infanticides, stabs her children to death in the family home (Brey 169). The crime of infanticide depicted in *A perdre la raison* along with the film's portrayal of one of its three main characters, Dr. André Pinget (Neils Arestrup), as the 'enemy' in the narrative, engages with and raises questions about contemporary socio-political dynamics in Belgium, particularly in relation to the legacy of francophone colonialism. Issues such as the legacy of colonialism, illegal immigration, and their impact upon contemporary Belgian society are explored in *A perdre la raison* vis-à-vis Dr. Pinget's relationship to infanticidal mother Murielle and her Moroccan-born husband Mounir (Tahar Rahim). These social and political issues include how the enduring legacy of francophone colonialism manifests itself in the exploitation, mistreatment, and limited rights as well as the lack of financial means, options, and resources of impoverished undocumented immigrants illicitly arriving in Belgium from former francophone colonized regions, in particular Morocco.

Rather than depict the gruesome murders of Murielle and Mounir's four children onscreen, the primary focus of *A perdre la raison* is an examination of the dysfunctional family dynamic in Murielle's household leading up to this horrific act. In doing so, *A perdre la raison* constructs Dr. André Pinget – the "patriarchal landlord and benefactor" (Edwards 2015: 181) of Murielle and Mounir – as the enemy in the film. Dr. Pinget brought Mounir to Belgium from his native Morocco; Mounir and Murielle then met in Belgium, fell in love, got married, and had four children (three girls and a boy) in rapid succession. Pinget pays for the family home – in which his medical office is located – as well as employs Mounir as his office manager (Block 2013: 17, 18; Brey 157).

Central to *A perdre la raison* is the enmity between Murielle and Pinget, the effects of which are disastrous for Murielle, setting in motion the events that culminate in the film's horrific denouement. Pinget is shown to be Murielle's enemy over the course of the film, as she is "prise dans les filets de Pinget [...] coupée de son savoir, de sa capacité à être. Elle entre dans une condition de femme inférieure à l'homme" ["caught in Pinget's net [...] cut off from her knowledge, from her capacity to exist. She enters into a condition of woman as inferior to man"] (Brey 2014: 162). Pinget's constant involvement in Mounir and Murielle's lives and his presence in their home occupies not only Murielle's living space but also her body and her mind. Pinget resides with Murielle and Mounir – and their four children – under the same roof, a living arrangement whose detrimental effects impact/exacerbate Murielle's emotional and mental state until she murders her four children:

> Murielle est elle aussi coincée par un mari qui est sous l'emprise d'un autre homme, qui l'empêche de s'exiler au Maroc, qui l'enferme dans un rôle de femme domestique et qui la coupe du monde. Pour mettre fin à cette domination, elle tue leurs enfants et fait une tentative de suicide.
>
> [Murielle is trapped by a husband who is under the influence of another man, who prevents her from exiling herself in Morocco, who imprisons her in the role of housewife and who cuts her off from the world. To put an end to this domination, she kills their children and attempts suicide.] (Brey 132)[1]

Not only is Pinget shown to be Murielle's enemy in *A perdre*, but also, he represents larger systems of patriarchal and francophone colonial oppression: he is the "métonymie du colon, qui s'approprie les membres d'une famille marocaine pour constituer sa propre famille, comme un colon puiserait ses ressources au Maroc" ["metonymy of the colonist, who appropriates the members of a Moroccan family to constitute his own family, as a colonist would draw his resources from Morocco"] (Brey 157). This recalls Anthony Lane's claim that *A perdre la raison* functions as "a parable for colonialism" (2013). The legacy of francophone colonialism is present in *A perdre la raison* through its references to/depictions of Mounir's birthplace of Morocco, especially in terms of illegal immigration from Morocco – which was a French Protectorate from 1912–1955 – to Belgium.

A perdre la raison explores illegal immigration from formerly francophone colonized regions – such as Morocco – to Western Europe through its portrayal of Dr. Pinget's arrangement of sham marriages for Mounir's two siblings (including his sister, who is married to Dr. Pinget), which allow them to leave their birth-

---

[1] All translations are mine unless otherwise noted.

place of Morocco in order to live and work in Belgium. This aspect of the plot of *A perdre la raison* recalls an earlier Belgian film which addresses illegal immigration, *Le silence de Lorna* (*Lorna's Silence*) (2008), which is written and directed by iconic Belgian auteurs Jean-Pierre and Luc Dardenne. The Dardennes' *Le silence de Lorna* depicts a criminal network in Belgium trafficking in phony marriages between Belgian citizens and illegal immigrants from Albania and Russia for the purposes of obtaining EU citizenship for participants in the scheme. However, as Daniel Fairfax notes, "critics [of *Le silence de Lorna*] have grumbled at various inaccuracies in the Dardennes' treatment of characters caught within the vagaries of EU immigration policy" (2013: 125).

From the late nineteenth until the mid-twentieth century, Belgium's colonial empire was primarily situated in Central and East Africa, namely, the Belgian Congo (1885–1960) and Ruanda-Urundi (1916–1962), respectively. Belgian's African colonies became the subject of numerous Belgian documentary films, such as those by André Cauvin (1907–2004), who "became a pioneer in ethnographic cinema with films made in the Belgian Congo" (Sojcher 2013: 20). Cauvin was "followed by film-makers such as Luc de Heusch, who was more mindful than Cauvin in associating a scientific rigour to his cinematic approaches" (Sojcher 2013: 20). Another example of a documentary about the Belgian Congo is 1934's *Terres brûlées* (*Burnt Earth*) by Charles Dekeukeleire (1905–1971) – "one of the founding figures of Belgian cinema" (Szaniawski 2013a: 45) – which functions as

> a visual diary documenting Captain Brondeel's expedition to the Congo, the first successful attempt to travel from Belgium to West Africa by truck (and which took almost four months). This was the director's first sound film, featuring memorable footage of Watuzis jumping. The film gave Dekeukeleire his legitimacy, but also showed his progressive approach to the local population of Africa, against the grain of the general patronizing colonialist mood that pervaded Belgian culture at the time (even if a late-1930s documentary, entitled *Black People Evolve/Les noirs évoluent*, certainly bears the hallmark of said patronizing attitude). (Szaniawski 2013a: 47–48)

However, along with Central and East Africa, Belgium also had a presence in North Africa in pre-Independence Morocco: from 1928–1956 Belgium was one of the European countries[2] that formed the Committee of Control administering the Tangier International Zone in Morocco. The current Moroccan diaspora and immigrant community in Belgium is substantial; according to Hassan Bousetta, "there is a general recognition that immigration has transformed Belgium into a fully-fledge [sic] multicultural society [...] Moroccans in Belgium come close to

---

2 Along with Britain, France, Italy, the Netherlands, Portugal and Spain.

being the largest immigrant community in the country" (2008: 397–398). Bousetta further notes that

> Moroccan immigrants in Belgium have been central to the migration debate since the mid-1960s. Initially attracted as guest workers, Moroccans have settled for good and developed one of the largest immigrant ethnic minority communities. With 81,000 people on the official records, Moroccans are ranked fourth amongst non-nationals, after Italians, French and Dutch. However, when ethnicity is taken into consideration rather than nationality, the estimated size of this community is more than triple this number [...] it is estimated that the Moroccan community represents a group of over 250,000 persons, ranking top with Italians. (398)

Furthermore, "Moroccans (and those of Moroccan origin) constitute the largest non-European community not only in [...] the capital city [Brussels], but also across Belgium. Their presence can be directly tied to the bilateral agreement of 17 February 1964 between Belgium and Morocco which brought a pool of cheap, manual labour to Belgium" (Costanzo and Zibouh 2014: 67–68).

That "Belgium belongs to a cluster of Northwest European countries that has a relatively long tradition of immigration" (Bousetta 397) is reflected by Belgium's cinematic production, since "Belgian cinema has opened itself [...] to a range of film-makers from the pool of immigrants and/or ethnic/cultural minorities who have come to reside in Belgium [including] several film-makers of the post-World War II generation from North African and Middle Eastern communities (as attested to by the success of Nabil Ben Yadir's comedy *The Barons/Les Barons*, 2009)" (Block and Szaniawski 2013: 7). Actor and director Ben Yadir (b. 1979, Brussels), is a "Bruxellois of Moroccan origin" (Costanzo and Zibouh 2014: 72–74).

By focusing on the members of Mounir's family who illicitly arrive in Belgium from Morocco, *A perdre la raison* considers aspects of the Moroccan diaspora in twenty-first century Belgium as well as illegal immigration to Belgium from former francophone colonial regions. In *A perdre*, contemporary Belgian society becomes a metonym for the former colonizing powers of Western Europe. This is further emphasized by the film's setting of Brussels, the capital city of the European Union.

With Niels Arestrup and Tahar Rahim incarnating the roles of sixty-something Caucasian Belgian physician Pinget and his twenty-something Moroccan-born protégé Mounir, respectively, *A perdre la raison* brings these two actors back together after they "had previously been cast together in Jacques Audiard's critically acclaimed French prison drama *Un prophète* (*A Prophet*) (2009), for which each won a César: Arestrup for Best Supporting Actor and Rahim for Best Actor" (Block 2013: 17).

It has been noted that in *A perdre la raison*, Arestrup and Rahim somewhat recreate their onscreen relationship/partnership from Audiard's *Un prophète* (*A Prophet*). For example, in *Un prophète*, Arestrup, as the older inmate, takes on the ambiguous role of protective father figure to the younger prisoner played by Rahim (Brey 159; Edwards 181, note 21). In addition to noting the similarities between the Arestrup-Rahim pairing in Audiard's *Un prophète* and Lafosse's *A perdre la raison*, Iris Brey (159) comments upon the incestuous tension between the two men in *A perdre la raison*:

> La relation entre le Dr. Pinget et Mounir frôle l'inceste [...] Lafosse réussit à retranscrire une ambiguïté entre les deux hommes. Il montre que ce besoin et ce désir d'être toujours ensemble, de vivre ensemble et même d'inclure Pinget pendant le voyage de noce de Mounir, dénote d'une relation quasi incestueuse.
>
> [The relationship between Dr. Pinget and Mounir verges on incest [...] Lafosse succeeds in retranscribing an ambiguity between the two men. He shows that this need and this desire to always be together, to live together and even to include Pinget on Mounir's honeymoon denotes a quasi-incestuous relationship.] (Brey 158–159)

Along with this quasi-incestuous relationship between Dr. Pinget and Mounir in *A perdre la raison* that Brey describes above, Lafosse observes of his film that it is "'the story of a young woman who meets a young man who is already attached to another man'" (Lafosse, qtd. in Dawson 2013: 60).[3] Indeed, according to Natalie Edwards, Mounir's "hints of homoeroticism with André become more and more evident" (181) as the narrative of *A perdre la raison* unfolds. Lafosse's and Edwards' comments here highlight the triangular relationship between Murielle, Mounir, and Pinget foregrounded in *A perdre*, and Murielle's position as "trapped in the claustrophobic environment where the triangular relationship between her husband, the doctor, and herself negatively impacts her" (Block 2013: 17). Although Edwards finds that in *A perdre*, Mounir is "more nuanced than may first appear [...] since he is clearly torn between his desire to please Murielle and André [Pinget] in earlier sequences," ultimately Mounir engages in a "progressive abandonment of Murielle" (2015: 181).

---

3 On these points, see also Brey: "Murielle est elle aussi coincée par un mari qui est sous l'emprise d'un autre homme" ["Murielle is also trapped by a husband who is under the influence of another man"] (2014: 132); "De même, il existe entre Pinget et Mounir cette tension entre le tabou absolu de l'homosexualité issu de la culture marocaine et le désir omniprésent d'être ensemble" ["Similarly, between Pinget and Mounir there exists this tension between the absolute taboo of homosexuality stemming from Moroccan culture and the ubiquitous desire to be together"] (159).

Like its predecessor, Audiard's French film *Un prophète*, Lafosse's *A perdre la raison* received numerous accolades, particularly from the Belgian film industry. Lafosse's film was selected as Belgium's entry for Best Foreign Language Film for the 2013 Academy Awards.[4] It won Belgium's Magritte Awards for Best Film, Best Director (Joachim Lafosse), Best Actress (Emilie Dequenne), and Best Editing (Sophie Vercruysse) in 2013, as well as the 2012 André Cavens Award from the Belgian Film Critics Association for Best Film of the Year. In addition, for her starring turn in *A perdre la raison* as Murielle, a mother driven to infanticide, Emilie Dequenne received awards such as the Cannes Film Festival's Un Certain Regard Award for Best Actress, the FIPRESCI Prize for Best Actress at the 2013 Palm Springs International Film Festival, and the Best Actress Award at the Saint Petersburg International Film Festival.

Considering the contributions Lafosse (b. 1975, Uccle, Belgium), *A perdre la raison*'s director and co-writer has made – and continues to make – to Belgian cinema, Jeremi Szaniawski considers him "one of the most talented voices to have emerged from Belgian cinema in the 2000s" (2013b: 130). Lafosse's filmography, as notes Szaniawski, comprises a "cohesive corpus of introspective, heavily psychoanalysed films [...] consistently centered around dysfunctional familial nexuses" (2013b: 130). Since *A perdre la raison* examines a dysfunctional family dynamic and situation that ultimately ends in infanticide, the film emblematizes the preoccupations of Lafosse's cinematic *oeuvre*.

As Edwards notes, *A perdre la raison* places this "infanticide in relation to current discourses of motherhood, incorporating postcolonial and historical aspects" (176) since the family tragedy is inextricably intertwined with the colonial question, according to Brey (159). Yet, as Brey observes of *A perdre la raison*, "l'infanticide ne va pas se situer au centre du film de Lafosse, c'est la lente descente aux enfers de Murielle qui va l'être, qui comme son prénom l'indique, va s'emmurer dans un schéma familial étouffant" ["rather than the infanticide, it is Murielle's slow descent into hell which is at the center of Lafosse's film; as her first name indicates,[5] she will be immured in a stifling family situation"] (2014: 153–154). So too does Edwards find that the emphasis of *A perdre la raison* is "not the act of infanticide" (176), since Murielle's murder of her four children happens off-screen, a deliberate choice made by Lafosse (Dawson 56–57), which is, as I have previously discussed, "a decision based on classical theatre

---

4 *A perdre la raison* was not ultimately selected for an Oscar nomination, unlike Audiard's *Un prophète*, which was nominated to represent France for this prize at the 82nd Academy Awards in 2010. The 2010 Best Foreign Language Film Oscar was awarded to *El secreto de sus ojos* (*The Secret in their Eyes*) (Argentina, dir. Juan José Campanello).
5 In French, "mur" means "wall."

aesthetics" (Block 18). Indeed, as previously noted, "the offscreen violence in *A perdre la raison* is narrated in the film's final scene, when Murielle calls the police and confesses her crime – also stating that she was planning to commit suicide but could not bring herself to do so" (Block 2013: 19).

Brey finds that Lafosse's decision not to display the murders of the children onscreen, but rather, to place them off-screen "minimise bien le pouvoir de la mère, pour possiblement amplifier l'identification des femmes avec cette mère, mais aussi, peut-être, pour minimiser sa faute" ["minimizes the power of the mother, to possibly increase women's identification with this mother, but also, perhaps, to minimize her wrongdoing"] (2014: 151). In addition, this prevents spectatorial voyeurism "suscité par le cas Lhermitte, puisqu'il ne montre jamais ce que le voyeur aimerait voir et utilise le hors-champ pour filmer l'infanticide" ["inspired by the Lhermitte case, because Lafosse never shows what the voyeur would love to see and instead uses off-screen space to film the infanticide"] (Brey 155).

Yet even if their murders occur at the end of *A perdre la raison* and are not shown to the viewer, the deaths of Murielle and Mounir's four children – three young daughters Jade, Sohane and Malika, and baby boy Ali – are announced from the film's earliest moments. *A perdre la raison* begins with an opening scene of Murielle who pleads, from a hospital bed, for her children to be buried in Morocco, the birthplace of Murielle's husband Mounir, the children's father. The next sequence is a shot of four small white coffins – containing the children's corpses – being placed into an airplane for burial in Morocco. The children, as revealed at the film's end, were all stabbed to death at home by Murielle, one after the other, and therefore, as Brey observes,

> en commençant son film par le dénouement, Lafosse évacue toute curiosité malsaine sur la mort des enfants qui avait été décrite en détail dans les journaux [...] Lafosse annonce clairement le sort des enfants, l'attente du spectateur pourra donc se focaliser sur autre chose.
>
> [By beginning his film with the denouement, Lafosse evacuates all salacious curiosity about the deaths of the children which was described in detail in the press [...] Lafosse clearly announces the children's fate, so that the spectator's expectation can be focalized on other things.] (153)

As Brey mentions above, one such element of the film on which the spectator's attention is focalized – other than the infanticide – is how *A perdre la raison* paints Murielle in a sympathetic light as a victim of circumstance rather than as a monstrous mother (Edwards; Brey 2014, ch. 3). Along with her psychological unraveling, Murielle experiences domestic violence at the hands of her husband Mounir as well as Pinget.

One of *A perdre la raison*'s most explicit scenes of domestic violence occurs towards the end of the film, after Murielle, who fell asleep from exhaustion, failed to prepare dinner. After Pinget has left to buy pizza for the household, Mounir slaps Murielle across the face, claiming that she is ungrateful for all that Dr. Pinget has done for them, demanding that she show Pinget respect by shouting, "he pays for everything and now he has to buy us dinner, too?"

Yet Mounir's demand in this scene that Murielle show Pinget gratitude contrasts with an earlier instance of domestic violence, when Mounir subjects Murielle to marital rape by forcing her to have sex with him on Pinget's bed (during the doctor's absence) and thus disrespects Pinget. Murielle protests that she does not want to have sex with Mounir on Dr. Pinget's bed because "she feels uncomfortable in André's room" (Edwards 181). Yet, as Edwards further observes, this scene is part of the larger metaphorical colonization of the women in the film by Pinget since "although Mounir physically rapes Murielle, André's actions towards Mounir's sister, mother and territory portray him as a metaphorical rapist of the former colony" (185) of Morocco. In Brey's estimation, this scene also indicates how Mounir reproduces Pinget's behavior towards Murielle, as he is her doctor and thus determines the fate of Murielle's body (160).

As demonstrated by these scenes of domestic violence, *A perdre la raison* does "present a compelling case for compassion" (176) for Murielle, as Edwards claims, since Murielle's "situation is beyond her control [and therefore] the viewer can do nothing but sympathise" (186). Thus, rather than depicting Murielle as monstrous, according to Brey, *A perdre*,

> au contraire, fait de Murielle une femme inoffensive, agent du *caring*, pour qui le spectateur a de la sympathie [...] une femme douce qui peu à peu se retrouve coincée dans un schéma de famille dysfonctionnelle.

> [On the contrary, [the film] makes Murielle an inoffensive woman, an agent of caring, for whom the spectator has sympathy [...] a gentle woman who little by little finds herself trapped in a pattern of family dysfunction.] (152)

This sympathetic characterization of Murielle is further evident in one of the film's most powerful sequences (Edwards 179), during which Murielle "breaks down [...] and cries uncontrollably at the roadside" (179) to a song on the car radio, Julien Clerc's "Femmes je vous aime" ("Women, I Love You") (1982). Clerc's eulogy to women proclaims:

> Femmes, je vous aime
> Femmes, je vous aime
> Je n'en connais pas de faciles
> Je n'en connais que de fragiles

Et difficiles
Oui, difficiles

[Women, I love you
Women, I love you
I don't know any easy ones
I only know fragile ones
And difficult
Yes, difficult].

Clerc's song, "un des classiques de la variété française, et propose une vision simpliste de la femme [...] une des chansons françaises les plus essentialiste sur les femmes" ["a classic of French popular music, which proposes a simplistic vision of women [...] one of the most essentialist French songs about women"] (Brey 169), in which he "sings about his love and fascination for women, how they are all unique, 'si douces' ['so gentle'] but 'si dures' ['so tough']" (Edwards 179), recalls Brey's discussion above of *A perdre*'s representation of Murielle as "une femme douce" ["a gentle woman"]. In addition, as I have previously noted of this moment in *A perdre la raison*,

> Clerc's song resonates with Murielle, as she feels unloved and abandoned while Clerc expresses love for and eulogizes women precisely for being, like her, fragile and difficult [...] Murielle, who identifies with such women, does not receive the reward of love that is, in Clerc's song, to be showered upon them [...] Her husband, who abuses her, is certainly not singing her praises. (Block 2013: 19)

Brey finds that the emotional depth of Dequenne's performance as Murielle in this scene is what led her to win the Un Certain Regard Best Actress Prize at Cannes in 2012 (169). Furthermore, in Edwards' estimation, "the length of the scene is almost unbearable, as we watch this isolated, desperate woman singing for almost four minutes about how other women are loved [...] Of course, we know from the structure of the film that no end to her suffering will eventuate" (179).

When Murielle listens to and sings along with Clerc's song "Femmes, je vous aime," she feels excluded from the community of women that he eulogizes. If the radio had instead played Françoise Hardy's song "Tous les garçons et les filles" ["All the Boys and Girls"] (1962), perhaps Murielle would have had a different reaction. She may have been able to seek comfort and consolation, as well as find commiseration with this female voice singing about how she feels unloved and abandoned as she moves alone through life, unlike all the other people of her age group: "Oui mais moi, je vais seule par les rues, l'âme en peine/Oui mais moi, je vais seule, car personne ne m'aime" ["Yes, but me, I walk alone in the streets, my soul in pain/ Yes but me, I go alone, since no one loves me"]. Perhaps Murielle would have found solidarity with Hardy's lyrics rather than experience the feelings of abjection brought about by listening to Clerc's "Femmes, je vous aime."

Moreover, of the sympathy that Murielle's suffering – including that on display in the "Femmes je vous aime" sequence – elicits in the film's viewers, Brey notes that

> le spectateur s'identifie à Murielle, personnage sympathique et attachant, et c'est là que réside la force politique du film [...] Lafosse réussit à faire de sa mère infanticide une mère à laquelle le spectateur peut s'identifier.
>
> [The spectator identifies with Murielle, a sympathetic and endearing character, which is where the film's political strength lies [...] Lafosse succeeds in making of this infanticidal mother a mother with whom the spectator can identify.] (140; 172)

As Edwards and Brey discuss above, it is not Murielle who is *A perdre la raison*'s antagonist. Murielle's heinous act of violence against her children, is, as the film's original French title suggests, an act perpetrated by someone who "took leave of her senses," or is of diminished mental capacity: "comme le rappelle le titre du film, elle a perdu la raison" ["as the film's title reminds us, she lost her mind"] (Brey 172). As Edwards observes of the murder of her children, "by the final scene in which she calls the children upstairs one by one in silence, we know that she has moved beyond the limits of the rational" (2015: 178), and she is, in Lafosse's estimation, "in a psychotic state when she carrie[s] out the murders" (Lafosse qtd. in Dawson 60).

Rather, the enemy depicted in *A perdre la raison* is Dr. Pinget, whose animosity toward Murielle increases throughout the film's narrative unfolding until its unbearable conclusion. *A perdre*'s Pinget is the enemy within, whose control over Murielle extends to her domicile, her mind, and her body, of which, in Brey's view, he has dispossessed her (131). Pinget, as "le colon qui domine Mounir et sa famille" ["the colonist who dominates Mounir and his family"] (Brey 159) and "the senior, white-haired patriarch [...] styled as the embodiment of France, colonising the Moroccan family, land and, especially, women" (Edwards 185), represents the larger patriarchal system that has colonized and victimized Murielle, akin to how it colonized and victimized Mounir's native Morocco. As notes Brey in her comparison of Medea and *A perdre*'s Murielle, whether "dans la pièce d'Euripide ou le film de Lafosse, la mère devient victime d'un système patriarcal" ["in the play by Euripides or in the film by Lafosse, the mother becomes the victim of a patriarchal system"] (131–132).

Indeed, Pinget exemplifies how "one man can be an occupying power," who "controls and corrupts even in his efforts to assist, plundering the sanity of his subjects" (Lane 2013) – most especially that of Murielle, which rapidly declines over the course of the film, setting in motion the events that lead to *A perdre*'s final moments when she murders her children before nearly committing suicide.

This dreadful turn of events brings to mind the real-life infanticide committed by Susan Smith in the United States in 1991, who "drowned her two young sons in a South Carolina lake [and] stated that she was planning to kill herself along with her two infant sons, but did not" (Block 2013: 18–19). In addition to recalling the Susan Smith case, *A perdre la raison*, although fictional, was, in Lafosse's own words in an interview for the film's press release "freely inspired" (*A perdre la raison* press kit) by the true event of the Lhermitte infanticides in Belgium (as discussed above). Lhermitte, who, like Murielle in *A perdre la raison*, had worked as a schoolteacher and whose husband, Bouchaïb Moqadem, was born in Morocco (akin to *A perdre*'s Mounir), received a life sentence. As Edwards observes about the intersection of *A perdre la raison* and the Lhermitte murders,

> Lafosse makes explicit the connection between his film and lived reality. As the final scene of *A perdre la raison* fades to black and the credits roll, we read 'Cette oeuvre de fiction n'a pas pour objet de relater avec exactitude le fait divers dont elle est inspirée' [i.e. 'This fictional film does not claim to accurately portray the events on which it is loosely based'] as a chilling reminder that this fictional representation is rooted in a real-life occurrence. (Edwards 186)

Indeed, as I have noted in a previous context, "parallels can be drawn between the Lhermitte infanticides and those in the fictitious film *A perdre la raison*," since

> Lhermitte, a former schoolteacher, and her husband, Bouchaïb Moqadem (born in Morocco), lived with Moqadem's Belgian sponsor/father figure, Michel Schaar, a doctor who had his medical office in their shared home. The similarities between *Our Children* and the Lhermitte case led Moqadem and Schaar to file a lawsuit against Lafosse, claiming violation of privacy and demanding to review his script, when the film's production was already underway (Lafosse refused). (Block 2013: 15)

Because Lafosse's *A perdre la raison* intersects with these real events of the Lhermitte infanticides, the film was met with controversy in Lafosse's native Belgium, where "despite receiving praise [the film] polarized critics and viewers [...] even more so because only five years separate the film from the actual Lhermitte murders, which impacted Belgian collective memory" (Block 17). Indeed, Brey observes that, "en adaptant un fait-divers qui avait secoué son pays, Lafosse a fait face à de virulentes oppositions comme si son film allait salir l'identité

Belge" ["in adapting a news item that shook his country, Lafosse faced virulent opposition, as if his film were going to besmirch Belgian identity"] (232).

Although *A perdre la raison* is based on the true event of the Lhermitte infanticides, Lafosse also likens the narrative of his film to a Greek tragedy (Dawson 58), which recalls that his decision not to show the children's murders onscreen is also reminiscent of classical Greek tragedy (which is recuperated by Jean Racine in his seventeenth-century French adaptations of Greek classics). Another element of *A perdre la raison* which is reminiscent of Greek tragedy is the presence of an augur, who appears, in Lafosse's film, in the form of a little boy, namely Murielle's pupil, who, after she yells at him and throws him out of the classroom, eerily predicts that she will do harm to her children. In this sequence, Murielle's "earlier maternal behaviour towards her pupils evaporates and [...] while heavily pregnant with her fourth child, she screams at a pupil unnecessarily. In a moment of sinister foreboding, which will not be lost on the viewer who knows the ending, the boy yells 'je plains votre gosse' ['I feel sorry for your child']" (Edwards 180). This pivotal moment in the film embodies the phrase "la vérité sort de la bouche des enfants" ("out of the mouths of babes") since this young boy is the only character in the film who seems to predict the tragic fate of Murielle's children at her hands.

Scholars and critics have furthermore compared *A perdre*'s protagonist Murielle to Medea. Brey considers *A perdre la raison* as "cette adaptation moderne du mythe de Médée [...] La Murielle dans *À perdre la raison* de Lafosse devient la résurgence de la Médée de la tragédie antique" ["this modern adaptation of the myth of Medea [...] The Murielle of Lafosse's *A perdre la raison* becomes the resurgence of the Medea of ancient tragedy"] (35; 137).[6] Lafosse notes that the genesis of his film was when he heard about the Lhermitte murders on the radio:

> [O]n the radio I heard about this real-life story of a mother – a teacher called Geneviève Lhermitte – who had killed her five children, one by one by cutting their throats, before attempting to commit suicide [...] what this woman did was unthinkable, unimaginable, I followed the case [...] I wasn't interested in telling the factual truth about what happened or showing the reality of what she did [...] People have asked me what is and what isn't true in the film. [...] it's a pure fiction [...] It's a Greek tragedy, and it's important to establish that from the beginning. (qtd. in Dawson 2013: 59)

---

[6] On this point, see also Brey (ch. 3; 131–140) as well as Edwards: "The condition of exile and the space of unfamiliarity that the mythical figure [Medea] was unable to overcome are echoed in *A perdre la raison*" (185–186).

Along with the element of Greek tragedy, another aspect of the Lhermitte case that intrigued Lafosse was the role played by Dr. Michel Schaar – Moqadem's sponsor/father figure – in Lhermitte's life and how Schaar's influence negatively impacted Lhermitte, Moqadem, and their children. According to Lafosse,

> [...] nobody seemed capable of seeing the power of the doctor in this story, the difficulty the Mounir character had resisting this man, and the consequences for his wife and family. People want to deny that it was anything to do with neocolonialism. The doctor pays for the house, the car, the holidays, the kids' clothes and he's the husband's boss: one has to ask why he is doing all this. People would tell me he had good intentions. The question for me to ask is: what is for the better and what is for the worse? What's scary is that the bad came out of the good: good intentions lead to the tragedy. (qtd. in Dawson 60)

Lafosse's *A perdre la raison* approaches these topics, including the neocolonial aspect, by foregrounding the fictional character of Dr. Pinget, who seems to play a similar role in the lives of Murielle, Mounir and their children as that of Dr. Schaar in the real Moqadem/Lhermitte household.

A perdre la raison focuses not only on Pinget's contentious relationship to Murielle, but also on how Mounir and Murielle gradually succumb into total dependence upon Pinget. According to Lafosse, "'the subject that really interested me was the loss of freedom for this young couple Murielle and Mounir, and how power was exerted over them by the doctor [Pinget]. What you have, in effect, is neocolonialism'" (qtd. in Dawson 60). Lafosse's claim here and above about neocolonialism is reinforced by Edwards, who finds that "the character of Murielle may be located in a specific geographical, historical and neo-colonial context" (186) as well as by Brey, who notes that Lafosse places "cette mère infanticide dans un contexte postcolonial" ["places this infanticidal mother in a postcolonial context"] (35–36).

In many respects, Dr. Pinget's relationship to Mounir and Murielle can be said to represent the legacy of colonial history in the present-day, since, as I have previously observed,

> remnants of the recent colonial past can be inferred in *Our Children*, as the white, Belgian, sixty something Dr. Pinget behaves as if Mounir, whom he had brought to Belgium, belongs to him and that Mounir 'owes' Pinget for his assistance in obtaining citizenship papers for his sister, as well as employment, lodging and financial support. A parallel can be drawn between the paternalistic Pinget and the European colons when Morocco was a French protectorate. Therefore, Pinget behaves as if he were the 'protector' of two individuals from Morocco, Mounir and Fatima [Mounir's sister]. Furthermore, Pinget is under the impression that his protectorate extends to Murielle, whom he also dominates financially and psychologically, stifling her. (Block 17–18)

Pinget's relationship to Mounir – and by extension to Murielle and their children – functions as a paternalistic arrangement that, as the film unfolds, increasingly recalls and mimics colonial oppression. As Edwards notes: "the representation of the legacy of colonialism and its connections with the maternal is [...] poignant in *A perdre la raison*. The vehicle for this depiction is the figure of André [Pinget] and his relationship to Mounir's Moroccan family" (185). According to Brey, in *A perdre*, "le dysfonctionnement familial est intimement lié à la question coloniale [...] il [Pinget] les domine" ["the family dysfunction is intimately linked to the colonial question [...] he [Pinget] dominates them"] (159).

Examples of how Pinget "dominates" the family, especially Murielle, include how he "controls every aspect of Murielle's life: he is her medical doctor, he robs her of her agency as a wife and mother [...] he forces Murielle to accept his dominion [...] Murielle's attempts at independence from Pinget are futile and immediately quashed, such as her desire to move her family to Morocco" (Block 18). Mounir's birthplace of Morocco functions as an escape for Murielle, where she experiences a respite from her troubles at home during a family trip there to visit Mounir's mother, Rachida (Brey 159): "les seuls moments où Murielle va sembler heureuse sont lorsqu'elle est avec sa belle mère, notamment lorsqu'elle lui rend visite au Maroc" ["the only moments when Murielle appears to be happy are when she is with her mother-in-law, notably when she visits her in Morocco"] (Brey 165).

Brey observes that Morocco represents "la seule terre d'asile possible pour Murielle" ["the only possible safe haven for Murielle"] (164), even though Morocco is "un pays qui a été colonisé, sous l'emprise d'une culture patriarcale très forte" ["a country that was colonized, under the influence of a very strong patriarchal culture"] (164). Murielle's hopes to move to Morocco – as she is fascinated by the country and its culture (161), which for her represents "un lieu d'utopie [...] alors que la culture marocaine pourrait, au contraire, symboliser l'oppression des femmes" ["a utopian place [...] while Moroccan culture could, to the contrary, symbolize the oppression of women"] (165)[7] – are dashed by Dr. Pinget. Yet Morocco will become the final resting place of Murielle and Mounir's children.

In its portrayal of Pinget, a Caucasian Belgian citizen who brings illegal immigrants from former francophone colonized regions to Belgium, the subject matter of Lafosse's *A perdre la raison* recalls some examples of Belgian cinema, such as the cinematic production of the internationally renowned iconic Belgian

---

[7] For further discussion of the representation of Morroco in *A perdre la raison* and its significance for Murielle, see Brey (161–171).

auteurs the Dardenne brothers, including their films *La Promesse* (*The Promise*) (1996), hailed as "Belgium Year Zero" by Dominique Nasta (2013: 113) and *Le silence de Lorna* (*Lorna's Silence*), as discussed above. These Dardenne films address similar issues in present-day Belgian society as those that are explored in Lafosse's *A perdre*.

For instance, the Dardennes' 1996 *La Promesse* (*The Promise*) – which "holds a place of unique importance in the annals of Belgian cinema," according to David Sterritt, as it "introduced the brothers as world-class auteurs" (Sterritt 2013: 118) – features Roger (Olivier Gourmand), a single father to his fifteen-year-old son Igor (Jérémie Renier). The relationship between Roger and Igor depicted in the Dardennes' *La Promesse* somewhat parallels that of Dr. Pinget and Mounir in Lafosse's *A perdre la raison*. Although "Le Dr. Pinget n'a pas d'enfant biologique" ["Dr. Pinget has no biological children"] nonetheless "il fait figure de père pour Mounir" ["he acts as a father to Mounir"] (Brey 157). Roger in *La Promesse* is "a trafficker who remorselessly exploits illegal immigrants in the Liège area" of Belgium (Nasta 113), employing them in dangerous jobs – such as construction work on his own house – while paying them exploitative wages and exposing them to harmful conditions, which become fatal for one of the migrants. Along similar lines as Roger in *La Promesse* , in *A perdre la raison*, Dr. Pinget also illicitly brings immigrants – members of Mounir's family from Morroco – to Belgium. Dr. Pinget does so by participating in and/or arranging phony green card marriages: he himself is married to Mounir's sister Fatima (Mounia Raouj) and later brings Mounir's brother, Samir (Redouane Behache), to Belgium through arranging Samir's marriage to Murielle's sister Françoise (Stéphane Bissot), again, in a fake green card situation. *A perdre la raison*'s emphasis on fraudulent marriages for illegal immigrants to Belgium recalls the Dardenne brothers' film *Le silence de Lorna*, which "foregrounds protagonist Lorna (Arta Dobroshi), an Albanian immigrant to Belgium, who is pulled into a vicious cycle of sham weddings orchestrated by the gangster Fabio (Fabrizio Rongione)" (Nasta 2013: 115).

As opposed to the undocumented immigrants in the Dardennes' *La Promesse* , who are forced to work as cheap labor and live in unsafe, substandard conditions provided for them by Roger, in Lafosse's *A perdre la raison*, Pinget gifts Mounir and Murielle a large home that comfortably houses them all together, and in which he himself not only resides alongside them and their four young children, but which also contains his medical practice.

However, this home, as Brey notes, becomes a prison for Murielle and her children, while simultaneously allowing Mounir and Dr. Pinget to live together, negatively impacting Murielle's role as Mounir's wife and the mother of his children (Brey 158–159). As I have previously stated, "Pinget, wielding power and control over the household, further alienates Murielle [...] the bond between the two men [Pinget and Mounir] makes Murielle feel estranged from their intimacy as she is left to raise her and Mounir's four children" (Block 17). Moreover, as Brey observes, Murielle "est complètement dépossédée de son corps, ce sont les hommes dans ce système patriarcal qui le contrôlent" ["is completely dispossessed of her body, since the men in this patriarchal system control it"] 159). Furthermore,

> Le corps de Murielle est utilisé à ses dépends [sic!], exploité jusqu'à ce qu'elle retombe enceinte. Là le corps reste en jachère jusqu'à ce qu'il puisse produire encore un autre fruit du désamour. Le corps incarne la terre dominée par le masculin, et renvoie le corps à un instrument pouvant produire des enfants.
>
> [Murielle's body is used at her own expense, exploited until she becomes pregnant again. There the body lies fallow until it can produce another fruit of hatred. The body incarnates the earth dominated by the masculine, and transforms the body into an instrument able to produce children.] (Brey 160)

This recalls Edwards' claim that in *A perdre la raison*, "the body of the mother is a contested space that is positioned uncomfortably between the two nations" (185) of Morocco and Belgium, and thus the film places "the representation of infanticide within a narrative of neo-colonialism" (185):

> Murielle's body is the perfect metaphor of the power of the patriarchal, colonizing force, since André [Pinget] exerts power, finances and influence over her body just as he does over Moroccan space. Read in this context, it is her status as a body of neo-colonisation that renders her position untenable [...] estranged from her French family and geographically, culturally and linguistically removed from her Moroccan family, Murielle is abandoned, misunderstood and powerless. (Edwards 185–186)

Murielle is further estranged from the quasi father-son pairing formed by Mounir and Pinget in *A perdre la raison*, since, according to Lafosse in an interview for the film's press kit, "these two men leave no room for Murielle" (*A perdre la raison* press kit). Moreover, according to Brey, "le manque de clarté autour des rôles joués dans la famille permet au Dr. Pinget d'avoir une emprise totale sur Mounir, et d'exclure Murielle de son rôle de femme ou d'amante" ["the lack of clarity around the roles played in the family allows Dr. Pinget to have total influence over Mounir, and to exclude Murielle from her role as wife or lover"] (158).

Dr. Pinget functions as Mounir's surrogate father, in what Lafosse, in an interview for the film's press kit, describes as an ambiguous relationship: "Doctor Pinget presents himself as Mounir's adoptive father but he isn't because he hasn't given him his name. That's why I would say instead that Mounir is Pinget's protégé, with all the ambiguity that entails" (*A perdre la raison* press kit). As in

Audiard's 2009 *Un prophète* (discussed above), in *A perdre la raison*, Rahim and Arestrup again "portray a co-dependent relationship between the older Dr. Pinget and his protégé Mounir" (Block 17).

The men's family ties in *A perdre la raison* are further strengthened by Pinget, who organizes a fake green card marriage between Mounir's sister Fatima and himself, in order to help her circumvent the intricacies of the immigration process from Morocco to Belgium. After Murielle's marriage to Mounir, she discovers – much to her surprise – that Pinget is married to Fatima, since Pinget has never cohabitated with his "wife" Fatima. Rather, as noted above, Pinget lives with Mounir and Murielle in the home in which his medical practice is also located. Edwards observes of Pinget's marriage to Fatima that this is a "relationship [...] clarified only when the family tell their story to Murielle after her wedding – and thus she is tied to them by law when she discovers it" (Edwards 185). Later in the film, Pinget arranges a green card or "paper" marriage for another relative of Mounir, namely his brother Samir. Pinget arranges for Samir to marry Murielle's divorced sister Françoise, so that Samir, along with his brother and sister, can leave Morocco to live and work in Belgium thanks to a marriage of convenience, like that of their sister Fatima.

These ties that bind Mounir and Murielle to Dr. Pinget are pulled even tighter by the marital arrangements between Pinget and Mounir's sister as well as between Mounir's brother and Murielle's sister: "les deux frères ont épousé les deux soeurs, et le père adoptif est en fait aussi le beau-frère" ["the two brothers married the two sisters, and the adoptive father is in fact also the brother-in-law"] (Brey 158). In Brey's estimation, this leads to repercussions for Murielle's status within the family: "Elle n'est plus épouse, elle n'est la fille de personne, elle n'est plus soeur mais belle-soeur puisque sa soeur fait un mariage blanc avec le frère de Mounir, et devient un être à qui il ne reste plus rien, à l'exception de ses enfants" ["She is no longer a wife, she is no one's daughter, she is no longer a sister but a sister-in-law because her sister entered into a green card marriage with Mounir's brother, and she becomes a being who has nothing left, with the exception of her children"] (162–163).

Thus, as Edwards states, by "marrying Mounir's sister to enable her immigration, employing Mounir, arranging the marriages of Murielle's sister and Mounir's brother, and buying a house in Morocco for the family [...] André [Pinget] has styled himself as the protector of Mounir's Moroccan family" (Edwards 185; see also Block 17, 18). Yet, not only is Dr. Pinget the self-styled "protector" of Mounir's family, but it is also as if Pinget were a puppeteer whose marionettes are the members of these families, but with the marionette strings tied around their necks:

> Toutes ces alliances glissées sur les doigts lors de ces mariages blancs, sont comme des cordes glissées autour du cou de chaque protagoniste qui se retrouve piégé par [...] Pinget [...] Ces alliances coupent la possibilité pour Murielle de se tourner vers l'extérieur puisque ses deux familles endogames sont contrôlées par Pinget.
>
> [All these wedding rings slipped on fingers during these 'white marriages' [e. g. green card marriages] are like ropes slipped around the neck of each protagonist who finds himself trapped by [...] Pinget [...]. These marriages prevent Murielle from turning towards the exterior, since these two endogamous families are controlled by Pinget.] (Brey 158)

At Mounir's brother Samir's wedding to Murielle's sister Françoise, Rachida (Beya Belal), the mother of Fatima, Mounir, and Samir, gives a heartfelt speech to Dr. Pinget in which she expresses her gratitude to him for all he has done for her family. As Edwards observes of Rachida, "her story hints at underlying suffering. No mention is made of her three children's father and she has clearly raised them alone and in poverty; her three children, especially the two sons, are desperate to leave Morocco for France [e. g. Belgium] and only when André [Pinget] appeared, we surmise, did this mother obtain the means to survive" (Edwards 183).

As opposed to Rachida's gratitude toward Pinget for his generosity, Murielle suffers under and is stifled by Pinget's constant presence and interference in her and Mounir's lives. It is as if Murielle, Mounir and by extension, their four children – as well as Mounir's sister Fatima and his brother, Samir – are Pinget's colonized subjects or possessions: "as 'parrain'/'godfather' of Murielle and Mounir's four children, Pinget functions as the head of this household, crushing any independence expressed by Murielle or Mounir" (Block 2013: 18). Not only is Pinget the godfather to Mounir and Murielle's children, but also, he is "agissant comme le paterfamilias dans sa propre maison où vivent le couple et leurs enfants" ["acting like the *paterfamilias* of his own house where the couple and their children live"] (Brey 157).

In the film, a conversation between Murielle and Dr. Declerck (Nathalie Boutefeu) – a colleague of Pinget to whom he has referred Murielle for counseling and therapy (Edwards 182) – demonstrates the depth of her subordination to Pinget:

> Murielle: Fatima, Mounir's sister, has been married to Dr. Pinget for years. Her name's Pinget but they don't live together and there's never been any problem.
> Dr. Declerck: You mean Dr. Pinget is this André that you often mention? Dr. Pinget, your family doctor? You live with your family doctor? [...] I can't work with a colleague who shares your life.
> Murielle: I don't live with him, he just shares our house.
> Dr. Declerck: Your family doctor sends you here, you're living with him, under the same

roof, okay. You go on holiday with him. He's your husband's adoptive father and your sister-in-law's husband. And he bought the house where he keeps on living with you.
Murielle: And he's bought a house in Morocco, too.
Dr. Declerck: I can't work with Dr. Pinget anymore.

Dr. Declerck's comments and observations in this scene demonstrate the numerous professional and ethical norms and boundaries that Pinget has crossed and broken in his interactions with Murielle and her family. Indeed, Pinget is fully aware of his professional and ethical transgressions, as he expressly forbade Murielle from telling Dr. Declerck that he lives with Murielle, Mounir, and the children, but rather to say that "qu'il était seulement son médecin traitant" ["he was only her attending physician"] (Brey 162). This dialogue between Murielle and Declerck also shows how unusual, problematic, and even disturbing Pinget's guardianship over Murielle appears to an outside observer who learns about her family situation and living arrangements.

In addition, in this scene, Murielle's excuses for Pinget's behavior towards her and her family show how he has colonized not only her home and her body, but also her mind, as she attempts to defend and justify his behavior to Dr. Declerck by claiming that, "I don't live with him, he just shares our house." Yet this statement is not accurate, as Pinget is shown throughout the film as an active member of the household and participant in the children's lives. Pinget's encroaching influence upon Mounir and Murielle is all encompassing and inescapable, exacerbating Murielle's already declining mental state as she is financially dependent on Pinget (Brey 162), since she no longer works as a schoolteacher: "Murielle devient l'esclave de la maison, Pinget lui dit d'arrêter de travailler pour mieux s'occuper du foyer et des enfants" ["Murielle becomes the slave of the house, Pinget tells her to stop working to better care of her home and her children"] (Brey 162). According to Edwards in her discussion of Murielle in *A perdre*, the "film shows her repeatedly enclosed in the dark kitchen and laundry room, juggling her household tasks against the backdrop of the screaming infants. Hardly ever venturing beyond the space of the home, she is gradually more confined in the expectation that she conform to the model of the perfect housewife" (180).

Of Murielle's relationship to Dr. Declerck, Edwards observes that as Murielle is "abandoned by individuals and institutions,"

> her only recourse is André's colleague, a psychologist who tells Murielle that her relationship with André imposes restrictions on the contact they may have. At the very end of the story [of *A perdre la raison*], she calls the psychologist [...] Speaking into the void of an answer machine, she says: 'J'ai des idées noires, j'ai peur pour les enfants [...] Je me sens emmurée ici.' ['I have dark ideas, I am scared for the children [...] I feel trapped here.'] André's

rage when he learns of this from the psychologist guarantees Murielle's silence and she kills the children shortly afterwards. (Edwards 182)

Pinget's control and "rage" against Murielle, as discussed above, manifests itself in his engaging in domestic violence against her. Some examples of the emotional abuse Pinget inflicts upon her include when he belittles her skills as a mother by telling her that she is an embarrassment to her children when she cheers loudly for them at a school play or that she looks ridiculous when she wears the *djellaba*, the traditional Moroccan gown that Rachida gave her (Brey 2014: 166). This is an item of clothing which, according to Brey, "représente la possibilité d'échapper à la Belgique, sa prison, pour apparentir au Maroc [...] un pays que Murielle perçoit comme synonyme de liberté" ["represents the possibility of escaping Belgium, her prison, to belong to Morocco [...] a country that Murielle perceives as synonymous with liberty"] (167–168).[8] This includes financial freedom, since the standard of living in Morocco is substantially lower than in Belgium. Therefore, Mounir and Murielle could live well there on only one income, unlike in Belgium, where they are forced to continue to depend upon Pinget's financial support indefinitely.

A perdre la raison portrays this convergence of the deadly "'factors and circumstances'" (Lafosse, qtd. in Dawson 60) – such as Pinget's acrimonious relationship towards and abuse of Murielle as well as the quasi-incestuous and homoerotic (Edwards 181) relationship between Pinget and Mounir – "'[that] combine to make somebody behave'" (Lafosse, qtd. in Dawson 60) the way Murielle does. Murielle's "growing psychological distress is presented as steadily more glaring" (Edwards 177), leading her on a downward "psychological spiral" (Edwards 178) that culminates in infanticide. *A perdre la raison* thus not only depicts Pinget as the enemy within Murielle's home, within her body, and within her mind, but also, in investigating "how a society could better protect the lives of the most vulnerable human beings in order to prevent their victimization" (Block 19), *A perdre la raison* brings Belgium's "recent tragic events to the forefront, interrogating the factors that triggered them" (Block 19) as well as how the legacy of francophone colonialism continues to be felt in present-day Belgium.

---

8 For further discussion of the significance of Murielle's *djeballa* in *A predre la raison*, see Brey (166–171).

Works Cited

"Interview with Joachim Lafosse" press kit for *A perdre la raison* <http://medias.unifrance.org/medias/66/56/79938/presse/a-perdre-la-raison-dossier-de-presse-anglais.pdf> (accessed 15 June 2017).

Block, Marcelline (2013) "Award of the Year: *Our Children/A Perdre la raison*," in *The Directory of World Cinema: Belgium*, ed. Marcelline Block and Jeremi Szaniawski (Bristol: Intellect), 15–19.

Brey, Iris (2014) *Les Mères déchaînées dans le cinéma français et francophone post-2000, chez Arnaud Desplechin, Christophe Honoré, Joachim Lafosse et Claire Denis* (PhD Diss., New York University).

Bousetta, Hassan (2008) "New Moroccan Migrants in Belgium," *Journal of Immigrant & Refugee Studies* 6. 3, 397–408.

Costanzo, Joseph, and Fatima Zibouh (2014) "Mobilisation Strategies of Individual and Institutional Actors in Brussels' Artistic and Cultural Scenes," in *Multiculturalism and the Arts in European Cities*, ed. Marco Martiniello (London and New York: Routledge), 56–82.

Edwards, Natalie (2015) "Obliged to Sympathise: Infanticide in *Il y a longtemps que je t'aime* and *A perdre la raison*," *Australian Journal of French Studies* 52. 2, 174–187.

Fairfax, Daniel (2013) "*Lorna's Silence*" in *The Directory of World Cinema: Belgium*, ed. Block and Szaniawski, 125–126.

Dawson, Thomas (2013) "Fear Eats the Soul," *Sight and Sound* 23. 6, 58–60.

Lane, Anthony (2013) "Beyond Control: *Elysium* and *Our Children*," <http://www.newyorker.com/magazine/2013/08/12/beyond-control> (accessed 15 June 2017).

Nasta, Dominique, with Mathieu Pereira e Iglesias (2013) "The Dardenne Brothers," trans. Marcelline Block and Jeremi Szaniawski, in *The Directory of World Cinema: Belgium*, ed. Block and Szaniawski, 111–116.

Sojcher, Frédéric (2013) "Small Country, Great Cinema? Anatomy of Belgian Cinema," trans. Marcelline Block, in *The Directory of World Cinema: Belgium*, ed. Block and Szaniawski, 20–23.

Sterritt, David (2013) "The Promise," in *The Directory of World Cinema: Belgium*, ed. Block and Szaniawski, 117–118.

Szaniawski, Jeremi (2013a) "Charles Dekeukeleire," in *The Directory of World Cinema: Belgium*, ed. Block and Szaniawski, 45–49.

Szaniawski, Jeremi (2013b) "Other Belgian Auteurs," in *The Directory of World Cinema: Belgium*, ed. Block and Szaniawski, 129–131.

Filmography

A perdre la raison (Our Children) (2012) Dir. Joachim Lafosse (Versus production).

Mario Ranalletti
The Past as Enemy in Argentine Cinema, 1983–2000

> I am afraid of the encounter
> with the past that returns to confront my life
> [...] But the traveler that flees
> sooner or later stops his walking [...].[1]

This chapter analyses how Argentine cinema during the transition to democracy after 1983 dealt with the figure of the enemy. As I want to argue, depictions of the enemy in the films here analyzed are not in principle contradictory to previous constructs: in the new democratic era, too, the enemy is still 'the subversive.' Indeed, the representation of the enemy in Argentine movies has always been connected to a larger topic, namely the representation of the recent past, and here especially of the 1970s. In this chapter, I want to show how representations of the enemy evolved mainly in consequence of the vicissitudes met by the social and judicial search for truth and justice after the repression during the last military dictatorship (1976–1983) in Argentina.

Novels, plays and films dealing with the dictatorship have emphasized how the junta legitimized their seizure of power as a 'war' against 'International Communism.' This is evident in high-impact films such as *La historia oficial* (*The Official Story*) (dir. Luis Puenzo, 1985), *La noche de los lápices* (*Night of the Pencils*) (dir. Héctor Olivera, 1985), *La República perdida* (*The Lost Republic*) (dir. Miguel Pérez, 1983) and *La República perdida II* (*The Lost Republic II*) (dir. Luis Gregorich and Miguel Pérez, 1984). However, there are also films with less impact in terms of audience but of high aesthetic quality, such as *Un muro de silencio* (*A Wall of Silence*) (dir. Lita Stantic, 1990), and *Garage Olimpo* (*Olimpo Parking*) (dir. Marco Bechis, 2000), which will also be considered here.

1 The Construction of the Enemy in Twentieth-Century Argentina

The figure of the enemy was a key element in Argentine political culture during the twentieth century. As an ideological construction, this figure nourished an

---
1 "To Return," Tango by Carlos Gardel (music) and Alfredo Lepera (lyrics), 1935.

https://doi.org/10.1515/9783110591217-013

imaginary of social destructiveness, creating a negative otherness: 'the subversive,' or 'the internal enemy.' For the upper and middles classes, this enemy threatened a national (and Catholic) Argentine identity. During the past century, the enemy's figure changed: the anarchists in the 1910s, the Jews in the 1920s, Communist workers in the 1930s, Peronist left-wing and Marxist guerrillas in 1960–1970. Since 1955, right-wing and religious extremists, through conferences, courses, informal talks, Catholic Church sermons, and spiritual retreats, brainwashed the military and police officers, using aggressive propaganda and mystifications of reality. The message was that the enemy was hidden in society, camouflaged among civilians and working every day to destroy Argentina's Catholic identity through different means. Given this, no negotiation was possible: the only solution was the enemy's total annihilation, for 'God and Fatherland,' as the indoctrinators claimed (O'Donnell 1988; Ranalletti 2001). In this imaginary of social destructiveness, the hidden enemy could be a school teacher, a college student, a housewife, a worker or a guerrilla fighter. It is important to take into account that it was not necessary to be a guerrilla member to be considered as a hidden enemy. This hidden enemy was named by many names: 'the Marxist subversion,' 'communism,' or simply 'the subversion.' This enemy, for the military and their civilian allies, was a 'local agent' of a global plot for world domination led by 'International Communism.'

The 1955–1976 period is marked by a progressive use of extreme violence by the armed forces and the police. The return of a Peronist government in 1973 launched a final escalation of violence. On 24 March 1976, the military took power. This military coup established the most repressive political system in Argentinian history. For the military and their civilian allies, the time had come to finish off the 'subversion.' A still undetermined number of people targeted as enemies (from 10,000 to 30,000) were abducted, tortured, and murdered. In most cases, their bodies were destroyed or secretly buried (CONADEP 1991). In December 1983, the military regime left power after its defeat in the Malvinas/Falklands War, and democratic elections were called. Many Argentinians realized that the military they had acclaimed in 1976 as 'saviors,' and praised as winners against the evil 'subversion,' were the same that the investigations of the press and the human rights organizations revealed as perpetrators of appalling crimes against humanity. Reports accusing the military of abducting babies, massacres, rapes, torture (even of pregnant women and children), destruction of detainees' bodies, and other atrocities began appearing in the media daily (Osiel 2002). These atrocities trigger many questions, which will divide society once again, most importantly: who should take responsibility for these crimes? Who should pay for them? (Malamud Goti 1996).

2 Looking over the Recent Past in Argentinian Cinema: From Enthusiasm to Disenchantment (1983–1990)

Argentine cinema of the first years of the new democracy tried to render a truthful narrative about a past plagued by violence. This cinema proposed a new version of the recent past, based on a dichotomizing scheme: the violence of the clandestine repression was the answer to the guerrilla violence. The first films hint at death, clandestine repression and violence rather than speaking about them directly. State terrorism is something only whispered about, narrated metaphorically, placed in an indeterminate time, and it is only comprehensible for those who have lived this experience. The cinema of those years represents a search for keys to an understanding of what had happened. The first democratic elections since 1952 decisively stimulated the film industry, now liberated from censorship (Burucúa 2009). In this narrative, which were the place and the representation of the enemy's figure?

The first film about the recent past that dealt with the issue of the country's enemy and had a great impact on the public was a documentary: *La República Perdida* (*The Lost Republic*), directed by Luis Gregorich and Miguel Pérez. Released on 1 September 1983, this film invited the audience to look back and reflect upon the past. *La República Perdida*, which originated with a team connected to the *Radical Civil Union*, the party that had won the elections of 30 October 1983, is a compilation based on research in film archives. The film proposes a dual perspective – 'right' and 'wrong' – on Argentine history between 1928 and 1976. It tries to define the right and wrong choices, with a clear political and didactic intention: to show to Argentinians the mistakes made in the past in order to prevent their repetition in the future. *La República Perdida* consists primarily of previously unreleased footage and archival documents (cinema and television newsreel, advertising, cartoons, photographs, magazine illustrations), but without interviews or testimonies; an off narration accompanies its 146 minutes, seeking to create an objective frame for the images. The research for the film (carried out when the military were still in power) rescued a large number of archival images the military would have considered dangerous and subversive.

The film offers a tour through twentieth-century Argentine history. It begins in 1928, with the second administration of radical president Hipólito Yrigoyen and ends in 1976, at the beginning of the last military dictatorship. The film highlights what it considers as assets and failures of the two most important political movements of the country: Radicalism and Peronism. *La República Perdida* tries to define the first as the democratic foundation of the political system and the second as representative of the laboring classes, but also as the source of antidemocratic attitudes.

La República Perdida had a significant impact on audiences, who appreciated the originality of its images. For Argentinians, it was the disclosure of that part of the national history which the military had tried to keep in the dark. Later, the film would be widely used by history teachers in high schools, besides being frequently screened on public television. In *La República Perdida*, the enemy is authoritarianism, represented by the *coups d'état* that took place in the country during the twentieth century (1930, 1943, 1955, 1962, 1966, 1976). Due to this repeated rupture of the institutional order, the Argentinians had lost their republic. The last Peronist government (1973–1976) plays a privileged role at the end of the film, appearing as mainly responsible for the 1976 *coup d'état*. The political intention is clear in the context of the concurrent electoral campaign: the enemy is the return of the past, that is to say, Peronism. The recent military dictatorship and its record of mass murder are only mentioned in the last two minutes of the film, with barely a reference to the disappeared. For *La República Perdida*, the enemy is the renewal of past 'mistakes': authoritarianism, political violence and military rule. One month later, a fiction film dealt with the period 1973–1976, providing one of the most important keys to understanding the fall into Argentina's last dictatorship. It is *No habrá más penas ni olvido* (*Funny Dirty Little War*), directed by Héctor Olivera and released a few days before the elections of 30 October 1983. Based on a novel by Osvaldo Soriano, and set in an imaginary country at no specific time period, Olivera's film is about the political struggle in a little village, "Colonia Vela." In this mostly metaphorical film, the references to State violence are stronger than in *La República Perdida*. The plot develops around Ignacio Fuentes (played by the popular Argentine actor Federico Luppi), the Peronist mayor of Colonia Vela, who is accused by some inhabitants of 'subversion.' The accusation states that the mayor is not a real Peronist, but an undercover Communist agent. Some people in Colonia Vela believe the accusation, while many others support the mayor, who does not take the accusations seriously himself, due to his staunch Peronist convictions, believing that the whole matter will soon be forgotten. However, as divisions between those who accuse the mayor and those who support him widen, the conflict turns violent.

Fuentes represents the enemy in the sense of a Communist hidden behind a false adherence to Peronism. It does not matter that the village has known him from times immemorial: the accusation is a stigma from which he will not be able to free himself in time. As a result, his unavoidable destiny is to be exterminated by the armed and police forces, who are trying to save the nation from falling under 'atheist and unpatriotic' Communism. This aim also justifies the violent means used by his opponents to overcome the destitution represented by the mayor. There is a parallel to *La República Perdida* in that the last Peronist government is to a large extent held responsible for the violence that Argentina was to see after the 1976 *coup d'état*. This is the violence that in *No habrá más penas ni olvido* quickly grows from insults and suspicions to murder and torture.

The extreme violence of the campaign against the mayor is uneasily mitigated by the use of humor and the grotesque. In one of the film's most famous scenes, when Fuentes and his allies are locked up in the Town Hall, surrounded by his enemies, Juan (played by Miguel Angel Solá) – one of Fuentes's allies – suggests requesting airborne help. Juan appeals to Cerviño (played by Ulises Dumont) – a drunkard who, when sober, piloted a fumigating airplane. Cerviño accepts to help Fuentes, and he uses as a "weapon" against the latter's enemies a load of dung which he drops on them from above. However, this intervention from the skies does not stop Fuentes's enemies from entering the town hall, killing some of the Fuentes group and taking the mayor prisoner. After that, Fuentes and all his followers will be tortured to death.

3 Argentina's Recent Past in the Box-Office: *La historia oficial* and *La noche de los lápices*

1985 was an important year not only because of the premieres of both *La República Perdida* and *No habrá más penas ni olvido*, but mainly because it witnessed an unprecedented event in world history, namely that for the first time a sovereign nation put its own former dictatorial regime to trial. It was a judiciary process which, taking as its inspiration the Nuremberg trials, would bring to light that the so-called 'war' against a 'subversive enemy' was in fact a clandestinely executed massacre.

The trial was the beginning of a long search for justice and truth about the campaign of illegal repression promoted by the Argentine State between 1974 and 1983, a process which, with several advances and setbacks, has continued until today. In this trial, hundreds of former detainees recounted to the judges their experience in the secret detention centers: kidnapping, rape, torture and many other kinds of violence and humiliations. Hundreds of perpetrators also declared themselves before the judges, denying the facts or claiming that their atrocious actions had been committed for the defense of the Homeland and the Catholic religion, both threatened by the 'subversive enemy.'

Towards the end of 1985, the court passed sentence against the perpetrators and demanded that investigations continued, considering the extent of the crimes. The horrors which the trial revealed caused Jorge Luis Borges, who had supported the military dictatorship, to write in the newspaper *Clarín:*

> Of the many things that I listened to that afternoon, and that I expect to forget, I am going to speak about the one that for me was the most shocking, so as to get rid of it. It happened on December 24. All the prisoners were taken to a room where they had never been before. Quite surprised they saw a long table set with tablecloths, china dishes, cutlery and wine bottles. Afterwards the delicacies (I repeat the guest's words) arrived. It was the Christmas Eve dinner. They had been tortured and did not ignore that they were to be tortured next day. The Lord of that Hell came and wished them a Happy Christmas. It was not a joke, it was not a way to explain himself, it was not remorse. It was, as I said before, a kind of innocence of evil. (1985)

1985 also saw the release of those films about recent Argentine history that have gained the greatest publicity until today: *La historia oficial* by Luis Puenzo, and *La noche de los lápices* by Héctor Olivera. Released on 3 April 1985, Puenzo's film – co-scripted with writer Aida Bortnik, and with a cast including a number of popular local actors – won the Academy Award for Best Foreign Language Film in 1986. It broke the box-office record in 1985, with 884,608 spectators and also became a document widely used in History and Civic Education classes.

La historia oficial is recognized as being one of the first films dealing with issues concerning the military dictatorship, like the 'stolen babies' or the civilian support to the military regime. The plot of the film devolves around the story of Gaby, a four-year-old girl. She is the adopted daughter of Alicia (played by Norma Aleandro), a high-school teacher of history. Alicia's husband is Roberto (played by Héctor Alterio), a wealthy businessman with close connections to the military. The couple and their daughter live in a quiet, comfortably ordered world. However, their almost idyllic world will be shattered by questions about the past, whose hidden truths become the 'enemy' in this film.

Alicia is changed by a meeting with her best friend Ana (Chunchuna Villafañe), who has returned to the country after a long exile. Their reunion brings back happy memories, yet it also confronts Alicia with the State terrorism when she learns that Ana was tortured by the military, before being forced to go into exile. This contradicts, for the first time, what Alicia has believed to know about the past, and she now begins to find gaps and contradictions in the story of Gaby as told by her husband. Some of the facts are incomplete and confused, and this prompts Alicia to look for information about the origins of the child. Little by little, Alicia begins to suspect that the girl's biological parents were made to disappear during the repression by the armed and security forces in 1976. Alicia connects the history of her family with the social context: the end of the dictatorship, and the subsequent claim for justice and truth about the 'disappeared persons' during the last military dictatorship. Alicia is searching for the truth, yet she is also afraid, trying not to think that Roberto has lied about their adopted daughter.

In the course of her investigations into Gaby's origin, Alicia meets the relative of a disappeared person, who has been looking for years for a child born in captivity. This meeting, and the influence of Benítez (Patricio Contreras), a colleague and teacher of literature, finally convince her that Gaby's history is different from the story told by her husband. With the information she has obtained from hospitals and police stations about disappeared people and babies born in secret detention centers, Alicia decides to confront Roberto. When his story is challenged, Roberto reacts violently, first accusing her of being credulous as to the propagandist lies of those defeated by the military in the recent 'war against subversion,' and physically attacking her when she persists.

La historia oficial is a dramatic film of classical structure, avoiding the tone and spirit of denunciation typical of political Latin American cinema. Tensions in the couple are a filmic representation of those that divided different sectors of Argentine society in the period of the return to democracy. The destruction of a false past and the eruption of the truth seem to put an end to the peaceful world of Alicia's family. Alicia's character is a metaphor of Argentine society, immersed in discovering the cruel truth about the recent past.

The film and its script have been criticized for what was considered the negative role given to the knowledge of the truth about the past. If the classical figure of the enemy as 'subversion' – hidden in society – appears in the film in several dialogues, it can be said that knowing the truth about the dictatorship is the most important 'enemy' in *La historia oficial*. Puenzo's film makes it clear that to know the truth is not a process free from vicissitudes (Guebel 1986). To know the truth hidden by Roberto unleashes brutal violence against Alicia, due to her yearning for knowledge. Alicia is overwhelmed by her discovery of the truth about the military government, her husband's lies, the illegal repression and the stealing of babies. Many commentaries saw in Roberto's violence against Alicia a kind of warning: could searching for the truth bring about violent reactions from the perpetrators? The film ends, and Gaby's history is not solved.

Another high-impact film dealing with the recent past and the figure of the enemy is *La noche de los lápices* (*The Night of the Pencils*), directed by Héctor Olivera. This film is based on a true story, the abduction of ten high-school students by a military-police joint task force, in the city of La Plata (Buenos Aires Province) on 16 September 1976, and on the investigations of journalists Héctor Ruiz Núñez and María Seoane. The students were activists in a social movement canvassing for a special bus ticket for students. They suffered imprisonment, torture and death. Only one of them, Pablo Díaz, survived and was released in 1980, his testimony being taken into account for the making of the film. The kidnapping was known to only a few people, direct family and friends, but has since become iconic of Argentina's recent political history.

For the first time, and as an important element of the story, a film for larger audiences showed without any ambiguities the violence of Argentine State terrorism: kidnapping, illegal incarceration and torture in secret detention centers. *La noche de los lápices* was filmed in the real homes of the kidnapped teenagers, in order to give more realism to the scenes. The film does not enter into the political profile of the teenagers, but focuses on the personality of each of them, creating clearly identifiable characters. It also shows an educational environment in complete turmoil, where the functions of adults are blurred, while the center stage belongs to the teenagers' activism.

The first third of the film still takes place in a cheerful atmosphere, supported by the aesthetic and narrative codes of Argentine cinema depicting families in the 1970s. However, when the 1976 *coup d'état* is announced, the mood of rejoicing is replaced by a gloomier one. The stiffness of adults' bodies and their stern gestures correlate with the dismal warnings about the changes the new military government is going to impose. The bodies of the teenagers, in turn, in constant movement during the first part of the film, now become violated bodies, subject to repression. The young people's joy and lack of prejudice are now regarded as synonymous with "atheist and antinational ideas," as is stated in a speech by the Head of one of the schools attended by the protagonists. The enemy, according to the film, is the young people's rebelliousness and the changes they propose: they have challenged a 'natural order' that casts them into a submissive role. The film had a great impact on audiences through close-ups of torture scenes in which the young age of the victims was foregrounded. Their bodies became the battlefield on which the perpetrators fought 'their' war to save the Homeland and the Catholic religion from the dangers represented by these young people. For the torturers, the enemy is not the young people themselves, but the 'communism' that manipulates youth, inciting them to protest and rebellion.

4 The Reply of the Perpetrators to the Judicial and Filmic Reviews of the Recent Past

La historia oficial and *La noche de los lápices* marked the end of a first period in the history of the movies made during the early years of the return to the rule of the law: the disclosure of horror. Argentine society was becoming fully aware of the extent of the repression and, above all, of the brutality employed by the military, who a short time before had been considered as 'saviors of the Homeland.' The military were no longer the heroes of the 'war against subversion,' but had been revealed to the public as torturers and murderers of people illegally detained. This change in outlook was not unanimous but intense, and it took place very quickly. To these changes, the military and their civilian allies reacted by exercising pressure on the government. Some members of the army and the police force charged with crimes against humanity refused to appear in court. Several active military officers demanded the end of the investigations about serious violations of human rights perpetrated during the last dictatorship. In order to achieve this aim, they organized three military rebellions between 1987 and 1989, which not only challenged governance but also cost human lives as some people died in the suppression of the rebellion. All the same, the rebellions promoted the passing of legislation that progressively satisfied some of the military's demands, for instance by establishing that judges could not start new proceedings but could only continue with trials already started. This legislation prevented many crimes from being investigated. Between 1989 and 1990, the Argentine government went even further, granting a far-reaching pardon to the perpetrators (Osiel 2000).

The military reaction had a profound impact on Argentine cinema. After *La historia oficial* and *La noche de los lápices*, other films continued to render Argentina's recent past. Other topics, other discourses, other aesthetics appeared, but without the impact on the audiences that Puenzo's and Olivera's films had made during 1985–1986. The enemy's representation in the movies becomes more elaborated and metaphorical. The main focus was no longer a search for pathways into the past in the attempt to understand it, but instead there was a turning to the artistic imagination in order to offer explanations enabling one to leave behind the time of the 'disappeared' and the mass killings.

In this second period, films dealing with the recent past and the representation of the enemy become introspective and more complex in their aesthetic proposals. The enemy does not appear clearly in their discourse, as in *La historia oficial* or in *La noche de los lápices*, but it is necessary to decipher hidden messages in the language and the gestures of those who lived through the recent traumatic past. The enemy is now oblivion, but also the unsettling possibility that the memory of the past might burst upon the present with destabilizing effects.

The forced exile of many Argentinians became one of the new concerns in Argentine cinema. Fernando E. Solanas' filmography of those years – *El exilio de Gardel. Tangos* (*Gardel's Exile. Tangos*) (1986), *Sur* (*The South*) (1987) and *El viaje* (*The Trip*) (1990) – represents very well the new filmic approach to the recent past. In these films, the turn to metaphor, to ellipsis and to allegory prevails over dramatic structure and the classical narrative strategy of the previously analyzed works. Solanas' cinema is a relic of the 1970s, as it were, out of place in the different atmosphere of the late eighties and early nineties. A key representative of Latin-American political cinema, Solanas in his three films frequently resorts to the absurd, the grotesque and the dreamlike in order to represent the past. His characters fight against lack of understanding and oblivion to the point of becoming ludicrous. The enemy in these films is not a real subject, or a political idea: it is oblivion and the reluctance on the side of Argentinian society to recognize the suffering of the dictatorship's victims.

Another interesting example of the changes in representing the enemy in Argentine cinema of the nineties is *Un muro de silencio* (*A Wall of Silence*), directed by Lita Stantic (1993), one of the best films about the forced exile of many Argentinians. With Lautaro Murúa and Vanessa Redgrave in the main roles, this film avoids any collective revision of history by restricting itself to the level of personal conflicts, rendering the past as ever-present in spite of a will to forget. The film's plot revolves around a trio composed by Kate Benson, a foreign filmmaker (V. Redgrave), Bruno Tealdi, a university teacher who lived in exile during the dictatorship (L. Murúa), and Silvia (Ofelia Medina), Bruno's former student, whose first husband – also a former pupil – was kidnapped and murdered by security forces. The three of them meet again for the project of making a film about the case of Silvia's husband, yet this idea is rejected by her as well as by her family. Her husband's disappearance is a part of her life that Silvia has decided to forget; however, Kate and Bruno believe that her story must be told and shared. Silvia's resistance is overcome when she thinks that she has seen her 'disappeared' husband in the street, and she becomes almost paranoid. The end of the film shows that the end of the traumatic past was only a fiction Silvia wanted to believe in, yet which loses its hold when that past reappears in the shape of her husband's 'ghost.'

Un muro de silencio represents the violence of State terrorism also through emotionally moving images. Mainly, however, it does so through turning to 'cinema within cinema': in the rehearsals for the shooting of Kate's movie, situations of torture, kidnapping, extortion and other humiliations suffered by the 'disappeared' and their families appear. In this movie, society is absent, and the conflicts which develop and are connected with the recent past are personal affairs, old stories that re-emerge as an unhealed wound. In Stantic's film, the enemy is the past which returns to disturb the present world the survivors of State terrorism have been able to build in a society that has excluded them from its priorities. *Un muro de silencio*, in spite of its pessimism, opens a window to hope. The end of the film shows Silvia's daughter entering upon a compromise with the past, in spite of the disputes of the adults.

Last but not least, there is another excellent and unique film I want to analyze here: *Garage Olimpo* (*Olimpo Parking*). Directed by Italian-Argentinian Marco Bechis, and released in 1999, this film had little success in the box-office. *Garage Olimpo* portrays the daily life in a secret detention center and shows the extreme violence and the humiliations suffered by the 'disappeared.' This gloomy film is intent on realism, while it fictionalizes the personal history of Marco Bechis as a detainee-disappeared in the "Club Atlético." The film's plot is outlined at the very beginning of the movie: María (played by Antonella Costa) is a social worker engaged in adult education in the poorer neighborhoods. Her father is dead, and her mother, to make a living for the family, rents out rooms in their house. María is under the observation of the secret military task force for her work and political activism. She is abducted from her home, in the presence of her mother, and taken to a hidden detention center. There, she meets Félix (Carlos Echavarría), one of her mother's tenants, who is in love with her, and one of the torturers. In Bechis' film, the 'enemies,' in the eyes of the perpetrators, are all the detainees, labeled as 'subversives': social workers, guerillas, teachers, housewives ... In several sequences, the film shows that the clandestine center is located in the middle of the town, among the everyday life of other Argentinians.

Garage Olimpo contains many references to the so called 'death flights,' when detainees, alive or dead, were thrown into the sea from flying planes, to places associated with the horrors (the film blends three detention centers – Club Atlético, Automotores Orletti, and the Navy War School ESMA – into one), and perpetrators like for instance frigate captains Jorge Acosta and Alfredo Astiz and the policeman Jorge Bergés. Bechis' film combines fiction and historical information in order to offer a modern psychological drama, the tension of which is determined by the connection between the torturer and his victim.

Garage Olimpo introduces the spectator to the sordid universe of the clandestine detention centers. It also brings in new questions and new issues associated with Argentina's recent past: torture as daily routine, the relations between perpetrators and their victims, the murdering of the detainees, and the presence of the perpetrators in the urban environment. All these are issues which had not been dealt with before, either in the cinema or in society. Bechis' film has the great merit of reversing the image of the enemy which the military had tried to impose, namely that of the subversive hidden in the heart of society, disguised as teacher or civil servant. Indeed, as the film makes clear, the enemy is the perpetrators, camouflaged as ordinary people, and represented by Félix, the tenant in love with Maria, who is kidnapped, tortured and, at the end of the film, placed under his 'protection' in the secret detention center.

Conclusion

The large majority of the Argentine people saw with joy and hope the return to democracy. In its wake, they also began to see conflicting interpretations of the recent past, in the press, in cinema and in literature. In particular, they came to realize that there was a hidden and utterly inglorious side to what many had called the 'war against subversion.' Many Argentinians believed that the military had taken power in that 'war' in order to preserve them from the dangers represented by the 'communist enemy.' The films produced during the early years of democracy showed that there had been no such war, but massacres perpetrated in secrecy.

The films analyzed in this chapter also showed to audiences that there was a lot more in that story. In these films the enemy is still, in general, 'subversion,' yet with the knowledge about the truth a new representation of the enemy appears. The films analyzed intimate that something about the past has not yet been fully revealed. In any case, however, the lies of the military and of those civilians who supported the 'war against subversion' were thoroughly eroded by these films, in spite of their political and ideological limitations. What they did show in particular was that the 'hidden' past was not a 'war against subversion,' which in fact never took place (Ranalletti 2010). The only real war was in 1982 against Great Britain, when the Argentine military were completely defeated. Even if this 'untold' may not be revealed explicitly, however, these films provide decisive inroads into widely accepted versions of the past. For the first time, questions about the fabrications of an internal 'war' were widely asked.

Early democracy cinema suggests that for Argentinians the 'enemy' is no longer 'subversion' but the knowledge of the truth about their recent past. Alicia, in *La historia oficial*, represents a society shaken out of their beliefs by the discovery that this belief had been constructed on hidden corpses or bodies thrown into the sea, and on heroic fictions. Interestingly, the films of those years as analyzed in this chapter create doubts in the spectator as to the possible consequences of the inrush of truth about the recent past. The knowledge of the truth about the 'war against subversion' may in fact produce further violence, as in *La historia oficial*, or disrupt the 'normal' world built after the clandestine massacres, as in *Un muro de silencio*.

However, as the sea often returns what it has taken, the bodies of the murdered thrown into the Rio de la Plata by naval officers were washed up on the coasts some time later. Early cinema after the return to democracy showed that the past had come back to confront Argentinians. According to the words of a popular tango, they were now forced to "stop their walking [...]" and face the truth.

Works Cited

Burucúa, C. (2009) *Confronting the Dirty War in Argentine Cinema, 1983–1993. Memory and Gender in Historical Representations* (London: Tamesis Books).
Comisión Nacional sobre la Desaparición de personas (CONADEP) (1991) [National Commission on the Disappearance of Persons]. *Nunca más. Informe*. [Report: "Never more"] (Buenos Aires: EUDEBA).
Guebel, D. (1986) "Preguntas sobre lo terrible" [Questions about the horror], *Humor* 181, 67.
Malamud Goti, J. E. (1996) *Game without End: State Terror and the Politics of Justice* (Norman: University of Oklahoma Press).
O'Donnell, Guillermo (1988) *Bureaucratic Authoritarianism: Argentina 1966–1973, in Comparative Perspective*, trans. James McGuire (Berkeley: University of California Press).
Osiel, M. J. (2000 [1997]). *Mass Atrocity, Collective Memory, and the Law* (New Brunswick and London: Transaction Publishers).
Ranalletti, Mario (2001) "El Cine frente a la Memoria de los Contemporáneos. Historia y Memoria en la Argentina sobre el Terrorismo de Estado a partir de dos Películas de Andrés Di Tella" [The Cinema Faces the Memory of Contemporaries. History and Memory in Argentina on State Terrorism in Two Andres Di Tella Films], *Historia contemporánea* 1, 81–96.
Ranalletti, Mario (2010) "Denial of the Reality of State Terrorism in Argentina as Narrative of the Recent Past: a New Case of 'Negationism'?," *Genocide Studies and Prevention. An International Journal*, 5. 2, 160–173.

Filmography

El viaje (*The Trip*) (1990) Dir. Fernando Solanas (Cinesur S.A.).
Garage Olimpo (*Olimpo Parking*) (2000) Dir. Marco Bechis (Classic).
La historia oficial (*The Official Story*) (1985) Dir. Luis Puenzo (Historias Cinematograficas Cinemania).
La noche de los lápices (*The Night of the Pencils*) (1985) Dir. Héctor Olivera (Aries Cinematográfica Argentina).
La República perdida (*The Lost Republic*) (1983) Dir. Luis Gregorich and Miguel Pérez (Noran S.R.L.).

La República perdida II (*The Lost Republic II*) (1984) Dir. Luis Gregorich and Miguel Pérez (Noran S.R.L.and Enrique Vanoli).
No habrá más penas ni olvido) (*Funny Dirty Little War*) (1983) Dir. Héctor Olivera (Aries Cinematográfica Argentina).
Sur (*The South*) (1987) Dir. Fernando Solanas (Cinesur S.A.).
Un muro de silencio (*A Wall of Silence*) (1990) Dir. Lita Stantic (Aleph Producciones S.A.).

Maria Kobielska
Who Attacked Whom? The Year 1981 in Twenty-First Century Polish Feature Films

Among the salient events of the past, which had most serious consequences for contemporary Poland's national memory, two seem to be crucial, namely, the Katyn massacre of 1940 (the mass execution of over 20,000 Polish prisoners of war by the NKVD (a Soviet secret police organisation), and the Warsaw Uprising of 1944 against the Nazi German occupants. The special position of both events in Poland's national memory confirms the traumatic foundations of Polish collective identity: the events which have shaped this identity, in the aspect of memory, are martyrological in their nature, and tell stories in which Poland, shown as the heroine of the memorial tales, is attacked, each time by a different aggressor. What is more, the trauma could not be properly worked through: the memory of Katyn was banned in the Polish People's Republic period (Kobielska 2016: 200 – 204, 216 – 217),[1] while the Warsaw Uprising commemoration was also misrepresented (Napiórkowski 2016: 16 – 27, 41– 50, 100 –109) because of the anti-Soviet character of the Home Army, absorbing most Polish underground forces during WWII. Consequently, the remembrance of Katyn and the Warsaw Uprising became a sign of resistance and protest against the post-war communist government.

As I shall argue, these two central events in the cultural memory of contemporary Poland must be complemented by martial law, introduced on 13 December 1981 by the Soviet-controlled government led by General Wojciech Jaruzelski, in order to curb the constantly growing force of the anti-communist *Solidarity* movement. The restrictions which came into effect with the introduction of martial law lasted, with different intensity, until July 1983. *Solidarity* was banned and its members were interned or jailed; severe restrictions in everyday life were introduced, including transport and communication, and the army became a presence in the streets. The number of fatalities claimed amounts to 90 people, including, among others, miners from the *Wujek* coal mine who were killed during strike-breaking actions (officially designated as 'pacification'). As later stated by representatives of the regime, martial law was introduced in order to restore peace and security and to prevent an armed intervention by the USSR; their opponents, on the contrary, claim that the only motif behind it was to suppress the opposition and stay in power.

---

[1] All translations from Polish are mine, M. K.

https://doi.org/10.1515/9783110591217-014

The year 1981 was to become particularly divisive for the Polish society as well as the national memory culture. Being a powerful experience of a generation and a touchstone for younger Poles, it yet could not fully adjust to the dominant patterns of Polish memory. As Lech Nijakowski puts it, the introduction of martial law stopped vivid discussions about the past led within the anti-communist civil movement, replacing it with a ritualization and mythologizing of the *Solidarity* memory (2008: 122). However, the impact of martial law was not so much to preserve the memorial division between 'us,' the real nation upholding the truth, and 'them,' the treacherous communists; instead, it created at least two other groups whose conflict has lasted until today. The split within the anti-communist movement was grounded on its destabilization, a loss of credibility and of trust in the leaders, and the ambiguity of the new situation, in which the question whether the introduction of martial law was legitimate could not find any final answer. These divisions even deepened during the 1980s and the transition years, when the former unity of the *Solidarity* movement became elusive, and the interests of those identifying with the anti-communist opposition became different according to beliefs, social position, class and capital.

The simple story about the united nation being attacked in 1981 by evil communists could not work anymore. Reactions to such a situation can be different: one will be trying to maintain it notwithstanding, presenting contemporary opponents as former enemies – communists or their secret agents, who not only introduced martial law, but also planned the tricky transformation of 1989. In such arguments, the vetting procedure became a powerful political tool, also against the leaders of *Solidarity*, especially Lech Wałęsa, who was accused of being not only a secret informant, but also a wilful collaborator of the communist Security Service (SB). On the other hand, the martial law is still a challenge to a narrative of success, in which a bloodless transformation, built on peaceful negotiations with the regime, started an outstanding and fortunate time in Polish history. Economic and social problems after 1989, outrageous within one narrative and non-existing within another, expand the controversies. Consequently, in the twenty-first century, opinions on the martial law amongst the general public can still serve as a proof of social divisions (Nijakowski 2008: 207) and as a symbol of a conflicting past.

With the developments of 1981, a thought-provoking situation arose as the enemy, external in the case of Katyn and the Warsaw Uprising, was now Polish. If the act of remembering always involves reconstruction and is always processual in nature, here the inscription of meaning and the definition of a framework for the understanding of events have been particularly obvious. This provokes key questions as to the concept of the enemy involved: how do we conceptualise and name the actors in the events, or, in simple terms, who attacked whom in 1981? What was at stake and what were the consequences of the events? And furthermore, what do the different stories about martial law say about the Polish culture of memory? What does the specificity of the 'enemy' or 'enemies' created within its frameworks tell us? I shall later analyse several sets of answers to these questions, i.e. the memorial narratives about the martial law, trying to show their conditioning and poetics. The selection of feature films about the martial law, analysed below, can be seen as representing different sides of the division, at times also commenting on it; hence, a detailed reading of these works will provide a more profound depiction of the split itself.

The proposed analysis shall demonstrate the general shape of the cultural memory of 1981 and possible shifts within it. Laura Basu's term "memory dispositif" may be useful in this context. The 'martial law films' are taken into consideration not only as cultural texts, in terms of their synopsis, film language and artistic shape, but also as ingredients constituting cultural memory via dynamic sets of various relations. Their tangle produces a memorial image (or images) of the central event of martial law, as Basu puts it, referring to Foucault and Agamben. They form a constellation producing a particular tendency within collective and cultural memory, generating complex mnemonic figures and intervening into identities (Basu 2010: 33–35, 41).

The moment which has become 'emblematic' of the 'martial law memory dispositif' was when on Sunday, 13 December 1981, viewers saw General Jaruzelski on their TV screens, announcing the establishment of the Military Council of National Salvation (WRON) and the introduction of martial law "in the entire state." Jaruzelski's face became a visual metonymy of the enemy, yet the functioning of this metonymy is somehow complicated. This is because that 'logo' of martial law has repeated itself with the greatest accuracy, and in all kinds of texts devoted to these events, to form a cliché; on the other side of this process of repetition is the emergence of an element that is prone to processing, in ways which sometimes depart really far from the initial form of the unambiguous emblem.

My choice to analyse the significance of 1981 on the example of contemporary feature film is not arbitrary, but is grounded in the ways cultural memory functions, and in the shape it has been taking on in twenty-first century Poland. On the one hand, film may reach wide audiences mainly because of the suggestiveness and clarity of its language, which constitutes an effective tool of communication and persuasion. On the other hand, and due to the high costs of its production, film is prone to being shaped by market tendencies and policies sanctioned by the state. Films, especially those devoted to history and memory, often depend on financial support offered by specialised state agencies (like the Polish Film Institute) or other cultural institutions.

In this context, the notion of a national cinema appears, understood, after Tadeusz Lubelski (and based on the concept by Jinhee Choi as well as Anderson's theory of imagined communities), as functional cinema, or cinema that encourages "the viewers to imagine themselves as people belonging to a specific society and culture" (Lubelski 2009: 9). Obviously, a major factor which enables such an imagining is a shared view of the past, of the same forms of memory and traditions perceived as one's own. In this respect, national cinema becomes a heritage cinema. As Andrew Higson put it, what governments will consider particularly important in this context is that "a strong national cinema can offer coherent images of the nation, sustaining the nation together at an ideological level, exploring and celebrating what is understood to be the indigenous culture" (2000: 63). Marcin Adamczak distinguishes two waves of high-budget historical "national super-productions" (2012: 72) in Polish culture: the first was created at the turn of the centuries and reaches back to events rendered in nineteenth-century literary classics, while the other originates from the years 2007–2009 and focuses on the history of the twentieth century. In this context, Adamczak lists *Katyń*, directed by Andrzej Wajda (2007) and *Generał Nil*, directed by Ryszard Bugajski (2009), but the wave is by no means limited to these examples. It brought with it an increasing interest in Polish cinema and an intensive turning to the past as a subject in Polish culture and the public sphere. The feature films of the period touch on the martial law, thus representing a tightly knit, but not homogenous, collection and, out of necessity, constitute the receptional contexts for one another. They can be treated as separate attempts to respond to the memorial situation as outlined above, in which, over 30 years after the events discussed, the question of how we remember them, and what actually happened, remains open and leads to further conflicts. However, they simultaneously form a constellation of the 'martial law memory dispositif.' A single image of the event, produced within this tangle, becomes merely a medium, a measure in the game where the stake is different and very contemporary: a due position not only in the memorial field, but in the general field of power. Its positioning in the social hierarchy and the economic and ideological post-transformation order, within the differentiation and assimilation structures, contains in itself a component that can be called the *view of the past*, demonstrated by an individual or shared by a group (or constructed by a text).

1 The Martyrological Pattern: The Martial Law as War

The first of the possible variants of the memorial tale about martial law is certainly the clearest and, perhaps, the simplest, as it uses black-and-white role divisions and martyrological identity patterns. Here, the term 'martial law' (*stan wojenny*) is made equal to the 'state of war' (*stan wojny*) – linguistically similar in Polish, although significantly differentiated. According to this story, the martial law was in fact a war in which the Poles were attacked by those in power, unwaveringly perceived as non-Polish and called representative of USSR interests. The widely used denotation of the period as a 'Poland-Jaruzelski war' concludes this way of its memorisation. This version of the tale is frequently associated with a rejection of the post-transformation shape of the Polish state, since it started with negotiations with the regime – the murderers of 1981. It adopts the martyrological language used with reference to martial law, tried many a time in Polish culture. In this point of view, usually paired with the national/conservative attitude, martial law is mainly seen through the prism of a brutal fight and persecution of heroic oppositionists by the murderous regime, which is well illustrated by Rafał Wieczyński's *Popiełuszko. Wolność jest w nas* (*Popiełuszko. Freedom is Within Us*) (2009).

I shall not analyse the movie in detail here, but only point to some of the most important determinants of the way in which the image of martial law is constructed in it. As a whole, the film is biographical or even hagiographic,[2] as defined approbatively by some of the commentators. The main character in the movie is the priest Jerzy Popiełuszko (starred by Adam Woronowicz), chaplain of the opposition in the 1980s, persecuted by the regime, murdered in 1984 by Security Service (SB) officials, and beatified as a martyr of the Catholic Church in 2010. The aim of Wieczyński's movie is to show the characteristics and position of the protagonist, "the national hero, the saint priest, the chaplain of *Solidarity* and the preacher," as pertinently described by Jan Pniewski in his comment (2009: 118). To the particular authority he has a priori as a priest, Popiełuszko adds recognition through a series of gestures and actions which prove infallible both in moral terms and in terms of prudence, assessment of the situation and effectiveness, and which permeate the movie. The hagiographic intention reaches its climax in the martyrological thread, shown in the progressing

---

[2] Some reviewers commented on the film as being an answer to an urgent need for Popiełuszko's hagiographic biography (cf. Szpulak 2009: 158).

oppression of the main character through increasingly brutal harassment and persecutions, until his gruesome assault and murder, ending with a scene showing Pope John Paul II engrossed in prayer over Popiełuszko's tombstone. The focus on these two irreproachable figures, generally perceived as authorities, has a persuasive function, making it difficult for the viewer to act with reserve or be sceptical about the pattern proposed by the film, represented by Popiełuszko and the Pope.

The movie presents the events of December as a war breaking out: an internee is lying provocatively, asking officials "What martial [law]? Gentlemen, who attacked us? Give me a weapon, I'm a real sharp shooter, I'll join you in defending our homeland." The comparison to war highlights the brutality of repressions whilst ridiculing the regime by showing how scandalous it is to attack one's own citizens, and by exposing the poorness of the pretexts to act. This representation mainly focuses on two images: the first introductory one is Popiełuszko's night ride through the snowy city, which is engulfed in chaotic anxiety, and filled with panic and violence. This manner of rendering the scene is continued in the depiction of the following day's events, showing emblems of martial law such as armed forces in the streets (and tanks and braziers), with General Jaruzelski's mandatory speech in the background, this time broadcast on the radio. The second of the above-mentioned images pictures the 'pacification' of the Warsaw-based steelworks, conducted as a regular battle, with elaborated scenes of gas-spraying and beating with truncheons, and with emphasis put on the desperate courage of workers defending the steelworks against the army. The battle scene will return in other fragments of the martial law sequence and in the outdoor collective scenes of suppressed manifestations in the streets of Warsaw in May 1982.[3] In *Popiełuszko*, this sequence constitutes a catalogue of different forms of noble and admirable opposition, demonstrated by impeccable characters who emphasise the peacefulness of their protests, organise themselves into mutual aid societies, help the prisoners, sing the Polish anthem when on trial and ensure medical assistance during demonstrations. Yet the central place in the catalogue is occupied by religious practice: rosaries and portraits of the saints are not mere emblems, but constitute distinctive features of the oppositionists (Mrozek 2009: 310).

Returning to the crucial question of the different versions of the martial law tale, it can be said that *Popiełuszko* in effect becomes an ideal or, as I see it, even an overdrawn example of a fabulously transparent martyrological narrative. It

---

[3] In the opinion of Andrzej Luter, these parts of the film made it a "great historical fresco" (2009: 56), joining the story of everyday life and dramatic events of the year 1981.

brings to life a collective entity, i.e. a community of irreproachable victims (the Polish nation), afflicted by trauma and experiencing cruel harm. Any bargaining, co-existence and negotiations of the victim with the absolute enemy (the torturer and the torturer's henchmen and heirs) should be impossible; the events were so significant and unambiguous that they may delineate a final, historical division into these two groups.

2 Against the Martyrological Pattern: The Decreased War

The anticipated war is also talked about a few months before 13 December by unionists from Wrocław – protagonists of Waldemar Krzystek's *80 milionów* (*80 Million*) (2011), yet this time, it is a very different war. The film avoids the previously described pattern by using two strategies: first, by drawing on the repertoire of comedy and, second, by showing an apolitical (if not de-politicised) history. It does not refer to the substance of the conflict between the brave *Solidarity* members and the regime which, due to its clumsiness and vagueness, is only a little hostile. Although the introduction of martial law serves as the end point of the whole story told by the film, it is present from the very beginning in the more or less enigmatic announcements, creating the pivot of the plot. Everyone is preparing themselves for martial law: heroes from the Wrocław *Solidarity*, their opponents and representatives of the regime, including the Security Service (SB). The most spectacular achievement of the "S" members is the withdrawal of 80 million zlotys from the Union's bank account, deposited there in order to secure the Union's operation after the introduction of martial law. Although denounced by the authorities as a bank robbery, this was in fact a normal cash transaction, made possible by the conduct of the bank's director, who notified the headquarters only after ordering the withdrawal, and to the skilful hiding of the cash at the seat of the curia (authorities of the Catholic Church in Wrocław).

The film's plot is constructed as a series of situations which expose, often with stock comedy techniques, 'howlers' by oppressors from the Security Service (SB), ridiculed by the underestimated unionists and their allies. Although brutal, the agents are easy to lead up: the only plans which they manage to accomplish boil down to beating up the workers. Their ineptitude and stupidity are enhanced by the braggadocio, self-righteousness and ridicule represented by the most distinctive of them, Captain Sobczak (Piotr Głowacki), who is recognised by the ostentatious and crude vulgarisms which he constantly uses. The unionists' smartness and wit make Sobczak's provocations backfire on him, with his eventual fall being rendered as in a comedy of errors. Rather than a loyal servant of the regime, the captain turns out to be a venal blackmailer, who claims money from the priests (who store the title 80 million zlotys) in exchange for his help, voices opinions that discredit him before his superiors or even insults them, forgetting that the conversation is being held in a room which is permanently tapped by his very own institution. By doing this, Sobczak excludes himself from the game (as this is what the events seem to be) of his own making.

The core of the internal conflict is virtually absent in *80 milionów*. The film only mentions in passing difficulties with supplies, and the reasons why *Solidarity* was established and why it was being constantly (yet ineptly) fought by the authorities are hardly indicated. Krzystek's film proves to be close to a picaresque novel: it presents an outwardly cheerful story about how the good and smart unionists outwitted their oppressors, deservedly making fun of them like Smurfs who keep laughing off Gargamel. After these preparatory sequences, martial law does not bring about a significant change in the tone of the narrative. Although *80 milionów* does introduce certain canonical images, such as tanks in the streets, detentions or ZOMO (Motorized Reserves of the Citizens' Militia) clashing with *Solidarity*'s demonstration, it is the atmosphere of a fête that wins, when the army is forced by the demonstrators to retreat, snowed under leaflets encouraging them to change sides. A tale about martial law thus becomes a tale about a victory of the good and the humiliation of a ridiculed enemy.

3 Against the Martyrological Pattern: History De-Heroised

In yet another variant of filmic tales about martial law, its inherent antagonistic potential is neutralised by employing a more general strategy of de-heroising.[4] With humorous elements scattered here and there, this strategy focuses on everyday life, showing the peculiar nostalgia for the Polish People's Republic. Among the feature films of the past few years, this strategy is most clearly evident in *Wszystko co kocham* (*All that I Love*) (2009) by Jacek Borcuch.

---

[4] According to Ewa Domańska, there are two general ways of showing the time of the Polish People's Republic in Polish culture: a tragic one and a de-heroised, comic version (2008: 167, 184–185).

The film's principle can be described as a pursuit of domestic realism,[5] with an emphasis on normality and the elimination of contrasts. It is a classic initiatory tale about first love, infatuations and misunderstandings with a bitter-sweet ending, in which the first sexual fulfilment of the characters entails grief when their paths have diverged. The story is set in provincial surroundings, rendered through very specific aesthetics as the scenery is discreetly filled with objects associated with the Polish People's Republic, like signboards and neon signs (today seen as gadgets) shown against the background of the Baltic shore. The incidents that make up the plot, i.e. the first successes of a punk rock band founded by four characters, the above-mentioned romance of one of them, the friendship between the boys or other situations in the characters' home space, are all small-scale situations which, whether funny, uplifting or sad, are in general all understandable, leaving the characters with clear and transparent opportunities to act.

The film ostentatiously excludes black and white judgement, which is particularly visible in the case of the protagonist's family: a father, member of the PZPR (Polish United Workers' Party) and Officer of the LWP (Polish People's Army) (Andrzej Chyra) becomes, in the martial law reality, an ally of the counterculture band of his sons, for which he is later dismissed from his post. Martial law could potentially lead to a conflict between the father, a military man, and the son, a punk singer (Mateusz Kościukiewicz), but this conflict melts in their warm relationship, based on mutual understanding. Similarly, it also seems that the situation in the country will put up a barrier between Janek, the son of a serviceman, and his girlfriend, whose father is an oppositionist, but these characters, too, reach an agreement during a romantic meeting on the beach.

If the severity of martial law was hyperbolised in *Popiełuszko*, in Borcuch's movie its image is constructed through the use of litotes. After the emblematic scenes showing Jaruzelski's TV speech in the main characters' house, the atmosphere is tense, but it soon turns out that the threads of everyday affairs will not be discontinued. It is during the martial law that one of the characters receives the long-awaited minibike, and another experiences sexual initiation by an older neighbour. From among the repressions, the biggest influence on their lives is

---

5 Krzysztof Kwiatkowski regards the film as apolitical, exploring the private and individual perspectives of the young protagonists, who are not interested in politics and the "great historical events" taking place around them (2010: 73). The reviewer's decision to situate *Wszystko co kocham* outside the mainstream in the remembrance of the martial law, however, misses the importance of the pattern of memory to which the film contributes, a pattern which is influential and politically relevant.

initially wielded by the curfew. The soldiers appearing in the streets would mainly warm themselves up by braziers or ask passing boys to bring them cigarettes in exchange for one pack rather than brutally harass the people, as shown in *Popiełuszko*. But the secure daily life of the family is eventually disturbed. Due to an envious neighbour's denunciations, a school concert is cancelled; the situation develops into a spontaneous protest rally, during which the students chant *Solidarity, Solidarity* and *WCK* (the name of the band). As a result, the protagonist's father is removed from the army for "providing aid and using military property for an anti-socialist manifestation." As it turns out, the worst that the characters suffer from the regime is the necessity to change their jobs and schools, move out or depart from their first loves which, although highly unpleasant, is not shown as a tragedy.

This image, presenting martial law as a bearable harm, one of many in life, which, although difficult, does not disrupt its course, is concluded in the final scenes. The protagonist, Janek, takes his revenge on the informer by breaking a windowpane and jumping on the roof of his car. This scene is saturated with wit and bravado, yet both the harm done by the neighbour and Janek's revenge are only minor dramas. *Wszystko co kocham* ends on a cheerful scene in which the boys, who have come to terms with the situation, sum up the course of events. Janek's friend Kazik (Jakub Gierszał) quotes the affirmative words of his father, who called their undertakings "the biggest protest in the *poviat* [district] since the beginning of the martial law." One will note that the father was previously presented as a hated perpetrator of domestic violence, which means that yet another conflict has been easily removed from the reality depicted. While in *Popiełuszko* the year 1981 means war, in Borcuch's film it is presented as a pretended war – an event which, although decisive for the characters' living conditions, is not fundamental, tragic or crucial for history (Rabsztyn 2010: 104). The enemy is not a torturer, but an incidental opponent of a small calibre, whose status is neither absolute nor generalised. And society does not become divided: those who seem to be in power may eventually turn out to be allies, and the romantic story of the first love proves stronger than the conflicts.

Narratives like this do not seem to contradict the martyrological pattern so much but to have in fact no points in common with it. The fundamental manoeuvre made by both narratives is a shift of the major subject of the utterance from the nation's martyrology to, e.g., day-to-day affairs; the image of the enemy, sharpened and hyperbolised in the first version, is blurred here and becomes not so dangerous. Such a shift, although with a different content, is also shown in Andrzej Wajda's film, *Wałęsa. Człowiek z nadziei* (*Wałęsa. Man of Hope*) (2013).

4 Using the Patterns: Wajda's Shift

Andrzej Wajda holds a special position as a director, especially where the cinema evokes memory, history and national identity. As written in the 1990s by Maria Janion, in his films Wajda creates an image of Polishness composed of an "idealization of the homeland on the one hand and the image of a vicious cycle, a dance macabre, a magic circle on the other" (1997: 10). Tadeusz Lubelski, an expert on the director's works (see his monograph *Wajda*), uses the same notions, pointing to the contribution of Wajda's output to the creation of a symbolic national imaginary and mythology, understood by Wajda himself as the artist's commitment to the society and its needs. As Lubelski puts it, "the important threads of the national history of the past twenty years took on the shape of images, which he brought to life in his films" (2006: 6) by presenting the "fictional variants [of such events] in all the wealth of the social and cultural background" (2006: 193), and by showing the connections between history and contemporary society's sense of identity. The same view was expressed by Ib Bondebjerg, who defined Wajda's movies as visualisations of the "explosive history and memory zones," "sensitive points and experiences" (2012: 38) of Polish history which the movies deconstructed, put to a debate, thought over and discussed anew, in still different forms. According to the common critical cliché, Wajda is a director or, metaphorically speaking, an "architect of the Polish imagination" (the phrase is so popular that it is difficult to trace who was the first to use it – see Wroński 2008: 1). Significantly, in his short commentary on *Wałęsa*, Ryszard Jabłoński described Wajda's role as that of a prophet who speaks to and on behalf of the entire nation (2014: 175–177).

As the sub-title of the film suggests, *Wałęsa. Człowiek z nadziei* (*Wałęsa. Man of Hope*) is set in the context of two other films directed by Wajda more than 30 years before, which are in fact his flagship movies, namely, *Człowiek z marmuru* (*Man of Marble*) (1976) and *Człowiek z żelaza* (*Man of Iron*) (1981). Both movies concurred to create a legend of the opposition of the Polish People's Republic, with its success represented by the strikes in August 1980 and the agreements hard-won in these strikes. Therefore, an attempt can be made to classify the film from 2013, the biography of the *Solidarity* leader, as a closing of the triptych: logical and understandable on the one hand, but surprisingly distant in time on the other. An interesting context here is created by one section of Wajda's filmic novella *Solidarność, Solidarność* (*Solidarity, Solidarity*) (2005), entitled *Człowiek z nadziei* (*Man of Hope*), according to which it was Wałęsa himself who suggested the title for the last part of the film triptych. The novella is composed of several selected scenes from *Człowiek z żelaza* and a conversation held in an empty screening room by Wajda, Wałęsa, Krystyna Janda and Jerzy Radziwiłłowicz (the latter two being the leading actors of the movie), seated in the first row. The documentary shots of triumph after the victory in the August strike and of crowds greeting Wałęsa, incorporated into *Człowiek z żelaza*, contrast with the long camera ride along rows of empty chairs, which introduces the subject of the loss of social confidence by *Solidarity's* elite after 1989. Wajda explains that for twenty-five years he was unable to shoot *Wałęsa. Człowiek z nadziei*, as it would have to be a film about a divided *Solidarity*, a *Solidarity* that lost the erstwhile governance of souls, which he did not want to do. What is interesting to notice here is a conflict between the image of Wajda as the 'architect' of *Solidarity's* imaginary, and the reservations which he voiced himself, out of concern for coherence, about the film which he eventually made in 2013.

The film about Lech Wałęsa has two protagonists: apart from the main character Lech Wałęsa (perfectly incarnated by Robert Więckiewicz), a major role in the film is only given to his wife Danuta (Agnieszka Grochowska). The plot of the movie starts in December 1970 and ends in 1989, with Wałęsa's famous speech before the US Congress. It uses a number of archival records, entwined through a precise montage with scenes shot by Paweł Edelman; with the help of digital technology, the figures of the actors were blended into some of the documentary footage, while other documentary material was smoothly made to merge with the film's own reality, suggesting for instance that scenes were shot by the cameras of SB officers on the screen. Beside the soundtrack composed by Paweł Mykietyn, songs of counter-culture bands of the 1980s were used. The general strategy of *Wałęsa* was to create an illustration of highly recognisable historical scenes (i.e. owing to the media). Without wanting to assess the effectiveness of this strategy with regard to the film's target groups, I believe that the pleasure of watching *Wałęsa* lies in recognising something well known and recollecting something which is already remembered, either from one's own experience or from the media. Even a most generous appreciation of Wajda's film would hardly claim that the national imaginary (or memory) it evokes was created by Wajda himself. It is more accurate to admit that he inserted the faces of his actors (as in the above-mentioned montage) into certain emblematic shots such as, for instance, the one of Lech Wałęsa on the Gdańsk Shipyard gate in August 1980 or the figure of his wife collecting the Nobel Prize in 1983 on his behalf.

As an astute analysis can show, Andrzej Wajda's strategy was oriented towards a different, and much more specific, aim than simply "directing the national imagination." What is interesting is that the commentators who took it upon themselves to indicate some general aim of the film would usually mention its potential educational and promotional use abroad. In their opinion, the movie was supposed to "explain the phenomenon of our victorious revolution to the world," "tell the world about our road to freedom," or formulate a (necessarily simplified) "universal message to a foreign recipient" (Baniewicz 2014: 120). Rather than an interpretation, it is a gesture which dismisses the interpretation, or even a sign of interpretational helplessness. However, a critical reading provides much more information about the subject. This movie about Lech Wałęsa, which seems to be a biopic at first, is in fact made up of a series of illustrations of well-known events in the last twenty years of the Polish People's Republic, forming neither a coherent story of a politician (or hero) nor a drama of an individual or a family. The only thread which is persistently pursued throughout the film and, at the same time, the only one in which I can clearly see the director's active decisions rather than an intention to follow the general scenario written by history, is a polemic against the mentioned controversies around the image of Lech Wałęsa stirred up by the vetting inspectors. The story, repeated in the Polish public debate in order to discredit Wałęsa, has several nodal points (such as his contacts with the Security Officers in the 1970s), to each and every one of which Wajda's film refers in a riposte. The thread culminates in a several minutes' sequence concerning the martial law.

As a whole, the sequence is based on the idea of making a film by confronting staged scenes with fragments of documents from the epoch. The fictional scenes are generally circumscribed, showing the protagonist (Lech Wałęsa) amidst his closest circle, while the documentary fragments provide a wider, panoramic view of the events at the end of 1981 and in 1982. For example, the scene which shows a raid of the Wałęsa family's flat by oppressors on the night of 13 December 1981 is followed by a fragment made up of documentary shots.

As was to be expected, Jaruzelski's speech announcing martial law has become the leitmotif of the film. Its visual rendering consists of hieratic shots of the general intertwined with documentary materials (or modelled to look like such), which, in very short scenes, show the most emblematic elements of the reality of December 1981, i.e. tanks in the streets, braziers, doors being forced open, and brutal apprehensions. Reviewing the range of such associations, this fragment creates an ironic effect by juxtaposing excerpts from the speech (and a disturbing musical motif in the background) with absurdly inadequate shots. "Our soldiers' hands are clean," says the general in the background of a scene full of violence, while the words "we want a great Poland; great through its achievements, culture and position in Europe" are heard whilst the viewers are being shown photographs of a horse-drawn cart filled with coal.

After the cut, Jaruzelski's voice still sounds from the radio in the car in which Wałęsa is being driven. In subsequent scenes, viewers are shown Wałęsa's confrontation with people who are outraged because of the introduction of martial law, his arrival in Arłamów, a village near the Soviet border where he was incarcerated, his conversation with Nawiślak, an SB captain (Zbigniew Zamachowski), scenes of everyday life and a meeting with one of the party's dignitaries (Grzegorz Przybył). Then, a documentary interlude follows, showing dramatic scenes of 'pacification' through the use of gas, water cannons and the militia's truncheons, and a longer scene presenting Wałęsa's meeting with a priest who supports him (Maciej Stuhr). Thereafter (in November 1982), Wałęsa is released from detention, after the death of Leonid Brezhnev, and returns to the coast. The grim, deserted atmosphere of an autumn night is suddenly transformed into one of joyful triumph when it turns out that the hero is being awaited in Gdańsk by a crowd of supporters with flags and banners.

Against the background of the martial law, Wałęsa is depicted in a twofold manner, as an indomitable (yet familiar) hero and as a martyr, which closely corresponds to the above-sketched shaping of his image in the film. The first of these two aspects is already present in the scene from the flat of Mr and Mrs Wałęsa, the meaning of which is stated straightforwardly by the character himself, when he tells his wife: "Wake up the kids. Let them see the communist government taking their father." As one of the most obvious and understandable scenes from the film, this scene is 'affixed with a caption,' like an emblem or a painting with the Stations of the Cross. From the very beginning, although aware of the danger of his situation, Wałęsa remains determined and undaunted by his opponents. A dismissive tone, expressive of the character's psychological advantage, is taken on by Wałęsa in all the scenes from Arłamów. For instance, he responds with a quick-witted joke to Nawiślak, who tries to intimidate him by threats of long imprisonment or even death. When Nawiślak says: "You know that our friends from the country of the rising sun keep asking whether it is indispensable that you stay alive?" Wałęsa replies: "Then I would certainly be beatified."

Beside the story of a hero who impresses everybody by his indomitability and endears himself by his sharp, simple wit, however, there is also that of Wałęsa as 'the martyr.' The latter is used to illustrate not so much the direct burden of repressions as the already mentioned accusations of collaborating with the Security Service (SB). The rejoinder, also already mentioned, gains prominence in the martial law sequence, while the opponents of Wałęsa, the alleged agent, appear more and more explicitly in the film. When Wałęsa, imprisoned by the Security Service officials in an unknown location, is recognised by some passing locals, they do not support him, as he may have expected. Instead, they surround his car, set about it with their fists, kick it, call him names and accuse him of triggering the dramatic situation in the country, trying to stop the car and letting out a stream of curses. The stylising of these aggressive figures as the only ones who do not belong to the authorities and yet distrust Wałęsa, is significant. They play the role of a collective character, a group of people with crooked faces, wearing heavy winter boots and caps pulled over their eyes and uttering incoherent and vulgar exclamations; also, they carry livestock (pigs) in the trunks of their cars, which is emphasized through a camera movement. Their hostility towards Wałęsa is thus associated with aggression and primitivism and takes on a class character, unexpectedly situating the protagonist outside of the proletariat.

The priest who visits Wałęsa in Arłamów (Maciej Stuhr) brings in a leaflet reading that "Lech Wałęsa is an agent of the Security Service, a hypocrite and a rascal of rascals," who, in December 1970, turned in his friends, and acted in cooperation with the government only to "lay the ground for the martial law." As the priest reveals, the flyers were distributed by the Security Service (SB). In this way, Wajda defines the historical origin of the later attacks on Wałęsa, averting the accusation that he acted in the interest of the enemy. What the above-mentioned scenes have in common is lengthy close-ups on Robert Więckiewicz's face, some of the very few in the entire film, when it has a look of concern, pain and disorientation rather than of wit or strength. (In the second case, Wałęsa turns back from the priest and breathes in deeply, the pervasive sense of dread being intensified by the extradiegetic music.) In my interpretation, Wałęsa as 'the martyr' is not a prisoner of the totalitarian regime (in this role he is a lively, witted protagonist), but a leader who has been deserted by some of his people, slandered by primitive aggressors and surrounded by libellers who only wait for him to make a mistake.

In view of the above, I should argue that the image of martial law created in *Wałęsa* is subordinated to the film's strategy, which is to lift Lech Wałęsa, as a figure of Polish public life, out of the vetting deadlock mentioned in the introduction (which is probably impossible). Here, I disagree with Joanna Krakowska, who calls the movie a dodge film that "creates a naïve, optimistic historiography" whilst "avoiding the necessity to face the Polish political obsessions and the social frustration" (81), passing over the "reason why the story is being told" (2014: 78). Indeed, the film does not explicitly show the said reason and does not take a stance in today's political disputes. However, this is not because it ignores the tensions created by Wałęsa's story, but because it rather tries to invalidate the dispute. The truth is that it does voice a clear viewpoint, through its attempt to show a situation in which one of the presented points of view will defend the status of unquestionability and default.

The focus of my interest, i.e. martial law, is presented here mainly through copying the well-known clichés such as Jaruzelski's speech, which is repeated so many times that it is robbed of any other meaning than its simple emblematic quality. With this brief referral to the reality of Poland at the end of 1981 and the beginning of 1982, *Wałęsa* shifts the subject of the discussion, making the legitimising of the protagonist as a familiar, non-problematic national hero after 1989 its main interest. The technique of interspersing fiction with archive materials can be perceived as a literal translation of the functions of the politics of memory into technological montage devices: it fills the gaps, thus building a decorative, strong image of the previously non-existent past. It seems that there are two enemies in *Wałęsa:* the regime, which is actually not clearly presented but signalled by an obvious cliché; and the plot against the protagonist, which is not explicitly shown either, but only implied.

Conclusion

Polish national cinema of the twenty-first century can be seen through the lens of a typical filmic form described as "film of national remembrance" (Mrozek 2009: 298), a model example of Higson's "strong national cinema." Andrzej Wajda's *Katyń* (2007) would be a standard model of the genre. Its definition covers addressing social commemorative needs (like improving the level of historical consciousness, filling the gaps of collective memory, commemorating forgotten heroes), aiming at building canonical forms of the collective memory of the group, and targeting a mass public seen as a whole nation. Such a film can serve as an instrument of patriotic education and of a politics of memory. In order to effectively create and sustain a national myth, it becomes a spectacle of very pronounced, unambiguous form, precisely defining good and evil, 'us' and 'them,' 'Polish' and 'alien.' Confronting the set of the 'martial law films' with this dominant tendency of 'films of national remembrance' shows a certain divergence. It is only *Popiełuszko. Wolność jest w nas*, with its martyrological frame, that can be described as one of a kind, intentionally aimed at showing the Polish nation as an unblemished community of victims. More ambiguous memory versions shown in *80 milionów* and *Wszystko co kocham*, decreasing and de-heroising what was a national trauma within the former pattern, create neither a mythical spectacle nor a lesson in history and patriotism. Wajda's audience is not conceived as a whole re-united nation; rather, *Wałęsa. Człowiek z nadziei* consolidates those who support its protagonist and the 'narrative of success,' while disavowing the adversaries.

It is certain that the memory of the martial law uses automatically repeated, highly recognisable clichés, which, however, give some room for semantically innovative processing. Furthermore, this very same memory turns out to be functionalised according to current needs; as such it was divided into versions which serve different strategies, clustered together in a non-communicative clinch and clashed, thus separating the field of memory with boundaries that are difficult to overcome. Jaruzelski's face may denote both an absolute enemy and terror, and something distant and not so important, or even a cliché with a blurred meaning. The martial law as a memorial construct is thus adaptable; as an entangled "memory dispositif" in Basu's understanding, it does not produce one clear-cut tendency, but a set of "highly individuated and fragmented identities" (Basu 2010: 38), conflicted figures and contradicting narratives. The 'martial law memory dispositif' is not a coherent ensemble, but a constellation, changing over time and adjusted to diverse contemporary uses. The 'enemy' created within it turns out to be a flexible memorial construct, created by different cultural practices of memory, which can be used either to mark its position in the trajectories of political disputes of the twenty-first century or to avoid taking such a place or, finally, to shift the narrative about the past towards an apolitical, personal or even nostalgic recollection.

Works Cited

Adamczak, Marcin (2012) "*Katyń* i *Generał Nil* a (długi) zmierzch paradygmatu," *Kwartalnik Filmowy* 77–78, 72–94.
Baniewicz, Elżbieta (2014) "Polityka jest obrzydliwa," *Twórczość* 1, 117–120.
Basu, Laura (2010) "Memory *dispositifs* and National Identities: The Case of Ned Kelly," *Memory Studies* 4, 33–41.
Bondebjerg, Ib (2012) "Confronting the Past. Trauma, History and Memory in Wajda's Film," *Images* XI. 20, 37–51.
Domańska, Ewa (2008) "Obrazy PRL w perspektywie postkolonialnej," in *Obrazy PRL-u*, ed. Krzysztof Brzechczyn (Warsaw: IPN), 167–186.
Higson, Andrew (2000) "The Limiting Imagination of National Cinema," in *Cinema and Nation*, ed. Mette Hjort and Scott MacKenzie (London and New York: Routledge), 57–68.
Jabłoński, Ryszard (2014) "A different Wajda?" *New Eastern Europe* 1, 175–177.
Janion, Maria (1997) "Jeruzalem słoneczna i zamknięty krąg," *Kwartalnik Filmowy*, 17, 5–12.
Kobielska, Maria (2016) "Endless Aftershock. The Katyn Massacre in Contemporary Polish Culture," in *Traumatic Memories of the Second World War and After*, ed. Jason Crouthamel and Peter Leese (London and New York: Palgrave Macmillan Press), 197–219.
Krakowska, Joanna (2014) "Czarnuchy," *Dialog* 4, 73–93.
Kwiatkowski, Krzysztof (2010) "Wszystko co kocham," *Kino* 1, 73.
Lubelski, Tadeusz (2006) *Wajda* (Wrocław: Wydawnictwo Dolnośląskie).
Lubelski, Tadeusz (2009) "Wstęp," in *Kino polskie jako kino narodowe*, ed. Tadeusz Lubelski and Maciej Stroiński (Cracow: Korporacja Ha!art), 5–9.
Luter, Andrzej (2009) "Popiełuszko. Wolność jest w nas," *Kino* 3, 56–57.
Mrozek, Witold (2009) "Film pamięci narodowej. Najnowsze kino polskie w dyskursie polityki historycznej," in *Kino polskie jako kino narodowe*, ed. Tadeusz Lubelski and Maciej Stroiński (Cracow: Korporacja Ha!art), 295–319.

Napiórkowski, Marcin (2016) *Powstanie umarłych. Historia pamięci 1944–2014* (Warsaw: Wydawnictwo Krytyki Politycznej).
Nijakowski, Lech (2008) *Polska polityka pamięci. Esej socjologiczny* (Warsaw: WAiP).
Pniewski, Jan (2009) "Portret hagiograficzny," *Przegląd Powszechny* 5, 116–118.
Rabsztyn, Tomasz (2010) "Punk, który nie dezerteruje," *Opcje* 1, 103–104.
Szpulak, Andrzej (2009) "Film zrobiony na kolanach," *Zeszyty Karmelitańskie* 2, 155–158.
Wroński, Paweł (2008) "Andrzej Wajda – architekt polskiej wyobraźni," *Gazeta Wyborcza*, 113, 1.

Filmography

80 milionów (*80 Million*) (2011) Dir. Waldemar Krzystek (Kino Świat).
Popiełuszko. Wolność jest w nas (*Popiełuszko. Freedom is Within Us*) (2009) Dir. Rafał Wieczyński (Kino Świat).
Wałęsa. Człowiek z nadziei (*Wałęsa. Man of Hope*) (2013) Dir. Andrzej Wajda (ITI Cinema).
Wszystko co kocham (*All That I Love*) (2009) Dir. Jacek Borcuch (ITI Cinema).

PART III: **Do Nations Need Enemies? Transcending/Perpetuating Nationalisms**

Daniel Reynaud
Redefining the Enemy in Contemporary Australian Anzac Cinema

In the words of pioneer historical film scholar Pierre Sorlin, historical cinema is "a reconstruction of the social relationship which, using the pretext of the past, reorganizes the present" (1980: 80). More concisely, Leger Grindon articulated that it "constitutes an address to the present" (1994: 1). Recent scholarship reinforces the idea of historical films addressing the concerns of the era that made them rather than the era in which the films are set (Cyrino 2000). Historical films also have complex interactions with notions of the individual and collective memory, and of national identity (Hughes-Warrington 2007: 81–83). Nowhere are these ideas more evident and applicable than in a study of Australian cinema on the central national narrative and myth of Anzac, built on the achievements of the Australians, as part of the Australian and New Zealand Army Corps (ANZAC), at Gallipoli in Turkey in 1915, and the later participation in France, Belgium and Palestine of the 'diggers,' as the Australians came to be known, throughout the rest of the war. The Anzac story on screen matches Sorlin's observation of historical films as indicators "of a country's basic historical culture, its historical capital" (21). Anzac cinema is embedded within the broad intertextual national processes of the memorialization of Anzac, and the concurrent socio-political and global contexts of the films have helped shaped the film representations of these Great War military conflicts, which act "as an apparatus of cultural memory" (Burgoyne 2009: 138).

This chapter examines the portrayal of the enemy in selected Australian film and television programs about World War One made since 1980. It begins by contextualising the representation of enemy with a quick overview of Australian war cinema during the Great War and the inter-war periods, before examining in detail the productions which occurred in two waves: 1980–1990, and 2010–2015. The first wave includes *Gallipoli* (dir. Peter Weir, 1981), *1915* (dir. Chris Thomson and Di Drew, 1982), *Anzacs* (dir. John Dixon, George Miller and Pino Amenta, 1985), *A Fortunate Life* (dir. Marcus Cole and Henri Safran, 1986), *Willesee's Australians: Private John Simpson* (dir. Henri Safran, 1988), *Always Afternoon* (dir. David Stevens, 1988), *The Alien Years* (dir. David Crombie, 1988), and *The Private War of Lucinda Smith* (dir. Ray Alchin, 1990). The second period includes *Beneath Hill 60* (dir. Jeremy Sims, 2010), *An Accidental Soldier* (dir. Rachel Ward, 2013), *Anzac Girls* (dir. Ken Cameron, Ian Watson, 2014), *The Water Diviner* (dir. Russell Crowe, 2015), *Gallipoli* (dir. Glendyn Ivin, 2015) and *Deadline Gallipoli* (dir. Michael Rymer, 2015). The themes that emerge revolve around shifting the identified enemy from that of Turk and German in Great War productions to the British in many of the productions of the 1980s, to an increasing empathy for the official enemy, and a problematisation of the whole notion of enemy in the later productions. In many cases, the concept of enemy is muted in Australian war cinema, as the fundamental issues revolve around the nature of the Australian identity and character, for which war is merely the backdrop, hence the enemy can be marginal to the cinematic preoccupations and themes which, as already indicated, reflect contemporary Australian beliefs and concerns.

The representation of the enemy in Australian Great War films follows an interesting and telling trajectory. The first films were made during the Great War itself and formed part of the national discourse in support of the war effort. Unsurprisingly, given the highly emotive propaganda fostered by militant government censorship of anything short of an aggressive pro-war stance, most films unequivocally took a pro-government line on their portrayals of the enemy. Typically, the enemy consisted of two groups, the official external enemy, Turk and German, and a subversive domestic enemy, in the form of spies and fifth columnists. Many of the films featured both. The first successful film was the short recruiting movie *Will They Never Come* (dir. Alfred Rolfe, 1915), where the enemy was not just the Germans but also indifferent stay-at-home young men in Australia gracing the sports fields instead of the battlefield. Two box-office hits in July 1915 dramatizing the Anzac landings which had taken place on 25 April 1915, *The Hero of the Dardanelles* (dir. Alfred Rolfe, 1915) and *Within our Gates* (dir. Frank Harvey, 1915), collectively featured treacherous Turks sniping at Red Cross workers and a villainous German spy who black-mailed a German-Australian into doing the spy's bidding.

A less xenophobic attitude towards the German as an enemy was evident in the movies *Murphy of Anzac* (dir. J. E. Mathews, 1916) and *The Joan of Arc of Loos* (dir. George Willoughby, 1916) and their reviews (cf. Reynaud 2007: 40–51), but any such trend was quickly shut down by the pervasive government censorship. Other films followed approved representations of the Germans as brutish Huns with 'Kaiser Bill' moustaches executing British nurses (*The Martyrdom of Nurse Cavell*, dir. John Gavin and C. Post Mason, 1916; *Nurse Cavell/La Revanche*, dir. W. J. Lincoln, 1916), and as women-ravaging, baby-killing invaders of Australia (*If the Huns Came to Melbourne* dir. George Coates, 1916; *Australia's Peril* dir. Franklyn Barrett, 1917). An oblique reference to the war effort was the spy thriller *The Enemy Within* (dir. Roland Stavely, 1918), which featured action-packed scenes of unidentified spies and a fifth-columnist group that was a thinly-disguised version of the reviled Industrial Workers of the World, an international socialist-anarchist-Marxist labour federation nicknamed the 'Wobblies' accused of anti-war activities in Australia by Prime Minister Billy Hughes' paranoid government.

Between the wars, Australian war films shifted to a predominantly heroic comic representation, to maximise audiences on the divisive subject of the Anzac legacy, which was contested between conservative and radical digger interest groups, and disliked by many civilians who were sick of the horrors and tragedy it represented (Reynaud 2007: 83–87). One Australian film-maker's mantra during the Great Depression was "when times are tough, make comedy" (Hall 1980: 117). Most war films of the inter-war period barely featured the official enemy in the form of Germans and Turks at all; rather, these appeared in imports as the villains whose capture formed the climax of the film. Australian productions were benign stories which emphasised the distinctively Australian character of the digger in contrast to his English counterpart, who was also positively represented. The films served as springboards for celebrating an Imperial Australian patriotism. The tacit enemy was actually radical republican anti-Imperial and anti-war sentiment, but which usually went unrepresented in the films. One amateur production, *The Spirit of Gallipoli* (dir. Keith Gategood and William Green, 1928) made the point more clearly, for "the enemy in the film was not the Turk but rather Australian indifference to the great Anzac achievement, an indifference that threatened to undo all that they have achieved for Australia" (Reynaud 2007: 108). Another adaptation of a German movie, *The Exploits of the Emden* (dir. Louis Ralph and Ken G. Hall, 1928) offered representations of Germans as chivalrous and sportsmanlike, winning praise for its "perfect fairness and impartiality" (*Sydney Morning Herald* 1928: 6). The last important war film of the era was released in 1940, and had its representations of the enemy attuned to the context of a new world war. With Turkey neutral in this war, *Forty Thousand Horsemen* (dir. Charles Chauvel, 1940) portrayed the Turks as honourable and respectful of the Anzacs, while the Germans were a throwback to the First World War, cast as arrogant, buffoonish and cruel villains.

Over the next thirty years, Australian cinema production suffered a serious decline, from which it tentatively began to re-emerge in the 1960s, reaching a full fruition of nationalistic period productions in the 1980s. A resurgence of Australian nationalism was deliberately fostered by successive governments, tapping into the young adult aspirations of a baby boomer generation which, having grown up in an era of peace, prosperity and American media, saw little relevance in the Imperial link. This immature nationalism built its identity on an aggressive differentiation from everything British, for which a repositioned, crudely Australian and anti-British Anzac legend emerged as a handy vehicle. Already, writers had tapped into the nationalistic potential of a distinctive Australian identity in the Anzac story, with one writer arguing that the nationalism born on Gallipoli "is a sentiment that is attractive to present-day temperaments" (McDonald 1983: 3), though not all writers conformed to the easy mythologising of the Anzacs taking place at the time. A couple of titles which represented the Anzacs in ways that challenged the myth formed the basis of screen adaptations, which preserved the independence of the literary text, thus resisting an overwhelming trend to the glorification of the Anzacs and the denigration of the British – the new enemy in Australian war films of the 1980s. On the whole, best-selling Anzac histories such as Bill Gammage's seminal *The Broken Years* (1974), Patsy Adam-Smith's *The Anzacs* (1978), and the Time-Life series *Australians at War* (1988) offered some discussion of the less savoury aspects of the Australians at war, but still tended towards the glorification of Anzac as a heroic national type. The once-contentious and evolving Anzac legend now entered a period of relative stability and widespread acceptance as a true representation of Australia's Great War participation.

The benchmark Australian film about the Great War remains *Gallipoli*, the best and most influential Australian war film, once even touted as a contender for the title of the best Australian film of any kind ever (Stratton 1990: 22). The film followed closely on the heels of *Breaker Morant* (dir. Bruce Beresford, 1980), which told the story of the execution of two Australian officers for war crimes by the British during the Boer War. *Breaker Morant* aggressively set up a binary between the Australians and the British, with the Australians representing a rough and ready common sense, decency and combat effectiveness and the British representing snobbery, bureaucracy and stupidity, while the Boers themselves, against whom both British and Australians were actually fighting, were almost inconsequential to the plot and barely represented at all. In many ways, the representations established by *Breaker Morant* became the template for Australian films of the 1980s, moving the concept of the enemy away from the combatant nation opposed to the Australians, instead showing them to be the British, the Imperial overlord under whose banner and authority the Australians fought.

Unsurprisingly, the enemy in *Gallipoli* was also essentially the British military hierarchy, while the Turks, ostensibly the enemy, were largely invisible. The movie placed responsibility for the deaths of Australian soldiers not on the Turks who fired the guns, but on the British officers who ordered the frontal attacks conducted with pointless stupidity and incompetence. The British were represented as being the opposite of the Australians, who exhibited all the virtues. British military incompetence did not stop them from exhibiting a patronising condescension, casually sipping their cups of tea at Suvla Bay, while the Australians were butchered in the diversionary attack at The Nek designed to keep Turkish pressure off British divisions supposedly outflanking the Turkish positions. The film portrayed a Colonel Robinson (a fictional version of the historical Australian Colonel Antill) who, in an upper-crust British-style accent, insisted that the attacks continue in the face of wholesale slaughter, while General Gardner, who ordered a halt to the pointless attacks, spoke in an unmistakeably Australian accent. Later, Weir disclaimed any intention of 'Pom bashing,' and regretted creating the impression that Robinson was British (1982: 42).

The film largely overlooked all other nationalities which might reasonably have been shown: the New Zealanders, who contribute two letters to the acronym Anzac, were absent – as they are from virtually all Australian Anzac cinema, while Egyptians were merely essential stock background figures in scenes set in the markets and brothels of Cairo, and Turks were glimpsed in the trenches at Gallipoli. Even the British rank and file, who formed the support troops to the Australian assault at The Nek, were absent, thus creating a simple dichotomy of the Australian soldier versus the British officer. The film's themes, concerning itself with issues of the Australian identity, meant that only Australians and British were relevant. As one critic perceptively noted, "*Gallipoli* is not so much about Australians in war as it is a celebration of the national ideology. It is largely about what is intrinsically Australian" (Freebury 1987: 7). The role of the British was as anti-type, exemplars of all the Old World failings that Australians had ceased to be in the Antipodes.

The other great popular screen representation of the Anzacs of that era was the miniseries *Anzacs*, which took rather a soap-opera approach to its treatment of the war, with a tendency to melodrama and cartoonish characters. In terms of reach and lasting influence, it was second only to Weir's *Gallipoli*, and DVD sales have continued strongly into the twenty-first century (Reynaud 2015: 194). As with *Gallipoli*, the real enemies in the miniseries were the English, as were the rare Australians who demonstrated un-Australian qualities. Indeed, one critic praised it specifically for advancing an Australian identity and rejecting a British one (Turner 1997: 232, 236–238). On the other hand, the formal enemies, that is to say the Turks and Germans, were rendered less demonic and given more sympathetic qualities, to the extent that they were portrayed at all. In fact one Anzac character was an ethnic German, acting as a window into the heart of the enemy. But, as with *Gallipoli*, the historical enemy was a shadowy figure necessary to make battle scenes functional rather than a source of active plot conflict. In practice, the opposition that the Anzacs faced came from the stupidity of British generals, the hypocrisy of Australian politicians, and the rare Australian soldier who failed to exhibit traditional Anzac values of mateship and a fair go.

The British were again the principal enemy. A critic wrote, "the British staff officers [...] appear incompetent or deliberately sadistic" (Mayer 1986: 64). Field Marshal Haig was an obvious target for British-bashing, especially as he had already been denigrated in British Prime Minister Lloyd George's post-war writings, and his reputation tarnished by historians like Alan Clark, Basil Liddell Hart and John Laffin, and in popular culture (for example in *Oh! What a Lovely War* dir. Richard Attenborough, 1969, and the later *Black Adder Goes Forth*, dir. Richard Doden, 1989). Lloyd George was given the floor in the series, allowing the wily Welshman to fire a few barbs at English incompetence that were pleasing to the Australian national consciousness of the 1980s. Haig was represented as patronisingly labelling the Australians 'colonial hooligans' who, since he could not execute them for crimes (the AIF did not have capital punishment), were sent to the Somme to 'quieten them down,' implying a deliberate use of the Anzacs as pointless cannon-fodder. While admitting they had been resourceful during the Boer War, he alluded to the Breaker Morant incident, saying "we shot a couple of them, as I remember." Other examples of British stupidity were highlighted by a general inspecting the front, exclaiming in wonder at the deep mud through which soldiers had been ordered to advance. Australian General Monash was represented as noting that their officer selection process was detrimentally affected by class considerations, thus affirming Australian egalitarianism over British class-consciousness. Even an otherwise popular Englishman in the Australian ranks, Bill 'the Pom' Harris, was chastised for failing to understand the Australian mindset when he labelled as 'mutiny' the mateship leading to the 60th Battalion's refusal to obey the order to disband. The archetypical larrikin Anzac, Cleary, played by Paul Hogan in the style of his 'Hoges' persona, exclaimed in frustration, "You still don't understand us, do you?," capturing the British-Australian binary at the heart of resurgent Australian nationalism, as exemplified in the Anzac legend of the era.

A few positive remarks were made about the British during the miniseries, sometimes noting their courage, but without restoring a sense of balance. Bill Harris may have been a former non-commissioned officer in the British Army, but he had deserted from it in the best Anzac anti-authoritarian manner. Characterised in advertising as "no whinging pommy bastard: he's a tough mate and a good soldier" (*Anzacs* file, National Film and Sound Archive), Harris clearly was on his way to transformation to a 'true-blue' Australian. Despite this tokenism of a good Englishman, the miniseries presented the British as the chief cause of problems for the Australians. Compared to them, the Germans and Turks appeared to be minor obstacles who would have been swept from the field if only the Australians had been in charge of affairs.

However, the British were not the only enemy of the true Australian. Included in the miniseries were several Australian characters who were negatively portrayed, each threatening to undermine the noble Anzac ideal. Cyril Earnshaw, a self-important windbag Australian politician, and his lacklustre son, Max, characterised the new Anzac legend of the 1980s, whereby the soldiers who fought were glorified while the politicians who brought war about were denigrated. In an era where post-Vietnam anti-war sentiment was still strong, this allowed the Anzac soldier to continue to hold the moral high ground, as a victim of the politicians rather than an agent of war. Earnshaw senior's 'Would to God' speeches marked him out as a figure of political hypocrisy and a target of satire, while his son was an inexperienced regulation-bound officer, commissioned on the strength of his political connections, who made a fool of himself in front of the men and other officers promoted from the ranks on merit. The other major figure of opposition to the Anzacs was the petty criminal soldier, 'Dingo' Gordon, described in promotional material as embodying "a contemptible side to the Australian character" (*Anzacs* file, National Film and Sound Archive). After deserting, Gordon was tracked down by his former mates and killed in a scuffle, thus showing how un-Australian disloyalty and self-interest was eliminated by the Anzac virtue of mateship.

The stereotypical portrayal of both the British and Australian enemy of the true Anzac seriously undermined the merit in doing so. Just as C. E. W. Bean, the official Australian war historian, labelled as untypical any Australian behaviour of which he did not approve, so also *Anzacs* constructed the less pleasant characters as being outside the norm, and thus not truly Australian. A critic noted that the series divided its cast "into 'real' Australians and the rest" (Mayer 1986: 64). To help make the moral issues clear, the reprehensible characters lacked any kind of positive qualities that might have made a viewer identify with them. The Germans and Turks received minimal coverage, but it was mostly positive. The character of Kaiser Schmidt acted as "the window through which we see and feel the German enemy, so that they are not caricatures" (*Anzacs* file, National Film and Sound Archive), which was a gesture towards attitudes to the enemy in the 1980s. More often, the perspectives of the Germans were used as puffs for the reputation of the Anzacs, as reports of German statements of Australian battlefield prowess were circulated among the Allies.

Two other productions of the 1980s tended toward the simplistic representation of the Anzac as virtuous, the enemy as sympathetic and the British as the villains, though both lacked the reach and the competence of *Gallipoli* and *Anzacs*. Simon Wincer's *The Lighthorsemen* (1987) was a less polemic presentation of the Anzac legend, and the portrayal of the English, while mostly conventionally stupid, lacked the venom of earlier productions. Both the Australians and the Germans mocked the British at various points in the film, while a prejudiced British general steadily opposed the Australian Light Horse attack that finally unhinged the stubborn Turkish defences. However, it showed positive qualities in two British officers; firstly General Allenby and secondly the foppish intelligence officer Meinertzhagen, whose upper-class-twit exterior concealed a brilliant military operator. The representation of the Turks and Germans was mixed. While some had the sense to admire the Australians, others demonstrated a British-like adherence to dogmatic stupidity – most evident in the character of Intelligence Captain Reichert, who fell for every one of Meinertzhagen's tricks, always overriding his insightful Turkish counterpart, Colonel Ismet. At the height of the battle, some Turks were represented as opening fire after having surrendered – this breach of military law was met by a justified massacre of the Turkish prisoners.

Henri Safran's *Willesee's Australians: Private John Simpson* (1987) was a forgettable episode in a television celebration of the bicentenary of European settlement. Conceived with jingoistic intent, its portrayal of the Turks was positive, showing them withholding fire and saluting Simpson for his daring work in rescuing the wounded, while representing the British in the blackest of colours, as wilfully stupid and criminally prejudiced against the Australians. Again, the function of the Turks was to highlight Australian merit and demonstrate by contrast how bad the behaviour of the Australians' ostensible Imperial brothers, the British, were.

Such was the Anzac jingoism of the decade that even critics were blinded, one scholar complaining that the "barrage" of Anzac productions merely "perpetuated the more uncritical, if comforting, myths about Australia's past" (Beaumont 1995: xix). Another chimed in, claiming that "every Anzac film blames arrogant British generals for Australian losses, and exonerates Australian leaders. Australia's egalitarian soldiers and society are contrasted with their class-ridden British counterparts." While conceding that "[t]here are elements of these films that gesture towards more complex and even critical tellings," he argued that "they are worked into the films so that the legend is reaffirmed" (Thomson 1994: 196–197). However, such sweeping generalisations overlooked a richer representation that occurred during the 1980s, admittedly in productions that failed to find audiences as large as either *Gallipoli* or *Anzacs*.

The miniseries *1915* featured a nuanced screenplay by Peter Yeldham based on the Roger McDonald novel of the same name. Its construct of the notion of enemy was more complex, and though the Turkish enemy was not featured, neither were they portrayed with any malice. What was more striking was an absence of anti-British sentiment. Instead of blaming the British generals for the suffering of the characters, more often their tribulations stemmed from their own poor choices or from the random mischance of war. For once, the biggest enemies of the Anzacs were the Anzacs themselves, as petty rivalries caused friction among them. As with earlier representations of Gallipoli, the series was more concerned with Australian identity, but for a change, the definition of this was not dependent on foregrounding an external enemy, either Turkish or British. In a similar vein, *A Fortunate Life* was also based on a book, this time the memoirs of West Australian Bert Facey. It also provided a nuanced representation of the concept of enemy, which was problematized. While British-bashing occurred in the miniseries, so also was there bashing of Australians, a point rarely made in other Anzac productions. The enemy was stupidity, from both British and Australian officers, and from civilians at home. In one scene set in Egypt, Australian officers left a unit to the devices of a drunken sergeant on an overland march, displaying professional neglect and incompetence. The British also came in for mockery, for their petty regimented ways and overbearing condescension, such as with an officer who would not help Facey even when it was in his power to do so and the need very evident, or the pointless bayonet drills conducted by petty-minded British sergeants. Once repatriated with war injuries, Facey ran the gauntlet of a series of exploitative, hostile, dismissive, and indifferent responses from Australian civilians, a new enemy in Anzac representation. On the other hand, in representing the Turks, the Australians were shown to refuse shooting at retreating Turkish soldiers after a failed attack, and during a burial truce a Turk offered Facey an orange. These incidents constructed the Turkish enemy as human, in many ways more sympathetic than elements of the British or Australian armies, or many Australian civilians.

The bicentennial year of 1988 also saw two miniseries screened which challenged the notion of friend and foe in Australian war cinema, *Always Afternoon* and *The Alien Years*. They shared a similar theme, being concerned with the treatment of Germans in Australia during the war years. Both represented the Germans in positive terms; technically, the enemy were German aliens (and even citizens) living in Australia, but actually the enemy was jingoistic Australian society in general and the Federal Government in particular. By shifting the focus from the battle front to the home front, both miniseries interrogated the national narrative of Anzac, and the new perspective made for uncomfortable viewing.

The Alien Years portrayed anti-German sentiment in Australia as having been deliberately cultivated by politicians keen to create a sense of fear to motivate civilians to support the war effort. One argued, "If we're to have recruits this country needs to feel threatened." But it was not merely politicians; policemen, camp officers and guards used petty bullying tactics, and civilians were shown treating the internees with crude racism. The miniseries juxtaposed the vindictive behaviour of Australians with that of the peace-loving German immigrants, many of them refugees from religious persecution in Europe. A good number were naturalised or married to Australians. One case was featured in the narrative: the eldest son of a German father and Australian mother joined the AIF, while his younger brother joined the German army, witnessing his brother kill two of his comrades in battle. Similarly, *Always Afternoon* explored the divided national loyalties of German-Australians. One character lamented, "My loving, lovely brother, who was Australian, was killed by Germans. My honest, gentle father, who was German, was killed by Australians. What language should I speak?" The sympathetic treatment of the Germans was helped by significant German funding but nevertheless was in keeping with a more tolerant age which did not see a wartime enemy as necessarily evil.

Both mini-series offer dramatically different constructs of the Anzac legend than had been conventionally told. *The Alien Years* director Donald Crombie described it as "a period in [Australia's] history of which many may be unaware – a period Australia should be quite ashamed of" (*The Alien Years* file, Promotional material, NFSA). Gone in these productions were the laconic, easy-going good-natured larrikins of the Anzac legend and in their place stood parochial and vicious Australians, imprisoning and even killing sober, hard-working fellow citizens at the behest of their own government, all in the name of fighting a just war. This unholy alliance of soldiers and civilians targeting peaceful aliens turned the Anzac legend upside down, portraying the Australians as the villains and the Germans as virtuous victims.

Ray Alchin's *The Private War of Lucinda Smith* (1991) took yet another turn in its portrayal of the enemy. While comedies of the war were produced between the wars, none had been attempted since. This miniseries came at a time when Australian audiences were tiring of a decade-long era of reverential period pieces, and it constructed the war as a bawdy comedy. Its unusual setting of the backwater theatre of German New Guinea offered a love triangle between an Australian chorus girl pursued by a German and a Britisher. While the German love interest was benignly represented, other Germans were stereotypically rigid. On the other hand, the miniseries poked fun at Australian prejudices, showing an Australian bar girl convinced that the amiable German lover would naturally be a rapist as portrayed in Allied propaganda. Uncharacteristically, Australian soldiers were portrayed more as 'Dad's Army' figures of fun, with a buffoonish officer, portly sergeant and incompetent men. Designed as a very unhistorical romp through the swamps of Melanesian New Guinea (and unmistakeably shot in Polynesian Samoa), the miniseries let some of the air out of the earnestness of the portrayal of both enemy and friend.

What followed was a twenty-year absence of Anzac from both the big and small screen – surprising in many ways, given the increasing popularisation of Anzac, with growing media coverage and political support, and ever-improving attendances at Anzac Day marches and at various pilgrimage sites around the world (particularly Gallipoli, Villers-Bretonneux and Kokoda), but this was perhaps reflective of the fact that the Anzac legend had stabilised, leaving little new to say about it on film. However, the Great War featured again in a new wave of Anzac productions from 2010, culminating in several releases to mark the 2015 centenary of the Gallipoli landings. In a search for audiences, most attempted tellings of the Anzac story that had escaped the public eye to date, selecting obscure units, such as miners, or under-represented figures such as nurses and deserters. These attempts largely failed. The reasons were variously attributed to a continuing national inferiority complex (Mathieson 2015), or a combination of a surfeit of Anzac programming, poor production values and television programming, and a national indifference to an overblown mythology (Phillips 2015). While none managed the impact of the earlier releases, these new productions demonstrated yet another subtle shift in how the enemy was represented.

The movie *Beneath Hill 60* heralded the return of Anzac to the big screen, the first since 1987. It told the story of an Australian tunnelling unit in Flanders, and while working in the traditions of the productions of the 1980s, it offered more subdued national stereotypes and projected a less polemic outlook than the classic productions of the golden era. It still managed to feature three officers as its key villains: one each of German, British and Australian origin, although it was possible to mistake the latter for an Englishman. Certainly, some critics did. The German and Australian colonels were characterised by a stubborn determination to stick to decisions made without the facts, while the British officer was patronising towards the colonials. On the other hand, another British officer somehow managed to stay pristinely clean while working around the diggings, and yet avoided the priggishness usually associated with a man who never seemed to get his hands dirty. As the representation of the British lost some of its condemnatory edge, a new common enemy emerged in Australian war film, in keeping with popular constructs of the Great War from Europe: that of the callous and incompetent Australian officer who placed his own decisions and comfort over that of military effectiveness and even the lives of his men.

In the claustrophobic settings of the tunnels, the enemy was a rarely-seen but constantly threatening presence. German tunnellers could be heard digging and even talking, and there was the constant threat of being blown up by counter-miners. Occasionally, German soldiers were portrayed, especially in scenes of raids on trenches. However, the film had one moment where it gave insight into the lives of the men on the other side, eavesdropping on a couple of German miners discussing home and loved ones. Soon after, they were trapped in an Australian counter-mining operation, setting up one of the most effective scenes of the film. One Australian, delighted at the success of their little explosion, flippantly joked that he had blasted the Germans all the way back to Berlin. Unlike the Australian characters in the film, the audience had come to know the unfortunate men, resulting in a poignant juxtaposition of the celebrations of one group over the death of another. While the Australian characters could rejoice in their work, the audience was set up to feel empathy (Reynaud 2010: 40.1–40.2).

The tele-feature *An Accidental Soldier* offered quite a radical redefinition of the enemy. Taking as its subject a pacifist baker who reluctantly enlisted in 1918 in the face of a shaming campaign in his West Australian hometown, its hero deserted during a battle, finding refuge with an older French woman before both were betrayed to the authorities. The enemy in this film was not the Germans, but the French authorities and French and Australian societies that forced men to war and hunted them down when they evaded it. Making an Anzac deserter the hero of a film flew in the face of the Anzac legend, where mateship ensured that a man did not let down the others in his unit. On the other hand, close news media coverage of the tragedies of war in recent Middle Eastern conflicts ensured that contemporary audiences were much more sympathetic to the hero's plight than might have been the case even during the immediate post-Vietnam era. The film successfully positioned the authorities searching for his whereabouts and the gossiping neighbours as the enemy, heightened by their suspicions over the French woman, whose husband was of German Alsatian origin. As with *Always Afternoon* and *The Alien Years*, the enemy in this film was this Anzac soldier's own culture. The war was not one between the rival empires of Britain and France on the one hand and Germany on the other, but rather between the ideologies of nationalistic hate versus humanistic pacifism and love.

The miniseries *Anzac Girls* followed the lives of five Anzac nurses, based on historical nurses who served in the war. With the nurses stationed behind the front, little was seen of the enemy, whose presence was manifested mainly through the stream of wounded men the nurses had to treat, although an occasional bombardment or aerial attack brought the enemy close. The enemies constructed by the miniseries consisted of the layers of hierarchy that constantly interfered with the capacity of the Australian nurses to perform to their potential. These hierarchies were the interlocking powers of Imperialism, sexism and militarism, meeting in the persons of various male British officers who had scant regard for Australian women nurses from a civilian background. Often the snobbery was exhibited by subsets of these powers, such as British hospital Matrons, or Australian officers. The episodes featured plenty of British-bashing, as the virtuous Anzac nurses battled snobbery, incompetence and condescension before triumphing in their roles.

While *The Water Diviner* fell rather short of an attempt to create a big-impact Anzac film capitalising on the name of its director and star, Russell Crowe, it also managed a significant reworking of the notion of enemy. Joshua Connor, the main character, travelled to post-war Turkey to find what had happened to his three sons, who went missing during the Gallipoli campaign. It was by far the most empathetic rendering of the Turks in Australian war cinema to that time, allowing audiences to engage positively with several key Turkish figures. One was the war widow Ayshe, the other half of the rather unconvincing love story, while the other two were Major Hassan and Sergeant Jemal, who helped Connor with his search for both the dead and living sons. Flashbacks of Gallipoli battles were shown, but the chief conflicts came from the Greeks in the Greco-Turkish War for Anatolia. In something of a throwback to Great War propaganda films, they served as typically villainous enemies, being represented more like atrocity-committing banditti than regular soldiers, and were not shown in any depth or with any sympathy. The Turks, on the other hand, were positively represented and worked as friends and emotional allies to Connor in his quest. The film created a sense of interdependence between the key Turkish and Australian characters.

If *The Water Diviner* was a box-office disappointment, then the miniseries *Gallipoli* was close to a disaster. Ratings fell so swiftly that the last few episodes of the seven-part series were hastily screened as double episodes. It trod such familiar territory that too few viewers were engaged as a result. Ironically, the series seemed to have pleased critics more than it did the general public. It combined the usual portrayal of British generals in comfortable circumstances sending men to their deaths (though to be fair, its British generals grew more human and sympathetic as the series progressed), with the newer version of Anzac, which portrayed the Turks quite sympathetically. When Mustafa Kemal ordered his men to die, the narrative framed it in a way that invited admiration; the same words in the mouth of a British general traditionally has been held up as typical British callousness towards the lives of colonials. In particular, the representation of the May 24 burial truce offered opportunities for Turks and Australians to interact. In virtually every case, it was the Turks who initiated friendship, offering gifts and sharing family photos, with the sometimes wary Australians warming up and responding positively. The net result was the creation of a bond of humanity between them. As the lead character 'Tolly' Johnson intoned in voice-over, "They were fathers, sons and brothers just like us. I didn't hate them anymore."

Deadline Gallipoli was the most recent representation of the First World War on Australian screens. It constructed a view of the war through the eyes of several historical war correspondents at Gallipoli, in particular Charles Bean. It overtly displaced the notion of the Turk as the enemy. One journalist opined, 'The enemy in the war is not the honourable Turk, but our incompetent leadership.' The miniseries followed the recent trend of showing the Turk in human colours, and giving them a voice. In one scene, a captured Turkish soldier confronted Bean while translating a Turkish news story which described the Allied invasion of Turkey. Queried by Bean over the term 'invasion,' the Turk tellingly replied, "What would you call it?" A closing scene of war museum relics showed a flute, which had featured earlier in the drama when a captured Turkish soldier was released after playing it. Poignantly, the Turk was shot by other Australians as he left the Anzac lines. The miniseries also positioned the enemy as consisting of any resistance to recounting the truth about the war. Often this resistance came about from senior military figures who did not want the truth reported; on other occasions a desire to smooth over awkward truths came from soldiers or even the journalists themselves, often prompted by a desire to save families from anguish.

Several interconnected issues emerge from a review of how contemporary Australian war films have represented the enemy. Firstly, there has been a significant shift away from the war films of the Great War and inter-war periods in how the Turks and Germans have been represented. They have evolved from villains, war criminals and subversives through a relatively neutral portrayal in the 1980s to the status of honourable combatants with a shared humanity in the most recent productions of the 2010s. Often, the enemy's words were appropriated to serve as encomium for Australian deeds, embroidering the Anzac legend with a more significant form of praise than any from an ally, and forming a most striking contrast with representations of British opinions of the Anzacs. In particular, the most recent productions reflected a populist sense of solidarity with the Turks, picking up on the widespread Australian perception of modern Turks being pro-Australian (Stanley 2013).

Secondly, while the Turks and Germans have remained the ostensible enemy in the films, the productions have tended to construct actual enemies who were not Turk or German. In the most popular productions of the 1980s, this enemy was most often the British, especially their high command, whose condescension, incompetence and downright wilful callousness was positioned as being the cause of most of the problems for the Anzacs. Occasionally, another populist whipping boy was added – that of politicians at home and abroad. A few productions problematized these simplistic representations, suggesting that Australians, military and civilian, government and non-government, officer and ranker, also contributed to the issues faced by the Anzacs, with behaviour that marked them as the enemies of the virtues of the Anzac soldier embodied by the myth. But these tended to be productions that failed to gain a mainstream audience, and in any case were often interpreted as being part of the mainstream. Reading all Anzac films as presenting stereotypes demonstrated the strength of the clichés in the Anzac legend. As we have seen, the more nuanced productions of the 1980s were often lumped together with their less subtle cousins by both critics and audiences, suggesting that dominant national narratives were key determinants in how individual representations were read. Productions that went against the grain suffered a double silencing of their reinterpretations: being overlooked by large audiences in the first place, and then being decoded as if they were more of the 'same old, same old,' and thus marginalised in value.

The more recent Anzac productions problematized the notion of enemy far more successfully than those of the 1980s, largely due to the fact that they spoke to an Australian audience that had moved on from the simplistic jingoism of three decades earlier. While there were still examples of blaming the British for problems, the nature of the enemy faced by the Anzacs was made more complex, and encompassed greater internal divisions and resistances. Not only were British and Australian hierarchies represented as the enemy, so also were the Anzacs themselves and the civilian societies of Australia and allied countries.

The third issue is the extent to which the ostensible enemy mattered. The productions of the 1980s hardly needed Turks or Germans, as their primary concern was rarely the war. They were statements about national identity, hence why the British were more often the enemy than Turks or Germans, as Australian nationalism of the era was focussed on cutting its family ties with Mother England. While this perspective did not completely die out, it was less dominant in the productions of the 2010s. 'Pommy-bashing' was replaced to some extent with a new need to construct the Turk as a friend and fellow human in the Anzac narrative, and to recognise alternative narratives in the Anzac story.

Contemporary Australian Anzac cinema has continued to wrestle with its representations of a central national narrative, continuing its ongoing "address to the present" (Grindon 1994: 1) on key matters of its "historical capital" (Sorlin 1980: 21). While the enemy is no longer presented in simplistic and antagonistic terms, the notion of enemy still retains strongly mythic elements which form part of the national construct of Anzac, including notions that the Australians preferred Turks to British generals, that the British were often butchers, and that because of Anzac, the Turks now have a high regard for Australians. In face of a national legend that continues to evolve, the next generation of Anzac cinematic representations will be interesting to observe.

Works Cited

Beaumont, Joan (1995) "Introduction," in *Australia's War, 1914–1918*, ed. Joan Beaumont (Sydney: Allen and Unwin), vii–xxii.

Burgoyne, Robert (2009) "Prosthetic Memory/Traumatic Memory: *Forrest Gump* (1994)," in *The History on Film Reader*, ed. Marnie Hughes-Warrington (London and New York: Routledge), 137–142.

Cyrino, Monica Silveira (2009) "*Gladiator* (2000)," in *The History on Film Reader*, ed. Hughes-Warrington, 176–184.
Freebury, Jane (1987) "Screening Australia: *Gallipoli* – a Study of Nationalism on Film," *Media Information Australia* 43. 1, 5–8.
Gerster, Robin (1987) *Big-Noting: The Heroic Theme in Australian War Writing* (Melbourne: Melbourne University Press).
Grindon, Leger (1994) *Shadows on the Past: Studies in the Historical Fiction Film* (Philadelphia, PA: Temple University Press).
Hall, Ken G. (1980) *Australian Film: The Inside Story* (Sydney: Summit Books).
Marnie Hughes-Warrington (2007) *History Goes to the Movies: Studying History on Film* (London and New York: Routledge).
Mathieson, Craig (2015) "Gallipoli's ratings fail highlights Australia's inferiority complex," *Sydney Morning Herald* <http://www.smh.com.au/entertainment/tv-and-radio/gallipolis-ratings-fail-highlights-australias-inferiority-complex-20150218-13hwz8.html> (25 May 2017).
Mayer, Geoff (1986) "Fair dinkum on the Western Front," *Cinema Papers* 55, 64.
McDonald, Roger (1983) "Who Owns the Great War?" *Age Monthly Review* 3. 9, 3–5.
Phillips, Richard (2015) "Australian audiences turn off Gallipoli TV war drama," *World Socialist Web Site* <https://www.wsws.org/en/articles/2015/03/13/anza-m13.html> (29 May 2017).
Reynaud, Daniel (2007) *Celluloid Anzacs: The Great War through Australian Cinema* (Melbourne: Australian Scholarly Publishing).
Reynaud, Daniel (2010) "Digging Up New Anzac Legends," *History Australia* 7. 2, 40.1–40.2.
Reynaud, Daniel (2015) "War," in *Directory of World Cinema*, vol. 19: *Australia & New Zealand*, ed. Ben Goldsmith, Mark David Ryan, and Geoff Lealand (Bristol, Chicago: Intellect), 193–196.
Sorlin, Pierre (1980) *The Film in History: Restaging the Past* (Oxford: Blackwell).
Stanley, Peter (2013) "Gallipoli: 98 Years On," <http://honesthistory.net.au/wp/gallipoli-club-peter-stanley> (15 May 2017).
Stratton, David (1990) *The Avocado Plantation: Boom and Bust in the Australian Film Industry* (Sydney: Pan Macmillan).
Thomson, Alistair (1994) *Anzac Memories: Living with the Legend* (Melbourne: Oxford University Press).
Turner, Graeme (1997) "ANZACS: Putting the Story Back in History," in *War: Australia's Creative Response*, ed. Anna Rutherford and James Wieland (Sydney: Allen & Unwin), 229–238.
Weir, Peter (1982) "The Birth of a Nation: An Interview with Peter Weir," *Cineaste* 11. 4, 41–42.

Filmography

1915 (1982) Dir. Chris Thomson and Di Drew (Australian Broadcasting Corporation).
An Accidental Soldier (2013) Dir. Rachel Ward (Goalpost Pictures).
The Alien Years (1988) Dir. Donald Crombie (Australian Broadcasting Corporation).
Always Afternoon (1988) Dir. David Stevens (Afternoon Pictures).

Anzac Girls (2014) Dir. Ken Cameron and Ian Watson (Australian Broadcasting Corporation).
Anzacs (1985) Dir. John Dixon, George Miller and Pino Amenta (Burrowes-Dixon Company).
Beneath Hill 60 (2010) Dir. Jeremy Sims (Lucky Country Productions).
Deadline Gallipoli (2015) Dir. Michael Rymer (Matchbox Pictures).
A Fortunate Life (1986) Dir. Marcus Cole and Henri Safran (Nine Network Australia).
Gallipoli (1981) Dir. Peter Weir (Australian Film Commission).
Gallipoli (2015) Dir. Glendyn Ivin (Nine Network Australia).
The Lighthorsemen (1987) Dir. Simon Wincer (Australian Film Commission).
The Private War of Lucinda Smith (1990) Dir. Ray Alchin (Resolution Films).
The Water Diviner (2015) Dir. Russell Crowe (Fear of God Films).
Willesee's Australians: Private John Simpson (1988) Dir. Henri Safran (Trans Media Productions).

Andrejs Plakans and Vita Zelče
The Fading of Enemy Images in Contemporary Latvian Cinema

In a 1972 book subtitled "notes of a film journalist," the popular Latvian émigré novelist and playwright Anšlavs Eglītis (1906–1993) offered an unusual account of his childhood and teenage experiences with 'Latvian' cinema specifically, and his later adventures in the motion picture world generally. His memoir was the result of his family's decision in the 1950s to finally take up permanent residence in Pacific Palisades, California, after almost a decade in German post-World War II 'displaced person' camps and then a stay of several years in Oregon in the United States. These wanderings had been preceded by a 1944 flight from Latvia to escape the country's reoccupation by the armed forces of the USSR. His historical descriptions, based largely on personal memory, of motion pictures and moviemaking in pre-WWII Latvia – the two interwar decades when Latvia was experiencing its first period of independence – included a detailed inventory of motion picture theaters in Riga and the films he saw in them, extensive descriptions of prominent European film stars, and the politics of the German and Russian film world. His observations about specifically *Latvian* filmmaking during the interwar decades, however, were remarkably terse: "Since there were virtually no Latvian films, the ubiquitous German film actors we saw at times seemed like our own" (Eglītis 1972: 3). The book, in other words, suggested that as Latvians were struggling to establish a recognizable national identity for their new country after 1918, the imagination of youngsters like Eglītis was being 'Europeanized,' rather than 'Latvianized,' by the films they saw because of the near-absence of Latvian actors, speaking Latvian, on the same screens.[1]

The situation Eglītis was highlighting in this memory-based description underlines the fact that the phrase 'Latvian cinema' in the country's first independence period (1918–1940) can realistically be used only in reference to foreign motion pictures shown in Latvian movie theaters. Feature films (referred to in the Latvian language as 'actor-films' [*aktierkino*], 'art films' [*mākslas filmas*], or in more recent discourse, "play films" [*spēlfilmas*]) made by indigenous Latvian moviemakers were so sparse as to be nearly invisible. Indeed, the first feature-length Latvian-made film that had considerable artistic merit and competitive

---
[1] The accuracy of his generalizations can be evaluated by reference to the two histories of early Latvian films by Pērkone (2008, 2016). Eglītis may have overstated the situation, but not by much.

potential did not appear until late in 1939, less than a year before in the summer of 1940 the country was annexed by and incorporated into the USSR.[2] As a consequence, the most productive phase of *Latvian* moviemaking to date, in both qualitative and quantitative terms, turned out to be the four decades (1945– 1985) during which the country's artists in all fields were under the strict control of the elaborate censorship system of the USSR. Even so, during the 1970s and 1980s, the Riga Film Studio (RFS; *Rīgas kinostudija*), became an important segment of the Soviet Union's film industry. RFS produced about seven percent of the entire Soviet film output, and its films attracted the third largest audience in the USSR (directly after the two leading Soviet-state producers *Mosfil'm* and *Lenfil'm*). Several of its detective films, comedies, melodramas, and musical comedies were seen by more than thirty million viewers.[3] At the same time, many of the RFS films contributed substantially to the maintenance of Latvian national identity, helping to sustain Latvian culture and language. Latvian filmmakers had learned the 'rules of the game' of the Soviet movie industry, as well as the required Aesopian language in films, both of which had also been mastered by many in the audiences of the time. In the whole Soviet period (1940 –1990), the RFS had created 214 feature films, around 1220 documentary films, more than 2000 newsreels, and around 60 animated films.[4] Of the twelve films included in the Latvian 'cultural canon' at this writing, only one – the silent feature films *Lāčplēsis* (dir. Aleksandrs Rusteiķis, 1930) *was not* made in the RFS Riga facilities of the Soviet period.[5] Yet, arguably, it was not until the post-1991 decades and the renewal of national independence that Latvian moviemakers became entirely free to pursue their calling wherever it might lead and to have

---

[2] The film in question is *Zvejnieka dēls* (*The Fisherman's Son*) (1939), directed by Vilis Lapenieks.

[3] RFS films were also sold to some fifty foreign countries, but there is little information about these transactions. The distribution of Soviet films abroad was a centralized and secretive operation since the income from sale of these films went directly to the state and not to the filmmakers and studios. The state, in turn, could use the moneys to support various political initiatives, such as, for example, sponsorship of communist parties in so-called 'enemy' countries of the USSR: see Goris 1982: 105 and Streičs 2006: 426– 427.

[4] For more on Latvian filmmaking in the Soviet period see Riekstiņš 1989; Sosnovskii 1976; Goris 1982: 102–118; Cāne 2014; and Matīsa 2005.

[5] Concerning the Latvian 'cultural canon,' see "Cinema" at http://www.kulturaskanons.lv/en/1/10/98/. It has to be noted that many of Soviet-period RFS films remain popular today among Latvian viewers. For example, a long-standing television-viewing ritual on John's Day (June 24; summer solstice) involves the 1981 film *Limuzīns Jāņu nakts krāsā* (*A Limousine The Colour Of Midsummer's Eve*) directed by Jānis Streičs.

their creations shaped primarily by their own artistic sense and their perceptions of the interests of a potential audience (Pērkone 2013: 536).

The post-1991 years, however, created other problems. The dominant concern now was what the nature of a 'Latvian national cinema' needed to be.[6] Politically speaking, the renewed 1991 Latvian state was conceived of as a *continuation* of the interwar Republic, with the Soviet period thought of as an unwelcomed interruption. Cinematographically speaking, post-1991 Latvian filmmakers had little to connect to by way of a Latvian filmmaking tradition stemming from the first independence period of a half-century earlier. The logically available connection was the Soviet era, but continuity with its filmmaking practices and output had to be handled gingerly. Another major difficulty was the vast supply of Western films to which the Latvian market was now open. As noted by a recent history of Latvian films in language that eerily resembles Eglītis' account of the interwar period, post-1991 filmmakers had to scramble to reconstruct 'Latvian' filmmaking because "[...] in the early 1990s Latvian screens were inundated with American products [...] there was a rapid drop in Latvian-made films and they became *almost invisible* in the generally available repertoire" (Balčus 2011a: 351; emphasis added). Consequently, post-1991 Latvian filmmaking has had to search for a new strategy for national uniqueness to accompany the country's re-orientation toward the west, the latter being marked by the 2004 accession of the country to the European Community and NATO, and by the opening of Latvian cultural space to cultural products, including films, from other countries.

Nonetheless, since 1991 Latvian moviemakers have shown no sign of wanting to surrender in the face of global competition and technological change, and have continued to make films meant to testify to the existence of a uniquely 'Latvian' cinematographic perspective on past and present reality. Moviemaking thus remains an essential part of the post-1991 renovation process of Latvian national identity that is still an unfinished task. Some changes, however, have become evident in the most recent years when it has become possible to talk about generational replacement. On balance, a new generation of film directors, who have obtained their professional education in western and Latvian cinema schools, appears to be making its mark in European cinematic space. The films of young directors have had success at international film festivals, e. g. at the Berlin Film Festival in 2013 a prestigious award was received by Jānis Nords for *Mammu, es tevi mīlu* (*Mommy, I Love You*), and in 2016 a film by Renārs Vimba called *Es esmu šeit* (*Mellow Mud*) also earned a prize. The international

---

6 The problem of conceptualizing cinema as 'national' is discussed by Higson 1989: 36–47.

composition of filmmaking teams and the engagement of non-Latvian actors in important film roles has become much more frequent: Ulrich Matthes in *Pelnu sanatorija* (*Exiled*) (dir. Dāvis Sīmanis, 2016), Sabine Timoteo in *Melānijas hronika* (*The Chronicles of Melanie*) (dir. Viesturs Kairišs, 2016), Edvin Endre in *Nameja gredzens* (*The King's Ring*) (dir. Aigars Grauba, 2017).

1 Contemporary Latvian Films Contextualized

The foregoing paragraphs will suggest that a properly contextualized analysis of such key terms as 'contemporary,' 'Latvian cinema,' and, indeed, 'enemy,' could become so extensive as to leave little room for a closer look at Latvian films themselves, which after all is the main objective of the present chapter. The recent evolution of creative impulses in even so small a European country as Latvia (2016 population ca. 1,900,000; proportion of ethnic Latvians ca. 65%) can be quite complicated, but the reader will have to obtain the basic information about the Latvian filmmaking profession from other sources, most of which, however, are in the Latvian language (Pērkone 2011, 2016; Brūveris 2014; Hogan-Brun 2009). In the present chapter, our focus will be much narrower, namely, on six relatively recent popular Latvian films to see what evidence is available for an assessment of enemy images (interpreting that phrase broadly). Our selection comes from the category of feature films because we judge this category to be relatively free of the directorial intent to persuade. These films are most likely to be expressive of the free play of the filmmaker's artistic imagination, unguided by ideological considerations other than perhaps concern for keeping alive a specifically Latvian filmmaking tradition. Also, these are generally films that have received some degree of international attention, some more and some less, which could be taken as testimony to their above-average quality.

The problem of 'the enemy' in these films also deserves some additional comment. Our premise is that feature-length films of this type will contain overt or covert 'conflict' of some kind, and that this manner of structuring the flow of images on the screen will involve some moral assumptions. With respect to conflict – the film context in which enemy images become relevant – Latvian real-life experience from the mid-nineteenth century onward has created a great mass of potentially useful conflict-ridden material for filmmakers to choose from. There have been at least four major regime changes and opposition to them, multiple attacks on the cultural self-affirmation of the Latvian intelligentsia, civil-war-like confrontations among Latvians as they participated in opposing great-power armed forces fighting over Latvian territory, involvement in the murder and repression of their fellow citizens, suspicion and distrust among the ethnic subpopulations of the Latvian state, and despair over the inability of inhabitants to incorporate into their thinking new values brought by systems-changes. The raw material, therefore, to enable filmmakers to interpret Latvian life in a Manichean fashion – in a 'children of light' versus 'children of darkness' manner – is plentiful, but, interestingly, post-1991 (contemporary) filmmakers have not felt obligated to create such a simple screen reality. Rather, their efforts have generally been two-fold, consisting, first, of creating images that remain within the socio-economic and cultural contexts that make movie themes immediately recognizable to *Latvian* audiences; that is, their movies are meant to continue a specifically *Latvian* tradition of filmmaking. The duality of friends and/or enemies enters films at the same time, if at all, as a part of the larger 'national' endeavor. Second, there has been a deliberate attempt to universalize these specifically *Latvian* images, to give them a larger significance, to infuse them with meanings that would move them beyond Latvian parochial concerns. Some analysts of recent European films have proposed a series of categories that can be used to analyze the interplay between global and national themes, and we shall adapt several of these for our own purposes (Aitkin 1996: 78–79). As the theoretical literature suggests, the focus on the 'national' is persistent everywhere. In these Latvian films, however, the parochial is merged with the larger intent of giving a particular film a broader appeal at least to a *European* audience. We shall examine these six films in terms of four separate problem categories: the Soviet past, the distant past, the human life cycle, and transitional states.

2 Dealing with the Soviet Past

The first grouping includes films that incorporate some or many of the extensive array of themes that for ideological reasons were largely excluded from filmmaking during the Soviet period but continued to smolder in the consciousness of Latvian audiences nonetheless and that broke into the open during and after the transformational years between 1988 and 1991.[7] These films could also be described as part of an effort to return *wholeness* to the historical narrative with which Latvians wish to portray their history. Unsurprisingly, these films directly or indirectly relate to World War II, during which the country experienced a double occupation (by the USSR and Nazi Germany) and at the conclusion of which

---

[7] After the death of Stalin in 1953, there was a persistent pushback among Latvian filmmakers directed at party-line censorship, but its successes tended to be unpredictable: see Pērkone 2011: 172–276.

it 'returned' to the USSR that had occupied and annexed it in 1940. While in other contemporary societies the World War II period has continued its inevitable retreat into the 'distant' past, in Latvia that war and the events in the years surrounding it have retained a remarkable contemporaneity.[8] Repeated trauma-creating events starting in the summer of 1939 and lasting to the war's end in 1945 contain a rich store of material for writers and filmmakers, particularly because for the many decades of the Soviet period only one interpretation of the entire period was permitted. The object facts of the matter are well known. In June 1940, Latvia was occupied by the USSR and annexed (in August) to it. During the following twelve months the pre-war Latvian political elite was decimated (executed, deported, imprisoned) and everyday life was sovietized. In June 1941, a mass deportation to the interior of the USSR of some 14,000 'undesirables' from Latvia capped the Soviet effort to cleanse the Latvian population of potential opponents of the new regime. The initially successful German invasion of the USSR in July 1941 brought a new occupying regime to the Baltic area and later in that year, the participation of several thousand Latvians in the Holocaust against the Jewish population. The year 1943 saw the creation of the Latvian Legion through the conscription of some 110,000 young men into the German armed forces and their participation in the ongoing war on the Eastern Front; at the same time, the Soviet Army created units comprised of young Latvians who had fled to the USSR ahead of the advancing *Wehrmacht*. By 1946 it appeared that the country had lost about one third of its 1939 population. Another massive deportation action – to rid the country of 'kulaks' (successful farmers) – followed in 1949, and the mid-1950s saw the end of the 'forest brothers' saga, i.e. the final surrender of those who in 1946 had 'gone into the forests' to continue armed opposition to the Soviet regime.

During the Soviet period of Latvian filmmaking, the war and its long aftermath offered a host of official enemy images: from the pre-1940 period of independence (the government as a 'bourgeois clique'), from the German invasion and the German occupation regime ('fascist' collaborators), from the anti-Soviet partisans ('bandits'), from the Latvian Legion ('Hitlerites') and from the Latvians who had fled to the West ('war criminals'). By contrast, Latvian filmmakers after 1991 have retreated from ideologically based stereotypes and caricatures in the direction of complexity, human tragedy, and ambiguity. In the process, they have rendered 'enemy' images much less categorical. In the title of the chapter, we have used the adjective 'fading' about the concept of 'the enemy' to highlight not only its relatively infrequent usage as an organizing principle for images on

---

[8] About the contemporaneity of WWII in post-1991 Latvia see Zelče 2011: 13–33.

the Latvian screen, but also to underscore the clearly marked tendency among post-1991 filmmakers (and other creators of visual and written cultural products) to refrain from thinking about portrayable reality, past and present, in this fashion.

The plot of the film *Baigā vasara* (*Dangerous Summer*; dir. Aigars Grauba, 2000), created sixty years after the depicted events, unfolds during several days preceding the June 17, 1940, occupation of Latvia by the Soviet Army, which was followed by Latvia's loss of national sovereignty later that summer. The main figures are two young irreverent radio journalists working for Radio Latvia, one of them (Roberts) emerging as the main character; a young Baltic German woman (Izolde) who is finishing her degree at the University of Latvia prior to departing for Germany (the vast majority of Baltic Germans having departed in October 1939); the actual Foreign Minister of Latvia of the time, Vilhelms Munters (1898–1967), Izolde's patron and probable lover; and Kārlis Ulmanis (1877–1942), the historical authoritarian leader of the Latvian state from 1934 to 1940, who is depicted as a helpless figure, heavily reliant on Munters and urging Latvians in a radio address to perceive ongoing events as taking place with the full approval of "the Latvian government." Munters is depicted as the inner enemy: he is in fact shown to be collaborating with the Soviets to steer Latvia into the USSR, while secretly planning to flee west together with Izolde and an Ulmanis-signed letter permitting him access to Latvia's government-deposited money in Western banks. The external enemy is, of course, the USSR, as symbolized by images of Russian tanks and Russian-speaking Soviet officials at diplomatic receptions. They are referred to in the dialogue among Latvians simply as "the Russians."

The dialogue in the film is conducted in Latvian and the film itself is replete with imagery of the Latvian countryside and urban areas, all of which, as well as the film's retelling of a crucial turning point in Latvian history, place it in the category of 'national' films. This inventive and in many ways ahistorical manner of depicting the last days of the Ulmanis government and of the 1940 Soviet takeover would never have passed even the first level of Soviet-era censorship: e.g. the arrival of Soviet tanks is not shown as being greeted by cheering Latvian masses, but as the result of brute force supported by a corrupt and amoral Foreign Minister (and his hard-drinking Russian wife) and by cynical Soviet diplomats. In the film, the Germans and even the Baltic Germans – who in the pre-WWII decades were perceived by many Latvians as one of the centuries-long historic enemies of Latvians – appear in a sympathetic light through the figure of Izolde (who nonetheless is somewhat opportunistic) and, with the image of the German steamer as the ultimate refuge of those fleeing the Soviet army and security personnel. One of the final images of the film consists of hundreds of would-be passengers (apparently without proper passports or tickets) rushing the embarkation bridge to the ship, as neatly-clad German sailors bar their entry. Ultimately, however, it is not the fate of the romantically involved personalities that is the main story: rather, the film is about the loss of Latvia's national sovereignty. By reference to this prize, the 'enemy' image in the film is conveyed in a gradated rather than absolutist manner: the Soviet military and plotting diplomats symbolize military superiority, but actual bloodletting (in the film) is minimal; the self-centered Foreign Minister Munters is amoral and venal; the indecisive President Ulmanis, who wants the population to pretend that all is normal, is depicted as, in a sense, allowing the takeover; and Roberts' chief at the Radio, who rushes out to buy a forged passport, can think of nothing else than flight. Thus both Russians and Latvians are in some sense collaborators in the country's final downfall. Izolde, who represents the Baltic German element, is more a victim than an enemy. Though imperfectly, the film delivers to the audience what might be termed the revisionist history of these events, since only a few personages – such as Roberts' uncle, who is helping Izolde escape, and Roberts' inventor friend at the radio station, who remains oblivious to the events around him – remain morally unscathed. Those in high office and those controlling Latvian military power are all morally ambiguous to various degrees, including officers of the Latvian national army, who remain powerless to override the President's decision not to resist.

The voice-over at the beginning of *Dancis pa trim* (*Three to Dance*) (dir. Arvids Krievs, 2011), is rendered by a present-day young Latvian describing his participation in an archeological dig in search of his grandfather, at a site in the Courland region in western Latvia where this unknown ancestor, before disappearing, had served in the Latvian Legion in the last year of WWII. The film is thus in effect a long flash-back, taking the audience to 1944–1945. The plot concerns four young Legionnaires, who are scheduled to be shot for their participation in a desperate attempt by one of the Legion's generals, Jānis Kurelis (1882–1954), to break free of German control and to create the core of a new Latvian national army. A young German officer, Ginters, is in charge of the prisoners and, among other things, is a Baltic German who has returned as an officer to the land of his youth, knows the Latvian language, and understands the local situation better than his superiors. Adding a symbolic dimension to the story, most of the action takes place in an old castle of the Livonian Order, which had been one of the chief power-wielders of the Livonian Confederation of the late medieval period on Latvian territory. The front-stage enemies in this film are clearly the high-ranking German-speaking officers (though not the Baltic German Ginters). The Russians remain offstage until the end, when Soviet planes bomb the castle and a small Soviet contingent makes a brief appearance and machine-guns the four young Latvian prisoners who have managed to escape from the castle prison during the turmoil. One of them, however, survives, is found by Latvian refugees on their way to Sweden, and after a lifetime in the US, returns to the scene of his wartime adventures in Latvia.

The film's plot is based on a 1959 novel by the Latvian émigré writer Valdemārs Kārkliņš (1906–1964), who, like Anšlavs Eglītis, fled Latvia in 1944 and in 1951 emigrated to the US to settle in Oregon.[9] Though most of the film's action is set in the past, the intent of the filmmaker is to suggest that young twenty-first century Latvians (the voice-over) are intent on filling the 'white spaces' of their personal histories (a grandfather in the Legion, a relative who has fled west) even when this means delving into the story of an organization – the Legion – that in the Soviet decades was officially condemned (and generally portrayed) as Hitler loyalists and war criminals. Just as in *Baigā vasara* so also in *Dancis pa trim* the dominant language is Latvian, with an admixture of German, and, in the brief episode at the end, Russian. This, and the setting of much of the action in the Order castle and in nearby farmsteads, locates the film in the 'national' category. Both films can also connect to the living memory of many (now elderly) Latvians, who remember the loss of Latvian statehood as well as the participation (by themselves or relatives) in the ill-fated Latvian Legion. The filmmaker takes the viewer back to the Kurelis episode, moving scenes back and forth between the duplicitous German military leaders; the Latvian General Kurelis and his staff, who harbor hopes that in 1944, just as in 1919,[10] the Western Allies will come to the aid of Latvians; the imprisoned Legionnaires, who are growing more desperate as the plot unfolds; and the maneuvers of Sandra, a love interest of one of the prisoners, to entice the Baltic German Ginters to help saving her Alfrēds. The Kurelis episode ends in disaster: German military leaders crack down on the 'Kurelians.' Initially tolerating the situation because the *Wehrmacht* is making its last stand against a rapidly advancing Soviet Army in the as yet unvanquished corner of the province – termed the 'Courland Kettle' or 'Courland Fortress' – and needing the Legion's manpower, the Germans finally arrest Kurelis, transport him to the Stutthof Concentration Camp in Germany, and execute or imprison his followers. Many of the Kurelians dis-

---

9 The close link between Latvian written literature and moviemaking began with the first major feature film *Zvejnieka dēls* (1939; see above), continued throughout the Soviet period, and entered the post-Soviet decades as a well-established tradition. The historical linkages between the several different branches of Latvian creativity – theatre, cinema, written literature – still needs systematic description.

10 See the description of *Rīgas sargi* below.

perse into the Courland forests, helping to initiate the post-war saga of the 'forest brothers.'[11]

Dancis pa trim embeds a personal story (the romantic triangle) within an altogether fantastic episode in the short history of the Legion (1943–1945), with these interlinked plots being further embedded in the larger story of the Courland Kettle. End-of-war panic and desperation prevents any of the characters from emerging cleanly as 'the enemy' or even as forthright and moral individuals. The Germans and Latvians are, after all, comrades-in-arms, fighting a common enemy, yet both have conflicting agendas: for the German army, withdrawal to the Fatherland is at this point the main concern; for the Latvian supporters of Kurelis, it is the renewal of the Latvian state. However, Latvian characters in the film are hardly positive heroes: the four imprisoned Latvian soldiers quarrel and fight with each other, the leaders of the Kurelians spin fantasies about resisting until liberation is brought by the arrival of "the Americans, the English, and the Swedes,"[12] the intervention of a Latvian Lutheran clergyman remains ineffectual, Sandra brings sexuality into play with the doubt-ridden Baltic German Ginters; and the Latvian farmer who earlier in the film provides a refuge to the four young 'deserters' worries less about their fate than about his own if his assistance were uncovered. An almost totally off-screen enemy is the advancing Soviet army, which becomes visible only at the end, when "the Russians" stop the four escapees, rob them of their watches, and after declaring that the "war is over" and that they should now be friends, shoot them in the back. Who is enemy and who is friend, who can be trusted and who not, and on which side the audience's sympathies should lie are questions that become harder to answer as the film goes on. Seemingly, the filmmaker appears more concerned with images that testify to the moral ambiguities of wartime, especially in the kind of extreme situation that clearly prevailed in the Courland Kettle.

3 The Uses of the Distant Past

A second category of post-1991 feature films has moved several steps farther back in time into the decades before World War II and brought to the screen a variety of stories unconnected with the direct personal experiences of residents of the twenty-first century Latvian state. If WWII themes, especially traumatic events,

---

[11] A thorough description of the Legion and the Kurelian episode can be found in Lumans 2006: 263–304, 367–370.
[12] In a dream sequence in the film, Sandra's subconscious creates a departing train bedecked with American flags.

could still be within living memory of many older people, the truly historic themes lie too far back in past time for audiences to have been personally involved. Nonetheless, historical events can still be components of Latvian collective memory – an element in a Latvian 'master historical narrative' – and as such can play a role in shaping the self-image of contemporary Latvians. In these films, one would expect positive stories, stressing accomplishment and agency – a demonstration that Latvians can succeed against insuperable odds. These films, in addition, can also be venues in which enemies could be portrayed in vivid ways. Yet two recent films proceeding in this direction and located in the relatively distant past, do not meet these expectations unambiguously.

Sapņu komanda 1935 (*Dream Team 1935*; dir. Aigars Grauba, 2012) takes the audience back to an actual historical event – the 1935 championship won by the Latvian national basketball team in the first all-European competition in this sport. The main character is the young Voldemārs Baumanis (1905–1992), who through a misspoken comment by a government sports bureaucrat from the National Sports Committee receives the assignment of creating and training a Latvian national team to compete in the first European basketball competition in Geneva. No funding for this venture is provided in the government's budget, however. Baumanis perseveres, chooses a rigorous trainer, assembles a team, puts it through a year-long training program, takes the team to Geneva and defeats stronger teams to gain an ultimate victory. The film portrays the effort of Baumanis' supportive family and other residents of his boarding house, the help of one of his wife's students whom she is tutoring in the French language, and, ultimately, the assistance of one other very important figure in the Latvia of the 1930s. The sports bureaucrats' machinations to ensure Baumanis' failure (for budgetary reasons) are trumped by a phone call from the country's authoritarian President, Kārlis Ulmanis, who demands the team be supported. The most emotional moments of the film come at the end, after the depiction of victory in Geneva. The final scenes of the film consist of short biographical sketches of each team member that report on their lives after the 1940 occupation. Some are killed in Soviet-era repressions and in the course of World War II; another commits suicide in a POW camp, and still others become refugees in the West. Only one of the Dream Team's members (Eduards Andersons, 1914–1985) lived out the rest of his life in Latvia, after returning there from deportation and imprisonment in the Vorkuta (Siberia) punitive camp.

The film has many of the outward features of 'national cinema' – the dialogue in Latvian, many shots of the capital Riga's recognizable sites (e.g. the front entrance of the University's main building, Riga's canals and parks) – rendering it easy for Latvian audiences to believe the story to be a part of their collective past of the pre-Soviet period. The story is indeed a success story, but the conflict involves almost no external enemies. This time, the enemy – if indeed the obstacles to Baumanis' efforts can be described as such – is entirely internal, appearing from the structure of Latvian society of the time and the psychology of the Latvians themselves. In spite of President Ulmanis' support, the sports bureaucracy finds ways to delay the release of funding to the team. The national team consists of capable players from several active Latvian amateur basketball teams, including that of the University of Latvia. Friction and snobbery between players who are university students (shown wearing fraternity regalia) and those who do not have this august status continually threaten the team's unity and impair friendly relations even during the train journey to Geneva. At the tournament, the Latvian team's practice sessions, housing arrangements, and even the dress code all appear to be arrayed against their success – all these problems being due to the shortage of funding. In Geneva, there are some signs of external animus. Even though the tournament's officials talk about the competition as being a substitute for war, the film implies that they seem to favor the well-financed teams from the larger countries, envisaging the Latvians as upstarts. The Latvian daily press at home reports on the team's progress variously as an example of Baumanis' folly or of national success: journalists, in other words, want sensational headlines to sell papers. Throughout, however, the spotlight is on the Latvian teams' internal struggles to achieve *esprit de corps:* international success ('agency') is shown to be achievable by the overcoming of self-doubt, lingering social prejudices and conflicts, and bureaucratic foot-dragging. The film's ending, however, makes clear that an external enemy was already lurking off-stage, as it were – the combined foreign policies of the totalitarian USSR and Nazi Germany, which in 1939 brought war to Europe, in 1940 brought an end to Latvia's national sovereignty, and later physically destroyed or scattered not only the Dream Team but a large portion of the country's other inhabitants.

The film *Sapņu komanda 1935* deals with an important national accomplishment – the basketball championship – that occurred about fifteen years after independent Latvia was proclaimed on 18 November 1918, while the next case study – another 'success story' – occurs during the year immediately after the proclamation, thus the immediate post-WWI period.

In *Rīgas sargi* (*Defenders of Riga*) (dir. Aigars Grauba, 2013), the year is 1919. World War I has already ended with an armistice, peace-makers in Paris are debating the future borders of Europe, the Bolsheviks under Lenin's leadership have taken power in Russia, and the embryonic Latvian government in Riga is having to cope with the continued presence on purportedly sovereign Latvian territory of foreign, though anti-Bolshevik, military contingents inimical to the idea of Latvian independence. One contingent is led by General Rüdiger von der Goltz (1865–1946), who answers to the new government of Imperial Germany; another is led by an adventurer, Colonel Pavel Bermondt-Avalov (1884–1973), a self-proclaimed defender of the now defunct "indivisible" Tsarist Russia. Their separate agendas are in conflict with those of the provisional Latvian government led by Kārlis Ulmanis. The Allies in Paris appear to want anti-Bolshevik military forces in the Baltic area, but must also reckon with the aspirations of the Latvian people and government. Ulmanis desperately seeks to persuade the residents of Riga to defend their city against the planned northward march of the combined von der Goltz/Bermondt armed forces, allegedly on their way to Petrograd to fight the Bolsheviks. Ulmanis' call for Latvians to defend Riga against the coming depredations of the combined von der Goltz/Bermondt forces is first met by skepticism even among his government colleagues, and certainly among many in the Riga population, who are ready to abandon the city. The fiery patriotism of the protagonists, a veteran, Mārtiņš, of the Russian Imperial army and his friends, inspires sufficient resistance to stop the enemy before it crosses the bridges linking the right and left banks of the Daugava River. The military action of the film recounts the failure of the enemy, the bombardment of the city by the enemy's biplanes, a successful guerilla-like counterattack by Mārtiņš and his friends against the entrenched enemy on the left bank, the arrival of Allied warships on the Daugava and their decision to support the Ulmanis government. In a flash-forward, at the end of the film the Allies are reported to have recognized Latvian independence. Also at the end, it is explained how in 1919 the new Latvian government created the Order of Lāčplēsis as the highest state award for service to the country. The film concludes with Mārtiņš' and his fellow fighters receiving the decoration and with a voiceover aimed at young viewers a moral is drawn, namely, that Latvia's independence is not a gift received for eternity but has to be fought for and renewed daily. *Rīgas Sargi* has turned out to be the most-viewed film in the decades since regained independence, with a viewing public that has already exceeded 200,000.

To many in a Latvian audience, the actual historical content of this film could have been familiar as part of the master narrative, learned in post-1991 school years, about the founding of the Latvian state, particularly the idea that the consolidation of national sovereignty required the expulsion of foreign armies from Latvian soil. The locale itself – the capital city – places the story firmly in the category of 'national cinema.' The defense of Riga thus joins other stories of Latvian military accomplishments of the period, notably the determined resistance shown by the Latvian Rifle battalions during WWI, as they defended Latvian (i.e. at that time, Tsarist Russian territory) from the German Imperial Army invading from the south; and the successes of the Latvian national army that confronted the armed forces of the Latvian Bolshevik government, which was in power in Latvian territory during the first half of 1919. In this master narrative the events of the year 1919 are frequently referred to as Independence Wars (*Neatkarības cīņas*), and the short chapter that involved von der Goltz/Bermondt-Avalov as *bermontiāde* (bermontiad), the latter designation in popular parlance lending the episode the semblance of a venerable crusade.[13] In the film, the enemy is a composite, or a collage: the wily von der Goltz uses the morally compromised and sybaritic Bermondt-Avalov ('a German' manipulating 'a Russian') to seek defeat of the upstart Latvian 'rabble;' on the Latvian side, self-doubt (even among high government officials) about the national will to resist has to be overcome by steadfast and heroic commonplace individuals before there can be success. The stance of the Western Allies is also described generally as morally ambiguous: it is said that they are waiting to see which of the 'local' combatants will triumph before deciding whom to support.[14] The enemy images in this film all have national coloration – primarily German and Russian – but, importantly, the behavior of the Riga Latvians themselves – many seemingly having little faith in national defense – modifies the absolutism of the portrayal. The audience are meant to have difficulties deciding which of the enemies is more of a hindrance to the Latvian national effort: the ego-driven commanders of the German/Russian military force or the self-doubting defenders of Riga.

4 The Utility of the Human Life Cycle

A third type of feature film clearly reveals the techniques used by Latvian moviemaking to retreat from the required ideologized tilt of Soviet-era films. These films employ stages of the human life cycle – childhood, adolescence, adulthood, old age – as the instrument for arranging images on the screen, and by means of this methodology, help to relativize reality. The following case study illustrates what the Latvian film specialist Zane Balčus described as the atmosphere in Latvian moviemaking around the pivotal year of 1991, namely, "a crisis of the moving image, a confusion in both aesthetics and content. Perceptions of the present were being sought through the prism of the past; there was also a search for national identity" (Balčus 2011b: 354).

---

[13] A detailed 'official history' of the von der Goltz/Bermont-Avalov episode is contained in Peniķis 1938: 5–215.
[14] At the same time, a brief series of frames in the film show an unidentified person distributing rifles from a truck to the 'Riga defenders' and voicing instructions in unmistakable native-quality English (while all other personages speak Latvian, German, and Russian).

Cilvēka bērns (*The Child of Man*) (dir. Jānis Streičs, 1991) started production during the more permissive final years of Soviet Latvia and finally came to the screen after the country had regained its independence in 1991. To ensure that the finished film would not 'belong' to the USSR (and later to the Russian Federation), the costs of the film – the so-called 'Moscow-financing' – were picked up by the two city governments in Latvia (Rēzekne un Daugavpils), and thus *Cilvēka bērns* became the first feature film of the renewed Latvian state. The director, Jānis Streičs, was even then one of a handful of old masters of Latvian cinema who had guided his earlier Soviet-era films through the existing censorship layers. Now, in the late 1980s, he could allow free play to his imagination. The film not only uses the viewpoint of a seven-year old boy (Bonifācijs Paulāns, or "Boņuks") but situates his life in an undefined period of the first independence pre-WWII decades in Latgale – the easternmost region of Latvia – where Roman Catholicism was more intense than in other Latvian regions and whose population has a distinct way of speaking the Latvian language (Plakans 2011: 49–70). The dominant atmosphere of the film shows spiritual hierarchy and social equality coexisting in a small farmstead-based community: the category of enemy is populated only by Boņuks' own active imagination, misunderstandings, and occasional misbehavior.

Two features especially made the film unusual by comparison to its predecessors of the Soviet era. First, it moved beyond 'national' uniqueness into 'subnational' uniqueness: the dialogue was entirely in Letgallian; and, second, the story was based on a novel with the same title published in 1956 by the exile writer Jānis Klīdzējs (1914–2000) who at that time was living in the US, having fled his native land in 1944. In effect, Streičs' film was aiming at the restoration of cultural wholeness, as it sought to reintegrate aspects of Latvian life that in the Soviet years had been carefully kept at arm's length and submitted to negative judgment: religiosity, a thriving Latvian literature in exile, life in the first independence period, and the primacy of community over class conflict. In his memoirs, Streičs emphasizes that in this period of Soviet collapse and the accompanying misunderstood euphoria about the release of creativity from censorship, he viewed as his 'enemy' the resulting wave of violence, coarseness, and pornography and therefore based his film on other previously unacceptable themes – humaneness, faith, and God (Āboliņa 2016: 367). The film was unquestionably in the 'national cinema' category; moreover, it seemed to relish the 'subnational.' Yet it was not nationalistic, because Streičs was using the viewpoint of childhood – the first phase of the human life cycle – to tell his story and by that means to exclude all adult conceptions of enemy. The 'bad' people in the film are bad only because Boņuks thinks they are and not because they are bad objectively. As a piece of 'national cinema,' however, the film was something of a prototype in its use of plot elements and settings recognizable in Latvian cultural life and in underscoring national identity: virtually all action on the screen is accompanied by singing or folkloric instrumental music, appealing to the notion that basically Latvians are a singing nation (Bula 2000; Smidchens 2013); the rural/urban differences are drawn sharply through recognizable symbols (automobile versus horses and spinning wheels), marking the connection between Latvian national character and rurality (Beitnere 2012); and the demonstration that a child's perception of reality is artistically valuable, which is a premise of an array of 'classics' in Latvian literature that starts in the pre-WWI years and runs to the present.[15] *Cilvēka bērns*, though, exemplified the positivist strain in this creative genre, whereas other feature films have used different aspects of childhood, using the same life-cycle approach.

5 Social-Economic Transitions as Context

A fourth type of feature film inserted its characters into a 'transitions' context, wishing to portray situations in which people do not have much control over the forces shaping their lives. An example of this category – *Kolka Cool* – can be viewed in one of several ways: as a tragicomedy portraying the entertaining side of social adjustment, as a realistic portrayal of everyday life in contemporary Latvia among certain social, age, or occupational subgroups, or as a story of universal themes that just happen to be playing out in a Latvian context.

The first word in the name of the film *Kolka Cool* (dir. Juris Poskus, 2011) needs explanation: *Kolkas Rags* (the Kolka Promontory) is the name of the peninsula that separates the Gulf of Riga from the Baltic Sea. In everyday Latvian parlance, the place-name *Kolka* is often used as a geographical reference to all of the northern part of the Courland (Kurzeme) region. The topographical title of the film, therefore, places it in the 'national cinema' category, as does the use of Latvian in the dialogue. Virtually all of the characters are young people (mostly in their early twenties) who, from one perspective, are depicted as spending their summer in a small community in Courland, engaging in various activities that their age group would consider 'cool.' Cigarettes, alcohol, 'hanging out,' using cars to replicate driving maneuvers seen on TV or in movies, sexual

---

[15] E.g. before WWI: Anna Brigadere (1861–1933), *Dievs, daba, darbs* ("God, Nature, Work") and Jānis Jaunsudrabiņš (1877–1962), *Baltā grāmata* ("The White Book") – childhood in traditional and modernizing Latvian farmsteads; in the Soviet/post-Soviet period: Vizma Belševica (1931–2005), *Bille* – childhood in pre- and post-WWII Riga; in recent years, Māra Zālīte (b.1952), *Pieci pirksti* ("Five Fingers") – childhood during Siberian deportation and after return.

relations, body training, provocative clothing among the young women and small sums of money as the source of conflict among the young men, brief encounters with the local police – all meaningless matters, leading nowhere – are the main features of this 'life-style.' From another perspective, these are young people trying to establish themselves in a 'backward' post-communist transitional country, the symbols of which surround their comings and goings: empty warehouses that no longer function, dilapidated apartment houses of the Soviet era, outdated automobiles, the Latvian dialogue peppered with Russian expressions, the omnipresence of unidentifiable 'Western' music on the radio. The atmosphere of near-desolation is enhanced by the fact that this community is rural.

As noted earlier, in the course of the twentieth century, Latvia experienced four major regime changes that brought home to the country's inhabitants the need to adapt quickly to new conditions and new values. Contemporary Latvian filmmakers have offered numerous examinations of the post-1991 transition, with the characters in such films groping for an understanding of the new realities that replaced the Soviet era. Social analysts documenting the nature of Latvian society since 1991 have concluded frequently that substantial proportions of the Latvian population were living in an unending state of *anomie:* unable to extricate themselves from directionless life-situations, they are permanently alienated from society at large.[16] *Kolka Cool* offers an interpretation from this perspective, but at the same time, hints at the possibility of hope. Enemies in any traditional sense are non-existent in this film, unless the term can be associated with the new, post-communist, society itself, the values of which the portrayed young people find difficult to internalize.

This 'transition' film succeeds in portraying life in post-1991 Latvia as bereft of extremes: conflicts seldom move beyond various kinds of low-level skirmishes of everyday life; they are minor at best, if not boredom-inducing. Threatening situations and enemies, if any, are either off-stage, or for the most part emerge from the personal characteristics of the main characters themselves rather than from obvious external threats as in *Rīgas sargi* and *Baigā vasara*. Given the 'flatness' of life, there is no heroism or faintheartedness because no situations develop in which such personal qualities can be manifested. Far from having happy endings, this 'transition' film promises no resolution of the depicted conflicts; life

---

16 Various recent publications in the series "Latvija: pārskats par tautas attīstību (Latvia: A Survey of National Development)" have dealt with the socio-economic bases of such alienation: see Zepa and Kļave 2011; Bela 2013).

continues in the form of repetitive small-scale difficulties with no progress in sight.

6 National Identity, 'Enemies,' and National Cinema

Even though a quarter century has passed since in 1991 Latvia regained its independence, vigorous public debates continue on many basic questions, which renders the country much like those other European nations that have been blessed with long uninterrupted national histories. One debate within the last decade involved the question of whether Latvian should remain the only state language, another flared up over changes to the Latvian constitution meant to clarify the role of Latvians in their multi-ethnic country. Yet another involved the nature of the connection to Latvia of the remarkably high proportion of citizens who have recently emigrated to other European Union countries in search of economic opportunities and have decided to take up long-term residence there. Questions of a collective and/or national identity continue to be reopened periodically, together with the auxiliary inquiries into the nature of Latvian culture generally, the identity of enemies, and, in one sector of the Latvian cultural world, into the somewhat less existential problem of what 'national cinema' has been and ought to be. The absence of unequivocal answers to perhaps unanswerable questions has not, however, been an obstacle to Latvian moviemakers continuing to make films that have all the earmarks of 'national cinema.' As a consequence, the variety of Latvian films within this general category is substantial, while the analysis of such variation remains in an early stage.

Nearly all contemporary theoretical literature about 'national cinema' implies the need for various forms of contextualization in order for the 'national' element in cinematic products to be properly isolated and identified.[17] If this recommendation is operationalized, then the analysis of cinema becomes, for that moment, an exercise in the writing of cultural history, and has to deal with the added complication that an historical approach creates, namely, the fact that all the conceivable contexts into which cultural products can be placed for analysis

---

17 Higson proposes that the study of the "cultural identity of a particular national cinema" should involve investigating "the ways in which cinema inserts itself alongside other cultural practices, and the ways in which it draws on the existing cultural histories and cultural traditions of the producing nation, reformulating them in cinematic terms, appropriating them to build up its own generic conventions" (Higson 1989: 43).

cannot themselves be assumed to be unchanging. The task of relating changing forms of cultural creativity to their changing socio-economic and political contexts more than doubles the difficulties of analysis, and this is particularly so in the case of national societies in which the beneficial indicators of fixedness, longevity, and permanence have not yet become firmly established. It comes as no surprise, therefore, that analysts of cinematic history have had to create a special typology for sorting the objects of their analyses: 'small cinema,' 'post-communist cinema,' 'national cinema,' and the like. All such categories suggest the existence of certain kinds of cinematic creativity that by virtue of their location are likely to be depicting behaviors and embodying values tentatively, with a heightened awareness that the only 'fixed' feature of the present is perpetual change.

Something like this heightened sensibility of the permanence of change is present in the Latvian films examined above. The fading image of the enemy in many of them appears to be a promising indicator that the traditional certainties about enemies are being held in check, or at least are being treated as variables. The most graphic portrayals of an enemy are contained in the films that deliberately bring to the screen those moments in the country's past when its residents came under direct attack – *Rīgas sargi*, for example, and *Baigā vasara*. In these the enemy is external: Germans or Russians or some combination of the two – in other words, the two neighbors that in the twentieth century sought mightily to establish hegemony over the Baltic littoral. Even in these films, however, the enemy image is hardly cut-and-dried, since they also portray some Latvians negatively (as potential traitors, collaborators, cowards, and the like). The category of 'enemy' therefore is not applied to specific ethnicities but is stretched to include persons of a variety of origins. In the films that seek to portray current everyday Latvian reality – an idealized past reality as in *Cilvēka bērns* or a harsh contemporary reality as in *Kolka Cool* – the enemy is almost exclusively internal – Latvians themselves, as it were: the lack of direction in small-town Latvian life in the example. Even in seemingly inspiring success stories as depicted in *Sapņu komanda 1935* it is *Latvian* behaviors and attitudes that form the main obstacles: bureaucratic intransigence, journalistic opportunism, and social prejudices among the basketball team's players. Most of the contemporary Latvian filmmakers whose films have been reviewed here were born in the Soviet era and, as if in reaction to that period's demands that enemies be unambiguous, seem to be determined not to replicate in their own work ideologically dictated enemy images. The presence of sub-textual intention among filmmakers renders interpretation problematic, however. The difficulties are really more in the nature of a dilemma involving mutually confuting goals. The desire to escape or transcend real or imagined Soviet-era uniformity – a worthy goal – stands alongside the continued desire to rebuild a 'national' Latvian cinematic tradition – another worthy goal. Hovering over the cinema of now-independent Latvia, however, are the accomplishments of Soviet-era Latvian filmmaking: the artistic quality of those films themselves (undoubtedly generated by the greater financial resources of that period), the size of the viewing audiences they attracted and still attract, and the public's awareness of Latvian films. Latvian cultural space is characterized by a distinct nostalgia, marked by the continued capacity of many of the films of the 1960–1980 period to be viewed as important events in national cultural and social life and by their ability to attract large audiences. Yet the size of the country, which in turn dictates the size of domestic cinematic audiences as well as the size of production resources, has inserted into the Latvian equation what, as mentioned earlier, one film analyst has termed the difficult and inescapable problem of "smallness" (Coates 2015). The more 'national' a film, the more obstacles it creates for itself for the goal of attracting a larger, perhaps international, audience. It remains to be seen whether in the Latvian case filmmakers, individually or collectively, will eventually succeed in cutting through such an assemblage of Gordian knots.

Works Cited

Aitkin, Ian (1996) "Current Problems in the Study of European Cinema and the Role of Question on Cultural Identity," in *European Identity in Cinema*, ed. Wendy Everett (Exeter: Intellect Books), 78–89.

Āboliņa, Daira (2016) *Jāņa Streiča maģiskais reālisms* (The Magical Realism of Jānis Streičs) (Rīga: Dienas Grāmata).

Balčus, Zane (2011a) "Latvijas kino sistēma atjaunotās neatkarības laikā (Latvia's motion picture system in the period of renewed independence)," in *Inscenējumu realitāte: Latvijasaktierkino vēsture*, ed. Inga Pērkone, Zane Balčus, Agnese Surkova, and Beate Vītola (Riga: Mansards), 331–353.

Balčus, Zane (2011b) "Filmu tematiskš un stilistiskās iezīmes 1986–2010" (The Thematic and Stylistic Characteristics of Films 1986–2010)," in *Inscenējumu realitāte*, ed. Pērkone, Balčus, Surkova, and Vītola, 354–374.

Beitnere, Dagmāra (2012) *Mēs, zemnieku tauta? Pašreferences latviešu kultūras paradigmā* (We, A Nation of Farmers? Self-Reference in the Latvian Cultural Paradigm) (Riga: University of Latvia).

Bela, Baiba (ed.) (2013) *Ilgtspējīga nācija 2012/2013* (A Sustainable Nation 2012/2013) (Rīga: Sociālo un politisko pētījumu institūts).

Brūveris, Klāra (2014) "The Latvian Accent: Metaphysical Migration in Contemporary Latvian Cinema," in *European Cinema after the Wall: Screening East-West Mobility*, ed. Leen Engelen and Kris Van Heuckelom (Lanham, Md.: Rowman and Littlefield), 125–139.

Bula, Dace (2000) *Dziedātājtauta: folklora un nacionālā ideoloģija* (The Singing People: Folklore and National Ideology) (Riga: Zinātne).

Cāne, Renāte (2014) *Latvijas dokumentālā kino komunikatīvo funkciju transformācija (1944–1990): Promocijas darbs* (The Transformation of the Communications Functions of Documentary Films in Latvia, 1944–1990) (Riga: Biznesa augstskola Turība).

Coates, Paul (2015) "Varieties of Smallness," in *European Visions: Small Cinemas in Transitions*, ed. Janelle Blankenship and Tobias Nagl (Bielefeld: transcript Verlag), 129–149.

Eglītis, Anšlavs (1972) *Lielais mēmais* (The Great Silent One) (New York: Grāmatu Draugs).

Goris, Aivars (1982) *Tauta savu dziesmu dzied. Apcere par Padomju Latvijas mūsdienu kultūrasdzīvi* (The Nation Sings Its Own Song. An Essay on Cultural Life in Contemporary Soviet Latvia) (Riga: Avots).

Higson, Andrew (1989) "The Concept of National Cinema," *Screen*, 30, 36–47.

Hogan-Brun, Gabrielle (2009) "Contesting Social Space through Language Education Debates in Latvia's Media Landscape," in *Discourse and Transformation in Central and Eastern Europe*, ed. Aleksandra Galasińska and Michał Krzyżanowski (New York: Palgrave Macmillan), 65–79.

Lumans, Valdis O. (2006) *Latvia in World War II* (New York: Fordham University Press).

Matīsa, Kristīne (2005) *Vecās labās... Latviešu kinoklasikas 50 spožākās pērles* (The Good Old ... The 50 Shiniest Pearls of Latvian Cinematic Art) (Rīga: Atēna).

Peniķis, M. (1938) "Latvijas nacionālās armijas cīņas ar Bermonta armiju 1919.g. rudenī (The Battles between the Latvian National Army and the Bermondt Army in the Fall of 1919)," in *Latvijas atbrīvošanas kara vēsture* (History of Latvia's Independence War), ed. M. Peniķis (Riga: Izdevniecība 'Literatūra'), Volume 2, 5–215.

Pērkone, Inga (2008) *Kino Latvijā 1920–1940* (Riga: Zinātne).

Pērkone, Inga (2011) "Estētika [Esthetics]," in *Inscenējumu realitāte*, ed. Pērkone, Balčus, Surkova, and Vītola, 172–276.

Pērkone, Inga (2013) "Personības Latvijas kinomākslā (Personalities in Latvian Cinematic Art)," in *Latvieši un Latvija. Vol. IV: Latvijas kultūra, izglītība, zinātne*, ed. Jānis Stradiņš (Rīga: Latvijas Zinātņu akadēmija), 521–538.

Pērkone, Inga (2016) *Latvijas pirmās filmas* (First Latvian Films) (Riga: Mansards).

Plakans, Andrejs (2011) "Regional Identity in Latvia: The Case of Latgale," in *Forgotten Pages in Baltic History: Diversity and Inclusion*, ed. Martyn Housden and David J. Smith (Amsterdam and New York: Rodopi), 49–70.

Riekstiņš, Elmārs (ed.) (1989) *Padomju Latvijas kinomāksla. Mākslas, dokumentālās unmultiplikācijas filmas* (Cinematic Art in Soviet Times: Feature Films, Documentary Films, and Cartoon Films) (Riga: Liesma).

Smidchens, Guntis (2013) *The Power of Song: Nonviolent Culture in the Baltic Singing Revolutions* (Seattle: University of Washington Press).

Sosnovskii, Immanuil (1976) *Kino Sovetskoi Latvii* (Filmmaking in Soviet Latvia) (Moscow: Iskusstvo).

Streičš, Jānis (2006) *Lāga dvēseļu straume* (A Stream of Good Souls) (Rīga: Dienas Grāmata).

Zelče, Vita (2011) "Par karu, vēsturi, un cilvēkiem (On War, History, and People)," in *(Divas) puses: latviešu kara stāsti* ((Two) Sides: Latvian War Stories), ed. Uldis Neiburgsand and Vita Zelče (Riga: Mansards), 13–33.

Zepa, Brigita, and Ēvija Kļave (eds.) (2011) *Nacionālā identitāte, mobilitāte un rīcībspēja2010/2011* (National identity, mobility, and capacity 2010/2011) (Riga: Sociālo unpolitisko pētījumu institūts).

Filmography

Baigā vasara (*Dangerous Summer*) (2000) Dir. Aigars Grauba (Platforma Filma).
Cilvēka bērns (*The Child of Man*) (1991) Dir. Jānis Streičs (TRĪS).
Dancis pa trim (*Three to Dance*) (2011) Dir. Arvīds Krievs (Kaupo Filma).
Kolka Cool (2011) Dir. Juris Poškus (FA filma/Moloko Film).
Lāčplēsis ("The Bearslayer") (1930) Dir. by Aleksandrs Rusteiķis (Aizsargu organizācija).
Limuzīns Jāņu nakts krāsā (*A Limousine The Colour Of Midsummer's Eve*) (1981) Dir. Jānis Streičs (Rigas Kinostudija).
Mammu, es tevi mīlu (*Mommy, I Love You*) (2013) Dir. Jānis Nords (Film Studio Tanka).
Melānijas hronika (*The Chronicles of Melanie*) (2016) Dir. Viesturs Kairišs (Mistrus).
Nameja gredzens (*The King's Ring*) (2017) Dir. Aigars Grauba (Platforma Filma).
Rīgas sargi (*Defenders of Riga*) (2013) Dir. Aigars Grauba (Platforma Filma).
Sapņu komanda 1935 (*Dream Team 1935*) (2012) Dir. Aigars Grauba (Platforma Filma).
Trimda (*Exiled*) (2016) Dir. Dāvis Sīmanis (Locomotive Productions).
Zvejnieka dēls (*The Fisherman's Son*) (1939) Dir. Vilis Lapenieks (Sabiedrisko lietu ministrija).

Francesca de Lucia
Looking for an Invisible Enemy in Israeli Film

The First Lebanon War, which started in 1982 and dragged on until the Israeli army's main withdrawal in 1985, continues to have an immense impact on the national collective memory, in ways that are not dissimilar to those of the Vietnam War for the United States. This conflict can be placed against the extremely complex background of broader Middle Eastern tensions, namely that of the Lebanese Civil War. It also carries ramifications that extend to the present day, since, most importantly, it contributed to the development of the Hezbollah.

The background of Israeli intervention in Lebanon is a protracted context of unrest and internal strife amongst the different political and religious components of Lebanese society, further complicated by the presence of hundreds of thousands of Palestinian refugees. The resulting civil war broke out in 1975, and would only conclude in 1990 (Traboulsi 2012). Israel's involvement in Lebanon was prompted by a Palestinian's attempted assassination of Schlomo Argov, the Israeli ambassador to Britain: "The attack on Argov coincided with renewed PLO shelling, from bases in southern Lebanon, of Israeli settlements along the border in northern Galilee" (Gilbert 2008: 503). The ultimate aim of this intervention was to stifle the presence of the Palestinian Liberation Organization in Lebanon and exert control on the area.

The First Lebanon War began as a supposedly brief operation in June 1982 but instead lasted for several years. Israeli troops withdrew from Lebanon in spring 1985, remaining only in buffer border areas, which were not evacuated until 2000. Writing as early as 1984, Zeev Schiff and Ehud Yahari note that

> as Israelis, we found ourselves dealing with a kind of war unprecedented in the history of the State of Israel, a war attended my many highly charged issues and questions that have never arisen in this country [...]. Israel's war with Lebanon was first and foremost a political venture [...]. (1984: 10)

This conflict represents a turning point in terms of the perception of Israel both at home and abroad. Unlike the Six Days War and the Kippur War (which, nevertheless, especially in hindsight, carry their own share of controversy),[1] the First

---

[1] The Six Day War (5–10 June 1967) pitted Israel against Egypt, Jordan and Syria, as the result of growing tensions between Israel and the Arab nations in the course of the 1960s. This conflict

Lebanon War is considered as the first purely aggressive, and consequently unjustified war initiated by Israel. It caused the country to lose global support and is sometimes interpreted as a 'loss of innocence.' Gilbert observes that "it was the first war in Israel's history for which there was no national consensus. Many Israelis regarded it as a war of aggression" (2008: 503–504). As illustrated by the contemporary press, Israel also began to lose support amongst allies abroad.[2]

Irit Kenyan also notes the difference of perception between the First Lebanon War and the military conflicts in which Israel had been involved earlier in its history: "a 'war of choice,' it seemed to run counter to the prevailing Israeli ethos, according to which the country went to war only when there was no other choice" (2014: 67). More relevantly, always according to Keynan,

> [this war] forced Israeli society to confront doubts previously repressed concerning Israeli Defense Forces (IDF) 'purity of arms,' the belief that the army always exercised restraint in its use of force and it resorted to violence only when necessary, avoiding hurting civilians, even at the risk of losing soldiers [...]. The doubts expressed in Israeli national discourse about the IDF's purity of arms escalated in the wake of the Sabra and Shatila massacre, which shook the Israeli public to the core. (2014: 67–68)

Indeed, the First Lebanon War has also become notorious for the Sabra and Shatila massacre. In this devastating episode that took place from 16–18 September 1982, a Lebanese Christian militia known as the Phalange, allied with Israel, carried out a mass murder of predominantly Palestinian refugees, whose number has been estimated from 700 to 3,500. The extent of the involvement of the Israeli Defense Forces in the massacre continues to be an object of debate, but a certain element of at least indirect complicity on the part of the IDF appears evident. The event prompted outrage both in Israel and abroad, leading to a political crisis and to the resignation of the then Minister of Defense Ariel Sharon, amongst oth-

---

started as a pre-emptive strike (LeBoer 2006). While Israel's survival was at stake, the war led to the occupation of the West Bank and the development of the settler movement (Gorenberg 2007). The Yom Kippur War began on 6 October 1973, when Egypt and Syria attacked Israel by surprise. The war lasted three weeks, after which "Israel emerged [...] however, more chastened than triumphant" (Rabinovich 2004: xv). Indeed, this conflict had a lasting impact on the country, leaving Israeli society with an increased sense of vulnerability and led to political shifts, eventually leading to the Labor Alignment losing its hegemony (Gilbert 2008).

2 See for instance Anthony Lewis, who, writing for the *New York Times* on 1 July 1982, points out that the then French president François Mitterand, "the best friend Israel has had in the Elisée Palace for years," had become heavily critical of the war and that "Israel's sweep on Beirut worried President Reagan and his White House advisers." In spite of his well-known pro-Israel stance, Reagan clashed with Prime Minister Menachem Begin as the conflict developed, "express[ing] outrage" for the bombing of Beirut (Weinraub 1982).

ers. Analyzing this situation, the novelist Amos Oz wrote with eloquent, bitter irony in *The Slopes of Lebanon:*

> Who is "guilty" of the mass murder at the refugee camps in Beirut? The guilty parties, the murderers, are our protégés, our pets, our allies – the Christian Phalangists. They and they alone. Who is "responsible"? The responsible party is the Begin government, and the Begin government alone. One who invites the Boston strangler to spend two nights in an orphanage cannot claim, when he sees a pile of dead bodies the next morning, that he had asked the man only to wash the ears and necks of the orphans. (2012 [1987]: 40)

The Sabra and Shatila massacre is at the center of Ari Folman's animated film *Vals im Bashir* (*Waltz with Bashir*) (dir. Ari Folman, 2008), and its echoes also permeate other Israeli films on the First Lebanon War. The complexity and controversy surrounding this event in Israeli history has unavoidable repercussions on its cinematic representations, in particular on the depiction of an elusive, sometimes incomprehensible enemy.

I shall focus on three recent films on the First Lebanon War: *Beaufort* (dir. Joseph Cedar, 2007), *Vals im Bashir* and *Lebanon* (dir. Samuel Maoz, 2009). Interestingly, the directors of these films are all veterans of the Lebanon War, something that draws yet another potential parallel with cinema on the Vietnam War, as visible for instance in the case of Oliver Stone. Felice Naomi Wonnenberg notes that these films, which have all received accolades outside of Israel, are part of the *yorim ve bochim* ("shooting and crying") genre. *Yorim ve bochim* narratives suggest that "people are aware of the problematic issues of war, yet still take part in it" (2013: 212). The expression is also used to refer to a well-established Israeli tradition of recollecting the experiences of soldiers at war.[3] These stories, whether fictional or fact-based, problematize both typical portrayals of the IDF and the broader role of the Israeli army. According to Wonnenberg, by showing soldiers as being self-doubting and emotional, the films return to a pre-Zionist view of the Jewish male.

The films tend to avoid direct portrayals of enemy figures, whether they be the Hezbollah or PLO. Rather, they explore the problematic blurring of notions of 'enemies,' 'civilians,' and 'allies,' as is obvious in *Vals im Bashir* and in *Lebanon*. This undefined enemy presence is also strongly associated with the landscape, which is often rendered in lyrical terms. In *Beaufort* especially, the enemy completely disappears into the verdant scenery, being reduced to the periodical shootings of deadly missiles. In this perspective, the threat to the soldiers ap-

---

3 *Yorim ve bochim* can be used in a pejorative fashion, as a way to indicate an attitude towards the IDF that is critical but does not suggest the taking of any real action.

pears almost as a natural calamity. This general view attenuates political controversies and analyses, bringing the focus on the characters of the soldiers. The three films all deconstruct the traditional themes of war movies, in particular that of the relationship between soldiers, as well as specific tropes of the IDF.

1 The Unseen Enemy in *Beaufort*

Joseph Cedar's 2007 film is based on Ron Leshem's 2005 novel *Im Yesh Gan Eden* (*If There Is a Heaven*), Leshem having coauthored the screenplay. It is significant to observe that *Beaufort*, which was made only a year after yet another highly controversial war with Lebanon, does not deal with the First Lebanon War proper, but with one of its lingering consequences, that is, the occupation of the medieval fortress of Beaufort, not evacuated until 2000. Thus, the second conflict in the area of Lebanon possibly prompted a cinematic reflection on the earlier war, starting however with a side development, rather than broaching the event directly. The narrative follows the lives of IDF soldiers before and during the evacuation of the Beaufort outpost. Its key character is Liraz Librati, the commanding officer, who is the narrator of Leshem's novel (where he is also called "Erez" after the cedars of Lebanon). Liraz is Sephardic and comes from the Northern town of Afula, his family presumably being working-class. In an interview contained in the extra contents of the DVD, Leshem notes that he set out to create a protagonist whose background was as different as possible from his own.

While the novel delves into the characters' pasts and their lives outside the base, the film erases these elements almost completely. Thus, the outpost of Beaufort becomes a remote, self-enclosed space inhabited by young men who have virtually no identity beyond their service in the IDF. The apparent calm of the outpost is periodically interrupted by missile explosions. In this perspective, the enemy, hazily identified as the Hezbollah, merges entirely with the landscape, whose luxuriant beauty is therefore rendered as treacherous. However, *Beaufort* makes no effort to give some insight or even a face to members of the Hezbollah; the explosions could almost be the result of a natural disaster. *Beaufort* obviously exploits the trope of the "Tartar steppe" (originally developed in a 1940 novel by the Italian writer Dino Buzzati that was made into a film in 1976), where soldiers waste away in a desolate area while waiting to confront an obscure, undefined enemy force. This aspect is reinforced by the presence of the eponymous "beautiful fort" originally built by the crusaders, implying a kind of ageless warfare. Through much of the film, Liraz appropriately endorses a traditional warrior ethos, often mentioning the 'heroism' of the Israeli army in Lebanon. His character undergoes a transformation in the course of the narrative, since he eventually does not succeed in fully endorsing the role of the paternal and efficient commanding officer. Liraz is unable to rescue a wounded comrade who begs for his help; subsequently he has a confrontation with the medic Koris, where he reflects on his position at Beaufort as the officer who presided over the evacuation of the outpost. Hence, the narrative presents the experience of soldiering as a personal one, rather than as a confrontation with external forces.

In spite of its lyrical and abstract elements, *Beaufort* is not entirely devoid of a political background and of more realistic aspects, signaled by the participation in the film of existing public figures such as the *Haaretz* journalist Gideon Levy. Early on, the soldiers discuss in disparaging tones the Four Mothers movement, which campaigned for unilateral withdrawal from Southern Lebanon. Raz Yosef notes that

> [...] the soldiers' masculinity is not only endangered by the enemy, but also by women: the Four Mothers movement – or, as Liraz calls them, the four "old ladies" [...]. According to the soldiers, the women's protest against the war has feminized the army, which in turn has undermined the fighters' military and masculine worthiness and disconnected them from the paternal authority of their commanders. The trauma of abandonment [...] is represented, therefore, as a crisis of heterosexual masculinity. (2011: 32–33)

The film hence summarizes an idea that Liraz develops at greater length in the novel, suggesting that not only the Four Mothers movement but Israeli civil society at large constitute a threat to the IDF and its work, almost on a par with external enemies:

> That band of females, those hysterical women who stir up trouble [...] Threatening to wear us all down. Trying to convince anyone that we, the fighters, are nothing but cannon fodder for a meaningless war, expendable tools. And the IDF, they claim, is blind and deaf, inciting us to war, sending these young men into the crossfire. We are those young men. Try to imagine the feeling. In those days you'd make your way home after a six week tour, and it was like that damned Lebanon was chasing after you [...]. A whole country of people who know fuck about the army, but they know better than anyone what needs to be done. At least they think they do [...] each of them adding his own contribution to the enemy's morale, to his honor [...]. I'd learned a long time ago that there was no chance to find peace and quiet when you went home. (Leshem 2005: 106–107)

In this context, the home front becomes indistinct from the war zone, if not, paradoxically, an area of greater distress than what Liraz in the novel calls the "snowy mountain" of Beaufort. The sense of paternal abandonment that Yosef notes is underlined more clearly, when Liraz watches an interview with the father of one of the soldiers killed at Beaufort. This man's comments are an essential rejection of the Zionist ethos: he claims paradoxically that he feels he has failed as a father by raising his son to be a member of an elite corps and not instilling him with a sense of fear. This represents a return to a pre-Zionist view of the world marked by caution and avoidance of danger, where endorsing the role of the armed combatant brings failure and destruction rather than security and honor.

While enemy forces remain unseen and ambiguous, *Beaufort* adheres to some conventional imagery of national identity. One of the symbols of the evacuation is the lowering of the Israeli flag, which Liraz insists on hoisting again when the soldiers end up staying an extra night in the fort. This gesture may be considered a simple safety measure, as indicated in the novel, or part of the role of historical "archivist" that Yosef attributes to the character. Equally meaningful in terms of symbolism is the attempt to remove the memorial plaque with the names of the soldiers killed at Beaufort; when detaching the plaque proves impossible, Liraz and his comrades come to the conclusion that those memorialized "want to stay." This suggests, once again, a sense of continuity with the mythical past of the fortress, as the IDF dead are associated with the fighters of different origins and time periods who have been present at Beaufort throughout its history.

In the end, unlike the protagonists of the original *Tartar Steppe*, the men of Beaufort do not grow old in the outpost. The film ends on a positive note, with the soldiers hugging each other and phoning their families to announce their return home. Only Liraz fractures this somewhat normative representation, since he stands in isolation, apparently dry heaving and weeping, implying his incapacity to tear himself entirely from Beaufort. In spite of hinting at some political elements, Cedar's film makes no effort to explore the broader context of the protracted conflict with Lebanon: "*Beaufort*'s Lebanon is not a country that the IDF invaded; it has no population that is caused suffering by the ongoing war; it has no history or autonomous existence beyond its function of servicing the tortured Israeli psyche" (Yosef 2011: 146). While this tendency partially subsists in later films, both *Vals with Bashir* and *Lebanon* make stronger attempts to envision the people in Lebanon and their role as enemies, or victims, of the Israelis.

2 Trauma and Guilt in *Vals im Bashir*

Ari Folman's *Vals im Bashir* is the most complex and innovative of the films taken in consideration in this chapter. The use of animation creates a sense of detachment from reality, elaborating a kind of paradox with the documentary endeavor of the film. Furthermore, *Vals im Bashir* questions the very notions of reality and memory, an idea that is underlined by the frequent use of oneiric elements. The film centers on an attempt, on the part of Folman, to reconstruct his memories of the Sabra and Shatila massacre. For this purpose, he interviews several other veterans, as well as drawing from interviews with prominent witnesses, such as the journalist Ron Ben Yishai, who telephoned Ariel Sharon to signal that the massacre was taking place, or an expert like the trauma psychologist Zahava Solomon. The visual technique resembles rotoscoping (tracing animation over live action), but instead the authors of *Vals im Bashir* combined traditional drawing techniques with the use of software. In this way, the film juxtaposes hyper-realistic figures with dreamscapes based on the characters' nightmares or hallucinations. Garrett Stewart observes that

> [...] the film's troubled bodies, heavy with dream and guilt, wad[e] through a lurid quagmire of deflected memory. The nightmarish atmosphere is offset by such hyper-cinematic gestures as warp-speed transitions between Dutch and Israeli locales or battleground overviews higher than any crane shot, steadier than any helicopter pan. In line with the developing ironies of psychic artifice in the film, these effects are not just associated with surrogate visual memories, they are surrogate cinema. (2012: 121)

Whereas Folman struggles to recover his memories, those of other soldiers emerge. The film's opening stages the recurring nightmare of Boaz, where mangy dogs run through the streets of Tel Aviv. Boaz explains that, because as a new recruit he was unable to kill people, his commandant forced him to slay twenty-six dogs which would otherwise have alerted villages of the presence of Israeli troops with their barks. This can be seen as the first incarnation of the enemy. The inhabitants of villages who rely on dogs to warn them do not appear, while the film leaves the dogs to stand in for them. At the same time, the film introduces a motif that will reemerge later, with the scene of the dead horses at the Beirut hippodrome: the dramatization of the killing of animals, which displaces the death of human beings, whether they be members of armed forces or civilians. The mention of a car containing a dead family, which is not shown directly, prefigures the victimization of civilians that will be central to the film. However, for the time being, this is just a passing reference, the focus remaining on the experience of the Israeli soldiers.

Boaz's nightmare leads to one of the iconic, recurring images of the film, that of emaciated, naked Israeli soldiers emerging from the sea to don their uniforms on the beach. Nicholas Baer observes that this kind of imagery deconstructs several motifs related to the founding of Israel, as well as to depictions of Jewish masculinity and Israeli soldiers. Because they are so physically slight, the soldiers evoke Holocaust survivors and, in particular, the Displaced Persons who were drafted in the *Haganah* or the IDF, sometimes before their arrival in

Palestine (2014: 102). Baer goes on to indicate that "7,800 former Displaced Persons joined the Israeli Defense Forces and these DPs [...] departed for the front lines soon after the founding of Israel on May 14, fighting in a war that would become associated with another exodus: that of Palestinian Arabs from their towns and villages" (2014: 103).

From this point of view, Folman adheres to a post-Zionist narrative, according to which "the Israeli state coerced and conscripted physically and emotionally vulnerable men, disacknowledging their traumatic experiences and forcing them to fill incongruous roles" (Baer 2014: 103). The reminiscence of the Independence War, in this perspective, alludes indirectly also to the Palestinian exodus or *Nakba*, and to the development of the Israeli-Palestinian conflict, of which the Lebanon war can be considered an offshoot. Folman here implies the idea that will be expanded throughout the movie, of the shifting view of Israeli Jews, especially in their roles of soldiers. Thus, the exploration of the impact of Sabra and Shatila challenges both perceptions of Israelis as underdogs and the myths of Jewish masculinity surrounding Zionist ideology. *Vals im Bashir* places much emphasis on the soldiers' fear, youth and inexperience. The element of water also remains persistent, suggesting not only the Displaced Persons (who have crossed the sea from Europe) turned into soldiers, but also a form of regression to childhood, if not to a prenatal state.

Representing members of the IDF as traumatized youths with little understanding of the geopolitical situation of which they are part unavoidably problematizes the representation of the enemy, especially in light of the intricacies of the conflict in Lebanon. The landscape, along with the soundtrack plays an important part in this context, becoming a stand-in for the mostly unseen Lebanese people. One of the interviewees, Carmi Cna'an, remarks on the beauty of the Lebanese countryside as he recalls his experience in a tank early on in the war. This scene is accompanied by Navadey Ha'Ukaf's song "Levanon, boker tov" ("Lebanon, Good Morning"), whose title obviously hints at Vietnam War movies. More significantly, the lyrics of the song suggest an almost thanatophilic romantic personification of Lebanon, of which the speaker says that it is "torn to shreds, bleeding in [his] arms," and subsequently states casually that "every day I have bombed Sidon / every day I have bombed Beirut / I got out alive but I could have died [...] / we bombed people we didn't know/ we probably killed some of them by mistake." Here, the murder of civilians is quickly dismissed, giving priority to the survival of the Israeli soldier. Furthermore, the mention of killing people "by mistake" foreshadows the devastating 'mistake' of Sabra and Shatila.

The enemy appears directly in one scene, as a young boy in an orchard holding a bazooka. Once again, the film highlights a potentially idyllic landscape while concentrating on one of the most amoral aspects of warfare, the use of child soldiers, which gives the role of combatant to the quintessential civilian. However, the figure of the boy remains a symbolic and abstract one. The experience of war, and its related confrontation with an enemy, is still to a great extent a highly personal and internal one in *Vals im Bashir*, even though the perspective shifts in the second half of the film, as Folman begins to discuss the Sabra and Shatila massacre and his own role in this event. The change in mood is signaled by the appearance of the "Bashir" of the title, the Christian Lebanese politician Bashir Gemayel, whose assassination triggered the Sabra and Shatila massacre as an act of vengeance. Cn'an likens the omnipresence of images of Bashir to his own idolization of David Bowie, and also attributes a kind of 'eroticism' to Bashir's followers. Thus, the intricacies of Lebanese political and religious divisions become analogous to the cult of celebrities, foreshadowing the incumbent disaster. The key sequence in the movie is that which gives *Vals im Bashir* its title, showing Shmuel Frenkel as he shoots a machine-gun in a crazed dance, to the accompaniment of Chopin's music:

> [O]n his own and terrified, he dances the title's waltz, firing randomly into buildings adorned with giant portraits of the just-assassinated leader. Although this macabre, poetically acute exhibition never happened, it is a poignant, perhaps necessary illustration of Folman's assertion that these young men are being led into a merry dance into oblivion for the sake of remote, distantly iconic, supernaturally machinating politicians. (Saunders 2010: 171)

The scene clearly aestheticizes warfare and, while it may be fantasy, it obscures any potential targets of Frenkel's effective shooting spree.

The final part of the film deals directly with Folman's resurfacing memories of Sabra and Shatila. Discussing once again with his friend Ori Silvan, he comes to the conclusion that the crux of his trauma derives from his taking on the "role of the Nazi," when he is the son of Auschwitz survivors. The journalist Ron ben Yishai also likens the refugees to iconic images of Jews in the Warsaw ghetto. The conclusion of the film blurs roles of enemies and allies, victimizers and victims as well as putting into discussion the traditional Zionist representations of Israeli and Jewish masculinity. Nevertheless, Folman's attempt to investigate Israeli responsibility in the Sabra and Shatila massacre, and in the First Lebanon War at large, remains ambiguous and problematic. *Vals im Bashir* ultimately emphasizes the responsibilities of high-ranking politicians, implying that the lower echelons of the army, which included Folman himself, had only limited autonomy and freedom to make moral choices. While they are not completely erased as in the case of *Beaufort*, the Lebanese still occupy a restricted role in *Vals im Bashir*, besides the symbolic image of the title character and the ominous presence of the Phalangists. Similarly, the enemy remains to a large extent elusive in Samuel Maoz's *Lebanon*, yet this is the film that gives more space to the Lebanese presence.

3 The 'I' of the Tank, the 'I' of the Camera: *Lebanon*

Lebanon is set entirely inside a tank, on the first day of the First Lebanon War. At a superficial glance, this film presents some obvious similarities with *Beaufort*, which are enhanced by the presence of some of the same actors, such as Oshri Cohen and Itay Tiran. More significantly, both films almost completely cut out the characters of the soldiers from any reality other than their service in the IDF and the environment they inhabit. However, the treatment of the experience of warfare is otherwise different, since *Lebanon* enacts a more direct deconstruction of traditional representations of the military and of the IDF in particular. In contrast to the lyrical background of the Lebanese forests, the setting of *Lebanon* is the claustrophobic interior of the tank. Interactions with the outside are limited to observations through the periscope and to the roof trap. Maoz rejects the trope of comrades in arms as a 'band of brothers,' which still appears, albeit partially deconstructed, in *Beaufort* and which even *Vals im Bashir* does not reject completely. In *Lebanon*, the soldiers in the tank constantly bristle against each other, experiencing limited bonding. Moreover, they not only have no understanding of the geostrategic context around them, but they express no patriotism or attachment to the IDF: they are trapped metaphorically as they are materially in the tank.

Lebanon is the most graphic of the three films, showing the impact of the war without the oneiric mediation of *Vals im Bashir* or the poetic abstraction of *Beaufort*. The only filter with the world is the cross-haired periscope of the tank, an eye which is parallel to the cinematic eye of the camera and, consequently, can be considered an 'I,' a narrator who interprets the world through this device. Wonnenberg points out that unlike Wolfgang Petersen's classic representation of submarine warfare in *Das Boot*, which also uses the periscope technique, "in *Lebanon* 'the other' is not a huge grey anonymous war machine but human beings, seen through the telescope in emotion-filled, extreme close-ups" (2013: 228–229). Thus Maoz's film reveals various Arab 'others' in different roles, shifting from victims to stereotypical terrorists, from prisoners to allies more terrifying than any enemy. The Lebanese are represented both as the victims of the IDF and as a potential threat. An early scene shows the Israeli officer Jamil coolly putting a wounded and mutilated man out of his misery. Later, an armed man whose face is covered by a keffiyeh holds a family hostage. These two contrasting images function like stock portrayals of respectively an anti-Israel and pro-Israel perspective, since in the first Israeli soldiers dispatch an innocent civilian in cold blood, whereas in the second they are confronted with an enemy unscrupulous enough to use civilians as a human shield, thus creating an impossible ethical dilemma, one that is evoked regularly in apologies of the state.[4]

The key element in terms of the representation of the enemy other, however, is the introduction of a Syrian prisoner of war. When he first appears, callously handled by Jamil, he is a pawn whose nationality puzzles the IDF soldiers inhabiting the tank, ignorant as they are of the complexities of the Middle Eastern conflict. His role, or rather his symbolic presence becomes more prominent as the narrative progresses, especially after the scene with the Phalangist. In *Lebanon*'s most disturbing sequence, a member of the Christian militia ascertains that none of the Israelis in the tank understand Arabic and then proceeds to give the Syrian prisoner an extremely graphic description of the rape, torture and mutilation that await him once the IDF hand him over to the Phalange. The prisoner then has no choice but to attempt desperately to seek the help of his uncomprehending captors. Interestingly, while the Phalangist's threats are subtitled, the Syrian's reaction is not, thus putting most of the audience in the position of the soldiers. The character of the Phalangist serves as a mirror image for Jamil, as both of them represent the destructiveness of the Israeli military intervention in Lebanon: the former is an ally who acts with thinly veneered savagery (his very presence indirectly foreshadowing the Sabra and Shatila massacre); Jamil, on the other hand, embodies cold and calculating violence, hypocritically disregarding warfare conventions by referring to an illegal bomb by a different name. Once again, *Lebanon* blurs and problematizes the notion of enemy, a notion that it reinforces in its conclusion.

In spite of its bleak and hyperrealist tone, *Lebanon* ends on a note of redemption. Unusual for a predominantly Jewish-made film, Christian and indeed Christological motifs appear. Christian iconography is introduced early on, when a gutted-out building reveals a traditional painting of the virgin and child. This suggests that the apartment was inhabited by Lebanese Christians, but, more importantly, prefigures the sequence where a disheveled woman is restrained by an

---

[4] For instance, even Amos Oz, who is known as a prominent left-wing intellectual, compared the situation of Israel and Gaza to that of someone who is being shot by a neighbor who holds a little boy in his lap (interview *Deutsche Welle* 2016).

Israeli soldier as she looks for her young, presumably dead daughter, thus embodying a kind of *mater dolorosa* figure. The end of *Lebanon* borrows elements from the Crucifixion. One of the soldiers helps the Syrian prisoner urinate (in an ammunition container, which the Israelis had previously used for the same purpose). Subsequently, the almost final shot is a close-up of the prisoner against the background of two pipes intersecting perpendicularly: along with the actor's thick dark beard and leaning head they create the sense of an *ecce homo* representation. A potentially humiliating gesture between a captor and his bound captive becomes a bonding and redemptive act. Wonnenberg observes that "this first of all human encounters, helping the enemy, the 'other' to 'fulfil his most basic human need,' as director Maoz called it, brings about the redemption. What the soldiers have been longing for throughout the movie finally happens: the fighting stops and, for the first time, they can emerge from the tank" (2013: 223).

The tank itself can be seen as a metaphor of the Middle Eastern conflict itself: a stifling, enclosed space in which both Israeli Jews and their Arab enemies have been trapped for decades. The Christological or Messianic element also appears in a less obvious, non-visual key through the death of Yigal, whose name, as noted by Raz Yosef, means "he will redeem" in Hebrew. It is significant that these moments of metaphorical sacrifice and atonement precede the dénouement of the film. *Lebanon* ends with the soldier Shmulik finally emerging from the tank, in the sunflower field that had appeared briefly at the very beginning. This represents survival, as well as the possibility of an exit from the oppressive situation of the Middle Eastern conflict.

Conclusion

Beaufort, *Vals im Bashir* and *Lebanon* depict disparate facets of the experience of the first Lebanon war, representing an effort to look back, with the hindsight of several decades, at a disruptive turning point in Israeli history. They all attempt to deconstruct in various ways the traditional images of the Israeli soldiers that are deeply rooted in Zionist ideology. At the same time, in their portrayal, the Arab enemy 'other' remains, to a greater or lesser extent, an elusive and vague entity. Furthermore, several critics point out that the strong focus on the Israeli soldiers with an emphasis on death or mental trauma suggests that they are seen as victims in a way that, as noted once again by Yosef, atones for Israel's collective national guilt.

Overall, the depiction of the First Lebanon War as visible in *Beaufort*, *Vals im Bashir* and *Lebanon* thus remains ambivalent. In a 2006 lecture (later collected in the volume *Writing in the Dark*), the novelist David Grossman investigated the necessity of

> [...] seeing the enemy differently. To think about the enemy then. To think about him gravely and with deep attentiveness. Not merely to hate or fear him, but to think about him as a person or a society or a nation that is separate from us [...]. To allow the enemy to be an Other, with all that entails [...]. Of course, it is not easy to read reality through our enemy's eyes. It is difficult and frightening to give up our sophisticated defense mechanisms and be exposed to the feelings with which the enemy experiences the conflict and how, in fact, he experiences us. Taking such a step challenges our faith in ourselves and our own justness. (2009: 54)

Interestingly, Grossman advocates here the idea of recognizing the enemy's 'otherness' rather than attempting to reject it. However, the representations of warfare found in the three films analyzed in this chapter hint at a process of 'thinking about the enemy,' yet fail to take on fully the challenge suggested by Grossman, since their portrayal of the enemy remains unfocussed. It is significant to note that *Vals im Bashir*, *Lebanon* and *Beaufort* were made in the relative aftermath of the Second Lebanon War that took place in summer 2006 as a conflict against the Hezbollah, being seen as a military failure for Israel (Harel and Issacharoff 2009).

While this conflict might have been still too immediate to be rendered in fiction, it could have elicited a reflection on the earlier war and the sense of historical repetition. Samuel Maoz himself points out in an interview that his desire to transform his own traumatic memories of the 1982 conflict (which involved shooting a man from a tank) into a film stemmed from the Second Lebanon War, and suggests that "it's no coincidence there have been three films about the [first] Lebanon war in as many years" (qtd. in Cooke, 2010). In the decades following the First Lebanon War, Israel confronted itself with shifting forms of warfare in which enemy figures often merged with civilians, as happened in the context of the First and Second Intifada. The continuing occupation of the West Bank has not only obviously had a devastating impact on Palestinian society but can be seen as damaging also for Israel in terms of politics, economy, collective psychology and international status.[5] In this perspective, modern Israel becomes the main threat against itself "its own worst enemy." Thus films that revisit a dramatic key episode of the country's history become part of a process of national introspection.

---

5 See for instance Daniel Bar-Tal and Izhak Schnell's volume (2014), which analyzes the consequences of the Occupation on Israel through the lens of politics, economics and psychology.

Works Cited

Bar-Tal, Daniel and Izhak Schnell (eds) (2014) *The Impacts of Lasting Occupation: Lessons from Israeli Society* (Oxford: Oxford University Press).

Baer, Nicholas (2014) "'Can't Films Be Therapeutic?': Cinema, Psychoanalysis and Zionism in Ari Folman's *Waltz with Bashir*," in *Mobile Narratives: Travel, Migration and Transculturation*, ed. Eleftheria Arapoglou, Monika Fodor, and Jopy Nyman (New York: Routledge), 97–110.

Cooke, Rachel (2010) "Samuel Maoz: My Life at War and My Hopes for Peace," *The Guardian* <https://www.theguardian.com/film/2010/may/02/israel-lebanon-samuel-maoz-tanks> (accessed 11 February 2017).

Gilbert, Martin (2008) *Israel: A History* (London: Doubleday).

Gorenberg, Gershom (2007) *The Accidental Empire: Israel and the Birth of the Settlements, 1967–1977* (New York: Holt Paperbacks).

Grossman, David (2009) *Writing in the Dark: Essays on Literature and Politics*, trans. Jessica Cohen (London: Bloomsbury).

Harel, Amos, and Avi Issacharoff (2009) *34 Days: Israel, Hezbollah and the War in Lebanon* (London: St Martin's Griffin).

Keynan, Irit (2014) *Psychological War Trauma and Society: Like a Hidden Wound* (London: Routledge).

LeBor, Adam (2006) *City of Oranges: Arabs and Jews in Jaffa* (London: Bloomsbury).

Leshem, Ron (2005) *Beaufort*, trans. Evan Fallenberg (London: Vintage).

Lewis, Anthony (1982) "At Home Abroad: The Consensus Cracks," *New York Times* <http://www.nytimes.com/1982/07/01/opinion/at-home-abroad-the-consensus-cracks.html> (accessed 11 February 2017).

Oz, Amos (2012 [1987]) *The Slopes of Lebanon*, trans. Maurie Goldberg-Matura (Boston: Houghton Mifflin Harcourt).

Oz, Amos (2014) "Lose-lose situation for Israel," *Deutsche Welle* <http://www.dw.com/en/oz-lose-lose-situation-for-israel/a-17822511> (accessed 17 September 2016).

Rabinovich, Abraham (2004) *The Yom Kippur War: The Epic Encounter That Transformed the Middle East* (New York: Schocken).

Saunders, David (2010) *Documentary* (New York: Routledge).

Schiff, Zeev, and Ehud Yahari (1984) *Israel's Lebanon War*, trans. Ina Friedman (New York: Simon and Schuster).

Stewart, Garrett (2012) "Screen Memories in *Waltz with Bashir*," in *Killer Images: Documentary Film, Memory and the Performance of Violence*, ed. Joram Ten Brink and Joshua Oppenheimer (London: Wallflower Press), 120–126.

Traboulsi, Fawwaz (2012) *A History of Modern Lebanon*. 2nd edition (London: Pluto Press).

Weinraub, Bernard (1982) "Reagan Demands End to Attacks in a Blunt Telephone Call to Begin," *New York Times* <http://www.nytimes.com/1982/08/13/world/reagan-demands-end-to-attacks-in-a-blunt-telephone-call-to-begin.html> (accessed 11 February 2017).

Wonnenberg, Felice Naomi (2013) "Sissy and Muscle Jew Go to the Movies," in *Contemporary Jewish Reality in Germany and its Reflection in Film*, ed. Claudia Simone Dorchain and Felice Naomi Wonnenberg (Berlin: De Gruyter), 205–230.

Yosef, Raz (2011) *The Politics of Loss and Trauma in Contemporary Israeli Cinema* (New York: Routledge).

Filmography

Beaufort (2007) Dir. Joseph Cedar (United King Films).
Lebanon (2009) Dir. Samuel Maoz (Ariel Films).
Vals im Bashir (*Waltz with Bashir*) (2008) Dir. Aril Folman (Film Gang).

Miri Talmon
Bonds Across Borders: A Fictional Enemy in Motion on the Israeli Screen

'The Conflict in the Middle East' and its associations of war and terror seem to be inextricably linked to any discussion of Israel and consequently of Israeli cinema and culture. Indeed, that conflict and its impact on Israeli society are a major preoccupation in Israeli culture, and the 'enemy' or in current discourse 'partner' – for war, and for peace – is always central in the corresponding discourse. Nurith Gertz contends that "throughout its history the Jewish-Israeli society used the Arab in order to define its own identity" (2000: 110). Her study of the myths in Israeli culture demonstrates how in a considerable number of cultural productions the key to the identity, desires and fears of Israeli society is held by the Arab.

In my discussion of representations of the Arab enemy in selected Israeli films I shall ask in what way these representations encode Israeli identity negotiations, anxieties and hopes. My discussion begins with a reflexive scene from *Khor Balevananh* (*A Hole in the Moon*) (dir. Uri Zohar, 1964) which allegorically re-presents the Arab-Israeli encounter in the land of Israel at the beginning of the twentieth century, when the first Zionist Jewish settlers came to a land already inhabited and cultivated by local Arabs. Following the analysis of this scene, which is pregnant with symbolic meanings, I shall then discuss three Israeli films, *Ha-Matarah Tiran* (*Sinai Commandos: The Story of the Six Day War*) (dir. Raphael Nussbaum, 1968), *Avanti Popolo* (dir. Rafi Bukai, 1986) and *Bikur Ha-Tizmoret* (*The Band's Visit*) (dir. Eran Kolirin, 2007). At three different points in Israel's (cultural) history, these films portray encounters between Israelis and their (former) Arab-Egyptian enemies. Their images of the Arab enemy and the dialogues between Israeli and Arab characters articulate pivotal concerns, anxieties, perspectives and attitudes of Israelis not so much with regard to their enemy as imagined on film, but rather with regard to themselves – as a nation and as subjects within this imagined community. While rendering encounters with the Arab enemy during war or in its aftermath, all the three films I shall discuss reflect an internal discussion concerning Israeli identity and memory. I shall focus on three instances of Israeli-Egyptian encounters in war and in its aftermath in order to demonstrate how the image of the Egyptian/Arab enemy underlies the construction of three different narratives from an Israeli focal position.

https://doi.org/10.1515/9783110591217-018

1 Primordial Encounters :
'Us' and 'Them' in Black and White

In a modernist, experimental manner, *Khor Balevananh* tells anew the story of the birth of the Israeli nation out of the desert – not only as the act of Zionist settlers, but also as an entrepreneurial trajectory of film production on a Western-like frontier. One of the most memorable scenes in this film strikingly illustrates the constructed nature of representations of the 'enemy' on film. In this scene, three 'Arabs,' cast by Jewish Israeli actors dressed in traditional Bedouin outfits, approach the fictional movie makers and Zionist entrepreneurs Tzelnik (played by Uri Zohar) and Mizrakhi (played by Avraham Heffner), imploring them to be given, for once, the role of 'the good guys' in the film they are making: "We always play the bad people, we would like for once to play good people!"[1] "Are you out of your mind?," Mizrakhi wonders, "How is it possible, you are Arabs!" "OK, we know," says the spokesman of the 'Arabs,' now shown in white contours over the black celluloid – literally and concretely 'in the negative,' rather than in black over white. "But for once, only this time, can we just play a small part?" – Tzelnik and Mizrakhi hide behind Mizrakhi's colonial hat and discuss the strange request, finally agreeing that the 'Arabs' should have just one scene. This, it turns out, is an Arab folk dance, a *Debkah*, in traditional Palestinian dress, yet in an absurd twist performed to the music and lyrics of an old Hebrew song: "El Yivneh Hagalilah" ("God will build the Galilee"). As they sing and dance in the absurd manner which characterizes this experimental modernist film, out of the blue as in old American Western films come Tzelnik, Mizrakhi and their Zionist Jewish crew, this time shooting at the Arabs with rifles instead of cameras. However, they then throw away their rifles and hug with the dancing Arabs. Once again, the Zionist settlers/movie makers and the 'Arabs' (in all their roles as local inhabitants of Israel/Palestine, as the 'settlers,' 'enemies,' and as the actors performing 'Hebrews' and 'Arabs') hug each other.

In a nutshell, this is a performative reflexive moment of the inception of the conflict between Israelis and Palestinians re-written, re-cast and resolved: the 'enemy' or, the 'Arabs,' are only (Israeli-Jewish) actors, playing a part; the shooting does not kill – it is just motion fiction; the 'Arabs' embrace and articulate the Zionist ideology of settling and building the Galilee, voicing the Hebrew-Zionist song while retaining their traditional authentic practices and folklore; all throw their guns away and hug. A happy ending. Peace. This scene estranges, ritualizes

---

[1] The translation of the dialogue is mine, MT.

and lays bare the complex relationship between Palestinian Arabs and Israeli Jews in an ideologically invested Zionist context. There is a de-familiarization of the Palestinian-Israeli conflict, not only by performatively and ritually enacting it, but also by reversing and overturning the roles of Jews and Arabs. The Arabs are not the ones who do the shooting, they are not the violent enemy. On the contrary, in this scene they are gentle rather than threatening, and at the mercy of the filmmakers, who decide whether they have any part in the story at all. Moreover, the Arabs here – as in other Zionist cinematic texts – represent what the Zionist transformed or the 'New Jew' strives to become: a builder, a farmer, a native indigenous to the land, a virile male, physically fit, a doer outdoors rather than a passive man of letters indoors. This cinematic encounter allegorically depicts the relations between Jews and Arabs as ambivalent and contradictory from the onset. On the one hand, the Arabs are conceived as successors of the ancient Hebrew forefathers, in the sense that they keep their practices as narrativized in the Bible alive: shepherds and farmers, living in the land of the Bible and maintaining its vibrant vitality and agricultural traditions. On the other hand, the Arabs carry diametrically opposed meanings as well, as they are the dangerous, threatening enemy who wish to destroy Zionist endeavor and expel Jewish settlers from the land; they stand for death and menace rather than life and renewal.

The meticulously constructed parody in white over black in the carnivalesque celluloid world of *Khor Balevananh* illustrates the problematics of film representations of enemies in particular – external or internal, and in general, of ethnic minorities and groups that threaten the cohesion, homogeneity or very existence of a nation. Moreover, the scene described above lays bare the unique apparatus of representation of the Arab in Israeli cinematic discourse. Representing minorities in terms of the opposition and contrast between black and white, stereotyping and allotting them narrowly circumscribed parts – the enemy, the terrorist ("we always play the bad people") – as well as symbolically annihilating them by not giving them any part at all on the screen, are well established practices in media and cinematic representations of minorities and enemies. In this particular case, the dichotomy of 'black' and 'white' lays bare the cinematic regime of representation of the Arab as enemy and opponent of Zionist endeavor and the Jewish-Israeli experience. The black and white materiality of the celluloid as used here exposes stigmatizing through the cinematic and cultural apparatus. It also exposes the performativity and formal distinction of black versus white as a construction of the medium rather than a natural fact. Arabs are the 'negative' of the Israeli image, the black alter ego of their whiteness, but also the desired 'other' representing authentic locality and indigenous spontaneity, thus rendering concrete subconscious yearnings of the Israelis. The ambivalence of attraction, revulsion and fear with regard to the Palestinian Arab rests on enduring textual and national histories. The biblical forefather Abraham has been preserved in the national memory and biblical textual mythology as a shepherd and a farmer, whose mirror image are the local Arabs encountered by the first Zionist settlers, as later recorded in the film *Hem Hayu Asarah* (*They Were Ten*) (dir. Baruch Dienar, 1960). They live the pastoral life of the Hebrew biblical forefathers, yet pose a threat to the very life the settlers wish to create in their ancient homeland, a peaceful pastoral life of work, freedom and renewal.

The cinematic encounter between Arabs and Jews in the Land of Israel/Palestine as parodically reconstructed in *Khor Balevananh* goes back to the 1880s, when Zionist settlers sought to revive a national Hebrew life and culture in the land of their forefathers and to live a sovereign life of freedom, dignity, productivity and cultural autonomy. However, as we know, the story developed very differently from any of the utopian narratives of national renaissance, mainly because of the conflict with the Arabs (the local Palestinians and the surrounding Arab states), who neither welcomed nor accepted the newly evolving cultural, communal and national entity in the territory of the Land of Israel-Palestine. This narrative of conflict, in which the Arab and Palestinian enemy has a major role in shaping Israeli collective memory and historiography, as well as anxieties and yearnings for a new, peaceful chapter of acceptance and containment, is in a constant state of negotiation and debate within Israel and beyond, in the media and in the arts.

2 Re-telling the History of War – Whose Story?

The three films selected for discussion refer to a major historic moment after which Israel would never be the same: the Six Day War in June 1967. Israel entered that war as a young David against a mighty Arab Goliath, as it were. It emerged not only victorious, but beginning a process of also becoming a delegitimized occupier of territories, violent aggressor and imperialist force beside a legitimate state defending its borders and very existence. The 1967 Six Day War was one of several military conflicts between Israelis and Egyptians, starting with the Israeli War of Independence of 1948 and the 1956 war in the Sinai Peninsula as part of the Suez Crisis, and followed by the 1968–1972 Egyptian-Israeli War of Attrition launched by Egyptian President Gamal Abdel Nasser, and the 1973 Yom Kippur War. A turning point in this serial drama of enmity, war and bloodshed dawned in November 1977, when Egyptian President Anwar el-Sadat initiated reconciliation with Israel. He called upon Israeli Prime Minister Menachem Begin to cease war and bloodshed, came to speak to the Israeli people in the *Knesset*, and became the first Moslem Laureate when he and Begin received the Nobel Peace Prize. Sadly, Sadat was assassinated in October 1981, before the complete withdrawal of Israel from the Sinai Peninsula in April 1982 as part of the peace treaty that had been signed between the two nations.

In 1968, immediately following the Six Day War, the film *Ha-Matarah Tiran* presented the narrative of an inevitable and heroic war of survival against an enemy whose aim was to annihilate the Israeli state and its Jewish inhabitants. In 1986, after the peace treaty with Egypt had been signed and the Sinai Peninsula returned to the Egyptians, the film *Avanti Popolo* adopted and embraced the focalization of Egyptian soldiers in the aftermath of the 1967 Six Day War, forsaken by their military commanders in the Sinai desert after the ceasefire. Focalizing on the imagined Egyptians as personalized and universalized human beings trapped in the absurdities of war, the film offers a pacifist counter-narrative to that of the 'enemy,' undermining conceptions of a heroic war as well as rendering the very experience of war as universally absurd and arbitrary, regardless of borders or nationalities. Finally, in the 2007 *Bikur Ha-Tizmoret*, the narrative of conflict and war is terminated and resolved by (cultural) reconciliation and mutual human acceptance. At a time of peaceful coexistence, the war becomes but a memory like an old photograph to be hung on the wall, rather than a haunting trauma.

Ella Shohat borrows Gérard Genette's concept of focalization in order to discuss Israeli cinema's Orientalist representation of history and the encounter between East and West in the Land of Israel-Palestine from 1930–1990. Focalization is theorized as the subject position, vantage point and perspective of diegetic characters, and thus "as the hinge that links the different narrative roles." Focalization allows for the structuring of identifications within the story world through the cognitive and perceptual grid of its "inhabitants," filtering our emotional experience and ideological judgements through characters as radiating "centers of consciousness" (Shohat 1990: 270). Shohat describes the primal encounters between Israeli heroes and their Arab enemies in Zionist Hebrew cinema, in particular in the genre she characterizes as heroic-nationalist films, as a battle filtered through images of encirclement. These encirclements focus spectators' attention and empathy on familiar Jewish protagonists defending themselves against alien, incomprehensibly violent Arabs (270). Such images of the few (Jews) against the many (Arabs), and of siege, she argues, play into the syndrome of traumatic memories originating in the European Jewish ghetto experience (271). The choice of the war genre to mediate most of the encounters between Jews and Arabs in heroic-nationalist films is not merely a reflection of the (historical and political) reality of war, Shohat claims. It also provides a hospitable textual environment for the underlying pride in the metamorphosis of the victimized passive Jew into a warrior in charge of his own destiny, faith, and survival (271).

3 First Encounter: The Six Day War (1967)

The film *Ha-Matarah Tiran* exemplifies Shohat's view of the ideological subtext in heroic-nationalist Israeli films.[2] The film articulates anxieties of annihilation in its opening expositional scene, then building the image of the (ultra-)competent Israeli warrior and mission-team through its plot. It tells the story of Israeli soldiers and cohesive military groups overcoming a lethal threat to their country by performing sheer impossible feats, and it does so through the spirit and vision underlying heroic-patriotic novels and films about the allies defending Europe against Nazi Germany during the Second World War. The linear trajectory of the plot works towards the elimination of an Egyptian radar station, a threat to Israel's security. This plot is similar to the film that seems to have inspired *Ha-Matarah Tiran* (or of which it may even be an outright remake): *The Guns of Navarone* (dir. J. Lee Thompson, 1961). This 'mission impossible' type of war film, adapted from the eponymous Alistair MacLean novel, is set in World War II. In *The Guns of Navarone*, a British commando are sent into the heart of Nazi-occupied Greece in order to destroy a massive German gun emplacement commanding a key sea channel. There is a conspicuous analogy between the destruction of the guns, which – according to the film's narrative logic – will help saving Europe from Nazi aggression, and the importance of destroying the radar station in the straits of Tiran for the survival of Israel. However, the fictional logic and its mythical undertones are motivated by a historical background, which reverberates in *Ha-Matarah Tiran* and is recognized by the film's contemporary viewers in Israel and internationally.

The opening scene of the film captures Israeli anxieties concerning an Egyptian attack and invasion. Historically, it is anchored in the days preceding the Six Day War, precisely speaking 22 May 1967, when President Nasser closed the Straits of Tiran to Israeli shipping and Egyptian media were full of threats against Israel. The film opens with a sequence of documentary footage and newsreels from May 1967 as seen on a television screen within the film. These

---

2 See also Nurith Gertz's discussion of nationalist-heroic films following the Six Day War in her study of Israeli cinema of the sixties (1993), and my own discussion of representations of the mission-oriented group of male warriors in Israeli cinema (Talmon 2001).

sights and sounds have become engraved in Israel's collective memory, recalling anxious anticipations of war after Nasser's closing of the straits, mobilizing his forces to the Sinai, and articulating his readiness to go to war with Israel in vehement public speeches on radio and TV. In the opening scene of Nussbaum's film, these documentaries of masses in the streets of Cairo supporting Nasser's militant declarations, and of military parades of tanks and battalions, are followed by the image of an Israeli woman waking up in horror, as if the documentary footage were a nightmare she experienced. Merging documentary footage broadcast in May 1967 by Egyptian media with the fictional Israeli wife of one of the film's protagonists, this opening scene creates the expositional setting for the motion fiction to come: a heroic 'mission impossible' type of war film, in which an Israeli team is sent to the heart of the Sinai and in which Egyptian forces are ready to be mobilized for a decisive war against Israel. The suicidal operation is presented as though its success were to determine the fate of the war with Egypt.

The Israeli film presents the typical mixture of heroic, masculine war films: the heroic soldiers and their solidarity and utter loyalty to their country and peers, their commitment to the mission, whatever sacrifice it necessitates, and the willingness of each member of the unit to make the ultimate sacrifice. This heroic and altruistic predisposition of the unit's members is complemented by the individual skills of each of them, which enable them to accomplish the seemingly impossible and fulfill their vital mission. Like the heroically patriotic Hollywood version of the 'mission impossible' type of war film (and especially Second World War film) therefore, this 1968 Israeli film creates an equally patriotic and heroic version of its own war and the Israeli army as represented by an "A Team," thus the tagline on the film's English poster. Before the antagonists are actually met on the battlefield, their generalized image as conveyed by the media has already been established as that of a horrifically violent, blood-thirsty mob in the streets of Cairo, seen on television or film theatre newsreels throughout Israel. Their aggression is rendered in the film through Egyptian propaganda broadcasts heard on Israeli radio as "The Voice of Thunder from Cairo" (in Hebrew: *Kol Hara'am me Kahir*).

Abstracted evocations of the Egyptian 'enemy' in the opening are fine-tuned and rendered more complex as the film proceeds. This is done in two ways: first, the plot builds towards a personal encounter between the Israeli soldiers and an Egyptian officer who is taken prisoner during the operation; secondly, the Israeli soldiers are shown not only to have highly individualized skills, but also to represent diverse ethnic and cultural backgrounds as well as diverse political affiliations and views, and consequently different dispositions regarding war and enemies. The most important distinction to be made in this respect, in this as well as in other Israeli films, concerns the ongoing heated debate within Israeli society on universal human ethics on the battlefield and in treating enemies and terrorists, as opposed to defending the nation's or one's own life at all costs, with security and survival becoming ultimate values in the face of terror and war. Hence, the dilemmas and contradictions involved in remaining morally just and sensitive while at the same time heroic and patriotic. What is at stake here is the ethical code which demands of every soldier not only to defend the nation and the lives of his own people, but also to respect and spare the lives of enemies as fellow human beings. In the film's narrative and drama, this dilemma and contradiction, and the universally human morally committed standpoint, is represented by the character of Moshe, nicknamed Moish.

As the mission team proceeds through the Sinai desert, they encounter four local Bedouins who attack them with guns and knives. The battle ends with the Bedouins' surrender, and an argument ensues whether to just let them go or take them captives. The more militant position is articulated by Eli, the member of the team who is a Holocaust survivor: according to him, the enemy is always lethal, Arabs are not likely ever to have mercy on Jews, and given the opportunity they will betray those who spared their lives. Earlier in the journey through the desert, as heated Egyptian calls to slaughter the Jews are heard on the radio, Eli, one of the commando, says to his comrades: "Kill the Jews, kill the Jews, that's what I hear through my life, they take God's role for themselves. I am the only one left from my family in Auschwitz." Later on, a debate ensues concerning the fate of the Bedouin prisoners of war, who before that were shooting at the Israeli soldiers. Eli insists that it is dangerous to let them go, and reminds his mates that a whole Israeli troop was killed by Arab militia in 1948 because they spared the life of an old Palestinian they had encountered and who gave them away.

Moish represents a different position, insisting that when the enemy is equipped with a rifle you need to defend yourself, but as soon as the enemy has no rifle, killing another human being is murder. The group decide to take the Bedouins' camels and leave them. The Bedouins summon Egyptian troops and another battle ensues, in which Eli is killed (as he dreaded), Moshe is wounded, and the also wounded Egyptian commander is captured. Hence, another subtext is added to the film's depiction of the Six Day War, a layer of meaning that is created through its portrayal of the Israeli-Egyptian encounter. The moral dilemmas which this encounter entails are rendered through the discussions within the Israeli unit and their conversations with their Arab prisoner. They concern the justification of war, moral attitudes of the Israeli army to their enemy and prisoners of war, and the very concrete and strongly defended value of a 'Purity of Arms' (in Hebrew: *Tohar Haneshek*) – an oxymoron which expresses the contradictory yearning for an ethically and morally 'pure' war.

The moments in the film when the action is stopped for the Israeli unit to debate among themselves are pregnant with meanings haunting Israeli society and culture. Instead of taking the heroic action that would clearly be justified as part of the film's plot, the Israelis on the screen in these moments represent real Israelis debating among themselves. What they articulate in fact is an internal discourse about the war, about its justification and the ethical and moral choices of the Israeli army at large and of each soldier in particular with regard to the enemy and to prisoners of war.

Since this is a typically heroic film produced in the aftermath of the Six Day War, its action-oriented narrative persists until the successful completion of the 'mission impossible.' The film thus presents an ideologically invested ending which not only validates the patriotic heroism and brave loyalty of the Israeli warriors and their sacrifice, but also portrays the Egyptian soldiers as determined, loyal, brave and no less patriotic. This makes the Israeli endeavor appear all the more justified. However, the interruptions of the action serve a vital function, rendering controversial discussions within the Israeli context as well as facilitating a dialogue with the imagined Egyptian enemy on the very justification of the war. Hence, the wounded Moshe, who remains to guard the wounded Egyptian officer Mukhamad Khalil, acknowledges his adversary's bravery after Khalil has tried to report to his Egyptian commanders, under his Israeli captors' 'nose,' of the Israeli team's (and his) whereabouts:

> Moshe: Tell me something, Captain. Isn't it a pity, with all the poverty in your country, why do you waste so much and make us waste so much on arms?
> Khalil: You took the land of my brothers and send them out to live like dogs without homes, I fight for them.
> Moshe: You could have solved the problem of the refugees a long time ago if you only wanted to, but you don't. Your leaders are more interested in keeping them as explosives for war. You cannot cope with the problems in your own country so you use us as an exterior enemy whom you can blame for everything.
> Khalil: Then why don't you take the refugees back?
> Moshe: And if we take them back, will you make peace?
> Khalil: You are imperialists, we have to finish you.
> Moshe: You've been brain-washed, Khalil. Finish us? Why? Do we have conflicting interests? Do we want to destroy you? Isn't there enough desert land that could be cultivated by you and by us?
> Khalil: We are in a state of war
> Moshe: (In Hebrew): Tzlalim.
> Khalil: What did you say?
> Moshe (lights Khalil a cigarette): Shadows, captain. That's what we'll all be if we don't learn to live in peace.
> Khalil: What are you talking about?
> Moshe: I am only dreaming.

Moshe sees Khalil not as the 'enemy' but as an equal, a rational and pragmatic man, who does his best as a commander, acting responsibly towards his men, the army he serves and his superiors.

4 Second Encounter: 1967 Revisited, the Enemy Revised

It is the summer of 1967. A ceasefire between Egypt and Israel has been declared. Three Egyptian soldiers, of the many who found themselves deserted by the Egyptian leadership in the Sinai Peninsula now conquered by the Israeli army, try to reach home through the desert. One of them is an officer, who insists they keep fighting in spite of the ceasefire. The others, however, refuse. Unlike their predecessors, the Egyptian soldiers in the 1968 film *Ha-Matarah Tiran* who keep fighting valiantly to see their Israeli enemy destroyed, the Egyptian soldiers in *Avanti Popolo* (1986) are not heroes but human beings, hot, thirsty, hungry, tired, and frightened. In the quarrel that follows their refusal to go on fighting, their commanding officer is killed. Khaled el Asmar (Salim Dau) and Gassan Hamada (Suhel Khaddad) bury him and continue towards the Suez Canal and Egypt, having rid themselves of their rifles and other equipment identifying them as Egyptian soldiers and burdening them on their walk through the desert. The actors do not speak Egyptian, but Palestinian Arabic, which Israeli spectators will not notice unless they have an Egyptian heritage (like a considerable number of Israelis) or speak Palestinian Arabic themselves (one fifth of Israeli society are Palestinian). They can also recognize the actors Salim Dau and Suhel Khaddad, who are Palestinian Israelis,[3] not Israeli Jews of Middle Eastern heritage, while it is obvious that the diegesis of the film is predominantly focalized on the Egyptians. Hence the film insists upon more authentic representations of the 'Arabs' on the one hand, and on identifications with the Arab-Egyptian enemy rather than the Israeli-Jewish soldiers in the drama on the other.

Later in the film, there comes a turning point when this symbolic role reversal becomes part of the drama. The point of view, so far consistently that of the Egyptian soldiers, suddenly changes as we see the Egyptians through the binoculars of an Israeli soldier. While in the nationalist heroic films focalization was consistently on the Israeli Jew (as seen through a Zionist ideological lens), *Avanti Popolo* makes issues of control and loss with regard to a point of view strikingly

---

[3] Ella Shohat argues that the casting of Palestinian Arabs in Israeli political films of the 1980s facilitated the self-representation of a Palestinian national identity (1990: 273).

conspicuous. In addition, the turnover of the point of view is followed by another remarkable reversal.

Khaled (against the commands of his religion, if he is a practicing Muslim) is completely drunk on some whisky that he and Gassan found in a UN jeep, together with a dead UN officer (which in itself is, of course, highly symbolic). He tries to reach for the water container of his Israeli captors – his enemies or rather, at this point, his fellow sufferers in the desert – and when refused faces them with this well-known monologue:

> "I am a Jew! Hath not a Jew eyes? Hath not a Jew hands, organs, dimensions, senses, affections, passions? Fed with the same food, hurt with the same weapons, subject to the same diseases, healed by the same means, warmed and cooled by the same winter and summer as a Christian is? If you prick us, do we not bleed? If you tickle us, do we not laugh? If you poison us, do we not die?"

Quoting Shylock, William Shakespeare's Jewish moneylender in *The Merchant of Venice*, Khaled assumes the role of a Jew. However, his speech also draws his audience's attention to the fact that they share basic human skills, flaws, constraints and qualities. Khaled's speech is interpreted by one of the Israeli soldiers as having "the roles mixed up." Nurith Gertz argues that the role reversal between Israeli Jews and Arabs manifested in this scene is typical of 1980s Israeli cinema, which reversed and switched Jewish and Arab identities. However, she argues, "upon the now reversed identities, it constructed, again and again, a bridge that unites Israelis and Arabs on a shared human basis" (1993: 111).

The encounter between the Egyptian and the Israeli soldiers occurs in a surreal setting, which highlights the absurdity not only of the fictional situation, but, as in the theater of the absurd, the absurdity of war as such. The wandering Egyptian soldiers, drunk on the UN officer's whisky, ride the UN jeep with the dead officer to the sounds of the Israeli Defense Forces' Anthem from the IDF radio broadcast. They approach the Israeli soldiers, who carry an umbrella in the blazing desert, to the sound of Belgian singer Adamo singing *Tombe la neige* ("The Snow is Falling") in French on the Monte Carlo radio station to which the Israeli soldiers' transistor is tuned. On top of all this, there is now also Shylock's speech, recited in English, and with much pathos, by the Egyptian soldier. Everything seems out of place, nothing appears to make sense, but then, as the sun sets, they all march together through the golden dunes of the Sinai desert, to the sounds of the Italian socialist anthem *Bandiera Rossa* (*Avanti Popolo*), which gave the film its title, from the Monte Carlo radio. As the six human figures march to the song of the red flag, and with the red sunset in the backdrop, they are unified in a magic moment which makes it impossible to distinguish between Israeli and Egyptian. United in the harmony of music and nature, as well as in the misery of thirst, hunger and homesickness, they become fellow human beings rather than enemies.

Later, as they all sit around their campfire and get to know each other, we learn about what the Egyptian Khaled and the Israeli Hirsch have in common. They are both aspiring theater actors. They both care about animals to the degree that even if they are starved, they will spare a rabbit rather than eat it. The most significant link between the Egyptians and Israelis, however, is that they have all become victims in a senseless cause, as the war has officially ended. This bitter analogy ends the film in a painfully determinist manner: as the sun rises in the morning, the Israeli soldiers walk on, and unable to read the warning signs in Arabic walk into a minefield. Only one survives. Khaled and Gassan hear the explosions and run to their rescue. Israeli forces, which had so far left the three soldiers to themselves, arrive and go after Gassan and Khaled, who frantically run towards the Suez Canal. Gassan is shot by the Israelis, while Khaled, who makes it into the water, is killed by bullets from both banks of the canal, Israeli and Egyptian. His spectacularly horrifying and pointless death at the end of the film turns him into another victim of the absurdity of war.

5 Third Encounter: Forty Years Later

The Israeli film *Bikur Ha-Tizmoret* dramatizes the encounter between Alexandria's police orchestra and the inhabitants of a small town in the southern desert of Israel, who have longed for some excitement to break the monotony of their lives. The desert, which serves as a backdrop in all the three films discussed here, provides an iconic site for the encounters between Israelis and Egyptians which they portray: as enemies and as human beings. In *Bikur Ha-Tizmoret*, however, this iconographic space for negotiations of identity also becomes the symbolic site of a quest for authenticity and personal fulfillment on both sides of the national divide between Egyptians and Israelis.

The film opens with the image of a white van arriving at an unidentified airport terminal. A man alights from the van and takes out of its back a big yellow Pilates ball, putting it next to him in the front of the van and then shutting the door again. He drives away, leaving a group of men wearing azure uniforms, later identified as the Alexandria Police Ceremonial Orchestra. This opening, which seems to make no narrative or dramatic sense, provides an exposition to the 'miraculous' arrival of the Egyptian orchestra at an Israeli town in the *Negev*, the southern prairie of Israel. In a later scene, the band descend from a bus in the middle of a vast desert, their azure uniforms reflecting the endless Mediterranean sky. Conspicuously out-of-place in the endless stretches of golden desert, their uniforms, dark blue suitcases and black boxes containing musical instruments appear almost surreal.

Blending the fantastic and hyper-realistic, these scenes establish the magic realist aesthetic lying at the core of the film. By juxtaposing and metonymically coupling disparate elements, the film creates a fairy-tale atmosphere in which the unlikely may happen, and carries with it the utopian promise of a better world. Like a surrealist painter, director Eran Kolirin produces unexpected visual and narrative juxtapositions, yet always bases the poesy of the 'magic' world on stark reality. He thereby makes us experience this magic as some marvelous absurdity which vanishes in thin air after one dreamy night. Thus, we cannot even be sure whether, in the context of the film, the magic actually happened or whether this was not rather rooted in our own imagination.

As William Earle argues, in surrealist films the flight from reality is necessary in order to experience reality effusively. In cinematic surrealism, the convergence of perception and imagination enables the imagination to give meaning to what is seen. This sort of convergence is essentially poetic, hence surrealist films, according to Earle, are visual poems (1987: 19–22). In this realm of cinematic poetry, where Kolirin locates his film, fresh perceptions of reality become possible. Kolirin's film estranges a spatial reality, a place culturally encoded in Israeli culture as "a development town" – a site which conventionally stands for "the place where nothing happens."[4]

Digital language and the symbolic law of the father are replaced in Kolirin's poetic universe by the pre-Oedipal, pre-language realm of analogical signs: music, gesture, intonation and untranslatable utterances which come directly from the soul's emotions and yearnings. Dinah, the film's protagonist, lives in Israel's southern periphery. She may therefore be one of many Israelis (including Kolirin's grandmother, according to his testimony, and the late President Shimon Perez) who in the 1960s and 1970s watched Egyptian movies (in Arabic) on Israel's first and only public television channel on Friday afternoons. Indeed, it is reasonable to assume that she shares an Arab linguistic and cultural heritage. Judging from her question "Masri?" (Arabic for 'Egyptian') when she first en-

---

[4] Development towns were the result of a national enterprise for the settlement and housing of the massive influx of immigrants and Jewish refugees from the Middle East and Europe into Israel in the first decade of the state's existence in the 1950s. While in retrospect this won the Israel Award of 1984 as a distinguished vital enterprise in the history of Israel's development, these small towns, which consisted mostly of housing projects built along Israel's borders, offered their inhabitants mostly marginality, unemployment, poverty and a sense of having been forsaken by the state and its center.

counters Tawfiq Zakaria, conductor of the Alexandria Police Ceremonial Orchestra, it is even plausible that she may have Jewish-Egyptian ancestors. Still, she seems to need translation when confronted with Tawfiq's Arabic, and for the Arab song which she has selected especially for him on the jukebox in the local restaurant. However, it is not the linguistic meaning of words and sentences Dinah seems to be attracted to, but the tactile, material, and sensual continuum of the Arab utterances and music.

The restaurant scene between Dinah and Tawfiq, set in a magic 'after hours' time,[5] brings home the film's message both through its comments on the limitations of language in inter-cultural dialogue, and through articulating Kolirin's own nostalgia. The song Dinah plays for Tawfiq on the jukebox ("everything beautiful/sweet reminds me of you") is not translated for the film's Hebrew-speaking audience (just like Dinah herself). The female singer's voice, the Arab melody and tonality and the instrumental color of this music all bring sweet memories and a sense of ultimate beauty to this magic dialogic moment. Written and composed by the Palestinian Israeli musician Habib Shkhade, the song evokes a world of cultural associations Israelis share with Arabs – associations of a lost and yearned-for cultural heritage of generations of Jews living in Middle Eastern homelands. These subconscious, repressed cultural longings associated with Arab culture, language and music cannot be accounted for in rational, digital language, notably that of public cultural discourses. The insistence on re-living and reviving Arab cultural traditions is a significant movement in Israeli culture. This yearning for an Arab heritage and nostalgia for a life in which Egyptian Arab movies were part and parcel of the lived culture is expressive of a utopian desire among Israelis to be an autochthonic part of the Middle East instead of a foreign European or 'Western' implant to be rejected and annihilated. As Kolirin puts it: "The film explores the desire to connect to the region – to people you don't know and who are part of it. It's about having a yearning for peace and also of being a part of what can make it happen." In his refusal to allow linguistic boundaries and historic adversity to come between these human beings,

---

5 The liminality of the nocturnal setting seems to quote both Martin Scorsese's 1985 *After Hours* and George Lucas's 1973 nostalgic *American Graffiti*. These intertexts shed light on the symbolic meanings of popular culture's underrated creative potentials, which Kolirin and his generational sensibilities seem to rehabilitate. In Lucas's film, the juke-box, the radio and the DJ wolf-man's commentary and songs express the emotions of teenagers in transition, during one magic last night of small town America in 1962. This is the eve of the loss of collective innocence, with JFK's assassination, the war in Vietnam, and the end of the world as Americans knew it ahead. Scorsese's film expresses the anxieties of American males on the verge of radically changing gender relations and resulting 'women on top' sensibilities in the 1990s.

Israelis and Egyptians, in the desert, Kolirin imagines a new Middle East which respects its traditional, classic Arabic culture, which all of its inhabitants – including Israelis – long for and are affiliated with.

In *Avanti Popolo*, the eponymous song serves as a temporary bond between the Egyptian and Israeli soldiers, forsaken in the desert and trying to find their way back home and get on with their lives. Two decades later, in *Bikur Ha-Tizmoret*, the Six Day War of 1967 as well as the 1973 Yom Kippur War are encoded as a suppressed memory in the Israeli psyche. The only moment in which there is an implicit allusion to Israel's wars is when the Egyptian group, invited to eat in Dinah's café, notice a portrait of Yitzhak Rabin, the Israeli chief of staff during the Six Day War, and a photograph showing Israeli soldiers on a tank, with a hand-written dedication to Dinah. The soldiers, ultimately victorious, may in fact have eaten in her café. One of the Egyptian band-members, eating there now, covers the photograph by hanging his hat on it. As Kolirin said in an interview: "I decided to hang a hat on politics and war" (the director's commentary soundtrack on the film's official DVD edition).

Still, the human bonds formed in *Bikur Ha-Tizmoret* are as fleeting as the enchantment of connecting to the sweetness and beauty of the Arab music and language. The magic of the night fades away as the morning comes and everybody returns to their dreary and isolated routine. However, this routine is now endowed with a new consciousness, the recognition of how trivial and unexciting most of life actually is. As the product of an intercultural encounter, this universal human recognition cannot be completely separated from the local political context. The scene in Itzik's nursery, in which Itzik suggests how his Egyptian guest Simon might complete his unfinished concerto, articulates his new understanding of his own life, which evolved during the Egyptian band's visit. He proposes to Simon neither to expect nor to create a grand finale. "It is about letting go," Kolirin states, and "it also reflects many questions about the concept of finding an ultimate solution, including the relationship between nations. It's all in the here and now and not necessarily in the grand finale" (director's commentary sound track on the film's DVD).

Conclusion

This chapter discussed the evolution of the story and image of the 'enemy' in Israeli cinematic discourse. I have traced this narrative through three distinct films, which are affiliated with three phases in the conflict between Egypt and Israel, as well as with different and dynamic contexts of production in the cultural history of Israeli cinema. In the process here outlined, the generalized and de-personalized Egyptian 'enemy' becomes a fellow human being, a foe turned friend, first entrapped, like the Israeli soldier, in the absurdity of war, and later in the eroding routine of everyday life and marriage. In the 1968 *Ha-Matarah Tiran*, produced immediately after the Six Day War, the Egyptian enemy is still created in the cliché image of a threatening enemy in a polarized national conflict. In 1986, following not only the 1979 peace accord with Egypt but also a long, bloody war in Lebanon and widening pacifist trends in Israeli culture, *Avanti Popolo* offers its viewers, Israeli and international alike, the Egyptian soldier's point of view and identifications. Furthermore, in the spirit of the post-Lebanon-War anti militarist backlash in Israel, heroism and patriotism are no longer relevant traits of soldiers and their enemies, and war is presented as a universal evil victimizing Egyptians and Israelis alike. *Bikur Ha-Tizmoret* (2007) illustrates not only how images of the 'enemy' have changed with regard to definitions of Israel's national policies and borders. The film also reflects a development from concepts of a distinct, external enemy, threatening and repeatedly attempting to annihilate Israel through war, to images of the 'enemy' as a 'partner' in peaceful co-existence, and a poet of the everyday. The 'enemy' has become an intimate brother of a longed for Arab culture which represents an object of nostalgia and the source of a more authentic identity for Israelis, whose heritage is rooted in the Middle East. The trajectory of the changing faces of the Egyptian enemy hence includes a dynamic narrative of Israel's own identity, collective memory, ethnic diversity, and discourses of place and cultural heritage. It is an evolving narrative which is turning black and white images into a wide spectrum of shades and colors, a rainbow, if you will, of the complex relations between Israeli Jews and the Arab cultural heritage of their Middle Eastern homelands as well as their Palestinian Arab brethren in Israel – the Palestinian members of Israeli society and culture.

Works Cited

Gertz, Nurith (1993) *Motion Fiction: Israeli Prose Fiction and Its Adaptation to Film* (Hebrew: *Sipur Me-hasratim: Siporet Israelit Ve'ibudeiha Lakolno'a*) (Ramat Aviv: The Open University of Israel Press).
Gertz, Nurith (2000) *Myths in Israeli Culture: Captives of a Dream* (London and Portland, OR: Vallentine Mitchell).
Shohat, Ella (1990) "Master Narrative/Counter Readings: The Politics of Israeli Cinema," in *Resisting Images: Essays on Cinema and History*, ed. Robert Sklar and Charles Musser (Philadelphia: Temple University Press), 251–278.

Talmon, Miri (2001) *Israeli Graffiti: Nostalgia, Groups and Collective Identity in Israeli Cinema* (Hebrew: *Bluz Latzabar Ha'avud: Khavurot Venostalgia Bakolnoa Ha'Yisraeli*) (Haifa: University of Haifa Press and Ramat-Aviv: The Open University Press).
William, Earle (1987) *A Surrealism of the Movies* (Chicago, Illinois: Precedent Publishing).
Utin, Pablo (2008) "Interview with Eran Kolirin," in: *The New Israeli Cinema: Conversations with Filmmakers* (Tel Aviv: Resling Publishing), 75–93.

Filmography

Avanti Popolo (1986) Dir. Rafi Boukai (A Micha Shagrir and Rafi Boukai Production).
Bikur Ha-Tizmoret (*The Band's Visit*) (2007) Dir. Eran Kolirin (July August Productions).
Ha-Matarah Tiran (*Sinai Commandos: The Story of the Six Day War*) (1968) Dir. Raphael Nussbaum (Aero Film).
Khor Balevananh (*A Hole in the Moon*) (1964) Dir. Uri Zohar (Geva Films).

Stephen Harper
Bosnia Beyond Good and Evil: (De)Constructing the Enemy in Western and Post-Yugoslav Films about the 1992–1995 War

For those old enough to remember its global media coverage, the horrors of the Bosnian War are condensed in a series of vivid images: bodies ripped apart by bombs and sniper fire, burning villages, columns of desperate refugees. What caused the conflict is much less clear – after all, the Bosnian War, which raged from the spring of 1992 until late 1995, is a massively over-determined event – although a few contributing factors are worth mentioning here by way of introduction. By the late 1980s, Yugoslavia was in dire economic distress, caused in part by its obligations to a savage International Monetary Fund 're-structuring.' Serbian, Croatian and Bosnian Muslim nationalisms had been growing for decades, exacerbating tensions in what had been, for most of the post-war period, a relatively peaceful multi-ethnic country. However, the break-up of Yugoslavia was also precipitated by the world's great powers. Germany, and especially Austria, encouraged the secession of Croatia and Slovenia in 1991, and there are strong suggestions that in the spring of 1992 the US encouraged Bosnia's president, Alija Izetbegović, to reject the Lisbon Agreement, a plan for the partition of Bosnia that might have prevented war (Tucker and Hendrickson 1993; Gibbs 2009: 108–112). Once the war had started, Western and other global powers defied a UN arms embargo by supplying arms to their regional client states. Indeed, the common claim that the great powers passively 'looked on' as the Bosnian War raged is largely mistaken. The US actively supported Bosnia as its client in the region, allowing arms to flow from Iran to Bosnia via Croatia and officially denied 'Black Flights' carrying arms and ammunition to Tuzla (NIOD Appendix II 2002: 145–174), although it was not until November 1994 that the US officially lifted its arms embargo. There is evidence that Britain also supplied arms covertly to Croatian and Bosnian troops (Curtis 2010: 211). The Bosnian Serbs, meanwhile, received Russian and possibly Romanian, Greek and Israeli arms via Serbia throughout the war (NIOD Appendix II 2002: 174–181). This was, in short, a complex, multi-sided conflict.

This chapter argues that screen fictions have tended to ignore this complexity, reinforcing the one-sided view of the war propagated by many Western journalists. It examines some of the best-known cinematic reconstructions of the war in both the West and the Balkans from the last twenty years, arguing that in both the East and the West the cinema of the Bosnian War, like Western news media accounts of the conflict, is heavily compromised by nationalism and racism and is strongly invested in the creation of enemy 'Others.' The chapter ends on a more optimistic note, however, discussing some less partisan treatments of the conflict that have emerged recently, especially from the countries of the former Yugoslavia.

1 The Construction of the Enemy in Western News Media

Responsibility for the myth of Western passivity lies partly with the news media. As Yugoslavia disintegrated into nationalist madness, a "paranoid public sphere" (as described by Adorno and Horkheimer 1972) arose in each of the country's former republics. News bulletins collapsed into absurd and crude propaganda. Western journalists, meanwhile, were mostly confined to their Sarajevo hotels, unable to report from the field and disastrously over-reliant on government propaganda. The conflict was a three-sided civil war, albeit an uneven one, the Serbs possessing more firepower than the Croats and Muslims and perpetrating hideous atrocities, from the brutal siege of Sarajevo to the Srebrenica massacre. But as the US tilted towards its client, the Bosnian government, the conflict was increasingly presented by Western journalists as a one-sided war of aggression waged by Serbs against Bosnian Muslims. The Western press transformed Serbian president Slobodan Milošević into a modern-day Hitler (Seymour 2008: 194), when in fact he was arguably less nationalistic than his opposite numbers in Croatia and Bosnia. Holocaust analogies became common, notably in the summer of 1992, when ITN's images of the 'thin man,' Fikret Alić, in the Serb-run detention camp at Trnopolje were exaggeratedly interpreted in the Western media as evidence of Nazi-style death camps. To be sure, these camps were places of real horror, violence and sometimes death; yet Western media virtually ignored Croat- and Muslim-run camps, although the Muslims ran twelve camps, the Serbs eight and the Croats five (Klaehn 2010: 56). As the Srebrenica massacre indicates only too well, the Bosnian Serb army was the best equipped force in Bosnia throughout the conflict and was thus capable of devastating atrocities against the civilian population; nevertheless, as Janine Clark reminds us, "terrible crimes were also committed *against* the Serbs – in Croatia, Bosnia and Kosovo" (2008: 675).

When the US and its NATO allies launched a devastating campaign to push back the Serbs in 1995, most of the Western news media condoned the attack, despite the thousands of refugees and deaths it created. Western journalists – even, and perhaps especially those of a liberal persuasion – were thus responsible for what Ed Herman and David Peterson call a "tsunami of lies and misrepresentations" (2007: 1). These misrepresentations were often justified by recourse to what British journalist Martin Bell called the "journalism of attachment," an allegedly new mode of affective reportage that aimed at infusing a suspect 'neutral' journalism with a proper sense of moral outrage, but which in fact became a license for over-simplification and one-sided reporting. As the BBC correspondent John Simpson noted, "a climate was created in which everything came to be seen through the filter of the Holocaust" (1999: 444–445), a situation that made criticism of the Bosnian government very difficult. A simplistic narrative emerged in which Serbs were cast as the sole villains of the war and Muslims its only victims, a framing that paved the way for NATO's eventual military intervention, and which has often been reflected, as I argue below, in even the most ideologically liberal films about the war.

2 Humanitarianism and Its Others: Liberal Filmmakers and the Bosnian War

Michael Winterbottom's *Welcome to Sarajevo* was released two years after the end of the Bosnian War and has become the definitive Hollywood treatment of the conflict. Based on the memoir of British foreign correspondent Michael Nicholson (1994), it focuses on the experiences of journalists in Sarajevo and in particular the quest of one of them, Michael Henderson, to evacuate a young girl from a Bosnian orphanage. The film has a documentaristic quality. Dramatic reconstructions of civilian suffering, including bloodied bodies strewn across the pavements of Sarajevo, are intercut with real television news footage, suturing Henderson's reports into the 'real world' of the Yugoslav wars. The children in the orphanage are presented to the viewer as part of Nicholson's news reports, speaking directly to camera with Nicholson's voiceover translation. It is an engaging technique that interpellates the audience as witnesses to the horrors of war through a cinematic rendering of the "journalism of attachment."

Nevertheless, *Welcome to Sarajevo*'s inclusion of actual news footage also reinforces hegemonic framings of the conflict that emphasize Serb villainy. There is a clip, for example, of one of Bill Clinton's public statements about the war: "history has shown us that you can't allow the mass extermination of people and just sit by and watch it happen." Later, television images of the Serb commander Radovan Karadžić are intercut with a speech delivered by George Bush, in which the former president asserts: "you can't negotiate with a terrorist." As the inclusion of soundbites from both Clinton and Bush suggests, the film reproduces the dominant US media-political script of the war. Serbs are depicted throughout the film as the war's sole aggressors – as raving psychopaths, in fact. There are also some striking reversals of historical fact: the Serb victims of the 1992 Sarajevo wedding massacre become, in the film, Croatians, while the rescued girl, in reality a Croat, becomes, in the film, a Muslim (Gocić 2001: 42–43). Throughout *Welcome to Sarajevo*, Muslims are the innocent victims of the war, Serbs are its villains, and journalists such as Henderson stand for the civilized values of multicultural Europe. This lionization of the Western journalist who goes beyond the call of duty is combined with an explicit endorsement of Western 'humanitarian intervention' when Henderson's flamboyant American colleague Flynn apologizes to his translator Risto on behalf of the US for "failing to deliver on those airstrikes." In *Welcome to Sarajevo*, Westerners are thus depicted as the actual or at least potential saviours of Yugoslavia.

In 1999, the BBC broadcast a two-part drama, *Warriors*, which follows the fortunes of British soldiers sent to Bosnia as UN 'peacekeepers' and which has become one of the most respected portrayals of the Western peacekeeping experience. It was written by Leigh Jackson and directed by Peter Kosminsky. As in many other Kosminsky dramas – *No Child of Mine* (1997), *The Project* (2002), *The Government Inspector* (2005) and *Britz* (2007) – a key theme is the betrayal of trust in authority. The drama's central thesis is that the UN's non-combat remit prevented the blue helmets from protecting the victims of the war and in many scenes, the soldiers can only look on in frustration as civilians are shelled or displaced.

The screenplay of *Warriors* is based on the transcripts of interviews conducted with more than 90 British soldiers and their families. In fact, the drama's depiction of war is considered so authentic that the film has been used in army training programmes to illustrate the dilemmas and challenges of peacekeeping. The television critics, meanwhile, went wild. *The Times*' Paul Hoggart, for instance, wrote that *Warriors* "was, quite simply, stunning – gut-wrenching, soul-searing, heart-rending, thought-provoking, sensitive, powerful, deeply disturbing and dripping authenticity" (1999: 12). Yet the drama's representational politics are problematic. Drawing comparisons between the Bosnian conflict and the Second World War, a Muslim woman, Almira Zec, advises Lieutenant Feeley that some form of Western intervention is required to prevent a repeat of the 1940s; "history is screaming at us," she tells him. But the use of WWII analogies to justify military intervention in Bosnia rests on two dubious assumptions: first, that Western military intervention is benevolent; and second, that WWII was a just war against fascism – a proposition that has been challenged by several scholars in recent years (Pauwels 2002; Baker 2008; Heartfield 2012) – and one which is unlikely to find favour in Dresden or Hiroshima. Nor is the drama's historical authenticity beyond question. Muslims here appear only as victims; this is especially problematic since *Warriors* is set in Vitez – an area of central Bosnia in which most of the fighting between 1992 and 1994 involved Muslim and Croat forces. The omni-presence of a slimy, racist Serb commander is also an historical distortion, since Serb forces were not active in the area (Žarkov 2014: 184). Kosminsky's productions have often been subjected to political censure for their radical challenge to establishment narratives; that *Warriors* drew no such attacks perhaps indicates how little it departs from the dominant narrative of the war.

Such one-sided representations of the war are not exclusive to Western productions. The most extensive treatment of the UN mission in Bosnia is *Alpha Bravo Charlie*, an epic fourteen-part TV drama about the Bosnian War directed by the acclaimed Shoaib Mansoor and broadcast by Pakistan Television to record-breaking audiences in 1998. The military-themed production was facilitated by Pakistan's ISPR (Inter-Services Public Relations), a body responsible for producing dramas and documentaries about the country's armed forces (Ansari 2011: 8). *Alpha Bravo Charlie*'s principal character is mild-mannered Gulsher Khan, a captain who is sent to Bosnia a few days after his marriage. Khan's unit is respectfully received by the Bosnian community, as rebuilding projects are begun and medicines, food and money are distributed. As in *Warriors*, the Pakistani soldiers form close bonds with the locals, especially their Bosnian translators, and Khan's burgeoning friendship with his translator Sandra is one of the drama's key storylines.

In one of *Alpha Bravo Charlie*'s emotionally most intense scenes Sandra reveals to Khan her family secret. As the camera slowly zooms in on her face, Sandra explains that her original name had been Selma, but that this was changed at the insistence of her stepfather, a Serb, who abandoned the family to join the army. Later, Sandra tells Khan a second story about her former boyfriend – also a Serb – who deserted her at the outbreak of the war but later returned to slaughter her entire village with a rifle. Having revealed the truth about her suffering at the hands of Serb men, Sandra becomes psychically emancipated and soon falls in love with Khan. She further tells Khan that the war is a "blessing in disguise" because "it has given us our identity; we had forgotten who we were. But now things will change, *inshallah*." The war – and specifically the Pakistani UN presence in it – enhances Sandra's sense of ethno-religious belonging. Sandra's only complaint is that the UN mandate does not allow arms. "Please don't give us food," she implores Khan, "it keeps us alive so that we can be killed by Serbs tomorrow." Instead, Sandra asks for weapons (Pakistan did in fact covertly provide arms to the Bosnian government during the war (NIOD Appendix II: 172; Haqqani 2005: 292)). Captured by Serb forces later in the series, Khan is shot dead in the second of two escape attempts, becoming a fondly remembered martyr in the drama's patriotic ending. *Alpha Bravo Charlie* thus celebrates the legacy of the Pakistani UN presence in Bosnia, casting the soldiers as heroic protectors of the global *ummah*.

All three of the productions discussed above reflect the mainstream 'Western' narrative of the Bosnian War. And it is important to note that their directors are all political liberals. Shaoib Mansoor's 2007 film *Khuda Kay Liye* depicts the wrongful detention and torture of a Pakistani terror suspect and strongly condemns the US war on terror. Winterbottom and Kosminsky are also liberal filmmakers who have been very critical of Western foreign policy since 2001. Winterbottom's docudrama *Road to Guantánamo* (2005) and Kosminsky's dramas *The Government Inspector* (2005) and *Britz* (2007) questioned the grounds for Britain's invasion of Iraq and the effects of the 'war on terror' on British citizens. In fact, all three directors have elsewhere demonstrated an anti-imperialist sensibility that is lacking from their films about Bosnia. Whether consciously or not, it seems that liberal filmmakers in the 1990s, like liberal journalists, helped to reproduce normative understandings of the war, reinforcing hegemonic definitions of the enemy 'Other.'

More recently, a Bosnian War drama has been made by Angelina Jolie – another prominent liberal public figure with a background in humanitarian work and a strong concern for the suffering of Bosnian women. Jolie's first foray into directing, *In the Land of Blood and Honey* (2011), is an award-winning film about a Muslim woman, Ajla, and a Serb policeman, Danijel, who date each other before the outbreak of the war, their friendship illustrating the multicultural harmony of pre-war Sarajevo. During the war, however, Ajla is transported with other Muslim women to a barracks where Danijel is a captain and where the women are repeatedly raped and reduced to 'bare life.' Danijel seems more kindly than his fellow soldiers, at least initially – but nevertheless confines Ajla to his quarters, where he rapes her. At the end of the film, seemingly tortured by his conscience, Danijel gives himself up at a UN checkpoint, confessing that he is a "criminal of war." That Danijel will be punished for his crimes is one of the film's progressive points; after all, in US cinema rape is often punished by vigilante reprisals rather than legal means, or not punished at all (Bufkin and Eschholtz 2000), and rapists are seldom shamed in films about rape in the Bosnian War (Bertolucci 2015).

Nevertheless, *In the Land of Blood and Honey* is deeply embedded within what James Der Derian (2001) calls the "military-industrial-media-entertainment network" (MIME-NET), and Jolie consulted with Wesley Clarke and Richard Holbrooke when researching the film. Perhaps unsurprisingly, given these associations, Jolie's film is strongly invested in establishing war guilt. Here again, Muslims are heroic resistance fighters and Serbs are cardboard cut-out villains; the regional Serb commander, Danijel's father Nebojša, is a blood and soil nationalist who smashes wine glasses as he pontificates about Serb greatness. Jolie even reconstructs ITN's infamous detention camp images in a scene where Danijel is driving through Sarajevo. Although the scene is meant to take place in the winter of 1994, Danijel drives past semi-naked prisoners resembling those featured in the 1992 Trnopolje footage and Jolie's camera lingers on one prisoner who bears a strong resemblance to Fikret Alić. By reviving an image that was widely interpreted as evidence of a fascist resurgence in Europe, Jolie draws an equivalence between Serbs and Nazis, exploiting the best-known image of the war for an ideological rewriting of history. Like the other screen dramas discussed above, *In the Land of Blood and Honey* may be a well-intentioned drama that expresses a broadly humanitarian ethos, but it tends to reproduce a simplified and stereotyped view of Muslim innocence and Serb villainy.

3 Hollywood Action Cinema: Masculinism, Militarism and the Psychopathic Serb

Action films about the Bosnian War have also played a role in enemy-construction, although often this has not gone much beyond using Serbs as episodic villains. Curiously, in Hollywood, this vilification has often taken a quite specific form, with Serbs depicted as pornography-obsessed sexual perverts. In Michael Bay's *The Rock* (1996), a box supposedly holding aid for Bosnian refugees turns out to be a Serb booby trap containing pornographic magazines and an explosive toy doll that spews sarin gas – a detail that inverts a real-life story from the same year, in which NATO officers found booby-trapped toys in a Bosnian Muslim training camp (Pomfret 1996: 25). Gustavo Graef-Marino's *Diplomatic Siege* (1999), meanwhile, depicts the invasion of the US Embassy in Bucharest by dead-eyed Serb terrorists, one of whom displays a penchant for pornographic gay magazines. And in John Irvin's *The Fourth Angel* (2001), Serb terrorists watch pornographic videos. These details revive a longstanding occidental association of the Balkans with sexual excess (think of Bram Stoker's *Dracula*); but they also serve the propaganda function of enemy construction, linking Serbs – and Serbs alone – with sexual depravity.

Other Hollywood actioners go further. John Moore's *Behind Enemy Lines* (2001) merits particular scrutiny as one of the few Hollywood action films to be set during the war itself. The film stars Owen Wilson as Lieutenant Chris Burnett, an American naval flight officer frustrated by the lack of opportunity for combat action. Eventually airborne on a reconnaissance mission over Bosnia, he deviates from his flightpath and is shot down in a demilitarized zone along with his pilot Stackhouse after photographing mass graves. The film's fetishization of the Americans' sophisticated surveillance technologies (Burnett refers to his aircraft's "shiny new digital camera") reinforces the preeminence of US high-tech, immersing the viewer in what Graham Dawson calls the "pleasure culture of war" (1994: 233–258). Burnett's photographs reveal that the local Bosnian Serb Army commander, General Miroslav Lokar, is conducting a secret genocidal campaign against the local population. Pursued by the Serbs in enemy territory, Burnett is eventually rescued through the belated efforts of Reigart – no thanks to Reigart's NATO superior, Admiral Piquet, an uptight Frenchman who represents pettifogging 'European' bureaucracy.

Piquet, who criticizes US unilateralism, is increasingly identified as the film's villain (Weber 2006: 62). The Serb soldiers, meanwhile, are heavily racialized "mono-dimensional demons" (Watson 2008: 55) who must be vanquished by angelic American forces. Cowardly and merciless and curiously unable to speak Serbo-Croat, the Serbs execute Stackhouse by shooting him in the back. And unlike the 'cool' white Americans and the Americanized, clean-looking Muslim youths who help Burnett during his ordeal, the Serbs are portrayed as "minstrels of mud and dirt" (Miskovic 2006: 450).

Burnett is successful in his mission and his photographic evidence results in Lokar appearing at the International Criminal Tribunal for the former Yugoslavia to face justice for his crimes. As in *Welcome to Sarajevo*, constructed news bulletins reinforce a pro-American perspective on the action. At an affective level, meanwhile, a high-octane rock music soundtrack shores up the assertion of US cultural hegemony. By these means, *Behind Enemy Lines* promotes a Manichean worldview in which US military masculinity, freed from "the constraints of multilateralism and diplomacy" (Ó Tuathail 2005: 361), guarantees moral clarity. It is therefore unsurprising that the film, although made before 9/11, was rush-released after the Twin Towers attack.

Serb screen villains often exhibit a backwardness and a desire to 'return' to the war, or to carry it on by other means, in order to avenge past humiliations. A well-known example is Victor Drazen, the chief villain of the first season of the Fox television series *24* (2001–2010), a Serb ethnic cleanser whose wife and child were killed during an undercover CIA operation. Yet a desire for revenge is not entirely the preserve of atavistic Serb villains. The heroes of male action melodramas are themselves typically wounded (and thus, etymologically, traumatized) figures (see Rehling 2009: 55–82) and the Western soldiers and journalists who return to Bosnia have their own grievances to avenge, even if they do so under the civilized pretext of bringing war criminals to justice.

From the late 1990s, as Western bounty hunters charged into the Balkans in search of war criminals, Western film and television dramas began to reflect their experiences in a series of 'back to Bosnia' narratives. The most high-profile of these, Richard Shepard's film *The Hunting Party* (2007), is set five years after the Bosnian War. It is based on an *Esquire* article by Scott K. Anderson (2000) about three journalists who hatch an unconventional plan to spend their holidays finding and arresting Radovan Karadžić ("It's payback time for that fuck," as one of the reporters declares). The posse of journalists ventures into what one of them calls "the heart of this Balkan madness" in order to track down "the most wanted war criminal in Bosnia," Dr Radoslav Boghdanović, also known as The Fox, and his bloodthirsty bodyguard Srđan.

The Hunting Party's central protagonist, Simon Hunt (Richard Gere), is an American TV journalist whose Bosnian girlfriend was raped and murdered by Boghdanović in 1994. Like Flynn in *Welcome to Sarajevo*, Hunt is a fearless journalist, stopping in the heat of battle to smoke cigarettes to a rock music soundtrack. But Hunt loses his composure – and consequently his job – during a live TV interview from Bosnia with his channel's veteran news anchor, Franklin. When Franklin, during a discussion of a massacre of Bosnian Muslims, tries to raise the question of Muslim responsibility for violence, Hunt explodes: "These people were butchered. Women were raped. Children were murdered. Come on, Franklin!" Hunt's outburst reveals his commitment to the "journalism of attachment." By contrast, the older anchorman Franklin embodies the conservatism of a compromised establishment and his vacillations compel Hunt to seek justice on his own terms. Like *Behind Enemy Lines*, then, *The Hunting Party* has a distinctly Oedipal subtext: the failure of paternal authority pushes Hunt, like Chris Burnett, to 'go rogue' and restore moral order by force.

The Fox and his bodyguard, meanwhile, are presented as Balkan Wild Men, animalistic avatars of a "volatile masculinity gone mad" (Longinović 2005: 38). The journalists eventually capture The Fox – no thanks to a laughably ineffectual UN police bureaucrat. Indeed, as in *Behind Enemy Lines*, US unilateralism trumps slow-moving, corrupt European diplomacy. That this unilateralism is covert and possibly illegal aligns the film with other Bosnian War thrillers, such as Mimi Leder's *The Peacemaker* (1999) and John Irvin's *The Fourth Angel* (2001), and reflects what Ross Douthat (2008) calls the "paranoid style" of post-9/11 Hollywood.

Although it is set in the US, Mark Steven Johnson's film *Killing Season* (2013) also focuses on the settling of old scores from the Bosnian War. Here Robert de Niro plays Benjamin Ford, a US Bosnian War veteran who has retreated to the Appalachian mountains in order to forget his wartime experiences. Ford is tracked down, however, by Emil Kovač, a sadistic Serb soldier who had been shot by Ford during the war and now seeks revenge on the American. Most of the screen time in *The Killing Season* is devoted to the brutal to-and-fro combat between the two men as they chase, torture and occasionally speechify to one another in a battle for physical and moral supremacy.

Critically maligned and a commercial flop, *The Killing Season* has incurred widespread ridicule for its raft of cultural solecisms (Kovač's un-Serbian name and incongruously Islamic beard being the favourite targets of the film's online detractors). More troublingly, Balkanist stereotyping abounds. As Dina Iordanova notes, the Balkans have often been viewed by Westerners as a place of "face-to-face sadistic fervour involving blood, spilled guts, severed limbs, tortured and mutilated bodies" (2001: 162). Kovač brings this savagery to America, his preference for a bow and arrow marking him as a pre-modern savage.

Also problematic is the film's opening depiction of the Bosnian War, which is provided by way of backstory. Purporting to depict the final stages of the conflict, the film shows the liberation of a Serb-run concentration camp – complete with Trnopolje-style barbed wire fence – as part of an American ground operation in which US infantry fight a close range battle with the Serbs. This 'Trnopolje liberation' scene is, of course, an invention: US ground troops did not enter Bosnia in 1995, let alone 'liberate the camps,' which in any case had been closed down by the end of 1992. Rather, the scene re-stages the Bosnian War for the purpose of establishing American heroism and Serb depravity. The allusions here to the liberation of the Nazi death camps (notably, a US soldier's discovery of a freight train carriage stuffed with corpses) also serve to re-temporalize the action: 1995 becomes 1945.

4 Constructing the National Enemy in Post-Yugoslav Cinema

Most Western films about the war have a superegoic character, calling for action to restore political and moral order in the Balkans. By contrast, Yugoslav and post-Yugoslav productions – especially Serbian films – often display a dark sense of humour and fatalism, exploring the nature of war in more ironic and allusive modes. The apparent elevation of poetics over politics in these Dionysian films (Gocić 2009) complicates and often confounds critical analysis. Interpretation is further complicated by the generic diversity of these films, which move beyond the drama and action genres favoured by Western directors to encompass satire, comedy and horror.

Unfortunately – and perhaps unsurprisingly – many directors from the former Yugoslavia have bent Hollywood's anti-Serb stick in the other direction, demonizing or at least marginalising Bosnian Muslim and other non-Serb identities. As several critics have argued, the cinema of the former Yugoslavia's most celebrated director, Emir Kusturica, betrays strong pro-Serb political sympathies. In the 1940s storyline in Kusturica's *Podzemlje* (*Underground*) (1995) – a film "supported and endorsed by government-controlled cultural institutions of Milošević's Yugoslavia" (Iordanova 2001: 122) – the heroes Marko and Crni "fight on relentlessly in occupied Belgrade, while the Slovenes and the Croats welcome Nazi troops, [and] Muslims and Croats steal weapons and money from the resistance fighters" (Magala 2005: 195). Nor does Kusturica, either here or in his subsequent Bosnian War film *Život je čudo* (*Life Is a Miracle*) (2004), acknowledge Serb atrocities in the 1990s. A great deal has already been written about Kusturica's nationalist affiliations, so here I shall only say that I agree with the majority of critics that Kusturica's films are as compromised by political bias as any Hollywood production.

A rather more complicated case is presented by Serb director Srđan Dragojević's tour-de-force *Lepa sela lepo gore* (*Pretty Village, Pretty Flame*) (1996) – the Urtext of Bosnian War cinema. Rich in symbolism and dripping in irony, this is arguably the most sophisticated film about the war. It is set in the Višegrad tunnel (also known as the Brotherhood and Unity Tunnel) in 1992, where a Serbian fighter, Milan, is trapped with his comrades, surrounded by Muslim soldiers. The film regularly flashes back to Milan's happy adventures with his childhood friend Halil, one of the Muslims now outside the tunnel; many of these adventures take place near the tunnel, which the boys will not enter, convinced that an ogre dwells there. The film also jumps forward to Milan's post-war experiences in hospital, where, consumed with thoughts of vengeance for the murder of his mother, he determines to kill a young Muslim patient. Milan's journey from amity to animosity illustrates the poisonous power of nationalism. Dragojević also shows the depravity of the Serbs, as they drunkenly loot and burn Muslim villages, proudly sporting the *kokarda*. Milja Radović (2009: 195) is therefore right to argue that the film highlights the idiocies of Serb nationalism; this is no doubt why the production was treated with suspicion by the Serbian elite and ran into significant problems with the authorities.

On the other hand, *Lepa sela lepo gore* also delivers a riposte to Western ways of seeing, expressing "frustration with the Western representation of the war, of Serbs and the Balkans in general" (Radović 2014: 51). This revisionist perspective is embodied by the figure of an American journalist who finds herself in the tunnel with the Serbs: blinded by Western stereotypes, she is initially horrified by the men; but her antipathy towards them lessens with familiarity. Elsewhere Dragojević goes even further, seeming to justify or at least minimize the scale of Serb atrocities. The film's only visible Muslim victim appears in a scene in which the Serbs loot a home, the dead body of its owner, Ćamil, appearing in the background of the shot. As Pavle Levi points out, Dragojević's camera only briefly shows Ćamil, eventually refocusing on the Serb soldier in the foreground and blurring out the victim behind him (2007: 148–149). It might be added that Ćamil appears not only in the background of this shot, but through a window, a distantiating framing that positions Ćamil as a mere 'representation' existing outside the Serbs' – and perhaps the viewers' – sphere of interest. Also problematic in *Lepa sela lepo gore* is the dismissive presentation of the effete anti-war demonstrators who protest in front of the military hospital, risibly chanting John Lennon's "Give Peace a Chance." Ultimately, then, *Lepa sela lepo gore* is an ambiguous text that criticizes some aspects of Serb nationalism while marginalizing Muslim suffering and the aspirations of the peace movement.

Many scholars of post-Yugoslav cinema regard *Ničija zemlja* (*No Man's Land*) (2001), directed by the Bosnian Muslim Danis Tanović, as an exemplary anti-war film that overcomes the sectarianism of other cinematic treatments of the war; but even here there are suggestions of nationalism. The film focuses on two combatants from opposing sides of the conflict – Čiki, a Muslim, and Nino, a Serb – who find themselves trapped between the Serb and Muslim front lines, as piranha-like international reporters seek to exploit the men's predicament and UN officials uselessly look on. Despite its welcome satire on the pretensions of Western journalism, however, *Ničija zemlja* frames the war and the trench-bound duo quite conventionally. The action in the trench is interspersed with a British TV news programme showing Radovan Karadžić threatening the Bosnian Muslims, and an argument between the film's two protagonists about the origins of the war identifies the Serbs as the only aggressors. The film's presentation of the unlikely trenchmates, meanwhile, is far from even-handed. The Bosnian Muslim, Čiki, is coded as the compassionate hero and his Rolling Stones tee-shirt reminds the audience that Muslims represent liberal, Western values. His Serb counterpart, on the other hand, is neurotic and duplicitous, attempting at one point to stab Čiki with his own knife. Notwithstanding the widespread critical assessment of *Ničija zemlja* as an anti-war film, then, Tanović, I would suggest, tends to present the Bosnian War as a morality tale of good Muslim and bad Serb.

5 Beyond Good and Evil: Deconstructing the Enemy in Post-Yugoslav Cinema

Where then to turn for an unpatriotic imagining of the Bosnian War in which enmity is overcome and the dividing lines between enemy and friend are dissolved, or at least de-emphasized? Here we might discuss three post-Yugoslav films about the Bosnian War that are very different to one another in tone yet which indicate potential lines of flight away from ethno-nationalism. Notably, some of the most sensitive films about the Bosnian War, such as Aida Begić's *Snijeg* (*Snow*) (2008) and Juanita Wilson's *As If I Am Not There* (2010), were directed by women and depict women's suffering during and after the war. The film that has attracted most international attention for its depiction of the after-effects of war trauma on Bosnian women is *Grbavica* (*Esma's Secret*) (2006). Written and directed by Bosnian Jasmila Žbanić, *Grbavica* is, along with *Ničija zemlja*, the most watched film in post-war Bosnia (Zajec 2013: 200) and its success led to the Bosnian government belatedly agreeing to provide financial support for the war's rape victims. A "film with very few men" (Pavičić 2010: 49), it tells the story of a working class single mother, Esma, and her wayward daughter Sara, who was conceived when Esma was raped during the war, but who has been brought up to believe that her father was a *šehid*, or war hero. The film alludes subtly to the nature of Esma's experiences during the war and critiques the sexist social norms of post-war Bosnia: Esma works as a waitress in a nightclub, and her abhorrence of the crass philandering of its patrons, together with her unease when in close proximity to men, hint at the nature of her prison camp ordeal and suggest that gender relations have barely changed in Bosnia since the war.

Unlike Angelina Jolie's film about war rape, *Grbavica* shows little interest in political demonization. The film's quiet social realism constitutes an implicit critique of the wild, self-Balkanizing cinema of Kusturica and Dragojević (Pavičić 2010: 48), as does Žbanić's distinctive use of cinematic space. In Kusturica's *Podzemlje*, the above ground/below ground dichotomy symbolizes the discrepancy between Yugoslavia's Communist superstratum and the deceived masses who live under its auspices. In *Grbavica*, this topography is reversed: Esma and Sara are often presented in hilltop spaces overlooking the Bosnian capital city from which Sara derives her name. In contrast with Kusturica's and Dragojević's enclosed spaces (basements, tunnels and graveyards), these locales convey a sense of possibility; and unlike the doomed, irredeemable characters of Kusturica and Dragojević, Esma and Sara are capable of change (Pavičić 49). Once Sara is apprised of her mother's secret, mother and daughter may begin a new life together.

Some other impressive post-Yugoslav films about the war focus on soldiers' as well as civilians' experiences of trauma. Kristijan Milić's *Živi i mrtvi* (*The Living and the Dead*) (2007), a Croatian-Bosnian co-production, follows Croat HVO soldiers fighting in the Croat-Muslim war of 1993. These scenes are intercut, however, with flashbacks to a previous generation of Ustaše-led soldiers fighting the Partisans in the Bosnian countryside during the Second World War. As the soldiers in the 1993 storyline stalk their Muslim enemies, they one by one lose their lives (sometimes to each other), all the while remarking upon the irony that they are now killing men with whom they went to school. This situation is mirrored in the Second World War scenes; in fact, some actors appear in both of the storylines, suggesting the essential commonality of soldierly experience across temporal and ethnic boundaries and invoking a 'hauntological' perspective on Yugoslavia's twentieth-century wars in which the dividing lines between past and present, friend and enemy become increasingly indistinguishable.

Somewhat similar in its downbeat atmosphere is *Neprijatelj* (*The Enemy*) (2011), directed by Serb Dejan Zečević and co-produced between Serbia, Republika Srpska and Croatia. *Neprijatelj* is a supernatural, allegorical drama with a distinctly Tarkovskian tone. Set in the immediate aftermath of the war, it begins with Serb soldiers, under the supervision of American IFOR troops, removing mines that they themselves had laid several years before. All of the men are damaged – whether by fear, aggression, or excessive religiosity – becoming increasingly abusive and eventually murderous towards one another. Searching a factory, the soldiers unearth a strange figure with the diabolical name of Daba, who has been walled into the building and who, disconcertingly, feels no cold, hunger or thirst. Initially, the chthonic Daba seems to be implicated in the violence, especially when the soldiers discover a mass grave underneath the factory, and at several points various frightened soldiers try – and fail – to kill him. Yet Daba tells the men that he deplores the killing of the war, remarking cryptically: "I am one of you." Indeed, as the film progresses it becomes clear that Daba is not the source of the growing tension among the men, but rather what Slavoj Žižek (1999: 121) calls an 'Id-machine,' an uncanny externalization of the soldiers' hostile proclivities. Craving an enemy, even after the end of the war, the soldiers have collectively conjured one up.

Daba epitomizes Zygmunt Bauman's figure of the Stranger: a liminal, 'undecidable' figure who is neither a friend nor an enemy and thus poses a threat "more horrifying than that which one can expect from the enemy" (1991: 55). For the soldiers, Daba is terrifying not because he is an enemy (enemies, after all, can simply be killed), but because his uncertain identity unsettles the binary categories of good and evil, friend and foe, that still define the soldiers' world. Like *Lepa sela lepo gore*, in which the Bosnian War is attributed to a malevolent ogre in a tunnel, *Neprijatelj* could be accused of supernaturalizing and thereby depoliticizing the war. Nevertheless, the film does offer a memorable philosophical deconstruction of sectarianism.

Conclusion

Through a critical textual analysis of an indicative selection of Bosnian War films, this chapter has argued that both Western and post-Yugoslav cinematic representations of the Bosnian War have tended to engage in enemy construction and political distortion. Hollywood and Bosnian films about the conflict, notwithstanding the often impeccably liberal credentials of their directors, have often reproduced images of Serb villainy and psychopathy. Such images draw their force from the international demonization of Serbs and Serbia in the 1990s. They also resonate with the longstanding stereotypes of Balkanist irrationality and turmoil described in the work of Maria Todorova (1997) and, in the case of Hollywood cinema, draw upon an American tradition of representing Slavs as coarse, drunken and violent (Golab 1980: 138–140). At the geopolitical level, meanwhile, the foregrounding of these images serves to elide the complexities of Yugoslavia's civil war, recasting the conflict as a one-sided war of Serb aggression – a characterisation that has been, and continues to be widely propagated in Western news media. On the other hand, filmmakers including Kusturica and Dragojević have elaborated their own tendentious and pro-Serb versions of the Bosnian War, the former going so far as to demonize non-Serb identities. Given this state of affairs, it is hardly surprising that many Bosnian War films have provoked angry and emotional responses from audiences and critics. Predictably, these responses have tended to bifurcate according to national/regional identity: Angelina's Jolie's *In the Land of Blood and Honey*, for example, has been praised by Western and Bosnian critics, but excoriated in the Serbian press; Kusturica's films, meanwhile, have often been lauded in Serbia but damned by Western critics. A quarter of a century after the end of the conflict, then, it cannot be said that the cinema of the Bosnian War has contributed greatly to processes of historical understanding or post-conflict reconciliation.

While there is no mechanical link between the creative personnel or production contexts of cinema, on the one hand, and representational politics, on the other, we might tentatively suggest that the films showing most resistance to the political demonology and geopolitical biases of Bosnian War cinema have some shared characteristics. Notwithstanding the problems with Angelina Jolie's *In the Land of Blood and Honey*, films with woman directors, such as *Grbavica*, have shown relatively little interest in apportioning national blame for the conflict and have focused primarily on the suffering caused by war, especially to its female victims. And although Kusturica's highly problematic international co-production *Podzemlje* might serve as a counter example, the anti-nationalist perspective of films such as the Serbian-Croatian *Neprijatelj* and the Croatian-Bosnian *Živi i mrtvi* perhaps suggest that the process of co-production can overcome the tendency to nationalist bias in the war film. At all events, the existence of such films shows that the cinema of the Bosnian War is capable of moving beyond the simple reversal of Western stereotypes and of challenging the sectarian discourses that have for so long disfigured both the region and its cultural representation.

Works Cited

Ansari, Javed (2011) "A Question of Image Building," *Slogan* 16. 8, 1.
Baker, Nicholson (2008) *Human Smoke: The Beginnings of World War Two, the End of Civilisation* (New York: Simon and Schuster).
Bauman, Zygmunt (1991) *Modernity and Ambivalence* (Ithaca, NY: Cornell University Press).
Bertolucci, Katherine (2015) "The Shame is on the Aggressor: The Image of Rape in Films about Bosnia and in the Films of Angelina Jolie," *Bright Lights* <http://brightlightsfilm.com> (accessed 13 September 2017).
Bufkin, Jana, and Sarah Eschholtz (2000) "Images of Sex and Rape: A Content Analysis of Popular Film," *Violence Against Women* 6. 12, 1317–1344.
Clark, Janine N. (2008) "Collective Guilt, Collective Responsibility and the Serb," *East European Politics and Societies*, 22. 3, 668–692.
Curtis, Mark (2010) *Secret Affairs: Britain's Collusion with Radical Islam* (London: Profile).
Dawson, Graham (1994) *Soldier Heroes: British Adventure, Empire and the Imagining of Masculinity* (New York and London: Routledge).
Der Derian, James (2001) *Virtuous War: Mapping The Military- Industrial-Media-Entertainment Network* (Boulder, CO: Westview Press).
Douthat, Ross (2008) "The Return of the Paranoid Style," *The Atlantic* <http://www.jmhinternational.com/news/news/selectednews/files/2008/04/20080401_Atlantic_TheReturnOfTheParanoidStyle.pdf> (accessed 13 September 2017).
Gibbs, David N. (2009) *First Do No Harm: Humanitarian Intervention and the Destruction of Yugoslavia* (Nashville: Vanderbilt University Press).
Gocić, Goran (2001) *Notes from the Underground: The Cinema of Emir Kusturica* (London and New York: Wallflower Press).

Gocić, Goran (2009) "The Dionysian Past and Apollonian Future of Serbian Cinema," *KinoKultura* <http://www.kinokultura.com/specials/8/gocic.shtml> (accessed 13 September 2017).
Golab, Caroline (1980) "Stellaaaaaa......!!! The Slavic Stereotype in American Film," in *The Kaleidoscopic Lens: How Hollywood Views Ethnic Groups*, ed. Randall M. Miller (Englewood, NJ: Ozer), 135–155.
Haqqani, Husain (2005) *Pakistan: Between Mosque and Military* (Washington, DC: Brookings Institution Press).
Heartfield, James (2012) *An Unpatriotic History of the Second World War* (Arlesford: Zero).
Herman, Edward S., and Noam Chomsky (1988) *Manufacturing Consent: The Political Economy of the Mass Media* (New York: Pantheon Books).
Hoggart, Paul (1999) "The Tormented Observers of an Uncivil War," *The Times* (22 November), 47.
Iordanova, Dina (2001) *Cinema of Flames: Balkan Film, Culture and Media* (London: BFI).
Klaehn, Jeffery (2010) *The Political Economy of Media and Power* (New York: Peter Lang).
Levi, Pavle (2007) *Disintegration in Frames: Aesthetics and Ideology in the Yugoslav and Post-Yugoslav Cinema* (Stanford, CA: Stanford University Press).
Longinović, Tomislav V. (2005) "Playing the Western Eye: Balkan Masculinity and Post-Yugoslav War Cinema," in *Eastern European Cinemas*, ed. Aniko Imre (New York and London: Routledge), 35–47.
Magala, Sławomir (2005) *Cross-Cultural Competence* (London and New York: Routledge).
Miskovic, M. (2006) "Fierce Mustache, Muddy Chaos, and Nothing Much Else: Two Cinematic Images of the Balkans," *Cultural Studies ↔ Critical Methodologies*, 6. 4, 440–459.
Nicholson, Michael (1994) *Natasha's Story* (London: Pan).
NIOD (Nederlands Instituut voor Oorlogsdocumentatie) (2002) *Srebrenica: A 'Safe' Area*, Amsterdam, NIOD.
Ó Tuathail, Gearóid (2005) "The Frustrations of Geopolitics and the Pleasures of War: *Behind Enemy Lines* and American Geopolitical Culture," *Geopolitics* 10, 356–377.
Pauwels, Jacques R. (2002), *The Myth of the Good War: The USA in World War II* (Toronto: James Lorimer).
Pavičić, Jurica (2010) "'Cinema of Normalization': Changes of Stylistic Models in Post-Yugoslav Cinema after the 1990s," *Studies in Eastern European Cinema* 1. 1, 43–56.
Pomfret, John (1996) "Bosnian Head of 'Terrorist' Camp Calls U.S. Concerns 'Very Silly,'" *The Washington Post* (15 March), 25.
Radović, Milja (2009) "Representation of Religion in *Pretty Village, Pretty Flame*," in *Exploring Religion and the Sacred in a Media Age*, ed. Christopher Deacy and Elizabeth Arweck (Aldershot: Ashgate), 189–202.
Radović, Milja (2014) *Transnational Cinema and Ideology: Representing Religion, Identity and Cultural Myths* (London: Routledge).
Rehling, Nicola (2009) *Extra-Ordinary Men: White Heterosexual Masculinity in Contemporary Popular Cinema* (Lanham, MD: Rowman and Littlefield).
Seymour, Richard (2008) *The Liberal Defence of Murder* (London: Verso).
Simpson, John (1999) *Strange Places, Questionable People*, rev. edition (London: Macmillan).
Todorova, M. (1997) *Imagining the Balkans* (Oxford and New York: Oxford University Press).

Tucker, Robert W., and David C. Hendrickson (1993) "America and Bosnia," *The National Interest* 33, 14–27.
Watson, William Van (2008) "(Dis)solving Bosnia: John Moore's *Behind Enemy Lines* and Danic Tanović's *No Man's Land*," *New Review of Film and Television Studies* 6. 1, 51–65.
Weber, Cynthia (2006) *Imagining America at War: Morality, Politics and Film* (London and New York: Routledge).
Zajec, Špela (2013) "*Esma's Secret, No Man's Land* and Consumption Patterns in War-Torn Territories," *Studies in Eastern European Cinema* 4. 2, 199–214.
Žarkov, Dubravka (2014) '*Warriors:* Cinematic Ontologies of the Bosnian War,' *European Journal of Women's Studies* 21 (2): 180–193.
Žižek, Slavoj (1999) "The Thing from Inner Space: On Tarkovsky," *Angelaki* 4. 3, 121–231.

Filmography

Alpha Bravo Charlie (1998) Dir. Shoaib Mansoor (Pakistan Television Corporation).
Behind Enemy Lines (2001) Dir. John Moore (Davis Entertainment).
Diplomatic Siege (1999) Dir. Gustavo Graef-Marino (Tapestry Films).
The Fourth Angel (2001) Dir. John Irvin (New Legend Media).
Grbavica (Esma's Secret) (2006) Dir. Jasmila Žbanić (Dogwoof Pictures).
The Hunting Party (2007) Dir. Richard Shepard (Intermedia).
In the Land of Blood and Honey (2011) Dir. Angelina Jolie (GK Films).
Khuda Kay Liye (2007) Dir. Shoaib Mansoor (Geo Films).
Killing Season (2013) Dir. Mark Steven Johnson (Nu Image).
Lepa sela lepo gore (Pretty Village, Pretty Flame) (1996) Dir. Srđan Dragojević (RTS).
Neprijatelj (The Enemy) (2011) Dir. Dejan Zečević (Biberche).
Ničija zemlja (No Man's Land) (2001) Dir. Danis Tanović (Noé Productions).
The Peacemaker (1997) Dir. Mimi Leder (Dreamworks).
Podzemlje (Underground) (1995) Dir. Emir Kusturica (RTS).
The Rock (1996) Dir. Michael Bay (Hollywood Pictures).
Warriors (1999) Dir. Peter Kosminsky (BBC).
Welcome to Sarajevo (1997) Dir. Michael Winterbottom (Miramax).
Život je čudo (Life Is a Miracle) (2004) Dir. Emir Kusturica (Mars Distribution).

Marek Paryż
Forbidden Bonding at the Time of the War on Terror: The Enemy as Friend in *Camp X-Ray* and *Boys of Abu Ghraib*

The year 2014 witnessed the release of two American feature films about the infamous detention centers for Islamic terrorists at Guantanamo and Abu Ghraib: Peter Sattler's *Camp X-Ray* (2014) and Luke Moran's *Boys of Abu Ghraib* (2014), respectively. Two thematically connected films may not be enough to establish a new direction in 9/11 cinema, but even if the simultaneous production of these two films was a coincidence, it was a meaningful one. They exemplify the search for ways of broadening the scope of cultural functions of feature films in the era of the War on Terror. They express the readiness of American filmmakers and audiences to closely explore and come to grips with the most morally disturbing aspects of the American interventions in the Middle East in the new millennium. As Robert C. Doyle observes, "The secrecy surrounding the prison facility at Guantanamo Bay has generated deep uncertainty and suspicions among many Americans who are concerned about an assault on the moral high ground" (2010: 332). A variety of film genres – war films, superhero movies, social dramas, Westerns, horror films and others – have been employed to discuss either directly or allegorically the condition of the post-9/11 United States and its citizens. The prison drama, the main genre vehicle in *Camp X-Ray* and *Boys of Abu Ghraib*, is an important addition to the conventions of 9/11 cinema because it is meant to address in a straightforward way crucial legal issues in the War on Terror. Stephen Prince writes:

> [...] the wars in Afghanistan and Iraq are part of this aftermath [of 9/11], as are the controversies over the administration's policy of designating terrorist suspects as illegal enemy combatants and holding them beyond the reach of civil and military law. The [Bush] administration's use of torture, forcible renditions, and secret prisons belongs to the legacy of 9/11, as does the expansion of domestic and foreign surveillance by the FBI, CIA, and NSA, often conducted without warrants. The Constitutional issues that arise from these novel policies are also part of the new climate of the post-9/11 world. (2009: 3)

The genre of prison drama furnishes a new perspective of examining individuals' involvement with a system that strictly delineates their spheres of functioning.

With regard to the presentation of the enemy, *Camp X-Ray* and *Boys of Abu Ghraib* attempt to transcend the convention whereby "[t]he image of an enemy is essentially an image of threat [...] represent[ing] an imminence of unwanted acts towards the self and motivat[ing] a subsequent need to remain vigilant, to plan defence or to actively engage in a pre-emptive first attack" (Vuorinen 2012: 3). The films under discussion present environments in which the power hierarchy in the War on Terror is as self-evident as it only can be, but at the same time the distance between its participants on the opposite sides has been reduced. Such closeness provides a basis for the investigation of how the clash of values that has had global dimensions manifests itself in interpersonal contacts and whether what happens on this interpersonal level confirms or undermines larger cultural imaginings. The reduction of distance between the self and the enemy also facilitates more direct ways of handling the problem of affects. The prison drama is among those 9/11 film genres that distinctly articulate the question about the recognition of the enemy.

Neither *Boys of Abu Ghraib*, nor *Camp X-Ray* has been a success with the critics or audiences, although the latter film, having premiered at Sundance Film Festival and featuring *Twilight* star Kristen Stewart and Peyman Moaadi, known from the Academy Award winning Iranian film *A Separation* (dir. Asghar Farhadi, 2011), has attracted a good deal of publicity. The reviews of *Boys of Abu Ghraib* have been almost unanimously negative. Brian Tallerico writes that it "has a few, brief insights into how boredom, anger and frustration helped fuel the rage that led to torture but the film couches it all in the filmmaking of TV-movie melodrama, draining it of all potential power and social context" (2014). Martin Tsai of *LA Times* points out the film's "glaring" omissions of "indelible details like the prisoners naked save for head coverings, menacing guard dogs, gleeful contract employees and overarching privatized military-industrial complex. Without planting such cultural signposts, the film hardly scratches Abu Ghraib's surface" (2014). Similar criticism has been targeted at *Camp X-Ray*, about which Amber Wilkinson of the *Daily Telegraph* writes that "[t]he macro-politics of Guantanamo Bay are kept firmly under lock and key in Peter Sattler's debut feature" (2014). The film has been described as a "naïve morality play" (McGovern 2014), a "fumbled Gitmo romance" (Brooks 2014) and, more appreciatively, "an obvious but strongly humanist drama" (Anderson 2014).

The opening of *Camp X-Ray* introduces an Arab man in a private apartment who is abducted while saying his prayers; we immediately see him sitting next to two other men, all three wearing characteristic orange uniforms and black hoods covering their entire heads, as they are being transferred by air and by sea – as the viewer will soon find out – to Guantanamo. Whether the Arab protagonist is a terrorist or not – there are some hints that he might be, but they are way too weak to be treated as evidence – he has been symbolically transformed into one. The short opening sequence is set around the time of the 9/11 attacks. Eight years later a young female private named Amy Cole (Kristen Stewart) arrives at Guantanamo to serve a term there as a guard. She socializes with the male soldiers as best she can, but her understanding of her position in the unit changes after a rape attempt by the Corporal (Lane Garrison) she directly reports to. This incident, for which she actually shares the responsibility, marks the beginning of the process of her estrangement. The uncomfortable situation in which she has found herself results, to an extent, in her readiness to be more open in her contacts with one of the inmates, Ali Amir (Peyman Moaadi). He targeted her the first time he saw her and introduced himself by throwing a so-called cocktail on her, a mixture of urine and faeces; nevertheless, after that, he has been making repeated attempts to involve her in conversations. Disillusioned about the fellow soldiers and the whole military system, on the one hand, and motivated by curiosity, guilt and even a sense of inferiority, on the other, Amy talks to Ali more and more often and begins to empathize with him. She puts her reputation at risk for his sake when she files a complaint against a superior soldier who forced her to assist him as he was watching Ali take a shower. In a conversation leading to the film's culmination, Ali poignantly tells her that he has no future because he cannot be sure that he will ever be released from detention, and even if he were, he would not be allowed to settle anywhere he would want to live. He takes out a blade he has managed to hide and puts it to his throat; Amy, instead of preventing his action, lets him decide whether he wants to – and is ready to – take his own life. He does not, and as he hands the blade over to Amy he grabs her hand and holds it, and she reciprocates this emotional gesture. This is their first handshake, and their last, as the woman's term is coming to an end.

Up to a point, in her daily service, Amy observes the rules of the military in a strictly professional manner. The film implies that she embodies a desired combination of professionalism and patriotism, and although she does not talk at all about how she feels about her country, her attitude shows a degree of engagement confirming her belief that her mission has a meaning. One of the early scenes at Guantanamo depicts the briefing of the guards before a new shift; the officer ends the briefing by calling, "Honor bound," to which the soldiers reply, "To defend freedom." At this very moment, Amy's expression bespeaks her pride to be where she is and her absolute conviction as to the reasons why she is there. For Cole, professionalism entails the ability to separate her private life from the set of relations that define her in the military environment. Early on in the film, we see her in her private room during a casual conversation with her mother via Skype, and in the scene that follows she is readying herself for service, putting on her uniform and tying up her hair. This is her way of assuring herself that her value as a soldier should not be perceived through the prism of her womanhood, as if she underwent a transformation every time she went on and off duty. She understands that a soldier on duty is expected to act with a certain automatism and that procedures exist so that a soldier does not have to think too much. Her initial attachment to the rules allows her to retain a simplified view of the world in which there are inevitable divisions and unequivocal hierarchies. Ironically enough, it is Ali who summarizes such a worldview during one of his tirades: "You locked us up here for years. For what? To show the world that you are good guy and we are bad guy?! Fuck you!" Her fundamental reassessment of the military environment leads her to overcome her automatized habits and to begin thinking critically about the larger situation she has been a part of. The subplots of her estrangement from the peers and of her acquaintance with a detainee have been integrated to the point when they provide crucial mutual motivation.

The rape attempt by Corporal Ransdell is an eye-opening experience for Amy, although the film evades the whole issue of rapes in the American army by suggesting a degree of the woman's responsibility for what happens. During a party with a lot of alcohol, Amy goes into the toilet and finds a pile of nude magazines stashed aside, and when Ransdell accidentally opens the door she holds up one of the magazines, points to a picture and asks him if this is what he wants. They embrace each other and begin to kiss. He pushes her hard against the wall and, suddenly alerted, she pushes him back with a seemingly equal force and walks out. She does not suffer any traumatic effects, but she knows that from now on things will not be the same. Ransdell takes it back on her a few months later when he uses a pretext to make her watch Ali take a shower, which is more than embarrassing for both the Arab detainee and the woman guard. When she files a complaint against Ransdell, she is rather shocked to hear the commander's implication that making a detainee feel "uncomfortable" is not a sufficient reason to take formal steps against the Corporal. In the end, she is the one who is treated with suspicion, especially as rumors have been spread about her making friends with the detainee. Her transfer to the night shift is a regular decision, but for her it obviously means punishment. She thus learns that the system will support Ransdell, who bends the rules to the limit defined by some tacit agreement, however out of keeping with the law, rather than her, who believes that rules should apply to both sides of the conflict. It is worth comparing briefly *Camp X-Ray* with *G.I. Jane* (dir. Ridley Scott, 1997), one of the few earlier American films that portray women in the armed forces. Whereas *G.I. Jane* is a narrative of gradual integration, *Camp X-Ray* is a narrative of continuous 'othering,' but both concern the problem of female empowerment. In the former film, the heroine achieves it by proving that her strength equals men's, and in the latter through small acts of disobedience which ultimately lead to an outright case of sabotage when Amy enables Ali to decide whether he will kill himself or not. As she was told on her first day at Guantanamo, a guard's responsibility is not to prevent the detainees from escaping, but from committing suicide.

Amy's experience of othering shows her as a sensitive person, and this in turn – given her role as a focalizer – enhances a perspective that humanizes the enemy. After throwing a cocktail on her, Ali is punished by being sent on what the guards call the frequent flyer program, which is a method of sleep deprivation: every two hours the detainee is moved from one cell to another for three days. It is she who decides whether Ali will be punished in such a way or not because the other guards ask her opinion and she says yes, although not without hesitation. She seems to be unsure as to the adequacy of this form of punishment, and when later on she sees Ali's complete exhaustion after he has been brought back to his cell, she immediately feels guilty, and from this moment on she tries to make little acts of compensation to him, especially by engaging in conversations, which she begins to enjoy. When Ali is still out of his cell, she enters it while another guard is conducting a routine search, she looks around and can see more closely his few personal belongings. She has crossed the threshold, both literally and symbolically, and she now realizes that the alleged enemy has a life she can somehow relate to. Importantly, this is the first situation that exemplifies how telling the film's sequential structure is: Amy's visit to Ali's cell happens directly after the rape attempt by Ransdell, highlighting the convergence of the stories of othering among the peers and befriending the enemy. The cell reveals so little about the inmate that Amy feels an imperative to find out more; therefore she secretly looks into his file in which she finds pictures of his badly bruised face and a register documenting his violent behavior. The fact that he has had several meetings with a psychiatrist suggests that his violence has a specific reason – vulnerability. She wants to help him in the only possible way, that is by listening to him and letting him see that she cares, but misunderstandings are inevitable. When Ali wants to give her a Sudoku he has drawn, she says that the rules do not allow this, upon which he flushes the piece of paper down the toilet and shouts angrily, "I was trying to be nice with you. I wasn't being asshole to you. I don't know why you are being asshole to me," ending with a diatribe against all Americans. The woman feels embarrassed and apologetic, and comes to see that the form of reciprocity she has offered is insufficient. Later on she tells him that she has been looking for a book he wants to read, which is not in the library, giving him to understand that she has done it for him. He appreciates her effort and apologizes for his irritating behavior. This scene, which can be seen as marking the beginning of their friendship, has an important structural function insofar as it brings the first part of the film to its conclusion. It is followed by shots of the Muslim detainees saying their prayers and the American soldiers honoring the flag, and the action moves onward by eight months.

Amy and Ali grow alienated from their respective groups to the point that, in a sense, they create a universe of their own. Obviously, such alienation manifests itself much more noticeably in her case as she functions among the fellow soldiers on a daily basis, whereas he is physically isolated from other inmates. However, there is a strong hint that he undergoes a similar emotional experience. The first episode that dramatizes the course of action in the second part of the film shows Ali playing football or, more precisely, kicking a ball inside a huge cage, while Amy is guarding him. Their casual conversation, which clearly they are both enjoying, is interrupted by the shouts uttered by another detainee from Ali's block, who is being led away by two soldiers. She says to Ali that the other inmates do not like him talking to her, and the moment she finishes her remark she hears a call from Ransdell; Ali can only repeat the words he has just heard from her. This signifies a relation of parity, which is confirmed by what happens in the immediate aftermath. Ransdell questions Amy about the subject of her conversation with Ali, and what follows is the shower scene that has already been mentioned. This disturbing occurrence strengthens the emotional bond between Ali and Amy because they have both found themselves in the position of victims – of humiliation in his case and of manipulation in hers. The punishment, arranged by Ransdell and suffered jointly by the two main characters, helps to define them in terms of their common humanity, and not through the prism of their respective cultures. Later on in the film, there is a brief shot of Amy kicking a ball against the cage, of course on the outside, as if she wanted to directly share Ali's experience. This act of impersonation shows that in their private universe the boundaries have become fluid. Ali also behaves at times rather unusually, for example we see him comb his beard before the beginning of Amy's shift, a small but meaningful gesture. The heroine more and more often acts in ways which are natural to her, but hard to understand for other soldiers, and this happens on formal occasions, as when she files a complaint against Ransdell, as well as on informal ones, as when she says to another soldier during lunch, "[i]t's not as black and white as they said it's gonna be." By far, the most symbolic expression of her alienation and disillusionment is her silence in response to the call "Honor bound," in a shot which is a repetition of the shot from the beginning of the film.

It is worth mentioning that the evolving relation between Amy and Ali has a dimension that brings to mind fairy tales; such associations are in place insofar as the film tells us that an impossible thing – a spiritual union of two people against all the odds – can happen. References to fairy-tale imaginings are straightforward in the film because the two main characters talk about Harry

Potter, the literary figure that fascinates the Arab man, which in turn intrigues the American woman who is not familiar with the Harry Potter cycle. On one of her first days on duty, Amy brings in a cart full of books for the detainees, and Ali starts a row with her because he has been waiting for the seventh volume of the saga for two years and it is still unavailable. This episode from the beginning of the film corresponds with the one that provides its closure: after finishing her term of service at Guantanamo, Amy sends a copy of the seventh book of Harry Potter to the camp's library with a dedication to a friend from "Blondie," the name by which Ali addressed her throughout the time of their acquaintance. In other words, allusions to a tale about magic constitute a frame for the narrative development. The film's focus on the extraordinary, if not altogether unreal, nature of what goes on between the two main characters results in a reduction or an evasion of a few crucial problems, including political ones.

Unlike *The Road to Guantanamo* (dir. Mat Whitecross and Michael Winterbottom, 2006), perhaps the best known film to date about the eponymous camp, *Camp X-Ray* does not raise any questions about the legitimacy of the system of detention facilities which was established in the wake of the War on Terror. *The Road to Guantanamo* tells the story of three British Muslim men who travel to Afghanistan to attend a friend's wedding and get arrested by the Americans on a charge of terrorism; they end up at Guantanamo, and their struggle to prove their true identities – and their innocence – is an indictment of the fundamental injustice of the cruel and myopic system they have become victims of. Michael J. Shapiro writes of Whitecross and Winterbottom's film, "Mixing a staged drama of the young men [...] with interviews of the actual victims, the docudrama powerfully contests the Bush administration's reassurances about the guilt of the detainees [...] and reassurances about humane treatment" (2009: 34). The criticism conveyed in *Camp X-Ray* concerns individual excesses sanctioned by the military establishment, and not the larger system of handling the alleged terrorists. The scenario wherein an honest and sensitive soldier confronts the unrelenting army machinery has recurred in war narratives since the First World War and provides a conventional vehicle for directing the action of *Camp X-Ray*. In this film, if the system is wrong, it is because of the shortcomings of the organization, and not because it serves a morally unacceptable purpose. Except for Ali, no other detainee on the block elicits Amy's – or the viewer's – sympathy. The film takes only brief glimpses of those other detainees – "a sea of mostly anonymous, screaming faces" (Sharkey 2014) – and they appear invariably scary, whether they utter wild shouts or remain suspiciously indifferent. Their coarse articulation sounds disquieting. One cannot say that the film denies their humanity; rather, it does not address such an issue, perhaps thus hinting that they should better stay where they are.

Camp X-Ray seems to implicitly support the existing system of detention, despite its undeniable imperfection, and this is best reflected in the fact that it does not answer the question whether Ali was a terrorist or not. Whatever happens in the course of action and however strong an emotional response the film is meant to elicit in the audience, the doubts aroused by the opening series of shots of Ali in his apartment linger on. The character walks past a television screen, showing huge billows of smoke around the World Trade Center, and goes into another room where he removes several cell phones from a plastic bag and arranges them in two rows on the table. There is a suggestive close-up of the telephones, establishing a metonymic as well as a symbolic connection with the televised image. The camera follows the silhouette, but does not reveal the face. The apartment is badly lit and everything happens, as it were, in dimness, as if the character were acting very cautiously. Furthermore, dimness metaphorically defines the viewer's position, making it impossible to determine his guilt or lack thereof. Accordingly, Ali can be an innocent man, a terrorist who undergoes a transformation thanks to his friendship with Amy, or a terrorist who plays his game to the very end. At the beginning of the film, the newly arrived guards, among them Amy, learn about the procedures and more practical ways of dealing with the detainees, and they hear the following warning, "They know the procedure better than you do. They will test you and they will best you"; it is not completely unlikely that the film illustrates exactly this. Ali appears to be able to read Amy's mind, to take advantage of her honesty, uncertainty and sense of inferiority. Having received an academic degree and having lived for a long time in the German town of Bremen, Ali has a much broader knowledge of the world than Amy, who has never been outside her country and has not attended college. Therefore, whenever they allude in their conversations to their backgrounds, he has an opportunity to remind her about his intellectual superiority. Ali refuses to explain himself before her, saying on one occasion, "I could tell you that I was not with Al-Queda or a terrorist or [...]. You wouldn't believe me anyway. Nobody believes me." In other words, he refuses to say what she wants to hear. What's more, this situation shows the extent to which their friendship depends on his ability to sustain her sense of guilt, which he does by implying that however exceptional their bond is, she is a part of the system that has crushed him. He wants her to see him as a man who believes in principles which are not those of fundamentalism, but of universal human dignity, "If I follow your rules this means you have the right to give me rules which you don't." The enemy, however tame, remains inscrutable.

While *Camp X-Ray*, by switching action from 2001 to 2009, safely bypasses the scandal which erupted when the most infamous cases of abuse of Muslim detainees by American military servicemen were revealed, *Boys of Abu Ghraib* deals directly with the problem of the use of torture at the American detention facilities for terrorists. The latter film spans the time from the summer of 2003 to the summer of 2004, the period when the most abusive cases of the mistreatment of inmates at the eponymous facility took place, leading to an international scandal in the spring and summer of 2004. The scandalous practices at Abu Ghraib came to be known as "the animal house on the night shift" and epitomized the excesses the American military system had fallen into in the War on Terror. In 2002, U.S. Defense Secretary Donald Rumsfeld approved of the use of the so-called enhanced interrogation techniques in order to collect the most crucial intelligence. These techniques were first implemented at Guantanamo, and the high-rank officer who supervised the operation was General Geoffrey D. Miller. As historian Alfred McCoy, author of *A Question of Torture* (2006), puts it in his commentary featured in the documentary film *Ghosts of Abu Ghraib* (dir. Rory Kennedy, 2007), General Miller "turned Guantanamo from a conventional U.S. military prison into a kind of *ad hoc* behavioral laboratory for the introduction and use of extreme techniques." In 2003, Miller was sent on a mission to Iraq to develop more effective methods of extracting information from the inmates at Abu Ghraib, a detention facility adapted from the Baghdad central prison where the opponents of Saddam Hussein's regime had been killed by numbers. What Miller's mission led to could be seen in the photographs that leaked to the media in the spring of 2004. An investigation and a series of trials followed, and eleven soldiers received sentences on the charge of dereliction of duty. General Miller consistently denied his inspirational role in developing methods of torture or abuse at Guantanamo and Abu Ghraib; he retired from the U.S. Army in 2006. The same year the American detention facility at Abu Ghraib was closed. *Boys of Abu Ghraib* tells little about this context; its makers may have assumed that it would be familiar to the film's audience. Therefore, instead of addressing, at least in part, the broader political implications of what happened at Abu Ghraib, the film puts emphasis on the drama of an individual caught in a situation that overwhelms and transforms him. The character in question is a young American soldier, and his contact with the enemy in the person of a detainee is decisive for the change he undergoes. Unlike in the case of *Camp X-Ray*, the viewers of *Boys of Abu Ghraib* learn for sure that the detainee is a former terrorist, the film thus entails a question as to the possibility of vindicating the evil committed by the American soldier. The portrayal of the enemy is indispensible for such a way of problematizing the film's central moral issue.

Their gender aside, the American protagonists of *Camp X-Ray* and *Boys of Abu Ghraib* share a few meaningful similarities with respect to background and personality. They both come from provincial towns and feel dissatisfied with the prospects that their environments offer them. However, they both join the army not out of calculation, but because they believe in ideals and in the necessity of action: we hear both of them say that they want – or once wanted – to make a difference. They are both honest and vulnerable human beings, unprepared for the confrontation with the horrific reality of the War on Terror they have known from television, unprepared to face the consequences of their own choices. Such a similarity cannot be accidental. The two films have been showcased as stories of initiation, although the protagonists stand not only for youth, but also for the commonplace, which facilitates the audience's identification with them. The protagonist of *Boys of Abu Ghraib* is 22-year-old Jack Farmer, whose squad has been assigned to the motor pool at Abu Ghraib. The soldiers soon find out that there is not enough work to keep them occupied, and their biggest problem turns out to be boredom. "We do not fight terrorists, we fight boredom," says Jack in a voice-over remark. He therefore volunteers to do night shifts as a guard in one of the detention blocks. The block is a part of the so-called "hard site," where "the craziest most fucked up people in the world" – as a fellow soldier tells Jack – have been kept. On his very first shift, Jack witnesses the cruel methods of "softening up" the detainees for interrogation, and although at first he doubts that this is all legal, he accepts the explanation he hears. In the course of his service as a guard, he engages more and more freely in conversations with an English-speaking detainee, and he unthinkingly disobeys very specific orders regarding contacts with the inmates. Such conversations soon become Jack's way of passing the time on duty, and he is truly disturbed to see Ghazi Hammoud, his Arab friend, being chained up for an interrogation. Before Ghazi's second interrogation Jack tries to speak for him and admits that he has "gotten to know this guy," which infuriates the other guards. And when they deliver the detainee back to his cell, they inform Jack that he has just confessed to planting a bomb that killed eighteen "innocent people." When Jack agitatedly asks his friend about this, he hears the most terrifying and hurtful words: "They were not innocent."

Whereas *Camp X-Ray* presents the detainees as aliens rather than as dehumanized beings, *Boys of Abu Ghraib* strikes the viewer through images of extreme forms of dehumanization. When Jack comes to the block to do his first shift, the first thing he sees is a detainee wearing a black cloth and a black hood and standing on a cardboard box, with electric wire attached to the fingers of both his hands. This is, of course, a reconstruction of one of the most memorable images of inmate abuse at Abu Ghraib, the picture of a "mock electrocution" of Ali Shallal al-Qaisi that was published on the cover of one of the May 2004 issues of *The Economist*. The guard who shows Jack around the block precisely and indifferently talks about "the extreme techniques": sensory deprivation, stress positions, loud music, isolation, and all of them will have been shown in the film. The detainees are addressed by nicknames invented by the guards, which signifies a denial of dignity and selfhood as well as the inmates' utmost subjection to the guards' will. The guard tells Jack, "You have to be aggressive, all right? If they sense weakness, you're in trouble," and it immediately turns out that aggressiveness means stark brutality. Jack is about to witness the humiliation of four detainees who have just gone through a period of sensory deprivation. Before going back to their cells, they are forced down to their knees, then one of them relieves himself and the guard pushes his face down into the pool of urine. The same happens to another of the four men as a punishment for making wild shouts. In the documentary *Standard Operating Procedure* (Errol Morris, 2008), Lynndie England, the woman soldier who appeared on the Abu Ghraib photographs holding detainees on a leash, says: "When we got there, the example was already set. That's what we saw. I mean, it was OK." Jack does not accept the situation so easily and he shares his doubts and qualms with the friends from the squad, but they do not understand his mixed feelings, identifying all the inmates with the type of terrorists they have seen on television. Their judgment of the detainees is quick and simple. Still, despite all the signals to the contrary, Jack continues to believe that at least very basic humane standards can be observed on the block. When he finds an older inmate unconscious, he starts resuscitation despite another guard's insistence that this is pointless. The fact that he already knows the smell of cocktail on his face does not change his attitude.

In both *Camp X-Ray* and *Boys of Abu Ghraib*, a guard's friendship with a detainee begins with the former's feeling of guilt. Ghazi is one of the four men whose humiliation Jack witnesses, and he draws Jack's attention because when the other three detainees start yelling, he does not join them and drops down motionless onto the floor. Jack feels qualms after the incident because he shares the responsibility for it, having been there and done nothing to prevent the abuse. On a later shift, Jack learns from Ghazi that one of the other detainees, nicknamed Jimmy Dean, has made a weapon. Jack searches Jimmy Dean's cell and finds nothing, then he angrily speaks to Ghazi, asking him if he enjoyed the show. Ghazi insists that Jimmy Dean does have a weapon and Jack is about to find out that this is true: when he approaches Jimmy Dean's cell to leave fresh toilet paper by the door, the detainee dashes forward, trying to stab him with a blade and missing. Jack now feels bad about misjudging Ghazi and wants to express his gratitude, which he does through his readiness to talk, and this means breaking an elementary rule. Later he even brings Ghazi some foodstuffs from the canteen, and they fraternize by complaining together about the taste. The feeling of gratitude is reciprocated, albeit only through verbal appreciation, but that is enough to make Jack feel rather special;

Ghazi says to him, "You treat everyone like a human being. I know you are a good man." And this is how Jack wants to think of himself. It can be said that certain emotional responses need to be triggered before communication between the two men on the opposite sides of the cell door becomes possible. For obvious reasons, the factor of language is crucial with respect to communication and, analogically to *Camp X-Ray*, *Boys of Abu Ghraib* features an Arab character who has a good command of English. This is a skill that allows the detainees to test their guards. It is not accidental that in the two films under discussion it is the detainees who initiate conversations with the guards whom they deem more sympathetic than others. Such situations invariably put the American guards at risk, but since they intuit no immediate danger, they let themselves be drawn into ambivalent relations. For the defeated, the use of the language of aggressors can be a symbolic form of weapon precisely because it helps create an aura of ambivalence.

While *Camp X-Ray* shows making friend with an enemy as a prolonged process, underscored by uncertainty, anxiety and tension, *Boys of Abu Ghraib* portrays it as a smooth course of events. After the incident with Jimmy Dean, Jack takes for granted everything Ghazi tells him, including compliments, such as "you're not like the other soldiers." Their handshake happens so naturally that it appears suspicious, and it happens early on in the film, ironically anticipating the terrible revelation of Ghazi's past. In any case, while the physical barriers inevitably separate the detainee and the guard, the psychological barriers disappear. Once the film's focus on the friendship of the two main characters has been established, the other detainees cease to play any roles in the plot. It is as if Jack and Ghazi have found a space of refuge to share. By far the most unlikely scene in the film shows them lying down on the floor on the opposite sides of the cell door and chatting the way friends do. Jack learns about Ghazi's two small children, and Ghazi about Jack's father, who failed to embody a role model for his son because of his modest achievement in life. They open themselves up to each other and talk about their innermost feelings, "Every second I am here I think about them," says Ghazi with his children in mind. Given his family experience, Ghazi puts himself in the position of one who can offer Jack advice and, having seen a photo of his girlfriend, he says that he should not wait too long to marry her. Last but not least, they tell each other jokes about former girlfriends. They explain to each other why they are at Abu Ghraib and, importantly, Ghazi only admits that he found himself in a wrong place at a wrong time: there was a bomb explosion to which the Americans connected him because they knew he had been educated as an engineer. In the end, when Ghazi calls Jack his "friend," the American is evidently glad to hear such an acknowledgment. This situation, emphasizing the closeness of the two men, is followed by a sequence of events that further confirms their bond, albeit with a tinge of cruel irony: Ghazi undergoes an interrogation, and Jack learns that his squad's term of service has been extended from six months to a full year. They are brutally brought back to the reality at precisely the same time.

One exchange between Ghazi and Jack is particularly meaningful in the light of the subsequent revelation of the former man's crime: in response to Ghazi's question about why he joined the military, Jack says that he wanted to do something important and adds that he is "a man of no regrets." Ghazi answers, "I know exactly what you mean," identifying himself as a man of no regrets, too. Only later on does the ominous sense of these words become apparent. When Ghazi confesses his responsibility for the bomb explosion to Jack, it is clear that he has been manipulating him emotionally all along. The fact is that the discovery of the truth about Ghazi would have taken much more time and effort if it had not been for the 'extreme techniques' of interrogation that he was subjected to. Jack reacts to the revelation with anger and fury, realizing that Ghazi has simply made a fool of him. Ghazi's sincerity and openness has been a mask he has put on to play a game at his expense because there was nothing he could achieve with his help. Therefore it cannot be determined for certain whether Ghazi's suicidal attempt after one of the interrogations was intended or enacted to make Jack feel even more guilty. In a way, by behaving humanely in relation to Ghazi, Jack has granted him a degree of moral superiority. It is as if, up to the time of the revelation, Jack had craved Ghazi's forgiveness for his inability to offer him any palpable help. And forgiveness is what he received when he heard from Ghazi, "There's nothing you can do. It's OK." The end of friendship signifies Jack's loss of innocence: Ghazi's deception puts things in perspective to the American soldier. On his next shift, Jack wants to prove that he is a different man, the kind of man – he now knows – he should have been from the beginning. He turns up the music and shouts to the detainees, "Rise and shine, motherfuckers! Everybody wake the fuck up! You no longer sleep on my shift! You do not nap, you do not take siesta, you do not rest your eyes, and you do not even fucking blink!" There is an exchange of meaningful looks between Jack and Ghazi: there is an expression of meekness on the former's face, and of anger, contempt and regained self-confidence on the latter's. And when the soldier notices that the detainee has closed his eyes, he darts into his cell, drags him out, taking the bucket for urine in his other hand, and forces his head into it, shouting "It's because of you!"

The brutal treatment of Ghazi is akin to catharsis for Jack, and he finally understands the meaning of his presence in Iraq. He says in voice-over narration, "Things seemed to move a lot faster after that night. I was able to start counting down the days again. [...] We tried our hardest to make the best of it." Apart from self-confidence and clarity of vision, these words imply a completion of the process of initiation. As we have seen in a number of classic American narratives of initiation, literary and cinematic, this process entails not only a newly acquired awareness of evil, but also – often enough – the readiness to embrace evil. Analogically to *Camp X-Ray*, in *Boys of Abu Ghraib* the enemy functions as a catalyst of the American protagonist's transformation. In Jack Farmer's case, the transformation has to do with acquiring the ability to victimize an Other, to execute power in extreme ways. This power is useless when Jack returns to civilian life, hence his disorientation that marks him as a victim this time. The concluding scene of the film shows Jack and his fiancée in a shopping mall, and they suddenly hear and see the news of prisoner abuse at Abu Ghraib echoing from dozens of television screens. On one of the pictures illustrating the news there is Jack forcing Ghazi's head into the bucket. The system will punish Jack for what it made him do, but for him this will also be a punishment for misjudging the enemy in the first place. *Boys of Abu Ghraib* thus ends like a cautionary tale.

Rajini Srikanth writes, "the construction of the detainees as 'the worst of the worst' and as incapable of suffering [...] has precluded the emergence of a publicly embraced politics of feeling with regard to their captivity" (2012: 136). Irrespective of their artistic merits or weaknesses, *Camp X-Ray* and *Boys of Abu Ghraib* are singular film achievements in trying to define possible frameworks, however selectively applied, for the "politics of feeling" that Srikanth talks about. They do so in markedly different ways, and this is an interesting aspect of their comparison. *Camp X-Ray* proposes a politics of compassion, understood as an emotion resulting from a fundamental inequality between the compassionate observer and the sufferer. As Lauren Berlant puts it, "compassion is a term denoting privilege: the sufferer is *over there*"; she further writes, "we cultivate compassion for those lacking the foundations for belonging *where we live*, and where we live is less the United States of promise and progress or rights and resources than it is a community whose fundamental asset is humane recognition" (2004: 3, original emphasis). Compassion thus fulfils a self-serving function in reasserting the essential humaneness of those who offer it. *Boys of Abu Ghraib* appears to carry more subversive implications with respect to the politics of feeling in suggesting, however briefly, that of shame. The idea is powerfully conveyed in the concluding scene in which Jack sees the picture of himself and Ghazi on myriad television screens. In the discussion of the difference between guilt and shame, June Price Tangney and Ronda L. Dearing observe that, "in guilt, our concern is with a particular behavior, somewhat apart from the self," whereas "[f]eelings of shame involve an acute awareness of one's flawed and unworthy self" (2004: 19–20). It is precisely such an image of the self that Jack – and, in a way, the viewer too – have been confronted with, and the protagonist's impulse to escape while there's nowhere to hide makes one ponder the deceptiveness of emotions that the identification with a film character generates.

Works Cited

Anderson, John (2014) "'Camp X-Ray': A Guantanamo Parable," *Wall Street Journal* <https://www.wsj.com/articles/camp-x-ray-too-much-makeup-too-little-worldview-1413483329?tesla=y> (accessed 7 February 2017).

Berlant, Lauren (2004) "Introduction: Compassion (and Withholding)," in *Compassion: The Culture and Politics of an Emotion*, ed. Lauren Berlant (New York and London: Routledge), 1–13.

Brooks, Xan (2014) "Review of *Camp X-Ray*," *Guardian* <https://www.theguardian.com/film/2014/jan/18/sundance-film-festival-review-camp-x-ray> (accessed 7 February 2017).

Doyle, Robert C. (2010) *The Enemy in Our Hands: America's Treatment of Enemy Prisoners of War from the Revolution to the War on Terror* (Lexington: University Press of Kentucky).

McGovern, Joe (2014) "Review of *Camp X-Ray*," *Entertainment Weekly* <http://ew.com/article/2014/10/17/camp-x-ray/> (accessed 7 February 2017).

Prince, Stephen (2009) *Firestorm: American Film in the Age of Terrorism* (New York: Columbia University Press).

Shapiro, Michael J. (2009) *Cinematic Geopolitics* (London and New York: Routledge).

Sharkey, Betsy (2014) "Flawed 'Camp X Ray' still exposes truths in war on terror," *Los Angeles Times* <http://www.latimes.com/entertainment/movies/la-et-mn-camp-x-ray-review-20141024-column.html%3e%20 (accessed 25 January 2017).

Srikanth, Rajini (2012) *Constructing the Enemy: Empathy/Antipathy in U.S. Literature and Law* (Philadelphia: Temple University Press).

Tallerico, Brian (2014) "Review of *Boys of Abu Ghraib*," Rogerebert.com. <http://www.rogerebert.com/reviews/boys-of-abu-ghraib-20145> (accessed 5 February 2017).

Tangney, June Price, and Ronda L. Dearing (2004) *Shame and Guilt* (New York and London: The Guilford Press).

Tsai, Martin (2014) "In 'Boys of Abu Ghraib,' echoing opinions about torture," *Los Angeles Times*. <http://www.latimes.com/entertainment/movies/moviesnow/la-et-mn-boys-of-abu-ghraib-review-story.html#axzz2xBS7kiPw> (accessed 7 February 2017).

Vuorinen, Marja (2012) "Introduction: Enemy Images as Inversions of the Self," in *Enemy Images in War Propaganda*, ed. Marja Vuorinen (Newcastle upon Tyne: Cambridge Scholars Publishing), 1–13.

Wilkinson, Amber (2014) "Review of *Camp X-Ray*," *Daily Telegraph*. <http://www.telegraph.co.uk/culture/film/filmreviews/10581385/Sundance-2014-Camp-X-Ray-review.html> (accessed 7 February 2017).

Filmography

Boys of Abu Ghraib (2014) Dir. Luke Moran (Vertical Entertainment).
Camp X-Ray (2014) Dir. Peter Sattler (Koch Media).
Ghosts of Abu Ghraib (2007) Dir. Rory Kennedy (HBO). YouTube. 1 November 2012. <https://www.youtube.com/watch?v=K-C2fVXuR6o> (accessed 7 February 2017).
Standard Operating Procedure (2008) Dir. Erroll Morris (Sony Pictures Classics) YouTube 17 April 2009. <https://www.youtube.com/watch?v=YooG1hrPNNg&t=21s> (accessed 4 February 2017).

Martin Löschnigg
Canadians and the Pacific War 1941–1945 in Anne Wheeler's *A War Story* and *The War Between Us*

The role of Canadian forces in the Allied war against Japan 1941–1945, and the impact of that war on Canada's Japanese community, have received little attention outside the country. Around 2,000 Canadians fought in the Pacific, most of whom were taken prisoners at the fall of Hong Kong (Stacey 1948). On the 'home front' meanwhile, Japanese Canadians living along the British Columbia Coast were subject to intense hostility and to repression under the War Measures Act – to expropriation, deportation and internment. In the eyes of the government, and of Caucasian Canadians at large, they had become the fifth column of the enemy threatening North America's Pacific Rim. Within the context of Second World War Canada, therefore, the 'Japs' represented an external as well as an internal enemy.

The present chapter discusses two films by Canadian director Anne Wheeler which deal with Canada and the war against Japan, approaching their subject from these different angles. *A War Story* (1981) chronicles the experiences of Wheeler's father, Dr. Ben Wheeler (1911–1963), who spent several years in a Japanese prisoner of war camp on Taiwan (then Formosa), having served as a medical officer attached to the British garrison in Singapore. Composed of newsreel footage, interviews and dramatic re-enactments, the film exposes the brutal treatment of the prisoners, many of whom were worked to death in a copper-mine near the camp, at the hands of the Japanese, and pays tribute to Dr. Wheeler's care for his men as a doctor and officer. His daughter's feature film *The War Between Us* (1995) deals with the deportation and internment of Japanese Canadians – many of them Canadian nationals – during the war. The film concentrates on the enforced relocation of a Japanese Canadian family from Vancouver to a village in the interior of British Columbia and their eventual 'repatriation' to Japan. Thematically as well as regarding their genres and scope, therefore, both films are in a way complementary. Together, they contribute to an assessment of Canada's participation in World War II, and shed light on the significance of that war for the shaping of a Canadian national sense of identity. As for *The War Between Us*, this film also (and perhaps even more importantly) reflects on Cana-

https://doi.org/10.1515/9783110591217-021

da's understanding of herself as a multicultural nation,[1] an understanding which has sometimes tended to the glossing over of a history of racially motivated discrimination especially against East Asian immigrants.

Born on 23 September 1946 in Edmonton, Alberta, Anne Wheeler is one of Canada's most acclaimed directors.[2] A prolific filmmaker, she has written and directed information, documentaries and drama mostly for Canada's *National Film Board* (NFB). Her films include adaptations of Canadian literary classics, like a two-hour television version of Margaret Laurence's 1975 novel *The Diviners* (1992), her second adaptation of Laurence after a 1985 television special based on Laurence's short story "To Set Our House in Order." In the same year 1985, her first dramatic feature film *Loyalties*, co-written with Saskatchewan writer Sharon Riis, was released. Set in Lac la Biche, a small town in Northern Alberta, *Loyalties* deals with the overcoming of cultural conflicts and of class barriers by personal friendship. Wheeler portrays the relationship between an upper-middle-class Englishwoman, Lily Sutton, who comes to live at Lac la Biche with her doctor husband under mysterious circumstances, and their hired housekeeper, Rosanne Ladouceur, a Métis woman. Dramatically charged and emotional in style, her film emphasizes the power of female friendship in the face of suffering and of adversity – a theme which is also prominent in *The War Between Us*. There, the relationship is that between a Japanese Canadian woman whose family are stripped of their livelihood and possessions and forced to live in a camp, and a white Canadian woman living in the town where the camp is built.

The emphasis on women's experiences is a hallmark of Wheeler's filmmaking: "I can't make films from any other perspective than a woman's perspective. That's who I am and proud of it" (qtd. in Cummins 2010: 22). This focus on female perspectives also characterizes one of Wheeler's most successful films, *Bye Bye Blues* (1989). Like *The War Between Us* and a *War Story*, the film is set during the Second World War. Inspired by the life of her own mother during the war (Wheeler 2012: 195–196), *Bye Bye Blues* tells the story of Daisy Cooper, a young wife and mother who returns to her prairie home after her husband has been posted to Singapore. When he is captured by the Japanese, Daisy becomes a

---

[1] Multicultural policies were implemented in 1971, under the prime ministership of Pierre Elliott Trudeau, father of the current Prime Minister. This was in response to increasing immigration from Non-European source countries, but also as an attempt to overcome the dualism between Anglo-Canada and Quebec. Multiculturalism became constitutional in Canada when in 1988 Ottawa passed the Canadian Multiculturalism Act, which "recognizes the importance of preserving and enhancing the multicultural heritage of Canadians." (http://laws-lois.justice.gc.ca/eng/acts/C-18.7/; accessed 7 September 2017).

[2] For a critical survey of Wheeler's films, see Lord 2002.

singer with a travelling dance band in order to support her family, and begins to assert herself as a woman. Wheeler both directed and wrote the screenplay that she adapted from the story of her parents during the war, fictionalizing the personal dimension already explored in the documentary on her father's imprisonment.

While Canadian troops in World War II were mainly deployed in Italy, Normandy, and the Low Countries, two infantry units were fighting in the defense of Hong Kong, and Canadian naval and special forces participated in various capacities in the Pacific and South-East Asia. In the Battle of Hong Kong (8 – 25 December 1941), 1,682 Canadian soldiers from the Winnipeg Grenadiers and the Royal Rifles of Canada ("C Force") fell prisoners to the Japanese. More than 40 other Canadians attached to British regiments serving in Asia, including Major Ben Wheeler, were also captured in the course of the war ("Prisoners of War in the Second World War"). Conditions in Japanese POW camps were notoriously brutal, with beatings, hard labour and inadequate food rations being the rule rather than the exception. Hundreds of Canadians died from illness or from slow starvation. Those who survived until Japan's surrender were often traumatized by their ordeal, harbouring bitter feelings against an inhuman enemy ("Canadian Prisoners of War").

The classic filmic account of Allied prisoners of the Japanese is, of course, David Lean's *The Bridge on the River Kwai* (1957). As Anne Wheeler has stated, her father, who did not normally talk about his war experience, was rather upset by that film. To him, *The Bridge on the River Kwai* was a "sham," since Lean had never experienced war himself (Wheeler 2012: 189). Also, one might add, the figure of the collaborator, Colonel Nicholson, was apt to inspire strong resentment among ex POWs, and his insistence on the privileges of officers clearly contrasts Major Wheeler's documented concern for his men. Wheeler died in 1963, when his daughter was still a teen. She knew very little of him, as she said (Thompson 2008: 102) and was 30 when she first became aware of the diary her father kept during his imprisonment (Wheeler 2012: 191). As a doctor, Wheeler had been allowed to keep a medical diary, yet had to be cautious as to what he recorded in it, since the diary could always be confiscated. All the same, it contained an on-going letter to his wife, about his hopes and fears, interspersed with the medical entries. Discovering the diary set Anne Wheeler on a search for her father's memory ("My father died when I was a teenager. Getting to know who he was as an adult became my quest"), and the perspective in *A War Story* is therefore "that of a daughter in search of a father" (191). As she acknowledges herself, "My perspective on what happened to him when I read this diary was limited" – from her own inexperience of war as well as from the self-censorship necessarily exercised by her father. However, 'censorship' also applied in the making of the documentary, as Wheeler was reticent about revealing some deeply personal matters contained in her father's diary-letter to her mother: "I censored my perspective because of the loyalty I felt towards my parents. My audience would get the truth but not the whole truth" (193).

A War Story, whose production started in 1979, is based on ample research. Wheeler conducted interviews with fellow prisoners of her father's when invited to a reunion in London and, by a stroke of luck, found "rare reels of Nitrate film disintegrating in cans," containing "original footage of the camps in Japan being liberated" in a London warehouse (Wheeler 2012: 192). On location in Taiwan, re-enactments of a prisoner working in the mine were shot with Wheeler's production manager, Dean Stoker, playing the role. These proved the first step towards the making of docudrama, "creat[ing] footage to match the limited archival footage I had found rotting in the British warehouse" (192). As Wheeler emphasizes, the only pre-liberation pictures of the camp her father was in "were taken by the Japanese for propaganda the one and only time the Red Cross arrived" (194). Further re-enactments showing Major Wheeler (portrayed by David Edney) and his men in the camp were filmed in a technique aiming at the historicity of archival material: "What we shot in Taiwan was treated to appear grainy, black and white, and in the process of decomposing like the footage I had rescued. I had crossed over to dramatic filmmaking" (195).

One man Wheeler says she interviewed when researching *A War Story* was a Japanese guard who, as it turned out, had been one of the torturers in the camp, and who admitted to having also tortured Wheeler's father. In "Perspectives on War," Wheeler indicates that this episode incited her to write a screenplay focusing on her father and this man, whom she had found in Japan years after the events (2012: 202). As it seems, this screenplay has not yet been realized, yet the episode is noteworthy because of the strong resemblance which its plotline bears to that of Jonathan Teplitzky's movie *The Railway Man* (2013), starring Colin Firth, Jeremy Irvine, and Nicole Kidman. *The Railway Man* is based on the true story of Eric Lomax (1919–2012), a lieutenant in the Royal Corps of Signals who was taken prisoner by the Japanese upon the fall of Singapore in 1942. Lomax was transported to Thailand, where he was put to work as an engineer on the construction of the Burma-Siam 'Death Railway,' and was tortured as a suspected spy by the Japanese military police, the Kempeitai, in particular by one Takashi Nagase. After many years, the former enemies met and became reconciled, as described in Lomax's memoir *The Railway Man* (1995), from which Teplitzky's film draws its title.³ As Anne Wheeler writes about discovering her fa-

---

3 Before, the story of Lomax and Nagase had been rendered in Michael Finlason's documentary

ther's torturer, "[t]hese are stories that could be lost and I feel a responsibility for them, as one of a few who have tried to understand these events from a human point of view. The war in the Pacific changed my life completely though I was not part of it" (2012: 202).

Wheeler's emphasis on how her own life has been affected by her father's war, and on the importance of preserving its memory, is illustrative of the situation faced by the "postmemory" generation as defined by Marianne Hirsch (2012). Despite their lack of first-hand experience, they are burdened with the personal or collective trauma of former generations, as well as with the cultural trauma which those generations' experiences have engendered. Bearing second degree witness to the experiences of previous generations, media productions like Wheeler's documentary produce what Alison Landsberg (2002) has referred to as "prosthetic memory" (see the "Introduction" to the present volume). The empathetic understanding which is created through Wheeler's filmic search is disseminated to the audience, influencing their conception of the past which is the film's subject – a process of dissemination which is greatly enhanced by Wheeler's techniques.

The blending of drama and documentary in *A War Story*, including "archival footage and photographs from many different Far East prisoner of war camps" (end credits), foregrounds the process of filmic mediation and of Wheeler's framing of her material. This has been anticipated by the film's leader, which shows the contours of a sleeping man in a tent (the fictionalized Dr. Wheeler), who then rises, lights a candle, looks at a photograph of his wife and child, and begins to write in a diary. In the following, the diary passages quoted in the film will be rendered through voiceover, as spoken by Canadian actor Donald Sutherland. In the next, symbolically charged scene a funicular is going downhill into the abyss of a dark mineshaft, the tracking camera following its downward movement along the rails. Dr Wheeler's (Donald Sutherland's) narrative sets in, moving from ironic understatement ("life, to say the least, is not pleasant") to accusation ("no day passes without someone getting a real beating up, for no reason except the sentries feel the urge") and resigned determination ("it's just inhuman [...] but I must fight on").

Cut. A dark screen and the sound of a siren introduce a flashback to the capture of Singapore,[4] rendered through Japanese newsreel footage and the voice-

---

Enemy, My Friend? (1993), which takes its title from Wilfred Owen's First World War poem "Strange Meeting."

4 On 15 February 1942. The time covered by *A War Story* extends to autumn 1945, when Wheeler's camp was liberated, with a coda giving glimpses of his life back in Canada in the 1950s. Several flashbacks relate the story of the director's parents before the war: Ben and Nellie Rose

over of Anne Wheeler herself: "More than 120,000 British subjects were taken prisoners. Ben Wheeler, my father, was one of them."⁵ Cut. The scene shifts to a veteran's reunion (voice-over Anne Wheeler) and, after another cut, to an account – accompanied by images of the landscape and traditional Japanese music – of the prisoners' three weeks passage, in a cramped 'hell ship,' to Taiwan. There, Major Wheeler and 525 other inmates were interned in the Kinkaseki POW camp in a mountainous region near Jiufen, in the north of the island, and were forced to work the copper mine in tropical heat.

The beginning thus establishes the basic structure of the film, which alternates between dramatic re-enactments and documentary, narrated by Donald Sutherland and Anne Wheeler respectively, and interviews with Dr. Wheeler's fellow prisoners. Prominent among these is former Sergeant Jack Edwards (1918– 2006), known for his efforts in tracking down Japanese war criminals, his campaigning for former servicemen and their widows in the Far East, and his memoir *Banzai. You Bastards!* (1994). Although Kinkaseki never achieved the notoriety of the Burma railway, it is still acknowledged to have been among the most brutal of the Japanese camps. Indeed, conditions as described by Anne Wheeler's interviewees were harrowing: working the mine, inmates were viciously beaten when they failed to fulfil the daily quota; many died from exhaustion or in rock-falls, from malnutrition, beri-beri and dysentery. Towards the end of the war, the survivors were marched to a new camp in the jungle, south of Taipei. Discounting some who had been transferred elsewhere, only 64 out of the original 526 prisoners made it to the Japanese surrender, "walking on the narrow edge between man and animal," as Edwards wrote: "All of us looked ghastly, eyes sunken, mere skeletons, covered with rashes, sores, or cuts which would not heal. Others too far gone to save were blown-up with beri-beri, legs and testicles like balloons" (cited from obituary in *The Telegraph*, 16 Aug. 2006).

Like the interviews, the camp scenes, filmed in blurry black and white to look like archival footage, and set mostly in the 'sick hut,' concentrate on Dr Wheeler's efforts as a medic to combat the effects of acid drips in the mine, bronchitis and infected feet, dysentery, oedema, starvation, worms etc. An inflamed

---

Wheeler were married in secret, living separately for two years until Wheeler graduated in 1935. In the same year, as the depression prevented him from setting up a practice of his own, he passed the entrance exam for the British Indian Medical Service, and the couple arrived in London. Shortly before their first child was born, Dr Wheeler had to leave for his posting in India, where his wife joined him in 1936. The family (now with three sons) were separated again when Wheeler was ordered to Malaya in 1941.

5 In fact, the Singapore POWs numbered about 80,000, with another 50,000 from the preceding Malayan campaign.

appendix is operated on with a razor blade, and without anesthetics. In the case of a man with a broken back, paralyzed from the chest downwards, Wheeler insisted that those in the sick barrack who could move kept massaging the man's legs to keep the muscles pliable. After some months, first improvements could be seen, and the man would eventually be able to walk. Above all, however, Dr Wheeler, according to his daughter's interviewees, tried to build up hope, fighting what he playfully referred to as 'disinclinitis' – the loss of any inclination to live, and the readiness to give up. His concern for the physical and mental survival of the men, and his personal courage standing up for them were rewarded by absolute "belief in him" (Jack Edwards), which made decisions as to whom to save, for instance when 'rest cards' could be given out, all the more terrible: "I have to play God in this camp, and I hate doing it" (Dr. Wheeler as quoted by Edwards).[6] In his diary, Wheeler noted: "broken-down, burned-out humans – may we never forget it, ever."

All interviewees emphasize the great solidarity among the men, their first concern being food and the hope of survival. The Japanese do not emerge as individuals; their cruel and humiliating treatment of the prisoners is repeatedly emphasized, and mention is made of suspicions that the prisoners were intentionally worked to death so that none should be left alive if the Americans invaded Formosa. Still, the Japanese are not demonized. Instead, Jack Edwards, in the final interview, provides some insightful comments on how he and his comrades were apparently perceived by their captors: "they [i.e. the Japanese] had nothing but contempt for us as men because they thought that individually we should either have been killed in battle or personally have committed suicide and honour would have been saved, and so as we were still alive, in their eyes we were virtually dead men, of no consequence, and should therefore be treated as such." Along the same lines, Dr. Wheeler notes in his diary: "I do not harbor the hate and resentment that I thought I would against the Japanese. Many had killed themselves rather than suffering the dishonor of being prisoner of war. Such a different philosophy of life and death!" Indicating the importance of dealing with traumatic experience by overcoming personal hatred, these sentences also provide the only motivational (and thus potentially personalized) remarks upon an external enemy who remains anonymous throughout the film. In consequence of this anonymity, there is a shift in emphasis to a de-personalized enemy in the shape of the general conditions in the camp, and in particular to an

---

[6] There are many parallels between Wheeler's story and that of the fictive Australian doctor Dorrigo Evans on the Burma Death Railway, the protagonist in Richard Flanagan's novel *The Narrow Road to the Deep North*, winner of the Man Booker Prize 2014.

'internal' enemy as represented by the psychological effects of these conditions on inmates, and their traumatic after-effects on the survivors. Emphasizing the strain on the minds of prisoners, the diary entries and interviews expound on the necessity of mental survival.

When there was hope of the Americans coming in 1944, Dr Wheeler noted in his diary: "the enemy, that is time, moves but slowly; how little a list of casualties tells the real story of war." In April 1945, another sick party was sent off to a camp in the jungle of southern Taiwan, with Wheeler being part of it. He was presented with a card bearing the signatures of the men remaining in Kinkaseki, and a quote from Christina Rossetti's "Remember:" "Better you should forget and smile / Than remember and be sad." On 29 August 1945, the war in the Pacific was over, and the film shows archival pictures of emaciated prisoners liberated by the Americans (Wheeler himself was weighing only 95 pounds). Clearly, these haunting images evoke associations with those of end-of-the-war survivors in the Nazi death camps, and these scenes become an indictment of de-humanized brutality in general. As Dr. Wheeler noted in his diary, the faces of the soldiers would always be with him, and he was asking himself how he would be remembered by them: "I tried to do the best by these men." The experience in the camp, as Jack Edwards states in the final interview, "brought out the best and worst in men [...] [Dr Wheeler] was fighting his war by trying to keep us alive and keep our spirits up." Nellie Wheeler had no knowledge whether her husband was alive or not until September 1945. When he eventually returned home in November of that year, the boat from which he disembarked at Victoria, BC, would return to the Far East with Japanese Canadians that had been expelled by the government (cf. Wheeler 2012: 199–200). Their story is the topic of Anne Wheeler's feature film *The War Between Us*.

In the years immediately before World War II, some 29,000 Canadians of Japanese ancestry – mostly first generation *Issei* and second generation *Nisei* – were living in British Columbia, concentrated in and around Vancouver. Nearly 80% of them were Canadian citizens or, technically speaking, British subjects like all Canadians, since Canadian citizenship did not constitutionally exist prior to 1947. After the attack on Pearl Harbor on 7 December 1941, and the Canadian declaration of war on the following day, they were regarded as a security threat and were categorized as enemy aliens under the War Measures Act.[7] This meant that

---

[7] Obviously, this meant that Japanese Canadians were not called upon to perform compulsory military service. Indeed, this had applied to Canadians of 'Oriental racial origin' even before Pearl Harbor. Upon request of the British, 119 Japanese-Canadian men of military age were permitted to join the Canadian forces in the Second World War, where they served as translators in intelligence units ("Japanese Canadians").

their citizenship rights, already restricted before the war (Japanese Canadians did not have the vote, and were barred by law from certain professions), were suspended (see Robinson 2009). Above all, however, large numbers of Japanese Canadians from the coast were removed to internment camps in the British Columbia interior and in the prairie provinces (see Sunahara 1981). Forced relocation went hand in hand with loss of employment, and the confiscation of businesses and personal property (see Adachi 1976; Roy 1990). In August 1944, the government under Prime Minister Mackenzie King stated that Japanese Canadians must either move east of the Rocky Mountains or opt for 'repatriation' to Japan once the war had ended (Roy 2007: 70). It was not until 1 April 1949 that these policies were repealed, and Japanese Canadians could again move to the 'protected zone' on the British Columbia coast (Roy 2007: 76; Adachi 1976: 343–344).[8]

As it is, fear of a threat represented by 'enemy aliens' loyal to Japan was really unfounded, since no act of disloyalty to Canada, of sabotage or espionage is on record.[9] Rather, these feelings were expressive of an undercurrent of racism and of the racially motivated discrimination which had characterized attitudes towards Japanese settlement on the West Coast since when it began in the 1870s (see Adachi 1976; Shibata 1977). Public awareness of this bleak chapter in Canadian history has been raised not least by literature and film, in particular by Joy Kogawa's autobiographical novel *Obasan* (1981), now standard reading in schools and universities nationwide. In this novel, Naomi Nakane, the author's *alter ego*, visits her widowed aunt (*obasan*) Aya and begins her research into the history of her family during World War II. Pressing her aunt to remember the paranoid hatred against the Japanese 'enemies,' her separation from her family and forced labour on a prairie farm, Naomi struggles to break the silence surrounding these events, especially also on the part of the victims.[10]

---

8 In 1988, an official apology was delivered by Prime Minister Brian Mulroney, and compensation was announced (see Omatsu 1992).
9 Newfoundland writer Michael Crummey's novel *The Wreckage* (2005) depicts the rare case of a returnee fighting on the side of the Japanese in the character of Noburo Nishino. A private in the Japanese Imperial Army, Nishino experienced racial hatred and discrimination growing up in British Columbia. He vents his desire for revenge through the sadism with which he treats Allied prisoners, by whom he is eventually beaten to death (see Grace 2012).
10 *Obasan* was made into a children's book, *Naomi's Road*, in 1985. Beside two sequels to *Obasan* (*Itsuka*, 1992, rewritten as *Emily Kato*, 2005, and *The Rain Ascends*, 1995), a number of other works by well-known Canadian writers have dealt with Japanese Canadian internment during World War II, for instance Terry Watada's short story cycle *Daruma Days* (1997) and Frances Itani's novel *Requiem* (2011).

Anne Wheeler's *The War Between Us* deals with the deportation and internment of the Kawashima family during the war. The film, whose characters and plot are partly based on real people and their stories, renders the Kawashimas' enforced relocation from Vancouver to the village of New Denver in the interior of British Columbia. There, the hostile relations between locals and internees gradually soften, and stereotypes are revised on both sides. All the same, the film ends on the Kawashimas' repatriation, under the War Measures Act, to Japan. Foregrounding a female perspective on the events through its protagonist Aya, the Kawashimas' daughter, Wheeler's film shows how political oppression and the experience of exile engender in her Japanese characters conflicting national and cultural allegiances.

Anne Wheeler became interested in the history of the Japanese when she moved to the West Coast in the 1990s ("It was curious to see the Pacific War from yet another perspective"), and tried to get the rights for filming *Obasan* (2012: 198). As it turned out, however, she received a script by Sharon Gibbon about Gibbon's mother, who had lived in the Slocum Valley of British Columbia when Japanese Canadians were located there. Her family had hired a young woman named Aya (the name of Wheeler's protagonist, and also of Kogawa's *obasan*) as a babysitter, and the two women became life-long friends. Both co-operated in telling the story of these years, and Gibbon herself had gone through numerous versions before offering it to Wheeler; thus, the "truth had lost its way," and the story was re-worked between Wheeler and Gibbon (Wheeler 2012: 198).[11]

The War Between Us opens with crosscuts alternating between the Kawashimas, a comfortably situated middle-class family in Vancouver, and the Parnums, working-class folk hard pressed for money, who live at New Denver in the rural interior of British Columbia. While the Kawashimas have just bought a car, proudly presented to the rest of the family by Mr Kawashima, owner of a small boat-works business, Ed Parnum has to confess to his wife that he is out of work again as the local mine has been shut down. The Kawashimas' new car has an important dramatic function: as they turn on its radio, they hear the news that all Japanese Canadians must register with the Royal Canadian Mounted Police (RCMP). Later in the film, they will be helplessly watching as the car is being driven by new owners. Like their house, it was appropriated and auctioned off by the government. When they appear before the officials, Mr. Kawashima, a veteran officer of the Canadian Expeditionary Force in the First

---

[11] Concerning Japanese Canadian women's experiences of displacement and internment in particular, see Sugiman 2004.

World War, is wearing his uniform, including his decorations for bravery, in order to underline his loyalty to Canada.[12] He is respectfully saluted, but is nonetheless registered as a 'Japanese National' – another moment of bitter irony, and another dramatically significant moment, as he will later burn the uniform and decorations in a highly symbolic act. His son and daughter, both born in Canada, are registered as Canadian citizens.

Gradually, the atmosphere tightens, leading up to the news of Pearl Harbor. Now, the Kawashimas' ID cards are all stamped 'Enemy Alien,' and the family have to face deportation. While Mr. Kawashima must hand over the house keys to the police, his wife and daughter are shown to be packing their belongings. Questions of identities and cultural allegiances are underlined again when Aya, always dressed in Western style clothes, like the other Japanese, holds a kimono against her body, thoughtfully looking at herself in the mirror – a scene which correlates to that of Mr. Kawashima wearing his uniform. Outside, the Kawashimas take a longing look at their home, maybe already sensing that it will be the last. As they are preparing to leave, they have racist insults shouted at them by young men driving past.

Meanwhile, cross-cuts to the Parnums and the New Denver villagers have prepared the audience for the conflicted encounters which are about to take place in these backwoods: the Parnums' elder daughter is shown reading to her mother from a newspaper article about the "ruthless" and "arrogant" character of the Japanese, and fear and resentment stir as the villagers are confronted with the government's plans of relocating 400 Japanese to New Denver. Lured by promises of electricity, a telephone service and jobs, however, they are soon won over by a wily government agent.

The arrival of the deported Vancouverites is heralded by a close-up tracking shot similar to the mineshaft scene at the beginning of *A War Story:* a dirt road is lapped up by a moving vehicle, signifying a journey into the unknown. The camera then shifts between long distance shots showing a lorry with people on its back, driving through bleak, rainy scenery, and close-ups of the Kawashimas on that lorry, with Ed Parnum driving. (Apparently, this is one of the new jobs which the villagers have been promised.) The camera's perspective thus changes from an anonymous, depersonalized rendering of the Japanese to an emphasis on their individuality, anticipating the development of mutual apprehensions once they have settled among the villagers. In the further course of the film, me-

---

12 During World War I, when Japan was an ally, a considerable number of Japanese Canadians volunteered in the hope of gaining previously denied citizenship rights in return for proving their loyalty, as did Black Canadians and First Nations. By the end of World War I, 185 Japanese Canadians served overseas in 11 different battalions (Walker 1989: 7, 12).

dium range shots that achieve a balanced visualization of individual characters on both sides become increasingly dominant. Perspective then tends to focus on the Kawashima family, with far fewer scenes in which the locals are among themselves. The *War Between Us* is thus complementary to *A War Story* also in the sense that the documentary contains only one instance of the (enemy) 'other's' perspective (their contempt for the prisoners), and this is related in an interview.

The arrival scene brings into focus the contrast between the well-dressed, urban Japanese who disembark from the lorries, and the rural backwater that will now be their abode. In its initial parts, Wheeler's film builds on the ironic reversal of racialized stereotypes, undermining supremacist notions of the non-white 'other' as backward or even primitive. Sometimes, the irony comes along in a rather heavy-handed manner. As the Japanese arrive, Marg, the elder Parnum daughter, is astonished to hear that "Some of them speak English." When Mas, the Kawashimas' son, approaches a group of local children for some information, he unthinkingly asks them whether they speak English. In reply, the 'natives' shake their heads in fright and run away. At the Sunday service, where one had expected to be among one's own again, the villagers are surprised to see many of the Japanese (including the Kawashimas) among the congregation, and a Reverend Yamamoto assisting the local minister.

As already indicated, much of the humour of the film arises from the incongruence of the class differences it shows with the stereotyped notions of 'white supremacy' ingrained in the villagers. The New Denver camp is one of the 'self-supporting projects' which housed middle-class families and others not considered as a great threat to public safety. When Aya is employed as a maid-servant by the Parnums, she is not sure whether she will be able to cook well on a wood stove, since she is used to gas. In one of the most memorable scenes, the Parnums are dancing and cheering as electricity has been installed, eliciting a cynical comment from the watching Mas that "The savages have discovered electricity." More importantly, however, there is an impression that through their solidarity, calm discipline and politeness, the Japanese are in many ways the 'better Canadians,' also in the sense that they demonstrate the best of the 'pioneering spirit' that is part of Canada's national mythology. This is illustrated for instance by the scene in which the Kawashimas (to the accompaniment of traditional Japanese music) walk towards the derelict shack which they have been allotted, and which they immediately start to clean and turn into a habitable abode. In another symbolic scene, the Parnums and some Japanese are tending to their vegetable gardens, next to one another but without speaking, the former with conspicuously poorer results than the latter.

I have discussed the opening scenes of Wheeler's film in more detail, since they are representative of her themes and of the techniques she employs in order to convey her humanitarian message. The remaining events may be briefly summarized here: gradually, hostility and (mutual) distrust erode, first between the Parnums and Kawashimas. Mary-Jean, the younger Parnum daughter, a girl too young for racism and an embodiment of uncorrupted 'natural sympathies,' acts as a mediator, and the growing *rapprochement* and mutual acceptance of the two families will culminate in the interracial marriage of Mas and Marg. Beyond their circles, there are tentative developments towards New Denver becoming something of a bi-cultural community. This is confirmed when a good portion of the local hockey team is shown to consist of Japanese – a wink at the role of the national sport as a test case for 'Canadianness.' However, the intercultural utopia is nipped in the bud when the Japanese must choose between relocation east of the Rockies or 'repatriation.'

The lynchpin of the improving interracial relations in the film is the friendship between the two women, Peg Parnum and Aya Kawashima. Aya (played by Mieko Ouchi) is reminiscent of the angelic females in Dickens: like Esther Summerson or Agnes Wickfield, she radiates warmth and sympathy, spreading comfort and cheer wherever she goes, and showing calm determination in adversity. Unlike in Dickens, however, there will be no happy end for her: as a dutiful daughter, she will go with her parents to war-torn Japan – in spite of a growing love-interest and the fact that, as she exclaims, "Japan means nothing to me!" Indeed, as Peg remarks, deflating the euphemism: "How can you repatriate someone to a place they've never been?" Aya's brother Mas, who has always most fervently embraced Canada (refusing to speak Japanese, as they enter New Denver, he also exhorts his family to "Speak English! We speak English in Canada!") has by that time already moved east with his bride-to-be. Upon the example of the Kawashima family, the film shows the effects of political and cultural oppression on its Japanese Canadian characters, namely divided loyalties and a crisis of identity which enforces unilateral cultural orientations rather than transculturation: having burnt his First World War uniform, Mr. Kawashima prays at a Shinto shrine. He has renounced Canada, turning to the old culture. As the ending of the film makes clear, this will be to the detriment of the villagers, too, who have reluctantly come to recognize the presence of the Japanese as humanly and culturally enriching. The concluding shots thus aim at conveying a sense of loss on both sides. As the Kawashimas are leaving New Denver, the camera turns to long exposure and motion, creating a blurry effect which suggests their "leaving only a ghostly trace of presence, suggesting a haunting-lingering-hovering sense of a past presence that cannot be attained or located" (Weiner 2014: 228). However, there is a note of optimism in that for the final shots the camera then shifts to Mary-Jean, who is wearing a kimono – presumably tailored by Aya from the cloth of her own. The coming generations will build multicultural Canada, striving to make a mutually beneficial co-existence of ethnoculturally different groups within the national frame come real.

If this is highly emotional (as is much of Wheeler's film), it stresses the fact that the overcoming of enmity must begin on a personal level. Sherrill Grace's judgment that "the film does not provide a happy ending, a resolution, or even a gesture of reconciliation" (2014: 316) therefore appears as somewhat too negative: true, the prospect of a reconciliation offered by the film's diegesis seems to be restricted to the personal sphere (another parallel to Dickens, incidentally), and may thus remain somewhat unsatisfactory, yet it does constitute an important step forward. Wheeler's depictions of both the Taiwan POW and British Columbia internment camps during the Second World War, and her cinematic translation of historical events in both films emphasize the transgenerational haunting which these events caused in each case. *The War Between Us* makes the audience face a long-suppressed racist episode in Canada's past, exposing the xenophobic hatred directed against an internal "enemy that never was" (Adachi 1976). Wheeler's film thus stands among other works of art, notably the works of literature mentioned earlier, which deal with the shadows of racially motivated discrimination in a country whose present (self-)image is grounded on the acceptance and cultivation of cultural plurality. Chronologically situated in the wake of its final institutionalizing, and in the midst of intensive discussions on the social implications of Canadian multiculturalism,[13] *The War Between Us* underlines the necessity of reconciliation with a view to the integration of ethnocultural groups into the Canadian multicultural spectrum. Its earlier 'companion piece,' as I would want to see it, *A War Story*, also addresses the necessity of exorcising the ghosts of the past, and it also points to the importance of overcoming personal enmity as a first step.

Works Cited

Adachi, Ken (1976) *The Enemy That Never Was: A History of the Japanese Canadians* (Toronto: McClelland and Stewart).

Bissoondath, Neil (1994) *Selling Illusions: The Cult of Multiculturalism in Canada* (Toronto: Penguin).

"Canadian Prisoners of War," *The Canadian Encyclopedia*, <http://www.thecanadianencyclopedia.ca/en/article/prisoners-of-war/> (accessed 7 September 2017).

---

13 See for instance Bissoondath 1994, Kymlicka 1998 and Taylor 1992.

Cummins, Kathleen (2010) "On the Edge of Genre: Anne Wheeler's Interrogating Maternal Gaze," in *The Gendered Screen. Canadian Women Filmmakers*, ed. Brenda Austin-Smith and George Melnyk (Waterloo/Ont.: Wilfrid Laurier University Press), 67–94.
Grace, Sherrill (2012) "Bearing Witness and Cultural Memory: *The Wreckage, Burning Vision*, and the War in the Pacific," in *Bearing Witness. Perspectives on War and Peace from the Arts and Humanities*, ed. Sherrill Grace, Patrick Imbert, and Tiffany Johnstone (Montreal and Kingston, London, Ithaca: McGill-Queen's University Press), 107–120.
Grace, Sherrill (2014) *Landscapes of War and Memory. The Two World Wars in Canadian Literature and the Arts, 1977–2007* (Edmonton: University of Alberta Press). [On Wheeler's *The War Between Us* see 314–319 and notes 505.]
Hirsch, Marianne (2012) *The Generation of Postmemory: Writing and Visual Culture After the Holocaust* (New York: Columbia University Press).
"Japanese Canadians," *The Canadian Encyclopedia* <http://www.thecanadianencyclopedia.ca/en/article/japanese-canadians> (accessed 7 September 2017).
Kogawa, Joy (1994 [1981]) *Obasan* (New York: Anchor Books).
Kymlicka, Will (1998) *Finding Our Way. Rethinking Ethno-Cultural Relations in Canada* (Toronto: Oxford University Press).
Landsberg, Alison (2002) "Prosthetic Memory: The Ethics and Politics of Memory in an Age of Mass Culture," in: *Memory and Popular Film*, ed. Paul Grainge (Manchester: Manchester University Press), 144–162.
Lord, Susan "States of Emergency in the Films of Anne Wheeler," in *North of Everything: English-Canadian Cinema Since 1980*, ed. William Beard and Jerry White (Edmonton: University of Alberta Press), 312–326.
Omatsu, Maryka (1992) *Bittersweet Passage: Redress and the Japanese Canadian Experience* (Toronto: Between the Lines).
"Prisoners of War in the Second World War," *Veterans Affairs Canada* <http://www.veterans.gc.ca/eng/remembrance/history/historical-sheets/pow> (accessed 7 September 2017).
Robinson, Greg (2009) *A Tragedy of Democracy: Japanese Confinement in North America* (New York: Columbia University Press).
Roy, Patricia E. (1990) *Mutual Hostages: Canadians and Japanese during the Second World War* (Toronto: University of Toronto Press).
Roy, Patricia E. (2007) *The Triumph of Citizenship: The Japanese and Chinese in Canada 1941–1967* (Vancouver: University of British Columbia Press).
Shibata, Yuko (1977) *The Forgotten History of the Japanese Canadians*, vol. 1 (Vancouver: New Sun Books).
Stacey, C. P. (1948) "The Canadian Army in the Pacific War," *The Canadian Army 1939–1945. An Official Historical Summary* (Ottawa: King's Printer), 289–309 (online: <http://www.cmp-cpm.forces.gc.ca/dhh-dhp/his/docs/CDN_ARMY_39-45_E.pdf> (accessed 7 September 2017).
Sugiman, Pamela (2004) "Memories of Internment: Narrating Japanese Canadian Women's Life Stories," *The Canadian Journal of Sociology* 29, 3, 359–388.
Sunahara, Ann (1981) *The Politics of Racism: The Uprooting of Japanese Canadians During the Second World War* (Toronto: J. Lorimer).
Taylor, Charles (1992) "The Politics of Recognition," in *Multiculturalism and "The Politics of Recognition,"* ed. Amy Gutmann (Princeton: Princeton University Press), 25–73.

The Telegraph (2006) <http://www.telegraph.co.uk/news/obituaries/1526416/Jack-Edwards.html> (accessed 7 September 2017).

Thompson, Peggy (2008) "'I like to work one on one:' Anne Wheeler," in *The Young, the Restless and the Dead. Interviews with Canadian Filmmakers*, vol. 1, ed. George Melnyk (Waterloo/Ont.: Wilfrid Laurier University Press), 95–114.

Walker, James W. St. G. (1989) "Race and Recruitment in World War I: Enlistment of Visible Minorities in the Canadian Expeditionary Force," *Canadian Historical Review* 70, 1, 1–26.

Weiner, Sonia (2014) "Double Visions and Aesthetics of the Migratory in Aleksandar Hemon's 'The Lazarus Project,'" *Studies in the Novel* 46, 2, 215–235.

Wheeler, Anne (2012) "Perspectives on War," in *Bearing Witness*, ed. Grace, Imbert, and Johnstone, 189–203.

Filmography

The Bridge on the River Kwai (1957) Dir. David Lean (Horizon Pictures).

Bye Bye Blues (1989) Dir. Anne Wheeler (Alberta Motion Picture Development Corporation, Allarcom, CFCN Television).

Loyalties (1987) Dir. Anne Wheeler (Alberta Motion Picture Development Corporation, Canadian Broadcasting Corporation CBC, Dumbarton Films).

The Railway Man (2013) Dir. Jonathan Teplitzky (Archer Street Productions et al.).

The War Between Us (1995) Dir. Anne Wheeler (Atlantis Films, Troika Films, Canadian Broadcasting Corporation CBC).

A War Story (1981) Dir. Anne Wheeler (National Film Board of Canada).

Jonathan Rayner
Lost Pasts and Unseen Enemies: The Pacific War in Recent Japanese Films

Since 1945, the history of World War II in the Pacific, and the record of Japan's aggression have themselves become battle grounds disputed by national and international commentators. As a result, the depiction of Japan's war in popular culture has been marked by obfuscation and ambiguity, with historical fact as much as a national perspective being contested by the creators of fiction, films, comics and animation. In many examples of post-war popular culture, representations of Japan's adversaries, most notably Americans, have been virtually absent, or have been limited to distant, dehumanised aircraft or ships on the horizon, the crews of which remain invisible and anonymous. In effect, the difficulty of portraying the war in Japanese cinema has become focused not on troubling representations of death (which can, on the contrary, be explored spectacularly and voyeuristically, with the full spectrum of cinematic effects and a concomitant exploitation of emotional and visceral impact (cf. Gerow 211) but on the necessary and identifiable presence of the adversaries and antagonists that Japanese wartime heroes can be seen to face:

> For the Japanese, it was important to construct a clear demarcation between the pre-1945 and post-1945 Japan because it needed to separate the 'polluted' past from the new present, as a springboard to construct a new narrative of postwar Japan [...] the postwar Japanese liked to portray themselves as victims of pre-1945 militarism [...] Moreover, the intensely myopic preoccupation of the Japanese with the 'self' came at the cost of ignoring the 'other,' namely the victims of Japanese aggression, especially in Asia. This was symptomatic of the incapability of the Japanese to come to terms with their own past. (Shimazu 101)

In Japanese war films made since 1945, a pervasive, national assumption of victimhood has functioned to obscure the victims and targets of Japanese aggression (the peoples of East Asia and their Western colonisers), while the deepening relationships with former adversary nations (primarily America) have made the portrayal of enemy combatants difficult and discomfiting. Such treatments also obfuscate, ignore or alter the origins of the conflict. Even *Nobi* (*Fires on the Plain*) (dir. Kon Ichikawa, 1959), a celebrated post-war example which represents unflinchingly the brutality Japanese troops showed towards Filipino civilians, ultimately places greater emphasis upon the suffering of Imperial Army soldiers abandoned to their fate far from home. The American enemy is only glimpsed from a distance, and is scarcely connected to the plight of Japanese soldiers.

In Japanese films the war can therefore appear as a de-contextualised drama rather than a narrative, represented with combatants but without combat, with consequences which lack original, apparent causes, and with heroes seemingly unopposed by tangible enemies. While similar characteristics, arousing comparable criticisms, have been discerned in Western war films (cf. Richards 2000), Japan's initiation of the conflict and (in the opinions of its neighbours) its apparent evasion of responsibility for it, have made this manipulation of the national past appear disingenuous, flawed or culpable. Far from marking a healthy separation from history, post-war Japanese attitudes have themselves 'polluted' the understanding of the past with the interests and interpretations of the present.

1 The Kamikaze and Japanese War Film

In two films addressing the problematic history of the Japanese *kamikaze* tactics adopted in 1944–1945, the effort of recovery of a stable national past is located within individual memory, familial history and the painstaking (re)discovery of lost relatives. *Ore wa, kimi no tame ni koso shini ni iku* (*For Those We Love*, a.k.a. *Assault on the Pacific: Kamikaze*) (dir. Taku Shinjô, 2007) and *Eien no O* (*The Eternal Zero*, a.k.a. *The Fighter Pilot*) (dir. Takashi Yamazaki, 2014) largely eschew representation of the enemy until climactic battle sequences showing deliberate, suicidal attacks upon American warships, which stand as moments of both national pride and personal mourning. The formidable contradictions apparent in these films' interpretation of Japan's war (in lamenting the destruction and loss of life suffered by Japan and her adversaries, and yet celebrating the patriotic sacrifices of the past which produced modern, peaceful and prosperous Japan) complicate the portrayals of the wartime enemies who are now essential post-war allies and trading partners. Therefore, within ongoing nationalist and pacifist discourses of the country's disputed past, and in the narratives of films representing versions of war history for contemporary audiences, the 'enemy' is frequently relocated within the militarist establishment, which may be identified as the instigator of Japan's war with fewer problems, and condemned as the source of the people's suffering. Yet in these films the continued honouring of the nation's war dead persists, both as a gratifying commemorative element for a loyal home audience, and as evidence of re-emergent militarism and a galling revisionist provocation for pacifist Japan and for the country's former enemies. As David Desser observes, Japan's war cinema has evinced

> [...] both an admirable attempt to come to terms with Japanese aggression against its neighbors and an almost simultaneous slippage into seeing the Japanese as no less a victim of

their own wartime actions [...] Saying that war is hell is not the same as saying that Japan's war aims led to hell. (2016: 74, 79)

These controversies of history appear most aggravated in films portraying the forms of 'special' (suicide) attack initiated and institutionalised during the last months of the Pacific War. Portrayals of willing self-sacrifice for the Empire had been the staple of many post-war Japanese films, particularly those representing Japan's war against Russia in 1904–1905 such as *Meiji tenno to nichiro daisenso* (*Emperor Meiji and the Great Russo-Japanese War*) (dir. Kunio Watanabe, 1957) and *Nihonkai daikaisen* (*Battle of the Japan Sea*) (dir. Seiji Maruyama, 1969). These commercially successful Russo-Japanese War films provided extravagant recreations of historical combat, in which dutiful soldiers laid down their lives willingly in the nation's cause. However, since they portrayed a more distant war in which Japan had been victorious, these films appear to have appealed to Japanese post-war audiences unproblematically as spectacular entertainment comparable to contemporary Hollywood war films, and may also have provided a focus for nationalistic pride without the danger of offending the country's former enemy and new ally, America. Indeed, the portrayal of a Russian enemy (albeit sympathetically in *Nihonkai daikaisen*), may have actually suited American opinion in the Cold War period. When the subject of the kamikazes of the Pacific War was addressed, as in *Taiheiyo no tsubasa* (*Attack Squadron*) (dir. Shûe Matsubayashi, 1963), the moral objections raised explicitly against suicide attacks within the narrative deflected criticism of the portrayal of willing self-sacrifice. The treatment of this subject in recent Japanese films, in a period when visits by politicians to the Yasukuni Shrine (which honours all Japan's war dead) provoke annual controversies, has compounded the contentious attitudes to conflict and war commemoration which have divided the country (cf. Martin 2016). In these films' attempts to articulate the purposes, meanings and after-effects of self-sacrifice as a key characteristic of Japanese identity, the identity of the enemy often becomes displaced, elided, or obscured.

2 *Ore wa, kimi no tame ni koso shini ni iku:* "the right way to lose a war"

Ore wa, kimi no tame ni koso shini ni iku (*For Those We Love*) dramatizes the kamikaze missions flown by Imperial Japanese Army pilots from the Chiran airbase in Kagoshima during the last months of the war. Chiran is a potent symbol of the kamikaze campaign, since many pilots departed from the base on their final missions and the site has since become a memorial and museum (Inuzuka 2016: 150–151). The film begins with the following title:

> I had the fortune to hear the poignant stories of the suicide corps recruits from Tomé Torihama, who had come to be known as 'Mother to the Kamikaze.' I was struck by the need to create a legacy attesting to the bravery and beauty of Japanese people back in those days. Shintaro Ishihara.

Ishihara's careers as a politician and governor of Tokyo were punctuated by frequent controversies regarding his right-wing views, including revisionist pronouncements on Japan's war history (Aoki 2014). As screenwriter and executive producer, Ishihara's statement of inspiration and intent connects his own memorialising effort with that of Tomé Torihama, the 'auntie' and mother figure to the youthful pilots who patronised her family restaurant. The role of the town and Tomé's restaurant in supporting the young pilots had been dramatized previously in *Hotaru (The Firefly)* (dir. Yasuo Furuhata, 2001). Tomé's reverential stance towards the "splendid, lovely young men" dominates the film, as her recollections of the war conveyed through voice-over and flashback pursue a persuasive and restorative agenda. Shots of young cadets engaging in competitive sports are interrupted by a cut to the grey-haired, smiling Tomé. Here, the editing and eyeline imply that she is looking on, in the physical presence of the young men, when in fact her vision of them actually reflects an imaginative, contemplative retrospection. As such this enshrining of Tomé as the custodian of the memory of the kamikaze (via the validation of her perspective and voice-over as the authentic account of the past) defines the film unapologetically as a first-hand emotional advocacy for the remembrance and recognition of the youthful pilots. Her 'view' brings the 'young men' insistently into the present.

However, these first memories of the young pilots' training are quickly succeeded by an historical episode which Tomé could not have witnessed: the briefing by Admiral Onishi at Mabalacat in the Philippines in October 1944, at which the strategy of 'special attack' became institutionalised (Inoguchi and Nakajima 1986: 420–422). The film's dramatization of this event foregrounds Onishi's ruthless imposition of kamikaze tactics, against his own and his subordinates' objections, as the only means to "protect our national identity through defeat and into the distant future." To overcome the other commanders' misgivings, Onishi asserts the necessity of the kamikaze campaign, not in order to win the war or even avoid losing it, but to "lose it the right way" to preserve national honour beyond the now-inevitable defeat:

I'm talking about Japan as a nation and the spirit of our people. One thing that must be said about this war is that we fight to free like-coloured people and races from the grip of the white man. This is beyond question: a just and valid purpose. This belief, this resolution, even though our struggle be defeated, for the honour of our nation, must be recorded correctly in the annals of history. To this end, young men must die. This is our only way.

Onishi's rationalisation of the adoption of kamikaze attacks accords with the dictums of contemporary propaganda: that far from engaging in a war of aggression and imperial expansion, Japan had responded protectively and responsibly against Western colonial control of Asia. The unqualified recapitulation of this justification in a film made in the twenty-first century exemplifies Japanese attitudes to and representations of war history which provoke accusations of disingenuousness. However, rather than simply evading Japanese accountability, this statement consciously aggrandizes the sacrifice of the kamikaze pilots, endowing their actions with a wider ideological integrity in addition to its stated importance in national defence. The deeds of the kamikaze are defined in sympathy with Japanese identity and official political morality, and in contradistinction from the corruption and iniquity of the Western enemy. However, the admiral's attempts to instil a nationalistic zeal are severely undermined when he admits that the kamikaze attack corps must be "voluntary in name alone." This stance is reaffirmed at the end of the Philippines sequence, which shows Onishi's subordinates repeating his unyielding doctrine to the first chosen 'volunteer,' Lieutenant Seki. Although he initially reacts with horror, Seki is persuaded to lead the first attack, to set an example for others to follow in safeguarding the "fate of the nation." Subsequently Seki's successful attack is represented by generic archive footage of kamikaze attacks.

As with the combination of persuasion and coercion credited to Onishi, the film's valorisation of Seki epitomises the contradictory stances adopted towards the role and character of the kamikaze. The admiral appears as both the mouthpiece for nationalistic dogma, which hedges historical fact and underpins the hero worship of the suicide pilots, and as the symbol of an inhuman totalitarian military establishment, held responsible for squandering lives to defer an unavoidable defeat. Similarly, Seki is shown to be a victim of military authority, a professional officer susceptible to the immoral manipulation of his superiors, and a heroic role model for the volunteers who succeed him. The film's depiction of the conscious selection of Seki as a regular pilot officer, to serve as an example for the drafted student pilots who made up the bulk of the kamikaze corps, condemns the military hierarchy even as it celebrates individual commitment and heroism in the national cause (Hill 2005: 4–5). In this way the kamikazes' enemies can be located internally and externally, and their heroic example can be commemorated and praised in victories over both.

Ore wa maintains these dual and contradictory claims throughout its subsequent narrative of the Army pilots nurtured by Tomé Torihama. The devotion of local civilians to the support of the Chiran pilots is shown to be both inspired and repaid by their willingness to die for the country. Tomé gives away her best kimono to get the ingredients for one pilot's requested final meal at her restaurant. Her daughter Reiko is a member of the group of schoolgirls recruited to work at the airfield, who learn the pilots' patriotic songs and copy their actions in making rising sun tokens with their own blood for the kamikazes to carry with them into battle. Witnessing the departure of one fighter group, civilians in the streets are shown kneeling and bowing in respect of their sacrifice. The connections between civilians and pilots are exaggerated when the schoolgirls and their teacher are amongst the victims of an American air attack on the base. Tomé's voice-over asserts their communal commitment: "The Special Attack corps weren't the only ones to die – Reiko's support team, the girls' volunteer corps, local soldiers, all took part in the sacrifice." This sharing of the kamikazes' martyrdom is also derived from a similar subordination to military authority: over archive footage of the bombing of Japanese cities and General MacArthur's re-invasion of the Philippines, Tomé's voice-over insists that beyond hearing rumours, "us common folk never knew how the war was really going." Being subject to curfews and censorship, the pilots and civilians alike are shown to be at the mercy of self-serving authorities, demanding obedience until death. Depictions of the reprimands and beatings meted out to pilots who show 'disloyalty' by returning from missions because of bad weather or mechanical failures, extend the unsympathetic portrayal of the military establishment requiring their sacrifice for notions of national identity, irrespective of the success they may be able to achieve.

The film's depiction of this reciprocity of care between civilians and kamikazes is foregrounded in the incident of Tomé's arrest by the Kempeitai (military police) for contravening rules on service personnel's mail. Pilots ask Reiko and Tomé to post letters to parents and relatives outside the base so that their final communications are not censored. When Tomé is detained and subjected to the same brutal treatment as the trainees, the pilots besiege the police station to demand her release. Even when she is freed, Tomé continues to antagonise the police commander by repeating her question: "Why do young men about to die deserve curfews and censors?" The enraged commander is only prevented from drawing his sword to kill her by sirens warning of an approaching air raid, in a moment which curiously conflates the internal and external adversaries against which the kamikazes, with Tomé's blessing and kinship, are seen to pit themselves. Tomé emerges from this confrontation surrounded and protected by her adoptive sons, with bruises which she labels her own "medals." In other episodes Tomé also appears to transgress convention or propriety in her support for the young pilots. For example she reunites one with his fiancée against his father's wishes and defies the curfew in her restaurant. In one troubling, explicit example of the film's historical stance, Lieutenant Kanayama, a Korean special attack volunteer, expresses his gratitude to 'Auntie' for treating him as an equal to the Japanese pilots: "I forget I'm Korean when I come here. You took care of me for so long, more so than my real mother." This representative of an 'inferior,' colonized people within the Asian 'Co-Prosperity Sphere' (the euphemism for Japan's empire-building agenda) attains an authentic status within the Imperial forces when he proves willing to sacrifice himself like a true Japanese citizen. The film appears to celebrate this Korean pilot's heroism and his loyalty to Japan, even though like other pilots he is also seen to be afflicted by doubts as to the meaning and purpose of his actions.

Tomé's nurturing activities, in defending the pilots' rights and well-being, combine her maternal and memorialising roles. As their supporter and spokesperson, she is the informed and privileged commentator whose knowledge and survival of this period of history are, the film suggests, invested with a national responsibility. In his last conversation with 'Auntie,' the youngest pilot, a nineteen-year-old named Kawai, passes on the years of life he forfeits to her. In the same conversation, Tomé assures him he will always be remembered. In the final attack sequence of the film, Kawai is seen to make a successful attack after his comrades have been shot down. Although mortally wounded, Kawai steers his plane into an American aircraft carrier, with his shouts of defiance and the diegetic sounds of battle replaced by elegiac orchestral music. In previous attacks, no kamikaze planes have been seen to actually hit ships: instead the action has been rendered through digitised recreations of World War II documentary footage, showing Japanese planes being destroyed in great numbers in futile attacks. By contrast, in the climactic attack the pilots are recognisable inside their planes, and in addition American ships (and their crews) are clearly visible for the first time. In succeeding, the youthful Kawai becomes the embodiment of the entire campaign, symbolically protecting and elongating Tomé's life in order for her to become the kamikazes' apologist and vindicator in and for the post-war world.

Following the attack the film records the inevitable end of the war, and the progression into the post-war world for which the kamikaze pilots died. Tomé and her family listen in disbelief to the Emperor's announcement of Japan's surrender, and witness American occupation troops destroying the few planes remaining at the base. Despite this concretisation of defeat, not least in the visible presence of Americans, the film's final definition of an enemy emerges from the recognition of the gap between past and present, and of the work of memory undertaken by Tomé and privileged by the film's narration. While survivors of the final attack are shown to be traumatised by their experiences and ostracised by civilians eager to forget the war, Tomé remains faithful to her nurturing of the pilots who lived as well as those who died. To help the troubled Lt. Nakanishi, who is burdened by survivor's guilt, Tomé visits the shrine erected at Chiran in memory of the kamikazes. As they gaze on the path lined with cherry blossoms (the "master trope of Japan's Imperial nationalism," Ohnuki-Tierney 2002: 3), the spirits of the dead pilots seem to appear before them, rejoicing and greeting them without recrimination. Tomé is comforted and Nakanishi consoled by the sight of these ghosts who, far from condemning the survivors and subsequent generations, appear contented and united in the afterlife. In completing its subjective war history and its personal reflection, the film's conclusion reiterates Tomé's uncritical, emotional honouring of the men and their memory.

3 *Eien no O:* "To succeed meant to die"

Ore wa locates its retrospective narrative within the experience and devotion of an emblematic individual whose act of memorialisation makes her a role model for later generations, who must be taught to remember and respect the war dead. By contrast, *Eien no O* (*The Eternal Zero*) is grounded in a familial investigative narrative, in which a secret past and a relative 'lost' in the war are recovered and rehabilitated, that positions the film poignantly within Japan's post-war negotiation (and negation) of its militarist past:

> Contestations over Japanese war memory are not only about the contents of textbooks or government apologies: they are real and current family dilemmas. Japan is made up of millions of families that all have members from the war generation. Given Japan's ongoing public war responsibility discourses, facing the past within the family frequently means asking difficult questions about grandparents' personal war guilt. (Seaton 2006: 60)

At his grandmother's funeral Kentaro, a directionless young man, discovers that she had a wartime husband who is never discussed at family gatherings. This lost relative is dismissed as a coward, who has been expunged from memory as a familial and national disgrace. With his sister Keiko he sets out to uncover the story of his vanished grandfather, interviewing surviving veterans who flew the iconic Zero fighter with him in a Navy squadron. Poignantly, the family funeral is dated diegetically in 2004, thereby multiplying the acts of retrospection which work to recover and redeem a symbolic history. Their enquiry carries several contradictory connotations of memorialisation and expiation: the unknown pilot, Lt. Miyabe was the same age as his grandson (26) at the time of his death as a kamikaze; his granddaughter is an author who sees the forthcoming sixtieth anniversary of the war as a lucrative writing opportunity; Kentaro, currently failing in his attempts to become a lawyer, hopes to find a sense of purpose through their investigation.

Having sought their grandfather's permission before embarking on their search, the siblings encounter hostility and experience embarrassment at the veterans' opprobrium for their lost relative. Miyabe is repeatedly condemned as a coward who cared only for his own survival and avoided dogfights, despite being a gifted pilot. However, their interview with Izaki, a terminally-ill veteran (and guardian of memory comparable to Tomé) initiates a return to wartime in a flashback in which Miyabe's actions are explained and exonerated. His love of life (also inseparable from love of his wife) leads him to shun combat for reasons of both personal survival and moral abhorrence. When he returns to the aircraft carrier *Akagi* after the attack on Pearl Harbour, Miyabe is shown to be alone in lamenting the absence of the key targets, the American carriers, while other pilots celebrate the destruction of the enemy fleet. Prophetically, he foresees Japan's inevitable defeat in the failure to destroy the enemy carriers in the attack. He also describes his horror at witnessing the loss of a bomber aircraft and its three-man crew, and voices his determination to survive the war.

Izaki admits to feeling loathing for Miyabe's selfishness in the midst of the nation's war, but the continuation of his flashback narration ultimately vindicates his superior officer. Miyabe and Izaki are next shown during the Imperial Navy's defeat at the Battle of Midway. Miyabe again seems endowed with prescience when he foresees the disaster which befalls the fleet, but nonetheless fights the attacking enemy planes with Izaki to protect their carrier. When his unit is ordered to undertake a long-range mission from the island base of Rabaul, Miyabe expresses his doubt that they can navigate, fight and return successfully, and is beaten by another pilot for his lack of martial spirit. However, when their wingman is forced to ditch his damaged plane on the flight back and dies in the sea, Miyabe tells Izaki of his anger at being forced to face a futile death, and restates the importance of survival for his family's sake. While the youthful Izaki demands that Miyabe allow him to crash his plane into an enemy ship should he be unable to return to base, the aged Izaki admits his understanding of Miyabe's desire to live. While openly expressing that such a thought at the time was "unthinkable," Izaki now sees it as the strongest declaration of love (for family and child) that a man of that generation could make. As in *Ore wa*, the authoritative veteran's narration in *Eien no O* eschews the origins of the war and the presence of the foreign enemy in exonerating and elevating personal and emotional motives within times of national crisis. Miyabe's ignominious reputation as a selfish coward is rectified and rehabilitated through recognition of his comprehensible and sympathetic desire for personal, romantic fulfilment, which is threatened by the enemies of Japanese militarism and the arbitrariness of war. Izaki's eventual acceptance of Miyabe's conviction, and his imitation of his superior's example in surviving the war himself, is vindicated (again in an echo of Tomé's narrational act) in his endurance to the present, epitomised and validated by the existence of his own family and his ability to correct the injustice done to Miyabe with his own recollection.

Having been inspired to find out more, Kentaro tracks down Takeda, an ageing businessman, who recalls meeting Miyabe as a flying instructor later in the war. Stories of their teacher's cowardice and his refusal to volunteer for kamikaze duty were known to his cadets. In training teenage reservists who have been conscripted only for special attack duty, Miyabe deliberately fails them in order to prevent their departure on missions. When a trainee is killed in a flying accident, their unit commander reviles the dead youth and denounces his lack of martial spirit. Miyabe speaks out in defence of the dead pilot and is severely beaten, but earns the understanding and respect of the other trainees as a result. Takeda recounts how a trainee crashed his plane into an American fighter to save Miyabe when he was attempting to lead enemy aircraft away from his students. The end of Takeda's flashback shows Miyabe with the cadet on the way to hospital, with both men exhorting each other to survive in order to "live and do good work for the sake of Japan." This recollection reinforces those of the other veterans, so Kentaro remains unable to understand his grandfather's eventual decision to undertake a kamikaze mission.

Poignantly, in finding his purpose in probing his family's hidden past, Kentaro isolates himself further from his contemporaries. Arriving late at a dinner with friends where a group holiday is being planned (ironically, all their suggested destinations – Hawaii, Saipan, and Okinawa – bear associations with the Pacific War, which the youthful members of the party are either unaware of or choose to ignore), Kentaro vigorously defends his relative and the kamikazes against their accusations of "romantic heroism" and "brainwashing," and comparisons with modern suicide bombers. However, in his attempts to distinguish the kamikazes patriotically and militarily from the fanaticism of terrorists, Kentaro confronts again his ignorance about his grandfather's motives for volunteering. A comment from Kageura, another former pilot who flew from Rabaul, only compounds the mystery. Kageura had hated Miyabe's perceived cowardice, but had seen him traumatised and transformed by their shared duty of escorting the kamikazes to their targets. When Miyabe finally volunteered for kamikaze duty himself, Kageura recalled how he angrily objected to skilled veterans being expended in a futile strategy: "Against overwhelming odds I'd gladly risk my life, but the Kamikaze had no odds. To succeed meant to die." Yet Kageura remembers that Miyabe swapped planes with another pilot on the morning of his final mission. Miyabe gave up his later model Zero to a younger pilot in preference for an earlier version of the fighter. Subsequently the younger pilot was forced to ditch because of engine trouble, and so was rescued after the mission. It appears that fate might have spared Miyabe after all, and that he could have survived the war.

However, on seeing the pilots' roster for the mission, Kentaro finally understands Miyabe's decision to volunteer, and the choice to swap aircraft. Although driven to volunteer by guilt over the deaths of his cadets, Miyabe had earlier promised his wife and child that he would return from the war, if he was wounded or even if he "had to be reborn" in order to do so. Revisited and reinterpreted flashbacks now solve the mystery of the past and reveal Miyabe's survival pact with Oishi, the cadet who saved his life. On the day of the final mission, Miyabe swaps his faulty plane with Oishi, assuring his survival and leaving a photograph of his family in the cockpit for him to find. At the end of the war, Oishi seeks out his leader's widow, and becomes her second husband, allowing Miyabe to keep his promise and maintain his principle of protecting his family, despite going to his death. Miyabe's act therefore merges the supposedly selfish and cowardly desire for survival with the altruistic saving of others and the safeguarding of family as analogies and parallels to the kamikazes' sacred, sacrificial and national duty. In a reversal of Kageura's understandable cynicism and a tacit reaffirmation of the kamikaze strategy, Miyabe's death meant that he succeeded. The achievement of Kentaro's understanding of his ancestor's heroism and selflessness is accompanied by a montage sequence which erodes the distinction between past and present in uniting the flashbacks, the veterans' voice-overs, and scenes from the end of the war which concretise the significance of Miyabe's symbolic and representative act. Included in this sequence is the broadcast of the Emperor's announcement of surrender, stating the need for the nation to "endure the unendurable" for a lasting peace for Japan. The threading together of wartime and peacetime in this sequence insists upon Miyabe's heroism, inferring his endurance of the unendurable in choosing death to save lives, and to safeguard his family by conferring its protection to an indebted surrogate. The film's final images, in which Kentaro appears to see Miyabe flying in his Zero over the cityscape of modern Tokyo, cements the film's connection between present-day Japan and the sacrifice of the past, and asserts the unbroken continuance of national values from one generation to another.

4 Contextualising the Cinematic Kamikaze

Despite, or perhaps because of, the controversy they inspired by their ambivalent treatment of the wartime past, these films became landmark commercial successes within the Japanese cinema. *Ore wa, kimi no tame ni koso shini ni iku* gained two billion yen from its Japanese release, while *Eien no O* earned more than eight billion yen, staying at the top of the Japanese box office for two months and in the process becoming one of the top ten highest grossing Japanese films of all time (cf. Schilling 2007, 2014). While it would be true to say that spectacular war films have always been popular in Japan (as in other countries), the spectacle of combat offered by these two films constitutes a negligible proportion of their overall duration. At the same time their recreation of kamikaze attacks, though arguably a selling point emphasized by their digital effects, represents the climactic resolution of their ambivalent deliberations on patriotic self-sacrifice. Their evasive or disingenuous arguments for peace and life, which are claimed to necessitate the pursuit of war and death, are resolved by the unequivocally heroic deeds of their protagonists in successfully executed attacks. The solitary, dedicated, selfless individual pilot is exalted as the unarguable victor over both the massed, anonymous enemies of wartime, and the Japanese enemies of past militarism and present indifference. In these respects, these treatments of the kamikaze phenomenon depart markedly from historical assessments of the late twentieth century, which claimed that the 'special attack' had been intended initially as no more than a short term expedient for the battle for the Philippines, and criticised the conception, operation and evaluation of the kamikazes strategically and tactically:

> Japan's suicide air operations mark the Pacific War with two scars that will remain forever in the annals of battle: one, of shame at the mistaken way of command; the other, of valor at the self-sacrificing spirit of young men who died for their beloved country. (Yokoi 1986: 473)

Ore wa engages in an act of national restoration, reaffirming heroic individuals through a narrative of personal recollection and commemoration. This is judged, by Tomé and presumably also by the film's screenwriter Ishihara, to be a necessary and expiatory task which restores war heroes to their proper place in national history. By contrast, *Eien no O* portrays the conduct of a familial-historical investigation, an attempt to recover fact and redeem a misprized individual. From a personal, socio-archaeological enquiry a national, cultural past is uncovered, with an emblematic extrapolation from one to the other: one family owes all to one man, and thus the country owes everything to him and his comrades. Both films are strident in their assertions of the essential validity of the truths they reveal or re-establish. Paradoxically, part of the reaffirmation of the men's heroism and of the country's obligation to them is the assertion of their own victimhood at the hands of the Japanese politico-military establishment. Their patriotism and sacrifice may be celebrated as fundamentally representative national traits, yet the connections created between the kamikazes and traditions of feudal loyalty (in *Ore wa*, for example, one pilot claims to be descended from the 'White Tigers,' the loyal samurai renowned for their service in the Boshin War) underline how contemporary Japan has (in error, it seems) progressed beyond, strayed from or pragmatically abused such honourable, historical precedents. If the truth of the past has been lost in a shameful obscuration, its restoration also appears to imply a perturbing retrenchment of conservative values. Within such a schema for circumscribed history and prescribed identity, the films' makers appear unabashed or unaware of the mendaciousness with which the past is treated.

Ishihara zeroes in on the ignorance of youth as a particularly worrisome feature of contemporary Japan. He relates a story told to him by a WWII pilot. The pilot, while standing on a commuter train, overheard a couple of young people talking: "'Hey, did you know that 50 years ago Japan and America were at war?' 'What? No way.' 'Idiot. It's the truth.' 'Are you serious? Who won?'" As Ishihara relates it, the pilot, hearing this, experienced such a shock that he had to get off the train and sit down on a bench on the train platform to recover. Here the victim is the pilot, and the countless other Japanese who suffered as a result of WWII. For Ishihara, the source of the problem is the lack of historical knowledge that leads to such confusion on the part of young people. What is striking about Ishihara's logic, however, is the limited way in which he portrays militarism, nation and youth. Rhetorically, it is quite powerful, but logically, it ignores as much history as the youths on the train (cf. Condry). Here the American adversary is almost irrelevant to contemporary Japan's obliviousness to its chronological past and its cultural traditions. The enemy is Japanese ignorance and identity loss: an ironic conclusion to reach given the long-running and rancorous clashes between left-wing and right-wing factions over the incomplete, inaccurate or partial accounts of Pacific War history endorsed by state-regulated school texts (see Ienaga 1993–1994; 2001). The disputable interpretation of the past which both *Ore wa* and *Eien no O* advocate is rendered unquestionable by the films' elliptical narratives, which foreground and portray the redemption of past and present through the recovery of a restorative truth. The pilots in both films are both distanced from militarism and yet anointed as patriots by their decisions to die so that others may live, replacing inevitability and victimhood with choice and heroism:

> This kind of almost tautological explanation for kamikaze actions is also the most inoffensive, because it largely isolates the dead from history. However, it also depends on the narration, as if kamikaze existed in order to be narrated as existing. As in [*Ore wa*], this effectively functions as self-justification for these movies themselves, reducing the kamikaze to a textual operation, as if their suicidal missions were essentially acts of narration but only about themselves [...] Yet the fact that these narratives aim to imbricate the act of narration (the films, the internal storytellers), the subject of narration (the kamikaze sailors or pilots), and the reception of the narration (the film audience or the survivors of the war) all in the same circular, unmediated textual process, purports to circumvent alternative interpretations. (Gerow 2016: 209)

Noticeably, it is not just the ignorance and indifference of younger Japanese which must be overcome by this narrative act, but also the obfuscation and silence of the intervening, parental and post-war generation which has implicitly failed to inform its offspring of wartime history. Kentaro's ignorance can only be corrected by a return to the original source of testimony in the veterans' flashbacks, which are treated as reverentially as Tomé's commemorations of the dead.

However, other types of enemies are also troublingly identified among those who oppose war, who attempt to evade duty or fail to honour the dead. At the outset of *Eien no O*, the condemnation of the lost grandfather's cowardice is unquestioned, as if the shamed individual has been scapegoated unproblematically for the defeat of the nation. If neither is discussed, both are implicitly denied. Conversely, the recovery of the emblematic Zero pilot as a multifaceted individual (a loving husband, an excellent pilot, a committed patriot and a sacrificial patriarchal figure, wedded to life but ultimately willing to die) provides a model citizen and hero essential to the construction of modern Japan. This realisation is confirmed by the paradoxical vision of the Zero over present-day Tokyo, apparently on its way to heroic destruction aboard an American ship in 1945. The film's conclusion thus consummates the incomplete recreation of the kamikaze attack seen at its opening, in which its outcome and identity of the pilot are deliberately occluded. That Miyabe is last shown smiling before the (still unseen) moment of impact, implies his transubstantiation in success, obscures his violent death, and confers immortality upon him and the fervent, enduring national values he has come to incarnate.

Conclusion

The casting of kamikazes as defenders, literally of 'loved ones' and allegorically of the nation and its inherent values, embeds these films within long-standing romantic and patriotic discourses surrounding Japan's wartime pilots. Dashing individualism and skill become entwined with personal bravery in the defence of Japan from American bombing raids, and moral superiority and integrity in the self-sacrifice of the kamikazes, in which pilots re-enact the loyalty of the feudal era samurai (Nakar 2003: 68). Just as the origins of Japan's war of aggression have been obscured by a rhetoric of liberation from and defence against Western imperialism, so the ferocity of 'special attack' is transmuted into a heroic defence of the tangible family, which stands in symbolic stead for the abstract nation. In their complex conflicts with personal conscience, imperial duty, individual desire and national authority, the cinematic kamikaze re-assert aspects of Japanese-ness even as they evasively redefine the adversarial enemy in the present as well as the past:

> [*Ore wa*] presents what might be called the Yasukuni Shrine version of the *tokkotai* story, in which the war was not an imperialistic adventure but an idealistic crusade to free Asia from Western domination. The pilots died not pointlessly but to protect their loved ones. They are not the local equivalent of suicide bombers but pure-spirited heroes who embody the Japanese tradition of self-sacrifice for the common good. And now they are gathered at Yasukuni Shrine, gods for all eternity, to be worshipped – and emulated. [...] Despite its problematic ideology and rambling story structure, [*Ore wa*] offers informed insight into the pilots' lives, including their fears and regrets, that makes them less like park statuary, more fallible flesh-and-blood. But it's also a rally-round-the-Hinomaru film that will warm the hearts of the boys on the sound trucks who long to re-launch that old Asian crusade. With any luck, Gov. Ishihara – and the rest of us – won't live to see it. (Richards 2000)

Schilling's suggestion that the re-emergence of World War II in general and the kamikazes in particular as cinematic subjects speak to aggressive nationalism in twenty-first century Japan may be derived from Shintaro Ishihara's inflammatory comments on the country's present-day territorial disputes with China (cf. Aoki 2014). Although the circular narrational acts of *Ore wa* and *Eien no O* might appear to elide the presence and identity of the enemy in their prejudicial returns to the past, it could be inferred that a third (regional, future) enemy is discernible alongside the anonymised adversaries of the Pacific War and the unsympathetic depictions of military authority. Additionally, therefore, these films' didactic evocation of Pacific War history and dutiful veneration of the kamikazes' victory over obscured foreign adversaries and modern indifference, can also be seen as an ominous, inculcatory patriotism for audiences of the Japanese cinema, at home as much as abroad.

Works Cited

Aoki, Mizuho (2014) "Controversial to the end, Shintaro Ishihara bows out of politics," *The Japan Times* <http://www.japantimes.co.jp/news/2014/12/16/national/politics-diplomacy/ishihara-bows-wants-war-china-compares-hashimoto-young-hitler/#.V83bFJgrLIU> (accessed 5 September 2016).

Condry, Ian (2007) "Youth, Intimacy and Blood: Media and Nationalism in Contemporary Japan," *Japan Focus* <http://japanfocus.org/-Ian-Condry/2403> (accessed 1 June 2010).

Desser, David (2016) "Under the Flag of the Rising Sun: Imagining the Pacific War in the Japanese Cinema," in *Divided Lenses: Screen Memories of War in East Asia*, ed. Michael Berry and Chiho Sawada (Honolulu: University of Hawaii Press), 74–100.

Gerow, Aaron (2016) "War and Nationalism in Recent Japanese Cinema: *Yamato*, Kamikaze, Trauma, and Forgetting the Postwar," in *Divided Lenses*, ed. Berry and Sawada, 196–219.

Hill, Peter (2005) "Kamikaze 1943–45," in *Making Sense of Suicide Missions*, ed. Diego Gambetta (Oxford: Oxford University Press), 1–42.

Ienaga, Saburo (1993–1994) "The Glorification of War in Japanese Education," *International Security* 18. 3, 113–133.

Ienaga, Saburo (2001) *Japan's Past, Japan's Future: One Historian's Odyssey*, trans. Richard H. Minear (Oxford: Rowman and Littlefield).

Inoguchi, Rikihei, and Tadashi Nakajima (1986) "The Kamikaze Attack Corps," in *The Japanese Navy in World War II*, ed. David C. Evans (Annapolis, MD: US Naval Institute Press), 415–439.

Inuzuka, Ako (2016) "Memories of the Tokko: Analysis of the Chiran Peace Museum for Kamikaze Pilots," *Howard Journal of Communications* 27. 2, 145–166.

Jin, Kim Hyung (2008) "Opponents try to block memorial for Korean kamikaze," *The Japan Times* <http://www.japantimes.co.jp/news/2008/05/10/national/opponents-try-to-block-memorial-for-korean-kamikaze/#.V9kQEpgrK00> (accessed 12 September 2016).

Martin, Alexander (2016) "Shinzo Abe Avoids Yasukuni Shrine as Japan Marks War Anniversary," *The Wall Street Journal* <http://www.wsj.com/articles/shinzo-abe-avoids-yasukuni-shrine-as-japan-marks-war-anniversary-1471237797> (accessed 5 September 2016).

Nakar, Eldad (2003) "Memories of Pilots and Planes: World War II in Japanese 'Manga,' 1957–1967," *Social Science Japan Journal* 6. 1, 57–76.

Ohnuki-Tierney, Emiko (2002) *Kamikaze, Cherry Blossoms and Nationalisms: The Militarisation of Aesthetics in Japanese History* (London: University of Chicago Press).

Richards, Jeffrey (2000) "(Loosely) based on a true story," *The Times Higher Education Supplement*, 16.

Schilling, Mark (2007) "'Ore wa Kimi no Tame ni Koso Shini ni Iku': An Ishihara weepy for the right," *The Japan Times* <http://www.japantimes.co.jp/culture/2007/05/25/films/film-reviews/ore-wa-kimi-no-tame-ni-koso-shini-ni-iku/#.V0GcoulFCP8> (accessed 22 May 2016).

Schilling, Mark (2014) "Flights of fancy – box office smash *The Eternal Zero* reopens old wounds in Japan with its take on wartime kamikaze pilots," *South China Morning Post* <http://www.scmp.com/lifestyle/arts-culture/article/1508179/flights-fancy-box-office-smash-eternal-zero-reopens-old> (accessed 11 November 2015).

Seaton, Philip (2006) "'Do You Really Want to Know What Your Uncle Did?': Coming To Terms with Relatives' War Actions in Japan," *Oral History* 34. 1, 53–60.
Shimazu, Naoko (2003) "Popular Representations of the Past: The Case of Postwar Japan," *Journal of Contemporary History* 38. 1, 101–116.
Yokoi, Toshiyuki (1986) "Kamikazes in the Okinawa Campaign," in *The Japanese Navy in World War II*, ed. David C. Evans (Annapolis, MD: US Naval Institute Press), 453–473.

Filmography

Eien no O (*The Eternal Zero*, a.k.a. *The Fighter Pilot*) (2014) Dir. Takashi Yamazaki (Toho).
Hotaru (*The Firefly*) (2001) Dir. Yasuo Furuhata (Toei Company).
Meiji tenno to nichiro daisenso (*Emperor Meiji and the Great Russo-Japanese War*) (1957) Dir. Kunio Watanabe (Shintoho).
Nihonkai daikaisen (*Battle of the Japan Sea*) (1969) Dir. Seiji Maruyama (Toho).
Nobi (*Fires on the Plain*) (1959) Dir. Kon Ichikawa (Daiei Film).
Ore wa, kimi no tame ni koso shini ni iku (*For Those We Love*, a.k.a. *Assault on the Pacific: Kamikaze*) (2007) Dir. Taku Shinjô (Toei Company).
Taiheiyo no tsubasa (*Attack Squadron*) (1963) Dir. Shûe Matsubayashi (Toho).

Contributors

Marcelline Block was educated at Harvard and Princeton. Among her publications are the first French to English translation of Jean-Pierre Bertin-Maghit's *Propaganda Documentaries in France, 1940–1944* (Rowman & Littlefield, 2016); *Fan Phenomena: Marilyn Monroe* (Intellect, 2015); *World Film Locations: Paris* (Intellect, 2011; Korean translation, Nangman Books, Seoul, 2014); *World Film Locations: Las Vegas* (Intellect, 2012); *World Film Locations: Prague* (Intellect, 2013); *World Film Locations: Marseilles* (Intellect, 2013) and its French version, *Filmer Marseille* (Presses universitaires de Provence, 2013), which she co-translated with Jean-Luc Lioult into French; *World Film Locations: Boston* (Intellect, 2014); and *Situating the Feminist Gaze and Spectatorship in Postwar Cinema* (Cambridge Scholars, 2008; 2nd ed., 2010), translated into Italian as *Sguardo e pubblico femminista nel cinema del dopoguerra* (Rome: Aracne editrice S.r.l, 2011/2012), volume 9 of the "Cinema ed estetica cinematografica" series of the Università degli Studi dell'Aquila. She coedited *An Anthology of French Singers from A to Z: Singin' in French* (Cambridge Scholars 2018); the first and second editions of *Geolinguistic Studies in Language Contact, Conflict and Development, Volume 1* (New York and Tokio: American Society of Geolinguistics Publications, 2017 and 2018); the second edition of *Plurilingual Perspectives in Geolinguistics* (New York City and Tokyo: American Society of Geolinguistics, 2016); *French Cinema and the Great War: Remembrance and Representation* (Rowman & Littlefield, 2016); *French Cinema in Close-up: La vie d'un acteur pour moi* (Phaeton, 2015), which was named a Best Reference Work of 2015 by *Library Journal*; *The Directory of World Cinema: Belgium* (Intellect, 2014) and *Unequal Before Death* (Cambridge Scholars, 2012), which were both awarded the Schoff Fund Publication Grant from Columbia University, and *Gender Scripts in Medicine and Narrative* (Cambridge Scholars, 2010), translated into Italian as *Prescrizioni di Femminismo. Emancipazione e stereotipi in Arte e Medicina* (Rome: Aracne editrice S.r.l, October 2014, "Le Sibille" series, edited by professors from the University of Naples, Federico II). Her chapters and essays about cinema, literature, and visual art appear in more than twenty-five books, and she is a contributor to numerous journals, including *Art Decades*, *Geolinguistics*, and *The Harvard French Review*.

Angela Brintlinger is Professor of Slavic Languages and Cultures at Ohio State University and author of numerous books and articles. Her monographs include *Writing a Usable Past: Russian Literary Culture 1817–1937* (Northwestern University Press, 2000) and *Chapaev and His Comrades: War and the Russian Literary Hero across the Twentieth Century* (Academic Studies Press, 2010). She has also edited several important collections, including *Madness and the Mad in Russian Culture*, with Ilya Vinitsky (Toronto University Press, 2007), *Chekhov for the 21st Century*, with Carol Apollonio (Slavica, 2012), and the forthcoming *Seasoned Socialism: Gender and Food in Late Soviet Everyday Life*, with Anastasia Lakhtikova and Irina Glushchenko (Indiana University Press, 2018). Her translations into English include *Derzhavin: A biography*, by Vladislav Khodasevich (University of Wisconsin Press, 2007) and the forthcoming *Russian Cuisine in Exile*, by Alexander Genis and Petr Vail (Academic Studies Press, 2018).

Francesca De Lucia is currently teaching in the Foreign Languages department of Minzu University of China. She previously worked as associate professor at Zhejiang Normal University in Jinhua. She holds a PhD from the University of Oxford, her thesis entitled *Italian American*

Cultural Fictions: From Diaspora to Globalization. She obtained a Master's degree (licence èn lettres) from the University of Geneva, Switzerland, and a Diploma in American Studies from Smith College, Northampton, Massachusetts. Francesca de Lucia's research involves ethnicity in American literature and film, with a particular focus on Italian Americans, Asian Americans and Jewish Americans. Her article entitled "The Impact of Fascism and the Second World War on Italian American Communities" was awarded the Geno Baroni Prize for the best historical article of 2008. Her work has also appeared in edited volumes such as *Transatlantic Encounters: Philosophy, Media, Politics* (Peter Lang, 2011) and *American Wild Zones: Space, Experience, Consciousness* (Peter Lang, 2016), as well as journals (*Italiana Americana, Polish Journal of American Studies, US Studies Online*).

Stephen Harper is Senior Lecturer in Media and Film Studies at the University of Portsmouth in the UK. He has published numerous books, chapters and journal articles on film and television images of war and conflict, cultural representations of mental distress, and many other subjects. His single-authored books are *Screening Bosnia: Geopolitics, Gender and Nationalism in Film and Television Images of the 1992–95 War* (Bloomsbury, 2017), *Beyond the Left: The Communist Critique of the Media* (Zero, 2012), *Madness, Power and the Media: Class, Gender and Race in Popular Images of Mental Distress* (Palgrave Macmillan, 2009) and *Insanity, Individuals, and Society in Late-Medieval English Literature: The Subject of Madness* (Edwin Mellen Press, 2003). Stephen also writes for non-academic publications and a selection of reviews and short articles can be found at his blog site www.relativeautonomy.com.

Janet Harris is an award winning documentary producer/director, having worked for many years at the BBC and as a freelancer with experience of working in Iraq in war and in post war. She filmed in Iraq as an embedded director with the British military for the BBC series *Soldier, Husband, Daughter Dad*, 2004 and for the BBC series *Fighting the War* 2003. Janet was last in Iraq in 2013 to make a documentary for the tenth anniversary of the invasion of Iraq for the BBC *This World Strand*, "Did My Son Die in Vain" (2014). She obtained a PhD from Cardiff University in 2012 and now lectures in Documentary and International Journalism at Cardiff. Her research interests include documentaries, war, Iraq, and conflict reporting. Her work has been published in *Disappearing War: Interdisciplinary Perspectives on Cinema and Erasure in the Post 9/11 World* (Edinburgh University Press, 2016); *Ford Madox Ford's* The Good Soldier: *Centenary Essays* (Brill Rodopi, 2015), *No Woman's Land: On the Frontlines with Female Reporters* (International News Safety Institute, 2012), as well as *Journalism Practice* (2016).

Gunnar Iversen is Associate Professor of Film Studies at Carleton University in Ottawa, Canada, and former Professor of Film Studies at the Norwegian University of Science and Technology in Trondheim, Norway. Iversen has published books and articles in many different languages, about Norwegian and Scandinavian Cinema, Early Cinema, Documentary, and Sound in Film and Media. He has co-written *Nordic National Cinemas* (Routledge, 1998) and *Historical Dictionary of Scandinavian Cinema* (Scarecrow, 2012), and co-edited *Beyond the Visual: Sound and Image in Ethnographic and Documentary Film* (Intervention Press, 2010). His research interests are Norwegian and Scandinavian Cinema, Sound Studies, Documentary, and Early Cinema.

Maryam Jameela is a second-year WRoCAH funded PhD Researcher in the School of English at the University of Sheffield. She received a Bachelor's degree in English Literature from the University of Sheffield and a Master's degree in Gender Studies from the University of Sussex.

She is currently developing a research project which seeks to use trauma theory to characterize lived experiences of the 1947 partition of India through archival study. Her PhD project examines intersectional representations of Desi women in post-9/11 cultural productions through comparisons of pop culture and governmental policy documents. She is particularly interested in critical race studies in film and literature, using affect theory and phenomenology. Some of her work can be found at *Forum*, *Brown Girl Magazine*, and various other publications.

Maria Kobielska completed her PhD in literary studies at the Jagiellonian University in Cracow in 2014. A member of the Research Center for Memory Cultures (JU), she teaches cultural studies and poetics at the Faculty of Polish Studies of the JU. Her research focuses on contemporary Polish culture from the perspective of memory studies, in particular the politics of memory. She is the author of a book on Polish memory culture in the twenty-first century, entitled *Polska kultura pamięci w XXI wieku: dominanty. Zbrodnia katyńska, powstanie warszawskie, stan wojenny* (IBL PAN, 2016). She has published extensively on Polish cultural memory as well as on the methodology of memory studies. Articles have appeared in in journals (*Teksty Drugie*, *Herito*, *Культура/Culture*) as well as edited volumes, including *Traumatic Cultures of the Second World War and After* (Palgrave Macmillan, 2016).

Noah McLaughlin is an Assistant Professor of French at Kennesaw State University, where he directs the Foreign Language Resource Collection and coordinates the Critical Languages Program. Along with all levels of French, he teaches courses about intercultural communication and competence as well as transnational cinema. He has publications in the fields of film studies, foreign language pedagogy, and popular culture, including the Rowman & Littlefield anthology *Bringing History to Life through Film*. He is the author of *French War Films and National Identity* (Cambria Press, 2010). He is currently researching the contemporary French biopic as well as the evolving roles of the Algerian War for Independence in Francophone cinema.

Martin Löschnigg is Associate Professor of English and Chair of the Section on Postcolonial Literatures in the University of Graz, Austria. He is vice director of the Graz Centre for Canadian Studies and a Corresponding Member of the Austrian Academy of Sciences. His research interests include narratology, autobiography, the literature of war and Canadian literature, and he has published widely on these subjects. Recent book publications include *The Great War in Post-Memory Literature and Film*, ed. with Marzena Sokołowska-Paryż (de Gruyter 2014, pb 2016) and *North America, Europe and the Cultural Memory of the First World War*, ed. with Karin Kraus (Winter 2015).

Niina Oisalo is a Doctoral Candidate in Media Studies at the University of Turku, Finland. She holds a Master of Social Science degree in International Relations from the University of Tampere and a Master of Arts degree from Brunel University London, majoring in Documentary Practice. Oisalo's PhD project *Transcultural Movement, Violence and Belonging in the Contemporary Nordic Documentary* explores the aesthetic and political operations of Nordic documentaries related to transcultural circumstances of colonialism, war and immigration. She has published in the *Journal of Scandinavian Cinema*, *Lähikuva* (a Finnish journal specializing in film and media culture). Oisalo's current research interests range from cinematic memory to Sámi documentary, ecocinema and the politics of imagining the Arctic in film.

Marek Paryż is Associate Professor and Chair of the Section of American Literature at the Institute of English Studies, University of Warsaw. He is the chief editor of the Polish *Journal for American Studies* and senior editor of the *European Journal of American Studies*. His articles have appeared in the *American Transcendental Quarterly, European Journal of American Culture, Zeitschrift für Anglistik und Amerikanistik* and other journals and collections of essays. He is the author of *The Postcolonial and Imperial Experience in American Transcendentalism* (Palgrave Macmillan, 2012), and co-editor of *The Post-2000 Film Western: Contexts, Transnationality, Hybridity* (with John R. Leo, Palgrave Macmillan, 2015).

Caroline Perret researches the impact of war on cultural production. She is particularly interested in art, illustrated books, literature, films and poetry in the historical, political, social and cultural context of the two World Wars both in Britain and France. Her work has been published in collections like *The Great War in Post-Memory Literature and Film* (De Gruyter, 2014); forthcoming publications include contributions to *Formulas of Betrayal: Traitors, Deserters, Collaborators in European Politics of Memory* (Palgrave Macmillan) and *Making Sense of Warfare Violence* (*European Review of History*). She has widely lectured in these fields, and is also a theatre critic.

Andrejs Plakans has been an emeritus professor of history at Iowa State University in Ames, Iowa since 2006. Born in Riga, he emigrated in 1944 and grew up in the USA, taking his PhD at Harvard University in 1969. His research interests include the social and demographic history of rural Eastern Europe, the history of the Baltic littoral, and various aspects of the history of modern Latvia. Recent publications include *The Latvians: A Short History* (Hoover Institution Press, 1995); *Experiencing Totalitarianism: The Invasion and Occupation of Latvia by the USSR and Nazi Germany 1939–1991: A Documentary History* (AuthorHouse, 2007); *A Concise History of the Baltic States* (Cambridge University Press, 2011; Russian translation *Kratkaya historya stran Baltii*, 2016), and *Historical Dictionary of Latvia* (Scarecrow Press, 2017, co-author Aldis Purs).

Holger Pötzsch is Associate Professor in Media and Documentation Studies at UiT Tromsø, Norway. His main areas of research are 1) borders and bordering practices with special emphasis on technology, 2) war films and games, and 3) the politics of cultural expressions and memory. In the first area, Pötzsch has studied how new technologies such as digital networks, dataveillance, biometrics, predictive analytics, and robotics have changed border locations and practices, and have impacted upon the way wars are fought and witnessed. His work on the issue has been published in, among others, the journals *New Media & Society, EPD: Society & Space, TripleC,* and *The Journal of Borderland Studies*, as well as the *Routledge Handbook of Media, Conflict & Security* (2016). The second field of interest focuses on how wars are represented in cultural expressions with main emphasis on Hollywood war films and AAA game titles. This part of his work has been published in anthologies such as *The Philosophy of War Films* (University Press of Kentucky, 2014) and in journals such as *Games & Culture, Game Studies, Nordicom Review,* and *Media, War & Conflict*. The third area of research comprises formal analysis into how cultural expressions invite particular understandings of shared pasts. In this area, his work has been published in the anthologies *Ethics and Images of Pain* (Routledge, 2012) and *Eastwood's Iwo Jima* (Wallflower Press, 2013), as well as in journals such as *Memory Studies* and *International Review of Education*.

Petra Rau is Senior Lecturer in Modern Literature at the University of East Anglia, UK. Her research areas are literature and film about war and fascism, travel writing, memory cultures and Anglo-German cultural relations. She is the author of *English Modernism, National Identity and the Germans, 1890–1950* (Ashgate, 2009) and *Our Nazis: Representations of Fascism in Contemporary Literature and Film* (Edinburgh University Press, 2013). Her edited collections include *Conflict, Nationhood, and Corporeality in Modern Literature: Bodies-at-war* (Palgrave, 2010) and *Long Shadows: The Second World War in Literature and Film* (Northwestern University Press, 2016). She is currently working on a family memoir.

Mario Ranalletti is an Argentinian historian and Professor at the Master and Doctorate Program in the Universidad Nacional de Tres de Febrero (Buenos Aires, Argentina). He took his PhD in history in 2006 at the Institut d'études politiques de Paris. His research is concerned with mass crime and extreme violence from an interdisciplinary and comparative perspective (Argentina, Bosnia, and Indonesia) and the rendering of extreme violence and its perpetrators in contemporary fiction films. His work has been published in *Destruction and Human Remains: Disposal and Concealment in Genocide and Mass Violence* (Manchester University Press, 2014), *A Companion to the Historical Film* (Blackwell Publishing, 2013), as well as in journals like *Amerika. Mémoires, identités, territoires* (2017), *Écrire l'histoire* (2014), *Anuario del Centro de Estudios Históricos "Prof. Carlos S. A. Segreti"* (2013), *Vingtième siècle. Revue d'histoire* (2010).

Jonathan Rayner is Reader in Film Studies in the School of English at the University of Sheffield, UK. His research interests and publications span Australasian cinema (especially Oz Gothic), genre films, auteur studies, the representation of naval history and war on film and television, and the relationships between landscapes and moving images. He is the author of *The Films of Peter Weir* (Bloomsbury, 1998/2003), *Contemporary Australian Cinema* (Manchester University Press, 2000), *The Naval War Film* (Manchester University Press, 2007), *The Cinema of Michael Mann* (Wallflower Press, 2013) and the co-editor of *Cinema and Landscape* (Intellect Books, 2010), *Film Landscapes: Cinema, Environment and Visual Culture* (Cambridge Scholars, 2013), *Mapping Cinematic Norths* (Peter Lang, 2016) and *Filmurbia: Screening the Suburbs* (Palgrave Macmillan, 2017) with David Forrest and Graeme Harper. His current research centres on aspects of the First World War centenary and analysis of the popular British magazine, *The War Illustrated*.

Daniel Reynaud is Associate Professor of history at Avondale College of Higher Education in NSW, Australia. His main research interests revolve around Anzac themes: cinematic representations of the Anzacs; and the Anzacs and religion. He has also published on history pedagogy and online teaching. His work has appeared in the *International Encyclopedia of the First World War*, *St Mark's Review: A Journal of Christian Thought & Opinion*, *Studies in Australasian Cinema*, and *Journal of Religious History*, as well as edited volumes, including *Secularisation: New Historical Perspectives* (Cambridge Scholars, 2014) and *The Great War in Post-Memory Literature and Film* (De Gruyter, 2014). He is the author of monographs, *Celluloid Anzacs: The Great War through Australian Cinema* (Vic Australian Scholarly Publishing, 2007), *The Man the Anzacs Revered: William 'Fighting Mac' McKenzie, Anzac Chaplain* (Signs Publishing, 2015), and *Anzac Spirituality* (forthcoming).

Marzena Sokołowska-Paryż is Associate Professor at the Institute of English Studies, University of Warsaw, Poland. She is the author of *Reimagining the War Memorial, Reinterpreting the Great War: The Formats of British Commemorative Fiction* (Cambridge Scholars, 2012) and *The Myth of War in British and Polish Poetry, 1939–1945* (Peter Lang, 2002). *The Great War in Post-Memory Literature and Film*, co-edited with Martin Löschnigg, appeared in 2014, re-issued in paperback in 2016 (De Gruyter). Her work has appeared in edited volumes, including *History of the Literary Cultures of East-Central Europe: Junctures and Disjunctures in the 19th and 20th Centuries* (John Benjamins, 2004), *Mnemosyne and Mars: Artistic and Cultural Representations of Twentieth-Century Europe at War* (Cambridge Scholars, 2013), *Horrors of War: The Undead on the Battlefield* (Rowman & Littlefield, 2015), *North America, Europe and the Cultural Memory of the First World War* (Universitätsverlag Winter, 2015), *Re-Imagining the First World War: New Perspectives in Anglophone Literature and Culture*, *The Great War: From Memory to History* (Cambridge Scholars, 2015), *From Memory to History: The Great War* (Wilfrid Laurier University Press, 2015), *The Long Aftermath: Historical and Cultural Legacies of Europe at War 1936–1945* (Palgrave Macmillan, 2016), as well as in journals, including the *Journal of War and Culture Studies* and *WLA: War, Literature and the Arts*. She is also an associate editor for *Anglica: An International Journal for English Studies*.

Miri Talmon, PhD, is a scholar of media culture, cinema, and television, who specializes in the research and teaching of Israeli culture and in comparative approaches to Israeli and American film and television cultures. She teaches at the Steve Tisch School of Film and Television at Tel-Aviv University. Miri Talmon is the author of several chapters and articles on Israeli television and cinema, of the book *Israeli Graffiti: Nostalgia, Groups and Collective Identity in Israeli Cinema* (Hebrew), and the editor, with Yaron Peleg, of the anthology *Israeli Cinema-Identities in Motion* (University of Texas Press, 2011).

Florian Zappe is Assistant Professor of American Studies at the Georg-August-University in Göttingen (Germany). He is the author of books on William S. Burroughs (*'Control Machines' und 'Dispositive' – Eine foucaultsche Analyse der Machtstrukturen im Romanwerk von William S. Burroughs zwischen 1959 und 1968*, Peter Lang, 2008) and Kathy Acker (*Das Zwischenschreiben – Transgression und avantgardistisches Erbe bei Kathy Acker*, transcript Verlag, 2013) and has published essays on a variety of topics. His research interests range widely from the theory and history of the avant-garde, critical and "French" theory, pop(ular) culture, the history of European and American cinema (with a focus on independent and experimental film), modern and postmodern literature to surveillance practices and their effects on our culture. Currently, he is working on a book project on the cultural history of atheism in America.

Vita Zelče is Professor in the Department of Communications Studies in the Faculty of Social Sciences at the University of Latvia in Riga. Her research interests include the history of media, cultural memory, social history, the history of women, and the politics of history-writing. Recent co-authored and co-edited books in Latvian in these fields include *The Last War: The Communication of Memory and Trauma* (Riga: Latvijas Universitāte 2010), *Embattled Memory: March 16th and May 9th* (Riga: Zinātne 2011), *(Two) Sides: Latvian Tales of WWII in Soldiers' Diaries* (Riga: Mansards 2011/2012). Her research on the present article was supported by a grant from the ERA.NET RUS+ project 'LivingMemories.'

Index

08/15 (dir. May)   128, 143
1915 (dir. Thomson and Drew)   253, 260, 268
24 (TV series)   334
80 milionów (dir. Krzystek)   239–240, 248, 250
80 Million (see 80 milionów, dir. Krzystek)
9/11 (terrorists attacks)   7, 13, 65, 91–95, 98–102, 334, 336, 345–346, 397
A perdre la raison (dir. Lafosse)   10, 197–213, 215–217
Die Abenteuer des Werner Holt (dir. Kunert)   130
Abu Ghraib (prison)   13, 345–346, 353–356, 358
An Accidental Soldier (dir. Ward)   253, 264, 268
Adam-Smith, Patsy (dir.)   256
The Adventures of Alënushka and Erëma (see Prikliucheniia Alënushki i Erëmy, dir. Gitis)
Afghanistan (War)   75, 77, 91, 114, 116, 345
After Hours (dir. Scorsese)   322
Aimée & Jaguar (dir. Färberböck)   130, 133
Alchin, Ray (dir.)   253, 262, 269
Algerian War   9, 164, 177–184, 186–188, 190–192, 194, 397
The Alien Years (dir. Crombie)   253, 261–262, 264, 268
All That I Love (see Wszystko co kocham, dir. Borcuch)
Alpha Bravo Charlie (dir. Mansoor)   331–332, 344
Always Afternoon (dir. Stevens)   253, 261–262, 264, 268
Amenta, Pino (dir.)   253, 269
American Graffiti (dir. Lucas)   322
American Sniper (dir. Eastwood)   6, 53, 58–59, 61–62, 64, 68–69, 71, 91
Andell, Pia (dir.)   148
Andy McNab's Tour of Duty   74, 81–82, 89
Anonyma: A Woman in Berlin (see Anonyma: Eine Frau in Berlin, dir. Färberböck)

Anonyma: Eine Frau in Berlin (dir. Färberböck)   8, 122, 133–141, 142, 143
Anzac Girls (dir. Cameron and Watson)   253, 264, 269
Anzacs (dir. Dixon, Miller and Amenta)   253, 257, 259, 260, 269
The Anzacs (dir. Adam-Smith)   256
Arendt, Hannah   69–70, 168
Argov, Schlomo (Israeli ambassador to Britain)   293
L'Armée des ombres (dir. Melville)   161
L'Armée du crime (dir. Guédiguian)   162
Army of Crime (see L'Armée du crime, dir. Guédiguian)
Army of Shadows (see L'armée des ombres, dir. Melville)
Der Arzt von Stalingrad (dir. von Radvanyi)   128–129, 139, 143
As If I Am Not There (dir. Wilson)   339
Ascenseur pour l'échafaud (dir. Malle)   181
Assault on the Pacific: Kamikaze (see Ore wa, kimi no tame ni koso shini ni iku, dir. Shinjô)
Assmann, Jan   1, 14, 56, 70, 130, 142
Astruc, Alexandre (dir.)   161
Attack Squadron (see Taiheiyo no tsubasa, dir. Matsubayashi)
Attenborough, Richard (dir.)   258
Au revoir les enfants (dir. Malle)   9, 163, 170, 172–174, 175
Audiard, Jacques (dir.)   200–202, 213
Auf Wiedersehen Finnland (dir. Suutari)   8, 145–147, 151, 154–155, 157
Australia's Peril (dir. Barrett)   254
Australians at War   256
Avanti Popolo (dir. Bukai)   12, 309, 313, 318–319, 323–325
Avoir 20 ans dans les Aurès (dir. Vautier)   181
Baier, Jo (dir.)   130
Baigā vasara (dir. Grauba)   11, 277, 279, 287, 289, 292

Bakhtin, Mikhail   53, 62
The Band's Visit (see *Bikur Ha-Tizmoret*, dir. Kolirin)
Banzai. You Bastards! (memoir)   366
Les Barons (dir. Yadir)   200
The Barons (see *Les Barons*, dir. Yadir)
Barrett, Franklyn (dir.)   254
La Bataille du rail (dir. Clément)   160
Battle for Haditha (dir. Broomfield)   6, 53, 64–68, 71
Battle of the Japan Sea (see *Nihonkai daikaisen*, dir. Maruyama)
Bauman, Zygmunt   340, 342
Bay, Michael (dir.)   333, 344
Beaufort (dir. Cedar, 2007)   12, 295–298, 301–302, 304–305, 307
Beaufort fortress   296
Bechis, Marco (dir.)   219, 229, 231
Beckermann, Ruth (dir.)   131, 141
Begić, Aida (dir.)   339
Begin, Menachem (Israeli Prime Minister)   294–295, 312–313
Béhat, Gilles (dir.)   182
Behind Enemy Lines (dir. Moore)   334–335, 344
Belgian Congo   199
Belševica, Vizma   286
Beneath Hill 60 (dir. Sims)   253, 263, 269
Beresford, Bruce (dir.)   256
Berri, Claude (dir.)   162
The Betrayal (see *Trahison*, dir. Faucon)
The Big Shave (dir. Scorsese)   178, 189–190
Bigelow, Katheryn (dir.)   64, 91
Bikur Ha-Tizmoret (dir. Kolirin)   12, 309, 313, 320, 323–325
Bin Laden, Osama   61
Bjørnstad, Anne (series creator)   34
Black Adder Goes Forth (dir. Doden)   258
Blumenberg, Hans-Christoph (dir.)   130
Boer War   256, 258
Boisset, Yves (dir.)   181
Das Boot (dir. Petersen)   302
Borcuch, Jacek (dir.)   240–242, 250
Borges, Jorge Luis   224
Bosch, Rose (dir.)   172
Boshin War   389

Bosnian War   12, 327–333, 335–337, 339, 341, 342
Bouchareb, Rachid (dir.)   162, 183
Boys of Abu Ghraib (dir. Moran)   13, 345–346, 352–356, 358, 360
Breaker Morant (dir. Beresford)   256
Brent av frost (dir. Jensen)   31, 33
Bresson, Robert (dir.)   161, 163, 169
Brick Lane (dir. Gavron)   7, 92, 97–102, 103
The Bridge on the River Kwai (dir. Lean)   363, 376
Brigadere, Anna   286
British Columbia   361, 368–370, 374
Britz (dir. Kosminsky)   330, 332
The Broken Years (dir. Gammage)   256
Broomfield, Nick (dir.)   6, 53, 64–69, 71
Brothers in Arms   73, 80, 82, 89
Bukai, Ralf (dir.)   309
Burma-Siam 'Death Railway'   364
Burnt by Frost (see *Brent av frost*, dir. Jensen)
Burnt Earth (see *Terres brûlées*, dir. Dekeukeleire)
Butler, Judith   57, 64, 70, 82, 107, 109–110, 118, 168, 174
Buzzati, Dino (dir.)   296
Bye Bye Blues (dir. Wheeler)   362, 376
Bykau, Vasil'   36, 42, 44
Caché (dir. Haneke)   183
Cameron, Ken (dir.)   253, 269
Camp X-Ray (dir. Sattler)   13, 345–346, 348, 351–356, 358, 360
Canadian Multiculturalism Act   362
A Captain's Honour (see *L'honneur d'un capitaine*, dir. Schoendoerffer)
Cartouches gauloises (dir. Charef)   183
Cauvin, André (dir.)   199
Cedar, Joseph (dir.)   295–296, 298, 307
Chabrol, Claude (dir.)   161
Le Chagrin et la pitié (dir. Ophüls)   9, 161, 163–164, 167–168, 170–172, 174, 175
Charef, Mehdi (dir.)   183
Chauvel, Charles (dir.)   255
Cher frangin (dir. Mordillat)   182
Chernyshevsky, Nikolai   51

The Child of Man (see *Cilvēka bērns*, dir. Streičs)
Chiran airbase (Kagoshima, Japan)   379
The Chronicles of Melanie (see *Melānijas hronika*, dir. Kairišs)
Cilvēka bērns (dir. Streičs)   11, 285–286, 289, 292
Clément, René (dir.)   160–161
Cléo de 5 à 7 (dir. Varda)   181
Cleo from 5 to 7 (see *Cléo de 5 à 7*, dir. Varda)
Coates, George (dir.)   254, 290
Cold War   5, 8, 20, 27, 30–33, 35, 122, 127, 142, 379
Cole, Marcus (dir.)   253, 269
collaboration   9, 22–26, 36, 159, 162–163, 167, 169, 172
collective enemy   77
The Colonel (see *Mon Colonel*, dir. Herbiet)
colonial oppression   10, 198, 210
colonialism   177, 194, 197–198, 210, 216, 397
communicative memory   56
compassion   66, 107, 204, 358
conspiracy thriller   31
Continuation War (Finland)   8, 148–149, 154
counter-memories   171
coup d'état (1976, Argentina)   222–223, 226
Le Crabe-tambour (dir. Schoendoerffer)   181
The Crazy Years of the Twist (see *Les Folles Années du Twist*, dir. Zemmouri)
Crimea, Russian takeover of   20, 42
Crombie, Donald   262, 268
Crowe, Russell (dir.)   253, 264, 269
Crummey, Michael   369
cultural memory   1, 3, 10, 53–54, 56, 146, 149, 155, 233, 235, 253, 397, 400
cultural phenomenology   7
Dancis pa trim (dir. Krievs)   11, 278–280, 292
Dangerous Summer (see *Baigā vasara*, dir. Grauba)
Dardenne, Jean-Pierre (dir)   199, 211
Dardenne, Luc (dir.)   199, 211
Daruma Days (short stories)   369

Days of Glory (see *Indigènes*, dir. Bouchareb)
de Palma, Brian (dir.)   68, 111
De Sédouy, Alain (dir.)   164
Deadline Gallipoli (dir. Rymer)   253, 265, 269
Defenders of Riga (see *Rīgas sargi*, dir. Grauba)
Dekeukeleire, Charles (dir.)   199
Delerive, Pierre (dir.)   182
Demy, Jacques (dir.)   181
deportation   121, 170, 276, 281, 286, 361, 370–371
Le Dernier métro (dir. Truffaut)   162
detention camp   328
Devigny, André   161
Dickens, Charles   373–374
dictatorship   10, 75, 219, 221–222, 224–225, 227–228
Dienar, Baruch (dir.)   312
Diplomatic Siege (dir. Graef-Marino)   333, 344
Dispatches: Battle Fatigue   73, 80, 83–84, 89
Dispatches: Battle Scarred   73, 89
Dispatches: Iraq – The Betrayal   73, 83–85, 89
Dispatches: Iraq – The Reckoning   82, 83, 85
Displaced Persons   299–300
displacement   13, 179, 370
Dixon, John (dir.)   253, 269
docudrama   332, 351, 364
Doden, Richard (dir.)   258
The Downfall (see *Der Untergang*, dir. Hirschbiegel)
Dragojević, Srđan (dir.)   337–341, 344
Dream Team 1935 (see *Sapņu komanda 1935*, dir. Grauba)
Dresden (dir. Richter)   131
Drew, Di (dir.)   253, 268
Drummer-Crab (see *Le Crabe-tambour*, dir. Schoendoerffer)
Duvivier, Julien (dir.)   161
Eastern Front (World War II)   121–123, 125, 128, 130–134, 137, 140–141, 276

Eastwood, Clint (dir.)   6, 53, 58–59, 61–62, 64, 68–69, 71, 91, 398
Edelweisspiraten (dir. von Glasow-Brücher)   130
Edwards, Jack   366–368
Eglītis, Anšlavs   271, 273, 279, 291
Egyptian-Israeli War of Attrition   312
Eien no O (dir. Yamazaki)   13, 378, 384–385, 388–391, 393
Eine Frau in Berlin (memoir)   133
Elle s'appelait Sarah (dir. Paquet-Brenner)   172
Emperor Meiji and the Great Russo-Japanese War (see *Meiji tenno to nichiro daisenso*, dir. Watanabe)
enemy image   1–3, 6, 11, 271, 274, 276, 278, 284, 289
The Enemy Within (dir. Stavely)   254
Enemy, My Friend? (dir. Finlason)   365
The Enemy (see *Neprijatelj*, dir. Zečević)
L'Ennemi intime (dir. Siri)   9, 177–180, 183–194, 196
Épuration   159, 173
Esma's Secret (orig. title *Grbavica*, dir. Žbanić)   339, 342, 344
The Eternal Zero (see *Eien no O*, dir. Yamazaki)
ethnic cleansing   121
Elevator to the Gallows (see *Ascenseur pour l'échafaud*, dir. Malle)
Exiled (see *Trimda*, dir. Sīmanis)
El exilio de Gardel. Tangos (dir. Solanas)   228
The Exploits of the Emden (dir. Ralph and Hall)   255
Eye in the Sky (dir. Hood)   91
Ëzhik v tumane (dir. Norshtein)   35–36, 38, 48, 52
Facey, Bert   261
The Fallen: Legacy of Iraq   74, 89
Die Fälscher (dir. Ruzowitzky)   130
Färberböck, Max (dir.)   8, 122, 130, 133, 135, 143
Faucon, Philippe (dir.)   183
Female Agents (see *Les Femmes de l'ombre*, dir. Salomé)
Les Femmes de l'ombre (dir. Salomé)   162

Ferroukhi, Ismaël (dir.)   162
Des feux mal éteints (dir. Moati)   182
The Fighter Pilot (see *Eien no O*, dir. Yamazaki)
Fighting Opium (see *L'Opium et le bâton*, dir. Rachedi)
Finlason, Michael (dir.)   364
The Firefly (see *Hotaru*, dir. Furuhata)
Fires on the Plain (see *Nobi*, dir. Ichikawa)
First Lebanon War   12, 293–296, 301–302, 304–305
First World War (Great War)   4, 9, 11, 123, 177–178, 185, 187, 191, 253–256, 263, 265–266, 282–283, 286, 351, 365, 370–371, 373, 398–399
The Fisherman's Son (see *Zvejnieka dēls*, dir. Lapenieks)
Flags of our Fathers (dir. Eastwood)   58–59, 71
Flanagan, Richard   367
FLN (National Liberation Front)   177–178, 181–183, 185, 188, 191
Die Flucht (dir. Wessel)   131
The Fog of War: Eleven Lessons from the Life of Robert S. McNamara (dir. Morris)   37
Les Folles années du Twist (dir. Zemmouri)   181
Folman, Ari (dir.)   295, 298–301, 307
For Those We Love (see *Ore wa, kimi no tame ni koso shini ni iku*, dir. Shinjo)
Ford, John (dir.)   187, 189
A Fortunate Life (dir. Cole and Safran)   253, 261, 269
Forty Thousand Horsemen (dir. Chauvel)   255
Four Mothers Movement   297
The Fourth Angel (dir. Irvin)   333, 335, 344
Français, si vous saviez (dir. Harris and De Sédouy)   164
Free Men (see *Les hommes libres*, dir. Ferroukhi)
Funny Dirty Little War (see *No habrá más penas ni olvido*, dir. Olivera)
Furuhata, Yasuo (dir.)   380, 393
Le Fusil de bois (dir. Delerive)   182
G.I. Jane (dir. Scott)   348

Gallipoli (campaign)   11, 253, 255, 257, 260, 264–265
Gallipoli (dir. Ivin)   253, 265, 269
Gallipoli (dir. Weir)   11, 253, 256–257, 259–260, 269
Gammage, Bill (dir.)   256
Gance, Abel (dir.)   178, 191
Gansel, Dennis (dir.)   130
Garage Olimpo (dir. Bechis) 219, 229, 231
Gardel's Exile. Tangos (see *El exilio de Gardel. Tangos*, dir. Solanas)
Garrel, Philippe (dir.)   182
Gategood, Keith (dir.)   255
Gavin, John (dir.)   254
Gavron, Sarah (dir.)   7, 92, 103
Generation War (see *Unsere Mütter, unsere Väter*)
generative mimetic scapegoating mechanism   9
Géricault, Théodore   178, 189–190
German New Cinema   125
Ghosts of Abu Ghraib (dir. Kennedy)   353, 360
Gibbon, Sharon   370
Girard, René   9, 15
Gitis, Georgii (dir.)   6, 36, 45–48, 50, 52
Glasow-Brücher, Niko von (dir.)   130
Glenaan, Kenneth (dir.)   7, 92, 103
Godard, Jean Luc (dir.)   164, 180–181
Göring's Baton (see *Göringin sauva*, dir. Andell)
Göringin sauva (dir. Andell)   148
The Government Inspector (dir. Kosminsky)   330, 332
Graef-Marino, Gustavo (dir.)   333, 344
Gramps in the Resistance (see *Papy fait de la résistance*, dir. Poiré)
Grauba, Aigars (dir.)   11, 274, 277, 281–282, 292
Grbavica (dir. Žbanić)   339, 342, 344
Great War   (see First World War)
Green, William (dir.)   255
Gregorich, Luis (dir.)   219, 221, 231
Grossman, David   305–306
Grossmann, Vasily   121, 142
Guantanamo (detention center) 13, 194, 345–347, 349, 351, 353
Guédiguian, Robert (dir.)   162
guilt   8–9, 13, 85, 109–110, 151, 174, 295, 298–299, 304, 333, 347, 351–352, 355, 358, 384, 387
Gulf War   74–75
Die Gustloff (dir. Vilsmaier)   131
Haas, Philip (dir.)   67, 71
Haditha   6, 64
Haganah   299
Hall, Ken G. (dir.)   255
Ha-Matarah Tiran (dir. Nussbaum)   12, 309, 313–314, 318, 324, 325
Haneke, Michael (dir.)   183
Harkis (dir. Tasma)   183
Harris, André (dir.)   164
Harvey, Frank (dir.)   254
Hedgehog in the Fog (see *Ëzhik v tumane*, dir. Norshtein)
Hem Hayu Asarah (dir. Dienar)   312
Hemingway, Ernest   38, 41
Herbiet, Laurent (dir.)   182
The Hero of the Dardanelles (dir. Rolfe)   254
heroism   22–23, 76, 287, 296, 317, 324, 336, 381, 383, 386–387, 389
Herzen, Aleksander   51
Heusch, Luc de (dir.)   199
Heynemann, Laurent (dir.)   181
Hezbollah, the   293, 295–296, 305
Hidden (see *Caché*, dir. Haneke)
Himmlerin kanteleensoittaja (dir. Huttu-Hiltunen)   148
Hirsch, Marianne   147–148, 157, 365, 375
Hirschbiegel, Oliver (dir.)   130, 143
La historia oficial (dir. Puenzo)   219, 223–225, 227, 230–232
historical consciousness   1, 248
historical film   3–4, 43, 53–54, 56, 122, 179–180, 192, 253
historiophoty   9, 177–179, 187
A Hole in the Moon (see *Khor Balevananh*, dir. Zohar)
Holocaust   122, 131, 147, 170, 185, 276, 299, 316, 328–329
Les hommes libres (dir. Ferroukhi)   162
Hong Kong, battle of   361, 363

L'Honneur d'un capitaine (dir. Schoendoerffer) 181
Hood, Gavin (dir.) 91
Hors-la-loi (dir. Bouchareb) 183
Hotaru (dir. Furuhata) 380, 393
Hugo, Victor 162
Hunde, wollt ihr ewig leben (dir. Wisbar) 128–129, 144
The Hunting Party (dir. Shepard) 335, 344
The Hurt Locker (dir. Bigelow) 64
Hussein, Sadam 74–76, 353
Huttu-Hiltunen, Heikki (dir.) 148
Ich war 19 (dir. Wolf) 130
Ichikawa, Kon (dir.) 377, 393
If the Huns Came to Melbourne (dir. Coates) 254
illegal immigration 197–200
In the Fog (see *V tumane*, dir. Loznitsa)
In the Land of Blood and Honey (dir. Jolie) 332–333, 341–342, 344
Independence War (Israel) 284, 300
Indigènes (dir. Bouchareb) 162, 183–184
Instrument of Himmler (see *Himmlerin kanteleensoittaja*, dir. Huttu-Hiltunen)
internment 361, 369–370, 374
intersectionality 91
Intifada 305
Intimate Enemies (see *L'Ennemi intime*, dir. Siri)
Iraq War 6, 58–59, 62, 64–65, 68, 73–75, 79, 82, 85
Iraq: The Legacy 73, 82, 84, 89
Irvin, John (dir.) 333, 335, 344
Ishihara, Shintaro (Japanese politician) 380, 388–389, 391
Iskyss (dir. Jensen) 31, 33
Israeli Defense Force (IDF) 294–300, 302–303, 319
Israeli War of Independence 312
Israeli-Palestinian conflict 300
Itani, Frances 369
Ivin, Glendyn (dir.) 253, 269
J'accuse! (dir. Gance) 178, 191
Japanese Canadians 13, 361, 368–371
Japanese military police (see Kempeitai)
Jaruzelski, Wojciech 233, 235, 237–238, 241, 245, 247, 249

Jaunsudrabiņš, Jānis 286
Jenseits des Krieges (dir. Beckermann) 131, 144
Jensen, Knut Erik (dir.) 31, 33
The Joan of Arc of Loos (dir. Willoughby) 254
Johnson, Mark Steven (dir.) 336, 344
Jolie, Angelina (dir.) 12, 332–333, 339, 341–342, 344
journalism of attachment 329, 335
Kairišs, Viesturs (dir.) 274, 292
Kamikaze 13, 378–391
Karadžić, Radovan 330, 335, 338
Kārkliņš, Valdemārs 279
Kätilö (novel) 148
Katyn massacre 233
Kauhanen, Pekka (sculptor) 146
Kazakh cinema (see national cinema)
Kempeitai (Japanese military police) 364, 382
Kennedy, Rory (dir.) 353, 360
Kettu, Katja 148
Khor Balevananh (dir. Zohar) 309–312, 325
Khuda Kay Liye (dir. Mansoor) 332, 344
Killing Season (dir. Johnson) 336, 344
King, William Lyon Mackenzie (prime minister) 369
The King's Choice (see *Kongens nei*, dir. Poppe)
The King's Ring (see *Nameja gredzens*, dir. Grauba)
Kinkaseki POW camp 366
Kipling, Rudyard 186, 195
Kirst, Hans-Hellmut 121, 142
Kiss of Ice (see *Iskyss*, dir. Jensen)
Kivihalme, Elina (dir.) 146
Klīdzējs, Jānis 285
Knopp, Guido (dir.) 130
Kogawa, Joy 369–370, 375
Kolirin, Eran (dir.) 309, 321–323, 325
Kolka Cool (dir. Poškus) 11, 286–287, 289, 292
Kongens nei (dir. Poppe) 23, 34
Kopelew Lew 121, 143
Korhonen, Timo (dir.) 147
Kosminsky, Peter (dir.) 330–332, 344

Krievs, Arvīds (dir.)   11, 278, 292
Krzystek, Waldemar (dir.)   239–240, 250
Kuka piru pimeässä näkee (dir. Soppela)   8, 146–147, 157
Kunert, Joachim (dir.)   130
Kusturica, Emir (dir.)   12, 337, 339–342, 344
Kyle, Christopher Scott   6, 58–64, 68–70
Lacombe Lucien (dir. Malle)   9, 163, 165–169, 172, 174–175
Lāčplēsis (dir. Rusteiķis)   272, 292
Lafosse, Joachim (dir.)   10, 197, 201–203, 206–212, 216–217
Laissez-passer (dir. Tavernier)   162
Lakhdar-Hamina, Mohammed (dir.)   181
Landsberg, Alison   4–5, 15, 53, 70, 365, 375
Lapenieks, Vilis (dir.)   272, 292
Lapland War   148–149, 151–152
The Last Metro (see *Le Dernier métro*, dir. Truffaut)
Latvian Legion   276, 278–279
Laurence, Margaret   362
Lean, David (dir.)   363, 376
Lebanese Civil War, the   293
Lebanon (dir. Maoz)   12, 295, 298, 302–305, 307
Leder, Mimi (dir.)   335, 344
Lelouch, Claude (dir.)   162
Léon Morin, priest (dir. Melville)   161
Lepa sela lepo gore (dir. Dragojević)   337–338, 341, 344
Letters from Iwo Jima (dir. Eastwood)   58, 71
Die letzte Schlacht (dir. Blumenberg)   130–131
Levinas, Emmanuel   68, 70
Liberté la nuit (dir. Garrel)   182
Liberty at Night (see *Liberté la nuit*, dir. Garrel)
lieux de mémoire   165
Life Is a Miracle (see *Život je čudo*, dir. Kusturica)
The Lighthorsemen (dir. Wincer)   259, 269
La Ligne de démarcation (dir. Chabrol)   161
Lilyhammer (created by Skodvin and Bjørnstad)   19, 34

A Limousine: The Colour of Midsummer's Eve (see *Limuzins Janu nakts krasa*, dir. Streičs)
Limuzīns Jāņu nakts krāsā (dir. Streičs)   272, 292
Lincoln, W.J. (dir.)   254
Link, Caroline (dir.)   130
The Little Soldier (see *Le Petit Soldat*, dir. Godard)
The Living and the Dead (see *Živi i mrtvi*, dir. Milić)
Lomax, Eric   364
La Longue marche (dir. Astruc)   161
Lorna's Silence (see *Le Silence de Lorna*, dir. Dardenne and Dardenne)
The Lost Republic (see *La República Perdida*, dir. Pérez)
The Lost Republic II (see *La República perdida II*, dir. Gregorich and Pérez)
Lotta Svärd (voluntary organization)   146
Loyalties (dir. Wheeler)   362, 376
Loznitsa, Sergei (dir.)   5, 36, 42–44, 49
Lucas, George (dir.)   322
Lucie Aubrac (dir. Berri)   162
Lund, Karianne (series creator)   33
Lupaus (dir. Vanne)   146
MacArthur, Douglas (General, United States Army)   382
male gaze   92
Malle, Louis (dir.)   9, 163–165, 168–170, 172, 175, 181
Malvinas/Falklands War   220
Mammu, es tevi mīlu (dir. Nords)   273, 292
Mansoor, Shoaib (dir.)   331–332, 344
Maoz, Samuel (dir.)   295, 302, 304–305, 307
Marie-Octobre (dir. Duvivier)   161
martial law (Poland)   10, 233–242, 245–249
The Martyrdom of Nurse Cavell (dir. Gavin and Mason)   254
Maruyama, Seiji (dir.)   379, 393
masculinism   333
Mason, Post C. (dir.)   254
Mathews, J. E. (dir.)   254
Matikainen, Ari (dir.)   147, 154–155, 156
Matsubayashi, Shûe (dir.)   379, 393

Max Manus (dirs. Sandberg and Rønning) 23, 31, 34
Max Manus: Man of War (see *Max Manus*, dirs. Sandberg and Rønning)
May, Paul (dir.) 128, 143
McDonald, Roger 256, 260, 268
Meiji tenno to nichiro daisenso (dir. Watanabe) 379, 393
Melānijas hronika (dir. Kairišs) 274, 292
Melville, Jean-Pierre (dir.) 160–161
memory dispositif 235–236, 249
metacinema 177, 178, 187, 192
The Midwife (see *Kätilö*)
Milić, Kristijan (dir.) 340
militarism 264, 333, 377–378, 386, 388–389
Miller, George (dir.) 253, 269
Milošević, Slobodan 328, 337
Les Misérables (dir. Lelouch) 162
Moati, Serge (dir.) 182
Mon Colonel (dir. Herbiet) 182, 184
Moore, John (dir.) 334, 344
Moran, Luke (dir.) 345, 360
Mordillat, Gérard (dir.) 182
Morocco 160–161, 189, 197–200, 203–204, 206–207, 209–210, 212–216
Morris, Errol (dir.) 37, 355, 360
Mother to the Kamikaze (see Torihama, Tomé)
Mulroney, Brian 369
multiculturalism 7, 362, 374
Mulvey, Laura 92–93, 103
Mummy, I Love You (see *Mammu, es tevi mīlu*, dir. Nords)
Muriel (dir. Resnais) 181
Un muro de silencio (dir. Stantic) 219, 228–229, 231, 232
Murphy of Anzac (dir. Mathews) 254
Nacht fiel über Gotenhafen (dir. Wisbar) 130–131
Nagase, Takashi 364
Nakba 300
Nameja gredzens (dir. Grauba) 274, 292
Napola (dir. Gansel) 130
The Narrow Road to the Deep North (novel) 367

national cinema 1–4, 14, 179, 236, 248, 273, 281, 283, 285–286, 288–289
national identity 1, 3, 8, 32, 113, 146, 243, 253, 267, 271–273, 284, 286, 288, 298, 318, 380, 382
nationalism 2, 5, 10–12, 29, 35, 49–50, 160, 174, 251, 255, 258, 267, 327–328, 337–339, 384, 391
neo-colonialism 212
Neprijatelj (dir. Zečević) 340–342, 344
Nesbø, Jo 19, 33
Der neunte Tag (dir. Schlöndorff) 130
New Denver, BC 370–373
Nicholson, Michael 329, 343
Ničija zemlja (dir. Tanović) 12, 338–339, 344
Night of the Pencils (see *La noche de los lápices*, dir. Olivera)
Nihonkai daikaisen (dir. Maruyama) 379, 393
NKVD 233
No habrá más penas ni olvido (dir. Olivera) 222–223, 232
No Man's Land (see *Ničija zemlja*, dir. Tanović)
Nobi (dir. Ichikawa) 377, 393
La noche de los lápices (dir. Olivera) 219, 223–227, 231
Nora, Pierre 165, 174
Nords, Jānis (dir.) 273, 292
Norshtein, Iurii (dir.) 35–37, 48–50, 52
Nowhere in Africa (dir. Link) 130
Nuit noire (dir. Tasma) 183
Nuremberg trials 223
Nurse Cavell (see *La Revanche*, dir. Lincoln)
Nussbaum, Raphael (dir.) 309, 315, 325
Obasan (novel) 369–370
occupation drama 22–23, 31–32
Occupied (see *Okkupert*, created by Lund, Skjoldbjærg, Nesbø)
October 17, 1971 (see *Nuit noire*, dir. Tasma)
The Official Story (see *La historia oficial*, dir. Puenzo)
Oh! What a Lovely War (dir. Attenborough) 258
Okkupert (created by Lund, Skjoldbjærg, Nesbø) 4–5, 19–24, 27–33

Old Man, The (see *Shal*, dir. Tursunov)
Olimpo Parking (see *Garage Olimpo*, dir. Bechis)
Olivera, Héctor (dir.)   219, 222, 224–225, 227, 231–232
Onishi, Takijiro (Admiral, Imperial Japanese Navy)   380–381
Ophüls, Marcel (dir.)   9, 162–165, 167–168, 170–171, 175
L'Opium et le bâton (dir. Rachedi)   181
Ore wa, kimi no tame ni koso shini ni iku (dir. Shinjo)   13, 378–379, 388, 393
Orient   96, 102
Orion's Belt (see *Orions belte*, dir. Solum)
Orions belte (dir. Solum)   31, 33
Our Children (see *A perdre la raison*, dir. Lafosse)
Outside the Law (see *Hors-la-loi*, dir. Bouchareb)
Owen, Wilfred   365
Oz, Amos   295, 303, 306
Pacific War   13, 361, 370, 377, 379, 386, 388–389, 391
Palestinian Exodus (see Nakba)
Palestinian Liberation Organization (PLO)   293, 295
Palestinian-Israeli conflict   311
Panorama: Basra – The Legacy   73, 82, 84–85, 89
Panorama: Bringing our Boys Home?   73, 80–83, 85, 89
Panorama: For Queen and Country?   73, 80–82, 84–85, 89
Panorama: Soldiers on the Run   73, 89
Panorama: The Battle for Basra Palace   73, 85, 89
Papy fait de la résistance (dir. Poiré)   162
Paquet-Brenner, Gilles (dir.)   172
Les Parapluies de Cherbourg (dir. Demy)   181
Paris brûle-t-il? (dir. Clément)   161
The Peacemaker (dir. Leder)   335, 344
Pearl Harbor   368, 371
Peckinpah, Sam (dir.)   187, 189
Le Père tranquille (dir. Clément)   160
Pérez, Miguel (dir.)   219, 221, 231
Peronist government   220, 222–223

Petersen, Wolfgang (dir.)   302
Le Petit Soldat (dir. Godard)   180
Phalange   294, 303
Philipp, Harald (dir.)   128
Platoon (dir. Stone)   68, 71, 180, 184–185, 190, 193
Plivier, Theodor   121, 143
Podzemlje (dir. Kusturica)   337, 339, 342, 344
Poiré, Jean-Marie (dir.)   162
Polish People's Republic   233, 240–241, 243, 245
political cinema   228
politics of feeling   358
Poorly Extinguished Fires (see *Des feux mal éteints*, dir. Moati)
Popiełuszko, Jerzy   237–238
Popiełuszko. Freedom is Within Us (see *Popiełuszko. Wolność jest w nas*, dir. Wieczyński)
Popiełuszko. Wolność jest w nas (dir. Wieczyński)   237–238, 241–242, 248, 250
Poppe, Erik (dir.)   23, 34
Poškus, Juris (dir.)   11, 286, 292
postmemory   147, 163, 365
Pretty Village, Pretty Flame (see *Lepa sela lepo gore*, dir. Dragojević)
Prikliucheniia Alënushki i Erëmy (dir. Gitis)   6, 36, 45–46, 48–49, 52
primary enemy   40, 77
prison drama   13, 200, 345–346
The Private War of Lucinda Smith (dir. Alchin)   253, 262, 269
La Promesse (dirs. Dardenne and Dardenne)   211
Promise (see *Lupaus*, dir. Vanne)
The Promise (see *La Promesse*, dirs. Dardenne and Dardenne)
propaganda   121, 123, 125, 133–134, 136, 139, 150, 162, 166–168, 174, 192, 220, 254, 262, 265, 315, 328, 334, 364, 381
A Prophet (see *Un prophète*, dir. Audiard)
Un prophète (dir. Audiard)   200–202, 213
prosthetic memory   5, 365
Puenzo, Luis (dir.)   219, 224–225, 227, 232
La Question (dir. Heynemann)   181

The Question (see *La Question*, dir. Heynemann)
R.A.S. (dir. Boisset)   181
Rachedi, Ahmed (dir.)   181
Racine, Jean   208
Le Radeau de la Méduse (Géricault)   178, 189–190
Radvanyi, Geza von (dir.)   128, 143
La Rafle (dir. Bosch)   172
The Railway Man (dir. Teplitzky)   364, 376
Ralph, Louis (dir.)   255
rape   8, 122, 125, 130, 132, 135, 138, 140, 204, 220, 223, 303, 332, 335, 339, 347–349
Real Story with Fiona Bruce   73, 80, 82–83, 85, 89
Redacted (dir. de Palma)   68, 71
repatriation   361, 369–370, 373
La República Perdida (dir. Pérez)   219, 221–223, 231
La República perdida II (dir. Gregorich and Pérez)   219, 231
Requiem (novel)   369
resistance   9, 20–26, 28–29, 32–33, 61, 128, 130, 132, 159–170, 172, 174, 185, 228, 233, 266–267, 283, 333, 337, 342
Resnais, Alain (dir.)   181
La Revanche (dir. Lincoln)   254
RFS (*Rīgas kinostudija*/ Riga Film Studio)   272
Richter, Roland Suso (dir.)   131
Rīgas sargi (dir. Grauba)   11, 279, 282–283, 287, 289, 292
Riis, Sharon   362
The Road to Guantanamo (dir. Whitecross and Winterbottom)   332, 351
The Rock (dir. Bay)   333, 344
Rolfe, Alfred (dir.)   254
Rønning, Joachim (dir.)   23, 34
Rosenstraße (dir. von Trotta)   130
Rothemund, Mark (dir.)   130
rotoscoping   299
The Round Up (see *La Rafle*, dir. Bosch)
Russo-Japanese War   379
Russo-Ukrainian conflict   49
Rusteiķis, Aleksandrs (dir.)   272, 292
Ruzowitzky, Stefan (dir.)   130

Rwandan genocide   13
Rymer, Michael (dir.)   253–254, 269
Sabra and Shatila massacre, the   294–295, 299, 301, 303
The Sacrifice (see *Les Sacrifiés*, dir. Touita)
Les Sacrifiés (dir. Touita)   181
Safe Conduct (see *Laissez-passer*, dir. Tavernier)
Safran, Henri (dir.)   253, 260, 296
Said, Edward   75, 85, 88
Saksalaisten sotilaiden lapset ("Children of the German Soldiers")   145
Salomé, Jean-Paul (dir.)   162
Sandberg, Espen (dir.)   23, 34
Sapņu komanda 1935 (dir. Grauba)   11, 281–282, 289, 292
Sarah's Key (see *Elle s'appelait Sarah*, dir. Paquet-Brenner)
Sarajevo wedding massacre   330
Sartre, Jean-Paul   177
Sattler, Peter (dir.)   345–346, 360
Schlöndorff, Volker (dir.)   130
Schoendoerffer, Pierre (dir.)   181, 191
scorched earth policy   121, 132, 149
Scorsese, Martin (dir.)   178, 189–190, 322
Scott, Ridley (dir.)   111, 348
Second Lebanon War   305
Second World War (WWII)   4, 5, 7–9, 19–20, 22–25, 27–32, 36, 42, 43, 46, 49–51, 58, 108, 122, 128, 145–147, 149, 154–155, 161, 168, 171, 177, 182, 185, 187, 200, 233, 271, 275–278, 280–281, 285–286, 314–315, 330–331, 340, 361–363, 368–369, 374, 377, 383, 389, 391, 396, 398
secondary enemy   77
sepia fascism   130–131, 133, 140–141
Sétif riot   183
Shakespeare, William   319
Shal (dir. Tursunov)   5, 35, 38–40, 49–52
shame   8–9, 19, 93, 99, 145, 148, 151–152, 155, 358, 388
Sharon, Ariel (Israeli Minister of Defense)   294, 299
Shepard, Richard (dir.)   335, 344
Shinjo, Taku (dir.)   378, 393
shooting and crying (see *yorim ve bochim*)

Le Silence de la mer (dir. Melville)   160
Le Silence de la mer (novel)   159
Le silence de Lorna (dir. Dardenne and Dardenne)   199, 211
Sīmanis, Dāvis (dir.)   274, 292
Sims, Jeremy (dir.)   253, 269
Sinai Commandos (see *Hamatarah Tiran*, dir. Nussbaum)
Singapore, fall of   364, 365
Siri, Florent-Emilio (dir.)   9, 177–180, 183–185, 187–194, 196
Sisters in Resistance (see *Soeurs de résistance*, dir. Wechsler)
The Situation (dir. Haas)   67, 71
Six Day War   12, 293, 312–314, 316–317, 323–324
Skjoldbjærg, Erik (series creator)   19, 33
Skodvin, Eilif (series creator)   34
Smarzowski, Wojciech (dir.)   14
Snijeg (dir. Begić)   339
Snow (see *Snijeg*, dir. Begić)
Sodan murtamat (dir. Korhonen)   147
Soeurs de résistance (dir. Wechsler)   162
Solanas, Fernando E. (dir.)   228, 231–232
Soldier Husband Daughter Dad (TV series)   74, 80–81, 89, 396
Solidarity movement   233–234
Solum, Ola (dir.)   31, 33
Solschenizyn, Alexander   121, 143
Sophie Scholl (dir. Rothemund)   130
Soppela, Mari (dir.)   8, 146–147, 151, 154, 157
Soriano, Osvaldo   222
The Sorrow and the Pity: Chronicle of a French Town under the Occupation (see *Le Chagrin et la pitié*, dir. Ophüls)
Sota ja mielenrauha (dir. Matikainen)   147, 154
The South (see *Sur*, dir. Solanas)
Soviet Union   27–28, 31, 35, 38, 121, 123, 128, 146, 148, 167, 272
The Spirit of Gallipoli (dir. Gategood and Green)   255
spy thriller   31, 181, 254
Srebrenica massacre   328
Stalingrad (dir. Vilsmaier)   122, 132, 144

Standard Operating Procedure (dir. Morris)   355, 360
Stantic, Lita (dir.)   219, 228–229, 232
Stauffenberg (dir. Baier)   130
Stavely, Roland (dir.)   254
Stevens, David (dir.)   253, 268
Stone, Oliver (dir.)   7, 71, 106, 114–115, 118, 190, 295
Strafbataillon 999 (dir. Philipp)   128
Streičs, Jānis (dir.)   11, 272, 285, 291, 292
Suez Crisis   312
Summer of '62 (see *Cartouches gauloises*, dir. Charef)
Sur (dir. Solanas)   228, 232
Sutherland, Donald   365–366
Suutari, Virpi (dir.)   8, 145, 151, 154–155, 157
Sweeney Investigates: Death of the Redcaps   73, 80–83, 85, 89
Taïda massacre   186, 188
Taiheiyo no tsubasa (dir. Matsubayashi)   379, 393
Taiwan   361, 364, 366, 368, 374
Tanović, Danis (dir.)   12, 338, 344
Tarantino, Quentin (dir.)   193
Tartar steppe (see Buzzati, Dino)
Tasma, Alain (dir.)   183
Tavernier, Bertrand (dir.)   162
Teplitzky, Jonathan (dir.)   364, 376
Terres brûlées (dir. Dekeukeleire)   199
terrorism   4–5, 20, 27–29, 32–33, 75, 93, 114, 221, 224, 226, 228–229, 351
They Were Ten (see *Hem Hayu Asarah*, dir. Dienar)
Third Reich   8, 122, 134, 153
Thomson, Chris (dir.)   253, 268
Three to Dance (see *Dancis pa trim*, dir. Krievs)
To Be Twenty in the Aures (see *Avoir 20 ans dans les Aurès*, dir. Vautier)
Tonight: Our Boys in Basra   73, 80–82, 84, 89
Tonight: War Wounds   73, 80–81, 85, 89
Torihama, Tomé (Mother to the Kamikaze)   380, 382

torture   13, 91, 115, 163, 169, 177, 180–184, 188, 193–194, 220, 223, 226, 228–229, 303, 332, 336, 345–346, 353
Touita, Okacha (dir.)   181
La Trahison (dir. Faucon)   183
transculturation   373
transition film   287
transnationalism   9, 177–179
trauma   12–14, 22–23, 59, 64, 79, 83, 86, 106, 113–117, 129, 133, 147–149, 151, 154, 170, 177, 178, 181, 187, 188, 228, 233, 239, 248, 276, 280, 297–301, 304–305, 313, 335, 339–340, 348, 363, 365, 367–368, 384, 386, 397
Trimda (dir. Sīmanis)   292
The Trip (see *El viaje*, dir. Solanas)
Trotta, Margarethe von (dir.)   130
Trudeau, Pierre Elliott   362
Truffaut, François (dir.)   162
Tuntematon emäntä (dir. Kivihalme)
Tursunov, Ermek (dir.)   5, 35, 38, 40–42, 50, 52
Ukrainian Insurgent Army (UPA)   14
The Umbrellas from Cherbourg (see *Les Parapluies de Cherbourg*, dir. Demy)
Un condamné à mort s'est échappé (dir. Bresson)   161
UN mission in Bosnia   331
Der unbekannte Soldat (dir. Verhoeven)   131, 144
Underground (see *Podzemlje*, dir. Kusturica)
Der Unhold (dir. Schlöndorff)   130
The Unknown Mistress (see *Tuntematon emäntä*, dir. Kivihalme)
Unsere Mütter, unsere Väter (TV series)   122, 132, 144
Der Untergang (dir. Hirschbiegel)   130–131, 133, 143
unwar films   146
V tumane (dir. Loznitsa)   5, 36, 42–44, 49, 51–52
Valon tuoja ("Bringer of light")   146
Vals im Bashir (dir. Folman)   12, 295, 298–302, 304–305, 307
Vancouver   361, 368, 370, 371
Vanne, Ilkka (dir.)   146
Varda, Agnès (dir.)   181

Vautier, René (dir.)   181
Vél d'Hiv   170, 172
Le Vent de la Toussaint (dir. Béhat)   182
Le Vent des Aurès (dir. Lakhdar-Hamina)   181
Vercors (novelist)   159–160
Verhoeven, Michael (dir.)   131, 141, 144
Vichy   159–160, 162–163, 166, 168, 170–171
El viaje (dir. Solanas)   228, 231
Vietnam War   77, 147, 180, 293, 295, 300
Vilsmaier, Joseph (dir.)   122, 131–132, 144
Volhynia (see *Wołyń*, dir. Smarzowski)
The Wages of War (see *Sodan murtamat*, dir. Korhonen)
Wajda, Andrzej (dir.)   10, 236, 242–245, 247–248, 250
Wałęsa, Lech   10, 234, 243–247
Wałęsa. Człowiek z nadziei (dir. Wajda)   242–244, 247–248, 250
Wałęsa. Man of Hope (see *Wałęsa. Człowiek z nadziei*, dir. Wajda)
A Wall of Silence (see *Un muro de silencio*, dir. Stantic)
Waltz with Bashir (see *Vals im Bashir*, dir. Folman)
War and Peace of Mind (see *Sota ja mielenrauha*, dir. Matikainen)
The War Between Us (dir. Wheeler)   13, 361–362, 368, 370, 372, 374, 376
war film   5–7, 22, 37, 53–58, 61, 68, 106, 110, 121–122, 128–131, 140–142, 160, 178, 189–190, 192, 254–256, 263, 266, 314–315, 337–338, 341–342, 345, 377–379, 388, 398
War Measures Act (Canada)   361, 368, 370
War on Terror   7, 13, 59, 63, 91, 93–94, 114, 332, 345–346, 351, 353–354
A War Story (dir. Wheeler)   13, 361–365, 371–372, 374, 376
Ward, Rachel (dir.)   253, 268
warrior ethos   296
Warriors (dir. Kosminksy)   330–331, 344
Warsaw Uprising   233–234
Watada, Terry   369
Watanabe, Kunio (dir.)   379, 393

The Water Diviner (dir. Crowe) 253, 264–265, 269
Watson, Ian (dir,) 253, 269
Wechsler, Maia (dir.) 162
Wehrmachtskinder 145
Weir, Peter (dir.) 11, 253, 257, 268, 269
Welcome to Sarajevo (dir. Winterbottom) 329–330, 334–335, 344
Wessel, Kai (dir.) 131
Wheeler, Anne (dir.) 13, 361–368, 370, 372, 374, 376
Wheeler, Benjamin, Dr., Major 361, 363–368
When Our Boys Came Home 73, 80–81, 83, 89
white supremacy 96–98, 102, 372
White, Hayden 9, 177, 179–180, 192, 194, 195
Whitecross, Mat (dir.) 351
Who the Devil Can See in the Dark (see *Kuka piru pimeässä näkee*, dir. Soppela)
Wieczyński, Rafał (dir.) 237, 250
Will They Never Come (dir. Rolfe) 254
Willesee's Australians: Private John Simpson (dir. Safran) 253, 260, 269
Willoughby, George (dir.) 254
Wilson, Juanita (dir.) 339
Wincer, Simon (dir.) 259, 269
The Winds of the Aures (see *Le Vent des Aurès*, dir. Lakhdar-Hamina)
Winter War 8, 146, 148
Winterbottom, Michael (dir.) 12, 329, 332, 344, 351
Wisbar, Frank (dir.) 128–131, 144
Within our Gates (dir. Harvey) 254
Wolf, Konrad (dir.) 130
Wołyń (dir. Smarzowski) 14
Wöss, Fritz 143
The Wooden Gun (see *Le Fusil de bois*, dir. Delerive)
The Wreckage (novel) 369
Wszystko co kocham (dir. Borcuch) 240, 241, 242, 248, 250
Yadir, Nabil Ben (dir.) 200
Yamazaki, Takashi (dir.) 378, 393
Yasmin (dir. Glenaan) 7, 92–93, 96–102, 103
Yasukuni Shrine (Japan) 379, 391
Yeldham, Peter 260
Yom Kippur War 294, 312, 323
yorim ve bochim ("shooting and crying" genre) 295
Zālīte, Māra 286
Žbanić, Jasmila (dir.) 339, 344
Zečević, Dejan (dir.) 340, 344
Zemmouri, Mahmoud (dir.) 181
Zero Dark Thirty (dir. Bigelow) 91
Živi i mrtvi (dir. Milić) 340, 342
Život je čudo (dir. Kusturica) 337, 344
Žižek, Slavoj 340, 344
Zohar, Uri (dir.) 309–310, 325
Zvejnieka dēls (dir. Lapenieks) 272, 279, 292

www.ingramcontent.com/pod-product-compliance
Lightning Source LLC
Chambersburg PA
CBHW031411230426
43668CB00007B/272